J.M.TuRneR
Halifax
1983 .

gift copy from
SCM Press for
articles on
'Hymns' and
'Charles Wesley.'

A DICTIONARY OF
CHRISTIAN SPIRITUALITY

A
DICTIONARY
OF
CHRISTIAN
SPIRITUALITY

EDITED BY

GORDON S. WAKEFIELD

Principal of the Queen's College BIRMINGHAM.

SCM PRESS LTD

1983.

Reprint 2004

Entirely New Edition

334 01966 4

First published 1983 by
SCM Press Ltd
26–30 Tottenham Road London N1

Filmset by Richard Clay (The Chaucer Press) Ltd,
and printed in Great Britain by
Fletcher & Son Ltd, Norwich

PREFACE

'Spirituality' is a word very much in vogue among Christians of our time. French Catholic in origin, it is now common to evangelical Protestants also. A recent course was criticized for lack of 'spirituality', meaning that the timetable included few periods for worship. The Orthodox might prefer to speak of 'mystical theology', as in Vladimir Lossky's title *The Mystical Theology of the Eastern Church* (where 'theology' is the contemplation of God rather than an activity of the discursive reason alone), or simply, as does Alexander Schmemann, of 'the Christian life'.

In all traditions, and in many non-Christian faiths and philosophies, the underlying implication is that there is a constituent of human nature which seeks relations with the ground and purpose of existence, however conceived. As Job says, 'There is a spirit in man.' For the Christian, as for Job, this Spirit is 'the breath of the Almighty', the Holy Spirit of God himself, and the activity the Spirit inspires is prayer. 'We do not even know how we ought to pray, but through our inarticulate groans the Spirit himself is pleading for us. . . .' (Rom. 8.26, NEB). But prayer in Christian theology and experience is more than pleading or petition; it is our whole relation to God. And spirituality concerns the way in which prayer influences conduct, our behaviour and manner of life, our attitudes to other people. It is often best studied in biographies, but clearly it shapes dogmas, inspires movements and builds institutions.

A Dictionary of Christian Spirituality attempts to give direct access to the whole development and present state of the subject. What is offered here is a series of succinct pieces, written by experts, often with a genius for compression, which will supply instant, accurate and thought-provoking information of high scholarship – some of it hot from the very latest research and evaluation – while whetting the appetite for further reading and study. That the first entry is 'Abandon' (in the sense of de Caussade), and the last 'Zen' gives some idea of the range. In between are articles which deal with the spirituality of every school and denomination throughout Christian history, giving indication of the rich varieties and innumerable types. Even where there is no direct entry the reader, by use of the cross-references, will find some insight. Though we have avoided a 'Who's who in Prayer', there are separate articles on nearly all the great spiritual theologians.

An effort has been made towards proper proportion. Orthodox spirituality is prominent, together with classic Catholic and Protestant, but what some would regard as deviations have their place. The developments of our own century – Feminism, Liberation Theology, the radicalism of the 1960s, Black Theology – are represented. There are American, Asian and African perspectives as well as Anglo-Saxon, while other religions cannot be ignored in any account of Christian spirituality today.

There has been a discovery in our time of the English mystics. Julian of Norwich is referred to again and again and not only in the specific articles. The Greek Fathers are undergoing a revival in the West. Not only does the study of the Oxford Movement establish its leaders' indebtedness, but the Methodist doctrine of Christian perfection is seen to have Cappadocian affinities, while for those whose main interest is not in historical derivations but in following the way to God, theologians such as Gregory of Nyssa, in spite of what some would find a quaint and archaic allegorizing, may correct Western misunderstandings of mysticism and offer a union of theology and spirituality which suits the Anglican temper of the Caroline Divines, the Cambridge Platonists and their modern heirs. The treatment of mysticism here is of particular importance. The greatness of the Carmelites remains undiminished, particularly that of St John of the Cross, another whose name occurs many times in these pages. His teaching may sometimes raise the question whether is he not as Buddhist as Christian; he is much nearer to Luther and the Reformation *sola fide* than could have been conceived at the time. A twentieth-century author whose influence emerges in this volume as even greater than I had imagined is the Anglo-American poet, T. S. Eliot.

The *Dictionary* should be of value to many different people, and not only students and scholars. Those who know Augustine's *Confessions*, Julian's *Revelations*, or *The Cloud of Unknowing* will learn more about them and their provenance; but they will also be introduced to works which have not undergone revival or been reproduced in paperback. The English Puritans, though they have attracted much scholarly attention since the last war, have lost popular influence; even John Bunyan has not his former standing in devotion. There is much about him here. John Milton, too, of perpetual fascination in faculties of literature, is prominent in the article on Puritan spirituality. Thomas Goodwin is forgotten now, yet his *Heart of Christ in Heaven towards Sinners* on earth teaches a devotion to the Heart of Jesus, and there are those who will be glad to read of it and perhaps unearth it from Goodwin's *Works*. Walter Marshall's *The Gospel Mystery of Sanctification* (1692) was precious in Alexander Whyte's Edinburgh at the turn of the century; it is the quintessence of Calvinist spirituality of which the cardinal concept was union with Christ; such a work is here set in its context. Richard Challoner (d. 1781), the Roman Catholic Bishop of Georgian England, is a writer who may be found edifying in a different age while, of the Tractarians, though the popularity of Keble's *The Christian Year* may have waned (one or two hymns excepted), Pusey is a mine of spiritual and sacramental power. There are many spiritual writers, ancient, mediaeval and modern, waiting to be enjoyed through this compilation.

The *Dictionary* is a product of ecumenism. It is doubtful if it could have been assembled in any period other than our own. I am grateful to many advisers and especially to the international team of more than a hundred and fifty contributors. The writing of dictionary articles is a distinctive art-form and often more difficult for experts than the writing of books. One of the special rewards has been the response and work of younger scholars, whose sharp minds and intense dedication fill one with hope for the years to come.

The Westminster Press of Philadelphia have been most helpful partners. James Heaney and his adviser, Professor Keith Egan of Marquette University, have elicited the majority of contributions from the USA and have ensured that the approach has not simply been that of an English editor. The latter's incisiveness and personal writings have been most valuable. The staff of the SCM Press have never failed in encouragement, hard work or patience. I must mention the obvious three – John Bowden himself, his secretary Rosamund Bacon, loaned to me for this purpose, and Margaret Lydamore, who has borne unflaggingly the heat and burden of copy-editing and proof collation. My wife deserves especial mention for she has not only been robbed of my company, but hammered out many of my own scripts.

For me, the privilege has been incalculable and the work a delight, even in the midst of many other preoccupations, and at the sacrifice of much free time. The *Dictionary* leaves me in the hope that it may be found of great usefulness and AMDG – to the greater glory of God.

GORDON S. WAKEFIELD

CONTRIBUTORS

Robin Aizlewood, *Teacher of Russian at Westminster School.* **Russian Spirituality**

George Appleton, *formerly Archbishop in Jerusalem.* **Petition**

Robert Atwell, *Chaplain of Trinity College, University of Cambridge.*
  Prayer for the Dead

Mariano Ballester, SJ, *Assistant General Director of the Apostleship of Prayer,
  Rome.* **The Apostleship of Prayer**

Annie Barnes, *formerly Reader in French Literature, University of Oxford, and
  Honorary Fellow of St Anne's College.* **Charles Péguy**

James E. Biechler, *Professor of Religion, La Salle College, Philadelphia.*
  Nicholas of Cusa

Peter D. Bishop, *Senior Lecturer in the History of Religions, Brighton Polytechnic.*
  Bhagavad Gītā; Bhakti; Taoism; Upanishads; Yoga

Lionel Blue, *Rabbi (Reform), Lecturer at Leobaeck College and Convenor of the
  Ecclesiastical Court of the Reform Synagogues of Great Britain.* **Jewish Spirituality,
  Judaism**

Gerald Bonner, *Reader in Theology, University of Durham.*
  St Augustine of Hippo; Bede

Maria Boulding, *Benedictine nun of Stanbrook Abbey.*
  St Benedict of Nursia; Benedictine Spirituality, Benedictines

John Bowden, *Editor and Managing Director, SCM Press.*
  Animals and Spirituality; Music and Spirituality

Sebastian Brock, *Lecturer in Aramaic and Syriac, University of Oxford, and
  Fellow of Wolfson College.* **Ephrem Syrus; Macarius the Egyptian; Syrian
  Spirituality**

Eluned Brown, *Senior Lecturer, Department of English Literature, University of
  Edinburgh.* **Joseph Hall; Samuel Johnson; Jeremy Taylor; Henry Vaughan**

Judith M. Brown, *Senior Lecturer in History, University of Manchester.*
  Ashram; Bede Griffiths

Raymond Brown, *Principal of Spurgeon's College, London.*
  Thomas Goodwin; John Howe; Preaching and Spirituality

Christopher Bryant, *Member of the Society of St John the Evangelist, St Edward's
  House, Westminster.* **The Psychology of Prayer; Unitive Way**

John Byrom, *Vicar of Swaffham Prior, Cambridge, and Honorary Canon of Ely.*
  Spiritual Reading

Gerard J. Campbell, SJ, *Director of Woodstock Theological Center, Washington.*
  St Ignatius Loyola; *Spiritual Exercises*

Reginald Cant, *Canon Emeritus of York.* **Evelyn Underhill**

Patrick W. Carey, *Professor, Department of Theology, Marquette University.*
  Jonathan Edwards

John Carmody, *Adjunct Professor of Religion, Wichita State University.*
Vatican II Spirituality

Wesley Carr, *Canon Residentiary, Chelmsford Cathedral and Director of Training, Diocese of Chelmsford.* **Angels; The Devil**

Rex Chapman, *Canon Residentiary of Carlisle and Bishop's Adviser for Education.* **Faith; Hope; Humility**

Benoit Charlemagne, *Priest and Member of the Capuchin Order.* **Poverty**

K. W. Clements, *Tutor, Bristol Baptist College.* **Martin Buber**

Walter E. Conn, *Professor of Religious Studies, Villanova University.* **Conversion**

Adrian James Cooney, OCD, *Master of Novices, Marylake Monastery, Little Rock, Arkansas.* **Lawrence of the Resurrection**

Lawrence S. Cunningham, *Professor of Religion, Florida State University.* **Simone Weil**

J. G. Davies, *Edward Cadbury Professor and Head of the Department of Theology, and Director of the Institute for the Study of Worship and Religious Architecture, University of Birmingham.* **Dance**

J. H. Davies, *Postgraduate Student, Corpus Christi College, Cambridge.* **Nature Mysticism**

W. R. Davies, *Principal, Cliff College, Calver, Sheffield.* **Glossolalia; Pentecostalism**

Daniel DiDomizio, *Associate Professor of Theology, Marian College, Wisconsin.* **French Spirituality; Sexuality**

F. W. Dillistone, *Fellow Emeritus, Oriel College, Oxford.* **Imagery, Images**

Francis Dorff, O Praem, *Priest of Daylesford Abbey.* **Spiritual Journal**

Eric Doyle, OFM, *Lecturer in Theology, Franciscan Study Centre, Canterbury.* **St Francis of Assisi; Franciscan Spirituality, Franciscans**

Benjamin Drewery, *Bishop Fraser Senior Lecturer in Ecclesiastical History, University of Manchester.* **Grace; Origen; Tertullian**

Elizabeth Dreyer, *Assistant Professor, Department of Theology, Catholic University of America.* **St Bonaventure; The Cloud of Unknowing**

Eamon Duffy, *Tutor and Director of Studies in History, Magdalene College, Cambridge.* **Richard Challoner; George Fox; William Penn; Quaker Spirituality; Recusancy, Recusants**

James D. G. Dunn, *Professor of Divinity, University of Durham.* **Fruit of the Spirit; Gifts of the Spirit; Experience of Jesus; Pauline Spirituality; Peace; Holy Spirit**

Keith J. Egan, *Professor and Chairman, Department of Religious Studies, St Mary's College, Notre Dame, Indiana.* **Fire; Spiritual Ladder; Water**

Harvey D. Egan, SJ, *Associate Professor, Department of Theology, Boston College.* **Consolations, Desolations; Indifference**

Carlos M. N. Eire, *Assistant Professor of Historical Theology, University of Virginia.* **Ars Moriendi**

E. Rozanne Elder, *Director, Institute of Cistercian Studies, Western Michigan University, and Editorial Director, Cistercian Publications, Kalamazoo, Michigan.* **William of Saint-Thierry**

Trond Enger, *Senior Lecturer, Halden College of Education, Norway.* **Pietism**

Gillian Evans, *Fellow of Sidney Sussex College, Cambridge.* **Fulbert of Chartres**

Sydney H. Evans, *Dean of Salisbury Cathedral.* **Anglican Spirituality**

Robert Faricy, SJ, *Professor of Spiritual Theology, Gregorian University, Rome.*
  Teilhard de Chardin
John Ferguson, *President, Selly Oak Colleges, Birmingham.*
  Mohandas Karamachand Gandhi
Antony Flew, *Emeritus Professor of Philosophy, University of Reading.*
  Extra-Sensory Perception; Humanism
Kenelm Foster, OP, *Catholic Priest of the Order of Preachers.*
  St Catherine of Genoa; St Catherine of Siena
Matthew Fox, OP, *Professor of Spirituality and Culture, Holy Names College, California.* **Creation-Centred Spirituality; Meister Eckhart**
George E. Ganss, SJ, *Professor Emeritus of Spiritual Theology and Director of the Institute of Jesuit Sources, St Louis University.* **Society of Jesus**
A. Raymond George, *Warden of John Wesley's Chapel, Bristol.*
  Friedrich Heiler; Prophetic Prayer
Mark Gibbard, *Member of the Society of St John the Evangelist, Oxford.*
  Dag Hammarskjøld
Brian Golding, *Lecturer in History, University of Southampton.*
  Gilbert of Sempringham
N. W. Goodacre, *Spiritual Director, Spiritual Counsel Trust.*
  Spiritual Direction; Retreats; Silence; Reginald Somerset Ward
R. W. Gribben, *Ecumenical Lecturer at Lincoln Theological College.*
  Methodist Spirituality; John Wesley
W. Jardine Grisbrooke, *lately Lecturer in Liturgy successively at The Queen's College, Birmingham and St Mary's College, Oscott.* **Nonjurors**
Robert T. Handy, *Henry Sloane Coffin Professor of Church History, Union Theological Seminary, New York.* **Christian Science**
R. P. C. Hanson, *Professor Emeritus, University of Manchester.* **St Patrick**
Richard Harries, *Dean of King's College, London.* **Penitence**
Alan Harrison, *Secretary, The Advisory Council for Religious Communities.* **Exorcism**
Brian Hebblethwaite, *Fellow, Dean of Chapel and Director of Studies in Philosophy and in Theology and Religious Studies, Queens' College, Cambridge; University Lecturer in Divinity, Cambridge.* **Incarnation**
Charles C. Hefling, *Assistant Professor of Theology, Boston College.*
  Austin Marsden Farrer
Michael Hennell, *Canon Theologian of Manchester Cathedral.* **Evangelical Spirituality**
E. Glenn Hinson, *Professor of Religion, Wake Forest University, Winston-Salem.*
  American Spirituality
Michael Hollings, *Parish Priest, St Mary of the Angels, Bayswater, London.*
  Intercession; St Thérèse of Lisieux
J. L. Houlden, *Lecturer in New Testament Studies, King's College, London.*
  Spirituality of the Bible
Francis H. House, *formerly Archdeacon of Macclesfield.* **Impassibility; Curé d'Ars**
Edgar N. Jackson, *Professor, Union Graduate School.*
  Harry Emerson Fosdick; Norman Vincent Peale
M. J. Jackson, *Vicar of St Mary's, Nottingham.* **Rastafarianism**
Eric James, *Director of Christian Action.* **Holiness**
Penelope D. Johnson, *Assistant Professor of History, New York University.* **Catharism**

John D. Jones, *Assistant Professor, Department of Philosophy, Marquette University*. **Catharsis; Neoplatonism**

Owain W. Jones, *Archdeacon of Brecon*. **Welsh Spirituality**

Alistair Kee, *Reader in Religious Studies and Head of Department, University of Glasgow*. **Death of God; Radical Spirituality**

N. H. Keeble, *Lecturer in English, University of Stirling*.
Richard Baxter; John Bunyan; Puritan Spirituality

Kosuke Koyama, *Professor of Ecumenics and World Christianity, Union Theological Seminary, New York*. **Asian Spirituality**

A. J. Krailsheimer, *Fellow of Christ Church, Oxford*.
Jansenism; Blaise Pascal; Trappists

Una Kroll, *Community Medical Officer*. **Transcendental Meditation**

William S. Kurz, SJ, *Associate Professor of New Testament, Marquette University*.
Koinōnia

M. J. Langford, *Professor of Philosophy, Memorial University of Newfoundland*.
Friendship; Providence

Ernest E. Larkin, O Carm, *Lecturer and writer*. **Discernment of Spirits**

Symeon Lash, *Lecturer in Biblical and Patristic Studies, University of Newcastle-upon-Tyne*. **Orthodox Spirituality**

Jean Leclercq, OSB, *Benedictine monk of Clairvaux*.
Humour; Meditation, Mental Prayer

Kenneth Leech, *Race Relations Field Officer, Board for Social Responsibility of the Church of England*. **Drugs**

Joseph T. Lienhard, SJ, *Associate Professor of Theology, Marquette University*.
Manichaeism; *Regula Fidei*; Rules

A. Quentin Lister, OP, *Professor of Theology, Pontifical University of St Thomas Aquinas, Rome*. **The Charismatic Movement**

Andrew Lockley, *Assistant Secretary, The Law Society*. **Communes**

R. Stuart Louden, *Minister Emeritus of the Kirk of the Greyfriars, Edinburgh*.
Robert Leighton; Samuel Rutherford; Olive Wyon

Andrew Louth, *Fellow of Worcester College, Oxford*.
Beatitude; Denys the Areopagite; Gnosticism; Greek Spirituality; Mysticism

John Macquarrie, *Lady Margaret Professor of Divinity, University of Oxford*.
Adoration; Ave Maria; John Baillie; Benediction; Celtic Spirituality

Dominic Maruca, SJ, *Professor, Institute of Spirituality, Pontifical Gregorian University, Rome*. **Roman Catholic Spirituality**

E. Ann Matter, *Associate Professor of Religious Studies, University of Pennsylvania*.
Marian Devotion

Moelwyn Merchant, *Professor Emeritus, University of Exeter and Canon Emeritus, Salisbury Cathedral*. **Spirituality and the Arts; John Donne; T. S. Eliot; Poetry of Meditation**

Anthony Meredith, SJ, *Tutor in Theology, Campion Hall, Oxford*.
Cappadocian Fathers

Margaret R. Miles, *Associate Professor of Historical Theology, The Divinity School, Harvard University*. **Detachment; Mortification**

Guerin C. Montilus, *Associate Professor, College of Lifelong Learning, Wayne State University, Detroit*. **Black Spirituality**

John A. Newton, *Superintendent Minister of the West London Mission of the Methodist Church.* **Edward King**

Aidan Nichols, OP, *Roman Catholic Chaplain, University of Edinburgh.* **Iconography**

Oliver Nicholson, *Junior Fellow, Dumbarton Oaks, Washington DC.* **Platonism; Plotinus; Proclus**

Gerald O'Collins, SJ, *Professor of Fundamental Theology, Gregorian University, Rome.* **Second Journey**

Diarmuid O'Laoghaire, SJ, *Visiting Lecturer at Milltown Institute of Theology and Philosophy, Dublin.* **Irish Spirituality**

Martin Pable, OFM Cap, *Director of Novitiate, Province of St Joseph, USA.* **Celibacy**

Parker J. Palmer, *Professor of Religion, Pendle Hill Quaker Study Center, Pennsylvania.* **Thomas Merton**

Geoffrey Parrinder, *Emeritus Professor of Comparative Study of Religions, University of London.* **Buddhism; Hinduism; Islam; Koran; Sufism**

Joan Petersen, *formerly Editor, SPCK.* **St Gregory I**

Richard M. Peterson, *Lecturer, Department of Theology, Marquette University.* **Hagiography**

John S. Pobee, *Head of the Department for the Study of Religions, University of Ghana.* **African Spirituality**

Leslie Price, *formerly Editor, The Christian Parapsychologist.* **Spiritualism**

Rosemary Rader, *Assistant Professor, History of Christianity, Department of Religious Studies, Arizona State University.* **Asceticism**

A. Michael Ramsey, *formerly Archbishop of Canterbury.* **Glory; Thanksgiving; Transfiguration**

Marjorie E. Reeves, *Honorary Fellow of St Anne's College, Oxford.* **Flagellants; Joachim of Fiore**

Michael Richards, *Rector of St Mary's, Cadogan Street, London and Editor, The Clergy Review.* **Jacqes-Benigne Boussuet; Francois Fénelon; Jeanne-Marie Guyon**

Nancy C. Ring, *Assistant Professor of Systematic Theology, Weston School of Divinity, Cambridge, Massachusetts.* **Conformity to the Will of God; Feminine Spirituality;** *Fuga Mundi*

Robert C. Roberts, *Associate Professor of Philosophy, Western Kentucky University.* **Søren Kierkegaard**

Edwin Robertson, *Minister of Westbourne Park Baptist Church.* **St Bernadette of Lourdes; Dietrich Bonhoeffer; Focolare; Charles de Foucald; Jocists; John XXIII**

Brother Roger, *Prior of Taizé.* **Taizé**

W. Rordorf, *Professor of Patristics, Faculty of Theology, University of Neuchatel, Switzerland.* **Sunday**

Geoffrey Rowell, *Fellow, Chaplain and Tutor in Theology, Keble College, Oxford and Canon of Chichester Cathedral.* **St Antony of Egypt; Coptic Spirituality; Egypt; John Keble; John Mason Neale; The Oxford Movement; Edward Bouverie Pusey; Thomas Traherne**

Norman Russell, *Priest of the London Oratory.* **Pierre de Bérulle; St Charles Borromeo; St John Climacus; F. W. Faber; St Philip Neri; Oratorians**

Max Saint, *formerly Parish Priest.* **St Cyprian of Carthage**

Philip Scharper, *Editor-in-Chief and General Manager, Orbis Books, New York.*
Dom Helder Camara; Ernesto Cardenal; Spirituality of Liberation

Graham Slater, *Principal and Tutor in Theology, Hartley Victoria College, Manchester.* **Experience**

S. S. Smalley, *Canon Residentiary and Precentor of Coventry Cathedral.*
Johannine Spirituality

Martin L. Smith, *Assistant Superior, Society of St John the Evangelist, Cambridge, Massachusetts.* **Richard Meux Benson**

Placid Spearritt, *Monk of Ampleforth.* **Augustine Baker**

C. E. Stancliffe, *Honorary Lecturer, Department of Theology, Durham University.*
St Hilary of Poitiers; St Columbanus; St Jerome

David C. Steinmetz, *Professor of Church History, Duke University.*
***Devotio Moderna*; Jean Gerson**

Emmanuel Sullivan, SA, *Ecumenical Officer, RC Diocese of East Anglia.*
Ecumenical Spirituality

Donald K. Swearer, *Professor of Religion, Swarthmore College, Pennsylvania.* **Zen**

Colin P. Thompson, *University Chaplain and Lecturer in European Studies, University of Sussex.* **Carmelite Spirituality, Carmelites; St John of the Cross; *Spiritual Canticle*; St Theresa of Avila**

E. J. Tinsley, *Bishop of Bristol.* **Imitation of Christ; *Kenosis*; Thomas à Kempis**

Ralph Townsend, *Warden of The House of St Gregory and St Macrina, Oxford.*
The Caroline Divines; John Henry Newman

David Tripp, *Ecumenical Lecturer in Liturgy, Lincoln Theological College.*
Covenant; Fasting; Lent; Love-Feast; Martin Luther, Lutheranism; Prayer Meeting; *Theologia Germanica*

Geraint Tudur, *Minister of Ebeneser Congregational Church, Cardiff.*
Howell Harris

Simon Tugwell, OP, *Regent of Studies, Blackfriars, Oxford.*
Dominican Spirituality, Dominicans; St Thomas Aquinas

J. Munsey Turner, *Superintendent Minister, Halifax Methodist Circuit and formerly Lecturer in Church History, The Queen's College, Birmingham.*
Hymns; Charles Wesley

A. R. Vidler, *Honorary Fellow of King's College, Cambridge.*
Henri Bremond; Friedrich von Hügel; Henri Huvelin; William Temple

Esther De Waal, *Lecturer in History, Canterbury School of Ministry and Tutor, The Open University.* **Family Spirituality**

Geoffrey Wainwright, *Professor of Systematic Theology, The Divinity School, Duke University.* **Eschatology**

Gordon S. Wakefield, *Principal, The Queen's College, Birmingham.* **St Aelred of Rievaulx; Affective Spirituality; *The Ancrene Riwle*; Lancelot Andrewes; *Anima Christi*; Spiritual Biographies; Jakob Boehme; Sir Thomas Browne; John Calvin; Calvinist Spirituality; The Cambridge Platonists; Confession; The Cross; *Disciplina Arcani*; Discipline; Disinterested Love; Philip Doddridge; Ecclesiology and Spirituality; Ecstasy; The English Mystics; English Spirituality; Eucharist; John Everard; Familists; Nicholas Ferrar; Francis de Sales; George Herbert; Holy War; Gerard Manley Hopkins; Icons; Lay Spirituality; Liturgical Spirituality; Love; Martyrdom, Martyrs; Miguel de Molinos; Moravian Spirituality; St Gregory**

Palamas; Perfection; Pilgrimage; The Psalms; Quietism; Jan van Ruysbroeck; Sacramentalism; Sacred Heart; Sacred Humanity; Saints, Sanctity; William Edwin Sangster; The Song of Songs; Spirituality; The Victorines; Vision of God; Juan Luis Vives; Isaac Watts; Leslie Dixon Weatherhead; Alexander Whyte

Roland C. Walls, *Brother-in-charge, Ecumenical Community of the Transfiguration.* **Enthusiasm**

Benedicta Ward, SLG, *Tutor in Mediaeval History, Centre for Mediaeval and Renaissance Studies, Oxford.* **St Anselm of Canterbury; Carthusian Spirituality, Carthusians; John Cassian; Cistercian Spirituality, Cistercians; The Hours; Monastic Spirituality, Monasticism; Richard Rolle; Spiritual Marriage**

J. Neville Ward, *Supernumerary Minister, Canterbury and Faversham Circuit.* **Abandon; J.-P. de Caussade; Contemplation; The Lord's Prayer; Rosary**

Kallistos Ware, *Fellow of Pembroke College, Oxford.* **Accidie; *Apatheia*; *Apophthegmata*; *Hesychasm*; Name of Jesus; Prayer to Jesus; *Philokalia*; Prayer of the Heart**

Alan Webster, *Dean of St Paul's Cathedral.* **W. R. Inge; Julian of Norwich**

Gerhard Wehr, *Writer, and Lecturer at the Diakonenschule, Rummelsberg, Nuremberg.* **German Spirituality; Heinrich Suso; Johannes Tauler**

James A. Whyte, *Professor of Practical Theology and Christian Ethics, University of St Andrews.* **Scottish Spirituality**

L. R. Wickham, *Vicar of Honley with Brockholes.* **St Athanasius of Alexandria**

Rowan Williams, *Lecturer in Divinity, University of Cambridge.* **St Bernard of Clairvaux; Dark Night, Darkness; Deification; Desert, Desert Fathers; St Ignatius of Antioch; St Irenaeus of Lyons**

Stephen F. Winward, *Minister of Four Oaks Baptist Church, Sutton Coldfield.* **Baptist Spirituality**

Richard Woods, OP, *Graduate Faculty, Institute of Pastoral Studies, Loyola University of Chicago.* **Abnormal and Psycho-Physical Phenomena**

ABBREVIATIONS

ANCL   Ante-Nicene Christian Library, Edinburgh 1864–

DACL   *Dictionnaire d'Archeologie Chrétienne et de Liturgie*, 1903

DHGE   *Dictionnaire d'Histoire et de Geographie Ecclésiastiques* ed A. Johnson and others, 20 vols and index 1937, Supplement 1944

DS   *Dictionnaire de Spiritualité ascetique et mystique* ed M. Viller, SJ, and others, 1932

DTC   *Dictionnaire de Théologie Catholique* ed A. Vacant, E. Mangenot and E. Amann, 1903–50

EETS   Early English Text Society

ERE   *Encyclopaedia of Religion and Ethics* ed James Hastings, 1921–

ET   English Translation

ET   *Encyclopedia of Theology. The Concise Sacramentum Mundi* ed K. Rahner, 1975

JRS   *Journal of Religious Studies*

LCC   Library of Christian Classics, 1953–

ODCC   *Oxford Dictionary of the Christian Church* ed F. L. Cross and E. A. Livingstone, 1974

PG   *Patrologia Graeca* ed J. P. Migne, 1857–66

SC   Sources Chrétiennes, Paris 1941–

TDNT   *Theological Dictionary of the New Testament* tr and ed Geoffrey W. Bromiley, 1964–

* An asterisk following a word indicates a separate entry under that or a similar heading.

Abandon

This term was used by certain seventeenth-century French writers for the trusting acceptance of God's providence and the co-operation with him in obedience which together were seen as essential Christianity. It has a positive relation to the teaching of St Ignatius Loyola *, St Francis de Sales *, Bossuet *, and particularly J.-P. de Caussade *, in whose *L'Abandon à la Providence Divine* it is expounded. In de Caussade's teaching 'self-abandonment' does not refer primarily to the renunciation of self-will that is so frequently urged in traditional ascetic theology. He takes much of that for granted in his own characteristic view of spiritual life, which is that the entire universal process, with all the beauty and misery that it contains, is to be seen by faith as God's love in action. Our personal situation at any given moment, being part of this process, is accordingly also an expression of God's loving care. God has allowed it to happen as the appropriate context of our now doing his will (which may of course be that we co-operate with him in altering it). Christian life is a matter of accepting the present disposition of things as from the hands of a loving Father and actively co-operating with him in doing his will as this is variously signified. Lived in this way life will come to be seen as God's drawing us to himself with the innumerable cords of an infinitely diverse net of love. De Caussade taught that this will not normally result in dramatic holiness but in a simple fidelity to the claims and opportunities of daily experience, often without perception of God's presence or certainty of his grace. But when anyone arrives at a habit of 'abandonment' there develops a sensitive faith that, even in adverse turns of events, everything within oneself and one's circumstances is connected, and involved in God's continual drawing or urging us to himself. Since life often does not look at all as if it is this kind of thing it is not surprising that de Caussade recommended a contemplative form of prayer, a prayer of 'unknowing' faith, of simple waiting on God and of repeated self-offering. He warns that such prayer will often be dry and humiliating, and that this must be accepted without perturbation and introspective concern about the prayer's correctness or acceptableness. If it is persisted in it will become a prayer without ceasing, a morally continuous contemplation, subsisting in intention even when the mind is apparently fully absorbed in the day's work, in the onset of pain, or in the radiance of the happy hour, so that 'in whatever state we are asked to whom we wish to belong in the bottom of our hearts, we are always disposed to reply "to God"'.

Since God is present in every experience, signifying his will and offering the grace in which his will can be done, there is virtually no essential difference between one experience and another. Abandonment makes irrelevant our customary preferential evaluation of the pleasant over the unpleasant. De Caussade made much use of this 'indifference' in his counsel about the way to peace in perplexity. He also taught, however, that in the search for perfection the Christian will find that disappointments, indeed everything that frustrates the natural self, form opportunities for receiving from God that deserve special attention. Such experiences, seeming to indicate God's absence, form dramatically convincing evidences of his presence when negotiated by faith and are in themselves the most effective exercises in detachment and the refining of our love of God into the love of God himself and not his gifts. There is no reason in anyone's desiring special religious experiences, states of prayer or opportunities of service. The difficulties that normally come to people, as God's providential purpose unfolds in their circumstances, 'open to them a far surer and swifter path than extraordinary states and works'.

L'abandon is not to be confused with simple acceptance, much less with resignation. It is that giving of oneself to God in which one wishes to do his will whatever the situation and at the same time not only accepts the situation as the current context for this but actively wills it, as it were endorses it, since faith interprets it not as mere happening but as divine providence.

J. NEVILLE WARD

Abnormal and Psycho-Physical Phenomena

Biblical and extra-biblical literature describe forms of human experience which, while differing significantly from normal, ordinary experience, are not considered to be illusions or delusions. Such extraordinary or paranormal experience has traditionally been regarded by theologians and spiritual writers as arising from supernatural, preternatural or natural sources. Intrinsically supernatural phenoma (miracles) are those caused by God alone, operating through human agencies. Preternatural phenomena are attributed to non-divine but superhuman influences such as those of angels or demons. Natural but extraordinary phenomena are considered to be the result of human powers operating in unusual modes or intensity, whether held to be common to but usually inactive in all persons or present in only some.

Traditionally the place, importance and significance of supernatural and preternatural powers and experience have been treated systematically in mystical theology. Natural but extraordinary experience, if related to the spiritual life, would also fall under mystical theology. Since the end of the nineteenth century, these and related but non-religious experiences have also been studied increasingly by scientists and philosophers such as William James, Henri Bergson and C. D. Broad. Parapsychology and paraphysics are gaining recognition as branches of science which investigate paranormal or extraordinary human abilities and experience, especially in so far as they are subject to laboratory observation and experimentation. Psychical research refers more broadly to the experimental field and to on-site investigation into spontaneous manifestations of such phenomena.

Truly charismatic (intrinsically supernatural), preternatural, and paranormal phenomena take the same general form –

either quasi-sensory perception (knowledge) or unusual motor phenomena (activity). The contents or objects of such experience are variable.

1. *Quasi-sensory perception* (often less satisfactorily referred to as extra-sensory perception * or E S P) may be either mind-to-mind contact or mind-to-object contact. The former is referred to as telepathy and signifies communication without physical mediation across spatial and even temporal boundaries which ordinarily preclude such contact. Transtemporal communication can be either precognitive (knowledge of future events) or retrocognitive (knowledge of past events). Such information can be obtained in both waking and dreaming states. Present events may be known at a distance by quasi-sensory experience which is visual (clairvoyance), auditory (clairaudience), or tactile (clairsentience). Other forms of quasi-sensory experience involve smell, taste and temperature sensitivity. In general, any ordinary medium of sense experience, or several together, may be a vehicle for quasi-sensory perception. Quasi-sensory perception differs from ordinary perception in that the existence, presence or activity of the object of perception cannot be verified directly at the time and place by the subject or by an observer. If such verification is supplied later, the event can be said to be veridical.

Mind-to-object contact is usually described as psychometry and refers to obtaining information otherwise unknown by means of contact or proximity with a material object. Water-divining and other forms of dowsing or radiesthesia such as the ability to locate lost objects, stolen material, precious metals, etc., are common examples.

2. *Unusual motor phenomena.* The ability to affect the material environment without physical intervention is referred to as psychokinesis (P K) or telekinesis. Phenomena may be grouped under three classes: moving stationary objects, stopping objects in motion, and effects on living tissue, whether beneficial or destructive. Levitation refers to the elevation of one's own body or another material object from a stable surface against the force of gravity. Other quasi-motor activities include feats of unusual strength or endurance, speaking in foreign languages unknown to the speaker (xeno-

glossy and glossolalia*), physiological changes such as luminescence, stigmatization and other marks on the skin (dermatographia), insensitivity or imperviousness to pain or injury (impassibility)*, lengthy abstinence from all food or drink (inedia), and certain types of dissociation reactions or trance behaviour such as rapture, automatic writing, mediumship, etc. Poltergeist activity or recurrent spontaneous psychokinesis (RSPK) and obsession are now generally attributed to unconscious effects of psychic disturbance.

3. *Emotional effects.* A wide range of emotional reactions may result from, accompany or even precede paranormal experience. Joy and peace seem to pervade experiences felt to be positively religious. Noxious experiences, such as demonic apparitions, ghosts, etc., produce fear, loathing and horror. The quasi-sensory perception of information lacking emotional value seems to produce little or no reaction other than surprise or mild agitation. Recent studies of extraordinary experience suggest that a religious dimension, whether perceived as benign or malignant, is often a function of interpretation, the phenomena themselves being subject to a wide range of possible meanings. The meaning, value and even incidence of such experiences are closely related, if not sometimes reducible, to social pressures such as high expectation, stress and religious fervour, as was evident in the witchcraft mania of seventeenth-century Europe and New England, nineteenth-century revivalist experiences, war time apparitions, etc.

In the practical order it is difficult and sometimes impossible to discern true charisms from preternatural and natural but extraordinary human abilities and experiences. It has thus been the custom among Catholic, Orthodox and Protestant spiritual authorities to regard all such manifestations with utmost caution and, in effect, to discourage their cultivation and exhibition. In general, extraordinary phenomena are not considered integral to the spiritual life but probable by-products of intense psychophysiological adjustments incurred during the course of spiritual development, particularly in its more advanced stages. The ultimate test of such events when they do occur has been whether they, first, produce an increase of charitable service to and within the community, and, second, preserve doctrinal integrity – negatively, in the absence of manifest departures from the essential beliefs of the community, and positively in authentic teaching and prophetic activity, especially the promotion of social justice.

E. Arbman, *Ecstasy or Religious Trance*, 3 vols, 1963–1970; R. Haynes, *The Hidden Springs*, 1973; E. Mitchell, *Psychic Exploration*, 1974; H. Thurston, *The Physical Phenomena of Mysticism*, 1952; A. Wiesinger, *Occult Phenomena in the Light of Theology*, 1957.

RICHARD WOODS, OP

Accidie

A term (Greek *akēdia*) signifying weariness, sloth, listlessness. It is first used as a technical term in Christian spirituality by Evagrius of Pontus, who listed it among the eight evil 'thoughts' (*Practicus* 12); St Gregory the Great* subsequently included it among the seven deadly sins (*Moralia* xxxi, 87, where it is termed *tristitia*, 'sadness'). Classic descriptions of accidie may be found in St John Cassian*, *Institutes*, Book 10, and in St John Climacus*, *Ladder* 13; for a mediaeval Western treatment, see St Thomas Aquinas, *Summa Theologiae*, II^a II^{ae}, q. 35. A form of ennui and apathy, it is the particular temptation of hermits rather than of monks in community. Since its attacks are most severe during the heat in the middle of the day, it is identified by Evagrius with the 'noonday demon' of Ps. 91.6 (90.6 Septuagint and Vulgate); he calls it 'the heaviest of all the demons'. It makes the monk restless, unable to concentrate on either work or prayer, and in an extreme form fills him with a longing to abandon the monastic life altogether. The virtue opposed to accidie is *hypomonē*, patient endurance or perseverance; the best weapons against it are manual labour, remembrance of death, and assiduous prayer.

A. and C. Guillaumont, *Evagré le Pontique: Traité Pratique ou Le Moine* (SC, 170–1), 1971, I, pp. 84–90, II, pp. 520–7; S. Wenzel, *The Sin of Sloth: Acedia in Mediaeval Thought and Literature*, 1967.

KALLISTOS WARE

Adoration *see* **Prayer (1) Adoration**

Aelred of Rievaulx, St

Very much in the tradition of Bernard of Clairvaux * and William of Thierry *, Aelred (or Ailred, 1109–1167) was born into the family of a Saxon priest at Hexham and spent much of his early youth at the court of King David of Scotland, where he entered into Norman culture. He was the official biographer of Edward the Confessor, and became Abbot of the Cistercian Rievaulx in 1147. He was a renowned spiritual writer, who is sometimes included among the English Mystics *. His works owe much to the *Confessions* and other writings of Augustine and are full of the passionate intensity of Bernard. He had something of a genius for friendship, and his conversion seems to have been to the love of God from a possibly inordinate earthly attachment and the fear of parting. His interpretation of the monastic rule is severe, but only because he wants monks to be set free for the divine charity. He was a scholar in the style of his day and burrowed in scripture and the Fathers to collect and develop themes, notably that of the Sabbath. There is much in Aelred's *The Mirror of Love*, I, 8 that is reminiscent of Abelard's hymn *O quanta qualia*; and it all starts from Augustine's *De Genesi ad litteram*. Aelred is not only more systematic than many contemporary and previous expositors; he identifies the sabbath rest with the entry into the love of the Father and the Son which is the peace promised in the Fourth Gospel.

Although he seeks to sublimate 'carnal concupiscence' by directing affections to the attractions of the Lord's flesh (and has a devotion to the childhood of Christ and is a precursor of those whose meditations enable them to be present as if in the body at each recorded event in the life of the Redeemer), he cannot escape the sheer delight of human friendship. No one more lyrically celebrates its joys and consolations, and his treatise on *Spiritual Friendship* is his *chef d'oeuvre*, a searching exploration by means of dialogue. It owes much to Cicero, and Aelred is never able to dismiss pagan philosophers as altogether vain – but it is theologically most remarkable in that it unites the discourses of the Fourth Gospel about *philia* with the mystical interpretation of the Song of Songs *. He writes of the spiritual kiss, 'given not by the touch of the mouth but by the affection of the heart', so that Christ himself kisses us in the love of our friends. Aelred's is indeed a spirituality of friendship, for friendship is the gift of God and the way to God. From the holy love with which we embrace our friend, we rise to the embrace of Christ. There is no eroticism in Aelred. We read him with none of the distaste with which Samuel Rutherford * may sometimes affect us. There is much here that our sex-obsessed age, which has gone far to making friendship impossible, needs to re-learn. It clearly comes from Aelred's own experience and spiritual struggles and shows how for him in the end *philia* triumphs over all.

See also **Friendship.**

Aelred, *De Spirituali Amica: Christian Friendship*, 1942; Eric Colledge, *The Medieval Mystics of England*, 1962; Charles Smyth, *The Friendship of Christ*, 1945, 1968; Aelred Squire, OP, *Aelred of Rievaulx: A Study*, 1969.

EDITOR

Affective Spirituality

This is the term used for the type or stage of devotion in which the feelings are not subdued, but love is directed towards God who inspires it by his own tenderness and regard for us in the humanity and passion of Jesus. It is the prayer taught by Bernard of Clairvaux *, and evidenced in the Franciscans *, the English Mystics * such as Julian of Norwich * and which is especially evident in the seventeenth-century. The English Puritans * furnish examples, though they used the adjective 'affectionate'. Augustine Baker * in *Holy Wisdom* writes of 'affective acts of the will' and the prayer is delivered from sentimentality by ascetic discipline and by the fact that in the truest Catholic spirituality it is not so much a 'falling in love with Jesus' at the outset of the Christian life as 'the mature devotion of the advancing soul. Catholic writers see it as the stage towards contemplation which succeeds mental prayer, in which the mind is not in absolute, tyrannical control, and words are few. It is the 'prayer of simple regard', of 'loving attention'. But it is not a prayer simply for non-intellectuals, or for those weary of thought. Martin Thornton has claimed an 'affective-speculative synthesis' as the clue to the understanding of English spirituality * and quotes C. C. J. Webb on Anselm * –

'No one has ever more strikingly shown how the disinterested search for metaphysical truth can be offered in the service of passionate devotion to God'.

Augustine Baker, *Holy Wisdom*, 1972; F. P. Harton, *Elements of the Spiritual Life*, 1931; Martin Thornton, *English Spirituality*, 1963.

EDITOR

African Spirituality

It is difficult to give a neat description of African spirituality for at least four reasons.

1. The problem of sources. In a largely illiterate continent, multiple traditions circulate orally and universal access to them is well-nigh impossible. There is considerable oral theology to be gathered and analysed. What is written down is often written from the viewpoint of the foreigner, the missionary, the Mission Home Board, etc. Church history needs yet to be written from the viewpoint of Africans, especially from the viewpoint of the African catechist who has been in the vanguard of mission.

2. The North Atlantic captivity of the African churches in the sense that African churches, having been evangelized from the North Atlantic, have been moulded by the traditions, norms, practices and usages of those parts, especially when the missionary doctrine of *tabula rasa* reigned supreme. The African churches reflect their Western origins *vis-à-vis* organization, polity, worship, discipline and even their ethos. Thus Roman Catholic and Protestant spiritualities of the North Atlantic are still evident in Africa. Liturgies, spiritual readings, theologies, music, etc. still have large components from the North Atlantic. The Book of Common Prayer of the Church of England is still used by Anglicans in Africa. In the Roman Catholic Church the Mass of the Roman Rite continues to be celebrated. Even when these have been translated into the vernacular, they are often sung to the Gregorian chant or German Airs, producing very incongruous pieces. The Lutherans hold on to *Confessio Augustana* and discuss political theology in terms of Luther's two kingdoms theology. African churches start with an assumed definition of Christianity. Even the Independent African Churches which represent, at least in part, a protest against the North Atlantic captivity of the church, retain North Atlantic and South European forms and usages. Thus the ecclesiastical titles of Metropolitan, Patriarch and Archbishop are not uncommon. Sartorial elegance of North Atlantic provenance is assumed by these churches without embarrassment.

3. The problem of the complex and elusive concept of Africanness. Africa, a large continent, takes 'all sorts and conditions of men', e.g. Caucasians such as the Afrikaaners and English who since 1652 and 1820 respectively have known no other home than Africa; Arabs, Aboriginal Bushmen, Berbers, Negroes, Hamites. Native Africans themselves bear the ineradicable marks of foreign influences such as Western culture, Christianity, Islam, etc., resulting to a certain degree in a crisis of identity. For all the diversities and uncertainties and the crisis of identity attaching to *homo africanus*, certain things are still characteristic of him: a religious ontology and epistemology, a sense of finitude which stands parallel to a sense of the omnipresence of mystery, communalism and extensive ceremonialism. These elements in one way or another inform the spirituality of *homo africanus*.

4. Various Christian traditions are represented in Africa. The two broad divisions of the Eastern or Greek Church and the Western or Latin Church are found. The Latin Church itself is further sub-divided into the Roman Catholic and Protestant Churches, the latter in an infinite variety. Each of these has its own type of spirituality, often with considerable influences from the North Atlantic.

Spirituality may be understood as 'the personal relation of man to God' (Sudbrack), the ways in which Africans appropriate – body, soul and mind – the salvific mission of Christ. Given the diversity of Africanness and the diversity of Christian traditions, we can only expect to find African spiritualities, in the plural.

A survey of some concrete historical problems on the African continent can assist in delineating African spirituality.

The historic churches have stressed rationality in religious life. Thus the 'spiritual' goes with what is intellectual. The intellectualization of Christianity is shown not only by the tomes of theological treatises and books to which theological students and the faithful are subjected in order to be adjudged worthy spokesmen of the church; but also by the insistence on the creeds as plumblines of orthodoxy. Discourse rather than dialogue becomes the mode of transmitting the traditions of the church. Thus the Christianity of the historic churches in Africa has tended to be an intellectual process compatible with 'mysticism of the obscure' and leading to 'esoteric "watering-down" of the spiritual' (Sudbrack).

In the predominantly illiterate and relatively technologically simple societies of Africa where religion is more danced out than thought out, heavy intellectual theology wears thin. Such rationalization and theologizing as there are come after experience. Consequently, at all levels in African churches there is rarely commitment to theology and theological education. Dialogue is preferred to discourse. The lyric is deeply appreciated, especially in the Methodist tradition, because it makes possible dialogue and because it is less of monologue. The lyric represents the fullest devotional expression of Christian worship in song which nourishes and sustains piety among the Africans. Similarly, the Independent African Churches characteristically celebrate rather than cerebrate the faith. Hence the stress on the irrational element in religion and the tendency to exaggerate the emotional nature of man, stressing commitment and free unanalysable acts. Thus African spirituality stresses the incalculable role of the individual and of commitment, action rather than reflection.

African mysticism, whether in traditional or Christian religion, is an experience of the divine while one remains on earth. African spirituality searches for deliverance capable of transforming one's terrestrial condition.

The historic churches from their North Atlantic origins deify individualism. God's challenge goes primarily to the individual; a person responds primarily as an individual. A person is saved as an individual. It is as an individual that a person affirms the baptismal creed. Luther and African Lutherans, for example, stressing the irreplaceable individuality of the believer, highlight personal conscience and direct approach to Jesus Christ through recourse to scripture.

Individualism has affected even the Independent African churches. The theology of direct access to God and the accessibility of the Bible to every individual so characteristic of the Protestant tradition has induced the fissiparous nature of these churches. Rather than an accredited priest opening up the scripture, an unknown quantity from nowhere just arises to expound the Bible and to start a church even without much formal training. Thus the individualism inherited from the Protestant churches in particular has been appropriated by the sects and is an element in the fissiparous nature of the sects. It is this that in part accounts for the fact that sects are not common in Roman Catholicism and high church Anglicanism where individualism is secondary and ritualism answers the emotional needs of iconic sacramental societies such as are in Africa.

The foregoing is only part of the picture. For there is evidence of dissatisfaction with individualism by Africans. African spirituality, starting from the traditional African epistemology which may be summarized as *cognatus sum, ergo sum*, i.e. I am because I am related by blood, stresses a sense of belonging. In the traditional African society the mystical life does not separate the individual from the community; rather it permits him to realize himself more fully in his daily life. This has been reflected in African Christianity. Three examples should suffice. 1. The funeral culture that has developed in Africa. People will give up everything for days and weeks so as to be present at the funeral, especially the Christian burial service of a relative, a friend or colleague in the office with whom they may not have had much contact. The Christian burial service becomes the focus for the expression of the sense of community. The community includes the dead in addition to the living. 2. The concept of the priest. In a village a Christian priest or minister is not just an officiant and mediator but a kind of lineage head, to whom both spiritual and secular problems are brought for advice and resolution. He is a type of community head, a general factotum. 3. The case of migrants to the cities. They often do not feel at home in the urban parish. So until they get established in the city, they attach themselves to a sectarian priest in a church. The congregation becomes the surrogate religious kinship group and the priest the head of the kinship group.

However, there is a certain ambiguity about this sense of belonging. Where it proves expensive and demanding materially, people are negative in their attitude to it. But where it cushions people against shocks and dehumanizing circumstances, it is most welcome.

Inherited Christian spirituality has a certain dualism which reflects the Pauline tension between spirit and flesh, e.g. II Cor. 2.6; 8.7. The spiritual arena is purified of all material concerns. This is reinforced by traditional African epistemology in which the soul represents permanence and continuity while the body represents change and decay. Consequently, there is a tendency to think the clergymen should live on next to nothing. A clergyman who shows interest in property is thought to be worldly and unspiritual. It is an affront to talk of a church making investments. In politics as in business it is often said 'keep religion out of politics and economics'. Politics and economics are said to be profane areas which are not for religious people. That is a dualistic heresy which denies the sovereignty of God over all life, though this attitude reflects a garbled version of eighteenth-century pietism.

However, alongside that dualism stands another tradition in which the sacred and the secular flow readily into each other as in the Bible and in traditional African culture where the borders of the sacred are much broader than in Western society. In the sectarian Musama Disco Christo Church, as in some historic churches, a menstruating woman is not to attend church. Christians persistently go back to native herbalists for healing because in their indigenous traditions there is nothing like unconsecrated medicine. Thus they find no satisfaction in the professional Western medical practice that leaves out references to the spiritual. In any case, many African Christians, as in biblical times, believe in spiritual forces behind any ailment, an idea which the Independent African Churches accept to their credit and advantage. Here, then, is the influence of traditional African culture in which a person merges with the world, seeing a religious dimension in everything. 'The essence of African spirituality lives in the feeling man has of being at once image, model and integral part of a world in whose cyclical life he senses himself deeply and necessarily engaged' (Zahan).

African Christian spirituality is very much Old Testament in texture and orientation. The values of family, hospitality and corporate personality are similar. Old Testament imagery and symbolism are appropriated and much appreciated. The exodus motif, for example, is much in use, especially when liberation and salvation are discussed. The Jerusalem or holy city motif is common in African songs to signify the hope of ultimate salvation. African Christianity, for partly the same reason, is very much legalistic in approach, following Jewish legalism.

African spirituality emphasizes joy. The sacred dance, which is a feature of many an Independent Church, is an attempt to express this joy in the Lord. The sombreness of the practices of the historic churches was precisely the problem for many Africans and led to schisms searching for satisfaction. The new music in African churches has taken on traditional African melodies and set them to Christian words to express uplifting and joyful music. The note of joy is seen as an outward sign of divine possession.

In African Christianity there is a focusing on the holy man. This is part of the sense of belonging, in which the minister of religion became lineage head, the protector and defender of the members of the group both physically and spiritually. The focus here is on the peculiar African creation of the catechist who is the unsung hero of African Church history. He was often a teacher or a lesser mortal who prepared the ground for the missionary or priest, nursed the congregation, won souls for the church and stayed with the people at the grassroots. He was the holy man on whom the Christian community was focused.

One of the most striking features of the African Church is the emergence of Independent African Churches and charismatic movements in the historic churches. The Independent African Churches are varied species in a single genre. Their varied names indicate their various emphases. Independent African Churches, Ethiopianist Churches, Pentecostal Movements, Spiritual Churches, Witchcraft Eradication Movements, Messianic Movements, Zionist Movements, Prophetic Movements, Separatist Movements and Syncretistic Movements. Common to all of these is an experiential supernaturalism which seeks for and believes in the promise of Christ to send his

Spirit. That is natural in a world which is full of spirits, having a religious ontology and epistemology. To that extent, the phenomenon is a protest against the historic churches' tendency to turn every manifestation of the Spirit into an official institution, equating every institution with charisma and further equating laws and institutions with spirituality. The leader and founder of the F'Eden Church of Ghana complains of the manifest 'lack of power', the sign of the presence of the Holy Spirit in the Presbyterian Church of Ghana and other historic churches. Some of them are a response to the endemic and chronic fear of evil spirits. All evil is in traditional society attributed to personal forces of evil. Consequently, religion is expected to offer protection against mishap which the Witchcraft Eradication Movements promise to do through exorcism. Furthermore, witchcraft belief reflects tensions within kin-groups. Therefore, the pilgrimage from the kin-group to the church is seen as the search for a new home where protection is offered against the evil machinations of members of one's own family. Finally, some of these Independent Movements are political movements donning religion. In Southern Africa where blacks are oppressed, the Zionist, Ethiopianist and Messianic movements have come into their own as escape routes and the hope of freedom. In these churches the Jerusalem motif is very strong. The present affliction makes them stress eschatological salvation and sometimes political liberation.

The phenomenon of the emphasis on the Spirit suggests that the African Churches have isolated the third person of the Trinity as the focus of religion, more so than Christ. Christ is ascended and now the Spirit is working. His work is in some sense continuous with the operation of spirits in traditional society.

These Independent African Churches are more commonly breakaways from the more Evangelical wing of Christianity, especially Protestantism. As was suggested above, it is in part the result of the theology of direct access to God. But there is the additional reason that Protestantism is too verbal and abstract for many in the iconic, sacramental culture of African societies. The ritualism of the sects then represents not only a protest against too much verbalism and abstraction but also an attempt to realize themselves as

active sacramental and iconic communities.

Christian spirituality in Africa represents a spectrum of traditions and the amalgam of biblical Christianity which is itself very semitic, Greek tradition, European and American traditions and African element. The culturing of Christianity in African soil has begun but is yet to come to fruition, especially in the historic churches.

See also **Black Spirituality.**

C. G. Baeta, *Prophetism in Ghana*, 1962; *Christianity in Tropical Africa*, 1968; D. Barrett, *Schism and Renewal in Africa*, 1968; (ed), *African Initiatives in Religion*, 1971; D. M. Beckmann, *Eden Revival Church*, 1975; Ram Desai, *Christianity in Africa as Seen by Africans*, 1962; A. Hastings, *Church and Mission in Modern Africa*, 1967; E. Fash-ole-Luke et al, *Christianity in Independent Africa*, 1978; J. S. Pobee, *Religion in a Pluralistic Society*, 1977; *Toward an African Theology*, 1979; H. S. Sawyerr, *Creative Evangelism*, 1967, A. Shorter, *African Christian Spirituality*, 1978; J. Sudbrack, 'Spirituality' in *Encylopaedia of Theology*, 1975; J. V. Taylor, *The Primal Vision*, 1963; D. Zahan, *The Religion, Spirituality and Thought of Traditional Africa*, 1979.

J. S. POBEE

Agape *see* Love-Feast

Alacoque, St Marguerite-Marie
see Sacred Heart

Albigenses *see* Catharism

Altizer, Thomas *see* Death of God

American Spirituality

American spirituality is an amalgam of elements imported from Europe blended with elements native to the American scene. Protestant and Catholic features have not yet congealed, but major church types – Mainline Protestant, Evangelical Protestant, Roman Catholic, Anglican and Orthodox – no longer exhibit clear dividing lines. General characteristics are:

1. *Diversity.* Protestant spirituality has exhibited diversity from the beginning; the American context has heightened this. Anglican, Roman Catholic and even Orthodox spiritualities, too, have evidenced the effects of a highly pluralistic culture, though their

anchorage in tradition has offset these to a considerable degree. Ecumenical engagement, in the meantime, appears to be producing a renewed appreciation of both traditional spiritualities and variety.

2. *Fluidity*. Accelerated change in modern technological society, pluralism and the modern ecumenical movement keep spirituality in constant flux. Among college students interest in mystical experience, whether Eastern or Western, is high. At the same time there is a return to traditional spiritualities.

3. *Individualism – corporatism*. Protestant spirituality in America has been highly individualistic, but this is changing. In the classical Protestant view the Spirit works directly through the individual will to effect obedience; thus there is less need for sacraments, priests, confessionals and other means. Since the Second Vatican Council*, however, both Protestants and Catholics have been shifting. As Catholics have moved towards the individualist end of the scale, Protestants have moved towards the corporatist. Accordingly, many now seek spiritual direction, speak favourably of formation, express appreciation for liturgical spirituality, employ means for spiritual growth and make retreats in monasteries or retreat centres operated by Catholic or Episcopal religious.

4. *Cognitive – Affective*. Inclined from the beginning towards cultivation of cognitive faculties through Bible reading, sermons and mental prayer, Protestant spirituality has struggled to find ways to develop affective faculties. Music and individual fervour in worship have supplied the chief means for this, as 'awakenings' have heightened affective concerns. Recently, however, American Protestants have rekindled interest in liturgical and sacramental spirituality as a way to achieve a better balance.

5. *Personal – Social*. Always highly personalistic and individualistic, American spirituality has gradually taken on greater social sensitivity. American saints of recent memory, for instance, would include Martin Luther King, Jr, the black Civil Rights leader martyred in 1968. During the turbulent 1960s, hymns and prayers as well as sermons and treatises assumed a strong social stance.

In the current ecumenical milieu, traditional assumptions underlying American spirituality require re-examination. 1. Should the accent be placed on justification or on sanctification? Except for Methodists or groups emerging from the same tradition, Protestants have emphasized the former, Anglicans and Roman Catholics the latter. Fearful of manipulation of individuals by ecclesiastical authorities, Protestants have interpreted justification in forensic terms as acquittal of the sinner by the merciful God and contested the Catholic emphasis on the power of the indwelling Spirit to transform and mould lives. With limited concern for sanctification, Protestant spirituality has tended to leave many in spiritual infancy. 2. Is grace to be understood as God's unmerited favour (the Protestant view) or as the power of the Spirit infused into the soul (the Catholic view)? Exclusion of the latter from Protestant spirituality has encouraged what Bonhoeffer called 'cheap grace', divine forgiveness without corresponding demand. 3. Are there different levels of saint-hood? Protestants have gone to great lengths to point out that the apostle Paul applied the word 'saint' to all Christians, and they have criticized the singling out of some as models of saintliness. The result is a reduction of Christian discipleship to a single level and superficial spirituality.

Diversity appeared early, for, while the Puritans controlled the New England colonies and Anglicans the South, the Middle colonies (New York, New Jersey, Pennsylvania and Delaware) had no numerically dominant group, consisting of Quakers, Baptists, Reformed, Presbyterians, Lutherans and numerous others. Alongside the more socially conscious spirituality of Puritans and Anglicans, therefore, there existed a more privatized piety of minority and non-conformist groups. Whereas Puritans and Anglicans laid down laws which would assure a devout citizenry or a holy commonwealth, non-conformist groups counted more heavily on enhancement of individual piety through gathering of the church or in family and individual devotion. The Friends or Quakers*, deserving of the label of 'Protestant contemplatives,' composed numerous treatises on spirituality. William Penn's* *No Cross, No Crown*, written during his imprisonment in the Tower of London in 1669, became a recognized classic of devotion in America.

The 'Great Awakening' (1730–1760) opened a new chapter in the history of American spirituality. Interrupting a period of religious indifference and decline, it challenged the deadening orthodoxy and orthopraxy of the day first in New Jersey among Dutch Reformed and Presbyterians and then in New England among Congregationalists. Subsequently throughout the thirteen colonies nearly every denomination experienced its effects in the form of conversions, renewal of commitment, recovery of vitality in church life, increased vigour in preaching, and expanded membership and participation. Not all approved the new style, but those who did shifted the accent from the orderly but subdued spirituality of their forbears to a spirituality stressing 'religious affections'. Jonathan Edwards *, pastor of the Congregationalist Church in Northampton, Massachusetts, set the tone for this with the publication of *A Faithful Narrative of the Surprising Work of God* (1937), *The Diary of David Brainerd* (1743) and *A Treatise on Religious Affections* (1746). In the second Edwards nominated Brainerd, a missionary to the Delaware Indians who literally threw away his life at the age of twenty-seven (1715–1742), as the American saint *par excellence*. In his very personal account of 'the surprising work of God' Brainerd united Puritan discipline and fervent evangelical experience with missionary zeal. This combination of qualities, meanwhile, gained near-canonical status as Moravian missionaries injected elements of German Pietism and the Wesleys and George Whitefield imported their holiness campaign. What the martyr and monk had been to Europe in the Middle Ages, the fervent-hearted missionary or evangelist became to America in the eighteenth and nineteenth centuries.

The chief variation on this spirituality would have been found among the Quakers, who continued to combine a contemplative piety with social action. Their model was John Woolman (1720–1772), whose quiet but revolutionary efforts against slavery and on behalf of the poor and oppressed anticipated modern concern by a couple of centuries. After 1787 no American Quaker owned a slave.

The American Revolution (1776–1781) and the frontier advanced further the varied, individualistic and experientialistic features of American spirituality. On the frontier, revivals characterized by fiery and emotional preaching, candid testimonies and experiential conversions handed on the stereotype developed in the Awakening. The experiential emphasis, fanned by the winds of the Enlightenment, touched even the more erudite and cultured segments of American population in the form of New England transcendentalism, represented by such noted literary figures as Orestes Brownson and John Greenleaf Whittier (1807–1892). Transcendentalism fostered a kind of nature mysticism.

Even in the frontier era, however, not all American spirituality fitted the individualistic mould. Numerous communitarian movements such as the Shakers, migrating from England in 1774, or the Amana Society, coming from Germany in 1842, openly rejected American individualism and opted for a disciplined and monastic spirituality featuring a combination of work and prayer similar to that of the Benedictine tradition. Most of these were also millenarian and declined as expectations of the immediate return of Jesus to earth faded. They never attracted a large following either.

American spirituality, nevertheless, did take on a stronger social consciousness during the post-Civil War era as the nation gradually industrialized and urbanized. Though individualistic piety, meshing well with the Enlightenment conviction that religion should be restricted to the private sphere, remained dominant, it revealed its weaknesses and inadequacies in 'those dark, satanic mills' and 'Hell's kitchens' of metropolis. On behalf of this 'social awakening' Charles M. Sheldon portrayed a different kind of saint, one who would ask, 'What would Jesus do?' and then follow *In His Steps*, the title of Sheldon's classic. Leaders such as Walter Rauschenbusch and Washington Gladden composed prayers and hymns for the social awakening, Gladden's 'Where Cross the Crowded Ways of Life' making a deep impression on the American religious conscience. A convert from Methodism, Father Isaac Hecker (1819–1888), meanwhile founded the Paulists, a missionary order devoted wholly to the service of Catholic immigrants streaming into the country.

Two other movements essentially concerned with spirituality, the Holiness and the Pentecostal*, emerged almost simultaneously with the social gospel movement. Though both rooted chiefly in Methodism and John Wesley's concern for sanctification, they went in opposite directions. The Holiness movement stressed discipline, the Pentecostal movement experience of the Spirit through tongue-speaking. They drew their constituency chiefly from the 'blue-collar' class which felt Methodism had left them behind culturally.

Two world wars, a depression, 'police action' in Korea and Vietnam, and rapid transition from a rural to an urban society impacted heavily on American spirituality in the twentieth century. As Protestant spirituality again bared its weaknesses in the face of these crises, new emphases appeared. Secular spirituality, responding to musings of Dietrich Bonhoeffer* (1906–1945), sought to bridge the gap between sacred and secular by way of a 'worldly holiness'. Since God is not 'out there', but 'the "Beyond" in the midst of our lives', we must meet him where he is at work in the secular city. To pray is to 'be with' people in friendship and service, to be 'the man for others'. Charismatic* spirituality, ascending the socio-economic ladder several rungs beyond Pentecostalism, headed in the opposite direction as it offered an alternative to formalistic and rationalistic religion. Quasi-oriental spirituality, attracting college youth especially, imported Eastern methods of meditation – Zen*, Transcendental Meditation*, Yoga* – which many hoped would ameliorate the dehumanizing and depersonalizing tendencies of Western science and technology. Traditional spirituality, especially of mediaeval variety, meantime recovered its appeal as the ecumenical movement blossomed anew during and after the Second Vatican Council. Protestants and Catholics alike acclaimed the writings of Bonhoeffer and Teilhard de Chardin*, Merton* and Martin Luther King, Jr, as their own.

Sydney E. Ahlstrom, *A Religious History of the American People*, 1972; Robert T. Handy, *A History of the Churches in the United States and Canada*, 1977; William G. McGloughlin, *Revivals, Awakenings, and Reform*, 1978.

E. GLENN HINSON

Ancrene Riwle, The

A rule for anchoresses or recluses which was written in the early thirteenth century, when such were a part of society and their lives not without the temptations of the professionally religious. There is indication that the *Riwle* may represent the English manifestation of a European women's movement of affective spirituality*.

The *Riwle* is not a mystical treatise but sets down principles of guidance for the solitary life in which mysticism would flower. It is vivid, witty, realistic and practical. It is divided into eight sections: 1. On Devotional Exercises; 2. On the Government of the Senses in keeping the Heart; 3. Moral lessons and examples; 4. Temptations and the means to avoid them; 5. On Confession; 6. On Penance and Amendment; 7. On Love or Charity; 8. On Domestic and Social Duties.

The rules are humane and proportioned. There is to be no excess of austerity or flagellation, but there are warnings against gossip and idle chatter ('cackling'). There is an interesting treatment of the seven deadly sins, which are compared to animals, which also have their whelps. Accidie* has eight of these – torpor, faintheartedness, dullness of heart, idleness, grudging and grumbling, sorrow for anything except sin, negligence, despair. The unknown author well understands that the solitary life may become more difficult as time passes and that God tests us more as we advance into holiness; yet 'in the end cometh great joy'. Love is the fulfilling of the law and the counsels of sisterly affection are written with gentle firmness. 'When you are united, the fiend cannot harm you . . . And if the fiend blow up any resentment between you, which may Jesus Christ forbid, until it is appeased none ought to receive Christ's flesh and blood . . . But let each send word to the other that she hath humbly asked her forgiveness as if she were present.'

M. Day, *The Ancrene Riwle* (EETS, orig series 225); M. B. Salu, *The Ancrene Riwle* (tr mod Eng), 1955.

EDITOR

Andrewes, Lancelot

Of the Puritan persuasion in early years, Andrewes (1555–1626) became both in his own lifetime and in his subsequent reputation the embodiment of all that was best and most beautiful in the spirituality of the English Church. Apologist for King James I against Cardinal Bellarmine, he was also a vigorous anti-Calvinist. Frequently preferred by royal favour, his holiness was not immune from an interest in rich revenues. He enjoyed great reputation as a preacher, his style, with its word-plays, linguistic elegance and conceits, totally different from Puritan plainness and perspicuity, though he has homely and humorous touches. He had great influence on T. S. Eliot*, whose 'Journey of the Magi', begins with a quotation from one of his sermons. His *Preces Privatae*, prepared for his own personal use and not published until 1648, provide daily devotions and are enriched with allusions and quotations from scripture and the Greek Fathers and liturgies. They are a chain woven of short sentences. In his chapel he used incense, altar-lights and the mixed chalice. He had in full measure the genius of his age in making prayer a lifting up of the mind to God, while never neglectful of compassionate pleading for the world.

See also **Caroline Divines, The**.

F. E. Brightman (ed), *Preces Privatae*, 1903; T. S. Eliot, *For Lancelot Andrewes. Essays on Style and Order*, 1928, pp. 13–32; J. P. Wilson and J. Bliss (eds), *Works* (Library of Anglo-Catholic Theology), 11 vols, 1841–1854.

EDITOR

Angels

The word means 'messenger'. In the Bible and later Jewish and Christian traditions angels are the messengers and agents of God. After the exile there is a sudden and not wholly explained development in Jewish thinking about angels. It appears that a new awareness of God's transcendence issued in a felt need for a system of intermediaries between God and man and an emphasis upon God's majesty, which is affirmed by the myriads of angels who worship him. Certain mighty figures, later known as archangels, appear in Daniel and the apocryphal books, and the process of naming the angels begins. A confusing variety of functions and names is found which is nowhere systematized, probably because angels were important in popular devotion. Generally,

however, angels worship God, bring messages to men and intercede for man with God. The vision of Isaiah (Isa. 6), which contains a number of unique features, seems to have significantly contributed to popular ideas about angels. The angelic hymn (see also Rev. 4.8) was used in synagogue worship and certainly by the fourth century AD is formally incorporated into Christian praise. The connection of earthly worship with that in the heavenly court is maintained liturgically to this day in the Sanctus. The winged seraphim seem to have been one source of the popular belief that angels have wings. Writers in the NT assume the OT background, but display a minimal interest in angels, usually stressing their limitations. So in Heb. 1 angels are inferior to the Son; in I Cor. 13.1 angelic language is displaced by the primacy of love; and in I Peter 1.12 angelic expectations are contrasted with the realities of Christian experience. The principalities and powers which feature largely in Col. and Eph. are in most cases, though not all, probably members of the angelic host. (On fallen and evil angels *see* **Devil**.) Col. 2.18 may imply a cult of angels, but the reference is more likely to be to a religious desire to worship with the angels in heaven. Angels are often confused with the saints (the term 'the holy ones' being used interchangeably for either) and the cult of the saints which sprang up in popular devotion was shared with the angels. Michael, the divine champion, and Gabriel, the messenger of comfort, become especially significant. The angelic hierarchy was described *c.* AD 500 by Denys the Areopagite*, sometimes known as Dionysius or pseudo-Dionysius, whose work underlies much mediaeval thought. Yet scholastic theology, even at its most speculative, is ultimately less interested in angels themselves than in what their existence might imply for the understanding of God and man. So, e.g., the concept of guardian angels, which may have Persian origins (Tob. 5.2) and which was believed to have been endorsed by Jesus (Matt. 18.10), is less concerned with the idea of personal protection than with affirming the dignity of each human soul. The Reformers seem not to have bothered much with the question, and angels more recently have been a feature of popular devotion and occasionally of apocalyptic fascination rather than of theological speculation.

G. A. Barton, 'Demons and Spirits (Hebrew)' *ERE*, IV, pp. 594ff.; Wesley Carr, *Angels and Principalities*, 1981; W. Grundmann, G. von Rad and G. Kittel, *'angelos'*, TDNT, I, pp. 74f.; H. L. Pass, 'Demons and Spirits (Christian)', *ERE*, IV, pp. 578ff.; O. Proksch, *'hagios'*, TDNT, I, pp. 88ff.

WESLEY CARR

Anglican Spirituality

If the word spirituality is to be used to indicate the recognition that the way we are with ourselves and the way we are with other people depends on the way we are with God, and that the way we are with God depends on our acknowledging the truth revealed through Christ of the way God is with us, then any study of Anglican spirituality emerging from the European ferment of the fifteenth and sixteenth centuries must first affirm the indebtedness of the Anglican understanding and practice to the biblical literature, the writings of the Fathers, the Rule of St Benedict and the liturgical use of scripture, and to the whole ethos of the mediaeval Latin church of the West. One touchstone of this indebtedness and continuity is the use of the biblical psalms in worship.

A rich inheritance of devotional literature enables us to observe over a period of four hundred years the kind of spiritual training which underpinned the outward practice of religion and the ideas which guided the day-by-day conduct of individuals with their neighbours. The awakenings and translations, the questionings and critiques that mark the period we label the Reformation, saw the English church bringing out of its treasure things new and old. The underlying assumption that persisted was that the basis for private prayer was liturgical. Revised forms of the mediaeval handbooks of devotion called *Primers* followed from the initiative in 1539 of John Hilsey, Bishop of Rochester. The *King's Primer* of 1545 led into the *Book of Common Prayer* of 1549. The increasing hold of the scriptures in English translation on the imagination of the emerging reformed congregations can be seen in the prayers written and published by Thomas Becon (*A Pomander of Prayer*, 1553) and John Bradford (*Private Prayers and Meditations*, 1559). The idea grew that

the words of scripture themselves even when twisted a good deal out of context have a special power in them. A deep sense of the dreadfulness of sin and fear of the wrath of God permeates these writings. The duty of living continually in the presence of God and of sanctifying every incident in the day's routine with prayer was placed firmly on the shoulders of every Christian. That there was a demand for books of this sort is proved by the evidence that more than eighty different collections of private devotions were printed during the reign of Elizabeth I. The Reformers staked the future of their work on a laity which was willing to accept both spiritual and intellectual responsibility.

A deep and widespread influence on personal religion for nearly two centuries emanated from the publication in 1612 by Lewis Bayly, Bishop of Bangor, of his book *The Practice of Piety, Directing a Christian how to walk that he may please God*, dedicated to Prince Charles, afterwards Charles I. John Bunyan* acknowledges its influence on himself. It had the form of a manual of popular theology as well as a handbook of devotion and shaped the religious views of middle-class English people whom the Reformers particularly wished to influence. In Richard Baxter's* opinion: 'Freeholders and tradesmen are the strength of religion and civility in the land.' The Puritans have left a significant ingredient within the complex of Anglican spirituality, notably love of the Bible, insistence on morality, strong sense of the individual's responsibility before God and demand for spiritual religion. (*See also* **Puritan Spirituality**.)

But as the seventeenth century opened out, writers on liturgy and prayer reaffirmed the validity of some of the insights and practices of the Middle Ages and found much to attract them in the doctrines and liturgies of the Eastern churches. Bishop Lancelot Andrewes'* *Private Devotions* reveal the variety of his sources. So too John Donne's* *Devotions upon Emergent Occasions*; so too the poetry and prose of George Herbert*. A recall to forgotten treasures came with John Cosin's publication in 1627 of *A Collection of Private Devotions in the Practice of the Ancient Church called Hours of Prayer as they were after this manner published by authority of Queen Eliza-*

beth 1556. The needs of Anglicans with catholic sensibilities were eventually met in more accessible form by the publication in 1650 of *Holy Living* by Jeremy Taylor*, to be followed in 1651 by *Holy Dying,* the two being subsequently printed together. John Wesley* read it when he was at Oxford and first began to doubt whether he was in a state of salvation. It started the quest that led to his conversion. John Keble*, who first studied it in 1817, described the experience as an epoch in his religious life. No book other than the Bible and the Book of Common Prayer has had a more profound and lasting influence on the distinctive inwardness of Anglican devotion. Joyful and exuberant genius radiates through the medium of his English style. There is no other book that so clearly expresses the essence of the classical Anglican understanding of the spiritual life with its insistence that there is no division between what is religious and what is secular. By grace our 'natural actions' may be turned into 'actions of religion'.

It is important to remember that Jeremy Taylor was writing to sustain members of a church in distress. An archbishop and then a king had been executed. The Book of Common Prayer was forbidden, the bishops proscribed and the orderly life of the church broken. At the same time hidden within this troubled church was a mystic whose writings only became known long after his death in 1674, Thomas Traherne*. In his *Centuries of Meditations* Traherne sees God in everything and everything praising God.

With the restoration of the monarchy, the healing of the church and the re-direction of its energies was greatly helped by an anonymous work published in 1657, reaching its twenty-eighth edition in 1790, entitled *The Whole Duty of Man.* John Wesley used and recommended it: candidates for confirmation were given it for their future guidance. The emphasis is on conduct rather than on belief, 'the plain way of holiness'. During the eighteenth century Anglicanism came to mean in doctrine, the Bible and the Prayer Book; in practice, *The Whole Duty of Man.* A book without vision or delight, it has played nonetheless an influential part in emphasizing 'that religion without morals is but superstition, that Christianity is not a set of beliefs but a way of life'.

The restoration of the monarchy was the signal for the restoration of the Prayer Book as the embodiment of the theological insights and devotional spirit of a church that understood itself as both catholic and reformed. A series of books written to revive understanding and sustain prayerful use of the Prayer Book marked the following century. There was Anthony Sparrow's *A Rationale on the Book of Common Prayer,* 1655; Thomas Comber's *A Companion to the Temple,* 1684; Robert Nelson's *Festivals and Fasts,* 1704; William Nicholls' *A Comment on the Book of Common Prayer,* 1710; George Stanhope's *Paraphrase and Comment upon the Epistles and Gospels . . . Designed to excite Devotion . . .,* 9th ed, 1775. Such expressions of Anglican piety centring upon the Prayer Book were appealed to a century later by Keble, Newman and Pusey as evidence that the aims of the Oxford Movement were no innovation.

The tradition of Jeremy Taylor's *Holy Living and Holy Dying* was taken up again in 1728 with the publication of *A Serious Call to a Devout and Holy Life* by William Law. This masterpiece of Christian seriousness lacked the range of the earlier writings of this style, but illuminated its diagnosis with vivid portraits of character-types. Law's *Serious Call* made a powerful appeal to the consciences of English people. The little community within which he lived at King's Cliffe in Northamptonshire recalls the better known family community of Little Gidding in the previous century (*see* **Ferrar, Nicholas**).

It was given to two very different men to break through the cool intellectualism and dry formalism that in the eighteenth century tended to reduce religion to little more than a code of behaviour. The first of these, William Wilberforce, was one of the most influential men of a period 'that matched great men with great events'. Convinced that Christianity required the response of the heart as well as of the head, he worked to make faith real and active in his outspoken book published in 1797, *A Practical View of the Prevailing Religious System of Professed Christians . . . contrasted with Real Christianity.* Widely read by men and women of all classes and translated into many languages, it would be hard to exaggerate its influence on the development of the evangelical element in Anglican spirituality in the nineteenth century. 'His book is the best explanation of his life, his life the best commentary on his book.' The second writer to evoke devotion that was warm and deep but never extravagant was John Keble*, whose poems *The Christian Year*, first published anonymously in 1827, had been through 140 editions before the copyright expired in 1873. In both writers deference to the Book of Common Prayer and its discipline is matched with personal devotion to the person of Jesus particularly called out by the recollection of his patient suffering on the cross. In this movement, whereby the feeling as well as the intellectual and formal elements in religion are developed, the widespread use of hymns in worship and personal prayer must not be forgotten; but always the ground-bass continuum of Anglican worship has been theological prayer. 'Pray theologically' was advice given by one theological college principal to generations of students. To an enquirer asking about the distinctive beliefs of Anglicans it would by no means be an evasive answer to say 'Study the Collects in the Book of Common Prayer.'

To generalize is to distort, but perhaps something of the essence of Anglican patterns of spirituality is indicated by the Prayer Book description of a Christian's duty as that of living a 'godly, righteous and sober life'. These principles recur. To live Christianly is the aim. In spirituality as in theology the Anglican Church has been the locus of a tripartite dialectic between the biblical literature, the experience of the church communities of the centuries and the critical guardianship of reason and sound learning. Openness to other traditions has further protected the Anglican way from either exclusiveness or fanaticism. The grandeur as well as the guilt of the human soul, fact as well as feeling, what is personal and what is of community have been held in reciprocal interplay within the framework of the church's life, in the confidence that growth in holiness requires the continual interweaving of the way we are with God, the way we are with ourselves and the way we are with others in the context of particular times and circumstances and working with the given raw material of an individual's genetic and psychological nature. Those who are acquainted with the sermons of Latimer (d. 1555), Andrewes (d. 1626), Donne (d. 1631), Taylor (d. 1667) and Tillotson (d. 1694),

to name but a few of the well-published preachers, will not easily underestimate the steady continuing influence on the shaping of Anglican spirituality of the weekly sermons in the parish churches throughout the centuries.

During the last century and a half several influences have effected change and development in Anglican sensitivity to the things of the Spirit. Among them we must identify the revival of variants of the Benedictine pattern of communities living under rule (some more contemplative; others more active in works of education and welfare); the training of men for ordination in theological colleges; the availability of retreats for laity and clergy; personal spiritual counselling; gatherings for conference, fellowship and prayer in such houses as Lee Abbey and Scargill. Books such as *Yes to God* by Alan Ecclestone (1974) and *Love's Endeavour, Love's Expense* by William Vanstone (1977) reflect contemporary perceptions.

To these considerations must be added the influence of the liturgical renewal that began in Maria Laach in Germany and Solesmes in France and penetrated the English consciousness by means of Gabriel Hebert's seminal book *Liturgy and Society* (1961). This thinking found expression in the movement towards the Parish Communion as the central act of worship on Sundays and this in turn has led to the publication of the Alternative Service Book 1980. Also during this period there has flowed into the bloodstream of Anglican search for true Christian inwardness a better knowledge and availability of classics of the spiritual life from mediaeval, reformation and counter-reformation Europe; a greater awareness of the mystical element in religion greatly stimulated by the researches, writings and retreats of Evelyn Underhill; an increase in opportunities for exchanges with members of the Orthodox churches of the East made possible by their enforced dispersion into Western countries.

More difficult to assess, but in no way to be overlooked, is the effect on Anglican spirituality of the spread of the Anglican version of Christianity first to the colonies and then to the wider ambience of dominions and empire. A useful exercise in comparative liturgiology would be to study the Alternative Service Book 1980 with other recent

Anglican revisions of the Book of Common Prayer. The growth of indigenous churches of the Anglican Communion in the Third World brings into the Anglican experience fresh interpretations of Christian response in art, music, dance, patterns of community and spontaneity less fettered by history. All this, together with 'pentecostal' expressions of prayer and praise in the older churches, opens up possibilities of faith response undreamed of by our forebears. More people than ever before are exploring methods of wordless prayer and contemplation, acknowledging the importance of bodily posture, seeking God in silence and simplicity.

In addition to titles mentioned in the text, see C. J. Stranks, *Anglican Devotion*, 1961; Martin Thornton, *English Spirituality*, 1963.

SYDNEY H. EVANS

Anima Christi

The prayer which begins 'Soul of Christ, sanctify me, Body of Christ, save me'. Attributed to Ignatius Loyola* because it stands at the beginning of his *Spiritual Exercises*, it is in fact much earlier, most likely fourteenth-century, since it is referred to in the diary of a German mystic, Margaret Ebner in 1344, and quoted on a doorway, erected in 1364, of the Alcazar in Seville. It is redolent of mediaeval devotion to Christ in his passion and was used to prepare for the Mass. It is of the same *genre* as the *Ancrene Riwle** and similarly conceives of Christ's wounds as hiding-places like clefts of a rock. There is no finer exposition of it than the Myrtle lecture of 1935 by the English Congregationalist Divine, Nathaniel Micklem.

Nathaniel Micklem, *Prayers and Praises*, 1941, frequently reissued; Herbert Thurston, *Familiar Prayers*, 1953, pp. 38–53.

EDITOR

Animals and Spirituality

Down the centuries the biblical and then the Christian tradition has been little concerned with animals for their own sake. By far the most attractive writing about them in the Bible is to be found in the wisdom tradition, which is international by nature, or in works like Ps. 104, which is usually thought to derive from an Egyptian original (writing of this kind is only equalled again in the Middle

Ages with St Francis of Assisi). Otherwise animals are mentioned most frequently in connection with laws of purity and sacrifices of various kinds. Even within the biblical wisdom literature there are virtually no extended animal fables; birds and beasts are usually mentioned in passing as illustrations.

From the patristic period onwards, however, Christian theologians, adopting the work of the naturalists of classical antiquity for their own ends, came to give animals Christian religious and spiritual significance. The *Physiologus* from before the fourth century AD is the ultimate source of the mediaeval bestiaries which proved so popular and from it such traditional symbols of piety and religion as the pelican and the phoenix originate. St Ambrose in the fourth century and St Isidore of Seville in the sixth enlarged on it and further refined its devotional content.

While intended as serious and factual commentaries on the animal kingdom, the mediaeval bestiaries, which were often attractively illustrated, owed more to the imagination and credulity of their creators than to direct observation. Fantasy is liberally mixed with fact – to those whose horizons were limited to the Western European world a unicorn or dragon was as reasonable as a whale or an elephant. And even where natural phenomena were observed directly, the interpretations of them were theological and moral rather than in any way scientific.

It might be tempting to write off the phenomenon of the bestiary as a quaint feature of mediaeval Christianity, outdated in the light of subsequent biology and the development of understanding of animal behaviour. However, to do so would be to ignore a not dissimilar phenomenon in the twentieth century. It seems that when they want to express some of the deepest and most elusive elements in human spirituality, using the word in its broadest sense, writers often feel drawn to use animal imagery, albeit in a far more sophisticated way than their predecessors in the Middle Ages.

A list of representative examples might begin with Kenneth Grahame's *The Wind in the Willows* (1908) and the cosmic encounter to be found in 'The Piper at the Gates of Dawn'; Margery Williams' *The Velveteen Rabbit* (1922) is a moving book about love and reality. The key character in J. R. R. Tolkien's great mythological saga *The Lord of the Rings* (1954–1955), with its theme of power and its misuse, is a hobbit, and while there are those who would hesitate to class hobbits as animals, they are certainly not human beings. Towards the climax, Richard Adams' *Watership Down* (1972) with its rabbit world comes close to Christian mysticism, and in *Duncton Wood* (1980), William Horwood explores a similar trend by creating a world of moles. Novels as they are, none of these works allows of direct and simple interpretation, but at the least they can be seen as evidence of a deep contemporary striving towards some kind of spirituality.

Possibilities of expression in the media world of cartoons and television are much more limited. However, even commercialism has not cheapened the often profound insights attributed to the animals in *The Muppet Show*, perhaps the nearest thing that we now have to the mediaeval bestiary, with a real community behind it. And finally, one way in which going to the dogs has not altogether proved a bad thing is that the trivial Mickey Mouse has been replaced as the most popular international animal character by a beagle called Snoopy, the subject of at least two semi-scholarly books which associate him firmly with the gospel tradition.

Like music*, the world of imaginary animals can be extremely, perhaps insidiously, powerful. Animal imagery is not enough to provide a spirituality in itself, and needs to be carefully controlled in case it deteriorates into sentimentality. However, its use does seem to unblock channels in the imagination which have previously been silted up by the conditioning of a scientific world-view.

JOHN BOWDEN

Anselm of Canterbury, St

Anselm was born at Aosta *c.* 1033. After a restless youth he entered the Norman abbey of Bec, was prior after Lanfranc, and finally abbot. He became Archbishop of Canterbury under William Rufus and Henry I. His public life was filled with dissension between himself and the king and he was twice in exile for his opinions. He died at Canterbury in 1109.

Anselm is best known as a theologian and philosopher of outstanding ability, but he also had a profound influence upon the spirituality of his age. In his *Prayers and Meditations*, composed at the beginning of his monastic life, he created a new kind of poetry, the poetry of devotion, for use in silent and private meditation. His prayers were lengthy, and written in the elaborate rhymed prose fashionable in the eleventh century. They are carefully constructed, and the choice of words has a deliberate intention for the work of prayer. Anselm begins with the use of words to stir up in himself the emotion of horror for sin, a compunction which is to lead to repentance and prayer for the help of God. He then proceeds, by a dialogue between himself, a saint, and Christ, to use words to increase in himself a sense of thanksgiving for the wonder of the mercy of God and therefore to increase the determination of his will to continue in God's service.

In the 18 prayers and 3 meditations which are now recognized as the genuine work of Anselm, there is a new and dynamic approach to prayer, which, however dated the language may seem, contains the basic teaching of compunction as the gateway to prayer and meditation on the scriptures, in a form which is individual and arresting. Many of Anselm's friends requested copies during his life, so that while they were meant for monks, they were also used by the laity. There are, for instance, early translations into Middle English, and the *Prayers* were used by Thomas Becket. Above all they received the flattery of widespread imitation, so that it has been impossible until this century to distinguish the genuine *Prayers* from the host of lesser imitations.

Anselm sent directions about the use of his prayers with the copies of them and a preface attributed to him also explains their use. They are to be read 'quietly . . . with deep and thoughtful meditation'; their purpose is 'to stir up the mind of the reader to the love or fear of God or to self-examination' (*Preface*). They are to be used as a starting point, as a basis for collecting the mind and sharpening its attention, so that it is drawn out of its lethargy and made open to the work of God. The *Proslogion*, a treatise well-known for the chapters which contain the so-called 'Ontological Argument', is also a meditation in this style, and its opening lines convey very well the method of Anselm's meditation: 'Come now, little

man, turn aside from your daily employment, escape for a moment from the tumult
of your thoughts, put aside your weighty
cares, let your burdensome distractions
wait, free yourself awhile for God and rest
awhile in him. Enter the inner chamber of
your soul, shut out everything except God,
and that which can help you in seeking him,
and when you have shut the door, seek him.
Now my whole heart, say to God, "I seek
your face, Lord it is your face I seek" '
(*Proslogion* 1). It is also in this treatise that
the fundamental concept of prayer for
Anselm is best expressed in his phrase 'faith
seeking understanding'; it is not only by the
effort of the discursive intellect that he sees
the soul as seeking God, but by the work of
prayer in which faith seeks understanding in
other and more profound ways.

Anselm, *Opera Omnia*, ed F. S. Schmitt, 6
vols, 1938–1961; tr by B. Ward of *Prayers
and Meditations* with the Proslogion, 1973;
G. Evans, *Anselm and Talking about God*,
1978; R. W. Southern, *St Anselm and his
Biographer*, 1963.

BENEDICTA WARD, SLG

Anthony, St *see* Antony of Egypt, St

Antony of Egypt, St

Traditionally ascribed the title 'the father of
monks', Antony (251?–356) was the son of a
Christian peasant farmer of Middle Egypt.
According to the *Life*, written by St Atha-
nasius*, at the age of about twenty Antony
responded to the reading of Matt. 19.21 ('If
you would be perfect, go and sell all that
you have and give to the poor; and come,
follow me') by giving away the land inherited from his father and going to live on the
desert margin of the village, seeking guidance from other hermits and holy men.
Endeavouring to pray without ceasing,
Antony experienced numerous temptations
in his quest for perfection. In the *Life* Athanasius describes many of the conflicts of this
spiritual warfare, as well as reproducing
Antony's teaching to his fellow ascetics
about the powerlessness of the demons and
their capacity to deceive.

In the latter part of his life Antony went
briefly to Alexandria to support Athanasius
in his campaign against the Arians, and then
withdrew to the Eastern desert, to a mountain cave not far from the Red Sea close to
where the monastery which bears his name
now stands. In the record of his life there
are accounts of his fasting; of his counselling
and healing of those who came to him for
help; and of the guidance given to others
who had withdrawn to the desert. For
Athanasius Antony was the first eremite,
who persuaded many to follow the solitary
life, so that 'there arose monasteries even in
the mountains, and the desert was made a
city by monks coming out from their own
and enrolling themselves in the heavenly
city'. As inspirer and guide of this monastic
movement Antony is presented as the prototype of the *geron*, *starets* or charismatic
'abba', a continuing characteristic of Eastern Christian monasticism.

In the seven letters ascribed to Antony,
which there are grounds for accepting as
genuine, there is a stress on the continuity
of God's redeeming work; and on the need
for men to be trained by the spirit of repentance so that they grow in discernment. A
few scriptural texts (Isa. 53.5; Rom. 8.15–
18, 32; and Phil 2.6–11) are emphasized and
referred to with great frequency. Although
there is spiritual warfare, it is not a war
against man's bodily condition, but against
demonic powers. When Athanasius described Antony as emerging from his twenty
years solitude, it is as a man 'all balanced,
as one governed by reason and standing in
his natural condition'. Athanasius' *Life of
Antony* was 'the first great manifesto of the
monastic ideal', and influenced the Christian
world considerably within a few years of its
writing.

St Athanasius, *Life of Antony* (tr R. T.
Meyer in *Ancient Christian Writers*, X),
1950; L. Bouyer, *La Vie de S. Antoine. Essai
sur la spiritualité du monachisme primitif*,
1950; D. J. Chitty (tr), *The Letters of St
Antony the Great*, 1975; D. J. Chitty, *The
Desert a City*, 1966; Benedicta Ward (tr),
Sayings of the Desert Fathers, 1975.

GEOFFREY ROWELL

Apatheia

A Greek term signifying: 1. in the case of
God, absence of passions, impassibility; 2.
in the case of human persons, mastery over
the passions.

The second usage of the word is Stoic in
background. *Apatheia* is employed in this

sense by Justin, but the first Christian author to adopt it regularly as a technical term is St Clement of Alexandria (see especially *Strom.* VI,9). It is frequently used by St Gregory of Nyssa and Evagrius, constituting for the latter the final aim of *praktikē*, the 'active life'. St Maximus the Confessor, drawing on Evagrius, likewise assigns a central place to *apatheia*, distinguishing within it four different levels (*To Thalassius* 55, *PG* 90, 544C). But certain authors, such as Origen and Theodoret of Cyrrhus, are deliberately sparing in their use of the word.

The precise meaning of *apatheia* depends upon the sense attached by the author in question to the word *pathos*, 'passion'. Some Greek Fathers, following Aristotle, regard the passions as neutral impulses, neither good nor bad in themselves, but becoming such according to the use that man makes of them. Theodoret, for instance, treats them as a necessary and useful part of human nature (*PG* 83, 952B). Those who take this view of *pathos* on the whole refrain from commending *apatheia* as an ideal; and, if commended by them, it tends to mean only the redirection of the passions, not their total elimination.

But other Greek authors adopt the Stoic view of the passions, looking on them as 'diseases' of the soul that are unnatural and intrinsically evil. Understanding *pathos* in this sense, Clement of Alexandria says that the truly good man has no passions (*Strom.* VII.11), while St John Climacus * insists that God is not the creator of the passions (*Ladder* 26). In such a context *apatheia* comes close to meaning their elimination. Occasionally, as for example among the Messalians, the word bears the yet more extreme sense of impeccability, a state in which one is no longer liable to temptation or capable of sin. But most authors exclude such a meaning: in the words of St Diadochus of Photice, '*Apatheia* is not freedom from attack by demons ... but to remain undefeated when they do attack' (*Cent.* 98).

Even in authors such as Evagrius, who take a Stoic view of passion, *apatheia* is not wholly negative, for he links it closely with *agapē*: it is not apathy (in the modern sense of the word), indifference, insensitivity – for which Evagrius would have used the words *akēdia* (*see* **Accidie**) or *anaisthesia* – but it is the replacement of lust by love; not the suppression of desire but its purification. Thus

St John Cassian *, transmitting Evagrius' teaching to the Latin West, translates *apatheia* as 'purity of heart'. Stressing its dynamic character, Diadochus speaks of 'the fire of *apatheia*' (*Cent.* 17), and Climacus terms it 'resurrection of the soul prior to that of the body' (*Ladder* 29). For such writers, then, it is not the absence of all feeling, but a state of reintegration and spiritual freedom, conferred by divine grace.

G. Bardy, in *DS*, I, cols 727–46; J. E. Bamberger, *Evagrius Ponticus: The Praktikos; Chapters on Prayer* (Cistercian Publications 4), 1970, pp. lxxxi–lxxxvii; A. and C. Guillaumont, *Evagre le Pontique: Traité Pratique ou Le Moine* (SC, 170–1), 1971, I, pp. 98–112; T. Rüther, *Die sittliche Forderung der Apatheia in den beiden ersten christlichen Jahrhunderten und bei Klemens von Alexandrien*, 1949.

KALLISTOS WARE

Apophthegmata

A term (from 'apophthegm', a terse, pointed saying) applied to the collections of early monastic material known in Greek as *Gerontikon* or *Paterikon*, in Latin as *Verba Seniorum*, and in English usually as *The Sayings of the Desert Fathers*. These contain anecdotes and maxims, originating for the most part from fourth- and fifth-century Egypt, and in particular from Nitria and Scetis; Abba Poemen and his disciples occupy a central place. Already before the end of the fourth century the earliest Greek collections of *apophthegmata* were circulating orally and had begun to be written down in a rudimentary form; the surviving major collections were virtually complete, in their present form, by the late fifth or early sixth century.

An apophthegm may begin with a monk's name: 'Abba Antony said . . .', 'A brother asked Abba Arsenius . . .'; or else it may be anonymous: 'An old man said . . .', 'The old men said . . .' The collections take two main forms: (1) alphabetical, with texts under the names of particular Desert Fathers or Mothers, and an appendix of anonymous sayings; (2) systematic, with texts arranged under themes (stillness, compunction, humility, etc.). Alongside the main body of material in Greek, collections of *apophthegmata* survive also in Coptic, Latin, Syriac, Georgian, Armenian and Ethiopian, often embodying texts not found in Greek.

The *apophthegmata* reflect the simple, practical wisdom of uneducated monks, mainly Copts, rather than the more systematic teaching of learned Greeks such as the Origenist Evagrius (although Evagrius also includes apophthegmatic material in his works). Pungent, human, lacking literary artifice and highly readable – often reminiscent of the stories told about Sufi and Hasidic masters – the *apophthegmata* convey, more vividly than any other source, the spirit of primitive desert spirituality.

See also **Desert, Desert Fathers.**

Texts: alphabetical – B. Ward, *The Sayings of the Desert Fathers* and *The Wisdom of the Desert Father*, 1975; systematic – H. Waddell, *The Desert Fathers*, 1936; Studies: W. Bousset, *Apophthegmata*, 1923; J.-C. Guy, *Recherches sur la tradition grecque des Apophthegmata Patrum*, 1962.

KALLISTOS WARE

Apostleship of Prayer
see **Prayer, The Apostleship of**

Aquinas, Thomas
see **Thomas Aquinas, St**

Ars, Curé d'
Jean-Baptiste-Marie Vianney (1786–1859) served for forty years as the curé of the obscure country parish of Ars near Lyons. During the last thirty years of his earthly life and ministry there he heard the confessions of many thousands of penitents a year. These included men and women from all parts of France and from all levels of society, from peasants to members of the government. Six thousand people attended his funeral, and he was canonized in St Peter's, Rome, in 1924 as the patron saint of parish priests.

He wrote no book, and study of notes taken of his sermons is unrewarding; but the testimonies of many of those who knew and loved him provide evidence of the characteristics of his spirituality. His main emphasis was on the love of God 'which, like an overflowing torrent, sweeps everything in its course'. 'Our faults are like a grain of sand beside the great mountain of the mercies of God.' 'Man being created by love cannot live without love: either he loves God, or himself or the world.' 'A pure soul with God is like a child with its mother. It caresses her, it embraces her, and its mother returns its caresses and embraces.' 'As earth can produce nothing unless it is fertilized by the sun, so we can do no good without the grace of the good God (which is) like the hand of a parent taking a little child.' 'The interior life is like a bath of love wherein one plunges.'

But his teaching was not sentimental. He led a severely disciplined and ascetic life himself, with a rigid timetable of mass, meditation, breviary, giving catechetical instruction and hearing confessions, with very little time for sleep or food and none for relaxation. On occasion he postponed giving absolution until the penitent had given evidence of repentance.

He constantly described sin as 'crucifying the good God'. The cross 'is what it has cost my Saviour to repair the injury my sins have done to God'. 'A God suffering, a God dying.' 'If you put fine grapes into the winepress there will come out a delicious juice: our souls, in the winepress of the Cross, give out a juice which nourishes and strengthens.' 'It is easy to understand that we are the work of God; but that the crucifixion of a God should be our handiwork, that is incomprehensible indeed.'

His personal spiritual life centred in the Mass and in the presence of Christ in the tabernacle. He had a great devotion for the Blessed Virgin Mary and the saints, especially his own patron saint Philomena, to whose prayers he habitually gave the credit for the miracles of spiritual and physical healing which people attributed to him. In this and other respects the outward forms of his piety were typical of many French priests of the period following the Revolution. He remained to the end of his life a very humble and unlearned man; but he was given extraordinary gifts of insight into men's characters and spiritual needs, deep compassion over the ravages of sin, and great skill in guiding penitents upwards on the spiritual way.

Henri Ghéon, *The Secret of the Curé d'Ars*, 1929; Alfred Mounier, *The Curé of Ars*, 1861, ET 1927; Francis Trochu, *The Curé d'Ars*, ET 1927 (abridged 1955).

FRANCIS H. HOUSE

Ars Moriendi

The term *Ars Moriendi*, or 'art of dying',
refers in a general way to texts dealing with
preparation for the moment of death. This
is a genre of practical, devotional literature
aimed at the laity, which first appeared in
the early fifteenth century, and, under various forms and numerous vernacular versions, remained popular into the 1700s.
Nineteenth and twentieth-century examples
of this genre exist, but they have been considerably less popular than their predecessors, and will not be treated here.

Though often mentioned in the same
breath with the *danse macabre* and other
aspects of late mediaeval interest in funereal
realism, the *Ars Moriendi* do not share in
the grotesque spirit of dancing skeletons and
rotting corpses. The tenor of most of these
texts is one of comfort: the dying man is
seen primarily as a faithful Christian who
needs to be prepared for the experience
beyond the grave by the assurances of a
loving God. On the whole, this literature
emphasizes the doctrines of grace and reconciliation over those of punishment and
damnation.

The origin of the *Ars Moriendi* has been
traced to the conciliarist epoch, more specifically to the Council of Constance (1414–
1418) which, as an attempt at reforming the
church in head and members, initiated pro-
grammes for educating the laity about religious matters. 'De arte moriendi', the third
part of Jean Gerson's * *Opus Tripartitum* (*c.*
1408) is the source of much of the earlier
craft-of-dying literature. Other important
sources are, of course, the Bible, the Fathers,
mediaeval liturgies, and later mediaeval devotional and doctrinal literature.

The generic title *Ars Moriendi* refers to
two versions of one text known as the *Tractatus*, or *Speculum, artis bene moriendi*. Both
versions share a basic structure and a central
theme. Most surviving manuscripts and
printed editions are of the longer version,
which is divided into six sections: 1. A collection of questions on death from Christian
authorities; 2. Advice to the dying person on
resisting the five sins of faithlessness, despair, impatience, pride and worldliness; 3.
Catechetical questions which must be
answered correctly in order to gain salvation; 4. Prayers and rules to assist in the
imitation of the dying Christ; 5. Advice to

those who are present around the deathbed;
6. Prayers to be said by those who are
present at the moment of death.

The shorter version of the *Tractatus* is
regarded as an abridgment of the longer.
Sections 1, 3, 4 and 5 of the longer version
are condensed and transposed into a
dramatic form: the struggle between angels
and demons for the dying person's soul.
While demons tempt the dying person to
give in to the five sins listed in the longer
text, the angels help him choose the opposing virtues of faith, hope, love, humility and
detachment.

The early *Ars Moriendi* texts are studied
as much for their iconographic value as for
their ethical and theological content. The
texts, which began to appear in xylographic,
or block-print, editions around 1465, often
contained eleven woodcuts illustrating the
death struggle: five depicting the demonic
temptations; five the angelically-inspired
virtues; and a final one showing the delivery
of the dying person's naked soul to an
angel.

The basic structure and content of the *Ars
Moriendi* remained largely unchanged until
the sixteenth century, when the forces of
humanism, Protestantism and the Counter-
Reformation gave rise to several innovations. The key assumption of the earlier texts
had been that one's eternal fate was decided
at the moment of death: 'salus hominis in
fine consistit'. The purpose of the treatise
was to allow the dying person to escape hell,
or even purgatory, by helping him or her
make a full, genuine repentance. The Renaissance added an extra dimension: the *Ars
Moriendi* should not only open the gates of
heaven at the moment of death, but also
show one how to live a good Christian life
before dying. The *Ars Moriendi*, then, is
transformed into an *Ars Vivendi*, and it
becomes a manual to be read not just at the
moment of death, but throughout the course
of one's life. This theme is already present in
some of Savonarola's sermons ('Predica
dell'arte del bene morire', 1496), but it
assumes a greater importance in the two
works of Erasmus, *De morte declamatio*
(1517), and *De praeparatione ad mortem*
(1533); and the one text of Josse Clichtove,
Doctrina moriendi (1520). In spite of this
change in focus, and in spite of a tendency
to cite classical pagan sources, these humanistic texts still adhere to the general pat-

tern of the earlier literature, especially in regard to the deathbed temptations. Erasmus' *De praeparatione* was translated into several vernacular versions, and it enjoyed a long and successful publishing history throughout Europe.

Protestantism may have rejected the key assumption of the mediaeval *Ars Moriendi*, that one's eternal fate is decided at the moment of death; as well as the existence of purgatory; but, surprisingly, it did not reject the literary genre of the craft of dying. Protestant *Ars Moriendi* texts expand on the humanistic theme, insisting that what matters most is the *Ars Vivendi*. To best prepare for death, one must persevere in faith throughout one's life. As the Calvinist *The Sicke Mannes Salve* of Thomas Becon (1561) clearly stated, a good life leads to a 'blessed end'. Because of their belief in election and their rejection of purgatory, Calvinists * focused on death as nothing to be feared, and as the entrance to everlasting joy. This ethos is revealed in Jean L'Espine's *Traicté pour oster la crainte de la mort et la faire désirer à l'homme fidele* (1583). Protestant treatises could also have a polemical and practical bent. Aside from denouncing and condemning Catholic belief and practice concerning death, some texts also include advice on how to write a good will and properly prepare for the welfare of one's survivors.

The Catholic Counter-Reformation produced a type of *Ars Moriendi* which combined the Renaissance focus on the art of living with a Tridentine reinterpretation of the traditional themes of the art of dying. Using the old themes and dramatic forms, the Counter-Reformation treatises place greater emphasis on the freedom of the will, the power of the sacraments, and the intercessory role of the church and the saints. Ignatius Loyola * was among the first to stress this type of devotion in his *Spiritual Exercises** (1548). Other Jesuits followed suit with a veritable flood of texts. Between 1540 and 1620, Jesuits authored 20 different *Ars Moriendi* titles; 139 followed between 1620 and 1700; and 101 appeared between 1700 and 1800. Among these, some of the more popular were Juan Polanco's *Methodus ad eos adjuvandos qui moriuntur* (1582), and Robert Bellarmine's *De arte bene moriendi* (1620), both of which went through several translations and editions.

To date, scholars have concentrated largely on the earlier mediaeval texts, and on France and England. Studies have focused primarily, though not exclusively, on two uses of the *Ars Moriendi*: 1. As a literary genre; or 2. As indices, through publishing records, of trends in popular piety. Much work remains to be done on the theological and ethical content of this vast corpus of devotional literature.

H. Appel, *Die Anfechtung and ihre Uberwindung in der Trostbüchern und Sterbebüchlein des späten Mittelalters*, 1938, pp. 63–104; P. Ariès, *The Hour of Our Death*, 1981; N. L. Beaty, *The Craft of Dying. A Study in the Literary Tradition of the* Ars Moriendi *in England*, 1970; T. S. R. Boase, *Death in the Middle Ages. Mortality, Judgment, and Remembrance*, 1972; Sister M. C. O'Connor, *The Art of Dying Well. The Development of the* Ars Moriendi, 1942; A. Tenenti, *Il Senso della morte e l'amore della vita nel Rinascimento (Francia e Italia)*, 1957, pp. 62–120.

CARLOS M. N. EIRE

Arts, Spirituality and the

Christianity has always maintained an ambiguous attitude to the arts as an expression of spiritual values and aspirations. On the one hand the church inherited from the Hebrew tradition a mistrust of all representation, of 'graven images'; but it is difficult to determine whether this was a prohibition against idols and idolatry, the setting up of Gods who had neither reason nor the senses, or a more metaphysical conclusion that the ineffable could not be incarnated, nor the unutterable given a valid imagery. This dilemma was intensified for the Christian church, since in Christ the ineffable was made incarnate, and indeed even for Israel there was a conflict between reprehension of the visual arts and a powerful dependence upon poetry and music to express the profoundest truths of spirituality.

The Puritan strain in Christianity periodically intensified this rejection of the visual and the sixteenth-century Homily, from Book II, 1571, characteristically entitled *Against the Peril of Idolatry*, sufficiently summarizes this line of thought; categorizing wall-paintings, sculptures and 'vestures', it goes on: 'When [the people] turn about from these preachers to the

books and schoolmasters and painted scriptures, shall they not find the lying books,
teaching other manner of lessons, of
esteeming of riches, of pride, and vanity in
apparel, of niceness and wantonness, and
peradventure of whoredom.' Iconoclasm
was a natural consequence, but among the
greatest poets and artists there was an intermediate position. One element in their
thinking argued from the worship of God,
the divine Artificer (even to such witty
extremes as Calderon's description of St
Veronica's kerchief as 'a self-portrait of
Christ the artist'); this tradition extends
from Leonardo's claim that 'the divine
power . . . of the painter transforms the mind
of the painter into the likeness of the divine
mind' to Coleridge's more Kantian standpoint in *Biographia Literaria* that, by the
echoing of the 'primary imagination', we
approach most nearly to the divine mind
when, that is to say, we are creative beings.
The Italian Academies of the sixteenth century even debated the primacy of the various
arts as expressions of the divine creativity,
exploring the functions of God as math-
ematical architect, as creator of landscape,
as artificer of form and as the final revelation of the Word. Leonardo in his *Notebooks* and best in his extended essay, *Il Paragone*, examines all the claims of architect,
painter, sculptor and poet and determines
at length in favour of the painter, since he
best expresses the divine gift of sight: 'O
excellent thing, superior to all others created
by God!' We should therefore have expected
that the comprehensive genius of Michelangelo would have been resolute in claiming this quasi-divine insight on behalf of the
artist, whether poet or painter. It is startling
therefore to find in two of his Sonnets
(XCIV and CXI) a clearly-stated retreat
from these claims of divinely inspired insight
and the adoption of a more 'mystical' stance.
In the first of these Sonnets Michelangelo
takes us aback with the phrase 'occhi in-
fermi' – 'weak eyes' – senses which fail 'from
temerity and foolishness' to pass 'from
things mortal to things divine'. The second
Sonnet is even clearer: 'Neither painting nor
sculpture may still that spirit turned to the
divine love which spread out his arms on
the Cross to enfold me.' We would do well,
of course, not to forget that Michelangelo,
before this expression of an artist's renunciation, had proceeded as far as any, in

word or image, to express that divine love.

Early Christianity, devoted as it was to
the Word, never forgot that it had been
made flesh, and whether in the direct simplicities of catacomb symbols (in cruciforms
or the vivid shorthand of the fish graffiti,
the Greek word Ichthus expressing the name
and titles of Christ) or in the austere splendour of Eastern or Italian mosaic. The mag-
nificence of Ravenna, the majesty of Christ
Pantocrator in Santa Sophia, were not
equalled in Christian iconography* until
stained glass added the further dimension of
translucence to Christian art, the suffusion
of a church interior with coloured light being
in itself a symbol of heavenly radiance, a
quality in this art form which we have re-
captured only in the last half-century.

With the triple impact of Reformation,
Renaissance and Counter-Reformation 'Tridentine sensibility', the terms of the debate
were altered. No longer were the arts merely
'illustrative', a bodying-forth for the illiterate in wall-painting, woodcut or glass of
concepts which the more sophisticated
gathered from the biblical words. The
baroque consciousness was more ambiti-
ously comprehensive. Its immediate forerunner we have seen in the 'Paragone controversy' of the Academies. But seventeenth-
century artists aspired to encompass a more
complex, ambiguous and penetrating spirituality. Two examples must suffice, from
poetry and music. When Robert Herrick
meditates on 'Good Friday: Rex Tragicus,
or Christ going to His Cross', he is prepared,
without unseemliness, to pick up the
theatrical reference in the word Tragicus and
to liken Golgotha to a stage and Christ
himself to the greatest classical actor:

> The Cross shall be my stage, and thou
> shalt there
> The spacious field have for thy theatre.
> Thou art that Roscius and that marked-
> out man
> That shall this day act the tragedian.

A powerful conjunction of concepts. Bach
carries still further the complex interweaving
of the arts to express spiritual truth. In the
chorale, 'Durch Adams Fall', the original
sin of Adam is heard both in the sombre
minor melody and in the descending chrom-
aticism of the bass line; in addition there is a
'visual' element in the score, as the middle
voices wind in a serpentine line, a symbol of

the agent of the Fall. The confluence of the arts in Herrick and Bach, indeed in all baroque artists from Monteverdi and Shakespeare to the music and art of the early eighteenth century, is the fine flowering of religious expression.

Since the Renaissance the relationship between spirituality and the arts has again been substantially 'illustrative', religious themes sharing the matter of the visual arts with classical subjects. In the latter half of this century, however, there has been at least a minor revolution in this relationship, with (among many others) Rouault, Matisse, Moore, Sutherland, Hepworth and Piper extending our awareness of spiritual values, in painting, sculpture, stained glass and tapestry, objects of meditation and not merely explication. And alongside these affirmative works there has been a related understanding that the exploration of dereliction is a valid part of spirituality; in this search, Eliot*, Pound, and Joyce in words, Picasso, Francis Bacon and their fellows in image, have marked the way to a new synthesis, to an understanding of the arts as instruments of a renewed spirituality.

See also **Music and Spirituality.**

MOELWYN MERCHANT

Asceticism

Human beings throughout history and in diverse cultures have generally engaged in a quest for self-identity and self-knowledge. Invariably the quest has involved a yearning and searching for 'the transcendent', something above, beyond, and outside the self, knowledge of which manifested to individuals the true meaning of human existence. The process of arriving at this experience of self-identity and identity of 'the other' has taken various shapes throughout history. Within the Christian tradition a variety of theories and practices of asceticism (from the Greek, *askesis*, 'discipline' or 'training') have loomed large as 'the way' to arrive at a knowledge of both self and God.

History provides evidence that asceticism is not a concept or practice unique to Christianity. Already during the Vedic period in Hinduism more than a thousand years before Christ, monks gathered in small ashrams where prayer, meditation, poverty, and detachment became a way of life. Also within certain Graeco-Roman philosophical schools and religious fellowships (e.g. the

Pythagorean), asceticism was considered essential for an individual's receptiveness to and communication with divinity. The motivation for certain ascetic practices was closely aligned to the belief that humanity had originally experienced a primordial state of perfection which was forfeited because of a transgression. By various ascetic practices the individual could be restored to a state where communication and union with the divine was again possible. Hence, in various religious traditions prior to and contemporaneous with the origins of Christianity a return to a primordial state of innocence and bliss triggered a number of ascetical practices deemed helpful or necessary in bringing about such return. Jewish communities such as the Essenes and Therapeutae likewise dedicated themselves to lives of solitude and activities conducive to a search for things heavenly, i.e., beyond the material world of the senses. The fourth century church historian, Eusebius (*c.* 260–340), saw these Jewish communities as the forerunners of the Christian ascetical movement prevalent in his own day (*Hist. Eccl.* 2.17).

But if the Christians were not the first to utilize asceticism in attaining their spiritual goals, the degree to which they systematized ascetical theory and practice was unparalleled in most other religious cultures. For the early Christians, asceticism became the most effective way of acquiring assurance of salvation. In the struggle for mastery over the temptations of the world, the flesh, and demonic powers, the soul could make its ascent to God from whom it had fallen by disobedience. From its inception Christianity attached importance to ascetic ideals as the most effective means for living a truly Christian life. The early Christian evangelists preached the coming of the kingdom, the otherworldly and apocalyptic message of Christ's imminent return. The anticipation of the end of time carried with it a sense of detachment from the things of the material world. The counsels of the Sermon on the Mount stressed the need for self-effacement in order to acquire the 'things of the Spirit' and the 'kingdom of God'. St Paul and others intimated their apocalyptic hopes when they advised freedom from the concerns and cares of marriage in order to spend more time in preparation for Christ's second coming. The motive for pursuing ascetic ideals was predicated on such injunctions as Christ's, 'If you would be my followers, renounce yourselves and take up your cross every day and follow me' (Luke 9.23). In fact, an ascetic life was seen as a mark of every true Christian. Many of the martyrdom accounts, for example, indicate the belief that asceticism was a prerequisite for gaining eternal life.

Within the early Christian congregations were groups of religious women living a type of ascetic life built on prayer, fasting, almsgiving, and good works. By the end of the second century the existence of such ascetic groups of men and women was one of the first things mentioned by non-Christian writers critically examining Christian beliefs and practices. There is also strong evidence that in the first and second centuries ascetic or encratite movements were already flourishing in Syria as an integral part of Syrian Christianity. The anthropological dualism of body and soul which became an important element in Egyptian asceticism at a little later date was not the major emphasis for Syrian asceticism. Syrian Christianity placed greater emphasis on ascetical practices as an aid in accelerating the coming of the *eschaton*, the final coming of Christ at the end of time. Writings such as Tatian's (*fl.* 150–170) treatise on gospel harmony (*Diatessaron*) indicate that Syrian asceticism was rooted in biblical images depicting radical poverty, necessity of prayer, and importance of 'life in the Spirit'. Celibacy* was an essential element in the ascetic way of life and some Syrian groups may even have required celibacy as a prerequisite for Christian baptism (*see also* **Syrian Spirituality**).

During the third and fourth centuries many individuals and small groups of ascetics also flourished in the wilderness areas of Egypt. One of the more famous solitaries, Antony* (*c.* 250–350), decided that since martyrdom was not to be his lot, he would spend the rest of his life as a solitary 'dying daily to self' in imitation of Christ, the first martyr (*Vita Ant.* 3). Antony and others saw the ascetic life as a type of martyrdom in intent, a daily exercising of the will and subduing of the flesh in imitation of the suffering Christ. This notion became paradigmatic for many solitaries, some of whom felt that through the gradual process of institutionalization the church was so accommodating itself to worldly society that it was losing the vision of true Christianity as defined by the scriptures. These ascetics saw their withdrawal from the rest of society as a necessary protest against a Christianity which they felt had separated itself from its original ideals and practices. According to the desert accounts ascetic practices included not only physical austerities (e.g., fasting, exposure to heat and cold, abstention from sexual activity, lack of sleep) but also mental discipline necessary to understand the nature of evil desires and thoughts so as to rid oneself of them. Evagrius of Pontus (346–399), one of the first Christian writers to use philosophical and theological terminology in describing ascetical experiences, descriptively lists eight fundamental evil thoughts which had to be eliminated if one wanted to become a true Christian: gluttony, lust, avarice, melancholy, anger, boredom, vainglory and pride (*Praktikos*). Evagrius contends that these thoughts are obstacles hindering prayer, the direct communication with God.

Places of silence devoid of the noise and temptations of the cities and its inhabitants became for many a solitary *abba* ('father') and *amma* ('mother') the exercising ground for becoming a true 'athlete of God'. Celibacy and poverty were an important part of the training conducive to attaining mastery over the concupiscences of the flesh. By subduing the natural desires for sexual activity and the acquisition of material objects the ascetics' desires and time would more easily be spent in the contemplation of spiritual matters, particularly in the individual's quest for unity with God. Although there were individuals whose fervour led them to an exaggerated disdain of human nature, most of the early desert accounts from Syria and Egypt warn against inordinately severe ascetic practices. These were seen as demonic devices resulting in egotism and false piety. Solitaries were repeatedly warned not to allow the means to the end to become a deterrent to attaining the end itself (*see also* *Apophthegmata*). The ascetics' training was against those forces both internal and external which took one away from the one thing necessary for eternal life, acquiring the fullness of life in and with Christ. Prayer, fasting, working with one's hands, and other practices of mortification were the training equipment used in the process of ensuring the simultaneous decrease of the individual and the increase of Christ.

According to literature of the late third and early fourth centuries hundreds of men and women went into the deserts or solitary places at the edges of the cities. There they would gather around a spiritual father or mother who had already acquired a reputation for wisdom after having undergone strict training in spiritual combat. After a period of time, during which the beginner consulted periodically with the spiritual director and lived a disciplined life of prayer, work and fasting, the ascetic would go farther into the desert alone to wage solitary battles against the demons. Often others would in turn attach themselves to the veteran ascetic and so the number of ascetic communities grew. In the early fourth century after Christians were allowed greater freedom to practice their religion and martyrdom became less accessible as the most perfect way to follow Christ, communities of men and women sprang up simultaneously almost everywhere. Although the eremitic (hermit) life still flourished in many areas there was a rapid growth of communal asceticism, i.e., a routinization of the daily life of the members of a community under the direction of a spiritual leader experienced in the principles and practices of asceticism. The basic orientation of the cenobitic life (from the Latin, *coenobium*, 'living in common') was similar to that of the desert solitary in that it was rooted in the evangelical precepts of renunciation, purity of heart, and *metanoia* or complete conversion towards God with all one's mind and heart. Cenobitic asceticism, however, was geared towards a life of mutual service, 'dying daily to self' amidst others in community where the commandment to love one's neighbour as oneself became a daily lived experience. Eventually, to the hermits' practice of poverty and celibacy were added obedience, stability within a specific community, and the conversion of one's way of life.

By the end of the fourth and the beginning of the fifth century the individualism of the solitary ascetics was gradually giving way to communal forms of ascetic life. The leaders or founders of the monastic communities (e.g., Pachomius, Amoun, Basil, Cassian *, Benedict *) saw great value in these support groups built on mutuality of goals. The quest for self-mastery was not rejected but

incorporated in a context of mutual service in creating an environment conducive to greater union with God. Withdrawal from the rest of society and entrance into a world of silence were still essential for returning to the Lord, but this was now accompanied by 'the labour of obedience' which 'will bring you back to him from whom you have drifted by the sloth of disobedience' (Prologue, *Rule of Benedict*). The various *Rules* placed less emphasis on ascetic feats and more on moderate means of discipline. Charity towards the other members of the community became a key to the development of harmonious life within the monastic family. The entire life of the monastic was to be an ascetic one, but rooted in an asceticism which stressed communal rather than individual aspects, sharing of monastic goods rather than personal possessions, celibacy rather than intimate affection for one person, and obedience to the will of another rather than addiction to one's own will (*see also* **Monastic Spirituality, Monasticism**).

Bishops like Basil (*c.* 330–379), Ambrose (*c.* 340–397), Augustine * (*c.* 354–430), and Gregory the Great * (*c.* 540–604) gave episcopal guidance to the ascetic movements within the church and encouraged moderate ascetical practices (e.g., works of charity, fasting, prayer) among the Christians in general. Such moderate practices were perceived as precepts of universal obligation for all Christians while the monastics' 'counsels of perfection' (celibacy, poverty, obedience, stability) were extolled as the means *par excellence* for advancing to greater degrees of holiness and re-establishing the original sacred order. Though the monastic movement as a whole contributed extensively to the spiritual life of the church's members by the inspiration it evoked through its actions and literature, the honour accorded it had at times the negative effect of minimizing the value of marriage and lay life.

During the Middle Ages in particular, when monastic communities were often gifted with large land-holdings and became engrossed in the care and maintenance of large feudal estates, there were periodic demands for reform both from within and outside the monastic communities. Records indicate that increased wealth was often responsible for the decrease in discipline and neglect of ascetical practices within monasteries. There were periodic outbursts and reactions against the laxities of specific communities and not too infrequently there were splits within the communities themselves, one group leaving in order to return to the more ascetic ideals of the founder. Many reformers founded new communities because they felt that those already established were no longer conducive to entering into an active spiritual relationship with God. Hence, Francis of Assisi * (1181–1226) urged a return to the simplicity and poverty of the gospels; Dominic (1173–1221) placed ascetic value on the discipline of rigorous study and preaching the word of God; the Canons Regular and Third Orders emphasized the importance of lay ascetic life centered around prayer and works of charity. Preaching, penance (e.g., fasting, giving up or sharing material possessions, making pilgrimages, persevering through daily trials), and prayer became the more popular forms of imitating the Christ of the gospels. There also developed during this time certain schools and systems of mysticism which claimed that the best way to arrive at true knowledge of God was through personally experiencing him, rather than primarily speculating about him as did the theologians, Mystics such as Meister Eckhart * (1260–1327), Teresa of Avila* (1518–1582), John of the Cross * (1542–1591), and Jakob Boehme* (1525–1624) emphasized great devotion to Jesus' humanity while at the same time urging detachment from creatures and creature comforts in order to understand more fully what that humanity involved. The means of acquiring a powerful experience of and unity with God was chiefly through watchfulness, i.e., being open to God's love by a cleansing of the heart from all things extraneous, by inner recollection, abandonment of self to God's actions, and persevering in hopeful anticipation of the final, eternal union with God (*see also* **Mysticism**).

At the time of the Renaissance and the Protestant Reformation there was a marked reaction against the ascetic ideal as the most excellent indication of the truly Christian life. Martin Luther * (1483–1546) and other reformers objected to ascetical practices on the grounds that they placed greater emphasis on works as necessary for salvation rather than on the gift of salvation made possible for all by the freely given grace of God. The cultic forms of asceticism which had become an integral part of the Mediaeval Christian tradition were replaced by greater attention to the word of God as expounded in the scriptures and by living out one's moral life by conforming to the ideals of like-minded believers (congregation). Hence in some Protestant areas monasteries were dissolved as a necessary measure for restoring marriage to a more respectable position than it had in a past which all too often ascribed second-class citizenship to those married. Although Roman Catholicism maintained monastic communities as an integral part of church structure, the tendency within the Protestant traditions has been to minimize and decentralize hierarchical structures as a means to eliminating divisive social stratifications evoked by such structures.

Since the last quarter of the nineteenth century, with the rise of such disciplines as comparative religion and psychology of religion, new ideals and practices of asceticism have gradually emerged. Interest in Eastern religions has led to the incorporation of certain meditative, disciplined practices aimed towards the development of interior harmony. The interest in modern psychology, anthropology and sociology has tended to replace the concept of body/soul dualism with emphasis on integration of the 'whole' person. The contemporary search is one for simplicity and peace in a world of sometimes confusing pluralism and alienation. The search for God is often seen as a necessary part of the search for self-identity and self-fulfilment. The communal aspect develops from an emphasis on responsive relationships symbolic of the God-soul relationship.

Within contemporary societies the traditional mistrust or contempt of the body is generally replaced by a common-sense form of discipline (e.g., being a vegetarian, exercising daily, finding the correct meditation posture). These practices are evoked by the conviction that by living a fully-integrated life one automatically curbs one's own egotistic impulses and desires. Virtue is seen not as a denial of something but an acceptance and affirmation of all that is most deeply human. Therefore body and soul are interdependent aspects of the integrated, whole Christian. That the individual's way to salvation includes dedication to the needs and sufferings of others is demonstrated by the increasing activities of social-justice activists whose Christian duties include everything from marching in picket-lines to teaching Third World victims how to fight injustice. The contemporary 'way' of the Christian ascetic has largely become that of structuring one's own perfection in the context of one's specific culture. According to the view of many contemporary theorists of asceticism, spiritual perfection is possible only as an outgrowth of human wholeness. Although this concept is not unique to the contemporary age, its all-pervading emphasis makes it a distinctive characteristic of twentieth-century spirituality.

Although there has never been a uniform definition or practice of asceticism throughout Christian history, the underlying motivation has always been that of overcoming the obstacles to the fulfilment of the gospel imperative to love God and love one's neighbour. The methods have varied in kind and degree of emphasis, but the universal aspiration of various people in different places and times has continued to be that uttered in the fourth-century eucharistic prayer of Serapion of Thmuis: 'make us truly alive'.

Owen Chadwick, *Western Asceticism*, 1958; Thomas M. Gannon and George W. Traub, *The Desert and the City: An Interpretation of the History of Christian Spirituality*, 1969; Margaret R. Miles, *Fullness of Life: Historical Foundations for a New Asceticism*, 1981; William Skudlarek (ed), *The Continuing Quest for God: Monastic Spirituality in Tradition and Transition*, 1982; Anselm Stolz, *L'Ascese Chrétienne*, 1948.

ROSEMARY RADER

Ashram

In Hindu religious experience ashram originally meant a forest dwelling where a person withdrew in later life after fulfilling the duties of parent and householder, to seek through peace and intense spiritual concentration a vision of and union with Reality as the source of all being. Disciples would gather round such a recluse who became known for his sanctity, treating him with great reverence as guru, or spiritual teacher who could enable enlightenment or 'realization' in those who subjected themselves to him, by virtue of his own experience of en-

lightenment. In modern usage ashram means a loose community of members and visitors gathered round a guru to seek an experience of God, from formal discourses, private conversations and counsel, and lengthy periods of personal and communal meditation. Modern Hindu ashrams began to appear from the late nineteenth century as part of a Hindu renaissance. They now exist in large numbers in India and abroad, reflecting a wide range of sects and doctrinal positions within Hindu tradition. This Hindu style of religious organization with its emphasis on contemplative spirituality, seeking the divine within the depths of each individual, began to influence Christians in India in the early twentieth century. That influence spread beyond India later in the century, adding a new dimension to Western Christian thinking and practice which ran parallel to a more general awakening of interest in Indian religions among people having no connections, or very tenuous ties, with the Christian churches.

Early Christian ashrams tended to be Protestant; founded by Indian Christians and foreign missionaries who, in contrast to earlier missionaries' condemnation of Hindu beliefs and customs, believed that the Holy Spirit has spoken in many ways through the centuries, and that the specifically Christian revelation could crown and fulfil, rather than destroy the deepest Hindu religious aspirations and perceptions of truth. They were also deeply perturbed that Christianity appeared a foreign import and could easily be seen as the ideological handmaid of British imperialism in India. Consequently those who lived in some of the early Christian ashrams wore *khadi* (hand-spun cloth) which was a badge of nationalist sentiment; and some openly worked with nationalist leaders such as Mahatma Gandhi *. Later in the century after India's independence the need of Christians to identify with nationalism ebbed as a source of inspiration for Christian ashrams and in its place flowed a deepening Christian awareness of the resources of Hindu spirituality * to inform and enrich Christian thinking and practice. Roman Catholic religious have been particularly prominent in advocating renewal based on ashram life, and in spreading the concept of 'inculturation', whereby Indian Christians are encouraged to draw on their Indian spiritual heritage to develop truly indigenous Christian ways of believing and praying. (For example, three Benedictines, Henri Le Saux, Francis Mahieu and Bede Griffiths*, created and sustained ashrams in southern India. Another publicist for Christian ashrams in India and abroad is Sister Vandana of the Order of the Sacred Heart, who lived for a time at an ecumenical ashram in western India.) The hall-marks of ashram life are exterior quiet and a simplicity which releases men from the burden of inessential concerns and possessions; a discipline combining meditation and worship with the labour necessary to sustain the community's life; and a flexibility and openness to seekers after God more possible than in Western monastic houses ordered by strict rule. Every ashram has a leader; but the leader's role is open to debate in the Christian setting. Many would say that no Christian can be to another Christian a guru in the Hindu sense; and that only Christ can enable a vision of God and union with God, and only he can require total obedience from the disciple. At the heart of the ashram experience is a quiet and disciplined waiting, in which one opens oneself to the presence of God, using symbols, meditative techniques, silence and conventional words of worship. However, the ashram movement has had its critics within the churches, particularly on the grounds that it undermines the distinctiveness of Christian revelation and underplays the significance of Christ, by its use of Hindu words and symbols, and its contemplative stress on the inward move ment of the individual soul to experience the immanent God.

Sister Vandana, *Gurus, Ashrams and Christians*, 1978.

JUDITH M. BROWN

Asian Spirituality

No spirituality can be thought of separately from its cultural background. At the same time it is by the force of spirituality that cultures continue to be meaningful. Spirituality is spirit in communion and in mutuality with culture. Japanese spirituality expresses itself in the Japanese language, as the language is defined by Japanese culture. Spirituality has 'personality', understood here as the ability to express itself through the use of symbols which it has itself created.

Within the vast geographical expanse of Asia, the rich cultural diversity in languages, customs, ethnic groupings, religious traditions and diverse economic levels has produced a variety of spiritual orientations. One can only think of Asian spirituality as a plural reality, as spiritualities; i.e., there are Asian Buddhist spirituality, Asian Islamic spirituality and Asian Christian spirituality. Even within Asian Buddhist spirituality there are different spiritual orientations as found in Theravada Thailand and Mahayana Japan. Similarly, Islamic spirituality as found in Pakistan and Indonesia shows delicate differences. Christian spirituality in Hindu India is significantly different from that of the Spanish Philippines.

There are important differences in the spiritual and intellectual life of Asians. The two largest and most ancient civilizations of Asia, India and China, exhibit sharp cultural contrasts. India places emphasis on the universals, minimizes specific particulars and finds creativity in the act of negation. China, on the other hand, prefers concreteness, particulars and practicality. Such clear cultural differences will be evident in the spiritual orientation of the two peoples. Gandhi* expressed the mind of India eloquently; 'Civilization, in the real sense of the term, consists not in the multiplication, but in the deliberate and voluntary reduction of wants.' In India there is a spiritual heritage that hinders her from adopting a strongly materialistic construction of human life, while such a heritage is relatively absent in the culture of the practical Chinese. Thus the symbolic life of India and China forms a distinctive contrast.

In spite of all these diversities, it is not impossible to think of a common base of Asian spirituality. This can be more easily seen if Asian spirituality is examined relative to Western spirituality. Conversely, the character of Western spirituality is made evident when it is compared with Asian spirituality. Asian spirituality is concerned with undifferentiated totality *before* creation, while Western spirituality is interested in differentiated totality *after* creation. Suzuki contrasts two poets of world repute, the Japanese Basho, and the English Tennyson:

When I look carefully
I see the *nazuna* blooming
by the hedge!

Flower in the crannied wall,
I pluck you out of the crannies,
Hold you here, root and all, in my hand
Little flower – but if I could understand
What you are, root and all, and all in all
I should know what God and man is.

In a cultural and spiritual sense this observation is helpful. Asia looks at the
flower, as it were, in its impression *before*
the creation, while the West examines in
detail the form of the flower *after* creation.
Asian spirituality is cosmological in the
sense that it is interested in the undifferentiated primordial image of all things,
while the West is eschatological in the sense
that nature's totality (cosmos) must be subject to eschatological (transcendent) judgment.

It is important to know that this eschatological moment is not indigenous to the
West. It comes from the biblical heritage
(Judaism, Christianity and Islam) which
came to birth on the western edge of the
great Asian continent. This eschatological
sense of discontinuity (differentiated) is the
element against which Asian spirituality
(undifferentiated) can be placed in contrast.
In general, the fundamental contrast between Western and Asian spiritualities is that
Asian spirituality is cosmological while Western spirituality is eschatological. Cosmological spirituality is also universal, but
the West, mainly because of the historical
presence of Christianity, has an eschatological element which is a 'scandal' to cosmological spirituality. While the cosmological spirituality proclaims that 'my help
comes from heaven and earth', eschatological spirituality would say 'my help comes
from the Lord who made heaven and earth'
(Ps. 121.2).

Just as there is a mutuality between Asian
spirituality and Asian cultures, there is a
mutuality between Asian spirituality and
Asian religiosity. When Asian spirituality
incorporates certain religious doctrines it
becomes Asian religiosity. Thus, for example, Hindu spirituality, at home with the
cyclical motions of the natural world,
becomes the context for the development of
the doctrine of *nirvana*, which teaches of
ultimate freedom from pain and from the
tedious cycle of birth and death. Spirituality
becomes religiosity when an ultimate value
is made into a religious formulation. Simi-

larly, the Japanese love of nature's vitality,
expressed in the image of 'sprouting reeds'
in the marshy land (the opening paragraphs
of the *Kojiki*), intimates the distinctive character of Japanese spirituality as a 'botani-
cal spirituality'. The image of 'sprouting
reeds' is a positive inspiration to the Japanese soul. Delight in images of this nature is
basic to the Japanese nature-worship religiosity known as the *'Way of Kami'* ('Shinto-
ism'). Another example comes from the
Chinese fascination with the movement of
air (*chih*). That the clean air ascends and
polluted air descends is a prominent interpretative principle in Chinese human experience. This has given the Chinese people
a cosmological religiosity. Asian spirituality
is rooted in such a primordial fascination
with the behaviour of nature, be it cyclical
movement, vitality of plants or movement
of air. Such a fascination is spiritual and
cultural since it is able to satisfy the human
need for self-identity in space and in time.
When these experiences are formulated into
religious words or doctrines, suggesting the
overcoming of cyclical existence, the struggle against mortality of life, or a systematic
discussion about the constituent elements of
the universe, then Asian spirituality assumes
the quality of Asian religiosity.

The contrast between cosmological and
eschatological spirituality may be further
expanded:

1. *In Asian spirituality there is no creatio
ex nihilo*. It is cosmological in the sense that
both the ideas of 'creation' and 'nothingness' are placed within the framework of
the totality of nature, not beyond it. They
are cosmologically, not eschatologically,
defined. The eschatology of Asian spirituality describes a critical moment within
the cosmic cycle of creation, maintenance,
dissolution, creation. Eschatology does not
confront the cosmos itself. The cosmic cycle
symbolizes the regularity, continuity and
predictability of time. Irregularity, discontinuity and unpredictability are foreign
to Asian spirituality, which has never appreciated the concept of *creatio ex nihilo*.
This observation is not just intellectual in
nature. It has been determinative to Asian
spirituality. Asian prayer is not eschatological, for instance. It is cosmological.
Prayer is a word directed to the impressive
totality of nature, not to Someone who is
discontinuous with nature. To use the word

of *Veda*, prayer is addressed to the self-generative cosmic heat (*tapas*). The question whether the doctrines of Theravada Buddhism on *nirvana* (absolute tranquility) and Mahayana Buddhism on the primal vows of the Boddhisattva (absolute mercy) would correspond to the philosophical and spiritual message of *creatio ex nihilo* cannot be discussed here.

2. *Asian spirituality is polytheistic*. The cosmos does not confront us with the choice between life and death (Deut. 30.19). On the contrary, it embraces all things and all possibilities. The image of embrace and not confrontation is more appropriate to cosmologically-oriented spirituality. The cosmos has many gods. The eighteenth-century Japanese scholar Motoori Norinaga writes: 'It is hardly necessary to say that it/god/includes human beings. It also includes such objects as birds, beasts, trees, plants, seas, mountains and so forth.' Asian spirituality sees many gods in the cosmos. No god is presented 'exclusively'. Truth is often portrayed in Asia as the totality of opposite principles, male–female, heaven–earth, day–night, and such truth is inclusive and is continuous with us. Exclusivity, on the other hand, is confrontational. Another way to say this is that in the West there is God ('The Lord who made heaven and earth') who knows perfectly what is good and what is evil (Gen. 3.5). God represents the ultimate moral principle relevant to all historical situations. This 'exclusivity' is foreign to Asian spirituality. We all receive instruction as to what is good and what is evil from the way of nature.

3. *Asian spirituality is not iconoclastic*. Asian spirituality does not judge idols in the way eschatological spirituality does. Asian spirituality accepts the culture of deification in which the line between the human and the divine (*Kami, deva*) is easily crossed. In the context of Asian spirituality idol makes comment on or even criticizes idol. Idolatry is not condemned from the view point of the transcendent God. The Psalmist makes this telling observation on idolatry; 'They exchanged the glory of God for the image of an ox that eats grass' (106.20). If 'the image of the ox that eats grass' does harm to humanity, Asian spirituality would make a critical comment. One of the most penetrating and well-argued critical words directed against human greed

comes from the sage of Asia, the Buddha. The Buddha would have protested that the ox, so long as it simply eats grass, is no problem. Only if the image is twisted to gratify human greed is there need for critique. But the criticism of Buddha is done apart from the first half of this verse, 'They exchanged the glory of God. . . .' Asian spirituality is not concerned with the glory of God. It accepts deification and idols. It is not iconoclastic. Here is a profound difference between East and West.

The history of Asian spirituality has not, however, remained isolated. In four major historical events it may be said that Asian spirituality has encountered eschatological spirituality, at least indirectly.

1. *Modernization*. The great efficiency introduced by modernization, in particular in the areas of science-based technology and the social economic theory of Marxism, has rapidly changed the general style of Asian life and challenged the traditional practice and expression of Asian spirituality. The cosmological piety of the people of Bali Island, Indonesia, for example, experienced a serious disruption when the Americans walked on the 'sacred' face of the moon in 1969. The articulate and impatient words of Marxism with its secular eschatological hope have shaken the patient spirituality of the cosmological orientation.

2. *Through Islam and Christianity*. The presence and expansion of the two universal faiths of strong eschatological orientation, Christianity and Islam perhaps provided the most direct encounters between Asian spirituality and eschatological spirituality. The evaluation of these encounters requires a careful historical investigation which, to my knowledge, has not yet been made. Such a study would have to cover the colonial period of Asia from the early sixteenth century to the early part of the present century which L. K. Panikkar called the 'Vasco da Gama' era. It is also important historically that the preaching of Christianity and Islam has continued in Asia since the year of Hiroshima, 1945, as many Asian countries were achieving political independence, including the emergence of the Chinese communist state in 1949. For the intervening three decades the eschatological message of Christianity and Islam has been preached to an Asia suffering from militarism, political totalitarianism, racial and ethnic conflicts,

hunger and poverty. In all these great complexities of history Asian spirituality is being encountered by the eschatological spirituality.

3. *Through ecological concern.* Asian spirituality as cosmological spirituality is basically ecologically oriented. In the time of brutal exploitation of nature, the cosmological piety is beginning to demonstrate its ecological conviction to humanity. In this context Asian spirituality is appearing as a substantial corrective to the world of eschatological spirituality. Asian spirituality prefers to see humanity living in harmony with nature rather than dominating over nature. It remains to be seen whether cosmological spirituality of Asia will contribute more to the understanding of the kingdom of God in this area than will eschatological spirituality. This is perhaps one of the most dramatic contexts in which the encounter between Asian spirituality and eschatological spirituality is taking place.

4. *Through anxiety about the possibility of nuclear destruction.* Anxiety over the possibility of the global destruction of humanity by nuclear weapons is occasioning the meeting of the cosmological and eschatological spiritualities as it calls both traditions into serious self-examination.

Asian spirituality is faced with the challenge of integrating cosmological spirituality and eschatological spirituality in such a way that cosmological spirituality can speak meaningfully through eschatological spirituality and eschatological spirituality through cosmological spirituality. The theological ground for that integration must be the theme of the suffering and hope of people. Cosmological spirituality and eschatological spirituality must be integrated *through* the suffering and hope of people. This suggests the need for an Asian *theologia crucis.* Asian Christian spirituality must respond to the words of Paul; '. . . we preach Christ crucified, a stumbling block to Jews and folly to Gentiles' (I Cor. 1.23). It is in its response to this challenge that the future of Asian Christian spirituality is located.

Tissa Balasuriya, *The Eucharist and Human Liberation*, 1979; H. B. Earhart, *Religion in the Japanese Experience*, 1974; Douglas J. Elwood (ed), *Asian Christian Theology*, 1980; Abraham J. Heschel, *The Sabbath*, 1951; Kosuke Koyama, *No Handle on the Cross*, 1977; Hajime Nakamura, *Ways of Thinking of Eastern Peoples*, 1974; Daisetz Suzuki, *Zen and Japanese Culture*, 1959.

KOSUKE KOYAMA

Athanasius of Alexandria, St

Athanasius (*c.* 296–373) was Bishop of Alexandria from 328. His vigorous assertion of Christ's Godhead and his rejection of the received interpretation of Godhead as admitting of degrees ('Arianism') led him to bitter controversy and five exiles from his see. All his surviving writings, in varying ways, reflect this conflict. His conviction that Christ is the eternal Son and Word of God who had taken a human body to rescue mankind from moral and physical corruption was expressed in powerful pamphlets like the three *Orations against the Arians* and *On the Incarnation.* The arguments Athanasius used were often defective, not only in logic, but also in what was later to be accounted orthodoxy; e.g. he took it for granted that Christ's conscious self was the divine Word and did not think that he had a human soul. However, his message, grounded in subtler and more wide-ranging reasonings by others, captured the church, overthrowing the hitherto accepted understanding of Christ. In this way he effected a lasting shift in Christian doctrine, guaranteeing that Christian spirituality should subsequently have as its theme for contemplation not a godlike hero winning for himself divine honours in his struggle with evil, nor a creating angel inhabiting a human frame, but the Son of God in flesh. He wrote little about the sacraments or private devotion. What pertains to spirituality in his works may be summarized under three headings.

1. *The human condition.* Man, a compound of flesh and immortal soul, is in God's image, reflecting God's rationality and, ideally, his stability. In fact, through Adam's sin men have lost the stability which is divine life and have become prey to sensuality and the idolatry which is subjection to devils.

2. *Divine intervention.* To restore the divine likeness (never wholly lost) the Word has entered the world, vivifying by his touch enfeebled and perishing human nature. Demonic powers retreat and human nature becomes what in Adam it ideally was. Moreover, Christ's mission is to make men

God's sons and to deify them, i.e. raise them to a higher spiritual level of real *rapport* with God. For all this only a Christ who is God in person could suffice.

3. *Christian asceticism.* Athanasius' *Life of St Antony* certainly represents more of his own convictions than those of the desert ascetic, Antony*. The purpose of the religious life is to restore the 'natural' state of man where the soul, governed by reason, controls the passions of a healthy body; it realizes the philosophers' dream amongst ordinary people. Asceticism brings supernatural faculties and the conquest of demons (viewed as essentially part of nature, not above it) in continuation of Christ's work; moreover, it makes a man a means of grace to others and to the church as a whole. This Christian asceticism is free from masochism. The need for divine grace is unstressed but presupposed: goodness requires a good will and the will is good when it is natural or normal; normality, and more, is God's gift in Christ.

St Athanasius on the Incarnation, tr by A Religious of CSMV, 1953; *Select Works and Letters* (Library of Nicene and Post Nicene Fathers), 1891; C. R. B. Shapland, *The Letters of Saint Athanasius Concerning the Holy Spirit*, 1951; G. L. Prestige, *Fathers and Heretics*, 1940.

L. R. WICKHAM

Attention see Contemplation

Augustine of Hippo, St

The spirituality of St Augustine (354–430) does not differ essentially from that of the Greek Fathers (*see* **Athanasius**; **Cappadocian Fathers**). Whether any direct influence existed cannot be conclusively established. Augustine's limited knowledge of Greek presumably precluded much direct acquaintance with Eastern theologians, but their ideas could have reached him through translations and Latin authors like St Ambrose, who read Greek fluently. However, the common background of the Bible, and the popular Platonism* of the later patristic age, would probably of itself have led Augustine and the Greek Fathers to a similar outlook. Thereafter Augustine's teaching, popularized in the writings of Gregory the Great*, dominated Western mediaeval spirituality, though supplemented in the ninth century by that of Denys the Areopagite* in the translation of John Scotus Eriugena, and of St Bernard* and his school in the twelfth. We may therefore fairly place Augustinian spirituality within the tradition of Western Christendom.

The question of Augustine's personal religious experience is controversial. Some scholars rank him among the greatest mystics; others deny that he was a mystic at all. Two passages in his *Confessions* (7, 10, 16; 7, 17, 23) describe ascents of his mind to God at Milan in 386, immediately before his conversion. The so-called Vision of Ostia, a meditation shared with his mother, Monica, just before her death in 387 (*Conf.* 9, 10, 23), has likewise been regarded as describing a mystical experience, notwithstanding Neoplatonic literary influence (see Paul Henry, *La vision d'Ostie*, 1938). These autobiographical passages constitute the primary evidence for regarding Augustine as a mystic. His exegesis of Ps. 41[42] has been understood as an account of mystical contemplation (*Enarr. Ps.* 41), while his *De Quantitate Animae* (33, 70–77), written in 388, nearly ten years before the *Confessions*, provides a description of the ascent of the mind to God which parallels that of *Conf.* 7, 17, 23. Similar descriptions occur elsewhere in Augustine (*De Gen. con. Man.* 1, 24, 42; *Doctr. Chr.* 2, 7, 9–11; *Trin.* 12, 15, 25). The problem about accepting them as evidence of personal experience is that they can also be understood as descriptions of human cognition, so that it is not clear whether Augustine is giving an account of contemplation or formulating an epistemological theory. The explanation appears to be that for Augustine the two processes cannot be separated (see Étienne Gilson, *Introduction à l'étude de saint Augustin*, [4]1969, pp. 311f.), which in turn suggests that his personal religious experiences, although involving a kind of supernatural enlightenment, were not mystical in the strictly theological sense of the word (see David Knowles, *The English Mystical Tradition*, 1961, pp. 25–9). What is certain is that Augustinian spirituality always includes an intellectual element. Despite the primacy of love in Augustine's theology, the ascent to God is a mental, as well as an affective and emotional, journey.

This raises the question of the degree to which Augustine was conditioned by Neoplatonism*. He never concealed the part which it played in his conversion (*Conf.* 7, 9, 13–15; *contra Acad.* 2, 2, 5; *Beata Vita* 1, 4) and an element of the intellectualism of Plotinus* remained to influence his theology throughout his life (e.g. *Doctr. Chr.* 2, 40, 60; *Civ. Dei* 10, 2). Nevertheless, Augustine recognized a fundamental division between Neoplatonism and Christianity through the doctrine of the incarnation, which Neoplatonism rejected (*Conf.* 7, 9, 14; *Civ. Dei* 10, 29; see Henry, op. cit., pp. 115–27).

The incarnation is at the heart of Augustine's theology. Christ is the mediator, by whom we come to God. 'The God Christ is the home where we are going; the man Christ is the way by which we are going. We go to him, we go by him; why do we fear that we should go astray?' (*Serm.* 123, 3, 3). 'By assuming man's nature he became the way. Walk by [him] the man and you come to God. By him you go, to him you go. Look not for any other way except himself by which to go to him' (*Serm.* 141, 4, 4; cf. *Conf.* 7, 18, 24; *Doctr. Chr.* 1, 34, 38; *Civ. Dei* 9, 15). Christocentricity dominates Augustinian spirituality and helps to explain the intensely personal note of the *Confessions*, the work which above all others gives an insight into Augustine's mind. It is true that in the *Confessions* God is addressed as the Father rather than the Son; but it is through the Son that Augustine is able to speak to the Father directly. 'Plotinus never *gossiped* with the One, as Augustine gossips in the *Confessions*' (E. R. Dodds). The influence of Augustine's personalism may be seen in works like St Anselm's* *Proslogion* and St Bonaventure's* *Itinerarium mentis in Deum*, in which meditation and philosophical argument are conjoined in typically Augustinian fashion.

Meditation and philosophical enquiry depend, however, on the study of scripture. Augustine, like all the Fathers, regarded the Bible as the inspired word of God, and it is significant that some of his most profound spiritual teaching occurs in the course of scriptural exegesis, notably in the *Sermons* [*Enarrationes*] *on the Psalms* and the *Tractates on the Gospel of John*. The scriptures are the means whereby we come to love God for his own sake, and men for God's sake; they inculcate the divine virtue of charity (*Doctr. Chr.* 1, 35, 39–36, 40; 2, 7, 10). Augustine admits that men may attain to

such a degree of perfection in faith, hope and charity as to be able to live as hermits without copies of the scriptures, but only because they have already reached this state through the scriptures (Ibid., 1, 39, 43).

Christ is the goal, Christ the way; the scriptures point the way to Christ; but this does not mean that the Christian life on earth is identical for all men. Augustine recognizes the classical distinction between the lives of action and contemplation, symbolized in the OT by Leah and Rachel (*Con. Faust.* 22, 52–57) and in the NT by Martha and Mary (*Serm.* 103; 104) and Peter and John (*Io. Ev. Tr.* 124, 5). While regarding the contemplative life as superior to the active because it is eternal, Augustine holds that perfection of contemplation is possible only in the life to come. In his monastic rule he emphasizes the active cultivation of charity in the common life rather than solitary contemplation, and in heaven the life of the saints is a social one (*Civ. Dei* 19,5).

Contemplation nevertheless is part of Christian living, even in this world, and characteristic of Augustinian contemplation is its interiority. 'Being admonished by all this to return to myself, I entered into my own depths, with You as guide; and I was able to do this because *You were my helper*' [Ps. 29(30), 11] (*Conf.* 7, 10, 16; cf. *Acad.* 2, 2, 4). Augustine's encounter with God is by a process of introversion, preceded by purging the mind of sensual images (*En. Ps.* 41, 7–8). This interior seeking produces self-knowledge (cf. *Sol.* 1, 2, 7; 2, 1, 1) and a consciousness of the deformation of the image of God in the sinful soul, which can only be reformed to wholeness by divine grace (*Trin.* 15, 28, 51. See G. B. Ladner, *The Idea of Reform*, 1967). Reformation is accomplished by participation in God, made possible by the mediation of Christ (*De Gen. ad Litt. Lib. imp.* 16, 57–60; *Trin.* 14, 12, 15). Participation is a Platonistic concept; but Augustine christianizes it, and brings it into harmony with catholic doctrine (see James F. Anderson, *St Augustine and Being*, 1965, pp. 54–60). Christ, being God and remaining wholly in his nature, became a partaker of our nature, so that we, remaining in our nature, might be partakers of his nature (*Ep.* 140, 4, 10; cf. *Enchir.* 28, 106; *Civ. Dei* 11, 12). From this doctrine of participation there is an easy transition to that of deification*, sometimes said to be peculiar to Greek theology. 'He who was God was made man to make gods those who were men' (*Serm*. 192, 1, 1; see Victorino Capánaga in *Augustinus Magister*, ii, 745–54). Deification is, however, by adoption and not of nature: 'If we have been made sons of God, we have also been made gods; but this is the effect of adoptive grace, not by generation by nature. For only the Son of God, our Lord and saviour Jesus Christ, was *in the beginning the Word, the Word with God, the Word that was God*. The rest who are made gods are made by His grace and not born of His substance that they should be the same as He, but that by favour they should come to Him and be *joint-heirs with Christ*' (*En. Ps*. 49, 2).

It is no accident that Augustine constantly urges the virtue of humility. 'God is already humble – and man is still proud!' (*Serm*. 142, 6, 6).

In addition to titles mentioned in the text, see: John Burnaby, *Amor Dei. A Study of the Religion of St Augustine*, 1938; Cuthbert Butler, *Western Mysticism*, ³1967; F. Cayré, *La contemplation augustinienne*, ²1954; Pierre Courcelle, *Recherches sur les Confessions de saint Augustin*, 1950; Ephraem Hendrikx, *Augustins Verhältnis zur Mystik*, Würzburg 1936; E. I. Watkin in *A Monument to Saint Augustine*, 1930.

GERALD BONNER

Ave Maria

Ave Maria is the name given to the commonest prayer addressed to the Blessed Virgin Mary, from the two opening words of the Latin form. In English, the prayer runs: 'Hail Mary, full of grace, the Lord is with thee; blessed art thou among women, and blessed is the fruit of thy womb, Jesus. Holy Mary, Mother of God, pray for us sinners now and in the hour of our death.' The first half of the devotion is a conflation, slightly edited, of the greetings addressed to Mary by Gabriel and Elizabeth in Luke 2, 28, 42. The version of the Vulgate is followed in the words 'full of grace' (*gratia plena*). The second half of the devotion cannot be much older than the sixteenth century. Like the Lord's Prayer, the Ave Maria is frequently used as an informal devotion. It also has its place in such devotional practices as the Angelus and the Rosary*. There are many musical settings, of which the most

famous are probably those of Schubert and Gounod.

JOHN MACQUARRIE

Baillie, John

John Baillie (1886–1960) taught in several American theological seminaries before returning to his native Scotland where he was professor at the University of Edinburgh from 1934 till his retirement in 1956. He was working at the time of the theological revolution initiated by Karl Barth and others, and welcomed many of the new insights, especially the stress on the initiative of God and the accompanying criticism of the humanistic bias of nineteenth-century liberal theology. But Baillie could not go along with the Barthian view that there is no genuine knowledge of God outside of the biblical revelation. He believed that all human beings have some access to the knowledge of God, and it is in the course of his wrestling with this problem that we can perceive his distinctive contribution to spirituality.

His two major theological works are *Our Knowledge of God* (1939) and *The Sense of the Presence of God* (1962). In the former of these, while criticizing the excesses of the Barthian position, he is critical also of the traditional natural theology on the grounds that our knowledge of God is not inferential but direct. We do not have to argue for the existence of God. We are aware of his presence, he discloses himself in the world and there is a general revelation open to all. Of course, Baillie is not for a moment disparaging the specifically Christian revelation of God, but he does hold that this revelation has taken place against the background of a diffused but genuine sense of God's presence. He claims that there is an analogy between this knowledge of God and our knowledge of other persons. No one argues for the existence of the other person – there has never been a time when we did not know of the existence of others, and to deny it would be an irrational solipsism. The sense of a divine presence in the world is further analysed and defended in his posthumous volume. Positivism in particular is attacked as a curtailment of human possibilities.

Baillie grew up in the north of Scotland, and it is tempting to see in his ideas the influence of the ancient Celtic spirituality*. A very important feature of that spirituality was precisely an intense awareness of the presence of God, and Baillie tells us that he cannot remember a time in his life when he did not know that presence. Again, at a time when great stress was being laid on divine transcendence, Baillie contended that there must be a proper recognition of the divine immanence, otherwise we would end up with a very distant God. This may have been partly due to his sense of balance in theology, but partly it reflects the spirituality of God's presence in the world. In Baillie's case, the ancient spirituality has become fused with a sophisticated theology. He once wrote that David Hume and Samuel Johnson * were each 'half men', the one a rationalist without spirituality, the other a spiritual person who lacked the critical faculty. That complaint came originally from Carlyle, and Baillie went far to heal the breach in his own person.

J. Baillie, *A Diary of Private Prayer*, 1937; *Invitation to Pilgrimage*, 1942.

JOHN MACQUARRIE

Baker, Augustine

Augustine Baker (1575–1641), of Welsh birth, became a Roman Catholic in 1603, and a Benedictine monk in 1605. After some years of pastoral work in England, he went to Cambrai in 1624 as spiritual adviser to a convent of English nuns. In 1633 he moved to the English monastery in Douai, and in 1638 returned to work in England. At Cambrai and Douai he composed some sixty treatises on spirituality, most of them designed only for specific small groups of readers. His ponderous and meandering style was to some extent lightened by Serenus Cressy in a brilliant digest published as *Sancta Sophia* in 1657 (*Holy Wisdom* in editions since 1890). Baker's reading was voluminous and eclectic, and his treatises make free use of many contemporary and earlier works, generally interpreting them from the standpoint of the apophatic tradition of Denys the Areopagite *. He was instrumental in preserving the texts and the teaching of several mediaeval English mystical works, notably *The Cloud of Unknowing* *.

Insisting that all Christians are obliged 'not only seriously to aspire to the divine love, but also to the perfection thereof suitably to their several states and vocations' (*Holy Wisdom* 1.1.1.11), he advises his read-

ers always to attend to the inner promptings of the Holy Spirit, making use of spiritual directors and books only so far as these prove profitable in the light of their own experience and reason, enlightened by grace. Any serious attempt at prayer must be accompanied by mortification of self-will. Baker much prefers 'necessary', i.e. inevitable, mortifications to voluntary ascetical practices (2.1.5), and offers sound and sensible advice to those troubled by scrupulosity (2.2.8–12).

He expects most people to begin the life of mental prayer by systematic meditation, using the imagination and the intellect to stimulate the desires of the will. But he also expects that this exercise will pall sooner rather than later for those, whether educated or quite unlearned, whose call is to union with God by internal prayer of the will, which he calls contemplation (3.3.1). He recommends 'forced acts', as it were short-circuiting the preliminaries of meditation and moving directly to the final declaration of desire to be united with God. These forced acts will be gradually displaced by 'aspirations' proceeding naturally, easily and constantly from the Holy Spirit (3.4.2). Forced acts and aspirations Baker classifies as active contemplation. They may be succeeded or punctuated by moments of passive contemplation or union, in which the soul experiences its own being and the being of other creatures 'only in that true being which they have in God, by dependence on him and relation to him, so that he is all in all' (3.4.6).

Baker has had a limited but constant following of readers who have found him a safe guide to liberty of spirit, helping them to be 'so absolutely resigned to the divine will, that whatsoever befalls them and all other creatures is most acceptable to them' (3.4.6).

Augustine Baker, *Holy Wisdom*, 1972; Anthony Low, *Augustine Baker*, 1970; Placid Spearritt, 'The Survival of Mediaeval Spirituality among the Exiled English Black Monks', *American Benedictine Review* XXV, 1974, pp. 287–316 (full bibliography).

PLACID SPEARRITT

Baptist Spirituality

It is almost four centuries since the Baptist movement began; and there has been development in space as well as in time. Baptists are now to be found in all five continents and in most countries. Their devotion has been influenced by prevailing belief and culture. Granted that there is this diversity, there are five characteristics of Baptist spirituality which are true for much of the time and in many places.

1. First, there is the emphasis on faith; a *personal response* to Christ is required of all. The classic of Puritan spirituality, *Pilgrim's Progress*, written in 1678 in Bedford Gaol by John Bunyan*, is the story of an individual. From the beginning to the end of the journey the pilgrim, Christian, is concerned with the salvation of his own soul. This concern is typical of Baptist piety. Baptists pray and preach for conversions. Baptism, the climax of conversion, is for those who have made this personal response. Through faith and baptism they enter the fellowship of believers. Taken together, faith, baptism and fellowship are distinctive of Baptist spirituality.

2. The Lord Jesus conversed with the Father in intimacy and freedom, and God has sent into our hearts the Spirit of his Son. *Freedom in prayer* was characteristic of the Separatists; their worship was predominantly charismatic. Reading from books was discouraged, spontaneity was highly valued. Today, the typical Baptist does not use a prayer book. At his daily prayers, morning or evening as fits the occasion, his prayer will be extemporary. Family worship – a chapter from the Bible followed by free prayer – was once widespread. Today some families read and pray, seated round the table, immediately after breakfast. Devout parents pray with their children as they are put to bed. In Baptist churches the place for extemporary prayer is the weekly prayer meeting. All the people present are encouraged to take part. There has been widespread criticism of extemporary prayer in the Sunday services; it can be long, boring, meandering, didactic, stereotyped. As a result, it is now being used with more discretion and discipline. But it has not been replaced. As an expression of the freedom of the Spirit, it has a valued and assured place in Baptist worship.

3. Baptists are a Bible-loving people, and their piety is rooted in and nourished by *the reading of scripture*. The Bible was the standard by which the Separatists judged all things, and was central in their gatherings for worship. In the eighteenth and nineteenth centuries, it was customary at the Sunday services not only to read, but also to make a running commentary on, or exposition of, a chapter of the Bible. Bible-reading was never confined to Sundays, and in most churches today there are mid-week meetings or house groups for Bible-study. At these the minister or leader explains the selected scripture or the people themselves share their insights. 'I saw him open the book and read therein.' The Bible was Christian's *vade mecum*; some people still carry it around with them for immediate use when needed. Many Baptists set aside some time every day for the devotional reading of the Bible. Some use explanatory notes on the text. The 'daily portion' of scripture, followed by extemporary prayer, is the staple diet of the devout Baptist.

4. The Bible and *preaching* go together. In *Pilgrim's Progress* Christian 'saw the picture of a very grave person . . . the best of books in his hand, the law of truth was written upon his lips'. The minister preaches from the Bible. In the old chapels, the lofty central pulpit was a symbol of the centrality of the word. It is still true that the focus of attention in a Baptist service is the sermon. Faith is evoked and devotion nourished by the preaching of the word. To name some of the great preachers of the nineteenth and twentieth centuries – Robert Hall, Charles Spurgeon, Alexander Maclaren, John Clifford, Harry Fosdick*, Billy Graham – is but to underline the importance of preaching for Baptists. The written, as well as the spoken word of the preachers, is their staple diet. The printed sermons of Spurgeon, sold at a penny, were the spiritual food of multitudes. Later, the books of F. W. Boreham and H. E. Fosdick found their way into countless homes and hearts. Baptists live by the word, spoken and written.

5. Bunyan concludes his description of the Christian minister with the sentence 'He stood as if he pleaded with men.' The depth of Baptist spirituality can be measured by the Baptist *zeal for evangelism*. Maps of the world were on the walls of the workshop of the cobbler, William Carey. His pamphlet *An Enquiry into the Obligations of Christians to use Means for the Conversion of the Heathen* (1792) was a trumpet call to world mission. Soon afterwards his memorable

sermon at Nottingham led to the formation of the Baptist Missionary Society. Baptist prayer meetings are a further example of this relationship between devotion and mission. The mid-week prayer meeting, in the nineteenth and early twentieth centuries, was the prelude to the Sunday evening evangelistic service. The people met to pray for the conversion of sinners. The same relationship was to be seen on the American frontier where Baptists achieved an unprecedented growth. Worship and evangelism were two sides of the same coin. At camp meetings and revival services lively singing, spontaneous prayer and Bible-reading were followed by emotional preaching with an appeal for personal response. The revival meeting has profoundly and enduringly influenced Baptist worship in many places.

These five characteristics are closely related and interdependent; together, they are the distinctive marks of Baptist spirituality.

STEPHEN F. WINWARD

Basil of Caesarea, St
see Cappadocian Fathers

Baxter, Richard
Richard Baxter (1615–1691), Puritan divine and prolific author, was episcopally ordained in 1638 and during the Interregnum prosecuted a renowned pastorate at Kidderminster. His work for a comprehensive church settlement at the Restoration was disappointed by the exclusivity of the Act of Uniformity (1662) which led to his reluctant withdrawal from the established church to become the leader of the moderate or 'Presbyterian' nonconformists. During the 1680s the term 'Baxterianism' came into use to characterize (and often to impugn) the eclecticism of his thought, the liberalism of his theology and the catholicity of his sympathies. On all divisive issues his eirenic temper consistently argued 'True mediocrity is the only way that's safe': Richard Baxter's Catholick Theologie (1675) sought to reconcile Calvinism and Arminianism, and he repeatedly advocated compromise on church polity along the lines of archbishop James Ussher's Reduction of Episcopacie unto the Form of Synodical Government (1656). Above all, he insisted on the inevitability, and therefore

the inconsequentiality, of opinionative differences. He strove to redirect men's commitment from ecclesiastical platforms, liturgical practices and doctrinal confessions to the sincere profession and practice of the Decalogue, Creed and Lord's Prayer. This 'catholic' or 'mere' Christianity, as he called it (a term taken up by C. S. Lewis), consisted in no more than, in St Vincent of Lérin's famous phrase, 'quod ubique, quod semper, quod ab omnibus creditum est' (what is believed everywhere, always, by everyone) and so extended fellowship across all denominational barriers.

Such tolerant acceptance that 'God hath not made our Judgments all of a complexion no more than our faces' was rare in an age of dogmatic partisanships and religious persecution. The same sensitivity to the complex individuality of every person informs Baxter's teaching on the Christian life, which refuses to prescribe an experiential norm as a model of conversion, or to offer a definitive list of marks of election, or to rely upon performance of specific duties as evidence of regeneration. Baxter looked rather to the sincere dedication of every faculty to Christ: to deny either the rational or the emotional in man is to impoverish the natural, and therefore the spiritual, life. He shared Puritanism's stress upon the everyday practice of Christianity and rejected monasticism, but warned 'We are fled so far from the solitude of superstition, that we have cast off the solitude of contemplative devotion.' His pioneering works of Christian apologetic argued that 'man is a rational creature' and Christianity 'a reasonable religion', but he recognized 'The Understanding is not the whole soul' and declared himself 'an Adversary to their Philosophy, that vilifie Sense, because it is in Brutes'. In The Saints Everlasting Rest (1650) Baxter, who was himself responsive to natural beauty, to music and poetry (especially George Herbert's*), boldly conscripted man's physicality as an ally in devotion. 'By arguing from sensitive delights as from the lesser to the greater' we may from sensual pleasure gain an intimation of heavenly bliss. Meditation upon the real, though imperfect, beauties and joys of the sublunary world would foster in those for whom anxious mortification alone constituted the Christian way a joyous devotion to its beneficent creator and increase the fervour of their prayer for the inconceivable, perfect joy of the beatific vision. He refutes the popular conception of the ascetic Puritan kill-joy: 'The *sense* is the natural way to the *Imagination*, and that to the *Understanding*: And he that will have no *sensible* and *natural* pleasure, shall have no *spiritual* pleasure.'

The Saints Everlasting Rest, 1650 (abridged J. T. Wilkinson, 1962); *The Life of Faith*, enlarged edn, 1670; *Poetical Fragments*, 1681 (introduced V. de S. Pinto, 1971); *Paraphrase on the Psalms*, 1692; *Reliquiae Baxterianae*, 1696 (abridged by J. M. Lloyd Thomas as *The Autobiography*, ed N. H. Keeble, 1974); *Practical Works*, 4 vols, 1707 (ed W. Orme, 23 vols, 1830); N. H. Keeble, *Richard Baxter: Puritan Man of Letters*, 1982; H. Martin, *Puritanism and Richard Baxter*, 1954; G. F. Nuttall, *Richard Baxter*, 1965.

N. H. KEEBLE

Beatitude

In recording the beatitudes by which Jesus pronounced his disciples blessed, the Evangelists use a Greek word (*makarios*) which means not ordinary happiness but rather the happiness of the gods. (The older English and German versions preserve this suggestion, though it is lost in later versions.) What Jesus is promising his followers, then, is not the happiness of fulfilled pleasure, but the bliss of communion with God. Understood like this the notion of beatitude links up directly with seeing the Christian life as assimilation to the divine, deification *: 'Blessed are the pure in heart, for they shall see God . . . When he shall appear we shall be like him; for we shall see him as he is' (Matt. 5.8, I John 3.2). And such has been the traditional understanding of beatitude in the Christian tradition. Both St Gregory of Nyssa and St Augustine *, to give two eminent examples, see in the beatitudes recorded by St Matthew in the Sermon on the Mount (5.1–12) a summary account of the Christian's ascent, in penitence and faith, to the transforming vision of God in which the Christian knows beatitude, that is, 'a possession of all things held to be good, from which nothing is absent that a good desire may want' (Gregory of Nyssa). Considerable ingenuity was exercised (and continued to be exercised – see Thomas Aquinas, *Summa Theologiae* II–I.69) – in detecting in the sequence of the beatitudes a progress from the recognition of one's need for God, to participation in the reconciling love of God ('Blessed are the peacemakers'). But in pronouncing blessed the poor, those that mourn, the meek, the hungry and thirsty, and those who are persecuted, Jesus points out the paradoxical character of Christian blessedness, a paradox which at its deepest is a reflection of the paradox of the cross: for 'the fellowship of the beatitudes is the fellowship of the Crucified' (Bonhoeffer). The beatitudes speak of the joy of the way of the cross, a joy that is embraced in accepting failure and suffering for Christ's sake; they speak too of the renunciation that detaches the soul from all that is not God, so that it finds its sole joy in him. Such an understanding of beatitude takes up the notion of blessedness found in the OT, especially in the Psalms, which speak of the blessedness of the poor, who have no one to look to for support but God Himself (see Pss. 1, 34, 40, 84, 112, etc.), and finds further development in St Paul, especially in II Cor., where God reveals to him that 'my grace is sufficient for thee: for my strength is made perfect in weakness' (II Cor. 12.9). In its fullness beatitude is eschatological, that is, it belongs to the final consummation, but the NT speaks of a blessedness which is known now in a partial and inchoate way. By their succinctness and prominence, the beatitudes suggest a charter for sanctity, and have continued to provoke reflection about that paradoxical quality: Kierkegaard * and Bonhoeffer * provide examples of such reflection in modern times.

ANDREW LOUTH

Bede

Although remembered today as the author of *The Ecclesiastical History of the English People*, the Venerable Bede (672/3–735) was, in the Middle Ages, particularly esteemed as a biblical commentator who, employing the allegorical method of scriptural exegesis, provided spiritual edification for his readers. A member of the monastery of Monk Wearmouth, County Durham, from the age of seven, he was later transferred to the twin-house of Jarrow and spent his life there. He appears to have been very happy, judging from the famous autobiographical sketch at the end of the *Ecclesiastical History* (V, 24). His great editor, Charles Plummer, called him 'the very model of the saintly scholar-priest', and his writings were the expression of the sort of pastoral care which he admired in his heroes, Gregory the Great*, St Aidan and St Cuthbert. Bede's religious profession undoubtedly influenced his thought, adding a distinctive monastic strain to the Augustinian spirituality which influenced him, like other Western mediaeval theologians. Although the Rule observed at Wearmouth–Jarrow was compiled by its founder, Benedict Biscop, Bede knew the Benedictine Rule and stands in the tradition of Benedictine spirituality*. Bede's goodness and personal charm – William of Malmesbury's description of him as 'most learned and least proud' will be endorsed by those who read his writings – should not conceal a fundamental austerity in his teaching. Like his master Augustine*, Bede recognized that creation, in itself, is good, but saw it as a temptation, if valued for its own sake. This wholly orthodox position prevented Bede in practice from effecting any real reconciliation of the secular and religious in his teaching, and however much he might esteem a Christian ruler like St Oswald, his ideal of Christian living was a retreat from the world into a monastery, like that of Queen Aethelthryth of Northumbria, who abandoned her husband to do so. For similar reasons Bede's profound scholarship was entirely subservient to theology and made no provision for any culture not specifically Christian. In this, of course, Bede was only typical of much mediaeval spirituality, and of his love and concern for other Christians, both clerical and lay, there can be no question. We may fittingly apply to him St Boniface's phrase: 'a candle of the church'.

Peter Hunter Blair, *The World of Bede*, 1970; M. T. A. Carroll, *The Venerable Bede: His Spiritual Teachings*, 1946, Felix Vernet, 'Bède le Vénérable', *DS*, I, cols 1322–9.

GERALD BONNER

Benedict of Nursia, St

As author of the *Rule* still followed today by Benedictines* and Cistercians*, Benedict (*c.* 480–547) is father of Western monasticism*. He lived in a chaotic world. The Roman Empire, crumbling from within, was overrun during the fifth century by barbarians. From 535 onwards Italy was again devastated by wars as the Byzantine Emperor, Justinian, attempted to reclaim it. Famine and brigandage were rampant.

Benedict was born at Nursia, the modern Norcia, north-east of Rome, probably of a patrician family. Sent to Rome as a youth to study, he was repelled by the city's moral laxity. Seeking solitude he fled to Effide, and later to Subiaco, where he lived an eremitical life in a cave for three years. A nearby community of monks persuaded the reluctant Benedict to emerge and be their abbot, but tension between their way of life and his culminated in an attempt to poison him. Benedict withdrew and returned to Subiaco, where disciples joined him in such numbers that he established twelve monasteries. Driven out again by the jealous hostility of a local priest, he migrated with a few disciples to Casinum, eighty miles south of Rome. On the summit of Monte Cassino, probably about 525, he founded his famous monastery. There he spent the rest of his life, celebrated for miracles and prophecy, often in conflict with the powers of evil and the lingering local cults of classical paganism, and beloved by the peasants of the war-ravaged countryside. There he wrote the *Rule* by which his influence has been diffused for more than fourteen centuries.

Book II of the *Dialogues* of Pope St Gregory*, written *c.* 593–594, is the only source for this outline of Benedict's life. Gregory's purpose is primarily moral and edifying rather than biographical in the modern sense. He presents Benedict's career in four successive cycles: in each there is a confrontation with sin or temptation, then a spiritual victory in which Benedict's virtue is manifested, then a new situation in which his influence radiates more widely. But greater influence is the occasion of a new confrontation with evil. Benedict thus grows through trials and temptations until he is set like a light on the high candlestick of Monte Cassino. He is the perfect type of *vir Dei*; his very name is a symbol; he is 'filled with the spirit of all holy men'. In him is embodied an ideal of conversion, contemplation and posthumous glory.

Artificially contrived symmetries, doublets within the *Dialogues* and obvious resemblances to earlier hagiographical or biblical models have raised questions about the historical value of Gregory's account. Popular legend and literary conventions, combined with Gregory's didactic purpose, have undoubtedly embellished the tradition, but it is conceded by most scholars that Gregory provides a core of reliable information. It is at least highly probable that the traditional ascription of the *Rule of St Benedict* to him is correct. Many of his personal characteristics can be divined from it; as Gregory says, this holy man could not teach other than as he lived.

John Chapman, *St Benedict and the Sixth Century*, 1929; J. McCann, *St Benedict*, [2]1958; A. de Vogüé and P. Antin, *Grégoire le Grand: Dialogues*, 3 vols, 1978–1980.

                          MARIA BOULDING, OSB

Benedictine Spirituality, Benedictines

'Benedictine spirituality' is here taken to mean primarily that which is discernible in the *Rule of St Benedict* (R B), and secondarily that which has developed through more than fourteen centuries of its use.

Recent scholarship esteems Benedict * less as an original genius and more in relation to the strong, diversified monasticism which had been developing for two hundred years before him. The writings of Cassian transmitted the eremitical spirituality of fourth-century Egypt to the West via Southern Gaul. The *Rule of the Master* (R M), probably composed in sixth-century Italy, stood in the same tradition. Benedict knew both; much of R B is verbally identical with R M, and most scholars support the priority of R M. But more community-minded traditions also influenced Benedict, especially that of Basil of Cappadocia, creator of a fraternal, socially conscious monasticism centred on the local church. Cenobitic groups flourished in fourth-century Egypt under Pachomius. Augustine's doctrine of relationships within the Body of Christ emphasized monasticism's communal, ecclesial character.

Benedict had so fully assimilated this inherited wisdom that he could isolate what was important and transmit its essentials in a simple, broad synthesis. He reduced the wordy R M by about two-thirds; the result is a short, clear code combining spiritual teaching with practical directives for most aspects of community life. R B is, according to Gregory, 'outstanding for discretion'. To a firm grasp of the principles it adds an unfussy flexibility about their precise application to particular situations, leaving much to the abbot's discernment.

The fundamental spiritual attitudes inculcated by R B are humility and unreserved obedience to God. The 'Work of God', as R B calls liturgical prayer, is to be performed with a reverent sense of God's presence and holiness, but the same awareness is to pervade monastic life at all times. Closely connected with it is the monk's consciousness of his own sin, weakness and need of God's mercy: a compunction of heart which is no craven fear but the confidence of a loved son. Prayer is expected to be so normal and inevitable a consequence of filial love and the habitual sense of God's presence that Benedict gives little specific instruction on it; though familiar with the mystical teaching of both the Desert Fathers * and Augustine * he is reticent on the matter. His objectivity is balanced, however, by a profound respect for human freedom and the mysterious diversity of persons. Benedict is less concerned with achieving uniformity than with the inner attitudes of his disciples. Obedience is to be given in purity of heart, the loving response of the ready listener.

The silence required by R B is therefore a positive, receptive attitude, necessary for the monk's habitual attention to the Word of God which rules all his prayer and activity. *Lectio divina*, or the prayerful reading in which he ponders the Word mediated through scripture or other books, is a powerfully formative practice, putting him into vital contact with the tradition from which he lives, and educating him in sensitivity to God's Word in his own life.

A monk's relationship to God is given tangible expression in the love, trust and obedience which bind him to his abbot. R B sees the abbot as a kind of sacrament of Christ. He is to 'temper all things so that the strong may have something to strive for, and the weak not recoil in dismay'. Benedict, however, complements R M's almost exclusively 'vertical' concept with a very demanding ordinance of fraternal relationships. There is no possible divorce between love of God and love of the brethren; the monks must be prepared for material dispossession, renunciation of self-will, mutual obedience, forgiveness and endless compassion with each other's weakness. Benedict reacts against the record-breaking individualism of the Desert Fathers, trusting in the inherent asceticism of common life, and in the stability he uncompromisingly demands, to bring his monks to perfect love.

The life is tripartite, a rhythm of prayer, work and *lectio*. Work, whether manual or mental, is integral to R B's spirituality, and is partly responsible for the wholeness often remarked in Benedictine life. Sane, humane and in a broad sense sacramental, R B realistically accepts the conditions man requires to grow and respond to God. The *Rule* is for the monk a practical application of the gospel to his celibate way of life in community, and brings him to a freedom of heart in which he can obey the Holy Spirit.

Most monasteries were eclectic until R B was imposed as a norm in the Carolingian Empire. Benedictine spirituality thereafter became formative in mediaeval Europe both for monks and nuns and for many who were educated or influenced by the monasteries. Important among its manifestations were the heavily liturgical Cluniac movement from the tenth to the twelfth century, and the Cistercian reform from the twelfth century onwards, which re-emphasized manual labour and developed the mystical elements (*see* **Cistercian Spirituality, Cistercians**). Missionary endeavour has been inspired by Benedictine spirituality from Boniface in the eighth century, through the post-Reformation English Congregation, to the Ottilien Congregation in Africa today. A significant contemplative emphasis among seventeenth-century English Benedictines, reacting against the discursive methods of prayer popularized by the Counter-Reformation, was associated particularly with Augustine Baker*, who perpetuated the tradition of the mediaeval English mystics and has remained influential.

Interspersed with periods of vitality and vision have been many instances of decline, when Benedictine spirituality has been weakened by adverse conditions or the mediocrity and inertia of human beings.

The spirituality of Benedictines has not always been synonymous with Benedictine spirituality, for by its very breadth and simplicity the latter has been hospitable to many 'spiritualities', often to its own enrichment. It can be claimed, however, that something recognizable has survived to be incarnated anew in many cultures and most parts of the world, a spirituality capable to some extent of being appropriated also by lay people. It

is scriptural, meditative, contemplative and fairly non-analytic in temper, normally embodied in a community life of prayer and work, lovingly respectful towards creation and productive of peace.

C. Butler, *Benedictine Monachism*, 1919; Timothy Fry (ed), *RB 1980*, 1981; David Knowles, *The Monastic Order in England*, 1963; Columba Marmion, *Christ, the Ideal of the Monk*, 1934; C. Peifer, *Monastic Spirituality*, 1966; A. de Vogüé, *La Règle de Saint Benoît*, 7 vols, 1972–1977; *La commaunauté et l'abbé dans la Règle de saint Benoît*, 1961; D. Rees (ed), *Consider Your Call*, 1978.

MARIA BOULDING, OSB

Benediction

This word is the latinate equivalent of the English word 'blessing', and covers approximately the same range of meaning. However, we generally use the word 'Benediction' for a formal or liturgical blessing. There are two common applications of the term.

1. When people are assembled together for worship, it is customary for the priest or president of the assembly to give them a blessing in the name of God, often at the time of their dismissal. Aaron and his successors were instructed to bless the people in the following terms (sometimes called the Aaronic blessing): 'The Lord bless you and keep you; the Lord make his face to shine upon you, and be gracious to you; the Lord lift up his countenance upon you, and give you peace' (Num. 6.24–26). In Christian worship, a trinitarian formula is more usual. A familiar example is the benediction at the end of the eucharist in the Book of Common Prayer: 'The peace of God, which passes all understanding, keep your hearts and minds in the knowledge and love of God, and of his Son Jesus Christ our Lord: and the blessing of God Almighty, the Father, the Son and the Holy Spirit, be amongst you and remain with you always.'

2. In the Roman Catholic Church and in some Anglican congregations, Benediction (or, more fully, Benediction of the Blessed Sacrament) is a solemn service of adoration. Theologically, it may be understood as an extension of the eucharist, and it often takes place after evening prayers, thus adding a sacramental dimension to the office. The

reserved sacrament is taken from the tabernacle or aumbry and is usually placed in a monstrance which stands on the altar. The monstrance is a vessel specially fashioned for this purpose, usually in the shape of the sun's disc surrounded by rays, and with a glass container in the centre, within which the sacramental Host is visible to the people. Eucharistic hymns are sung, and Christ is praised and adored in his sacramental presence. The priest then takes the monstrance and, as the sacrament is censed, he makes the sign of the cross over the people. Further prayers and praises are offered, and then the sacrament is returned to the aumbry. This simple but beautiful service conveys in an impressive way the sense of the divine presence, and also has a missionary function of extending the blessings of the eucharist to those who are on the fringes of the church.

J. Macquarrie, 'Benediction of the Blessed Sacrament' in *Paths in Spirituality*, 1972.
                                    JOHN MACQUARRIE

Benson, Richard Meux

A disciple of Dr Pusey and Student (i.e. Fellow) of Christ Church, Oxford, Benson (1824–1915) founded in 1866 while vicar of Cowley the Society of St John the Evangelist, the first Anglican religious community for men. He exercised his decisive influence through an indefatigable ministry of preaching, retreats, missions and spiritual direction and through more than twenty books. Among these spiritual commentaries on scripture predominate, notably *The Final Passover* on the Passion and Resurrection narratives and *War Songs of the Prince of Peace* on the Psalms, some of them based on liturgical lections. The biblical character of his spirituality is very marked and has roots in his evangelical heritage and his devotion to the Hebrew language; daily meditation on scripture in the context of liturgical life is the basis of the spiritual discipline he aimed to foster. Equally striking is the patristic quality of his teaching, the integration of theology and spirituality, orthodoxy and life. 'The contemplation of theological mysteries is the very foundation of that practical life of holiness whereby we are to appropriate the gift of divine joy.' Foremost among these mysteries is the 'Tri-Personal Being of God', 'the circulating Act of the Divine Life'. Salvation is participation in the very life of the trinity through union with the ascended Christ in the Holy Spirit, inaugurated in baptism and renewed in the eucharist. All prayer, from the divine office to the heights of contemplation, springs from the Holy Spirit and is participation in the eternal prayer of Jesus which is diversified through all the members of his Body. Because 'community is the life of God', man made in his image can attain his true destiny only in a renewed society, the communion of saints. Benson repudiates the post-Constantinian accommodation of the church to the 'world' and its unregenerate power-structures; the gospel demands a confessing church with a prophetic stance over against society, dependent not on size or wealth but on the ascended Lord alone. His severe ascetical and moral teaching and stress on spiritual warfare in the radical tradition of monasticism looks to an approaching era of persecution and martyrdom. *Followers of the Lamb* and instructions to the SSJE published posthumously, such as *The Religious Vocation*, show the bearing of these themes on religious communities which are microcosms meant 'to realize and intensify the gifts, to realize the energies belonging to the Church'. 'It is the contemplative life gazing up to God and doing battle with Satan, which is the essential character of all Christian life.' Their work of mission and service flows out of their contemplative engagement since to be drawn by prayer into the life of God is to be caught up in the 'divine onflow of love', the continous pouring out of the Holy Spirit to act in the world. Holiness is essentially self-communicative.

Martin L. Smith SSJE (ed), *Benson of Cowley*, 1980.
                              MARTIN L. SMITH, SSJE

Bernadette of Lourdes, St

Baptized Marie Bernarde Soubirous, oldest of the six children of a miller, and affectionately called 'Bernadette'. By her visions of the Blessed Virgin Mary she made her home town of Lourdes a new place of pilgrimage for the world.

She was born in 1844 and brought up in poverty. At the age of fourteen she experienced eighteen apparitions of the Virgin at Massabielle Rock, near Lourdes. This vision of Our Lady of Lourdes was of 'the Immaculate Conception'. It was accompanied by several miraculous sensations, all of which were carefully investigated later. On one occasion, a miraculous spring of water was revealed to her; on another, she was commanded to build a church at a specified spot. These phenomena are part of the mediaeval piety which had been made popular again during the early years of the nineteenth century. The experiences of this peasant girl matched the popular piety of the day encouraged by such eminent figures as F. W. Faber* in England and Mgr Gaston de Ségur in France. The vision itself of the Immaculate Conception was also consonant with the popular demands which had led to a proclamation by Pius IX in 1854. The piety of the period was concentrated upon Christ and his mother, but soon became wildly popular in relation to Mary, almost to the extent of Mariolatry.

Bernadette was herself part of this, but in a quiet modest sense. Her visions roused popular enquiry and she suffered much from constant questioning and publicity. To escape from this and develop her own spiritual life she joined the Sisters of Nôtre Dame at Nevers, and remained there until her death in 1879. She was beatified in 1925 by Pius XI and canonized in 1933. Her feast day in France is 18 February, but this is not part of the universal calendar; in some parts of the world it is observed on 16 April.

The new devotional trends of the mid-nineteenth century of which Bernadette was a part were related to the advance of Ultramontanism, but the pietistic expression of these trends was unfortunate. Its good intentions were no protection against mediocrity and bad taste, as can be judged by its many artless hymns and insipid devotional writings. It drew too much of its inspiration from suspect sources, e.g. legends of the saints, whose critics tended to be taxed with rationalism. The accent was too often on the observance of a moral code enjoining an individualist and legalistic type of morality. This stress on individual devotion narrowed the perspective of many who had already lost contact with the Bible and the liturgy. But it was a good reaction to the attenuated Christianity, verging on Deism, which had grown up in the eighteenth century. The stress on regular confession, the exhortation to more frequent communion, the attention

given to the essentially sacramental character of Catholicism, the intense concentration on the Infant Jesus in the manger or on the Sacred Heart, all focused attention on the reality at the centre of Christianity. It was the rediscovery of Christ which led to a renewal of devotion to his Mother.

Bernadette was the most famous of those who saw visions of Mary, but not the first. Almost all the apparitions were in France. They were apparitions which gave further impetus to the mounting tide of Marian devotion among the mass of clergy. The apparitions to Catherine Labouré (1830) began what has been called 'the epic of the miracle-working medallion'. Bernadette had started what became the miracle cures of Lourdes. The Roman Catholic Church has since tried to get both into perspective and control the excessive expectations and claims.

André Ravier, *Bernadette*, 1981.

EDWIN ROBERTSON

Bernard of Clairvaux, St

The most versatile and widely influential leader in the early Cistercian movement, Bernard (1090–1153) was also a prolific writer on contemplation and the soul's pilgrimage. The core of his doctrine can be found in some of the shorter works like the treatise *de diligendo Deo* (*On Loving God*) or the *de consideratione* (*On Consideration* – or perhaps better, *On Meditation*); but it is stated at its fullest in the sermons on the Song of Songs, a magnificent sustained commentary on a book already treated by Origen* and Gregory of Nyssa as an allegory of the spiritual life. Although Augustine* and Gregory the Great* are clearly important influences on his thinking and terminology, he also had some acquaintance with Origen and other Eastern Fathers – perhaps at first-hand: there is good evidence that the library of the abbey of Clairvaux in Bernard's lifetime contained translations of a surprising number of Greek writers. However, although he probably knew some of the writings of Denys the Areopagite*, there is no real trace of indebtedness to the *Corpus Areopagiticum* in any serious degree.

Thus the title 'Last of the Fathers', often applied to Bernard, is intelligible enough. He stands at the end of a long tradition which saw reason and faith as fused together in a single intuitive loving act. To be 'reasonable' was to activate (or allow to be activated) in oneself the image of God, that capacity for conformity to the divine archetype, the eternal Word and Wisdom, which is alone truly rational. Hence Bernard's sharp hostility towards Abelard, who seemed to be reducing reason to dialectical technique and faith to 'judgment', *aestimatio* (see the pamphlet, *Against Some Errors of Abelard*).

So in common with most of his predecessors, Eastern and Western, Bernard thinks of Christian discipleship and Christian prayer as beginning with self-knowledge – which is the knowledge both of the divine image and of one's own empirical distance from the realization of this image. This is humility; but on its own it is 'cold' humility, not of itself saving or transforming. It must be kindled into warmth and love by the displaying to us of the divine compassion in Jesus (Sermon XLII on the Song of Songs). God humbly and lovingly gives himself into our hands, and so shows us and created in us the mature humility of faith – free and thankful self-surrender, to God and to each other (this is the key to the meaning of obedience in the monastic life). In this way, fear yields to love, winter to summer (Sermon LVII.2, on the Song of Songs, *de dil*. III.8, Letter 109, etc.).

And compassion in turn leads to the loving, longing contemplation of God for his own sake. The more we discover of him, the more we find remains to be discovered; so that we never become absorbed into God, united with his nature, but are united with his loving will. This is what 'deification' means (*de dil*. X.27): we are restored to our nature as God's image when we mirror the love of Father and Son – when we by will and grace reflect that eternal and natural harmony. As for Greek writers like Maximus the Confessor, the process is seen as the temporal analogue of an eternal fact; we attain or grow into what God the Son eternally and unchangeably *is*. And this, incidentally, should remind us that, although Bernard is often credited with encouraging and intensifying devotion to the humanity of Jesus, it is always the *eternal* Sonship of Jesus which is the focus of his theology of redemption.

It should be noted, too, that Bernard, like Gregory the Great (and like several of his own Cistercian contemporaries such as William of St Thierry*), avoids any facile disjunction between contemplation and action. The fruit of contemplation is always properly the nourishment of the entire church (e.g. Sermon IX on the Song of Songs); and the fruit of loving and compassionate action, the sharing of gifts given, is properly an increased longing for and openness to the graces of contemplation (e.g. Sermon LVII on the Song of Songs). The contemplative life is – and can only be – a life in and for the sake of the church.

Various works in the *Cistercian Fathers* series; B. Scott James (tr), *The Letters of Saint Bernard of Clairvaux*, 1953; E. Gilson, *The Mystical Theology of Saint Bernard*, 1940; Benedicta Ward (ed), *The Influence of Saint Bernard* (esp. articles by A. Louth and M. Smith), 1976.

ROWAN WILLIAMS

Bérulle, Pierre de

Pierre de Bérulle (1575–1629), diplomatist, reformer of the clergy, and cardinal, was the founder of the 'French school' of spirituality. Born of an old family, he was educated by the Jesuits* and at the Sorbonne. After 1594 he came under the influence of Madame Acarie's circle, which included Benet of Canfield and Dom Beaucousin. The latter became his spiritual director and encouraged him to publish his first work, the *Brief Discours de l'abnégation intérieure* (1597). In 1599 Bérulle was ordained to the priesthood and in 1601 was appointed Royal Almoner. Zealous for reform, he established the Spanish Carmelites in Paris in 1604. His main work, however, was the founding of the French Oratory in 1611 on the model of the Oratory of St Philip Neri* with the chief difference that the French fathers devoted themselves to controversy and education. The most important writings of Bérulle's maturity are the *Discours des Grandeurs de Jésus* (1623), the *Elévations sur l'Incarnation* (1625), and the *Elévation sur Sainte Madeleine* (1627). In 1627 Bérulle was awarded a red hat for his diplomatic work. But in 1629 he was disgraced for opposing Richelieu's foreign policy and died later in the same year.

Drawing eclectically on the Greek Fathers, the Flemish mystics and contemporary Jesuits, Bérulle evolved a powerful christocentric spirituality of adoration.

Christ, after his various 'states' on earth (birth, hidden life, public life, etc.), is now in 'a new permanent state in heaven' in which he offers perpetual homage and sacrifice to the Father as the perfect 'servant' and supreme high priest. The goal of the spiritual life is to reproduce in the Christian the adoration and servitude of Christ himself – for only the Son can truly adore the Father – by imitating his 'states'. Christ is to be to the Christian almost what the Word is to the flesh. Bérulle even speaks of the 'annihilation of the Christian'. 'I wish the spirit of Jesus to be my spirit,' he says, 'and his life my life.'

This total assimilation to Christ is realized partly through meditating on his earthly 'states' – Bérulle has a well-developed sense of the humanity of Jesus to balance his emphasis on the Word – and partly through receiving the eucharist, which in its union of earthly and heavenly is a 'copy' of the incarnation. Through the eucharist the life of the head of the mystical body flows into the members and divinizes them. But perfect self-renunciation is necessary in order not to put up any barrier.

In this way the believer's manner of life itself becomes an act of worship. It is significant that Bérulle's favourite word for prayer is 'elevation'. Adoration, self-oblation and servitude (the last term expressing a Dionysian sense of hierarchy) lead to a participation in the eternal sacrifice of Christ in intimate union with him.

Unfortunately, Bérulle's attempt to force his spirituality on the Carmelites*and Oratorians* by imposing a vow of servitude to Jesus and Mary led to some bitterness. This did not prevent his being considered a saint on his death, but the process for his canonization was halted because the passive aspects of his teaching found favour with the Jansenists*. His influence was nevertheless extensive, especially among Oratorians and Sulpicians.

Oeuvres complètes, ed F. Bourgoing, 1644; ed with corrections by J. P. Migne, 1856. The editio princeps was reprinted photographically in 1960. The most useful studies are by P. Cochois, Bérulle et l'école française (Maîtres spirituels), 1963; J. Dagens, Bérulle et les origines de la restauration catholique, 1952 (with an excellent bibliography); M. Dupuy, Bérulle. Une spiritualité de l'adoration, 1962; F. Guillén Preckler, Bérulle aujourd'hui 1575–1975. Pour une spiritualité de l'humanité du Christ, 1978; A. Molien, DS, I, cols 1539–81; J. Orcibal, Le Cardinal de Bérulle. Evolution d'une spiritualité, 1965.

NORMAN RUSSELL

Bhagavad Gītā

An important Hindu scripture, the Bhagavad Gītā forms part of the great epic of the Mahābhārata. As scripture it is theoretically regarded as smriti (what is remembered) rather than śruti (what is revealed), and so is of lesser importance than the Vedas. But in practice the Bhagavad Gītā is probably the best known piece of Hindu religious writing, and its influence is very great (see Hinduism).

The Bhagavad Gītā ('Song of the Lord') was compiled between the second century BC and the second century AD. Its story is set at the beginning of a battle between two related groups in north India, the Pāndavas and the Kauravas. Arjuna, a Pāndava prince, recognizes in the ranks of the opposing army many of his own kin, and is horrified at having to do battle with them. His chariot driver, who is later revealed to be none other than Krishna, the eighth avatāra of Lord Vishnu, persuades him that his duty as a warrior is to fight, and that his duty, or dharma, must take precedence over other considerations. The Gītā, which comprises 700 of the Mahābhārata's 100,000 stanzas, is largely in the form of a dialogue between Arjuna and Krishna, with Krishna's words occupying the greater part of the text. Krishna's speeches include many references to Sāmkhya philosophy, and to the crucial importance of Hindus following the dharma of their own caste. So strong is the emphasis upon jati dharma that some scholars have taken the Gītā to be in part a tract against the Buddhists, whose lack of concern for caste obligations appeared for a while to threaten Hindu society.

The Gītā suggests three possible routes to liberation, or salvation. One is jnāna yoga, the way of wisdom based on an understanding of the ancient texts and teaching handed down by gurus. Another is karma yoga, the way of action in which a person does what is right (according to his dharma) without fear of the consequences or expectation of reward. Such disinterested action, known as nishkāma karma, forms an important part of the Gītā's message, and was central to Mahatma Gandhi's* teaching on non-violent resistance. The third route to salvation is bhakti yoga, or loving devotion to a personal God (*see* **Bhakti**). This in the end is presented as the most effective means of spiritual progress, and because of this emphasis the Gītā has been, and remains, an important text for devotional religion in India. Although the Gītā has received a variety of interpretations, it seems likely that its major contribution to Indian spirituality has been in its advocacy of self-surrender to a God of grace.

The importance of the Gītā for bhakti is heightened by the description in chapter 11 of a theophany in which Krishna reveals himself in his divine form to Arjuna. The theophany is awesome, but it reveals a loving, personal God who saves people by his grace.

The Gītā has been translated into many languages, and is well-known in the West. It also provides an important scripture for Western sects associated with the worship of Krishna.

E. Arnold, *The Song Celestial*, 1961; A. L. Basham, *The Wonder that Was India*, ³1967; J. Mascaro, *The Bhagavad Gita*, 1962; R. C. Zaehner, *Hindu Scriptures*, 1978,

PETER D. BISHOP

Bhakti

Bhakti is a popular form of Hinduism* which lays emphasis upon loving devotion to a personal God, and finds expression through worship, dance, song, and pilgrimage.

Bhakti religion in India is found in two main forms, Vaishnavism and Śaivism.

Vaishnavites worship Lord Vishnu, either directly or through his consort Lakshmi or his avatāras. Avatāra means literally 'one who descends', and it is in Vaishnavism that there developed the doctrine of successive descents of Lord Vishnu into the world. The main Vaishnavite tradition teaches that there are ten avatāras, of whom one is still to come. But the Bhāgavata Purāna lists as many as twenty-two avatāras, and a school of Bengali Vaishnavism extends the number to twenty-four. The avatāra doctrine differs from the Christian idea of incarnation in a number of important respects, not least in

the notion that avatāras need to come into the world repeatedly in order to counter threats to the stability of society or the breakdown of moral and religious law. The best known of the avatāras of Lord Vishnu are Rāma and Krishna. Krishna, who may have been in origin a local god of south India, but whose story appears in the Sanskrit Bhāgavata Purānas, is especially important in bhakti religion. The stories of Krishna include accounts of his amorous adventures, particularly with his favourite love Rādhā, and are taken to be analogies of divine-human love. A more restrained picture of Krishna is found in the much earlier text of the Bhagavad Gītā*. Vaishnavism was expressed by the Ālvārs, who were poet-saints in the Tamil country between the seventh and tenth centuries AD. The poetry of the Ālvārs, collected in the Nālāyiram, expresses a strong devotion towards Lord Krishna and teaches that salvation is available to all by grace, regardless of caste. Vaishnavite devotionalism and Hindu philosophy were reconciled by Rāmānuja in the eleventh century in his system of Visishtadvaita, which taught that there is a personal God who is in the world as the soul is in the body. A fourteenth-century member of the Rāmānuja school was Rāmānanda, who used the name of Rāma for God and admitted people to his school of fervent devotional worship regardless of their caste background. In the early sixteenth century a Bengali, Chaitanya, inspired a new Vaishnavite movement of fervently emotional religion directed towards Krishna. Chaitanya taught the value of Nām Japa, or the chanting of the name of Krishna, as a means of achieving salvation.

Śaivism is a form of bhakti religion in which Lord Śiva is the object of worship. Śaivism is strongly monotheistic, and regards Śiva as both creator and destroyer of the world. A common image of Śiva portrays him as Natarājan, or Lord of the Dance, engaged in a cosmic dance of creation and destruction. The terrible aspects of Śiva are particularly illustrated in his consorts, Durgā and Kālī.

An important school of Śaivism which developed in south India from the seventh century AD is Śaiva Siddhānta, which has a number of points of similarity with Christianity. Śaiva Siddhānta teaches that salvation comes from reliance upon God as saviour, stresses the greatness of divine love, and has a deep sense of sin.

In the West bhakti has appeared chiefly in the form of Krishna cults, although in their Western manifestations these are only a partial reflection of Indian bhakti.

R. G. Bhandarkar, *Vaisnavism, Śaivism and Minor Religious Systems*, 1980; M. Dhavamony, *Love of God According to Saiva Siddhānta*, 1971; W. D. O'Flaherty, *Hindu Myths*, 1975; A. K. Ramanujan, *Speaking of Śiva*, 1973.

PETER D. BISHOP

Bible, Spirituality of the

This subject would have appeared, and may still appear, to most Christians to involve, if not a tautology, then almost a definition: what else is the Bible if not spirituality? Whether interpreted allegorically in patristic and mediaeval times or by less formal ways of spiritual exegesis, even the least propitious parts of the Bible have served as vehicles of prayer: God's word to man, the written revelation, may be used as the basis for man's approach to God, whether by way of direct quotation, as in the recitation of the Psalter, or by meditation, as in the imaginative reconstruction of gospel scenes with a view to affective prayer and resolution. As far as private prayer is concerned, other parts of the Bible have in practice played a less conspicuous part than the Psalms and the Gospels; but almost all of it has had a share in that nourishment of Christian prayer, by imagery and word, which the liturgy provides, through both direct reading and allusion or quotation in prayers and others forms. In all such use of the Bible the tendency is to be indiscriminate and unitive. Taken simply as God's word, it speaks with one voice and there is no attention to variety of background, historical period and authorship.

Historical criticism points to a different approach. It begins by analysing the material in terms of literary genre and historical origin. On this basis, only certain parts of the Bible should be viewed as spirituality, that is as arising out of prayer or designed for use as prayer. Not that the classification of the material is straightforward, especially in an area as loosely defined as this. The first creation narrative (Gen. 1.1–2.4a), for example, may be read

now as myth or as doctrine, but it is hard to believe that it was not composed in a spirit of profound concentration on God as the comprehensive and purposive creator on whom all depends absolutely.

Within the Bible itself, there is an evident tendency for material to change in use, so that its function in later OT times was often different from that of its original composition. In particular, there is a twin movement towards the more *popular* and the more *individual* use of material whose original purpose was probably to accompany royal ceremonies and public acts. Many of the psalms may have undergone such transitions, well before the continuing of the process in Christian use (e.g. Pss. 2, 72, 93, 97, 110). A penitential lament like Ps. 51 came already in later Judaism to acquire the character of an act of personal devotion rather than of formal liturgy.

With that development went a movement towards the spiritualizing of external elements. The king's enemies became spiritual forces assailing the soul. Political warfare turned into moral struggle. The history of Israel, with its tale of God's saving acts, became the possession of the individual as he uttered his praise as a member of God's people. The human heart became the forum where God's relationship with his people was worked out, over a wide range of emotional and theological possibilities. Again, the psalms provide the most striking examples, notably those which include historical material, such as 78, 105 and 106.

Israel's history provided the most distinctive and persistent note in OT spirituality. It gave to it that corporate and national character which survived the tendencies to interiorize and personalize the use and application of forms of worship. This element found its most typical expression at the festivals, which were seen as commemorating various aspects of the Exodus from Egypt. The liturgical form in Deut. 26.5–11 gives a vivid impression of this fundamental aspect of Jewish piety.

Whatever their subsequent use in Jewish devotion, the original setting of the psalms was in connection with the worship of the Temple. Pss. 84 and 122 exemplify devotion which centres on the Temple itself. However, there are clear signs that the role of that worship, in particular the sacrificial system prescribed in the Law, was at times in dispute, even before the Exile in Babylon in the sixth century BC prompted the growth of a spirituality which was independent of it (but cf. Ps. 137). Other moral and spiritual priorities are asserted in oracles of pre-exilic prophets (Isa. 1.12–17; Micah 6.6–8) and have left their mark in some of the psalms (40.6–8; 51.16–19).

While the psalms form by far the richest quarry for OT spirituality and developed as both formative and expressive of Israel's awareness of God, prophetic and historical books often include material which is similar in character to the psalms and sometimes identical with them, e.g. I Sam. 2.1–10; II Sam. 22; Jer. 17.7f. There was much cross-fertilizing between various elements in Israel's religious life.

OT prayer is marked by directness and frankness. Kings, psalmists and prophets speak to God with familiarity, presenting their requests out of a sense of their place as members of his household. See, for example, II Kings 19.15–19, with its candidly military and political motivation; and II Sam. 7.18–29, with its appeal to God's own interests as bound up with David's dynastic ambitions. There is indeed frequently an assumption that God is on his people's side. They, or their leaders, can approach him confidently and enter into discussion with him. Prayer is chiefly petition, mingled with praise which is close to flattery. Sometimes, however, as in Isa. 6.5 or Job 42.1–6, there is a sense of being overwhelmed by the awesome holiness and power of God. And in Jeremiah, for example, there is recognition of the pain and anguish which attend God's service (20.7–18). The pre-exilic prophets in particular see God as threatening towards his disobedient people and as seeking their repentance (Amos 2.6ff.; Hos. 4.1ff.; Isa. 1.2ff.; Jer. 18.13–17). In later Christian terms, what is relatively rare is the element of disinterested adoration or a sense of gradual ascent to a God who is obscured from man and hard of access, unless he makes himself known as an act of grace. In other words, what later came to be recognized as mysticism is rare. It is, however, by no means lacking: see Ex. 33.17–23; I Kings 19.9–14; Pss. 42, 63, 84; Isa. 6.1–8; Ezek. 1.4–28. This last passage was the source *par excellence* of later Jewish mysticism.

In broad terms, the OT testifies to two contrasting aspects of spirituality; hope and confidence on the one hand, crisis and conflict on the other. The former aspect appears in the greater number of the psalms and in the appeal to Israel's history as the sign of God's sure favour to and presence with his people. The latter appears in the prophetic protest against disobedience and complacency and in the awareness of suffering as the lot of God's people. The tension between the two is worked out supremely on the personal level in the Book of Job, but also in writings like Ps. 22 and Isa. 53.

In the NT, early Christian spirituality manifests itself in a variety of ways. There are two generally accepted instances in the Pauline letters of hymnody, whose existence is testified in Col. 3.16 and Eph. 5.19, as well as in the Letters of Pliny (X.96). These are to be found in Phil. 2.6–11 and Col. 1.15–20. Both passages are regular if not strictly rhythmical in structure, both are detachable from their contexts. There is no agreement whether either is by Paul himself or, at least in part, taken over by him from earlier Christian use. If the latter is the case, they bear witness to lofty and doctrinally elaborate Christian poetic writing at a very early stage – and by hands otherwise unknown. These writings, and especially the former, may be seen as, in a general sense, credal. They are summaries of belief about Christ's divine mission. Yet they are also rightly viewed as expressions of praise and devotion.

The same combination of what later became differentiated as doctrine on the one hand and spirituality or liturgy on the other – formulas stating belief and formulas expressing prayer – is to be found in the blessings or thanksgivings which, after the initial greeting, open most of the Pauline and other letters in the NT. A brief formula of thanksgiving was conventional in Hellenistic letter-writing. In Christian hands, it has been elaborated, under the influence of Jewish formulas of blessing (i.e. blessing or praising God), by the addition of material appropriate to the purpose of the letter. In II Cor. 1.3ff. and I Peter 1.3ff., the 'blessing' form itself is used. In some cases, Paul develops the thanksgiving by way of specific petitions (Rom. 1.10; Phil. 1.4; Col. 1.3; cf. I Thess. 1.2).

There is other hymnic material. Eph. 5.14 may give us an early baptismal acclamation. The Revelation to John contains many hymn-like statements which are chiefly doxological in character; that is, they are ascriptions of glory to God or to Christ. They are likely to witness to the liturgical prayer of the writer's church, though, as we have them, they are closely related to their context (e.g. Rev. 5.12; 7.12; 19.1).

The oldest Christian prayer known to us is to be found in I Cor. 16.22 (cf. Rev. 22.20): Maranatha, Our Lord, come. It focuses attention on the eschatological character of early Christian faith and prayer. They prayed in the hope and expectation of the End, centring on Christ's appearance. The same emphasis dominates the Lord's Prayer*. The origins of this prayer are in dispute, some even holding that it is a composition of the evangelist Matthew on the basis of statements to be found elsewhere in the tradition of Jesus' preaching: certainly it represents the gist of that preaching put in prayer-form. But if we suppose it to be a formula going back behind the written Gospels, we face the question of its original form. It exists in two early versions, in Matt. 6.9–13 and Luke 11.2–4. On the usual theory of Gospel composition, these derive from a common source (Q), and Luke's version, simpler and shorter, is likely to be closer to that source and so to the prayer's origin. However, both versions show signs of the style and religious interests of the evangelist concerned, and the context in each case (for Matthew, teaching on the basic duties of piety, for Luke, teaching, in an almost idealized setting, on dependence on God's generosity) is almost certainly his work. Whatever the solution of these problems, the thrust of the prayer is single, not multiple as its several petitions seem to indicate. Though Luke's version ('Give us *each day* our daily bread') has a tendency to apply it to daily Christian existence, this is likely to be a movement away from its original intention, which was wholly directed to the coming of the kingdom of God, that is the full revelation of his purposes which Jesus himself proclaimed and inaugurated. This same emphasis is present also in the stories of the Last Supper (Mark 14.25; I Cor. 11.26), which, as Paul's concern in I Cor. 10.16f. and 11.16ff. shows, was the sometimes problematic focus of much early Christian devotion.

If that devotion was, at least to begin with, eschatological in direction, it was also largely (despite the Lord's Prayer, directed to God as Father) christological: Our Lord, come. Jesus was seen as God's agent for bringing in the much longed for kingdom. In this sense too, early Christian prayer was wholly the expression of early Christian belief. Jesus would bring about – had already begun to bring about – the consummation of God's purposes for the world and for his people. Also, more personally and in the present, there is no doubt that Paul's spirituality was thoroughly Christ-centred (Gal. 2.20; Phil. 1.21). This was a matter of experience as well as of hope.

The early Christians' understanding of Jesus was close to the heart of their spirituality, not only narrowly in terms of their forms of prayer but in the wider sense of their manner of approach to God. From this point of view, the Gospels, each taken as a whole, may be seen as expressions of spirituality. It has become customary to read them as doctrinal or religious documents, each representing a particular viewpoint current in the early church. But, as we have seen, doctrine and spirituality are not much distinguished at this time, and these four outlooks may be viewed appropriately as 'spiritualities'. It is indeed neither fanciful nor unhelpful to see in the various Gospels, in rudimentary form, spiritual outlooks which have subsequently become both more firmly distinguished and of central significance in Christian history. Thus (to give the barest outline of a sketch), Matthew, with his sense of Christian life thoroughly mapped out by both old law and new, yet infused with the presence of Christ, is not different in essence from that form of Christian discipleship which centres on steady and willing obedience to a monastic rule or its like. Mark's dismissal of the Jewish Law in favour of the central demand of the kingdom has his heirs in those who set the gospel continually against all other forces, which seem always to be its rivals rather than its helpers. Luke's piety, centred on Jesus and the Christian fellowship, and with a strong sense of the continuity of both from Israel of old, speaks to those for whom wide, tolerant acceptance of all reasonable aids to the gospel seems legitimate, provided the religious centrality of Jesus is maintained. John's more obviously structured and comprehensive picture of Jesus' significance as the expression of God's being and purpose may be seen as the first of those whose spirituality must always seek integration with the concerns of the intellect, while still centred on Jesus as the clue to the disclosure of God's mind and as the way to union with the Father.

J. Jeremias, *The Prayers of Jesus*, 1967; J. Lowe, *The Lord's Prayer*, 1962; H. Ringgren, *The Faith of the Psalmist*, 1963; J. T. Sanders, *The New Testament Christological Hymns*, 1971; C. Westermann, *The Praise of God in the Psalms*, 1966.

J. L. HOULDEN

Biographies, Spiritual

The OT in some ways anticipates the West European or American novel. But the NT shows little interest in life stories as such. The Gospels are not biographies of Jesus Christ, but narrative proclamations with an underlying theological aim. We are given information about Christ's contemporaries only in relation to him and the beginnings of his church. Lives of Christ will intermittently be in fashion but they have to depend on imaginative reconstructions of his childhood and daily life as an adult. The danger is that they may either be sceptical or sentimental and either way governed by presuppositions, which lack hard evidence. The most satisfactory result would be obtained by setting Jesus in his cultural context, and continuing the story of his influence in subsequent centuries, 'the historic Christ in his fulfillment'.

The story of Paul's conversion is told more than once in the NT and he himself illustrates his theology from his own experiences as well as recounting what happened to him, in self-defence, or to affirm God's providence or Christ's love. But he does not systematically write his life and no one tells us what his end was.

Christianity is concerned with people and stories of what happened to such as Perpetua and Polycarp, the young mother and the aged bishop, were very popular, not least in the age of the martyrs though there was so much concentration on the witness unto death that, apart from the conversion, the life was not treated in detail. Augustine's *Confessions* (397) of the same genre as the spiritual autobiographies of pagan philosophers told of an inward odyssey. Cast in the form of prayer, like many pagan works,

with long quotations from the psalms, it is a searching psychological examination, as well as a record of an intellectual quest. Augustine* might not have written as he did ten years earlier in the aftermath of his conversion. He has by now had time to realize that conversion is not enough (cf. Peter Brown, *Augustine of Hippo,* 1967, ch 16).

John Bunyan's* *Grace Abounding to the Chief of Sinners* is from another age and a less exalted pen, but it is a powerful and searching account of his inward struggles and sufferings before he found assurance in Christ. For him there was no philosophy to inspire or depress, no learned companionship. Even the love and joy of the Bedford Baptists could not bring him the peace he craved; he was alone before God with a book in his hand.

When lives are written for edification the record may be falsified and fact and legend not distinguished This was notoriously so in the Tractarians' *Lives of the Saints*. Today hagiography* is almost impossible because of critical method and psychological suspicion. Faults are discovered and exposed, and moral failings cannot be ignored; witness the recent lives of Paul Tillich, Karl Barth and Martin Luther King. The Christian reader must learn to withstand the shock and sorrow of depressing, even scandalous 'revelations', neither gloating nor brooding, which would be signs of a like tendency to evil, but thanking God for all that is true and good, while learning some of the hard realism of Luther's saying: 'always a sinner, always penitent, always justified'.

EDITOR

Black Spirituality

The Western concept of spirituality is not always appropriate when used outside its original cultural context. It is heavily influenced by a particular system of philosophy inherited from the Greeks and formulated by Aristotle and Plato. The concept is implicitly antithetical in that it opposes spiritual reality to the corporeal. Knowledge, however, is relative, and dependent upon the nature and conditions of specific culture (= cultural relativism). Therefore, philosophical, ethical and metaphysical truths stem from groups holding them. Greek dualism must not be taken as the universal paradigm of human logic and rationality (De Queiroz). Certainly, this Western concept of spirituality is ill-fitted to define the African reality.

In the West, this concept describes the personal relations of the Christian, as individual, with God. It concerns the soul. The African systems do not pose a dichotomy between spiritual and corporeal (body), and spiritual and material (matter). The African mind grasps both realities as a whole. An African myth says that life and death are both sides of the same seed which is existence. The world is perceived as a unity and reconstructed as interacting parts.

African holism subsumes the constituent parts of the inner and outer world as a totality. Thus, male and female conjoin their entities to generate life. This produces the African mythical egg. Throughout Africa the egg symbolizes cosmic generation, androgyny and perfection. The yolk represents the female entity; the white, the male constituent; and the shell and its membrane symbolize the placenta. Androgyny is the beginning and end, alpha and omega. Thus, human as microcosm comes to the world androgynous or unified. The rituals of initiation disjoin the sexual elements and bestow upon individuals masculinity or femininity.

The essence of African androgyny is the opposite of Aristotelian and Platonic dualism. Androgyny is integrative, inclusive and afferent (= inward), while dualism is fragmentating, disintegrative and efferent (= outward). In terms of relations with God, the consequences are as follows: God, as both genitor (male) and genitrix (female), is manifest in the ancestor (also genitor and genitrix), the founder of the phylum. The ancestor mythically reflects the androgyny of God. The people commune with God by conforming to the ethical and religious paradigms set by the ancestors as mediators. Humans are not born with an internal split (original sin) as in the Christian myth. Instead, humans are born internally unified. The rituals of passage bridge the external and cosmic gap. They insert the individuals into space and time. Community as continuation of the ancestor's life in space and history is the frame of reference in which individual destiny is worked out. Each individual is inserted into these dimensions, space and time, through birth rites such as the burial of the placenta and umbilical cord, the house-cleaning after childbirth, the child's first haircut, the first outing of the mother and child, and later the imposition of the name. Evil, and especially sorcery, may be defined as any threat to cosmic integration and the community well-being. This is why rituals of reconciliation have such importance in African community, for conflict must be resolved and unity restored.

God, as the ordering power of the cosmos, is revealed through the spirits. These spirits are not genitors, they are managers of the world. The rites of devotion to them aim at re-structuring, renewing and reinforcing the cosmic order in its continuity. No act of devotion is self-centred. The subjects benefit from the renewal of the cosmic or community order. Human perfection does not lie in bridging any mythical gap between heaven (nirvana) and earth. Instead, humans as microcosms are restored in the rejuvenation of the macrocosm. In other words, man reaches perfection through his integration into the cosmos, not through individual asceticism. The sense of human well-being derives from holistic interaction with the cosmos as a unity.

As a consequence, how one lives in *this* world, whether one upholds the values contributing to the common good, is central in African thought. Life holds such significance that death itself is converted into life through very elaborate and sophisticated funeral rites. These ceremonies enact the rebirth of the departed into the community and the ancestors who head the phylum. These funeral rites, then, are birth rites inverted.

The essential dimension of African mysticism is precisely its rootedness in life. Related to spirituality, mysticism refers to direct communion with God as ultimate reality and truth. At various stages in his life, an African participates in rituals which bring him in touch with this reality. Semantically, mysticism implies insight, penetration and discernment. From its Greek root, mysticism refers to mystery as ultimate truth. This new knowledge is generated through silence and meditation, humility and retreat. Mysticism also refers to *logos*, the word as androgynous genitor of cosmic order. These categories are fundamental in African mysticism. The *logos* is experienced especially through rituals of initiation which force the initiate to retreat, silence and communion with the inner world in the forest which represents the space of mystery. The *logos*, as ordering power, also occurs through rituals of the epiphany of the spirits through the effacement of the mediums. This epiphany or 'possession', which is both an effacement and a resurgence (of a new personality), is not an individualistic act. It has vital meaning in the community generating *communal* insight, truth and penetration, and reinforcing life in its ultracosmic dimension. The elders, out of touch with this world, and conversing only with the inner world of spirits and ancestors in unintelligible words (*logos*), culminate the ideal of African mysticism. Each previous ritual, throughout human existence, enacts this ideal. These rituals develop communication between community and the inner world.

This is the ancestral heritage that the Africans lost by conversion to the Christian myth with its Greek philosophical and theological structure. It is 'the loss of the ancient religious systems with the coherent vision of the world which was their support' (Mweng). With the loss of myths and rituals fully and structurally significant, there is also the loss of social, aesthetic, emotional, metaphysical values and fulfillment. The inaccessible character of Christian doctrine, with its esoteric dogma, symbols and metaphors, keeps this religion and its spirituality foreign to the African world. Islam* is more adaptive, and penetrates more deeply into the African life.

Christianity in the African world gave birth to prophetic religions on the Black continent, and, in America, to the birth of Black sectarianism, all of which are religions of protest. Both Black prophetism and sectarianism (= the re-actualization of the African *logos* [= word] as ordering power) aim at stopping African depersonalization at home and in the diaspora. They inspire Black responsibility as they produce a new synthesis through Christ, the Black Messiah. The Africanization of such fundamental Christian concepts as God, changed into Black God (the Rastafarians*); Messiah, into Black Messiah (Cleage); Christ, into Black Christ (Kimbangu); angels, into Black angels (Harris); ended the era in which Blacks (or Africa) allowed the West to define the cosmos (= universe) for them. This process is an African attempt to de-Christianize (= de-Westernize) Christianity. It is historically an attempt to re-valorize Afri-

can images and paradigms. The reaffirmation of the African *logos* (= word) renews the ancient African cosmological order through a new vision of Christ as the spiritual substitute for the ancestors and spirits. This is the rise of a new cosmogenesis and a new order.

See also **African Spirituality.**

L. Barrett, *The Rastafarians*, 1977; R. Bastide, *Les Amériques noires*, 1967; *Le sacré sauvage*, 1975; J. Beattie and J. Middleton (eds), *Spirit, Mediumship and Society in Africa*, 1969; G. Bond, W. Johnson and S. S. Walker (eds), *African Christianity: Patterns of Religious Continuity*, 1979; H. A. Carter, *The Prayer Tradition of Black People*, 1975; A. B. Cleage, *The Black Messiah*, 1969; G. M. Haliburton, *The Prophet Harris*, 1973; A. Hastings, *A History of African Christianity, 1950–1975*, 1979; P. M. Hebga (ed), *Personalité africaine et catholicisme*, 1963; B. Holas, *Le séparatisme religieux en Afrique noire*, 1965; C. E. Lincoln, *The Black Muslims in America*, 1961; A. A. Mazrui, *World Culture and the Black Experience*, 1974; J. S. Mbiti, *Concepts of God in Africa*, 1970; K. A. Opoku, *West African Traditional Religion*, 1978; G. E. Simpson, *Black Religions in the New World*, 1978; S. S. Walker, *Ceremonial Spirit Possession in Africa and Afro-America*, 1972; G. S. Wilmore and J. H. Cone (eds), *Black Theology: A Documentary History. 1966–1979*, 1979.

GUERIN C. MONTILUS

Boehme, Jakob

A German Lutheran of humble origins, a shoemaker by trade, whose mystical experiences in his thirties resulted in theosophical writings of great obscurity and immense influence. A natural religious genius from childhood, with an exultant longing for some link with the mysteries of the universe, Boehme (1575–1624) sought to escape from the confines of scholastic Lutheranism and institutional Christianity with its unhappy divisions. How he acquired his knowledge is uncertain. His teaching has affinities with the Swiss physician and alchemist Paracelsus (d. 1541) and with Rhenish mysticism. But a genius is sensitive enough to pluck ideas out of the air and too great a preoccupation with his sources is fruitless. There are undoubted psychological similarities between Boehme and George Fox*, though decisive theological differences. Boehme conceived of God the Father as the *Ungrund* or Urgrund, 'the bottomless abyss', unfathomable, amoral, yet containing the possibilities of both good and evil. There thus seems to be a dualism in God reproduced in the creation. Christ, God the Son, is light and wisdom and the way to salvation, though only by what Louis Bouyer had called a painful 'tearing apart', so that the good is seen in contrast to evil and the final unity of all things is possible through union with Christ. Human character is determined by the constellation of the stars during conception and pregnancy, but this does not mean that man cannot enter the union which makes him conqueror and brings him to heaven. The Holy Spirit is the expression and expansion of God into human life.

Boehme's fervently expressed teaching excited many, men as different as Charles I, the Cambridge Platonists*, the Quakers*, Isaac Newton and, in the next century, William Law. John Wesley* condemned him totally as obscure ('. . . an inexcusable fault in a writer on practical religion') with no proofs of his hypotheses and contradictory of 'Christian experience, reason, scripture and himself'. But in Germany he had some influence on Hegel, while the twentieth-century Russian theologians, Bulgakov and Berdyaev are his debtors. It is not difficult to see why. Bouyer distinguishes three appealing elements: the religious significance he gave to the material cosmos; his deeply tragic sense, 'not only of human life but of cosmic and even divine life' — Russians would feel a natural affinity for this; and 'the extremely bold way in which the possibility of a communication of the divine life to man was explained in an effective participation of the Creator in the life of the creature'.

There is not a great deal in English, though Boehme's works were translated by J. Ellistone and J. Sparrow, 1644–1662. In addition is C. J. Backer, *Prerequisites for a Study of Jacob Boehme*, 1920, and a useful account in Louis Bouyer, *A History of Christian Spirituality*, vol 3, 1969, esp. pp. 164–8.

EDITOR

Bonaventure, St
The foundational structure of the thought

of Bonaventure (1217–1274) can be seen in the three-fold movement of emanation, exemplarism and return. All things proceed from the Creator, resemble him as vestige, image or similitude, and have as the ultimate goal to return to union with God. Because of sin, persons are 'bent' and in need of grace in order to grow in likeness to God. Faith is the cornerstone of the spiritual life which is seen as a hierarchical process of reform and elevation to God. Bonaventure uses the well-known phases of purgation, illumination, and perfection to describe the spiritual life which he images as a journey of the soul into God. The first stage, the rectification of one's fallen state, involves the theological and cardinal virtues; in the second stage, the gifts of the Holy Spirit operate to make the virtuous life easier; perfection is facilitated by the beatitudes which lead one to a state of joy and repose. There is continuity and dynamic unity among the various stages. They are recapitulative inasmuch as the activities of each stage continue to have a place at later stages of the spiritual journey. The operations of the journey include prayer by which one receives grace, a life of virtue by which one becomes righteous, meditation which leads to knowledge, and contemplation which ends in wisdom.

Bonaventure's understanding of the spiritual life is intimately connected with that of his theology in general. The *raison d'être* of theology, for Bonaventure, is union with God. As a theologian and professor at the University of Paris and later as General of the Franciscan Order, Bonaventure's thought attests to the profound way in which he valued the intellectual life. The intellective and affective dimensions of the spiritual life should never act in isolation from one another. The goal of theology and of the Christian life is wisdom, which can refer to the illumination of the understanding or to a more direct, affective, experiential knowledge which comes from union with God. The journey begins in faith, leads to illuminating knowledge and culminates in an affective union. In union, the soul leaves the intellectual operations quieted in order to move beyond them to mystical peace. 'The very best way to know God is the experience of His sweetness; it is far better, nobler and sweeter than intellectual research' (*3 Sentences*, 35.1). Although Bonaventure sees the spiritual journey as the sphere of every

Christian, few reach the crowning heights of mysticism – the experience of ecstasy. In this state everything is left behind: 'It still remains ... to pass beyond and above not only this world but moreover the soul itself' (*Itinerarium mentis in Deum*, 7.2). At the summit there is but union in love. This experience lies hidden and is ineffable; it is both illuminating and suffused with darkness. The faculties are silent and the *affectus* alone watches.

Bonaventure's spirituality can be described eminently as christological and trinitarian. Christ is the exemplar *par excellence* in whom all creation is grounded and reflected. The Trinity, mirrored in all reality, is seen as a fountain of plenitude. The Word is the Father's perfect expression of overflowing goodness, and the soul returns to union only through the Son. The Spirit sends gifts which make possible the spiritual journey towards the union of the spouse and the beloved. The Spirit's gift of wisdom in its highest form, i.e. the wisdom of faith, unites all other types of wisdom, provides an experiential knowledge of the divine goodness and allows for the contemplation of God as he is known in himself by faith and as he is loved for his own sake in charity. This highest state of Christian wisdom is a rapture of the heart and mind in God by a mystical union of charity and can be obtained solely by the grace of the Holy Spirit.

In Bonaventure's spirituality, the crucified Christ lies at the beginning, is the means and the final consummation of the journey. Bonaventure's emphasis on the crucified reflects one key way in which his thought is influenced by the tradition of St Francis *. Bonaventure's masterpiece of spirituality, the *Itinerarium mentis in Deum*, clearly reveals this theme which is at the heart of the Franciscan way. The journey begins with a recollection of Francis' mystical experience and reception of the stigmata on Mount Alverno and ends with a mystical sleep with Christ on the cross. In his poetry and other spiritual treatises the cross is never far from sight. Bonaventure's spirituality also follows the way of Francis in its reliance on scripture, in its attention to nature as a sign of God's presence and power, in the important role given to poverty and humility, in its language which is filled with expressions and imagery of the tender love of God and the soul.

In addition to the influence of Francis which is paramount, Bonaventure also inherits and incorporates into his sytem ideas from Augustine *, Denys the Areopagite *, Bernard * and the Victorines *. He is also known for his rather developed theology of the 'spiritual senses' in which, in the sphere of the spiritual, the soul hears, sees, touches, smells and tastes the sweetness of God.

Because of the unity of Bonaventure's world-view, it is difficult to consider one aspect of his thought without reference to the others. However, the spiritual life which leads to an affective union with God, has a primacy in that it is foundation and end of all reality. Outside this journey in which all reality will become one with God, nothing makes sense. 'If you wish to know how these things may come about, seek grace not learning, desire not the understanding, the groaning of prayer not diligence in reading, the Bridegroom not the teacher, God not man, darkness not clarity, not light, but the fire that wholly enflames and carries one into God through transporting unctions and consuming affections' (*Itinerarium*, 7.6).

Saint Bonaventure, *Itinerarium mentis in Deum; De triplici via; Soliloquium; De perfectione vitae ad sorores; Lignum vitae; Collationes in Hexaemeron*, II and XVIII; *3 Sentences*, q. 23, 24, 26, 35, in *Opera Omnia*, Quarrachi, 10 vols. 1882–1902; *S. Bonaventura*, 1274–1974, 5 vols., 1974; J. Bonnefoy, *Une somme bonaventurienne de théologie mystique*, 1934; J.-G. Bougerol, *Introduction to the Works of Bonaventure*, 1964; E. Cousins, *Bonaventure and the Coincidence of Opposites*, 1978; *Bonaventure* (Classics of Western Spirituality), 1978; G. Tavard, *Transiency and Permanence: The Nature of Theology According to St Bonaventure*, 1954; Z. Hayes, *The Hidden Center*, 1981.

ELIZABETH DREYER

Bonhoeffer, Dietrich

Born 4 February 1906, in Breslau, Germany, Bonhoeffer was a Lutheran theologian, early involved in the ecumenical movement and a leader in the struggle of the Confessing Church against the nationalist and racist views of National Socialism. After serving German-speaking congregations in London (1933–1935), where he came under the influence of Bishop Bell of Chichester and the Anglican religious communities, he returned to Germany to lead a preachers' seminary in Finkenwalde (near Stettin) and formed a religious community (House of Brethren) around it. He refused exile in America, despite danger to his life, returned to Germany for the war years and joined political resistance to Hitler. He spent his last two years in various prisons and was executed at Flossenbürg, 9 April 1945.

He was strongly critical of the church for its failure to deal with the evils of racism and circulated letters as long as he was able, to maintain the spiritual life of his former students during the period of war and the church struggle. He continued writing during his two years in prison and these letters have profoundly influenced the postwar development of theology in Europe, America and the Third World.

His teaching on prayer, the religious life, the role of the Christian and the Christian community in the world are bound up with his theological understanding of Christ and the church. In this teaching, he tried to work out a new range of ethical attitudes to replace the 'ethics' of earlier times.

1. In his lectures on *Christology* (ET 1966, revd 1978), unfinished in 1933, when he was much troubled by the rise to power of National Socialism and the election of Adolf Hitler as Reich Chancellor, he defined his view of the place of Christ in the Christian experience. These lectures dealt with Christ as the centre of human experience, by whom alone that experience can be understood, the centre of human history, by whom alone that history can be interpreted, and the centre of nature, whose meaning is found in Christ alone. The lectures also dealt with the real presence of Christ in the word, the sacrament and the community.

2. In his book, *Life Together* (ET 1954), privately circulated to those of his Finkenwalde community after it had been closed by the Gestapo in 1937, he described the privileges of community life, not as the wish dream of an ideal, but a divine reality. Christ is present in such a community by the love of its members for one another. He advocated a disciplined and regular reading of the Bible as a means of holding the community together. In this he was much influenced by his brief visits to Kelham and Mirfield communities in England, where he was impressed by the disciplined use of the psalms in worship. He startled his fellow-Lutherans by advocating not only monastic-like communities, but also confession before communion. After confession to one another and the obtaining of forgiveness, the 'day of the Lord's Supper is an occasion of joy for the Christian community'.

3. In his *Letters and Papers from Prison* (ET 1953, revd 1971), many addressed to and discussed with Eberhard Bethge during his two years in prison at the end of his life, apart from his criticism of the church and proposals for the renewal of its structure, he developed startling new lines in theology, giving currency to such phrases as 'religionless Christianity', 'man come of age', 'secular holiness'. He argues for the autonomy of man, who having reached his maturity must learn to 'live in the world as though there were no God'. Human maturity is to learn to be human and responsible, not to be rescued by God from the consequences of one's own mistakes. He taught that God needs man as the instrument for accomplishing his renewal of the world. He develops these themes in letters, poems, fragments of novels and of plays.

Eberhard Bethge, *Dietrich Bonhoeffer: Theologian, Christian, Contemporary*, 1970; Mary Bosanquet, *The Life and Death of Dietrich Bonhoeffer*, 1968.

EDWIN ROBERTSON

Borromeo, St Charles

St Charles Borromeo (1538–1584) was Archbishop of Milan and one of the great reformers of the Catholic Church in the sixteenth century. As the second son of a noble house he was destined for an ecclesiastical career from an early age. He rose rapidly at the court of his uncle, Pius IV, being made cardinal at the age of twenty-two and prefect of the Secretariat of State. The death of his elder brother in 1562 was the turning-point of his life. Refusing his parents' request to return to the lay state and succeed his brother, he decided to commit himself to the priesthood. In 1563, after an Ignatian retreat which left an indelible mark on him, he was ordained priest and then bishop. Although nominated Archbishop of Milan in 1564, he had to petition the Pope for three years before being allowed to reside in his see. Once in Milan, however, he worked indefatigably against much opposition to implement the reforms of the Council of Trent. The holding of provincial and diocesan synods and the erection of seminaries gradually transformed the life of the clergy. At the major seminary in Milan (which became the pattern for seminaries all over Europe) students were not only to follow a regular course of studies but were to set aside a period of mental prayer and make an examination of conscience daily, as Borromeo did himself. The Archbishop not only established the new orders of the Jesuits*, the Theatines and the Barnabites in his diocese, but also founded an order of episcopal helpers who became known as the Oblates of St Charles. He made frequent visitations throughout the province, convinced that the first duty of a pastor was to know his flock. (His model in this respect was John Fisher, Bishop of Rochester.) He was a most effective preacher, preparing his sermons carefully after much meditation but delivering them extempore. In them he encouraged the practice of prayer, the frequentation of the sacraments, and the making of retreats and pilgrimages. Nor were practical works neglected. He founded homes for the destitute, orphanages, hospitals and even banks where money would be lent to the poor without interest. Even in his lifetime Borromeo was influential throughout the Catholic Church and he still remains the model of a good pastoral bishop.

Opere complete di S. Carlo Borromeo ed G. A. Sassi, 1747, reprinted 1758; *S. Caroli Borromaei Orationes XII* ed at the request of Paul VI for the Fathers of Vatican II, 1963. The standard biography is by S. Sylvain, *Histoire de Saint Charles Borromée* (3 vols), 1884. See also C. Castiglioni, *DS*, II, cols 692–700; R. Mols, *DHGE*, XII, cols 486–534 and *New Catholic Encyclopedia* 2, pp. 710–12; and for a readable life in English, M. Yeo, *A Prince of Pastors, St Charles Borromeo*, 1938.

NORMAN RUSSELL

Bossuet, Jacques-Bénigne

Ordained priest at twenty-eight, Bossuet (1624–1707) owed his spiritual formation and thus his concern for the poor, together with a certain pruning and simplification of his vigorously exuberant talent, to St Vincent de Paul. Based in Paris from 1659, he

gained a reputation through his preaching and became tutor to the Dauphin in 1669, which task occupied him until 1681, when he became Bishop of Meaux. His teaching was expounded through his Lenten sermons, funeral orations, tutorship of the Dauphin, debate over the recovery of church unity, scholarly, philosophical, moral and spiritual controversy, personal meditations and correspondence.

As one of the great exponents of post-Tridentine and baroque spirituality, Bossuet is remarkable for his classic presentation of the living authority and power of the Word of God. He declared in his sermon for the second Sunday in Lent (1661/6), that 'the truth of Jesus Christ is as really present in the preaching of the Gospel as the body of Jesus Christ is in the blessed sacrament', illustrating his theme abundantly from the Fathers and making clear the depth of obedience to which all who hear the Word are individually called. A twentieth-century theology would bring out the single continuity of Word and sacrament more than Bossuet's parallelism enabled him to do, but on their dynamic relationship and on the sovereignty of the Word his teaching has perennial force. His sermons still attract students as outstanding examples of Counter-Reformation rhetoric, in the currently rehabilitated sense of the term.

Bossuet's *Exposition de la Doctrine de l'Eglise Catholique*, written with irenic intent, was so moderate and so liberal a statement that many Protestants refused to recognize it as authentic, in spite of papal and widespread episcopal approval; it is one of the few works of controversy that is still readable in a time when ecumenical *rapprochement* has become general. His desire to promote unity led also to an exchange with Leibniz, which broke down over the acceptance of the authority of Trent.

Bossuet does not emerge with credit from the controversy over Quietism* and the eventual condemnation by Rome (though in terms less severe than he desired) of the spiritual teaching of Madame Guyon* and of Fénelon*. Temperamentally ill at ease with what seemed to him to be a dangerously obscure and irrational doctrine, he sought by personal influence and by vehemently polemic writing (*Relation sur le Quiétisme*) to discredit them, succeeding to the extent of making a wide sector of public opinion suspicious of mysticism for many years to come.

His *Méditations sur l'Evangile* and his *Elévations sur les Mystères* give a better idea of his doctrinal profundity and the moving, even lyrical, eloquence with which he could give expression to his faith.

Oeuvres ed F. Lachet, 31 vols, 1862–1866; T. Goyet, *L'Humanisme de Bossuet*, 1972; Jacques le Brun, *La Spiritualité de Bossuet*, 1972; E. E. Reynolds, *Bossuet*, 1963; J. Truchet, *La Prédication de Bossuet*, 2 vols, 1960.

MICHAEL RICHARDS

Bremond, Henri

Henri Bremond (1865–1933) was a French historian of Christian spirituality and man of letters. Like two of his brothers he joined the Jesuit* Order. He served his novitiate in Britain and became keenly interested in English religious personalities, such as J. Keble*, J. H. Newman*, George Eliot and Matthew Arnold, who became the subject of his early writings. Finding himself too restricted as a Jesuit he left the Order in 1904 and thereafter was a secular priest dedicated to literature and scholarship. His eminence as a man of letters was recognized in 1924 by his reception into the Académie Française. He was a close friend of several of the Catholic modernists, notably G. Tyrrell, A. Loisy, F. von Hügel* and M. Blondel. The full extent of his sympathy and agreement with them, particularly with Loisy, was not revealed till after his death. He never concealed his distaste for the rationalism of the scholastic theologians, and he incurred ecclesiastical censure on more than one occasion, e.g. for the part he took in Tyrrell's funeral in 1909. But when pressed he always submitted since he was determined to remain in the church, and the issues at stake in the modernist controversy were not his main concern.

Though he himself disclaimed having mystical experience, it was the mystical element in traditional Christianity and in religion generally that chiefly interested him and to which he attached overriding importance. His principal work was the many volumed *Histoire littéraire du sentiment religieux en France* (1915–1932). This is an unfinished history of French spirituality from the seventeenth century onwards which is enlivened throughout with colourful portraiture of, and quotation from, both well-known and forgotten men and women of prayer. It was the 'devout humanists' whose attractiveness Bremond delighted to portray. He stood for world-affirmation and was antipathetic to the Jansenist* strain in French catholicism with its severe and rigid puritanism. Thus he espoused the cause of Fénelon* in his famous controversy with Bossuet* about Quietism* and he wrote favourably about Fénelon's friendship with Madame Guyon* as he had already done about the relations of St Francis de Sales* with Madame Chantal.

His writing so sparkled with wit and irony that the solemn guardians of orthodoxy always viewed him with suspicion and were inclined to charge him with frivolity. Many of his contemporaries found him to be at once fascinating and enigmatic. But there is no doubt that his teaching about the paramount value of *pur amour* (disinterested love*) was very seriously intended.

André Blanchet, *Henri Bremond 1865–1904*, 1975; Jean Dagens and M. Nédoncelle, *Entretiens sur Henri Bremond*, 1967; Emile Goichot, *Henri Bremond, historien du sentiment religieux*, 1982; Henry Hogarth, *Henri Bremond: the life and work of a devout humanist*, 1950.

A. R. VIDLER

Browne, Sir Thomas

A doctor of medicine, born in London, but living most of his life in Norwich, Browne's (1605–1682) best known work is *Religio Medici* (1636). S. T. Coleridge (1772–1834) described this as a 'delicious' book. He also refers to Browne's 'egotism' which he finds 'natural and becoming', and which helps to fix Browne as a 'Renaissance' man of individuality and 'gusto'. Browne's whole philosophy is that of an acute and tolerant observer of nature and of the human condition. He observes the faces of those he visits, how they change, and may take on at various times the lineaments of forebears and relatives, especially in death. He is fascinated when urns containing what he believed to be Roman ashes – they were in fact Anglo-Saxon – were unearthed at Walsingham. He belongs to the morning of the scientific age. He wrote a vast exposé of 'vulgar and common errors' – *Pseudodoxia Epidemica*.

Yet some superstitions still cling. He believes in witchcraft, convinced that not to do so is atheism.

Browne adheres to a seemly and moderate Laudian ceremonial, yet within conformity to order and beauty in worship, he allows his intellect to range, and refuses to make the way of salvation 'narrower than our Saviour did'. Neither relics nor miracles are necessary to faith. He does not crave to have been present at Christ's tomb, nor to have seen him in the body; he covets the beatitude of those who have not seen and yet have believed.

He is no mystic with the ardour of an intense personal religion, though he loves to entertain mystical thoughts and to express them in the 'organ notes' of numinous prose. All harmonies – even tavern songs – make him feel religious; but there is no 'immediacy', no direct revelation, no 'showings' as with his Norwich precursor Julian*, no inward voices. He is too interested in finding out why grass is green and blood is red to gaze transported at his Crucified God and be lost in him.

He may be called a 'devout humanist' and, following the thought of Bonaventure* and others, man is for him the 'Great Amphibium', dwelling in two worlds at once, a marvellous being, a microcosm of nature. 'There is all Africa and her prodigies within us.' The world, however, in spite of its fascination is a hospital, or hospice, 'a place not to live, but to die in'. There is a curious jostling of old ideas and new; but he propounds wise and eloquent moral maxims, and writes, in the authentic Christian tradition: 'This, I thinke is charity, to love God for himself and our neighbour for God.'

Geoffrey Keynes (ed), *Works*, 4 vols, 1964; *Selected Writings*, 1968; R. H. Robbins (ed), *Pseudodoxia Epidemica*, 2 vols, 1981.

EDITOR

Bruno, St
see **Carthusian Spirituality, Carthusians**

Buber, Martin
Buber (1878–1965), perhaps the most famous modern Jewish thinker, emphasized man's two-fold attitude to the world, signified by *I–Thou* and *I–It*. In *I–Thou*, man addresses his world or neighbour as *Thou*, and allows himself to be addressed as *Thou*

in turn. This is the relation of mutual personal encounter, dialogue, communion. In *I–It*, he regards his world as an *It* – the attitude of observation, description, usage, seen at its most detached in scientific analysis. Both attitudes are necessary, but it is in *I–Thou* that man is genuinely human. 'All real living is meeting.'

The most profound *I–Thou* relation is with God, the Eternal *Thou* who can never become an *It*. God cannot be grasped in descriptive concepts and definitions, but only addressed in personal encounter. This obviously bears on prayer, worship and the spiritual life, and has influenced modern Christianity at least as much as Judaism. But paradoxically, for Buber 'spirituality' was a suspect term, in view of four main considerations:

1. 'Spirit' does not belong to the individual person, but lies *between* persons in the *I–Thou* relationship. Spirit is the liberating event which opens persons into the mutuality of acceptance and dialogue. True spiritual existence is therefore communal, not isolated and individual.

2. Our relation to God is not alongside or additional to all our other relations and activities. God is not encountered apart from the world – 'Creation is not a hurdle on the way to God' – and it is through each and every *Thou* that we may meet the Eternal *Thou*. Prayer is the gathering up of the totality of existence into relation with God, and means the hallowing of the everyday world. Buber was here greatly influenced by the Hasidic Judaism of central Europe.

3. There can be no preparation or prescription for the occurrence of an *I–Thou* encounter, whether with another person or with God. It must be awaited in openness. Spiritual exercises or cultivation of an 'inner life' are irrelevant to the moment of sheer awareness of 'the Presence', and the particular form or *Thou* through which the divine *Thou* may meet us cannot be predicted.

4. Nor can this encounter be preserved in continuity through cult or ritual. Cult comes to replace the pure relation which man can preserve 'only if he realizes God anew in the world according to his strength and to the measure of each day'.

Buber was not a mystic, if mysticism implies absorption of the self into the divine. The *I* is preserved in the immediate relation with the divine *Thou*. From a Christian incarnational and sacramental standpoint it must obviously be asked if the encounter with God can be so freely detached from particular forms. But the *I–Thou* relation is now, by adoption, a widely accepted part of Christian terminology.

Martin Buber, *I and Thou*, 1937; *Between Man and Man*, 1973; *The Eclipse of God*, 1953.

K. W. CLEMENTS

Buddhism

Buddhism began in India in the fifth or fourth centuries BC with the teaching of Gautama, who came to be called the Buddha, 'enlightened'. He was one of many religious teachers and seekers and himself sat under notable authorities. A similar but more ascetic contemporary movement was Jainism, whose leaders are Jinas, 'conquerors', and who survive in India with some three million adherents. Buddhism flourished in India for about a millennium and a half and then was virtually wiped out there by reviving Hinduism* and iconoclastic Islam*. There has been some revival of Buddhism in India among outcastes, but long ago it became the most successful early missionary movement, stretching right across Asia.

Buddhists believe that there have been Buddhas past, so that Gautama came in a long succession, and there will be Buddhas to come, notably the eschatological figure Maitreya. In this, Buddhist belief resembles that in Hindu avatāras. But this plurality is modified by the conviction among Southern Buddhists that Gautama is the only Buddha is this present very long world aeon. It is said that if there were more than one Buddha now their followers would disagree, and also that the world would not be able to bear the weight of two Buddhas.

Buddhism seems to be an exception among world religions, rejecting belief in God, the soul, supernatural grace and the value of material life. It presents 'a stunning problem', says Melford Spiro, but he found it to be 'a pseudo-problem' because Buddhists differ very little from people in general. Buddhists do not believe in a supreme creator God, since the world rises and declines in an eternal round, but there may be a chief of gods who is the first in each world cycle and called Brahma like a Hindu god. Buddhism is not a-theistic, since many gods appear in its myths, though they are secondary figures attendant upon the Buddha. The Buddha himself is not one of the gods; he is far above them, 'the god beyond the gods' and 'the teacher of gods and men'. In practised religion images of the Buddha are innumerable, in every temple, pagoda and home, receiving the adoration of the faithful. It follows that Buddhism is not self-salvation, as it is sometimes presented in the West, but it is a revelation of eternal truth by the omniscient Buddha and salvation depends on his wisdom and grace.

Buddhist notions of soul or self are similarly complex. In the second sermon attributed to him the Buddha spoke of 'the marks of non-self'. There are five bodily and mental elements (*skandhas*): body, feeling, perception, impressions and consciousness, and none of these is the soul because all suffer and die. Edward Conze says that 'the Buddha never taught that the self "is not", but only that "it cannot be apprehended"'. This is the assertion also of the canonical Questions of King Milinda, though it then goes on to deny that there is any being which passes from one body to another in reincarnation; the link between the two is the deeds (*karma*). Even more indefinable, yet real, is nirvana, 'blowing out' of desire, the goal of Buddhist effort. It is not in one of the many heavens but far beyond, not indicated by form or duration, explanation or simile; yet 'there is nirvana'.

The Buddhist analysis of the human condition, from his first sermon, is the universality of suffering, its cause in desire, cure in cessation of desire, and method in the Noble Eightfold Path of mental and moral discipline. This seems a pessimistic analysis requiring world-renunciation. Its primary followers are the Sangha, the Order of monks and later of nuns, and in traditional Buddhist countries they provide a clerical class engaged in education of the young and guidance of the old.

Whether or not Buddhism began with a select group of world-renouncers, with an ethic rather than a religion, it soon developed religious features. The first lay followers are said to have uttered the Threefold Refuge: 'I go to the Buddha for refuge, I go to the Dharma (doctrine) for refuge, I go to the Sangha for refuge.' Like Hindu affirmations of going to a god for refuge, this triple formula is uttered many times a day down to the present. The ordinary Buddhist tries to renounce self but to enjoy existence by following Five Precepts: non-injury, not stealing, chastity, not lying, and temperance.

There were many sectarian divisions in developing Buddhism and two major schisms remain, with sub-sections, in Theravada and Mahayana. The Theravada, 'doctrine of the elders', reject the name Hinayana, 'small vehicle', given by their rivals. They prevail in five countries of south-east Asia: Sri Lanka, Burma, Thailand, Kampuchea and Laos. Here there are many beautiful buildings for worship: pagodas, dagobas and wats, which contain relics of holy people and are the objects of visits for veneration and meditation. Worshippers bring flowers, cloth rosettes, paper lamps and incense sticks (joss sticks). Money is put in boxes and bells are struck to announce arrival. The faithful join hands before their faces, bow, kneel and prostrate at images of Buddha and shrines. Prayers are uttered in time of need.

If Buddhist philosophy is regarded as agnostic, its worship is as central as in other religions. It is called *puja* like Hindu worship, consists of offering gifts and acts of adoration. Liturgy and scriptures are chanted, with physical acts of reverence, and incense is burnt. There is inner worship of contemplating Buddha or another holy being which has been compared to the Christian 'prayer of contemplation'. In addition to individual or family visits to pagodas there are special public services and ceremonies, with processions and distribution of sacred food, and pilgrimages are made to special shrines and holy mountains. Regular festivals mark the events of sacred story, the birth, renunciation, enlightenment and nirvana of the Buddha. Other festivities combine Buddhist with older indigenous ceremonies which have been thinly adapted to the official religion.

Northern Buddhism in China, Tibet, Korea, Japan and Vietnam is Mahayana, 'greater' or 'universal vehicle' of salvation. This teaching was set out in the scripture, the Lotus of the True Law or Lotus Sutra, about the second century A D, which has been called 'the gospel of half Asia'. Here the glorified Buddha, sitting on a vulture

peak in the Himalayas, and called by his clan name Shakyamuni, addresses thousands of disciples, Bodhisattvas and gods. He offers salvation to all who worship him, so that the prayer of a single believer will bring deliverance to all his company. This doctrine of universal grace and faith spread from India across Asia and incorporated many divine beings.

The Lotus Sutra introduces the concept of Bodhisattvas, 'enlightenment-beings', who take vows to defer their own nirvana until all beings are saved. Notable is Avalokita, the Lord who surveys, who in China became Kwanyin and in Japan Kannon, the Lady giver of children. In Kyoto there is a temple of a thousand Kannon images said to be forms assumed for the benefit of mankind. New Buddhas began to appear at an early date. Amitabha or Amida, a Buddha of 'Infinite Light', rules over the Western Paradise and calls believers to his Buddhafields. In Japan he is represented by a great bronze figure at Kamakura. Vairochana or Roshana, from a Hindu title for the sun, was regarded as coming from an original Adi-Buddha, and is represented in the world's largest bronze statue at Nara. The Buddha-to-come is very popular, often depicted as a fat jolly figure with money bags. There are countless other Buddhas and Bodhisattvas, so that the original Gautama was overshadowed if not eclipsed. The thirteenth-century Japanese reformer Nichiren, who opposed the faith-grace cult of Amida and tried to return to the original Buddha, got no farther than the vulture peak of the Lotus Sutra.

As there are many objects of worship in Buddhism so there are innumerable temples and pagodas. Alongside the monks and nuns, orders of priests developed and congregational worship was organized in new movements. Mahayana came to dominate in Tibet and Korea, mingled with Taoism * and Confucianism in China, and formed Two-fold Shinto in Japan. Although religion was much attacked under Chinese communism, recent relaxation of oppression has revealed much of the hold that Buddhism still has there and in Tibet. Some monasteries, images and paintings are being preserved and pilgrimages tolerated. In Japan most people look to both Shinto and Buddhism, especially women.

Buddhist houses have a Buddha-shelf,

which is often an elaborate shrine with a central image or painting, in front of which incense and flowers are offered. In temples priests perform liturgies, chant Buddhist texts, including wishes for national and universal welfare, while the laity may come in the evening to light joss-sticks and candles. In Tibet and Nepal prayer wheels of various kinds are set in motion, to aid in repetition of texts. Worship is paid to great Buddhas and Bodhisattvas and there are many stories of their answers to prayer.

Prayer beads are widely used in Buddhism, a common type having 108 beads, but there are some with many more for telling over great names of Buddhas. Formulas of invocation may begin with the Hindu word O M, as in the Tibetan *Om mani padme hum*, 'hail to the jewel in the lotus', or *Namu Amida Butsu*, abbreviated as *Nembutsu*, 'homage to Amida Buddha', in Japan. Relics, images and scriptures were early fetched from India, and pilgrimages are still made to sacred mountains and places associated with heroes of the faith. There are commemorations of events in the lives of Buddhas and festivals of the dead. In Japan Buddhism with its many texts became adapted to funeral ceremonies, while Shinto kept the life-giving occasions of birth, childhood and marriage.

In Mahayana developments Buddhism split into sects or schools. Pure Land Buddhists direct devotions to Amida in the Western Paradise, emphasizing salvation by faith alone which is comparable to bhakti* in Hinduism. Ch'an in China, which became Zen* in Japan, is said to have taken its name from the Sanskrit word for meditation, *dhyana*. Meditation is practised by all Buddhists but especially by Zen monks who use it for direct enlightenment independently of knowledge or scriptures, though chapters of the Lotus Sutra are used in meditation. 'Enlightenment experience' was expected at any time in activities suffused with meditation and so Ch'an-Zen greatly influenced the arts: painting, calligraphy, flower arrangement, tea drinking, archery and even swordsmanship. T'ien-T'ai (Japanese Tendai) Buddhist sects, named after a monastery on mountains of that name in China, sought to reconcile different schools of Buddhism both in their devotions and practices.

Powerful modern Japanese sects go back to the reformer Nichiren. Soka Gakkai, 'creative-value-study society', has both religious and political activities, with millions of followers. Rissho-koseikai, 'righteous and friendly society', is notable for great temples and meetings and for sessions of pastoral counselling. Such movements appeal to many young people, organizing huge public processions like carnivals, and worshipping the glorified Buddha in adoration and meditation.

Noah S. Brannen, *Sōka Gakkai*, 1968; Edward Conze, *Buddhist Scriptures*, 1959; *Buddhist Thought in India*, 1962; Richard F. Gombrich, *Precept and Practice*, 1971; Raymond Hammer, *Japan's Religious Ferment*, 1961; Paul Levy, *Buddhism: a 'Mystery Religion'?*, 1957; Melford E. Spiro, *Buddhism and Society*, 1971.

GEOFFREY PARRINDER

Bunyan, John

John Bunyan (1628–1688), open communion Particular Baptist minister and author of *The Pilgrim's Progress*, was, by his own word, 'of a low and inconsiderable generation', his family 'being of that rank which is meanest and most despised'. He was brought up in Elstow, Bedfordshire, to be a 'brasier' or tinker. Contact with Puritan radicals during his service in the Parliamentarian army (*c.* 1644–1647) may have been partly responsible for inducing the prolonged spiritual crisis he later recounted in his classic spiritual autobiography *Grace Abounding to the Chief of Sinners* (1666). In 1655 he joined John Gifford's Baptist church at Bedford, and began 'in private' and 'with much weakness and infirmity' to 'discover my Gift'. The following year, he 'was more particularly called forth, and appointed to a more ordinary and publick preaching the Word', which brought him into conflict with the Quakers. These controversies resulted in Bunyan's first publications, *Some Gospel-Truths Opened* (1656) and its *Vindication* (1657), which were followed in 1659 by the fullest exposition of his covenant theology, *The Doctrine of the Law and Grace Unfolded*.

At the Restoration in 1660 Bunyan was imprisoned under the old Elizabethan act against conventicles, and continued in detention, though with some freedom of movement, until Charles II's Declaration of

Indulgence was issued in March 1672, two months after Bunyan had been elected pastor of the Bedford church. During this imprisonment (there was a second, brief term in 1677), Bunyan continued writing: by his death he had some sixty works of practical and controversial divinity to his credit. His repeated claims in these treatises that he had not 'borrowed my Doctrine from Libraries. I depend upon the sayings of no man. I found it in the Scriptures of Truth,' and his defiant assertions, 'I never went to school to *Aristotle* or *Plato*' nor knew 'the Mode nor Figure of a Sylogism', are in accord with the anti-scholasticism of the radical Puritan tradition. He had, in fact, received at least an elementary education and knew Luther, Foxe's *Book of Martyrs* and some standard works of Puritan divinity, but it remains true that the role of 'humane learning' in his works is insignificant beside their uncompromisingly biblical inspiration, their experiential intensity and their trenchant directness of expression.

These qualities could be paralleled elsewhere in Puritan writing, but *The Pilgrim's Progress*, the most popular work of Christian spirituality ever written in English, is unparalleled. It was the unpremeditated product of an inspiration so compelling that Bunyan put aside the tract he had in hand (probably *The Heavenly Footman*, 1698) in order to develop the anecdotes, exempla and moral types characteristic of Puritan homiletics into a sustained allegory. The result was the dramatization of Calvinist conviction through the universal medium of the quest or journey image, familiar to Bunyan both from the Bible (particularly the Abraham legends, the Exodus saga and their interpretation in Hebrews) and from the folk tales and romances he admitted reading in his youth, but combined, in his work, with a sharply observed realism, both psychological and circumstantial. Encouraged by its unprecedented success, Bunyan went on to its sequel, *Mr Badman* (1680), the more ambitious multi-level allegory, *The Holy War* (1682), and the second part of *The Pilgrim's Progress* (1684). Literary historians discern in these works the nascent novel genre, but for Bunyan fiction remained a means, not an end, to 'make a Travailer' of his reader along the way to the Heavenly Canaan which, though it lies open to every person of faith, runs unavoidably through the wilderness of this world with its vicissitudes, uncertainties and moral complexities.

George Offor's three volume edition of *The Works* (1853; 1862) is currently being replaced by the Clarendon Press's complete Oxford English Texts edition of Bunyan, comprising 12 volumes of *Miscellaneous Works*, general editor Roger Sharrock, 1976–, and separate editions of *The Pilgrim's Progress*, [2]1960, *Grace Abounding*, 1962, *The Holy War*, 1980 and *Mr Badman*, 1983. The standard biography is John Brown, *John Bunyan*, revd F. M. Harrison, 1928; *see also* G. B. Harrison, *John Bunyan: a study in personality*, 1928; O. L. Winslow, *John Bunyan*, 1961; Monica Furlong, *Puritan's Progress*, 1975. *The Church Book of Bunyan Meeting* was edited in facsimile by G. B. Harrison, 1928. Bunyan is related to different aspects of the Puritan tradition in John Tindall, *John Bunyan: Mechanick Preacher*, 1934, and U. M. Kaufmann, *The Pilgrim's Progress and Traditions in Puritan Meditation*, 1966. His theology is the subject of Richard L. Greaves, *John Bunyan*, 1969. Henri Talon, *John Bunyan: the Man and his Works*, ET, 1951, and Roger Sharrock, *John Bunyan*, 1968, have a literary bias, as have Roger Sharrock (ed), *John Bunyan: a Casebook*, 1976, and Vincent Newey (ed), *The Pilgrim's Progress: Critical and Historical Views*, 1980. Coleridge's suggestive annotations on the *Progress* are printed in *Coleridge on the Seventeenth Century*, ed Roberta Florence Brinkley, 1968.

C. Hill.   N. H. KEEBLE
G. Wakefield.

Calvin, John

The most formidable, intellectually, of the Protestant Reformers, whose influence may not inaccurately be compared to that of Karl Marx in later centuries. In temperament Calvin (1509–1564) was shy and withdrawn, 'a poor, timid scholar', yet capable of warm friendships. The extent of the calumny and misrepresentation he has attracted is itself impressive, though among his contemporaries, many of his opponents honoured and respected him. He has often been attacked for doctrines which were equally those of the Catholic Church, notoriously double predestination; charges of cruelty, though some stick, could be advanced with even more justification against Catholic inquisitors and English bishops; to say he was a dictator is historical nonsense. Prodigiously learned in the scriptures and the greatest patristic scholar of his age, he was trained also in the law and was a superb organizer. Born in Picardy, he was intended for the priesthood, but did not proceed beyond the tonsure. His spiritual awakening and vocation to restore the church to its original purity occurred in 1533. He had some years of struggle and conflict, and a period of exile at Strasbourg before he returned to Geneva in 1541, where he was not infrequently at odds with the governing Council and at times harassed by the disorderly. His authority was pastoral rather than political. He was a minister of a congregation and a preacher of eminence, who so believed in the unity of word and sacrament that he would have had holy communion every Lord's Day had the Council permitted it. He promoted the Geneva Psalter, most of the tunes being written by Louis Bourgeois, whom Calvin sponsored. He fostered education, industry and Protestant ecumenism, and had joined in conferences with Roman Catholics when there was still hope of reconciliation before the Council of Trent. His *Institutes* (*Christianae Religionis Institutio*), first published in 1536, in Latin, and thereafter much amplified and revised with a definitive edition in 1559, remain one of the classic works of systematic theology.

His was a severe morality, and he was particularly against sexual irregularities and blasphemy, but neither he nor his theology should be blamed for what a later age has found repulsive in Scottish Sabbatarianism, New England witch-hunts, Western capitalism, or South African apartheid.

See also **Calvinist Spirituality**.

John Calvin, *Institutes of the Christian Religion* ed J. T. McNeill (LCC XX–XXI), 1961; *Theological Treatises* ed J. K. S. Reid (LCC XXII), 1954; G. E. Duffield (ed), *John Calvin*, 1966; R. N. Carew Hunt, *Calvin*, 1933; J. Mackinnon, *Calvin and the Reformation*, 1934; T. H. L. Parker, *Portrait of Calvin*, 1954.

EDITOR

Calvinist Spirituality

The Christian life starts in the Divine initiative, in God's gift of Jesus Christ as our sanctification, our prophet, priest and king. Predestination, or election, is not the 'focal theme', but union with Christ. The former is the essential presupposition and affirms the sovereignty of God, that our whole salvation begins with his grace and ends with his glory, but spirituality is our participation in what God has done for us in Christ. We are made 'very members incorporate in the mystical body of his Son' as Cranmer's eucharist has it.

The union is a great mystery – this is what the term 'mystical' means in Reformed theology. Authors influenced by Calvin all speak of its reality. It is no mutual relation of separates. We are 'bone of Christ's bone and flesh of his flesh'. The NT speaks of it in metaphors of the utmost intimacy – vine and branches, bread and water. It is as the hypostatic union of the Father and the Son in the Godhead. The mystery is the more awesome in that the glorified Christ is in heaven and yet it is to him that we are united. The Holy Spirit makes this possible '. . . though it seems an incredible thing that the flesh of Christ, while at such a distance from us in respect of space, should be food to us, let us remember how far the secret virtue of the Holy Spirit far surpasses all our conceptions and how foolish it is to wish to measure its immensity by our feeble capacity. Therefore what our mind does not comprehend let faith conceive, that the Spirit truely unites things separated by space' (*Inst*. 4.17.10). On our part, the union is effected by faith, but since faith is the creation of the Holy Spirit in human hearts, this is only another way of affirming the work of the third person of the Trinity. Calvin grows lyrical about faith. It is complementary to the love of God in the 'mystical' contemplative Catholic tradition. It enables us to penetrate the heavens, it brings the very life of Christ into our souls, it means that we, while still on earth, may live the life of heaven.

By the very language used, it is clear that the sacraments also are instruments of this mystical union. The two Gospel sacraments of baptism and the Lord's Supper were instituted by Christ to make the union effective in the life of the church. They are its visible signs, material reminders of the reality of the union, ways by which Christ assures us of his perpetual presence and that all that he is and has is ours. Baptism must not be denied to infants ('Suffer little children to come unto me') for they are in the New Covenant just as they were, by circumcision, in the Old, and we must not make Christ's religion narrower than that of the Jews. Infant baptism is the sign that the union is the Holy Spirit's work, not ours. We are passive at the beginning of regeneration; faith does not create the Covenant; the Covenant creates faith. But the visibility of baptism is important. It should always be administered in the congregation and should inspire the most solemn thoughts in the witnessing worshippers, and encourage them to the 'improvement' of their own baptism in Christian lives.

The Calvinist doctrine of the Lord's Supper demands the concept of what T. F. Torrance has described as 'eschatological distance', the fact already noted as of great importance in Calvinist theology that Christ is now in heaven and will be there until the last day. In the eucharist the Holy Spirit lifts us up to be with him. The manner of his presence is inexplicable – hence the heresy of transubstantiation – but the secret must lie, not in the descent of Christ, but in our being raised to be with him. 'He is not here; he is risen'; but we may go where he is gone. Here again, in sacramental theology, is the juxtaposition of the indispensable work of the Holy Spirit and the effectiveness of the faith which he implants in us. The sacrament is the means whereby, through both, we ascend. It is, in fact, the portrayal or acting out of the whole Christian life. Faith is essential to this sacrament. 'Christ himself is the substance of the Supper; but men do not receive more from the sacrament than they gather with the vessel of faith' (*Inst.* IV 14.9.17). The wicked do not receive Christ. The sacrament is efficacious only in the elect. The Lord's Supper constitutes the church, which is a eucharistic community, but word and sacrament must never be sundered, for – and this is paralleled in Augustine – it is the word which gives the sacrament its power, makes it more than dumb show, and creates the fellowship of the faithful.

'Outside the church there is no salvation' is as much a tenet of Calvin as of Cyprian *. But there is, in Calvinist divines of the sixteenth and seventeenth centuries, some confusion as to the precise relation of the mystical union to the institutional church in the world. Calvinism adheres to the distinction between the church visible and the church invisible – the church 'as it really is before God – the church into which none are admitted but those who by the gift of adoption are sons of God and by sanctification of the Spirit true members of Christ'. But we are not the judges, and therefore, although we shall be constantly sensible of its defects and of its need of reformation, we must not dissociate ourselves from the visible fellowship. In fact, although not all members of the visible church belong to the invisible, it seems as though the reverse is not true. To believe in the Holy Catholic Church 'relates in some measure to the external church', the world-wide communion of those who affirm the historic creeds, are loyal to word and sacrament and acknowledge due authority, which includes what Calvin calls observing the ministry. This undoubtedly means submission to the preaching of the word, a keen and not uncritical but always worshipful listening to those who, like the apostles, are called not to be 'lords of faith but helpers of joy'.

Discipline * is a *sine qua non* of the church. There must be good order, though presbyteral is more scriptural than that of bishops and priests. Discipline follows logically from preaching and pastoral care and much of it has to do with the resolution of cases of conscience. The role of the minister as 'confessor' is not abolished in Calvinism. It is not a matter of 'every man his own priest', but of the royal priesthood of the faithful. The grille goes and the sacrament of penance, but not the authority to remit and retain sins. It is here that the charges of cruelty and undue severity cannot be denied throughout Calvinist history, and Calvin himself resorted too much to the OT in the punishment of offenders. Yet he considered the penitential system of the early church too hard and was not a rigorist. Penitence *, sincerely professed, was enough for full restoration to Church fellowship, and the early church was excessive in banishing sinners from holy communion for years, and sometimes for life. This was to thrust them into hypocrisy and despair – a just indictment of some Catholic discipline.

Prayer is the principal exercise and expression of faith. Even pagans may find their prayers sometimes answered, but the Christian prays in response to God's grace, and he does so with confidence that he will be heard. Calvin and all his successors deal at length with the parts and problems of prayer. There is stress on the importance of thanksgiving. Prayer is best in the words of scripture – 'speak to God in his own holy language'. Calvinist devotion is ordered not 'enthusiastic', yet Roman and Anglican Prayer books were apt to be deemed insufficient, almost a trifling with God, wishes rather than prayers. True prayer is earnest, intense, a wrestling with God, or a pleading with him, as preaching is a pleading with men. And sometimes Calvinist prayers have been 'sermons to the Almighty', a sad degeneration born out of the longing and the necessity to pour out the whole heart. When it comes to intercession, compassion always gets the better of logic. An English Calvinist bishop could pray 'Give thy gospel a free and joyful passage through the world, for the conversion of those who belong to thine election and kingdom'. William Perkins (1558–1602), a redoubtable Cambridge Calvinist, says that we may pray for mankind particularly – for any one by name, or by country, however evil; it may, in spite of all appearances, be God's will to save them. But we ought not to pray collectively for all sorts and conditions of men, for there will be some beyond salvation. A subtle and unsatisfying logic. William Gouge (1575–1653) is better – the ground of prayer is the judgment of charity not of certainty. And he quotes with approval the English litany – 'That it may please thee to have mercy upon all men'. And prayer is a sign of our union with Christ. It must be offered in his name. And no one of the elect is ever cast out of his prayers. 'The smoke of his incense ascends for ever and he will intercede to the utmost till he hath saved to the utmost' (Thomas Goodwin).

Catholics have often felt that Calvinism is, like winter, awe-inspiring but bleak, covering the spiritual landscape with frost. This cannot be supported if Calvinist spiritual writers are studied as a whole. They have not been blind to the wonders, beauties and joys of creation, they have not stifled the arts of music and poetry in particular, and they have sustained family life and family prayer, and not only in bourgeois homes; witness Burns' 'the Cottars' Saturday night'. At best there has been high seriousness combined with deep if not often

ecstatically expressed joy; courage too, boldness of spirit, fear of God rather than men. Calvinist spirituality would find it difficult to see sanctity in whisky priests as portrayed by Graham Greene, or in a Geoffrey Beaumont accompanying the gospel with gin and cigarettes (see Harry Williams, *Some Day I'll Find You*, 1982). The worldly wise will always suspect that Calvinists are hypocrites and sometimes be proved right; but more often this may be because the latter implicitly condemn 'the world' and inflame a bad conscience. That publicans and harlots may enter the kingdom before the 'unco guid' is a hard saying for those who believe that Christ rescues us from vice and the slavery of evil habits, and would turn 'sordid and bitter dwellings' into households of his love. The Christian life must always swing between the poles of freedom and discipline. And if the Calvinist tradition has sometimes been too hard on permissiveness, so has the Catholic, which has often failed at the other extreme, and in its notable humanity left people and societies with a tincture of grace, rather than released a mighty flood of moral revolution.

See also **Calvin, John.**

J. D. Benoit, *Direction Spirituelle Protestantisme: Étude Sur La Légitimité d'une Direction Protestante*, 1940; *Calvin, Directeur d'Ames*, 1944; J. C. McClelland, *The Visible Words of God: A Study in the Theology of Peter Martyr*, 1957; Walter Marshall, *The Gospel Mystery of Sanctification*, 1692; T. F. Torrance, *Kingdom and Church*, 1956; R. S. Wallace, *Calvin's Doctrine of the Christian Life*, 1959; B. B. Warfield, *Calvin and Calvinism*, 1931.

EDITOR

Camara, Dom Helder

Dom Helder Camara (b. 1909) is Roman Catholic Archbishop of Olinda and Reçife in North-east Brazil. He entered the seminary in 1923, was ordained priest in 1931, and Auxiliary Bishop of Rio de Janeiro in 1952.

During the Second Vatican Council (1962–1965) Dom Helder organized informal meetings with bishops from around the world who shared his concern that the church be a church of the poor, a servant church. Small at the beginning, the group grew to several hundred bishops by the end of the Council, and exerted great influence upon Pope Paul VI.

In 1964 two events occurred that shaped both Brazil and the Catholic Church: a military junta seized power and Dom Helder was named Archbishop of Olinda and Reçife, the poorest region of the country.

For almost two decades the two forces were on a collision course. The junta, under successive generals, labelled the efforts of Dom Helder 'communist' and 'subversive'. Yet as champion of the poor and advocate of non-violent social change, Dom Helder became a world figure. He received the Martin Luther King Jr International Peace Prize in 1970, and was twice nominated for the Nobel Peace Prize. In 1973, when Henry Kissinger and Le Duc Tho received the Nobel Prize for terminating the Vietnam War, Dom Helder was awarded the People's Peace Prize – $300,000 raised by Europeans angered by the choice of the Nobel Committee.

In Brazil, however, Dom Helder remained officially a non-person. The media were forbidden to mention his name, except in false charges or derision. His only means of reaching the more than one million members of his diocese was a daily five-minute homily at 6.0 a.m. over Radio Olinda. The government dared not touch Dom Helder himself, but it could and did with impunity persecute Dom Helder through his close associates. Priests and nuns were jailed, tortured, and in a few cases murdered, together with hundreds of lay men and women. Only with a gradual move towards a restored democratic government in 1982 did the repression ease.

As a voice for the voiceless, Dom Helder has been heard through much of the world. As a skilled organizer, he pioneered the formation, first, of national bodies of bishops in his native Brazil, then of regional bodies of bishops throughout Latin America. Such national and regional groups were endorsed by the Second Vatican Council and have become a marked feature of the postconciliar church.

Among those who have most inspired him Dom Helder cites Gandhi* and Martin Luther King Jr, who led him to preach and live non-violence in a violent land; and Teilhard de Chardin*, who helped him see that 'at all times hope has the last word'.

In spite of his international prominence, Dom Helder is an extremely simple man, totally available to the people of all classes

who flock to him literally day and night. At the heart of his spirituality is ability to listen to the Spirit speaking through others, speaking through events, speaking through the ants which live in the bushes of his tiny garden, speaking through starlight and storm. For him, as for all the great mystics, the whole of creation is the Creator's seamless robe.

His spiritual legacy is found most clearly in his 'Meditations', written between 2.0 and 4.0 a.m. every morning since his seminary days. These meditations have been translated into every language. Poetic in form, profound in content, deceptively simple in diction, they are unique in the treasury of Christian spirituality.

Helder Camara, *The Desert is Fertile*, 1976; *A Thousand Reasons for Living*, 1981; Mary Hall, *The Impossible Dream: The Spirituality of Dom Helder Camara*, 1979.

PHILIP SCHARPER

Cambridge Platonists, The

It is not clear that they were ever a party in the church, but they form a definite group, who were all in the Platonic tradition rather than the Augustinian; that is, they believed that a purified reason could bring the soul to the vision of God, rather than that human nature was a mass of perdition, which needs a miracle of grace, received through the institutional church, to recreate and redeem it. Their undoubted number includes Benjamin Whichcote (1609–1683), John Smith (1618–1652), Henry More (1614–1687) and Ralph Cudworth (1617–1688). Peripheral are Nathanael Culverwell (?1615–1651) and Peter Sterry (?1613–1672), who strike many of the same notes, but are perhaps Calvinist* more than Platonist*. John Norris (1657–1711), though he was an Oxford man, and later, is very much of the Cambridge temper.

They have an unflagging faith in reason. 'The spirit of man is the candle of the Lord' (Prov. 20.27), which does not deny prevenient grace, since God himself lit the candle; nor does it take away all mystery; candlelight is not the full blaze of day, and its gentle flickering enhances the sense of an unknown beyond immediate perception in the room in which it shines. But the Cambridge Platonists feared irrationalism, superstition (even though More believed in witchcraft) and the tyranny of ecclesiastical systems. 'If ever Christianity is exterminated it will be by Enthusiasme' (More). Christianity is not 'Mystical, Symbolical, Aenigmatical, Emblematical; but uncloathed, unbodied, intellectual, rational, spiritual' (Whichcote). There is no opposition between rational and spiritual, 'for spiritual is most rational' (Whichcote). The negative way in which reason and its concepts are discarded is not for them, nor do they enter a 'Cloud of unknowing' – the candle must not be put out.

Theology is a Divine life rather than a Divine Science (Smith), and the great truth of the Christian faith is that God is love. '(God) ... enclaspeth the whole world within his outstretched arms, his soul is as wide as the whole universe, as big as yesterday, today and forever' (Cudworth). The Cambridge Platonists will not make any distinction between *agape* and *eros*. The latter is the Neoplatonic term; the former from the NT. The clear vision of God is 'the privilege of intensely loving souls' (Clement of Alexandria), and John Smith adapts Plotinus*: 'As the Eye cannot behold the Sun ... unless it be Sunlike, and hath the form and resemblance of the Sun drawn in it; so neither can the Soul of man behold God ... unless it be *Godlike*, hath God formed in it, and be made partaker of the Divine Nature.' Deification*, as in the Greek Fathers, is a key notion. The incarnation is the greatest honour that could be done to human nature. 'The Son of God came into it' to raise it to all possible perfection (Whichcote).

They are through and through ethical theologians. Mystic ecstasies, if vouchsafed, are not ends in themselves. Deification is not a state of being lost in God; it is to love as God loves, to be merciful as he is merciful; which is why the Platonists show comparatively little *odium theologicum*. More's anti-Catholic polemic is sometimes sheer bigotry, and Norris attacked the Quakers, whose 'Inner Light' must not be confused with the Platonists' candle, since it is a pneumatological concept drawn from the experience of the Holy Spirit in untutored lives, not the notion of a philosophical élite. But for their time, and indeed for any time, the Platonists reveal outstanding magnanimity, and John Smith excels them all.

There is one particular theme of Plato-

nism which is stressed by these theologians; what Cudworth calls God's 'Gayety and Festivity'. Peter Sterry says: 'Spiritual joy is the laughter of the Divine love, of the Eternal Spirit which is in our spirits,' and Culverwell, deploring those who look upon religion as a rigid and austere thing, with 'never a summer day after it', assures them that grace does not mean to take away joy, but to refine it, not to quench the light but to snuff it, that it may burn brighter and clearer. We are to give our heart to God that he may make it happy, with a happiness which stretches its capacity to the full.

Rosalie L. Colie, *Light and Enlightenment. A Study of the Cambridge Platonists and the Dutch Arminians*, 1957; H. R. McAdoo, *The Spirit of Anglicanism*, 1965, pp. 121–96; C. A. Patrides (ed), *The Cambridge Platonists*, 1969, 1980.

EDITOR

Canticle, Spiritual
see Spiritual Canticle

Cappadocian Fathers

Traditionally Christianity in Cappadocia owed its spread, if not its birth, to the missionary zeal of Gregory Thaumaturgus (*c.* 213–270), a disciple of Origen* and the teacher in the faith of Macrina, the grandmother of two of the Cappadocian Fathers, Basil (330–379) and Gregory of Nyssa (*c.* 330–395). The third Cappadocian, Gregory of Nazianzus (329–389), a friend of the two brothers, studied with the former at Athens (351–356) and together with him compiled a collection of the writings of Origen known as the *Philokalia**. The early influence of Origen on all three Cappadocians is clear in their treatment of the nature of and means towards the acquisition of spiritual perfection.

1. All of them assume that there exists in each one of us a natural desire for God for the release and realization of which the whole ascetic and mystical enterprise exists (cf. Basil, *Regulae Fusius Tractatae* 2. i; Gregory of Nazianzus, *Oratio* 32.21; Gregory of Nyssa, *De Instituto* VIII, 1.40, 7ff.). The end of the process of purification is called divinization (cf. Basil, *De Spiritu Sancto* ix.23; *Naz. Or.* 2.22; 73 and *passim*). Gregory of Nyssa, characteristically, never uses the expression and only rarely the idea

of divinization, probably because he thought it tended to obscure the unbridgeable chasm that separates Creator from creature.

2. Divinization (*see* **Deification**) is largely thought of in terms of (*a*) moral perfection, leading to likeness to God and (*b*) knowledge of God, conceived of, above all, as a spiritual and transcendent reality.

(*a*) The first stage, often termed 'purification' and described in language that echoes both Matt. 5.8 ('Blessed are the pure of heart, for they shall see God') and the Platonist* demand for likeness to God (cf. especially Plato, *Theaetetus* 176b and Plotinus, *Ennead* i, 2, 5; i, 6, 9) requires great effort (cf. Basil, Prologue to *Reg. Fus. Tra.* 2; Nyssa, *De. Instituto* VIII, 1, 45, 3). The assumption that underlies the whole treatment of the need for purification is that 'like can only be known by like', a principle that finds expression in both biblical and Platonist sources (compare II Cor. 3.18; I John 3.2 with *Republic* 490aff.). Gregory of Nazianzus, probably the most Platonic of all three, is particularly full of such language (cf. *Or*. 2.74; 7.17; 16.14; 18.4), though it also occurs in the *De Virginitate* of Gregory of Nyssa (esp. ch. 11). Both Gregory of Nazianzus in his *Second Theological Oration* (s. 2) and Gregory of Nyssa in the *Life of Moses* use the symbol of the mountain with which to describe the purification and upward movement of the human spirit in its quest for the knowledge of God.

(*b*) In Basil, as distinct from the other two, the knowledge of God in which the progress of ascent culminates is intimately connected with the illumination provided by the Holy Spirit. In him this enlightening, divinization and the action of the Holy Spirit are nearly inseparable (cf. *De Sp. S.* ix.22–23; xvi.38; *Epp*. 226.3; 233.1). In Gregory of Nazianzus the climax of the process of moral cleansing is described in highly intellectual terms, nor is there any obvious role left for the body. For him, as for his disciple Evagrius, there is a marked tendency to assimilate theology to prayer. This is clear from the fact that the true theologian needs to purify himself in the same way as the ascetic and arrives at a knowledge of God as 'intellectual spirit' in both cases (compare *Or*. 7.17; 21 and *Or*. 28.2; 3: 32.15: 39.8). In this and in other respects Gregory of Nazianzus is the most Origenist of all the Cap-

padocians. Both insist on the character of God as 'mind' (compare Origen, *De Principiis* i.I.6 and Gregory of Nazianzus, *Or*. 16.9: *Ep. Theol*. 1.49), and both describe the growth towards God in the manner traditional since Aristotle (cf. *Eth. Nic*. X.vii) as a two-stage progress of 'action' and 'contemplation' (cf. Origen *In Lucam*. i.3: *In Jn*. fr. 80 and Gregory of Nazianzus *Or*. 4.113). The influence of such a way of speaking upon Evagrius is clear from the opening sections of his *Praktikos*. In Gregory of Nyssa's earliest spiritual writing, the *De Virginitate*, and in a (?) later work, the *De Instituto*, the two-stage pattern of virtue and contemplation of spiritual reality is largely reproduced. So, in *De virginitate* 11 he argues that anyone who has cleaned the eye of the soul is able to perceive spiritual beauty and so leaves behind him his attachment to things of the body. Both the language used and the pattern described are reminiscent of the *Symposium* of Plato (210–212), where the ascent of the soul from physical to spiritual beauty is outlined. In both cases the object of desire and the climax of the movement upward are termed absolute beauty.

3. The generally Platonist and spiritualizing account of the perfecting of the Christian is modified in three important respects by Basil and Gregory of Nyssa.

(*a*) Basil, besides being an ascetic, was also a founder of a monastery at Annesi on the shores of the Black Sea (cf. *Ep*. 2), and for the monks he wrote among other spiritual writings two sets of Rules, the *Longer* and *Shorter*. They are important for their marked moderation, which distinguishes them from the Egyptian monachism of Antony* and Pachomius and from the austerities of his friend Eustathius of Sebaste. Basil stresses the need for both work and prayer and insists on the importance of charity and obedience. Central for the future of the monastic movement is his insistence on the importance of community and the danger of a solitary attempt to live out the ideal of perfection (cf. on these last two points *Longer Rule* 6, 7).

(*b*) Gregory of Nyssa towards the end of his life abandoned the Platonism of the *De Virginitate* in favour of a spirituality which took more seriously the centrality of the distinction between creature and Creator upon which his reply to the challenge of the Neo-Arians rested (cf. *Contra Eunomium* i.270ff.). Man, even in his spiritual side, being always necessarily a part of the created order, is unable to escape the time sequence to which creation assigns him. He can neither become eternal himself nor escape from the realm of time (cf. esp. *Hom. VII on Ecclesiastes*). Besides convincing us of the total otherness of God and of the impossibility of ever seeing him face to face, these homilies lay a great stress on the need to make ourselves more like God by our growth in virtue. God himself *is* virtue for Gregory, a view from which Plotinus dissents (cf. *Ennead* i.2.1 with *Eccl. Hom.* VII. V.407.1: *De Vita Moysis* i.7). The *De Vita Moysis* and the *Comm. on the Song of Songs* develop the doctrine of the infinity of God and argue that as God is infinite, the only way in which we can become like him is by a never-ending growth and progress in virtue. Sometimes he connects this vision with Phil. 3.13 ('Forgetting what lies behind I strain forth to what lies ahead'). Cardinal Daniélou called this whole pattern one of *epektasis*. In *De Vita Moysis* the vision of God on the mountain leads to the conclusion that the only way of realizing the vision is by following God endlessly. In section ii.152ff. of that work, seeing God and perpetual following are made equivalent.

(c) Despite the profound difference introduced into the concept of perfection by such a scheme it still lies recognizably within a classical framework. Some scholars, however, notably W. Jaeger and R. Staats, have argued that there exist very marked similarities between Gregory's *De Instituto* and the *Great Letter* of Macarius *, a document almost certainly of Messalian provenance. Indeed the bulk of the evidence is in favour of an influence exerted on Gregory rather than by him. This means that there exists in him a strain of thought that is quite foreign to his customary Hellenism, one that stresses the importance of feeling and the experience of the Spirit, as central to if not constitutive of the life of the Christian. Staats has also argued that Messalian influence can be found in the final chapter of the *De Virginitate*. The welcome that Gregory apparently gave to enthusiastic religion of this sort should modify a too intellectualist assessment of his writing.

4. The body, the resurrection and the sacraments do not play a large part in the spirituality of any of the Cappadocians. This is partly, no doubt, because their surviving writings are not expressly concerned with these issues. It should, however, be noted that strongly though they were influenced by Origen, none of them held the doctrine of the pre-existence of souls and all of them, especially Gregory of Nyssa, lay stress on the bodily integrity that results from the resurrection of Christ (cf. *Oratio Catechetica* 16). Even so, when Gregory of Nazianzus discusses the final end of the body, it is merely to say that it will be so transformed by the soul as to be freed from the elements that are normally associated with it, the 'flesh being raised above on the wings of reason' (*Or.* 16.15; cf. *Or.* 2.17). Although Gregory of Nyssa devotes *Oratio Catechetica* 33–37 to a discussion of baptism and the eucharist, it would be unfair to pretend that even in him the main accent does not fall on the spiritual qualities of faith and conversion, and their prerequisite, free will, without which growth towards God is impossible (cf. *Or. Cat.* 39; *De Vita Moysis* i.1–5).

See also **Deification; Perfection; Vision of God.**

There is no general study of the spirituality of the Cappadocians. The best treatments are to be found in the *Dictionnaire de Spiritualité*, Paris 1937 (under the names of Basil, Gregory of Nazianzus and Gregory of Nyssa, by G. Bardy, J. Rousse and M. Canevet, respectively).

On Basil: W. K. L. Clarke, *St Basil the Great, A Study in Monasticism*, 1931; *The Ascetic Works of Basil the Great*, 1925. On Gregory of Nazianzus: Anna-Stina Ellverson, *The Dual Nature of Man, A Study in the Theological Anthropology of Gregory of Nazianzus*, 1981; D. F. Winslow, *The Dynamics of Salvation, A Study in Gregory of Nazianzus*, 1979. On Gregory of Nyssa: D. L. Balas, *Metousia Theou*, 1966; H. U. von Balthasar, *Présence et Pensée, Essai sur la philosophie religieuse de Gregoire de Nysse*, 1942; J. Daniélou, *Platonisme et Theologie Mystique. Doctrine spirituelle de Saint Gregoire de Nysse*, [2]1944; W. Jaeger, *Two Rediscovered Works of Ancient Christian Literature: Gregory of Nyssa and Macarius*, 1954.

ANTHONY MEREDITH, SJ

Cardenal, Ernesto

Ernesto Cardenal (b. 1925) is an unusual

combination of priest, poet, mystic and political activist.

Educated in his native Nicaragua and Mexico, he took graduate courses in literature from 1947–1949 at Columbia University in New York City. Here he came upon the writings of Thomas Merton*, who had become a Roman Catholic while a student at Columbia, and had entered the Trappist* monastery at Gethsemane, Kentucky in 1941.

Cardenal himself underwent what he called a 'second conversion', the realization that 'God reveals himself as love before which all human loves fail'. He entered Gethsemane in 1957, where Merton was named his spiritual director.

Merton gradually became convinced that for Cardenal the surest communication with God was not through the solitary contemplation of a Trappist monk, but through contact with people. After two years at Gethsemane, Cardenal left the Trappists and returned to Nicaragua where he was ordained priest in 1965.

A year later he established a Christian community at Solentiname, a group of rocky islands within Lake Nicaragua, whose inhabitants are poor farmers and fishermen.

Nicaragua was still the personal fiefdom of the Somoza family, one of the most brutal of Latin American dictatorships. The biblical reflections of the farming and fishing families identified Herod as Somoza, and their vision of the kingdom of God on earth impelled them to political revolution. The biblical reflections of the peasants were published in Spanish, then translated into English and German. Cardenal's own poetry was translated into every major language. In October 1977, Somoza's National Guard ravaged Solentiname, burning the homes and killing many of the unarmed peasants.

Cardenal took refuge in Costa Rica. Free now to travel, his poetry readings in North America and Western Europe awakened people to the savagery and corruption of Nicaragua's despot, and gained, if not support, at least understanding of the Sandinistas, armed revolutionaries dedicated to Somoza's overthrow.

Overthrown he was, on 19 July 1979. Within the new Government of National Reconstruction, Ernesto Cardenal was named Minister of Culture, a post which he describes as essentially 'priestly', because it deals with total human development 'through poetry, music, publications, cinema and sports'. The bloody revolution over, new wars must be waged – against ignorance and illiteracy and, the great enemy, individual and societal selfishness. 'If the revolution had wanted to take a different direction,' says Cardenal, 'it should have placed all this in the hands of a militant atheist.'

On 12 October 1980 Ernesto Cardenal became the first South American to receive the prestigious Peace Prize of the German Publishers' Association. His acceptance speech is almost a précis of his spiritual vision that all things created are united to God through his love. Even revolution must therefore be a qualitative social change, a *metanoia* leading towards love.

The primary vision is ancient; only its expression in poetry, influenced by Ezra Pound, and a rhetoric tempered by revolution and its aftermath, is seemingly new.

Ernesto Cardenal, *Apocalypse and Other Poems*, 1977; *Love*, 1981; *Psalms*, 1981; *The Gospel in Solentiname*, 4 vols, 1982.

PHILIP SCHARPER

Carmelite Spirituality, Carmelites

The Order appears to have been founded by St Berthold *c.* 1155, who settled on Mount Carmel with other hermits. Carmelite tradition, as expressed in the thirteenth-century *De institutione primorum monachorum*, tells of a succession of monks on the site from Elijah onwards, according to some Fathers the founder of monasticism. Arguments about the Order's antiquity continued till the end of the seventeenth century, but the succession from Elijah is now regarded as legendary.

The strict Rule, enjoining long periods of prayer, was drawn up by Albert of Jerusalem 1206–1214, to provide an appropriate framework for the eremetical life on Carmel. The community remained there for a while after the Christians were defeated in 1187, but abandoned it during the thirteenth century and sought refuge in Europe. Mount Carmel was not resettled by the Order until 1631. In 1229 the Carmelites were placed among the mendicant orders by Gregory IX, and in 1247 the Rule was revised to accommodate a more active life, which included preaching and teaching. The Order spread gradually, though never attained the numbers of the Dominicans* or Franciscans*. It remained cenobitic. Monasteries were founded in cities and university towns, and the first English house was established at Aylesford, Kent, in the mid-thirteenth century. The Carmelites later became noted opponents of Wyclif. During the generalship of John Soreth in the fifteenth century the first Carmelite nuns were instituted in the Low Countries, and soon became established in Italy, Spain and France.

As in many other Orders, attempts were made during the fifteenth and early sixteenth centuries to reform communities where life had become lax, though none made a lasting impression on the Carmelites. However, Teresa of Avila*, already a Carmelite for many years and feeling an increasing need for a return to a stricter life, founded the first house of Discalced Carmelite nuns in Avila in 1562, with consequences she can hardly have foreseen. She went on to make seventeen foundations, and through the work of her fellow-Carmelite John of the Cross* fifteen were established among the friars. The Reform provoked great hostility from some within the Order, and both suffered for their labours, John being imprisoned for eight months and Teresa wearing herself out in travelling, ecclesiastical politics and battles which she usually won. After her death serious differences arose within the Reform, especially under its first vicar-general Nicolás Doria; St John himself died in disfavour. The formal separation of the Discalced from the mitigated Carmelites took place in 1592. However, the Reform was to prosper, spreading rapidly into the Low Countries, France, Central Europe and the New World from Spain and Italy and attracting many recruits of deep spiritual gifts. Tomás de Jesús (1564–1627), the leading interpreter of Teresa in the next generation, restored the eremetical life with the founding of Carmelite 'deserts'.

The Order's theological tradition was predominantly Thomist (see **Thomas Aquinas, St**), but interpreted through the English theologian John Baconthorpe (d. 1346) and Michael of Bologna (d. 1416). The main theological achievement of the Discalced belongs to the *Salmanticenses*, who between 1631 and 1701 produced a theological course in the form of a vast commentary on Aquinas. The Order has a traditional devotion to Mary, and was a strong defender of the Immaculate Conception before its definition. The dress is a dark brown habit, brown scapular and white mantle. Other Carmelite saints are St Mary Magdalen of Pazzi (1566–1607) and St Thérèse of Lisieux*(1873–1897).

Carmelite spirituality has been profoundly influenced by St John and St Teresa; indeed, they represent its classic fomulation and, some would say, stand at the peak of the mystical tradition of the West. Both wrote poems, St John's of the highest order; their teaching is developed in their prose works, and it is here that St Teresa particularly shines, with her colloquial style and her imaginative use of metaphor. Very different in character and background, and with some discrepancies between them in doctrine, their teaching on prayer is nevertheless complementary. Theirs is an affective spirituality, stressing the need to leave behind the world of natural knowledge and to reach out with love towards God in the darkness of faith. Both probe and interpret the different states of prayer, especially the higher reaches, in a way not previously attempted or bettered since. They are sceptical about the experience of supernatural phenomena, as these are not the goal of the mystical journey, which is God alone, beyond all sensory perception and image, as the naked human spirit is lifted into union with the divine essence which created it. This union, granted by God to very few, anticipates in this life the joys of the beatific vision.

Their most enduring contribution is perhaps two-fold: one, the ordering, classifying and analysis of many distinct stages in the life of prayer and the experiences which accompany them; the other, the clear distinction they draw between various states of meditation and the passive infusion of contemplation. St John gives the classic signs of the moment when the transition from·one to the other approaches (*Ascent* II.13–14): inability to meditate and aridity in consequence; desire for nothing other than God; and pleasure in solitude and a 'loving attention' to God. Both teach an intensely pure form of mystical prayer, which in its highest forms abandons all intermediary aids; and they constantly stress the need for humility, since spiritual pride is the gravest of all dangers. Hence the emphasis on the fruitful effects truly God-centred prayer has on the lives of its practitioners, and on the dangers of self-deception.

The influence of Carmelite spirituality has increased during the twentieth century as the writings of St John and St Teresa have become more accessible. Their orthodoxy and the authenticity of their teaching, sometimes suspect in their own time, is underlined by their recognition as Doctors of the Roman Catholic Church, and the influence of St John of the Cross on Pope John Paul II is well known.

J. B. de Lezana, OCC, *Annales Sacri, Prophetici et Eliani Ordinis Beatae Virginis Mariae de Monte Carmeli*, 4 vols, 1645–1656; *Constitutiones Fratrum Discalceatorum Congregationis S. Eliae Ordinis Beatissimae Virginis Mariae de Monte Carmelo*, 1638; *Monumenta Historica Carmeli Teresiani*, Teresianum, 1973–; L. van den Bossche, *Les Carmes*, 1930; David Knowles, *The Religious Orders in England*, 3 vols, 1948–1959; R. McCaffrey, OCC, *The White Friars*, 1926.

COLIN P. THOMPSON

Caroline Divines, The

Behind the political and constitutional issues which were dividing England during the reign of the early Stuarts in the first half of the seventeenth century, a group of holy men, writers and thinkers, set about proclaiming what they believed Anglicanism to be. These men came to be known as the Caroline Divines, and they owe allegiance to the work of John Jewel, Bishop of Salisbury, and Richard Hooker, who by their learning had defended the church both against Rome and Puritanism* during the reign of Elizabeth I. The Caroline Divines, by their lives as well as their writings, did much to give quality and strength to the Church of England in their time.

It is interesting to note that in the nineteenth century the revival of principles of High Church Anglicanism (which drew much inspiration from the Divines) centred on Oxford: but in the seventeenth century the movement centred on Cambridge. The main names in the group we call the Caroline Divines were all Cambridge scholars:

Lancelot Andrewes*, Richard Montague, John Cosin, Thomas Fuller, Jeremy Taylor*, George Herbert* and Nicholas Ferrar*. William Laud was the only Oxford man among them. Other names often associated with the group are those of Anthony Sparrow, Herbert Thorndike and Thomas Ken. They were not a team, unlike the men who led the Oxford Movement*. They rarely met each other, but each in his own way combined personal sanctity, scholarship, poetry and a dedicated life. Their spirituality has the combined qualities of discipline, austerity, devotion and simplicity.

The Divines appealed to the Tractarians in the first place as a source of High Church principles, of doctrinal coherency and consistency in the Church of England. The Divines produced works of immense scholarship on the development of doctrine. But the Tractarians also read the spiritual and devotional literature of the Divines, and it is to this that we shall refer in this article. An extensive selection of the writings of the Caroline Divines can be found in P. E. More and F. L. Cross (eds), *Anglicanism* (1935); and more complete editions of their works are in the *Library of Anglo-Catholic Theology* and the Parker Society editions of Anglican writings. The sermons of the Divines, both from a spiritual and literary point of view, are among the glories of the English language.

The Divines conceived of Christian discipline as ordered by the formularies and liturgies of the church. John Cosin (1594–1672) outlined the precepts of the church in *A Collection of Private Devotions* (1627); they included the observance of appointed festivals and holy days, the keeping of fast days, the observance of established ecclesiastical customs and ceremonies, attendance at the daily offices of the church, and the frequent reception of the sacrament, with humble devotion, especially at Easter. William Laud (1573–1645), the only one of the Divines to become Archbishop of Canterbury, a man who knew the machinations of ecclesiastical politics, used to pray in his *Private Devotions* (ed F. W. Faber, 1838) for the Church of England in particular: 'O merciful God, bless this particular Church in which I live; make it, and all the members of it, sound in faith and holy in life . . .' The clergy were expected to be exemplary in discipline. Laud would pray: 'Lord, give me grace, that as oft as they shall come in my way, I may put them in remembrance whom I have ordained, that they stir up the gift of God that is in them by the putting on of my hands . . .' *The Rule and Exercise of Holy Living* (1650) of Jeremy Taylor (1613–1667) expected a practical but demanding spiritual discipline: '. . . although it cannot be enjoined that the greatest part of our time be spent in the direct actions of devotions and religion, yet it will become, not only a duty but also a great providence, to lay aside, for the service of God and businesses of the Spirit, as much as we can . . . No man is a better merchant than he that lays out his time upon God, and his money upon the poor.' Both in public, ordered by the Prayer Books of the church, and in private, perseverance in the practices of a holy life were held in high esteem. The *Greek Devotions of Bishop Andrewes* (tr J. H. Newman, 1843) were lengthy formal prayers used in private. They consisted in an order for Matins, Evening Prayer, and a course of prayer for the week under the five headings of confession, prayer for grace, profession, intercession and praise, each one with an introduction. George Herbert (1593–1633), the poet of the Divines, caught the spirit of Caroline discipline in his poem entitled 'Obedience'.

> O let thy sacred will
> All thy delight in me fulfill!
> Let me not think an action mine own
>   way.
> But as thy love shall sway,
> Refining up the rudder to thy skill.

The discipline of body and mind necessarily led to austerity in the lives of the Divines. There is a seriousness and spareness in their spirituality which bespeaks a search for truth and humility. They wanted only the bare essentials, so that the glory could be God's. In *Holy Living* Taylor used to pray for necessities: 'Lord, turn my necessities into virtues; the works of nature into the works of grace, by making them orderly, temperate, subordinate, and profitable to ends beyond their own proper efficacy . . . let my body be a servant of my spirit, and both body and spirit servants of Jesus . . .' The spiritual life was a delight, but it was also a labour. Bishop Andrewes (1555–1626) said in his *Latin Devotions* (tr J. M. Neale, 1844) that 'he who prays for others, labours for himself'. Prayer had the austerity of

study, and study the austerity of prayer. Andrewes would pray before reading the scriptures: 'Open thou mine eyes, that I may see wondrous things in thy law: take away, O Lord, the veil from my heart while I read the scriptures.' Taking away the veil was the quest of austerity. It left the Christian with a bare dependency on God. *The Poems and Translations of Thomas Fuller D D* (1608–1661) contain a prayer which asks for bareness: 'Lord, what particulars we pray for, we know not, we dare not, we humbly tender a blank into the hands of almighty God; write therein, Lord, what thou wilt, where thou wilt, by whom thou wilt . . .' He expresses the same search for bareness in a prayer which puns on his own name: 'My soul is sustained with a dusky colour. Let thy Son be the scope. I'll be the Fuller.' Laud's austerity has the shrewdness of the ecclesiastical politician. The *Private Devotions* contain a prayer for prosperity, in which he prays that he may be made worthy of the place to which he has been raised in the church, 'that all my endeavours may be to make truth and peace meet together. In this course give me understanding to discover my enemies, and wisdom to prevent them . . .' But the austerities of abstinence, fasting and penance bring also self-knowledge: 'I am become a monster to many,' prayed Laud, 'but thou art my sure trust. O be thou my anchor forever.' The austerity of life at Little Gidding, the little community founded by Nicholas Ferrar (1592–1637), can be seen in the religious dialogues recited in the great room during the Christmas of 1631–1632. The origin of the religious exercises contained in *The Story Books of Little Gidding* was in Ferrar's compilation of divine interludes, dialogues and discourses, planned by him for the purpose of weening his family from Christmas games. They began on All Saints' Day, and on the holy days of Christmas they repeated and acted these Christian histories, taken from both ancient and modern historians.

Qualified by austerity, the Divines espoused the traditions of Christian devotion. The matrix of their devotion was the eucharist. Bishop Richard Montague (1577–1641) represents the Caroline attitude to the sacrament of the eucharist in *A New Gag for an Old Goose* (1624): '. . . we acknowledge right willingly, and profess, that in the blessed sacrament . . . the body and blood of our Saviour Christ is *really* participated and communicated; and by means of that real participation, life from him and in him conveyed into our souls.' Real participation was one of body and spirit. Hence they defended outward gestures of devotion. In a speech on church ritual, Laud testified: 'For my own part, I take myself bound to worship with body as well as in soul, whenever I come where God is worshipped . . . Bishop Jewel . . . approves all, both the kneeling and the bowing, and the standing up at the Gospel . . . they are all commendable gestures, and tokens of devotion, so long as the people understand what they mean.' They maintained a devotion to the saints. In a sermon of 1642 Cosin described the memory of the saints as precious among us, that their persons should be glorified, their praises sung, their virtues revered, their names blessed; so long as the name of God and Jesus Christ is held precious above them all. *The Story Books of Little Gidding* contain a hymn for St John the Evangelist's Day, written by Ferrar, which represents Caroline devotion to the saints:

Thy holy faith we do profess;
Us to thy holy fellowship receive.
Our sins we heartily confess:
Thy pardon therefore let us have.
And as to us thy servant gives
Occasion thus to honour thee:
So also let our words and lives
As lights and guides to others be.

The devotional writing of the Carolines emphasized the centrality of the incarnation in Christian spirituality: the incarnation revealed to men in Jesus Christ, the Word incarnate, in the sacrament of Christ's body and blood, in the revelation of Christ's continuing presence in the holy example of the saints. Their devotion therefore shied from abstraction and strove to show itself in the fruits of love and charity. The Carolines were above all pastors and bishops, and their devotion led to pastoral service. Prayer is concerned not only with the heavenly, but also with the earthly, as George Herbert's poem, entitled 'Prayer', seeks to express:

Prayer, the Church's banquet, Angels' age,
God's breath in man returning to his birth,
The soul in paraphrase, heart in pilgrimage,

The Christian plummet sounding heav'n and earth.

With all their learning and ecclesiastical influence, the spirituality of the Carolines celebrates above all the simplicity of the relationship between God as creator and man as his creature. 'As every man is wholly God's own portion by the title of creation,' wrote Taylor in *Holy Living*, 'so all our labours and care, all our powers and faculties, must be wholly employed in the service of God.' God is wholly in every place, bounded only (as Taylor put it) with cords of love. The Christian can no more be removed from the presence of God than from his own being. 'Faith pours forth prayer,' wrote Andrewes in the *Latin Prayers*, 'let it be poured forth in prayer.' Faith constrains the mind from over-reaching itself in Caroline spirituality. Man is given the gift of rationality, a tool he should use in his search for God; and he is a finite creature, privileged with the ability to glimpse the infinite. In this their spirituality is akin to that of the early Fathers of the Church, whom they read and knew intimately. Bishop Montague's remark on eucharistic theology in *A New Gag for an Old Goose* combines learning with simplicity: 'We have learned that revealed things are for us; secret things are for God. Therefore we wonder, why the world should be so much amused at, and distracted with, those inexplicable labyrinths of consubstantiation and transubstantiation, which only serve to set the world in division; nothing to piety, nor yet information.' There is a pragmatism here which, far from being the consequence of any unimaginative spirituality, bears the virtue of intellectual humility. A short prayer of Thomas Fuller gives a striking image of the character of Caroline spirituality:

Hard is my heart, Lord, to my grief, I feel
Be you the Loadstone, it shall be the steel.

R. D. TOWNSEND

Carthusian Spirituality, Carthusians

The Carthusian Order was founded in the eleventh century in Italy as part of the reform of monastic life, which had a particularly marked tendancy towards solitude.

This was for the Carthusians also combined with a certain kind of apostolic zeal which has continued until today, in which concern for love of neighbour became an integral part of the prayer which was based on the love of God. The continuity and strength of Carthusian spiritually remains remarkable.

The Carthusian Order was founded by St Bruno, who was born about 1030 in Cologne. He was master of the cathedral school at Rheims and later chancellor of the cathedral; about 1077 he first resolved to leave his academic career and serve God in prayer and solitude. Eventually he went with some friends who shared his ideals to Molesmes in the diocese of Langres, where they joined St Robert of Molesmes, the future founder of the Cistercians *, then living with a group of men who had been hermits in the forest of Colan. Deeply influenced by accounts of the ideals and practices of Egyptian monasticism, Bruno left that part of the group which was intent on establishing the monastery that was to become Cîteaux, preferring to explore the ideals of Nitria and Scetis (*see* **Desert, Desert Fathers**) in which solitaries lived in individual houses, though near enough to one another for mutual support. With six companions, Bruno placed himself under the care of the devout Bishop of Grenoble, Hugh, who encouraged them to settle in the mountain desert of the Chartreuse. On the feast of St John the Baptist, the patron of hermits and asectics, the group formally began their monastic life, 3,136 feet above sea-level, in simple wooden huts near a chapel. 'Christ's poor men who dwell in the desert of the Chartreuse for the love of the name of Jesus' was their own description of themselves. In order to preserve the isolation of each hermit, a group of lay-brothers was added to the Order, living together and serving the hermits. The hermits said their Offices in their cells, took their meals alone and worked alone, meeting only for the Offices of Vespers and Vigils, and for the eucharist on Sundays and festivals. Poverty, austerity and silence supported their ideals of solitude and simplicity. The solitude of the Chartreuse rigorously excluded visits by outsiders, especially women, and they were equally firm in declining the use of rents and tithes with the obligations they brought to their recipients.

The Carthusians have never been renowned as scholars or for great mystical writings, though some of them have made genuine contributions to the Christian spiritual tradition, for instance, Guigo I with his *Meditations*, Guigo II in *The Ladder of Monks*, Adam of Dryburg with his *Fourfold Exercise of the Cell*, Denis the Carthusian and St Hugh of Lincoln. It is suggested that the author of *The Cloud of Unknowing* * may have been a Carthusian, and certainly his works, like other mystical writings, were popular among the members of the Order. The real contribution of the Carthusians, however, to Christian spirituality does not lie in their writings but in their lives. The laconic inscription on their graves '*Laudabiliter vixit*' points to the essentially plain and unemotional character of Carthusian commitment, whose worth lies in lives which are lived on the frontiers of eternity, whether finding their passage through in a unknown death in the infirmary or in the more dramatic death such as that of the English Carthusians whose martyrdom is described by Maurice Chauncy. These are men who, like the early monks, have deliberately chosen to make the inner experience of loneliness which lies in the heart of every man the centre and pivot of a whole life, conforming the outer circumstances to the inner realities, in the search for God from whom only will come their salvation: 'for he with whom God is, is at no time less alone than when he is alone' (William of St Thierry, *The Golden Letter*, IV). This life is lived in the conviction that wherever one part of torn and broken humanity is before God, his redeeming action is available for all. As St John of the Cross * says: 'An instant of pure love is more precious in the eyes of God and more profitable for the Church than all other good works together.'

The Carthusian Order includes some houses of nuns, but the Order has remained relatively small, and the houses usually number only twelve inmates at a time. In the twelfth century they were admired by many of their contemporaries, such as Peter the Venerable, Guibert of Nogent, St Bernard of Clairvaux *, and William of Saint-Thierry *; the latter wrote his famous treatise on solitude and prayer for the Carthusians of Mount Dieu, the *Golden Letter to the Brethren of Mount Dieu*, the first phrase of which summarizes their original spirituality and ideals: 'To the brethren of the Mount of

God, by whom the eastern light and ancient light and ancient Egyptian fervour of religion are brought into this Western darkness and cold of France, namely the pattern of solitary life and form of heavenly conversation.' Carthusians claim that their Order has never been 'reformed because never deformed', and their austerity and remoteness have become a legend. The headquarters of the Order is at present in Parkminster in Sussex, England.

Texts: Dom Maurice Laport, *Aux sources de la Vie cartusienne*, 8 vols., 1960–70. See also Maurice Chauncy, *The Passion and Martyrdom of the Holy English Carthusian Fathers: The Short Narration*, 1935; David Knowles, *The Monastic Order in England*, 1963, pp. 374–91; J. Leclercq, 'St Bruno, Guigo and the Chartreuse', in *The Spirituality of the Middle Ages*, Vol. 2 of *A History of Spirituality*, ed Leclercq, Vandenbroucke and Bouyer, 1968, pp. 150–61; E. M. Thompson, *The Carthusian Order in England*, 1930.

BENEDICTA WARD, SLG

Cassian, John

John Cassian was born *c.* 360, probably in the Roman province of Scythia minor, and he was brought up in an affluent and pious family. *C.* 392, he sought admission to a monastery near the Cave of the Nativity in Bethlehem, with an older friend, Germanus. A visitor to the monastery shared the cell of Cassian and Germanus, and was later recognized as a famous ascetic from Egypt, Pinufius, who had fled from his monastery at Panephysis, fearing fame and praise. Cassian and Germanus were deeply impressed by their visitor, and in 385 they asked leave to visit Egypt themselves. They spent seven years visiting the monks of Egypt and talking with them; they returned to Bethlehem and then made a second visit to the desert, which they left during the Origenist controversies. Cassian visited Rome, then settled as a monk in Marseilles, where he wrote his most famous works, the *Institutes* and the *Conferences*, based on his experiences in Egypt. He died in 435.

The writing of John Cassian on the incarnation, whereby he presented the views of Nestorius to the West, were condemned as heretical, but his books on monasticism were widely read and became one of the major influences in the formation of Western monastic spirituality. In response to a request from the monasteries of Gaul, he expressed what he knew of Egyptian monasticism in terms appropriate to his readers and attempted to convey the principles and practices of the desert in terms familiar to the Latin West. He is one of the great theorists of monasticism, following his master, Evagrius, concerned not only with what the monks did but with why they did it. In his works, the practical and theoretical aspects of monastic life are inextricably mingled. The theory behind the monk's way of life is presented by Cassian in terms of an inner journey, which begins with the fear of God, and passes through compunction to renunciation of self, and flight to the desert. There the monk begins the life-long battle with his passions by establishing the life of Christ within himself, by the singleness of heart that seeks only God and the perfection of charity which proceeds from that centre. For the monk, Cassian presents the means to this end as unceasing prayer, from the first stages of meditation to the 'prayer of fire' which is a gift of God: 'it is not a perfect prayer in which the monk is conscious of himself or understands his prayer' (*Conferences* IX, 31). This prayer is nourished by the scriptures and in particular by the psalms. Cassian sees the ascetic life of a monk in terms of the discipleship of the gospel, whereby the monk is united with Christ crucified, as an anticipation of the kingdom of God. Through this union with the incarnate Lord revealed in the scriptures, the monk learns to have a 'single eye' with which to see God only as his goal.

The influence of Cassian upon Western monasticism cannot be overstated. In his works the Greek terminology of Evagrius is translated into Latin providing a permanent vocabulary for prayer; the structure for progress in prayer which he outlines also provided a lasting basis for the discussion of spirituality. The *Institutes* and the *Conferences* were recommended by St Benedict's *Rule* (cap. 73) and have therefore provided a major item in monastic reading for centuries in the West.

See also **Monastic Spirituality, Monasticism.**

Cassian, *Institutes* and *Conferences*, ET by E. C. S. Gibson, 1894 (incomplete); *Insti-*

tutes, Fr tr by J. C. Guy, 1965; *Conferences*, Fr tr by E. Pichery, 1964–1965; Owen Chadwick, *John Cassian*, 1968; L. Cristinai, *Cassien*, 2 vols, 1946; J. C. Guy, *Jean Cassien, vie et doctrine spirituelle*, 1961.

BENEDICTA WARD, SLG

Catharism

The name of Cathari, or Cathars, has been given to men and women who lived in Western Europe during the Middle Ages and believed in dualism – the existence of two antipathetic, creative principles: a good creator who formed positive spirit and was at war with an evil creator who brought into being negative matter. The origin and transmission of this belief has been much debated and is still in question. However, it is clear that dualist theories had an ancient, pre-Christian tradition which in the teachings of the Persian spiritual leader, Mani, in the third century AD, and in Gnostic religious myths, had presented a challenge to early Christianity. The orthodox attack led by Augustine of Hippo (AD 354–430) deflected dualist ideas from the increasingly Christian Mediterranean world of the late antique period so that dualism found a more receptive climate in the Balkans and the Near East.

In the mid-tenth century, Bogomil, a priest in Bulgaria, attracted a band of followers with his dualist theology; he taught that God had driven from heaven his rebellious son along with a host of misled angelic followers. This prince of darkness had created the material world and had imprisoned the fallen angels' souls in human bodies. Bogomil urged his followers to live a simple life so as to detach themselves from the wickedness of the material world in which they lived. The next major appearance of dualism occurred in the eleventh century in Western Europe; these believers in dualism were called Cathars. A hot, scholarly debate has long raged whether the Cathars were directly influenced by the Bogomils or were primarily an indigenous sect. Most scholars will at least acknowledge that some Bogomil teaching affected Catharism, and that by the mid-twelfth century close ties existed between the two groups.

Two major strains of dualism developed in the Middle Ages. That espoused by Bogomil is called moderate, monarchist, or mitigated dualism in which the evil creator, Satan, was formed by God, the good creator; the other system known as radical, absolute, or Dragovitsan dualism posited that the two creators were coeternal so that neither one was derivative of the other. Absolute dualism was to win general acceptance in the southern half of France, Languedoc.

In the middle of the twelfth century, Catharism reached Languedoc, and because a considerable number of its adherents lived in the city of Albi, the Cathars of Languedoc came to be known generally as Albigenses. Catharism spread rapidly through all levels of the population and was perceived to threaten orthodox Christianity. At first Cistercian preachers tried publicly to debate with the Cathars. These efforts were signally unsuccessful so that the church, goaded by the assassination in 1208 of the papal legate, Peter of Castelnau, turned to armed repression. In 1209 Pope Innocent III proclaimed a crusade against the Albigenses which was led at first by Simon de Montfort. The taking of the mountain retreat of Montségur in 1245 ended the last stage of the Albigensian Crusade, a bloody campaign which had been marked as much by the greed of the northern crusaders as by their genuine religious convictions. The Inquisition established in Languedoc in 1233 further rooted out Cathar sympathizers so that by the end of the thirteenth century, only small pockets of heretics survived in Languedoc and northern Italy.

The Cathars believed in a life of asceticism to free the spirit from the bonds of matter. A small number of both men and women became the Cathar élite – called perfected people by the Catholics, and 'Good Christians' or 'Good Men' by the Cathars – people who had received the sacrament of the consolamentum and who lived a demandingly ascetic life as celibate vegetarians. Perfected women usually retired to Cathar convents, while perfected men travelled in pairs to preach, teach, and baptize with the consolamentum. Most Cathars, however, were 'believers' whose lives were not religiously rigorous but who listened to the perfected preach and intended to accept the consolamentum at death. The bitterness with which the Catholic Church attacked the Cathars was overtly for their rejection of the sacraments and key doctrines like the incarnation, but indirectly for their challenge to the growing wealth and worldliness of the church as well as the threat they posed to patriarchal power by the inclusion of women among perfects as well as believers. By the end of the Middle Ages, the combined forces of secular and religious power had eradicated Catharism from Western Europe.

The sting of the later name 'Puritan' lay in its being a translation of 'Catharus', though the English Puritans were totally different from the mediaeval Manichees.

E. L. R. Ladurie, *Montaillou: The Promised Land of Error*, 1978; M. Lambert, *Medieval Heresy*, 1977; S. Runciman, *The Medieval Manichee*, 1961; W. L. Wakefield, *Heresy Crusade and Inquisition in Southern France 1100–1250*, 1974.

PENELOPE D. JOHNSON

Catharsis

Catharsis, purgation or spiritual purification refers to the events and processes by which an individual is cleansed and freed from those impediments – sensible, intellectual, and spiritual – which block the quest for authentic existence and union with God. (This catharsis should not be confused with the catharsis which Aristotle thought tragedy provided; namely, a certain cleansing and release from various emotions though aesthetic means.) Christian and non-Christian writers alike insist on the essential importance of catharsis or purgation for progress in spiritual life. Plato's allegory of the cave is a classic description of purgation in a non-Christian framework. For Plato, philosophy itself purifies the soul to effect its restoration from injustice to justice.

Progress in spiritual life is traditionally described as following three ways or stages. The purgative way is the initial stage in which one is freed from attachment to worldly, sensible things and in which the senses and sensible appetites are disciplined and mortified. The next stage, the illuminative way, is characterized by a contemplation or knowledge of God. This stage for some individuals is succeeded by the unitive way*: the ecstatic union of the soul with God in the darkness of unknowing in which the soul is radically transformed in God so that God alone shines in the soul. The passage from illumination to unity is marked by a further purgation, the 'dark night of the soul', in which one is freed from all intellection, will, and desire and, ultimately, self-consciousness.

Unless totally and completely transformed in God, a condition which Christians generally attribute only to Jesus, the individual will to some degree fluctuate within the three ways. Further, elements of each way are to some extent present in the other ways; e.g. an individual in the purgative way also experience some illumination and union with God. The purgative way is common both to the process of ethical perfection (e.g. Plato) and mystical life. The dark night of the soul is restricted to mystic life. It is more dreadful than the purgative way for the individual who has made great progress in contemplating God is suddenly afflicted with stagnation, despair and intense feelings of being abandoned by God.

The teachings of St John of the Cross* on purgation will be summarized because of their prominent role in much Christian and, especially, Catholic theology. Catharsis or purgation is necessary for the soul to be freed from the disorder wrought by sin. Such purgation necessarily involves suffering and pain as the individual is deprived from his or her attachments to things other than God. Purgation, which is always accompanied by grace, assists the individual in becoming centred solely on God. Catharsis takes place in two nights – the dark night of the senses and the dark night of the soul. The dark night of the senses usually takes place in the transition from the purgative to the illuminative way, the dark night of the soul in the transition from illumination to unity. Purgations in these nights are of two kinds: active and passive. In active purgations or nights the individual labours to remove sinful habits and seeks to discipline him or herself to do only God's will. In passive purgations or nights the individual undergoes purgations at the hand of God. Such purgations engender a feeling of helplessness and despair in apparently being abandoned by and unable to achieve union with God. Such purgations are often accompanied by purgative contemplations in which the individual experiences a loving knowledge of God together with an awareness of his or her own wretchedness before God.

See also **Dark Night, Darkness**

JOHN D. JONES

Catherine of Genoa, St

Saint and mystic. Born at Genoa, May/June 1447; died there, 14/16 September 1510.

Catherine's family, the Fieschi, were among the greatest in Genoa; her father, who died before her birth, had been viceroy of Naples. Catherineta, as she was called, grew up tall, beautiful and intelligent, but of a nervous, hypersensitive temperament. At sixteen, as a pawn in family politics, she was married to Giuliano Adorni who was unfaithful and neglected her. After ten unhappy years she underwent a religious conversion (March 1473) and began two practices which she continued for the rest of her life – that of daily communion and that of nursing the sick in the city's largest hospital, the Pammatone. By this time Giuliano's extravagance had brought him to penury. What was less to be expected, his wife's conversion was soon followed by his own. Having agreed to live in continence, the pair first took a small house by the Pammatone hospital and later two rooms within its walls. Giuliano became a Franciscan tertiary. He died in 1497. Meanwhile Catherine laboured away in the hospital, with particular heroism during the great fever epidemic of 1493. In 1490 she was put in charge of the female wards and proved an excellent administrator. From 1493 dates her close friendship with young Ettore Vernazza, a Genoese lawyer to whom we owe many details of her life and conversation. But down to 1499 she remained strangely isolated, spiritually. Though a daily communicant, she only rarely went to confession and did without any spiritual direction. This state of things ended, however, in 1499, when she at last found a priest, Cataneo Marabotto, to whom she could open her heart freely. He remained her confessor and, in some sense, director until her death, after much physical agony, in September 1510.

The main source of information about Catherine, and of the works ascribed to her, is an anonymous compilation made after her death and published at Genoa in 1551 as her *Life and Teaching* (*Vita e Dottrina*). The *Life* would seem to have been the work, in the main, of Marabotto. The doctrinal part contains the so-called 'Treatise on Purgatory' – originally forming one chapter of the *Life*, and a 'Spiritual Dialogue' in two parts (now commonly printed as three). F.

von Hügel's* position in his great pioneering work on Catherine was that she wrote neither of these works exactly as we have them, but that the substance of the 'Treatise' was authentic; as for the 'Dialogue', it was all the work of E. Vernazza's daughter Battista. The entire subject has been reconsidered – in the light, in part, of fresh evidence – by U. Bonzi da Genova, OMCap who, while agreeing in the main with von Hügel about the 'Treatise', is firmly of the opinion that Catherine was the author of Part I of the 'Dialogue'. This last point is interesting in itself, but more important is the agreement of the two major Catherinian scholars as to the substantial authenticity of the little work on purgatory, this being the foundation of Catherine's reputation as mystic and theologian. She saw purgatory as the continuation and completion of a process that begins in this life; the process of suffering endured by every soul drawn simultaneously by love for God and love of self. Of this suffering she says and concisely shows that it is *necessary*, granted those conditions, and that for every soul that enters the afterlife with some desire for God in preference to self, this suffering *must* end in perfect joy, because there is now nothing between the soul and the self-giving Absolute Goodness except the residual effects of past self-love.

Catherine of Genoa: Purgation and Purgatory, The Spiritual Dialogue (Classics of Western Spirituality), 1980; U. Bonzi da Genova, OMCap in *DS*, II, cols. 290f.; *S. Caterina da Genova*, 2 vols, 1960–1962; F. von Hügel, *The Mystical Element of Religion*, 2 vols. [2]1923; R. Ombres, OP, 'The Theology of Purgatory', *Theology Today*, No. 24, 1978.

KENELM FOSTER, OP

Catherine of Siena, St

Saint; born at Siena *c*. 1347, Catherine Benincasa was one of the many children of a Sienese dyer. At the age of twelve she vowed her virginity to Christ and at sixteen was admitted into a Dominican lay sisterhood. Later she was to tell her confessor, Raymond of Capua, OP, that she had never learned anything from men or women about the way of salvation, 'but only from the ... sweet bridegroom of my soul, the Lord Jesus Christ'. Nevertheless her Dominican connection was of the utmost importance, for two reasons. First, it gave her extraordinary spiritual and intellectual apostolate the backing of a religious order of unsurpassed prestige and authority in the church. Secondly, the Dominican ideal of 'communicating things contemplated' (Aquinas, *Summa theol.*, 2a2ae. 188, 6; 3a. 40, 1 ad 2) exactly suited Catherine's approach to Christ as 'the sweet First Truth', the Word made flesh 'to give ... knowledge of the glory of God' (II Cor. 4.6; cf. John 1.18). We shall see presently how Catherine envisaged this gift of knowledge.

After three years of strict seclusion Catherine began her public life, probably in 1368, at the command, as she believed, of Christ himself. It falls into three periods: 1368 to the summer of 1374; thence to November 1378; thence to her death on 29 April 1380. The first period, spent entirely in Siena, saw the formation round her of a 'family' of friends and disciples, both men and women, clerics and layfolk. This represented a shift in the direction and expression of her charity: hitherto concentrated on the poor and the sick, it became increasingly doctrinal as she grew more conscious of her vocation as teacher and counsellor. So the great series of her letters began (*c.* 1370), dictated to secretaries chosen from her 'family'. Before long these letters began to touch on public affairs, beginning with the contemporary project of a crusade against the Turks. That issue receded, however, as Catherine became involved successively in two more urgent matters: the conflict between Florence and the Holy See, 1375 to July 1378, and the Great Schism, which began in September 1378. Both issues stimulated her intense desire for a reform of the church; but whereas in the former her chief immediate concern was to reconcile the Holy See with the Italian laity – with whose grievances she had much sympathy – once the Schism began every other consideration took second place in her mind to the unity of the church and the authority of Urban VI. Her first call was now to the clergy – a recall to obedience. For her the indispensability of the church – and so of its unity – consisted in this, that it is the medium through which the blood shed on the cross for sinful man is available to sinners individually. The church holds the keys of the blood', the blood 'reaches us through

the ministers of Holy Church'. The church only exists *in function of* the Blood. And with this we return to that 'knowledge' of God that the incarnation, as she understood it, reveals. The God so revealed is Father, Son and Holy Spirit, but viewed especially in relation to man – as creator and, since man's lapse into sin, above all as recreator. This recreation works by love, the supreme manifestation of which is the blood shed on the cross. The way to God starts here – in an awareness of his love through that sign of it. But this awareness, Catherine never tires of insisting, presupposes self-knowledge.

Catherine of Siena: The Dialogue (Classics of Western Spirituality), 1980; Raymond of Capua, OP, *The Life of Catherine of Siena*, 1980, K. Foster, OP and M. J. Ronayne, OP, *I, Catherine* (tr of 60 letters and a part of the *Dialogo*), 1980.

KENELM FOSTER, OP

Caussade, J.-P. de

Jean-Pierre de Caussade (1675–1751) entered the Jesuit novitiate at Toulouse in 1693, was ordained priest in 1705 and professed in 1708, and throughout his life was much appreciated as a teacher, preacher and confessor. For some years he gave conferences to the sisters of the Order of the Visitation at Nancy and undertook the spiritual direction of several of them. Notes of these conferences, together with examples of his extensive correspondence, were preserved but remained unpublished for many years. In 1861 they were published by H. Ramière, in the form of a treatise followed by many of the letters in which de Caussade sensitively applied and expounded his teaching, under the title *L'Abandon à la Providence Divine*.

De Caussade published one book, in 1741, *Instructions spirituelles, en forme de dialogues, sur les divers états d'oraison, suivant la doctrine de Bossuet* (translated as *On Prayer*). This is a set of dialogues, almost an elaborate catechism, on the subject of contemplative prayer, which endeavours to show that such prayer is not subject to the current official criticism of Quietism* but is, when correctly understood, in keeping with the teaching of Bossuet*, Bishop of Meaux, the distinguished and energetic opponent of Quietism. It includes Bossuet's brief instructions towards practising the prayer of simple recollection and attention to God.

His teaching is derived from the spirituality of St Francis de Sales * (especially in the *Treatise of the Love of God*), has much in common with that of St John of the Cross * and the Carmelite * school, and owes its attractive practicality to his own experience of the life of faith and all that he learned from the penitents he so imaginatively counselled.

There is little interest in exceptional states of prayer and complex analysis of the route to perfection. Perfection is open to all here and now by God's grace, since it resides in our self-giving to God's providence and doing his will as it is signified to us. Whatever our present situation happens to be, it is to be seen as God's will for us in the limited sense that he clearly consents to its being the context of our present service to him. Because God is present in every situation, clearly or obscurely, under the disguise of something he wishes us to do, bear or enjoy for his sake, his will for us is further to be seen as our doing that which he wishes to be done in it. De Caussade spoke of each passing moment as being the veil of God and so also, when scrutinized and interpreted by faith, the unveiling of God. He gave the term 'the sacrament of the present moment' to this understanding of time and continually expounded the Christian life as an active and passive co-operation with God moment by moment. The kind of prayer he recommended is a prayer of simple waiting on God, of discernment of his presence, and of co-operation with him in the doing of his will.

See also **Abandon.**

J. P. de Caussade, *Self-Abandonment to Divine Providence*, tr Algar Thorold, 1959; *On Prayer*, tr Algar Thorold, 1949.

J. NEVILLE WARD

Celibacy

Celibacy in the Christian tradition is understood as the choice to remain unmarried in order to devote oneself completely to God and his concerns. It implicitly includes the will to renounce all deliberate sexual activity. In communities of religious life, this decision is usually professed publicly in the vow of chastity. Such a vow can also be made privately by Christians who choose to remain in secular life. Since the eleventh century, the Roman Catholic Church in the West has required its priests to remain celibate. In the East the legislation is somewhat different: married men may be ordained, but those who are already ordained priests or deacons are not allowed to marry.

It is generally agreed that Christ presented the ideal of celibacy to his disciples in Matt. 19.10–12. After listening to his teaching on the indissolubility of marriage, the disciples exclaim: 'If that is the case between man and wife, it is better not to marry.' To which Jesus replies: 'Not everyone can accept this teaching, only those to whom it is given to do so. Some men are incapable of sexual activity from birth; some have been deliberately made so; and some there are who have freely renounced sex for the sake of the kingdom of God. Let them accept this teaching who can.'

In reflecting on the spiritual values of celibacy, theologians and spiritual writers usually group them under three headings: christological, ecclesial, and eschatological or prophetic. The christological value begins with the existential fact that Jesus himself lived in a state of celibacy. In doing so, says Pope Paul VI, he opened to mankind a new way of holiness, 'in which the human creature adheres wholly and directly to the Lord, and is concerned only with him and his affairs' (Encyclical on Priestly Celibacy, 1967, n. 25). By embracing celibacy, then, the Christian endeavours to be closely conformed to Christ, sharing in his very lifestyle.

The ecclesial value of celibacy is seen in the fact that it frees one from the obligations of marriage and family life. But this is not supposed to foster selfishness or isolation. Rather, it is assumed that the celibate will devote his or her energies to the loving service of God's people. Ideally, the celibate's capacity for love is not thwarted but rather purified and broadened to embrace those who might otherwise be forgotten.

The eschatological value of celibacy is based on the New Testament notion that 'in the resurrection they neither marry nor are given in marriage' (Matt. 22.30). Celibacy is believed to be a sign of the world to come, where sexual relationships will be transcended and 'God will be all in all' (I Cor. 15.28). Recent writers, taking a more incarnational approach, translate this into the prophetic language of protest. In a culture where sexual gratification is presumed to be an absolute necessity, celibacy witnesses to an alternative value system based on the gospel. It raises questions about the culture's basic assumptions. One who freely chooses celibacy affirms that nothing is more important in life than 'the love of God which comes to us in Christ Jesus' (Rom. 8.39).

It is readily acknowledged today that celibacy is a special charism whose presence in the individual needs to be carefully discerned. Hence there is continuing controversy in the Roman Catholic Church over whether celibacy should be a universal requirement for ordained priesthood. In any case, spiritual writers are careful not to exalt celibacy in a way that denigrates marriage. There is recognition that both marriage and celibacy are authentic Christian vocations, and that both are needed to express the full mystery of God's presence and love in the world.

D. Goergen, *The Sexual Celibate*, 1974; E. Schillebeeckx, *Celibacy*, 1968; A. Van Kaam, *The Vowed Life*, 1968.

MARTIN PABLE, OFM Cap

Celtic Spirituality

Today the Celtic peoples occupy only a few inhospitable areas on the Atlantic seaboard of Europe, and their ancient languages and distinctive culture are in danger of being swept away. It is hard to believe that in the so-called 'Dark Ages' preceding the end of the first millennium, the Celtic realms kept alive a strong tradition of Christian learning and piety. Ireland was indeed at that time a 'land of saints and scholars'. It is harder still to believe that a thousand years earlier Celtic tribes were in possession of large tracts of the European continent. From the earliest times, the Celts appear to have been a deeply religious people and there are many remains of their pagan cults, as well as accounts of their mythology. They were a rural people, and their religion was very much a religion of nature. It would seem that for the Celt every spring, river, lake, mountain and forest was a sanctuary, so that, like other early peoples, they dwelt in a sacral environment. This in turn meant that every act of daily life was invested with religious significance. The names of some of the early

deities have been preserved. One important figure was the god Lugh, said to have been the master of all skills. His name can still be discerned in many of the place-names of Western Europe, notably Lyons (Lugdunum). Among goddesses, Brigitta had a strong following and her name will come to our notice again shortly.

When Christianity came to the Celtic realms, there was no sharp break with the past. The old sanctuaries continued to be frequented, though now their numinous properties were ascribed to local Christian saints rather than to pagan divinities. A good example is the widespread cult of St Bridget among the Christianized Celts, for it is clear that she had inherited the prestige that had belonged to the pagan Brigitta. At Govan church, now within the city of Glasgow, there are interesting evidences of the smooth transition from the old ways to the new. The churchyard is circular in shape, preserving the form of an ancient stone circle, though the stones themselves have long since disappeared. Within the church, an ancient stone shows the cross incised upon one side, while on the back is a representation of the sun's disc.

Perhaps the most important heritage which Celtic Christianity received from the old religion was the profound sense of the immanence of God in the world. If the Christian doctrine of creation is (as some theologians have claimed) supposed to de-divinize the natural world, this certainly did not happen among the Celts. They remained very much aware of a divine presence in all nature, and it is this sense of an all-pervading presence that is characteristic of their Christian piety.

A theological basis for this immanentist spirituality was provided by John Scotus Eriugena (810–877), the greatest thinker produced by the Celtic church. His major work, *De Naturae Divisione*, begins from an inclusive concept of 'nature' which is held to embrace both God and the creatures. On this view, there can be no dualistic separation between God and his world. God is in all things and is said to be the true essence of all things. They are not external to him, because for God 'making' is the same as 'being'. A favourite word with Eriugena is 'theophany', and it would not be going too far to say that for him the world is a theophany. It is true that he was deeply influenced by Neoplatonism, yet one could say that his was a truly Celtic theology. Only long after his death was his teaching condemned because of alleged pantheistic tendencies, but modern scholars have rehabilitated Eriugena and have claimed him as a forerunner of Whitehead and other modern thinkers who have looked for a dialectical way of understanding the relation of God to the world.

The combination of the sense of transcendence and otherness with that of God's involvement and immanence may also reflect the social organization of the Celts. In Ireland, the High King (a title often transferred to God) had his abode on the Hill of Tara, exalted above the plain yet close enough to be sharing the life of the people.

The expression of Celtic Christian spirituality has come to us in a wealth of poems and hymns. The simplest of them are little more than spells to keep away illness or other misfortunes, and it would be hard to determine where magic ends and genuine piety begins. Other poems celebrate the power, beauty and mystery of nature; others invoke the divine blessing at the crucial moments of life – birth, marriage, the blessing of a new house, the approach of death; still others, perhaps the most typical, are for the events of daily life and work – getting up, kindling the fire, going out to work, returning home, the family meal, lying down. It is very much a down-to-earth spirituality. In all these simple happenings, there is an awareness of the presence of God and of the saints. Peter and John and Christ himself are with them in the fishing boat. The Trinity is invited to lie down with them when they go to bed at night. In both Scotland and Ireland, one can still meet persons who claim to have had visions of Christ or the saints, so vivid is their sense of presence.

While it is true that Celtic spirituality has been bound up with a way of life which is now virtually extinct, it does not follow that it has become only a historical curiosity or that there is nothing that can be learned from it in the modern age. We often hear the plea for a spirituality that will impinge on everyday life, and Celtic spirituality certainly did that. Admittedly, everyday life in an industrial and computerized society is vastly removed from what it was among people whose lives were spent in farming and fishing. But it may be that the theological basis of that old spirituality, namely, an understanding of God as deeply involved in his creation, can generate a new spirituality appropriate to new social conditions.

A. Carmichael (ed), *Carmina Gadelica*, 5 vols, 1900ff.; M. Dillon and N. K. Chadwick, *The Celtic Realm*, 1967; P. MacCanna, *Celtic Mythology*, 1970; G. R. D. McLean (ed), *Poems of the Western Highlanders*, 1961.

JOHN MACQUARRIE

Challoner, Richard

The son of a Protestant wine-cooper of Lewes in Sussex, and a Catholic mother, Challoner (1691–1781) was prepared for first communion by John Gother and sent by him to study for the priesthood at Douai in 1705, where he remained as student and then professor till 1730 when he went to work as a missioner in London. He quickly established himself as a director of souls as well as an efficient administrator, and on the feast of St Francis de Sales (29 Jan) 1741 was consecrated as assistant bishop to the Vicar Apostolic of London, whom he succeeded in 1758.

Challoner's ministry was modelled on that of his patron St Francis de Sales*, and of St Vincent de Paul, whose ideals he urged on his priests: strict personal asceticism, accessibility to the poor, emphasis on teaching and spiritual direction through the confessional. He was the author of over sixty separate works – polemic, instruction, prayer-books, catechisms, biblical translations and paraphrases, books of meditations, martyrology and hagiography.

His instructional and devotional writing conforms closely to the Salesian pattern evolved by the secular clergy in the seventeenth century, and handed on to him by Gother. He translated the *Introduction to the Devout Life* (1762) and published several collections of meditations modelled on it, of which the best known are *Think Well on't* (1728) and *Meditations for Every Day in the Year* (1754). These lack the poetry of his model, and are drably written, but they drew on older English as well as continental authors, and have considerable religious power: they remained in print for the next century and a half. He included extracts from Francis de Sales in his most famous work *The Garden of the Soul* (1740), a book of prayers and instructions in the tradition of the *Manual* and of William Clifford's *Little Manual of the Poor Man's daily devotion*. This was a distillation of the sober piety which had characterized English Catholicism for two hundred years. It went through ten editions in his lifetime and, modified beyond recognition, remained in print into this century. The rest of his devotional work recapitulates all the main emphases of recusant piety. His genteel modernization of the Douai Bible (1749–1750) drew heavily on the A V and remained the standard Catholic translation till the 1950s. He translated Thomas à Kempis, St Augustine's *Confessions*, the *Life* of St Teresa – all recusant favourites. He reissued the *Manual* and many of Gother's writings. His *Britannia Sancta* (1745) and *Memorial of Ancient British Piety* (1761) provided British hagiography while *Memoirs of Missionary Priests* (1741–1742) drew on a huge range of printed and M S S sources to provide a moving and still historically valuable account of Catholics executed since the Reformation. Challoner's piety was intense but muted in tone, tinged with the moralism of his century but deeply christocentric and firmly rooted in scripture, and sacramental observance. His work was aimed at ordinary men and women, its tone practical.

'Mental prayer, by way of meditation, is very easy, even to the meanest capacities; it requires nothing but a good will, a sincere desire of conversing with God, by thinking of him, and loving him. In effect, the great business of mental prayer is *thinking* and *loving*; and who is there that can even live without *thinking* and *loving*?'

See also **Recusancy, Recusants.**

Edwin Burton, *The Life and Times of Bishop Challoner*, 1909; E. Duffy, *Challoner and his Church*, 1981.

EAMON DUFFY

Charismatic Movement, The

The Charismatic Renewal Movement is a modern world-wide movement, predominantly lay, now found among members of all the major Christian denominations, including the R C Church. Its distinctive feature is an emphasis on practice of the charismatic gifts described in the N T (cf. I Cor. 12–14), normally preceded by the spiritual experience called in Pentecostal terminology the 'baptism in the Holy Spirit'. It emerged as an identifiable movement at the beginning of the 1960s in the United States and Great Britain, then in other Western European countries and finally all over the world, including the Third World (e.g., Latin America, where it often overlaps the proliferating new *communidades de base*). One reliable estimate puts numbers at 11,000,000.

This movement is to be distinguished from the 'outpouring of the Spirit' in the early 1900s, especially at the Bible School of Charles Parham, Topeka, Kansas in 1901 and at the Azusa Street Mission in Los Angeles in 1906–1909, which resulted in early 'classical' Pentecostalism* and in the establishment of Pentecostal Churches, such as Assemblies of God and Pentecostal Holiness Churches. These newer 'pentecostals' or 'charismatics', as some preferred to call themselves, were convinced that they should remain in their own churches, although to varying degrees they borrowed theological ideas and worship styles from classical Pentecostalism.

In this early period, the characteristic of people from the mainline Protestant Churches in Europe or America receiving the 'baptism of the Spirit' was the private nature of their experience, usually alone or among a few others at a Bible camp, a house prayer meeting, sometimes during a period of crisis, i.e., generally a time when they experienced their own helplessness and a need to reach out to the Spirit for power to live the Christian life and witness. Subsequently, many of them experienced isolation, misunderstanding and often rejection by family or friends and even pastors, and were astonished and more than delighted to find others who had had similar experiences. Often prayer partnerships would follow or little prayer groups mushroomed in homes, at work and in university circles.

Various circumstances contributed to the spread of the Charismatic Movement. One of the earliest was the Full Gospel Businessmen's Fellowship International, founded in 1952 by Demos Shakarian. This is an international, inter-denominational group which preaches on the Holy Spirit's blessings and gifts. Members usually meet in public restaurants. A talk and witness by some well-known speaker follows the meal, and an invitation to prayer. Now this group also broadcasts on TV and has two magazines.

In the US, the media have played an important role in the spread of the movement in the 1960s and 1970s. Well-known networks of charismatic TV stations include Pat Robertson's Christian Broadcasting Network (CBN), Jim Bakker's Praise the Lord Network (PTL) and Sister Angelica's Eternal Word Network (which is RC); there are also many books, tapes and records of music, e.g. by 'the Fishermen' from the Church of the Redeemer, Houston, Texas, and the Word of God Community, Ann Arbor, Michigan.

An early pioneer in the area of healing in the US was Agnes Sanford, author of several books, and founder of a school of pastoral ministry to train ministers, priests and laity, in 'healing of the memories' techniques. Later, she practised all the traditional pentecostal charisms in her ministry. Others in this field included Anne White, Ruth Carter Stapleton and Barbara Shlemon, the first Catholic.

In the 1960s also, from Fort Lauderdale, Florida, the Holy Spirit Teaching Mission began to send out speakers and authors such as Derek Prince, Don Basham and Bob Mumford for charismatic teaching and witnessing on 'the circuit'. Much the same work was done by the Fountain Trust in Britain, led by Michael Harper. Very soon representatives from each of the denominations became known to the charismatic fellowship, e.g. Dennis Bennet and Graham Pulkingham (Episcopalian), Michael Harper (Anglican), Larry Christenson (Lutheran), Harald Bredeson (Dutch Reformed), Rodman Williams (Presbyterian), Tommy Tyson (Methodist), and, of course, 'Mr Pentecost', as he was called, David Du Plessis, former Secretary of the Pentecostal World Conference. Women in this ministry included such as Corrie ten Boom, Catherine Marshall and Katherine Kuhlman, well-known for her healing services.

When Roman Catholics entered the movement, (beginning in 1967 at Duquesne University, Pittsburgh) they brought a new dimension of social organization, and much of their theology, which they sought to reconcile with the movement's patterns of worship. They rapidly published many books on charismatic themes. As more and

more Catholics began to receive the 'baptism in the Spirit', often now in organized groups of 'Life in the Spirit Courses', a National Service Committee was established and national and international conferences were hosted at South Bend (University of Notre Dame), leadership conferences were held at Ann Arbor (site of University of Michigan), a world catalogue of prayer groups appeared, and a regular international magazine, *New Covenant*, with many books and tapes. In 1976 an International Communications Office, created in the USA in the 1970s, transferred to Brussels, later moving to Rome in 1981.

At least some of the RCs in the movement were quickly manifesting the full range of traditional Pentecostal practices: glossolalia* (which had attracted so much attention initially), prophecy, healing, deliverance, etc. But by the early 1970s there was also widespread interest in community commitment, covenants, leadership, teaching, ecumenical outreach and social action. In the USA these themes were treated at the annual National Conferences at Notre Dame and Leadership Conferences in Ann Arbor. Many covenant communities began to spring up, such as Word of God (Ann Arbor), Alleluia Faith Community (Augusta, Georgia) and the Community of St Patrick's (Providence, Rhode Island). Others in Europe followed in Dublin, Brussels and France.

One of the reasons the movement spread so successfully among RCs was its connection with the universities (e.g., Duquesne, Notre Dame, University of Michigan, etc.). Also, it so happened that some preachers such as Francis MacNutt (who was to become perhaps the most influential speaker and author in the Catholic renewal, especially in the healing ministry) received the 'baptism in the Spirit' just prior to embarking upon a series of scheduled retreats in various monasteries and religious houses. Thus, the 'good news' was passed on to a cadre of preachers and to men and woman working in spiritual direction, etc., and the network of religious orders naturally lent itself easily to a rapid dissemination of the new Pentecostal fire.

Initially, the established churches adopted a Gamaliel 'wait-and-see' policy, finally giving a cautious approval with warnings of several 'dangers'. In 1969 Bishop Zaleski was commissioned by the American bishops to do a study of the charismatic movement in the USA and this resulted in a positive assessment by him and by an annual confirmation by US bishops, who became increasingly positive. Unofficial papal approval came in 1975 when 10,000 charismatics were received in Rome by Paul VI, largely through the liaison and sponsorship of Cardinal Suenens of Malines, Belgium. Later meetings with Paul and John Paul II consolidated this approval. Over the years, the Protestant denominations and the Orthodox Church have added their approval, or issued norms, such as the 'guidelines' of the United Methodists in 1975. Together with the cautious approval, however, there seems to be a growing tendency to routinization, at least among RCs. Certainly, this movement is rather more middle-class than the earlier working-class classical Pentecostalism.

Since 1972, the Vatican has been in conversation annually with representatives of the classical Pentecostal and Neo-Pentecostal movements, with theologians from both sides contributing. At their second exploratory session in November 1971, they had agreed on this statement: 'The essence of Pentecostalism is the personal and direct awareness of the indwelling of the Holy Spirit, by which the risen and glorified Christ is revealed, and the believer is empowered to witness and worship with the abundance of life as described in Acts and the Epistles. The Pentecostal experience is not a goal to be reached, nor a place to stand, but a door through which to go into a greater fullness of life in the Spirit. It is an event which becomes a way of life in which often charismatic manifestations have a place. Characteristic of this way of life is a love of the word of God, and a concern to live by the power of the Spirit.'

Walter Hollenweger, *The Pentecostals* (ch 1), 1972; Kevin and Dorothy Ranaghan, *Catholic Pentecostals*, 1969 and *As the Spirit Leads Us*, 1971; John Sherrill, *They Speak in Other Tongues*, 1964; David Wilkerson, *The Cross and the Switchblade*, 1964.

A. QUENTIN LISTER, OP

Charity *see* Love

Christian Science

The 'discoverer and founder' of Christian Science was Mary Baker Eddy (1821–1910),

who grew up in New England at the time when transcendentalist thought was widespread. After a fall on the ice in 1866, she claimed that by a remarkable healing experience she was led to the discovery of how to be well and how to cure others. Interpreting the Bible from this perspective, she published in 1875 the first edition of what later became *Science and Health with Key to the Scriptures*. The book was to go through many revisions and it remains, together with the King James (Authorized) version of the Bible, the central authority among Christian Scientists. Also in 1875 the first Christian Science society was organized; in 1879 'The Church of Christ (Scientist)' was chartered with headquarters in Boston. The 'Mother Church' continues as the world headquarters of the movement; other Christian Science churches are branches. There are no ordained clergy, but 'readers' conduct services, while 'practitioners' treat those seeking cure by prayer.

Christian Science rests on the premiss that God is all in all, God is divine Mind. Mind (synonymous with Spirit), Soul, Life, Truth, Love, Principle, is all that exists. Mind's expression of itself is man, who as the idea and image of God is immortal and perfect. Spirit being all, matter is unreal illusion and is nothing. Inasmuch as evil has to do with matter, it too, along with disease, sin and death, is unreal. Death is an illusion of mortal sense, and may continue to appear until destroyed by spiritual sense. Sin is belief in the real existence of other minds than the divine Mind. Sickness too is false belief; suffering exists only in the mortal mind. To the Christian Scientist, healing is a religious function, for disease and illness as delusions of the human mind can be destroyed by the prayer of spiritual understanding. The faith of Christian Science is claimed to be not *primarily* to heal physical disease but to regenerate human thought through spiritual understanding.

Sydney E. Ahlstom, 'Mary Baker Eddy', *Notable American Women, 1607–1950: A Biographical Dictionary*, vol. 1, pp. 551–61, 1977; Charles E. Braden, *Christian Science Today*, 1958; Robert Peel, *Mary Baker Eddy: The Years of Authority*, 1977

ROBERT T. HANDY

Cistercian Spirituality, Cistercians

The Cistercian Order, so called from its first house at Cîteaux, was founded in 1098 by a group of monks led by Robert of Molesmes with the avowed intention of following the Rule of St Benedict more closely than had been possible in their previous monasteries. Cîteaux founded other houses but its rapid expansion came only after Bernard and his companions became monks there in 1112; two years later, Bernard was sent as abbot to the new foundation at Clairvaux. By the end of the twelfth century, 530 Cistercian abbeys had been founded; these were grouped together by the constitution, the *Carta Caritatis*, drawn up by Stephen Harding in 1119.

The aim of the founders of Cîteaux to pursue a simpler form of monastic life within the tradition of the text of the *Rule of St Benedict* was amplified and expanded in the next generation, particularly by the overwhelming influence of Bernard of Clairvaux*. The spirituality of the Cistercians cannot be separated either from the general currents of devotion operating in the twelfth century in Western Europe or from the genius of St Bernard. It must therefore be seen in its context of both these factors and any particular themes which are called 'Cistercian' should be understood as inclusive rather than exclusive of the general tradition of Christian spirituality. With this in mind, there are certain themes that appear both in the life and in the writings of the Cistercians. First, there is the concept of monastic life as a separation from the world by a group intent on the same way of life. This group-solitude distinguished the first settlement at Cîteaux, and continued in the other foundations, which were away from towns and exclusive of all but members of the group. This ideal of corporate solitude is connected with two other traits of Cistercian spirituality: one of these is the idea of the 'Order', the solitary groups connected by bonds of filiation with one another, to form the 'Cistercian Order', in which could be distinguished a 'Cistercian Spirit' as a distinctive form of the monastic spirituality. Secondly, the use of unused land on the edge of civilized life, exclusive of external contacts, meant that manual labour received greater emphasis than in other monasteries

and ensured both that a great deal of land was worked by the Cistercians and that they employed the *conversi*, the lay brothers, for this purpose. The institution of the *conversi*, men who were neither ordained nor choir monks but were fully members of the community with less obligation to choir, gave a certain non-intellectual slant to the Cistercian ethos. It also formed part of the next Cistercian trait, emphasis on the simplicity of devotion and a more personal christocentric approach to the relationship between the soul and God. The aim of the monastic life as led at Cîteaux and its related houses was the union of the soul with God, through a life of obedience to the rule and customs of the Cistercians, with a particular emphasis on the ascetical practices of silence, fasting, manual labour and poverty. This personal aspect of prayer was given detailed analysis by St Bernard especially in his treatise *On Loving*, and by William of St Thierry* in *The Enigma of Faith*. Its best-known product is the Marian hymn, traditionally sung by the lay brothers after Compline each night, the *Salve Regina*, reflecting perfectly the tender devotion of the Cistercians to Christ and his Mother, in terms of personal love and dependence. The interiorized devotion of the early Cistercians is reflected in their less formal writings by an interest in the interior miracle of conversion, seen in terms of images and signs, rather than in external miracles and wonders. In particular the devotion and sanctity of the lay-brothers was frequently described in terms of personal contact with the angels and saints in a world of intense awareness of significance in every act or event. The use made of the Cistercian monks in episcopal and even papal positions indicates the respect felt for this way of life in the church, although such work has traditionally been regarded by themselves as alien to their vocation.

The later Cistercians were subject to new pressures and assumed different responsibilities. The development of sheep farming led them into a greater involvement with trade and this in turn diminished the early emphasis on both disengagement from society and on corporate poverty. The Trappists* provided a particular emphasis in Cistercian spirituality, one which flourished in Europe and in America, while the Cistercians of the Regular Observance have also developed in other ways, particularly by involvement with teaching and parish work.

Louis Bouyer, *The Cistercian Heritage*, 1958; Louis Leckai, *The White Monks*, 1953; Thomas Merton, *The Silent Life*, 1957; Many translations of major Cistercian works are published by Cistercian Fathers, Kalamazoo, Michigan, USA.

BENEDICTA WARD, SLG

Clairvoyance
see **Extra-Sensory Perception**

Climacus, St John

John Climacus (*c.* 579–649), a monk of Mt Sinai and the author of *The Ladder of Divine Ascent*, has since the seventh century been the most popular spiritual writer of the Orthodox world. He entered the monastic life at the age of sixteen, attaching himself to a spiritual father called Abba Martyrius. When Martyrius died, he withdrew to a hermitage at Tholas, some five miles from the main monastery at the foot of Mt Sinai. After forty years of solitude at Tholas, John was elected abbot of the main monastery. It was during this period that he wrote *The Ladder* at the request of a neighbouring abbot, John of Raithu.

John was writing for monks, but in so far as a monk is a layman who is trying to live the demands of the gospel to the full, his work has always appealed to a wider audience. He treats of separation from the world, the practice of the virtues and the attainment of the likeness of God, organizing his material under the image of Jacob's ladder (cf. Gen. 28.12). Others had used the image of the ladder before him, but John developed it further, giving it thirty rungs, one for each of the hidden years of Christ.

At the heart of monastic spirituality is the remembrance of death, which puts earthly concerns into their correct perspective. The monk constantly mourns for his sins, but his sorrow is interpenetrated with joy, 'like honey in a comb'. In some, compunction is manifested physically by the gift of tears. The physical is not contrasted with the spiritual, but only the corrupt with the incorrupt. The monk's task is the sanctification of soul and body together: 'Everyone should struggle to raise his clay, so to speak, to a place on the throne of God.' What hinder him are the passions, which in *The Ladder*

are simply distorted natural impulses which have to be redirected towards God. The goal of the struggle is dispassion, not a blank impassivity but a total openness to love without any impediment of self-regard.

In the life of prayer the spiritual father is of paramount importance, for the way of self-direction leads to disaster. The spiritual father – the 'shepherd', or 'healer' in John – not only guides his disciples but even bears the burden of their sins. John discourages loquaciousness in prayer and the use of sensory images. He is the first to use the expression the 'Jesus Prayer' (*see* **Jesus, Prayer to**) for a repeated short prayer invoking the name of Jesus, though he does not prescribe any specific formula. By such prayer a man attains to stillness, which is a state of unceasing, wordless prayer. The hesychast, or man of stillness, whose whole life has become prayer, is flooded with the love of God and is even transfigured with uncreated light. This state is not a static one, for since the love of God is inexhaustible progress in perfection is eternal (*see* **Hesychasm**).

John's work is a synthesis of previous monastic teaching, combining the intellectualist tradition of Evagrius Ponticus with the unity of body and soul of the Macarian homilies (*see* **Macarius the Egyptian**), and also drawing on Diadochus of Photice, Mark the Ascetic and John Cassian*. But the whole is infused too with the fruits of his own experience, his shrewd insight into the human soul, and his monastic sense of humour.

The Greek text of *The Ladder of Divine Ascent* and of a second, shorter work of Climacus, *To the Shepherd*, is in *PG*, 88, cols 632–1208; ET by Lazarus Moore 1959, revd, with the addition of *To the Shepherd*, 1978; ET by C. Lubheid and N. Russell of *The Ladder* only (Classics of Western Spirituality), 1982, with introduction by Kallistos Ware; *see also* G. Couilleau, *DS*, VIII, cols 369–89.

NORMAN RUSSELL

Cloud of Unknowing, The

The Cloud of Unknowing is regarded as one of the outstanding spiritual treatises of fourteenth-century England. The debate about its authorship remains unresolved. There is some consensus that it was written by a priest, perhaps a Carthusian, at the request of someone who was seeking direction in the spiritual life. This may account in part for its individualistic tone, although the author may also have had a broader audience in mind. Also written by this same author are three other original works: *Letter of Privy Counselling*, *Letter on Prayer*, *On Discerning of Spirits*, and three translations: *Denys Hid Divinity*, *The Pursuit of Wisdom*, and *Letter on Discretion*.

The Cloud of Unknowing is part of a larger spiritual movement in fourteenth-century England which includes writings such as the *Ancrene Riwle**, the *Fire of Love* by Richard Rolle* (d. 1349), the *Scale of Perfection* by Walter Hilton (d. 1396), the *Shewings* of Julian of Norwich* (d. 1442), and the controversial biography of Margery Kempe (d. 1440). This English spirituality is characterized by its freshness, concreteness and joy – notable because in other spheres, the period was marked by social, political and ecclesiastical turmoil. The Hundred Years' War was raging, the Great Schism had taken place, the Peasants' Revolt had begun in 1381 and society was suffering the effects of the Black Death.

The Cloud of Unknowing is an example of apophatic or negative theology. The author relies heavily on the thought of Denys the Areopagite* – even the title is taken from Denys's *Mystical Theology*. The language of *The Cloud* is vigorous and eloquent, revealing a forceful and original thinker. The work is written in the north-east Midland dialect used by Chaucer and is marked by enthusiasm, humour, vivid expression and literary beauty. Its closely reasoned arguments, its reliance on faculty psychology, and its development of Augustinian theology of the reciprocal action of grace and the human will suggest the influence of scholastic thought in the vein of Thomas Aquinas*. *The Cloud* also relies on the inheritance of the Victorines* and is suffused with biblical imagery.

The Cloud contains a detailed and practical explanation of the author's views on the method of contemplative prayer. He explicitly states that he is writing for those who have been called to the contemplative life, although he does not disdain the active life and sees in its inward dimension a participation in the work of contemplation (Prologue). The way to perfect contemplation is the way of negation. The first task is to separate oneself from the world and crea-tures by leaving them behind in the cloud of forgetting. This is accomplished by meditation on one's sins and on the passion of Christ. Everything of the senses is to be left behind and even the self with its spiritual faculties must be abandoned. Contemplation is concerned with God alone.

Beyond the cloud of forgetting is the cloud of unknowing which stands between the contemplative and God. This cloud can be pierced only by 'naked intent' or a 'blind stirring' of the will. This naked impulse shoots up like 'a sharp dart of longing love' to penetrate the cloud so that the soul might experience direct union with God. The soul is moved by intense desires and longings which signal the call to contemplation. Although the intellect plays an important role in the way of union (especially in the spiritual sight which one gains through faith), nevertheless it is the affective power which operates in the unitive stage. Only the blind stirring of love can beat on the dark cloud of unknowing on the way to union with God.

In the earlier stages one must exert a great deal of effort in the struggle to banish all thought and distraction and to restrain them below in the cloud of forgetting. This toil, which is extremely arduous, will prepare the way for grace, for God's action on the soul, which is the awakening of love (ch. 26). The author suggests that the seeker of union gather all desire into a simple word such as 'God' or 'love' in order both to keep distractions in the cloud of forgetting and to beat upon the cloud of darkness above (ch. 7). But the contemplative work of love is ultimately the gift of divine activity and even the desire for union is possible only if the gift is already present in some way (ch. 34). The *Cloud* also stresses the importance of the discernment of spirits. Without honesty and guidance, the beginner especially is easily led astray and deceived by illusion and pseudo-experience (ch. 45). The sacrament of penance is seen as a source of purification for the contemplative and helps to prepare him/her to begin the work which will culminate in ecstatic union with God (ch. 15, 28, 35, 75). Study, reflection and prayer must be cultivated by 'beginners and those a little advanced'. Reading, thinking and praying are interdependent activities that must be seen as a unity. One cannot progress to higher stages without attention to the word of God.

The final goal can be fully experienced only through grace and the miracle of love. 'No one can fully comprehend the uncreated God with his knowledge: but each one, in a different way, can grasp him fully through love' (ch. 4, 70). The transcendence of God makes it difficult to know him by way of reason. The superior way to God is the way of mystical or hidden knowledge which is intuitive and ineffable. God lies beyond the cloud of darkness and unknowing and the will alone can attempt to pierce it with its naked impulse of love.

In spite of its emphasis on seeking God by way of unknowing, the *Cloud* has a distinctly christological focus. It begins with an invocation to the Trinity, suggesting that the goal of contemplation is union with God, one and three, in whose image man/woman is created. The author directs his readers to turn to Jesus and his love to find help in the contemplative work (ch. 4, 7, 22). The contemplative shares in Christ's redemptive suffering: 'Whoever wishes to follow Christ perfectly must also be willing to expend himself in the spiritual work of love for the salvation of all his brothers and sisters in the human family' (ch. 25). It is the Lord Jesus Christ himself who calls us in the Gospel to the perfection of every human virtue. We are to be perfect by grace as he is by nature (ch. 15). But the ultimate contemplative experience for the author of the *Cloud* is one of humility and nothingness, beyond interior and exterior senses, beyond intellectual and even spiritual faculties. 'And so keep on working in this nothingness which is nowhere and do not try to involve your body senses or their proper objects . . . "The most divine knowledge of God is that which is known by not-knowing"' (ch. 70).

See also **English Mystics, The.**

P. Hodgson, critical edition of all works by author of *The Cloud*, 2 vols, 1958: J. Walsh (ed), *The Cloud of Unknowing* (Classics of Western Spirituality), 1981; W. Johnston, *The Mysticism of the Cloud of Unknowing*, 1967; D. Knowles, *The English Mystical Tradition*, 1961; E. Colledge, *The Mediaeval Mystics of England*, 1961; C. Pepler, *The English Religious Heritage*, 1958; J. Walsh (ed), *Pre-Reformation English Spirituality*, 1965.

ELIZABETH DREYER

Columbanus, St

Columbanus, or Columba the Younger (perhaps born *c*. 540, perhaps *c*. 560, d. 615, and not to be confused with Columba of Iona), entered St Comgall's monastery of Bangor (Ulster), later becoming head of the monastic school. After some years he desired the greater ascetic renunciation of *peregrinatio*, 'pilgrimage': i.e. leaving his native Ireland to spend the rest of his life as an exile in a foreign land. He therefore crossed to Gaul in 591 and settled in the Vosges wilderness at Annegray, founding additional monasteries at Luxeuil and Fontaine to house the influx of disciples. His retention of Irish customs antagonized the Gallic bishops. Later he also offended the king, hitherto his protector, by refusing to condone royal concubinage; and in 610 King Theuderic ordered his deportation. However, Columbanus evaded this and eventually made his way to Italy. There he founded another monastery at Bobbio, where he died.

Columbanus' life expresses his ascetic teaching; for he saw this life as but a journey leading to the life to come. As travellers (or 'peregrini'), we should sit light to this world, which perishes, and hasten on to our true fatherland in heaven. His Christianity is biblically grounded. He sees the Bible as providing norms to live by, not inspired mysteries to be interpreted spiritually. 'This is the truth of the Gospel, that the true disciples of Christ crucified should follow Him with the cross.' They should walk as Christ walked, in poverty and humility, stripping themselves of all earthly desires and possessions. Then, once earthly things are forgotten, perpetual love of God will take their place.

Despite the harshness of Columbanus' ascetic demands his teaching in many ways reflects an optimistic view of man. There is no yawning gulf fixed between God and man. Rather, Columbanus emphasizes that God created man in his own image and likeness; and, by rightly using the virtues implanted in his soul, man can attain likeness to God. The key is love: 'For [man's] love of God is the restoration of His image. But he loves God who keeps his commandments' – especially that of loving others. Columbanus thus insists on the literal following of Christ and his commandments, which may require harsh toil; but 'if we suffer together with Him, together we shall reign'. 'For who is really happier than he whose death is life, whose life is Christ ... to whom heaven is made low and paradise opens ... who obtains ... joy for sorrow ... and God for mortality?' As this illustrates, Columbanus regards asceticism only as a means to an end. The focus is on God, and often his sermons slip into moving prayer.

Columbanus made a lasting impact on Gaul, especially in those areas which, after the Germanic invasions, were only nominally Christian. The disciples he attracted set afoot a monastic revival in northern Gaul, spreading the Rule of Benedict combined with that of Columbanus. Lay Christianity was also stimulated by his forthright Christian witness, and by his introduction of private penance (public penance having fallen out of use). By making laymen think about their sins, private confession and penance helped to form their Christian awareness.

Columbanus' spirituality is best sampled at first hand: his writings are edited with English tr, good introduction and bibliography by G. S. M. Walker, *Sancti Columbani Opera*, ²1970, though some scholars dispute Columbanus' authorship of some of the works included; *Columbanus and Merovingian Monasticism*, ed H. B. Clarke and M. Brennan, 1981; J. F. Kenney, *The Sources for the Early History of Ireland*, vol I, 1929; F. Macmanus, *Saint Columban*, 1962.

C. E. STANCLIFFE

Combat, Spiritual see War, Holy

Communes

There is a rich communal tradition within the Christian church. Acts 2.42–46 and 4.32–35 offer a picture of the first Christians sharing their goods (or the proceeds of sale) for the benefit of one another and of the poor as part of their life of prayer and praise and brotherhood.

From early on in the history of the church the monastic orders' primary structure was the communal group. Others too, following the Reformation, embraced the communal model as a way of living, which was thus brought within the Protestant tradition.

An early mid-European group were the pacifist Hutterians, an Anabaptist sect taking their name from Joseph Huter.

Largely separatist for four centuries, the Hutterians have endured persecutions in various countries in which their communities have settled. Their early mentor Peter Riedemann set forth in 1540 in his *Rechenschaft* the communitarian practices which the Hutterians have ever since regarded as based on the life of early Christians. The Hutterians still prosper in North America. In England, the turmoil of the seventeenth century threw up both the withdrawing Little Gidding community and the politically committed Diggers. Little Gidding was born out of the urge of Nicholas Ferrar*, then in public life, and others, to develop a community with a rhythm of work and worship. The Diggers (though they were frustrated by the antipathy of the local inhabitants), tried on Cobham Common in Surrey to build a community whose co-operative principles would serve as a model for England under the Commonwealth.

For the Diggers communitarianism was the very basis of their Christian life. For the Shakers, on the other hand, who also lived communally, a millenarian emphasis was more important. The Shakers were founded in the mid-eighteenth century by Mother Ann Lee, whom her followers regarded as The Woman of the Apocalypse (Rev. 12). Their early ecstatic worship (which gave them their name) led to prosecutions, and was later ritualized in dances. The Shakers bonded together in communities for mutual support against a hostile world.

Sociological theory emphasizes the role of community living as a means of confirming and supporting the minority views of the members of all such groups. This analysis is applied to contemporary Christian communes which are often set over against a secular world. However, the recent growth of communes owes a good deal to 'secular' influences as well as to the Christian tradition and in particular to the utopian socialism of thinkers like Robert Owen. Although some communities have been established after the Second World War (Taizé* in France, Focolare* in Italy, La Poudriere in Brussels, Laurentiuskonvent in Germany) and in the 1930s Dietrich Bonhoeffer* had led the German Confessing Church seminary at Finkenwalde on communal lines, it was only in the wake of the 'youth revolutions' of 1967–1968 that communes sprang up in any number. The common factor of recent Christian communes has been by and large the sharing of life's material necessities, simplicity, a devotional discipline and a commitment to others. Unhierarchical structures, impermanence and a holding back from complete community of goods, which had all been features of 'secular' communal groups of the late 1960s and subsequently, percolated through to the new Christian groups also.

Perhaps the first such groups were those founded in 1969 in Blackheath, South London and Newhaven in Edinburgh, which grew out of the membership of the Student Christian Movement. They were committed to working for political change. At about the same time the Ashram Community was born. Originally inspired by the thinking of Methodist theologian John Vincent the Ashram Community established houses in deprived areas, where residents (often professionally qualified) also worked and were involved in neighbourhood activities such as youth and play-groups, advice centres, local politics and housing problems. In France and Italy, and even more in Latin America, hundreds of so-called 'base communities', also operating on a neighbourhood basis, have grown up and exist in uneasy tension with the hierarchy of the Roman Catholic Church to which their members usually belong. This pattern of neighbourhood involvement was a common one for Christian communities working in the 1970s for social justice, but Christian communes have also been active in the fields of personal evangelism, the care of the mentally and physically handicapped, farming and reconciliation.

While most contemporary groups have no more than a dozen members, the membership of two British groups founded in the 1970s has grown to three figures. The associated groups of the Post Green Community in Dorset and the Community of Celebration on the Isle of Cumbrae have been in the forefront of the thinking of the Charismatic Movement* and greatly influenced by the life of the Church of the Redeemer, Houston, Texas. The other large community in the UK is based on the Baptist Chapel at Bugbrooke in Northamptonshire, where over 500 members share a community of goods under a strict community discipline, hierarchically organized.

Communities based on particular local churches were increasingly in evidence in the later 1970s but often lasting for a few years only and with a transient membership. Root Groups, sponsored by USPG, the Anglican missionary society, offer an opportunity to people between 18 and 30 to live communally in a parish for a year. A significant factor in the growth of communities in local churches was the increased emphasis on the corporate life of the church. In this way, communal life has been absorbed into the mainstream of the churches and is no longer the fringe activity it was even a few years ago.

Andrew Lockley, *Christian Communes*, 1976.

ANDREW LOCKLEY

Communities *see* **Communes**

Confession *see* **Prayer (2) Confession**

Confession, Practice of
see **Penitence**

Conformity to the Will of God
Since the apostolic age, women and men have endeavoured to live in fidelity to God as revealed in Christ Jesus. This is the meaning inherent in the expression 'conformity to the will of God'. This endeavour has been mediated by the specificity of the world-view operative in the Christian community in which these persons lived.

Those communities acting out of a neoplatonic mind-set interpreted Christ's message to be perfect as his heavenly father is perfect (Matt. 5.48), as demanding less regard for the material and more attention to the immaterial aspects of life. Thus, continence was to be preferred to genital expressions of sexuality and voluntary poverty to riches. Such communities produced persons remarkable for their fidelity to God in Christ Jesus. Among them may be numbered Clement of Alexandria, Augustine of Hippo* and Denys the Areopagite*.

Those communities acting out of a more Aristotelian mind-set interpreted the injunction to perfection as necessitating an integration of body and spirit. Although Thomas Aquinas* was the major Christian interpreter of such a view, the mediaeval context in which he lived precluded a decisive departure from the spiritual practices of earlier Christianity. This fact must not cause one to see as unimportant the major change in motivation and attitude which this shift in world-view initiated.

The Protestant Reformation retrieved the incarnational insight that immersion in the realities of this world was desired by God. Thus, a monastically oriented spirituality was complemented by a sense of vocation to work in the everyday world to bring this world itself to a new perfection. Calvin* and his descendents are exemplars of this spirituality.

The modern philosophic turn to the subject has fostered a spirituality of conformity to God's will that views faithfulness to the demands of one's human impulses towards knowing and loving, towards self-transcendence, as conformity to God's will. In such a context, the traditional dichotomy between the typically Roman Catholic emphasis on a spirituality modelled on the monastic ideal, and the Protestant emphasis on a spirituality based on worldly involvement has been relativized. Perfection is viewed as embracing that life-style which most enables the Christian to respond with increasing love to the knowledge of God which is born of faith. Dorothy Day, Dietrich Bonhoeffer*, Maurice Blondel and the monks of Taizé* have emerged from such a spirituality.

Although one's world-view and religious tradition heavily influence the expression of one's fidelity to God in Christ, there are, nevertheless, several elements that are common to all those seeking to conform their lives to God's will. Thus, the Christian life may not be reduced to one's historical situation.

First among these elements is prayer, which has consistently been viewed as the mode of communication between God and the person. Prayer, nourished by the scripture, reveals to one the overwhelming love God has for his people and elicits response. This response, although always mediated by one's particular historical perspective, enables one to become free of the various biases and limitations generated by that perspective. In this freedom, one determines what it means to love God with one's whole heart.

A second element common to all endeav-

ours to live in accordance with God's will is love of neighbour. This is not viewed as subsequent to the love of God but indigenous to that love. Thus, mediaeval spirituality emphasized hospitality, Reformation spirituality emphasized fair business practices, and modern spirituality is at least beginning to emphasize a deprivatized notion of loving one's neighbour which constrains the Christian to take cognizance of the systemic oppression of whole groups of people. Political and liberation theologies* are born of this insight, an insight which is shared by Protestants, Catholics and the Orthodox.

Finally, discipline directed towards developing the interiority demanded by the self-transcendence necessitated in living in conformity to the will of God is characteristic of all attempts to live in conformity to God's will.

NANCY C. RING

Consolations, Desolations

The OT attests that Israel as a nation and in selected individuals experienced both the consoling presence and the desolate, seeming absence of Yahweh. The Messiah was to be Israel's consolation (Luke 2.25); Israel's rejection of him led to her desolation (Luke 21.20). Jesus' Spirit is now the permanent source of his consoling nearness. Those in Christ can and should console each other (Rom. 1.12).

Virtually all spiritual writers have discussed God's warm, peaceful, joyful, encouraging visitations which effect tears of love, repentant sorrow, a desire for heavenly things, prompter service of God, and affectively intensify faith, hope and love. The seeming absence of Jesus' Spirit produces feelings and thoughts of gloom, discouragement, sadness, confusion, disquiet, torpor, a movement towards earthly things and a tendency towards loss of faith, hope and love.

God, the good angels, the evil angels and the self ascetically or mystically effect consolations and desolations to lead a person to or away from salvation. Rules for the discernment of spirits disclose the sources of these movements and help a person to find God's will (Ignatius of Loyola).

Essential consolation ('substantial devotion'), or the courage to seek and do God's will despite affective fluctuations, must be distinguished from transitory consolations facilitating God's service, but which are neither free nor necessary. Desolation may come from tepidity, God's desire to teach humility, to strengthen essential consolation, or from God's mystical purgation (dark nights of the senses and spirit). The dangers of consolation are vanity and pride; of desolation, discouragement.

H. Egan, *The Spiritual Exercises and the Ignatian Mystical Horizon*, 1976; H. Martin, 'Désolation', *DS*, III, cols 631–45; L. Poullier, 'Consolation Spirituelle', *DS*, II, cols 1617–34; J. Toner, *A Commentary on St Ignatius' Rules for the Discernment of Spirits*, 1982.

HARVEY D. EGAN, SJ

Contemplation

In its Christian use this word normally denotes the kind of prayer in which the mind does not function discursively but is arrested in a simple attention and one-pointedness. In meditation* the mind reflects on some Christian truth or passage of scripture or personal experience, using words and ideas in more or less logical progression, with the aim of reaching fuller understanding and personal appropriation of the truth considered, or working through some experience in the light of Christian faith in order to come to some decision, awareness of God's will or re-affirmation of faith. In contemplation the mind functions in the opposite way. Words and thoughts in logical progression, reflections with the aim of coming to fresh insight or decision, are exactly what the mind does not want, and indeed it finds them a hindrance. What is desired is the opportunity simply to express to God one's loving, hoping, trusting, thanking, in as few words as possible. These few words tend to be repeated many times. The repetition has the effect of steadily reducing their meaning and serviceableness. A time comes when a deeper desire is revealed to the person praying. What began as fragmentarily verbalized loving or thanking becomes more than anything else an offering, though without this self-giving being mentally considered or understood.

In the literature of Christian prayer, the movement from meditation to contemplation has been treated as a progression to be expected under certain qualifying conditions. Contemplation has been seen as a state reached by degrees and only possible to those whose practice of meditation is extensive but mysteriously beginning to dry up. This gradualistic concept has also played an important role in the understanding of contemplation itself which, in the classical texts, is seen as characterized by stages, variously named, culminating in an ecstatic union with God and one for which even such a term as 'spiritual marriage' has been employed. Extensive commentary and exposition of the work of such writers as John Cassian*, the author of *The Cloud of Unknowing**, St John of the Cross*, St Teresa of Avila* and St Francis de Sales*, form the continuing study of contemplation as part of mystical theology. It is often technical and obscure. The twentieth century has seen the development of another kind of literature of the subject, inspired by the modest aim of helping ordinary people to learn a contemplative style of praying. At certain points the two naturally overlap. *The Cloud of Unknowing* and the work of J.-P. de Caussade*, for example, seem to be accessible and congenial to many people. The last twenty years have seen such an awakening and revival of interest in meditation and contemplation that it can be considered a significant movement of the Spirit in our time. This revival is not confined to the Christian church and did not in fact begin within the church but in tentative, comparatively uninformed, exploration of Eastern forms of contemplative prayer. The interest continues and is represented by such enthusiasm as is associated with the Transcendental Meditation* (strictly a style of contemplation) of the Maharishi Mahesh Yogi, while specifically Christian forms are illustrated by the movement known as the Julian Meetings (named after the mystic Julian of Norwich*), an unstructured network of ecumenical groups of people who meet to learn together Christ-centred contemplative prayer.

A more flexible and less doctrinaire understanding of contemplation than that which characterizes traditional ascetic theology is probably more congenial to our time. It is possible that some people are naturally disposed to contemplate at the beginning of their Christian life. The teaching of prayer at local church level could well make room for this and be released from the obsession with petition and intercession, unimaginatively interpreted, that has unfortunately dominated it for too long. It is increasingly being suggested now that intercession itself, when better understood, is constructively seen as a form of contemplation.

Christian contemplation needs Christian meditation, in the sense of reflection on the great Christian image which is Christ himself, his truth, and all that has been well thought and said and done in his name under the guidance of the Spirit. Without this, contemplation could eventually become a not particularly Christian exercise, not necessarily objectionable for that reason but simply a very different matter and perhaps nearer to Transcendental Meditation which seems to be associated with no system of belief, seldom leads to increased awareness of spiritual reality, and has a rather loose relation to the intellectual and emotional life of the practitioner.

Contemplation and meditation, main sources of nourishment in the life of faith as they are, need each other. Contemplation alone is volatile, can lose touch with earth and the word made flesh, needs some ballast of analysis and self-reference. Meditation alone can be ponderous, may succumb to self-preoccupation, needs the leaven, the freedom, of wordless loving. Even so there is, as in all spirituality, an element of mystery. Not all who love Christ, not all who want God, hear the call to prayer. And the relation between prayer and the spiritual and emotional maturing of the one who prays is not easily discerned and established. St John of the Cross, perhaps because of this, said 'at eventide they will examine thee in love'.

John Chapman, 'Contemplative Prayer', *Spiritual Letters*, 1944.

J. NEVILLE WARD

Conversion

The Christian understanding of conversion as a moral–religious reality finds its roots in the OT: the history of Israel is the story of a people repeatedly being called to conversion, called to turn back to its covenant with the God it has adulterously abandoned. David is the model of how this call to conversion works in the individual sinner's life

(II Sam. 11–12). The story of Job, who comes to recognize the mystery of God, underscores the fundamental truth that even the just person is called to conversion.

John the Baptist continues the prophets' call to conversion in the New Testament. And after John's arrest, Jesus takes up the call and makes it central to his preaching: 'The time has come . . . the reign of God is at hand. Be converted and believe in the good news' (Mark 1.15).

The key biblical words for conversion are *naham* and *shub* in Hebrew, and *metanoia* and *epistrophe* in Greek. If conversion means a radical turning, or a redirection of one's life, the first word in each pair, emphasizing repentance, specifies a turning *from* (sin), while the second indicates a turning *towards* (God). Emphasis on conversion as repentance for sin has probably kept Christians from thinking of Jesus as having experienced conversion, even though he did present himself to John for baptism. It has been the extraordinary experience of Paul on the road to Damascus, rather, that has dominated Christian thinking about conversion in the NT (especially accounts in Acts). Many contemporary theologians, however, realizing the full *religious* depth of conversion beyond the moral, recognize in Jesus' response to crises in his life and ministry a transformation of faith, a rethinking of his relationship to the Father that defines the very essence of religious conversion.

Though rooted in the prophetic call of the OT, and absolutely fundamental to NT teaching, conversion was by no means an exclusively Judaeo-Christian reality. Indeed, the early Christian meaning of this fundamental reality was elaborated in a cultural context of mutual influence where it shared the term *epistrophe* with Middle- and Neoplatonism as well as with Stoicism and Gnosticism. Judaism and Christianity might have been alone among ancient Mediterranean religions in demanding conversion, as A. D. Nock claims, but philosophic conversion as the object of education, a moral–intellectual 'turning of the soul', was already established with Plato (*Republic* VII, 518D).

The philosophic search for truth becomes the Christian yearning for God in St Augustine *, whose *Confessions* recount his intellectual, moral and religious conversions.

Indeed, the *Confessions*' eloquent articulation of the profound *experience* of interior transformation has given St Augustine a pre-eminent place in Christian spirituality. Though mediaeval spiritual writers like Meister Eckhart * continued to focus on the experience of Christian life, the dominant scholastic mode of theology effectively lost the experience of conversion in the metaphysical analysis of faith, grace and justification. Luther best marks the return of conversion as experienced to a central place in reflection on the Christian life. However else they differ, Luther * and St Ignatius of Loyola * share the reality of conversion in their personal experience as well as in their analyses of the spiritual life. Despite the enormous influence of Ignatius' *Spiritual Exercises* * on individual lives, however, it would be some four centuries before formal Roman Catholic theology was ready to recognize in the experience of conversion the significance which had become a primary characteristic of Protestant theology.

Philipp Spener and Pietism in Germany, John Wesley * and the founding of Methodism in England, and Jonathan Edwards * and the Great Awakening in New England are only three of the many names and events that would have to be mentioned in any complete survey of conversion in Protestantism. More than anything else, perhaps, these were responsible for the popular religious revivalism that carried into and through the nineteenth century. Even the high Anglican divines like Pusey *, who held to baptismal regeneration, did not dispute in most cases the need of 'a solid and entire conversion'.

It was in the revivalist context at the beginning of this century, then, when psychology was still in its infancy as a science, that William James' classic *Varieties of Religious Experience* (1902) established a presumption in favour of adolescence as the common time for conversion. Despite C. G. Jung's later emphasis on the religious quality of the mid-life crisis, most psychological studies of conversion have followed James in seeing it as an essentially adolescent phenomenon.

Only in recent decades has developmental psychology – notably the psychosocial life-cycle approach of Erik Erikson – reoriented the psychological study of conversion by relativizing the identity crisis associated with adolescent conversion as just one of several critical turning points in the larger personal context of the life-cycle. From this perspective, conversions of adolescence and youth (even those expressed in religious language) appear to have a distinctly moral emphasis. At the same time, the older adult's crisis of integrity v. despair not only echoes Jung, but correlates closely with contemporary theological analyses of specifically religious conversion as the total reorientation of one's life through unconditional surrender to God in Jesus Christ – a surrender of one's claim to absolute autonomy. If the gospel makes it clear that this interior transformation must be realized in justice and love of neighbour, contemporary theologians have clarified that these must take social structural as well as interpersonal shape.

Rooted in biblical and historical sources, nourished by theological sensitivity to personal and social experience and supported by psychological approaches attuned to personal development and the possibilities of self-transcendence, the contemporary discipline of Christian spirituality is in the process of effecting a critical retrieval of conversion as the foundation of authentic Christian life.

P. Aubin, *Le problème de la 'conversion'*, 1963; E. H. Erikson, *Childhood and Society*, [2]1963; C. G. Jung, *Modern Man in Search of a Soul*, 1933; J.-M. LeBlond, *Les conversions de saint Augustin*, 1950; A. D. Nock, *Conversion*, 1933.

WALTER E. CONN

Coptic Spirituality

The spirituality of the Coptic Church, whose tradition claims St Mark as its founder, has been powerfully shaped by the heritage of Alexandrian Christianity (and by the influence of St Cyril in particular), and by the traditions of desert monasticism. The traditional founders of both the eremitic and coenobitic forms of the religious life, St Antony * and St Pachomius, were both natives of Egypt, and this has given both the hermit and the monastic community a special role in the Coptic Church, whose bishops all come from the monastic priesthood.

The monastic offices and their associated

hymns, and the celebration of the eucharist forms the centre of the traditional worship of the church, with the liturgy being celebrated rather more frequently (and with more frequent reception of communion by greater numbers of the faithful) than in the Byzantine tradition. There is likewise a fuller congregational participation in the liturgy, and the chants and texts of the hymns, the music of which it is often claimed is in direct continuity with the music of ancient Egyptian temple music, are widely known and appreciated.

From the time of Moslem domination, and particularly in times of persecution, the desert monasteries have been both a place of refuge and a source and focus of Coptic devotion. That role continues today. In recent years there has been a notable revival in the Coptic Church, a major feature of which has been the renewal and growth of the monastic life, with associated retreats and pilgrimages. Inspired by the writings of the Desert Fathers and other early teachers of Christian prayer, there has been renewed writing and instruction about prayer by spiritual leaders, such as the late Pope Kyrillos VI, Pope Shenouda III and Father Matta el-Meskeen. This teaching is strongly scriptural and has been influenced to some degree by the work of Protestant commentators of an earlier generation, such as Matthew Henry. The long history of martyrdom in the Coptic Church has given the martyrs and their relics a prominent place in worship and devotion and contributes to the monasteries being places of pilgrimage.

The biblical tradition of the Flight into Egypt has been elaborated and accorded an important place in popular piety, with many places of pilgrimage associated with the Virgin Mary and the Holy Family, both in the Delta and in the Nile Valley. The powerful defence of the title *Theotokos* ('God-bearer') by Cyril of Alexandria has led to a strong tradition of Marian devotion in the Coptic Church. The many Marian hymns draw on a rich typology from the OT in celebration of the mystery of the incarnation and Mary's place within it. The significant appearances of the Virgin at Zeitoun between 1968 and 1970 are reminders not only of the place of Mary in Coptic devotion, but also of the importance of visions and a mysticism of light within popular Coptic piety. There is likewise a strong belief in miracles and in a ministry of healing and exorcism.

See also **Desert, Desert Fathers**.

A. S. Atiya, *A History of Eastern Christianity*, 1968; O. Meinardus, *Christian Life and Thought in Egypt*, 1970; *Monks and Monasteries of the Egyptian Desert*, 1961; I. H. el Musri, *The Story of the Copts*, 1978; De Lacy O'Leary, *The Saints of Egypt*, 1937.

GEOFFREY ROWELL

Cosin, John *see* **Caroline Divines, The**

Covenant

1. *Relationship of mutual commitment, created by exchange of promises.* In the OT, covenant (*berith*) imagery derived from Middle Eastern custom and the ritual of treaty-making. The form of the treaty was: (i) statement of the identity of the initiator; (ii) recital of events leading to the treaty; (iii) statement of relative obligations of the parties; (iv) invocation of divine sanctions. The terms varied with the relations between the parties – between equals ('parity-treaty'), imposed by a greater upon a less ('vassal-treaty'), initiated by a lesser to secure protection of a greater ('submission-treaty'). Covenant imagery was also used of friendship (I Sam. 18.3), marriage (Prov. 2.17).

2. *God's gracious commitment to his elect people and the whole creation.* The concept of God's commitment to his people is the key to OT religion and theology. God identifies himself as God of the Exodus (Ex. 20.2); Israel therefore owes him a life of holiness in worship and social ethics (Ex. 20.3ff.). The covenant-making consists of: (i) declaration of God's identity and will; (ii) agreement of people to obey; (iii) seal of covenant sacrifice (Ex. 20–24). The human side of the covenant is marred by failure (I Kings 19.10, Jer. 11.3, Ezek. 15.69 and *passim*) but can be renewed by reiterated allegiance (II Kings 11 and 23). The divine side is attested by religious and social institutions (Sabbath, sacrifice, temple, priesthood, royal house); there is prospect of a new covenant in which each soul knows God personally (Jer. 31). This complex of ideas is extended to that of a covenant between the Creator and the life of the entire creation ('Noachian' covenant, Gen. 9).

In the NT, Jesus mediates the promised

New Covenant by his death (I Cor. 11.25, Mark 14.24, Matt. 26.28), rising and ascending (Heb. 12.24) and his gift of the Spirit (Acts 2.33). Through him, there is now access to (covenant-relationship with) God for all peoples (Rom. 5.2, Eph. 2.18). The concept is developed to describe successive stages, 'dispensations', in God's progressive gracious plan for the whole universe (Rom. 9.4, Gal. 4.24, Irenaeus, Cocceius and 'Federal Theologians', and in Christian evaluation of non-Christian prayer and worship); also used by Duns Scotus of God's faithfulness in honouring the sacraments whenever they are celebrated ('occasionalism').

3. *Mutual commitment of members of a gathered church* (*in Protestantism*). The English Separatist Robert Browne, in his *Booke which sheweth the Life and Manners of all true Christians* (1582), describes how the local church must be 'planted and gathered' by means of a covenant with two sides: there is God's 'promise to be our God and Saviour, if we forsake not his government by disobedience. Also his promise to be the God of our seed, while we are his people. Also, the gift of his Spirit to his children as an inward calling and furtherance of godliness.' The human side is that 'we must offer and give up ourselves to be of the church and people of God. We must likewise offer and give up our children' and dependent minors; 'we must make profession that we are his people by submitting ourselves to his laws and government'. He also, in his *True and Short Declaration* (1583?), describes the making of such a local church covenant: 'There was a day appointed, and an order taken, for redress of the former abuses, and for cleaving to the Lord in greater obedience. So a covenant was made, and their mutual consent was given to hold together. There were certain chief points proved unto them by the Scriptures, all which being particularly rehearsed unto them with exhortation, they agreed upon them, and pronounced their agreement to each thing particularly, saying, "To this we give our consent . . ." ' Such a corporate covenant with God, implying a new relationship among those making it on the human side, has been adopted in modern ecumenism, as a commitment to closer fellowship and recognition without immediate organic union, between churches of one tra-

dition (e.g. Indian Baptists) or of differing traditions.

4. *Commitment of the individual soul to God*. The covenant pattern of ideas is found in initiation, Jewish and Christian; instruction–decision–admission is the plan of Jewish proselyte baptism, adopted in the Christian baptismal liturgy. Renewal, reaffirmation, or appropriation of baptismal vows is typical of monastic, reforming or renewal movements (monastic profession, Lollards, Luther, Puritans, Loyola, Wesleys). Confirmation and eucharist have been interpreted as variously renewing the baptismal covenant, especially in Anglican spirituality (Beveridge, Secker). Personal covenants to seal conversion-experience figure largely in Puritan biography and counsel. J. and R. Alleine and P. Doddridge offered model covenant prayers. Wesley adopted the Alleines' prayer ('. . . thou art now become my Covenant-Friend, and I, through thy infinite grace, am become thy Covenant-Servant'; cf. Ignatius of Loyola's *Suscipe, domine*), and used it as a corporate prayer, leading into holy communion, as the core of what became British Methodism's Annual Renewal of the Covenant. Similarly, renewal of baptismal vows, climax of parish missions, was introduced into the Roman Easter Vigil rite in 1955.

J. Alleine, *An Alarm in Unconverted Sinners* and R. Alleine, *Vindiciae Pietatis*, both reprinted in Wesley's Christian Library, vols 14, 30; K. Baltzer, The *Covenant Formulary*, ET 1970; P. Doddridge, *The Rise and Progress of Religion in the Soul*, [2]1854; F. Gavin, *The Jewish Antecedents of the Christian Sacraments*, 1928; G. E. Mendenhall, *Law and Covenant in the Ancient Near East and in Israel*, 1955; A. Peel and L. H. Carlson (ads), *Writings of Robert Harrison and Robert Browne*, 1953; T. Secker, *Lectures on the Catechism of the Church of England*, [2]1840; D. H. Tripp, *The Renewal of the Covenant in the Methodist Tradition*, 1969.

DAVID TRIPP

Creation-Centred Spirituality

The Creation-Centred spiritual tradition begins its spirituality with the theme of original blessing rather than original sin. Unlike the Fall/Redemption tradition, it emphasizes cosmic grace and humanity's divinization more than psychological introspection. It takes delight in the holiness of all being and avoids dualistic theisms by its images of panentheism – God in us *and* us in God. Its basic psychology, one of trust of body, imagination and cosmos, is based on a microcosmic/macrocosmic synchronicity with the universe rather than on ego psychology. Passions are a blessing, and humility (from *humus*, earth) means to befriend our earthiness. Its explicit goal is not contemplation as such, but compassion as in Luke 6.36: 'Be you compassionate as your creator in heaven is compassionate.' It understands compassion not as an ethical duty or as a feeling-pity-for, but as justice – 'compassion means justice' said Meister Eckhart – and as celebration. The principle meditation discipline in this tradition is 'extrovert meditation', i.e. centring by way of giving birth. Thus art is the most essential form of meditation – it is in the creative act that humanity's image of God – the primary Artist and Creator – is best remembered. Art is 'the way of the prophets' that empowers the *anawim* to self-expression and liberation. Dualism is the sin behind all sin and its expression in perverse creativity – i.e. sadism or masochism – is considered to be the most demonic use of the image of God: The use of human creativity to curse instead of to bless with.

Instead of the three-fold path which Plotinus * named as purgation, illumination and union, the Creation-Centred spiritual tradition names the spiritual journey in four paths: Via Positiva: Creation; Via Negativa: Letting Go and Letting Be; Via Creativa: Birthing; Via Transformativa: New Creation of Compassion and Social Justice. This fourfold path is not one of climbing up a ladder, but is a holistic spiral emanating from the core of creation – the *dabar* or creative energy of God.

While the disciplines of the art of savouring, of letting go, of creating and of carrying on social justice are of paramount importance in this tradition, asceticism is not. 'Asceticism is of no great importance' writes Meister Eckhart. Why not? 'Because it creates more instead of less self-consciousness and ego.' Humour, paradox and dialectic are important elements of this tradition. Instead of identifying the via negativa with asceticism, the Creation-Centred spiritual tradition understands it as a radical letting go of all images, all names, all role-playing to 'sink' into darkness where the 'God without a name' dwells and where our depths lie, for 'the ground of the soul is dark' (Eckhart).

The Creation-Centred spiritual tradition is in fact the oldest spirituality in the Bible. The Yahwist author (J) of the Hebrew Bible is creation-centred, as is much of the historical books, the prophets and wisdom literature as well as Job and Song of Songs *. The NT, too, is rich with creation theology. Eastern Orthodox spiritualities have generally been a source for Western proponents of the Creation-Centred spiritual tradition. Creation-Centred spiritual theologians in the West have included: St Irenaeus *, St Benedict *, Pelagius (the Celtic tradition is profoundly creation-centred), St Hildegarde of Bingen, St Francis of Assisi *, St Thomas Aquinas *, Mechthild of Magdeburg, Meister Eckhart *, Julian of Norwich *, John of the Cross *, George Fox *, Teilhard de Chardin *, M. D. Chenu, Thomas Berry, Rosemary Ruether, Jon Sobrino. Since Newton, the creation-centred tradition has been kept alive more by prophetic poets, musicians and artists than by theologians in the West. But with Einstein's opening up again of the mysteriousness of micro/macro universe, physicists, eco-scientists and others appear eager for the prophetic mysticism of a creation spirituality. Latin-American liberation theologians hold much in common with Creation-Centred spirituality (*see* **Liberation, Spirituality of**). Native American spirituality and Taoism * would be examples of Creation-Centred spirituality outside the Biblical tradition. Creation-Centred spirituality has deep roots in pre-patriarchal traditions as is clear from feminist research into these traditions by Ruether, Rich, Daly, Harrison, Starhawk.

R. Bly, *News of the Universe*, 1980; M. Fox, *Breakthrough: Meister Eckhart's Creation Spirituality in New Translation*, 1980; *Original Blessing: A Primer in Creation-Centred Spirituality*, 1983; (ed), *Western Spirituality: Historical Roots, Ecumenical Routes*, 1979; R. Ruether, *New Woman, New Earth*, 1975.

MATTHEW FOX, OP

Cross, The

The making of the sign of the cross is

attested as early as Tertullian* (c. 200): 'at every forward step and movement, at every going in and out, when we put on our clothes and shoes . . . in all the ordinary customs of every day life we trace the sign (de C Mil 3). Augustine believed it necessary to all sacramental acts, but its prevalence in the mediaeval church caused the Reformers mostly to repudiate it, though it is permitted with a restricted interpretation in the Book of Common Prayer, and has prevailed in Lutheranism. Bonhoeffer* testified to its helpfulness according to Luther's instruction at morning and evening prayers.

The cross as the Christian symbol, prominent in art and architecture, dates from Constantine's vision before the battle of the Milvian bridge and his conversion to Christianity. His mother, Helena, according to a later tradition, discovered the relic of the true cross in Jerusalem, but Egeria, on pilgrimage in the mid-fourth century, knows nothing of this though she describes the 'holy wood' in its gold and silver box, and the ceremony of veneration on Friday of the 'Great Week'.

Because of its militant Constantinian associations, the cross was for some centuries the symbol of Christ's victory and the Christian's warfare. It is not the painful instrument of the Man of Sorrow's humiliation but as in the *Dream of the Rood*, is decked in gold and jewels. 'It was no felon's gibbet/Rather it held the gaze of holy souls.' It is the mighty tree which 'the young warrior', God himself, climbed. Earlier, Venantius Fortunatus (d. c. 600) in the Latin hymns *Vexilla regis prodeunt* and *Pange lingua* had celebrated the glorious battle of Calvary and apostrophized the cross as the tree of redemption, with other analogies too. 'For him the terrible transom-beam of the instrument of Manumission is seen as a Roman steelyard exactly weighing the price' (David Jones, *Epoch and Artist*, 1959, p. 261).

By the Middle Ages, the cross was more often the crucifix and there was devotion to the suffering Saviour (*see* **English Spirituality**) including the Five Wounds (cf. also Charles Wesley's* hymns) and the Sacred Heart*. Much art was a realistic and terrible representation of Bonhoeffer's aphorism: 'Only a suffering God can help.' This continued and became even more prominent after the Catholic Reformation and the

Council of Trent, and exercises of meditation, Ignatian and others, were made before the crucifix.

The bare cross itself was still a symbol richly charged as in Donne's* poem 'The Cross', which was written in protest against those iconoclastic Reformers who replaced the cross in English churches by the Royal Arms, and which finds the sign of the cross everywhere and inescapable, in nature, in every stroke of the swimmer, ship's masts, birds' wings, 'the Meridians crossing the Parallels'.

Reformed Christianity disliked images and 'visual aids' in devotion. The approach was more intellectual and in some ways more spiritual than that of Western Catholicism or Eastern Orthodoxy. Reformed divines painted word pictures of Christ's passion and sang hymns about the cross. Thomas Adams, an eloquent Puritan, preached a sermon in which he presents 'a faire and lovely crucifix, cut by the hand of a most exquisite carver, not to amaze our corporall lights with a piece of wood, brasse or stone curiously engraven to the increase of a carnal devotion, but to present to the eye of the conscience the grievous passion and tender compassion of our Saviour Jesus Christ' (*Workes*, 1630). John Dod (1550–1645) declares that the crucifix makes no difference between Christ and the thieves, 'but if we would see an image of Christ, look upon poor Christians . . .' (*On the Commandments*, 1604). John Bunyan* epitomizes classic Protestant devotion, which has been echoed in the sentiments of twentieth-century liberal theology, when Christian's burden rolls from his back at the cross and he sings:

Blest Cross, blest Sepulchre!
    blest rather be
The Man that there was put to
    shame for me!

J. A. W. Bennett, *Poetry of the Passion*, 1982; Gorden Huelin, *The Cross in English Life and Devotion*, 1972; Louis Martz, *The Poetry of Meditation*, 1954; C. E. Pocknee, *The Cross and the Crucifix*, 1962; G. S. Wakefield, *Puritan Devotion*, 1957; John Wilkinson (ed), *Egeria's Travels*, 1971.

EDITOR

Curé d'Ars *see* **Ars, Curé d'**

Cyprian of Carthage, St

Cyprian's sanctity is shown by the completeness of his conversion in middle life when he was a wealthy lawyer at Carthage, his wisdom as bishop in dealing with the disciplinary problems arising from the Imperial persecutions, his courageous leadership during the plague, and his martyrdom or 'Coronation' in 258. The evidence is contained in his fifty-nine letters, six synodical directives, his tracts *Concerning the Lapsed, On the Unity of the Church, On the Lord's Prayer*, and in the eye-witness account of his martyrdom. Cyprian was twelve years a Christian and ten years a bishop.

At his baptism he gave his money to the poor and his estates to public uses.

In the Decian persecution (249) Cyprian was persuaded to sustain his church from a place of concealment. Some Christians stood firm, suffering death, mutilation, imprisonment or forced labour. Others lapsed by sacrificing to Caesar or surrendering the scriptures. The problem of the lapsed became acute when certain Confessors claimed the right to issue certificates readmitting apostates to the eucharist. Cyprian insisted that reconciliation await the return of peace; then each case would be considered by the bishop in council. To act prematurely was to ensure disorder, desecrate the sacrament and dishonour the bishop. Meanwhile Cyprian was willing to permit penitents to be communicated *in articulo mortis*. The strength of his judgment rests on the seriousness of apostasy, the need for public recantation, and the danger of schism in arrogant self-righteousness. 'He cannot have God for his Father who does not have the church for his Mother' (*On the Unity*, 6).

Persecution temporarily ceased with the death of Decius and the outbreak of the plague. Cyprian called Christians 'to act in a way worthy of their birthright' and himself led a noble work of relief. His exposition of the Lord's Prayer dates from this time. It owes something to Tertullian*. *Our Father* is the corporate prayer of the church; 'since we are God's children let our deeds be consonant with our words'. We ask that God's Name may be hallowed and his Kingdom come *within us*; for where else does he not reign? 'Thy will be done' means both done and borne – we ask that we may prefer nothing to Christ, who preferred nothing to us. We pray for bread and for forgiveness, the primary needs of body and soul. 'Do not extend your prayer beyond necessity.' The last petitions, for deliverance from temptation and from the power of the Evil One, are all we need to make when we are too tired or too ill to pray more; so Augustine* understood Cyprian to say. The letters on the eucharist (63) and baptism (73) are of the same period. 'The sacrifice we offer is the passion of love ... The infant is not to be debarred from grace: he has in no way sinned except that being born in Adam after the flesh he has contracted the contagion of the ancient death.' Cyprian denied the validity of baptism by heretics, but African rigorism yielded to the Roman view; the unorthodoxy of the minister does not hinder the efficacy of the sacrament.

The Valerian persecution (257) sought to destroy the church by destroying its leaders. Cyprian was decapitated on 14 September 258. He chose to die among his own people, avoiding apprehension whilst the Proconsul was absent from Carthage. 'God asks not for our blood but for our faith.' Martyrdom itself is no proof of sanctity. He had received the certainty of his own 'coronation' a year previously. Among his last written words were these to Fortunatus: 'If God's soldier ... is called away without attaining martyrdom, the faith which is ready to welcome it will not lose its reward. The crown is given for field-service in time of persecution: in time of peace it is given to him who is certain of God's word.' On the scaffold Cyprian did not give the inspired word that the people expected. His serenity was its own message.

Augustine's deep veneration for Cyprian appears at the end of *De Baptismo*. 'The radiance of Christian charity everywhere gleams forth in this man.'

E. Wallis (ed), *Cyprian's Works*, Ante-Nicene Fathers, vol 5, 1978; E. W. Benson, *Cyprian*, 1897.

MAX SAINT

Dance

Dance as a form of religious devotion has been and is universal both in time and space. Evidence for it in prehistory is provided by cave paintings; it was a normal feature of

Egyptian and of Classical Greek religion; it was central to Shaker practice; it has never ceased to be an element in Hindu worship and at the present day it is found throughout the world: in Africa, Australia and North America; in Israel, where Jews dance with the Torah; in Spain, where choristers dance before the high altar at mass. To the dancer, it is not a diversion but a making visible of the invisible movement of the spirit – no Pueblo Indian, to take one example among many, would ever dance without an intense preparation through fasting and prayer.

The attitude of Christianity in the past has been somewhat ambivalent. No one could forget the many examples recorded in the OT, with pride of place given to David gyrating before the ark – an action that was a solemn ritual and not a mere gambolling for joy (II Sam. 6.14). The Psalms in particular treat dance as a normal part of worship (149.3). The Fathers, however, under the later Roman Empire when dancing had degenerated to a lascivious spectacle, were by no means enthusiastic. Influenced too by Neoplatonism and its tendency to exalt the soul above the body, many of them sought to discourage the practice, but they were unable to suppress it. Throughout the Middle Ages, and indeed up to the nineteenth century, churches and cathedrals gave it regular space.

In the twentieth century dance is becoming more and more recognized as a means not simply of recreation but of spirituality, it being understood as a religious exercise whereby the interior homage rendered to God may be externalized. Without doubt dance can express adoration, praise, supplication, spiritual joy; it can become a prayer, articulated not by words but by the movements of a person's whole body. Since worship is not only the offering to God of ourselves as bodies (Rom. 12.1), but also of the best we are capable of, the gift of dance, equally with other creative talents, such as music, painting, architecture, may become an oblation.

Within a congregational setting dance can be not only a part of the liturgy, in the sense that it itself is the vehicle of worship, it can also take the form of a dance-drama to explore and present the meaning, for example, of parables or OT stories. This is to draw attention to the mimetic aspect of dance, which may take balletic form, but modern

or free dance is equally appropriate. It is particularly so when what is envisaged includes both a dance-choir and an entire congregation. It is scarcely necessary to point out that if dance can contribute to public worship, it can also play a role in private devotions. Such a mode of spirituality corresponds to a biblical view of God as a living being, not static but dynamic, the one who according to Jewish eschatology will himself, when the kingdom comes in its fullness, lead his people in a triumphant dance.

Doug Adams, *Congregational Dancing in Christian Worship*, 1976; E. L. Backman, *Religious Dances in the Christian Church and in Popular Medicine*, 1952; J. G. Davies, *The Secular Use of Church Buildings*, 1968; (ed), *Worship and Dance*, 1975.

J. G. DAVIES

Dark Night, Darkness

'God is light and in him is no darkness at all' (I John 1.5). Texts such as this have made some Christian writers hesitant about speaking of the ascent to God in contemplation as an advance into darkness. Yet, from Philo onwards, the Judaeo-Christian contemplative tradition had come to look on the story of Moses' ascent of Mount Sinai as an image of the maturing soul; and Moses, in Ex. 19 and 20, goes into cloud and darkness to meet God.

'Darkness' (*gnophos*, as opposed to *skotia* or *skotos*, which usually have very negative connotations) serves as a metaphor both for the unfathomable transcendence of God and for the blindness of the human understanding confronted by God – though it is a mistake to look for absolutely clear and watertight distinctions between the two. Some writers see *gnophos* as culpable ignorance, spiritual obstinacy or immaturity; others simply as the unavoidable condition of the understanding while still in the shadow of the body (Origen's image); and others again as a kind of liberation from the obstruction of images and ideas.

This last interpretation is characteristic of Gregory of Nyssa, who is the first to combine the 'cloud' of Exodus with the 'night' of the Song of Songs*, the darkness in which love is consummated. As we learn that the divine nature is not to be held or grasped, eludes all definition, we learn that to know

God is a matter of longing, love and active discipleship, not a preserve of the mind alone. The darkness of our experience of God is a revelation of his inexhaustibility, and so it stirs the growth of endless yearning, self-transcendence. Thus from initial light – the illumination of conversion – we move into a 'luminous darkness', as we become increasingly free of attachment to created objects and goals, material or mental.

But it is Denys the Areopagite * who gives fullest expression to the idea that darkness is itself both the condition and the quality of true knowledge of God. Dionysius does not bother to distinguish *gnophos* and *skotos*, and can speak, in a famous passage in the *Mystical Theology*, of God sending out a 'ray of darkness', with which the self-forgetting self is united. Beyond both affirmative and negative language concerning God lies the 'darkness' of an encounter with what cannot be named or imaged, in the ecstasy of self-transcendence where we meet the self-transcending, 'ecstatic' love of God. As Vladimir Lossky noted, Denys' language unites the notions of God's self-communication, as light, and his essential unimaginability and inexhaustibility, as darkness. The paradox affirms that Christian speech is incurably dialectical. No attempt to resolve it even by supposing that there is both a communicable and an incommunicable 'part' of God will do. The illumination is *itself* a revelation of the dimensions of inconclusiveness, challenge and questioning in all talking about what we refer to as God.

In the Christian East, the imagery of light more and more dominated the mystical writing of the Byzantine period; but in the West, the later Middle Ages saw a striking retrieval of the Dionysian language of 'divine darkness'. Both Tauler * and Ruysbroeck * speak of the 'night' of contemplation, and the English *Cloud of Unknowing* * develops the picture of the soul suspended in prayer between two 'clouds': below is the cloud of forgetting, the veil which hides created concerns and lesser loves; above, the cloud of unknowing, the darkness of God which can be passed through only by the 'dart of longing love' answering the obscure ray of grace which kindles it like a 'sparkle from the coal'.

But Tauler and Ruysbroeck, more than any earlier writers, stress also that the darkness in question is not only a blockage to knowing: it is, equally importantly, a blockage to feeling. The 'night' is thus also an experience of emotional or 'affective' aridity – an image almost interchangeable with 'desert'. Thus Tauler, in a Passiontide sermon, speaks of the 'incomprehensible wild *desert*, where no one finds either way or mode, for it is above all mode' and of the 'hidden *darkness* of the modeless God'. Darkness and desert alike stand for the contemplative's experience of basic disorientation, which appears at first as a total undermining of the self's reality and value.

The clearest systematization comes in John of the Cross *. Taking (like Gregory of Nyssa) the nocturnal imagery of the Song of Songs as his starting point, he divides the night into three parts. There is the growing obscurity of the 'night of sense', in which the self concentrates its desire on God alone rather than any external ends. But the darkest part of the night is the 'night of spirit' (what is usually called the Dark Night of the Soul) in which the self is stripped even of any remaining spiritual gratification and of every consoling image of itself. Only beyond this does the dawn of illumination break into final union.

These are not conceived as straightforwardly successive states. They overlap and interact a good deal, and both 'nights' have active and passive aspects (struggle and receptivity together). John can use the language of 'annihilation' to describe what is happening in the night of spirit, yet it should be remembered that he consistently presupposes throughout the reality of a freely consenting human will. The final stage of the self's utter transparency to grace is not a merging into a kind of cosmic consciousness. Thomas Merton * compares the process to the Zen *enlightenment, a simple wholeness of response, attained by the 'dark night' of a systematic breaking-down of the picture of the self or mind as detached and omnipotent problem-solver. There are valid parallels here, though John is far readier to see the 'night' as something forced on us, not by a spiritual master according to technique, but simply by a combination of outer circumstances, an inner honesty about the necessary formlessness of our experience of God, and a consequent suspicion of intellectual or spiritual satisfaction, of ideas *or* feelings suggesting achievement and finality.

The sense of dereliction involved in the night of spirit (John refers here to Jesus' cry from the cross) is sensitively explored by later writers, notably Augustine Baker* in the seventeenth century and J.-P. de Caussade* in the eighteenth. The positive interpretation of these negative experiences was one of the issues in the heated debate between the Wesleys* and William Law, though John Wesley in old age was to come round to something much closer to John of the Cross's view. Among twentieth-century writers, Abbot John Chapman is perhaps the best interpreter of this theme; though it has also become immensely important in some modern religious poetry – Eliot's* *Four Quartets*, the later R. S. Thomas, Geoffrey Hill.

John Chapman, *Spiritual Letters*, 1935; A. Cugno, *St John of the Cross*, 1982; Vladimir Lossky, ' "Darkness" and "Light" in the Knowledge of God' in *In the Image and Likeness of God*, 1975; A. Louth, *The Origins of Christian Mystical Theology*, 1981; Thomas Merton, *New Seeds of Contemplation*, 1963; *On Zen*, 1976.

ROWAN WILLIAMS

Dead, Prayer for the
see **Prayer for the Dead**

Death of God

The slogan 'the death of God' generated a dramatic, colourful and often heated debate in America in the period 1963–1967. Historically the phrase might be used in the context of the Atonement, but it was given a distinctive and abrasive meaning in the work of Friedrich Nietzsche (1844–1900). It may have been reflection on his personal journey from youthful belief to later unbelief which led him to speak of the 'death of God'. Strident atheism of the seventeenth and eighteenth centuries assumed that belief in God could be demonstrated to be false on purely logical grounds. Nietzsche had no interest in such an approach. He declares that, 'it is our taste which now decides against Christianity, not our reason'. In his own time a change in experience and consciousness had come over Europe, with the result that belief in God had died. The intentionally shocking phrase 'the death of God' is a metaphor which describes

cultural fact rather than a logical conclusion.

The modern use of the phrase stems from the publication in 1961 of Gabriel Vahanian's book entitled *The Death of God*. Although Vahanian was not advocating Nietzsche's position, there was an appropriateness about using the metaphor, since Vahanian was dealing with a cultural movement in post-war America. In the fashionable religiosity of the time he saw true religion to be the first casualty. In this Vahanian was discarding the 'hard' line of Nietzsche for the 'soft' use of the phrase which was found in the early Barth's rejection of the God who was used to justify capitalism and war. It is time, Barth claimed, 'to declare ourselves thorough-going doubters, sceptics, scoffers and atheists in regard to him . . . He is dead.' In the flood of books, articles, lectures and sermons of the 1960s dealing with the 'death of God' it was normal to adopt this 'soft' use, to declare dead a false conception of God or a false attitude towards God.

The 'death of God theology' would not have had the impact which it did on the basis of this 'soft' use. The pace was set by three theologians who seemed to use it in its original 'hard' sense. Their positions were completely different from one another but they all seemed to begin from the same premise, the fulfilment of Nietzsche's cultural prophecy, 'the report that the old God is dead'.

The most complex and creative of the three was Thomas Altizer, a professor both of English literature and of religion, in whose thoroughly dialectical works can be seen the influences of Blake, Hegel, Nietzsche and Eliade. If the sense of the presense of God is lost for many in the midst of modern secular culture, it is tempting to attempt to rectify the situation by turning the clock back, by seeking to re-establish the conditions of a previous religious life. Altizer not only considers this unlikely to succeed, but proposes an interpretation of the incarnation which shows why God is dead and how the sacred must now be pursued through the profane. To accept the full implications of God becoming man may in the end lead to a new consciousness of God. William Hamilton constructs no metaphysical model in describing the death of God. The influence of Bonhoeffer* is clear. His writings are disarmingly autobiographical, as he describes the process by which his own religious life gradually changed, till he came to recognize that he no longer had any consciousness or experience of God. He does not argue his position, nor advocate it, yet his words articulated the experience of many Christians. In this time of waiting for God to return he still feels that he belongs within the Christian community. In contrast to these relatively 'soft' uses of the phrase 'death of God' we have the more abrasive presentation by Paul van Buren. He declares that the *word* 'God' is dead. Although he claims to be adopting the functional analysis of the later Wittgenstein, his positivist guide-lines are those of Flew and Braithwaite. Against these self-imposed constraints he later struggles when he seeks to justify a special normative function in life for the 'Jesus-story'.

None of the main contributors to the 'death of God' theology provided a solution which was widely acceptable, but they each claimed that loss of belief in God is widespread even within the church and that new forms of spirituality are therefore required. The remarkable response to their work, among clergy and laity but more extensively in the media and throughout society at large, is a measure of the importance of these claims.

Thomas Altizer, *The Gospel of Christian Atheism*, 1967; *Radical Theology and the Death of God*, 1968; Paul van Buren, *The Secular Meaning of the Gospel*, 1963; William Hamilton, *Radical Theology and the Death of God*, 1968; Alistair Kee, *The Way of Transcendence*, 1971; Bernard Murchland (ed), *The Meaning of the Death of God*, 1967; Friedrich Nietzsche, *The Complete Works of Friedrich Nietzsche*, ed Oscar Levy (vol 10 *The Joyful Wisdom*, vol 11 *Thus Spake Zarathustra*); Gabriel Vahanian, *The Death of God*, 1961.

ALISTAIR KEE

Deification

The word has acquired a very suspicious sound in the ears of perhaps the majority of Western Christians, partly as a result of the claims of mediaeval and sixteenth-century sectarian and apocalyptic groups to be united in essence with God (and so incapable of sin). Discussion of the subject has also been a good deal hampered by the confusion of doctrines of deification with speculations about a divine and uncreated 'core' of the human soul.

The only biblical text which seems to bear directly on deification is II Peter 1.4, where the destiny of Christian believers is described as becoming 'partakers of the divine nature'. However, other passages (such as Rom. 2.7; II Tim. 1.10) speak of Christians being endowed with the divine property of 'incorruption' – freedom from the tendency of the finite world to disorder and disintegration. There is an unmistakable borrowing here from the vocabulary of Hellenistic religiosity; and it is not confined only to the later parts of the NT.

At the same time, however, early Christianity was developing a doctrine of incorporation into Christ through the indwelling of 'Spirit': what distinguishes Christians is their right to relate to God as Father, in the way that Jesus did (Rom. 8). And this can also be expressed in terms of Father and Son 'making their home' in the believer (John 14.23). Thus the Christian is taken into a relation of unlimited intimacy with God; and for the Johannine tradition, this relation exists as an eternal reality in God's life, because the Word is in relation to God (*pros ton theon*) from the beginning (John 1.1), and the Son shares the Father's glory before the world is made (John 17.5). The 'glory' and 'eternal life' given to the believer consist precisely in sharing this relationship.

Thus there are two strands making up the classical patristic view of deification. One, the more obviously available convention in the religious language of the day, thinks primarily in terms of a communication of divine attributes, the other in terms of participating in an intra-divine relationship. These are not seen as contradictory by the Fathers, though we can learn a good deal about the general cast of a writer's thought by observing which strand predominates. They are brilliantly synthesized in Origen*, for whom the human goal is to return to the soul's pristine state of union with the eternal Logos, a condition of immutable rational contemplation of the Father, a perfect reflection back to God of his own inner rationality. For the tradition stemming from Origen, therefore, deification is very closely linked with the shedding of the 'passionate' (and thus unstable) part of the empirical soul, and the restoration of the soul's primitive purity as *nous gymnos*, 'naked understanding'. This scheme is most fully elaborated in the writings of Evagrius Ponticus at the end of the fourth century.

Other writers in the fourth and fifth centuries avoid this model, with its hints of a doctrine of the pre-existence of souls. Cyril of Alexandria and Augustine show far more concern with the theme of adoptive sonship and the restoration to human beings of a divine image which consists most profoundly in the capacity for free and loving response to the Father's initiative. For Augustine in the *de Trinitate*, the final restoration of the image occurs when, by the grace of Christ and incorporation into Christ, the powers of the *mens* (the whole process of our inner life) come to have God for their object. It is God who then defines and determines the soul's active reality, so that the soul reflecting upon itself cannot but see God. This is 'deification' by means of perfect *relation* with God.

Deification had played a major role in the fourth and fifth century christological debates (Christ must be God if what he imparts to us is divine life). This made it necessary for the Eastern Christian world from the Council of Nicaea onwards to distinguish carefully between Christ's 'natural' sonship and our incorporation into it by will and grace. Maximus the Confessor, in the seventh century, claimed that we may be by grace all that God is by nature; but this occurs only through God's free self-emptying in the incarnation, enabling and prompting our self-emptying in reply. So in Christ and in Christ's people there is a movement of mutual interpenetration (*perichōrēsis*) between divinity and humanity; not that the natures are confused or mingled – the *acts* (*energeiai*) of both interrelate, and human nature is transfigured by being permeated with the loving, self-giving action of God. For Maximus, as for earlier writers like Gregory of Nyssa in the fourth century, deification meant taking on the characteristic modes of activity of God (compassion, self-surrender) rather than simply sharing a set of abstract and static attributes (incorruptibility, etc.): shared attributes can only be interpreted as a dimension of shared activities, otherwise deification would mean fusion directly with the divine nature in its transcendence.

This formed the basis of the theory associated with Gregory Palamas*, Archbishop of Thessalonica in the fourteenth century, which distinguished sharply between God's essence and his *energeiai*: the essence is simple, indivisible, not capable of being shared, the energies are multiple and sharable. Deification is union with the divine acts or operations, the rays streaming out from the inaccessible source. The 'Palamite' system was linked with a strongly realist view of the transfiguration of the whole person: the saint's spiritualized senses can perceive the uncreated light (the light seen at Jesus' transfiguration), and the saint's body may itself radiate the same light. This has been a very important theme in Eastern Orthodox spirituality up to the present day.

The Western tradition has generally preferred Augustine's* approach, systematized by Thomas Aquinas*: deification occurs when the formal object of will and understanding is God, so that God determines entirely what is loved and grasped by the soul (this is what is sometimes called 'intentional' union). But this does not at all preclude a theology of comprehensive 'substantial' transformation, the reconstruction of the human spirit at its very roots – indeed, properly understood, the concept of 'intentional' union demands and presses towards such a theology. St John of the Cross* builds on Aquinas' foundations in his account of the state of union.

The revival of Catholic mystical theology at the end of the nineteenth century, and the recovery by theologians such as Scheeben of the patristic and early mediaeval understanding of grace as the indwelling of the Trinity helped to awaken interest in this area; and this was further stimulated in the present century by the Orthodox theological renaissance, and the extraordinary and fruitful 'retrieval' of Maximus and Palamas by writers of the calibre of Staniloae and Lossky. Some Orthodox scholars see the 'transcendental anthropology' of Karl Rahner as coming closer than most Western theology to the classical language of deification; Hans Urs von Balthasar has also – in a very different way – utilized Eastern as well as Western perspectives on deification in his theology of divine beauty and its communication to us in Christ. There are valuable leads here for the use of the 'deification' tradition in constructing a contemporary

theology and spirituality of Christlike freedom – freedom dependent on relation with
the Father, yet 'divine' in its own authority,
creativity and capacity for self-giving and
compassion.

A. Louth, *The Origins of the Christian Mystical Tradition*, 1981; Vladimir Lossky, *The
Vision of God*, 1963.

ROWAN WILLIAMS

Demons *see* Devil, The

Denys the Areopagite

The Areopagitical Corpus is a body of writings which purport to have been written by
the Denys (or Dionysius) who became a
Christian as a result of St Paul's speech on
the Areopagus in Athens (Acts 17.34), but
which were probably written towards the
end of the fifth century and bear the mark
of the influence of the late Neoplatonism* of
such as Proclus* (410–485). They first appear at the beginning of the sixth century
cited by Monophysites in controversy with
the Orthodox, and though initially rejected
by the Orthodox, very soon their spiritual
power was felt and they were accepted as
authentic. The writings (which are presented
as the surviving works of a more extensive
corpus) consist of the *Divine Names*, the
Mystical Theology, the *Celestial Hierarchy*,
the *Ecclesiastical Hierarchy* and ten letters.
They all have a single ultimate aim: the
union of the whole creation with God by
whom it was created, a union in which the
created order will attain perfection, or
become divinized, as Denys is fond of
saying. This union is the final stage of a
three-fold process of purification, illumination and union: the famous three ways of
the mystical tradition, found first in this
form in Denys.

The different works expound in different
ways how this goal is achieved. In the *Divine
Names* it is told how our praise of God may
be perfected: the various ways in which God
manifests himself, first as the Blessed Trinity, and then through the various divine
attributes, beginning with goodness and
ending with unity, are explored. This knowledge of God through affirmations about
him drawn from creation and the scriptures
is called *cataphatic* theology. In the two
works on the hierarchies the glittering
beauty of the created order, as it consciously

praises and serves God and seeks to be
united with him, is explored. The celestial
hierarchy consists of three orders of celestial
beings, each of three ranks: seraphim, cherubim and thrones; dominations, powers and
authorities; principalities, archangels and
angels. The ecclesiastical hierarchy is also
presented as a triad of triads: first a triad of
liturgical rites or mysteries: baptism, the
eucharist or synaxis, and the mystery of oil;
secondly a triad of sacred ministers, the
threefold apostolic hierarchy of bishops,
priests and deacons; and finally a triad of
those who receive their ministrations: the
monks, the laity (called the contemplative
order), and catechumens, penitents and the
possessed, who are all excluded from the
celebration of the sacraments. These two
hierarchies – the celestial and the ecclesiastical – themselves are represented as the
lower ranks of a triad, the pinnacle of which
is God himself, the Blessed Trinity, or the
Thearchy (as Denys habitually calls him).
Hierarchy is defined as a 'sacred order and
knowledge and activity which is being assimilated as much as possible to likeness with
God and which, in response to the illumina-
tions that are given it from God, raises itself
to the imitation of Him in its own measure':
the whole system of the hierarchies describes
a society of angels and men, mutually supporting and supported, by which the whole
society is raised to union with God and so
enabled to radiate as perfectly as possible
the inexhaustible glory of God. The hierarchies are static: that is, they are not a
ladder of ascent, but a graded hierarchy of
beings, at every level of which creatures find
union with God by fulfilling their vocation
as perfectly as they may. As far as mankind
is concerned this means that an ordered
sacral society fulfils its vocation in the
celebration of the liturgy through which all
are drawn into union with God and all are
vehicles of God's love for his creation. The
theology of the hierarchies is called *symbolic*
theology, for in the liturgy a symbolic reality
is disclosed through which God is borne to
his creatures. But in his treatment of both
cataphatic and symbolic theology Denys is
at pains to show how they point beyond
themselves, for all affirmations fall short of
God, and the most important aspect of
understanding symbols is in passing beyond
them to the reality they disclose (something
more evident when there is no natural simi-

larity between the symbols and what they symbolize, for which reason Denys prefers 'unlike symbols').

Both cataphatic and symbolic theology point beyond themselves to the theology of negation, *apophatic* theology, which is the subject of the short but powerful treatise, the *Mystical Theology*. In this the soul passes beyond anything it can perceive or know into the darkness where God is: it is reduced to 'complete speechlessness' and 'united in its highest part in passivity with Him who is completely unknowable, it knows by not knowing in a manner that transcends knowledge'. This is the divine darkness, the cloud of unknowing: and Denys both draws on the development of this theme by earlier writers such as Philo and Gregory of Nyssa, and is himself a powerful influence on later tradition. In the darkness the soul learns to relinquish its own activity and to submit to God who himself brings about union. Denys speaks here of a 'suffering' of divine things, of an ecstasy in which the soul goes out of itself and is united to 'the ray of divine darkness which is beyond being'. But his dominant thought here is that this is a union of love: the soul in its love for God knows God's love for itself and is united with him.

Apophatic theology is the acme of Denys' theology, but it establishes and does not undermine cataphatic and symbolic theology. Underlying all three theologies is the realization of the unknowability of a God who is therefore 'known in all things, and apart from all things . . . Therefore everything may be ascribed to Him at one and the same time, and yet He is none of these things.'

Good, complete tr into French by M. de Gandillac, 1943; text and tr of *Celestial Hierarchy* in SC, 58, *bis* (with good bibliography); R. Roques, *L'Univers dionysien*, 1954, and his articles on *Contemplation* and *Denys* in *DS*, II, cols 1885–1911; III, cols 243–86; H. U. von Balthasar, Herrlichkeit II/1, 1962, pp. 147–214; E. von Ivánka, *Plato Christianus*, 1964, pp. 225–89.

ANDREW LOUTH

Desert, Desert Fathers

Early monastic writers like Peter Damian sometimes speak of the monastic life as having its origins in the withdrawal to desert places of OT saints like Elijah. John the Baptist was also invoked as a primitive 'monk', and the Jewish *therapeutae* described by Philo in the first century (a group not unlike the Dead Sea sect) were thought by mediaeval authors to be Christian recluses, living lives of celibacy and discipline in remote places. For all the lack of historical perspective here, such notions were not entirely absurd. The ideal of withdrawal to the wilderness was not a Christian invention; for apocalyptic Judaism (picking up certain themes in prophetic literature, notably in Hosea and Jeremiah), the desert was a place for the renewal and purification of the covenant community. Israel had first received the Torah in the wilderness, and the flight to the desert could be a return to its sources, stripping away the corruptions of state and cult. The wilderness is also the place of refuge, for prophets like Elijah and protesters like the Maccabees: the community led out into the wilderness is gathered under God's protection, shielded from the assaults of the godless. All this is built into the ideology of the Dead Sea sect, and obviously left its mark on Jewish Christianity (Rev. 12.14). And Jesus' own sojourn in the desert is clearly, for the evangelists, a recapitulation of Israel's period of trial and temptation after the Exodus, and thus a radical renewal of the covenant.

Origen * interpreted the desert wanderings of Israel as a type of Christian spiritual life, characterized by separation from sin and passion, withdrawal from the world and growth through wrestling with temptation (*see* his famous Homily XXVII on Numbers). But there were probably already in Origen's day some Egyptian Christians who lived out this 'separation' by literal withdrawal from society. When in about 269 the young Antony * received his call to poverty and asceticism, there were some recluses from whom he could learn. But it was his own withdrawal, in the 280s, to the 'inner desert', well beyond the reach of his fellows, which established a new Christian convention – a physical flight from human society to confront the deepest human tensions and fragilities in solitude.

Antony emerged from a long period of complete isolation to become the centre of a group of disciples; and by the end of his long life (*c.* 355) the Egyptian desert was quite heavily populated with ascetic communities, varying in style from the very tightly-organized monastic townships established by Pachomius in Upper Egypt to the looser federation of smallish groups in the north (in areas around the Nitrian lakes, and at the Wadi el Natroun, usually called the 'desert of Scetis'). The popularity of the movement owes something to the legalization of Christianity by Constantine; martyrdom had been the crowning symbol of Christian detachment, but, now that this had ceased to be available, monasticism took its place. It has been said, with some reason, that the monastic movement was a protest – half-conscious – against too facile an accommodation between church and world. In that sense, it was an 'apocalyptic' phenomenon, as much as the Qumran community had been.

The desert was seen as a place teeming with hostile spirits, and a major part of the early monk's vocation was repeated confrontation with the destructive and deceptive power of the demons. Sometimes this might mean spending time in the ruins of a pagan shrine, exposing oneself to the wiles of the evil spirits who had been served there. More often, though, it was a matter of learning to discern between authentic and inauthentic 'religious experiences' – acquiring a degree of suspicion of vivid or consoling visions and revelations, easily manufactured in the extreme conditions of hunger and isolation, learning to endure faithfully, in boredom, depression, frustration, without taking refuge in the devilish lure of dazzling spiritual dramas (angelic voices and visitations, etc.).

Thus the desert is a place for overcoming illusions and purifying desire. All the great monastic teachers of the fourth century, Macarius, Poemen, Moses, the more intellectual and philosophical Evagrius, agree in insisting that true solitude means a refusal to imprison others in your own projections – or, in their terms, a refusal to 'judge the brethren'. And this often means in practice a ready flexibility in interpreting and directing the spiritual lives of others. The novice puts himself under the guidance of an 'old man' (gerōn), the abba, 'father', of a small circle, and accepts the abba's word and example as absolutely God-given; but correspondingly the abba must have a profound sensitivity to the varying needs of those in his care (a point stressed heavily in the monastic rules of both Basil and Benedict,

in a more structured setting). The characteristic literary form generated by this pattern of life is to be seen in the *Apophthegmata Patrum*, the *Sayings of the Fathers*, extant in a large number of differing versions and languages (in its earliest form dating from the first quarter of the fifth century) – a loose compilation of anecdotes and *obiter dicta*, often beginning with the novice's request for instruction ('Give us a word, Father'). (*See Apophthegmata*.) From the same period come the more literary and polished summaries of the teaching of the Fathers by John Cassian*, in his *Conferences* and *Institutes* – the main means by which the desert tradition was transmitted to classical Benedictinism*.

Most monastic reform movements in the mediaeval West looked back to a 'desert' ideal and made a point of geographical withdrawal to inaccesible spots. One rather special case deserves mention, though, as opening up a rather different interpretation of the tradition. In the thirteenth century, an association of hermits based on Mount Carmel in Palestine and looking to Elijah as their first founder gradually turned themselves into the Order of Carmelite* friars. However, their originally eremitical nature was never wholly forgotten, and the great sixteenth-century reform of the Order attempted to secure, for the fathers and sisters of the reformed observance, a balance between apostolic activity and withdrawal to a 'desert', an isolated retreat house, at regular intervals. Similar provision was made for the Capuchin branch of the Franciscans*. Thus the possibility was established of integrating the 'desert experience' into a religious life more closely involved with ministry in the world than that of the first monks. And in our own age the prophetic figure of Charles de Foucauld*, with his lonely witness and death in the Sahara, has inspired the experiments of the Little Brothers and Sisters of Jesus in combining a serious and demanding contemplative life (including regular lengthy retreats) with work alongside the poor and deprived – especially (in Europe) the victims of the industrial and inner-city 'deserts' and their attendant demons.

Thomas Merton* has written extensively about the contemporary need for a critical contemplative perspective on the illusions of 'advanced' consumer society, and suggested that such a society will only recognize its desolation and its vulnerability to self-deceit so long as there are those ready to confront the emptiness and the temptation to consoling projections with commitment and honesty – to create a 'desert' of solitude in which the desert of society can clearly see both the extent of its sickness and privation and the hope of living through it in faithful candour and compassion. And this is a task not restricted to those who are 'institutionally' contemplatives: as more than one of the Desert Fathers recognized, certain aspects of the desert vocation belong to the calling of all Christians.

See also **Monastic Spirituality, Monasticism**.

Peter Anson, *The Call of the Desert*, 1973; Derwas Chitty, *The Desert A City*, 1966; Thomas Merton, *Conjectures of a Guilty Bystander*, 1965; *Raids on the Unspeakable*, 1966; René Voillaume, *Seeds of the Desert*, Benedicta Ward, *The Sayings of the Desert Fathers*, 1975.

ROWAN WILLIAMS

Desolations
see **Consolations, Desolations**

Detachment
Detachment, or non-attachment, is a difficult but important concept in the history of Christian spirituality. Frequently discussed misleadingly as primarily the abandonment of certain objects and/or relationships, its meaning for the spiritual life has come to be misunderstood as a denigration of those objects and relationships. The insight behind the injunctions to detachment of spiritual leaders, not only within the Christian tradition, but also in many of the religions of the world, is that of the impossibility of committed love and service to God if one is enslaved – emotionally or by habitual dependence – to objects or relationships. In the Christian tradition, admonitions to detachment are found in the teachings of Jesus, in St Paul (see, for example, Col. 3.9–10; Eph. 4.22–24), and are a prominent feature of the teaching of patristic and mediaeval authors. The concept of detachment was criticized and reinterpreted by the Protestant reformers and reaffirmed in Roman Catholic monasticism. A secularized version of recognition of the importance of detachment takes the form, in contemporary life, of a critique of the aggressive acquisitiveness of modern society.

The practice of detachment does not have as its object rejection of any created good, but rather aims at correcting one's own anxious grasping in order to free oneself for committed relationship to God. Although a temporary sacrifice of particular objects and/or forms of relationship to which an individual is compulsively attached may be an important stage in coming to understand the attachment, only objects or relationships towards which one is unable to prevent compulsive addiction should be permanently given up.

Meister Eckhart*, a fourteenth-century German mystic, describes detachment as a process of stripping oneself of everything that defends or conceals the centre or 'core of the soul', the place of experience and knowledge of God. His agenda of identifying and relinquishing habits, rituals and practices, social conditioning, feelings, and ideas is preliminary to a spontaneous regathering of these in constellation around the new centre of the self which has been constituted by an experience of God. After this process of stripping and gathering, Eckhart taught, the person will be less likely to *identify* herself or himself with either objects or relationships. Eckhart's description of the meaning and importance of detachment is characteristic of the description of many spiritual leaders. His insistence that, when one is not attached to characteristic patterns of thought and behaviour, created goods no longer prevent but actually 'point you to God', is an important correction of the view that the need to reject implies a pejorative estimation of the goodness and beauty of creation and other human beings.

'Depouillement', *DS*, III, cols 455–504; Owen Chadwick (ed), *Western Asceticism* (LCC), 1958; Donald Nicholl, *Holiness*, 1981.

MARGARET R. MILES

Devil, The
The idea of a chief evil spirit is widely attested in late Judaism and in Christianity. Before the exile there are hints of a primitive view of such a being (e.g. Azazel in Lev. 16 and Lilith in Isa. 34.14), but Satan remains

strictly a non-demonic adversary (Job; Zech. 3.1ff.; I Chron. 21.7). The exile, however, seems to have created an increased awareness among the Jews of the transcendent holiness of God, which produced a new interest in angels* and in demons. Yet although a variety of names is assigned to a large number of angels, in the case of evil spirits it appears that names are primarily given to one figure only, whose hostility is undeniable but whose exact role is not consistently portrayed – Satan, Belial or Mastema. He becomes progressively not just the adversary (Satan) of man but also God's enemy, and he disrupts all relationships between man and God. So he is regarded as the tempter or seducer and, though less frequently, the destroyer. Hebrew religion, however, did not surrender its long-held belief that God is himself the source of everything, good and bad alike (Amos 3.6; Isa. 45.7), and this hostile figure was not allowed to become the sole explanation for the existence of evil. As a result his relationship to demons is never wholly clarified.

Much Christian belief about the devil derives not from the OT but from intertestamental Judaism. Two major traditions about the fall of the angels are developed. The first is taken from Gen. 6 according to which the sons of God (who are regarded as angels) lusted after the daughters of men and produced a race of giants whose offspring were the demons which plague mankind. The alternative view is that the fallen angels are those who offered their allegiance to Satan, who even before the creation of the world dared to challenge God's supremacy. He was expelled from heaven and is thus in the end impotent as the accuser of men before God but powerful in his attacks on God's people. The former tradition is the more important for Jewish thought and retains a considerable influence in early Christianity. Gradually it is supplanted by the second view which contains a stronger sense of direct conflict between God and Satan, good and evil. A further influence on Christian thought may come from the community at Qumran, where Belial is regarded as a powerful enemy of God, the temper of men and the prince of spirits.

In the Gospels Jesus is also presented as in conflict with the demons, who are opposed to God's kingdom; as tempted by Satan; and as speaking of Beelzebub, the prince of demons. Christians are personally caught up in a similar struggle (e.g. I Peter 5.9; James 4.7), but the conflict is also interpreted on a larger scale between two ages or worlds. At times the devil is given lordship over one of these. In John 12.31 he is the prince of this world and in I Cor. 5.5 Satan is the agent of death into whose hands an erring Christian may be consigned. The mysterious prince of the power of the air (Eph. 2.2) may be a fearsome conflation of this idea with the concept of the tempter. The principalities and powers mentioned chiefly in Col. and Eph. are probably not demonic in themselves. In Eph. 6.12, however, they are linked with the devil and his seductions and so become part of his malevolent army. Generally in the NT the devil's activity is to hinder the work of God (I Thess. 2.18) and to deceive the Christian (I Cor. 7.5), but in the end God's supremacy is not in doubt (Rom. 16.20; Rev. 20).

After the time of the NT the devil becomes more prominent in Christian thought and practice and a sense of prevailing evil seems to increase. Exorcisms are offered as evidence of God's greater power in this life or death struggle, but the power attributed to the devil also grows. This process can be traced in the baptismal liturgy. Mankind was sometimes regarded as the devil's property and the question of how atonement was made became crucial. A response to this question was made in terms of a ransom which may be paid to the devil or of a divine trick whereby the devil, himself the chief of deceivers, is outwitted. It should be noted, however, that there was no one view of the atonement in the early church and that modern objections to these notions are also to be found in some writers of the period.

In the Middle Ages there was much scholastic speculation about the devil, chiefly about the exact reason for his fall and whether he could be saved. Parallel with this a widespread popular belief may be discerned, which sometimes produced an anti-church cult of Satan. The Reformers do not question the devil's existence, but they develop a strong sense of personal responsibility for error and tend to internalize the struggle between good and evil. In the church today firm belief in the devil and in demonic powers may be found alongside complete scepticism. Many seem able to affirm the almost personal power of evil in the world without necessarily associating this with the figure of the devil.

H. A. Kelly, *Towards the Death of Satan*, 1968; E. Langton, *The Essentials of Demonology*, 1948; T. Ling, *The Significance of Satan*, 1961; J. B. Russell, *The Devil. The Perception of Evil from Antiquity to Primitive Christianity*, 1977.

WESLEY CARR

Devotio Moderna

The *Devotio Moderna* was a movement of mystical piety which began in the Netherlands in the fourteenth century and spread throughout the Rhineland into Northern France and Germany and even eventually into Spain and Italy. The movement was associated primarily with the Brethren of the Common Life and the Canons Regular of St Augustine in Dutch and German-speaking territories. The word *devotio* has the general meaning of the 'service of God'. It is called modern in contrast to the mystical piety of the Benedictines* and the Mendicant Orders, especially the school of mystical theology associated with the names of Eckhart* and Tauler*.

The founder of the movement was Geert Groote (1340–1384). He was born in Deventer, studied arts, canon law and theology in Paris, and held benefices in Utrecht and Aachen, though without having received holy orders. His principal subject was probably canon law and his writings show the influence of his legal training. As a result of a conversion in 1374, he renounced his career as a canon lawyer, gave his home to a group of women who became the first Sisters of the Common Life and retired to a monastery at Monnikhuizen near Arnhem. He refused the priesthood because of his humility and only consented to become a deacon in 1377 in order to be able to preach. The last years of his life were spent as an itinerant missionary and preacher. His violent language was little to the taste of the ecclesiastical authorities who in 1383 forbade him to preach. He died the following year.

His brief life did not prevent him from gathering and training many disciples. His letters show that he exercised a wide and deep influence. He left behind him a considerable number of autobiographical, ascetic and practical writings. His temperament was practical rather than speculative. He gave primacy to will rather than to intellect and showed little interest in theory as such. While he read the Rhineland mystics, he remained suspicious of their hunger for ontological union with God. He was more concerned with the reform of moral abuses in the life of the church.

Groote viewed contemplation more simply than the Rhineland mystics. Contemplation loses its intellectual aspect and is identified in practice with the perfection of love. Groote conceded, moreover, that not everyone admits such perfection is possible. Further precision in this matter seemed to him superfluous. The single thing on which he insisted (and in this respect he showed some affinity with Rhineland mysticism) is the necessity of a preparatory surrender to God, of spiritual poverty, and of the affective practice of virtues. The faithful soul on its way to the heavenly Jerusalem should imitate the humanity of Christ. The contemplative life is not exalted over the active. Both ways lead through the humanity of Christ to his divinity.

The *Devotio* began as a lay movement. Groote gathered around him a circle of friends for whom he served as a kind of spiritual director. The first and principle disciple of Groote was Florent Radewijns (1350–1400). On the order of Groote he became a priest. At Groote's death, he became the director of the first houses of the Brothers and Sisters of the Common Life established at Deventer. The Brethren of the Common Life differed from the Mendicants and the older monastic orders in their stress on the purely voluntary character of their life together. While they were frequently indistinguishable in their manner of life from mendicant friars – that is to say, they embraced a life of poverty, celibacy and obedience – they did not bind themselves to that life by a monastic vow. They could leave their house, therefore, at any time without incurring an ecclesiastical penalty. Their spiritual life was marked by conscious inner devotion, frequent brief periods of meditation during the day, particularly before each new activity, and a concern to prevent through constant inward meditation the liturgical worship of the church from lapsing into merely formal exercises.

The first houses of the Common Life were opposed by the clergy who had opposed

Groote. But Radewijns persisted in his efforts to set the houses on a firm footing and in time the opposition died down, though there were always whispers that the Brethren were heretical and had affinities with the Beghards and Beguines. In 1387 a new step was taken with the foundation of a house of Canons Regular in Windesheim. Radewijns became the head of a vast congregation which finished by absorbing the monastery of Groenendael and the many houses affiliated with it in Germany and France. The Canons Regular and the Sisters of the Common Life more than the Brethren were marked by a desire for an *artior vita*, a stricter life. This desire created a sympathetic bond between the Windesheimers and the observant congregations of the older mendicant orders.

While the *Devotio Moderna* was represented by such important authors as Geert Zerbolt van Zutphen (1367–1398), Gerlac Peters (1378–1411), Joannes Vos de Heusden (1391–1424), Hendrik Mande (1360–1431) and Joannes Mombaer, (1460–1501), the best known writing from this movement is *The Imitation of Christ*, now generally attributed to Thomas à Kempis* (1380–1471). One finds in this writing the characteristic stress on affective devotion and on the contemplation of the humanity of Christ which marks the movement as a whole.

Thomas does not appear to admit the possibility of enjoying here below even a fleeting vision of the divine essence. The contemplation which certain privileged souls enjoy on earth is a vision of an inferior order, different from the vision of the blessed souls in heaven not only in duration but also in its very nature. While Thomas knows and describes a mystical vision of divine truth, his interests lie elsewhere. What is important for Thomas is obedience, union of the will of the disciple with the will of God, the imitation of Christ – in short, a form of the spiritual life open in principle to every Christian. The *Imitation* summarizes the principal tendencies of Christian spirituality in the fifteenth century. After an excess of speculation, there is a return to a clear and simple ideal. There is a return to the absolute primacy of love, to simple conformity to Christ and to the practice of the virtues associated with humility.

The connection of the Brethren of the Common Life with Northern Humanism has probably been exaggerated by some scholars. Aside from Erasmus the *Devotio Moderna* had little contact with Dutch humanists. While the Brethren ran schools, copied manuscripts and later started printing firms, they did not attend universities and so stood outside academic life. John Pupper of Goch, Wessel Gansfort and Gabriel Biel are the exceptions which prove the rule. Goch was a secular priest, Gansfort was on friendly terms but never a member of the Brethren, and Biel only joined the Brethren after he had already attended the university and served as a cathedral preacher. In the sixteenth century the piety of the *Devotio Moderna* was absorbed by Erasmians, by Jesuits, even by the Benedictines and the mendicant orders. While the last house of the Brethren was not closed until the nineteenth century, the *Devotio Moderna* as an independent movement came to an effective end during the Reformation period. The great period of its life was the fourteenth and fifteenth centuries.

Albert Hyma, *The Christian Renaissance*, 1925; R. R. Post, *The Modern Devotion* (Studies in Medieval and Reformation Thought 3), 1968.

DAVID C. STEINMETZ

Direction, Spiritual

The pastoral guidance of souls by counselling and prayer through the illumination, grace, and power of God the Holy Spirit. Certain men and women have been given this 'gift' which enables them to act as guides and counsellors on the spiritual way. Devoted souls benefit greatly from this ministry.

Père Grou says in *The Hidden Life of the Soul*, 'He who really desires to give himself to God, should weigh well the advantages of having guidance from another, because the best and wisest men are blinded as to their own inward life, and the holiest and best fitted to direct others would not effect to direct themselves.'

The spiritual director is a physician of souls, one who seeks to diagnose the condition of the soul with its graces and ills, and to assist it into the way of growth. He is not primarily a judge, nor at any time a dictator. He is a spiritual father/mother concerned with the welfare of his/her children.

There is no authoritarianism in spiritual

direction. It should not be followed blindly; guidance of every kind should be checked against conscience, holy scripture, church teaching, the dictates of common sense, and relevant circumstances. It is a sign of deterioration in spiritual direction if force of any kind is used.

Spiritual direction since the Reformation has combined the hearing of confessions with spiritual counsel. The father of this post-Reformation teaching is Francis de Sales*, whose penitent Madame de Chantal always had opportunity for talk with her 'director'.

Reginald Somerset Ward*, who began this form of spiritual direction in the Church of England during the 1914–1918 war, always allowed time for talk and discussion as well as for confession. The *prie-dieu* and one chair (for the priest), gave way to the *prie-dieu* and two chairs (one for the penitent and one for the priest). The whole transaction is considered to be 'under the seal', thus establishing confidence between priest and penitent. Since Vatican II* the Roman Catholic Church has started to develop this same kind of counselling technique, priest and penitent in a room with table and chairs.

What is the relationship of psychiatry to spiritual direction? Today the two go 'hand in hand' when there is confidence between the clergy and doctors. When psychiatric aid is needed the penitent will consult the doctor and later re-establish relationship with the priest. Spiritual counsellors by their gifts, training, and insight, are able to know when to advise help from a psychiatrist. The seal of confession might appear to be at risk but this is not so because medical records concern areas of ill-health in body, mind and spirit, rather than sin. Doctors, like clergy, exercise discretion about their patients and their work.

Psychological study in this century has revealed a close link between fear and moral failure (sin). This has greatly increased the demand for counselling, and 'secular' institutions like the Westminster Counselling Centre in London have sprung up in major cities. This link between spiritual need and moral and social failure has been widely studied in Frank Lake's Clinical Theological Centre in Nottingham. Many of his patients, passed on by clergy, have returned to normal religious practices with renewed zest and insight after receiving help and healing from the Centre.

Spiritual direction is not necessary for all souls but it is very desirable for some and it can be a great help to many others. Those whose prayer is mystical in character specially need it because their consciousness of God is such that without 'direction' they could become afraid, depressed and self-centred. Counselling helps them to find a spiritual equilibrium. Then there are the specific manifestations of light, colour, sense and smell together with locutions and shewings, all of which need an expert in the spiritual life to interpret them. Fears concerning these kinds of spiritual insight have in the past led to misunderstanding and witch hunts. The Bible warns against wizardry which is very often the deteriorated and undirected working of mystical prayer.

The most positive use of spiritual direction is in two specific areas: understanding ourselves in the light of God, and growth in the life of faith and prayer. The counsellor helps the soul to see itself and through direction shows the way to fullness and joy. The arts of meditation*, intercession* and contemplation* have to be learned. The life of prayer has to be maintained and sustained over the years if maturity and insight are to come. These gifts of grace are not achieved by our own efforts. We learn to stay in the light and love of God so that he can achieve them in us.

Frank Lake, *Clinical Theology. A Theological and Psychiatric Basis to Clinical Pastoral Care*, 1966; Kenneth Leech, *Soul Friend*, 1979; Reginald Somerset Ward, *A Guide for Spiritual Directors*, 1957.

                                N. W. GOODACRE

Discernment of Spirits

Discernment of spirits is a biblical charism (*diakrisis pneumaton*, I Cor. 12.10) and patristic virtue (Greek *diakrisis pneumaton*, Latin *discretio spirituum*), whose object is to identify the presence or absence of God in given human activity. The 'spirits' are affective movements within the person, and they are evaluated in their orientation or direction according to the gospel principle, 'You will know them by their fruits' (Matt. 7.16). Discernment of spirits is thus a means to discern the presence or absence of the Spirit.

In the tradition the source of the movements is ultimately God or the devil, acting through outside agents like angels or demons or through the good or evil principles of spirit and flesh within the human being. Whatever the theological categories they are outside the actual discipline of discernment, since the project is not a speculative description of causes, but a practical judgment and decision about life choices. The process is experiential and inductive; it is wisdom rather than science. Discernment is, thus, open to new developments in theological understanding such as the insights today of depth psychology and social analysis.

The Desert Fathers* evolved teachings on discernment that were systematized by some outstanding spokesmen like John Cassian* (d. 432–435?) and John Climacus* (d. 649) and later codified by Ignatius of Loyola* (d. 1556). The locus classicus for the tradition is Ignatius of Loyola's *Spiritual Exercises**, his manual for retreat directors, especially in the sections entitled, 'Rules for understanding to some extent the different movements produced in the soul and for recognizing those that are good to admit them, and those that are bad, to reject them' (Puhl translation, nn. 313–336). The two sets of rules, one for beginners (the 'First Week'), and the other for the truly converted, whose lives show spiritual freedom or 'indifference' (the 'Second Week'), supply a handy reference for summarizing the tradition.

In the unconverted or newly converted, the affective movements are too unstable to act as positive indicators of God's presence or will. It is important to be in touch with them and to own them, hence the importance of self-knowledge and humility. But the immediate task at this stage is integration of the affectivity in the total personality and the direction of one's life according to sound, moral norms amid the fluctuations of euphoric and depressive feelings.

Discernment of spirits properly speaking goes beyond this alertness to feelings and living by general norms prudentially applied. It seeks to read the movements of the sensible and spiritual affectivity in a positive way, i.e. as signs of the influence of the Spirit or a counter-force. This is possible in the Second Week, because the affectivity now registers in an immediate, uncensored way the reaction of the whole person. Specifically the feelings now show the consonance or dissonance between the present experience and the spiritual orientation of the person. The criteriology of these affective responses is precisely the tradition of discernment. 'Consolation' reinforces the orientation towards God, 'desolation' opposes that fundamental option. The challenge is to identify true consolation and desolation and properly interpret associated choices.

Discernment takes place in the context of divine love experienced (Rom. 5.5) and delicate self-knowledge. But it looks for convalidation outside the individual and in the community, often in the person of the spiritual director.

C. Floristan and C. Duquoc (eds), *Discernment of the Spirit and of Spirits*, 1979; E. E. Larkin, *Silent Presence, Discernment as Process and Problem*, 1981.

ERNEST E. LARKIN

Disciplina Arcani

Christians suffered severe, if intermittent, persecutions for three centuries. They also lived in a world of mystery religions. Both facts encouraged some concealment of their rites and beliefs from pagan society. Catechumens were allowed to hear scripture and sermon, but were dismissed before the Prayers of the Faithful, including the Lord's Prayer, and the eucharist. In some centres, such as fourth-century Jerusalem, the preparatory instruction of catechumens seems to have been primarily ethical and the sacraments or 'mysteries' were not explained until they had been baptized and received into the full worshipping life of the church. In contemporary Milan, the Lord's Prayer and the words of institution would be passed over in the reading of the lessons, if the uninitiated were there.

The leaders of the Oxford Movement* seized on this secret (Lat. arcane) discipline of the early church and taught a doctrine of 'reserve in communicating religious knowledge', partly in reaction from Methodist and evangelical openness. There was a touch of romanticism in this. 'Beauty is shy' (Keble): 'Nature withdraws from human sight/The treasures of her light' (Isaac Williams). So, clouds and darkness are round about the holy God, as they were about Jesus, transfigured, and ascending into heaven. After his passion, he showed himself to his disciples and not to the world. There was a particular revulsion from the raucous and blatant preaching of the cross. Isaac Williams deems it deplorable that 'the highest and most sacred of all Christian doctrines is to be pressed before and pressed home to all indiscriminately', a sentiment which is paralleled in Goethe (*Wilhelm Meister*).

There is in the gospels 'the Messianic Secret', Jesus's reluctance to be acknowledged as Messiah, and have his praises sung as such by those he had cured; and also the puzzling words of Mark 4.10–12, which suggest that the disciples are the initiates who understand the mystery of the kingdom of God, whereas those outside have to be content with parables, which are not lucid 'human interest' stories to make everything clear, but riddles which may but darken their minds the more.

There will always be some temperaments for whom the arcane is endlessly alluring, who feel that intelligibility is reductionist and John Wesley's* 'plain truth for plain people' inadequate to the mystery at the heart of the universe; *Christianity not Mysterious*, the Deist John Toland's title (1696), will be deficient in both intellectual and spiritual excitement, denying the poetic, and limiting God. This undoubtedly accounts for the fascination for some doctrinally orthodox Christians of an esoteric writer such as Jakob Boehme*. In *The Genesis of Secrecy* (1979), subtitled 'on the interpretation of narrative', Frank Kermode, a Cambridge Professor of English Literature, has examined St Mark's Gospel, rather in the spirit of Austin Farrer*, as a work of literature. 'Mystery' is a recurring theme in the Gospel from Chapter 4 onwards and it is the unwillingness to accept this which constitutes the silliness and stupidity of the disciples, Peter at Caesarea Philippi and on the Mount of Transfiguration, and the women at the tomb. What we find in the Gospel is 'something irreducible yet perpetually to be interpreted; not secrets to be found out one by one but Secrecy' (p. 143). Admittedly Kermode's conclusion is somewhat weary and dispirited – books, like the world, are 'hopelessly plural, endlessly disappointing'. Helen Gardner's severe criticism of him derives from her very Christian conviction that interpretation is not all, nor is the interpreter master of the text. Beneath the Gospel lies a substratum of event and fact, what E. C. Hoskyns would have called 'rough,

crude history'. The lure of the esoteric may darken counsel and lead to confusion, fantasy and in the end despair; yet to lack the capacity for the spiritual and unearthly side of religion (and of life) is a grave defect. One of J. H. Newman's* compelling characteristics was that, in contrast to his contemporary, Dean Stanley, he had a tremendous sense of 'the awfulness of things unseen'. There was something *sui generis* in his profound seriousness and reverence about everything that touched religion. Christianity will always need in its corporate life as well as in the individual lives of its adherents, the right balance between proclamation of an 'open secret', declared in Christ, and reverence and restraint before incommunicable mystery.

In the twentieth century, the notion of *disciplina arcani* has been revived through the influence of Dietrich Bonhoeffer*, who taught a 'worldly holiness', which did not remove the Christian from the painful ambiguities of political action, or deny the legitimacy of human happiness or of human mastery of the forces of nature as God's vicegerent. But beneath the humanism there must be a discipline of devotion, founded on scripture and the long inheritance of personal faith. This must be arcane in that it is not constantly advertised, both because Pharisaic trumpeting is unchristian and because there are those who are not yet ready for God's final word and whose birth into Christ could therefore be abortive.

EDITOR

Discipline

In its narrower usages this refers to mortification*, the austerities, particularly of the monastic regime, and sometimes to the scourge of knotted cords with which the religious whipped themselves to drive out sensual desire or afflict chastisement for their sins. Also, it might help to identify them more closely with the flagellated Christ. Von Hügel* knew of a nun who, in order to try to compel a former pupil to break off an illicit love-affair, threatened to scourge herself until she stood in a pool of her own blood each day the liaison lasted.

Discipline also refers to the rules governing membership of some communions. *The Apostolic Tradition of Hippolytus* (*c.* 215) lists crafts and professions forbidden to Christians, while catechumens are expected to have 'lived piously' and 'honoured the widows'. Calvinist and Methodist churches among the mainstream have sought to require definite adherence to certain rules with powers of excommunication or exclusion in the event of lapse. At times in the churches of the former tradition this has been extremely severe with penalties imposed by the civil power, and/or denunciation before the assembled congregation. The minister's powers of discipline are grave and help to account for the awe in which that office is held in, e.g. the Church of Scotland. Methodist history, from the time of the Wesleys * onwards, is strewn with instances and controversies about those who have 'ceased to meet', and each year each church, or 'society' is expected through its appropriate committee to review the membership roll and erase the names of those who have not conformed to the minimum requirements of, for example, attendance upon the 'means of grace'. In a liberal age and among Christians pledged to be 'the friends of all, the enemies of none', this is a hard and often offensive task. There is much enquiry as to what the conditions of church membership should be and a perennial tension between formalism and freedom, rigorism and humanism, a tension found in the NT itself. What is generally conceded is (a) the way must not be made narrower than Jesus made it, and (b) just as poetry is a 'desperate discipline' (Richard Church) so the Christian life cannot be one of 'uncharted freedom', and the very generosity of the divine love demands an absolute dedication in return.

J. H. S. Burleigh, *A Church History of Scotland*, 1960; F. P. Harton, *The Elements of the Spiritual Life*, 1931; K. E. Kirk, *The Vision of God*, 1931; Ronald Knox, *Enthusiasm*, 1950, pp. 422–548; Methodist Conference Office, *The Constitutional Practice and Discipline of the Methodist Church*; R. C. Mortimer, *The Duties of a Churchman*, 1951.

EDITOR

Disinterested Love

There is a sixteenth-century Spanish sonnet of unknown authorship, which is more familiar as an English hymn translated from the Latin and wrongly attributed to the Jesuit St Francis Xavier. It declares that if there were no heaven and the soul were consigned to deepest hell, the love of God would be its own reward. Such disinterestedness became a feature of Christian spirituality during the Middle Ages. It is of no concern to Augustine and cannot but be embarrassed by the teaching of Jesus, but Cicero's *De Amicitia* (which had wide provenance and among others influenced Aelred of Rievaulx *) asserts that the love of friends must be disinterested, and Abelard and the Cistericians thought of God as our everlasting friend whom we should love for his own sake and his absolute goodness whatever he may do with us. This flowered in the late sixteenth and seventeenth centuries and is seen in the teaching of St Francis de Sales *, though finely balanced.

It had its opponents all along, but it was finally condemned in a papal brief *Cum alias* of 1699, after an ugly and embittered controversy between Bossuet *, Bishop of Meaux and Fénélon *, Archbishop of Cambrai. The latter was the apostle of pure love set forth in his *Explication des Maximes des Saintes*. It is easy to be attracted to his personality and his teaching, especially when one is aware of the depths to which his enemies stooped and his own record as a compassionate and charitable prelate. In retrospect the condemnation seems justified. Not only does disinterested love deny hope *, and love *, if mutuality is in some ways essential to it; it is unchristianly individualistic, for though I may not seek for reward for myself and rather be with Christ in hell than without him in heaven, assuming that there could be heaven where he is not, I must wish for the salvation and beatitude of others and for the triumph of the kingdom of God. When it is not the hyperbole of the lover of God, it is a spirituality of absorption in the Divine and, though individualistic and élitist, paradoxically leads to the loss of self in God. Yet it may have calmed if not removed the obsessive fear of death and damnation which oppressed so many souls in seventeenth-century Catholicism. 'Fear was swallowed up by being allowed to triumph unopposed, by the acceptance of the worst possible outcome – but that outcome is in the hands of God, and God is love' (John McManners). And it is rehabilitated in de Caussade's * 'abandonment to Divine Providence'.

John Burnaby, *Amor Dei*, 1938; R. A. Knox,

Enthusiasm, 1950; John McManners, *Death and the Enlightenment*, 1981; D. D. Williams, *The Spirit and Forms of Love*, 1968.

EDITOR

Doddridge, Philip

A Dissenting Divine in the succession of Richard Baxter* and John Howe*, Doddridge's (1702–1751) chief pastorate was at Castle Hill, Northampton, to which he transferred an academy for Dissenting ministers of which he had just become Principal. Although under the disadvantages of nonconformity, his friendships ranged wide. He had considerable influence at Oxford and Cambridge and even began some 'talks' with Archbishop Herring with a view to interchange of pulpits between the church and Dissenters. These foundered as so often since at the point of episcopal ordination. He was a great letter-writer, while his catholicity of spirit could include Baptists, Arians (Unitarians) and John Wesley*. Love of Christ was for him a surer test of orthodoxy than precise formulation. His piety is exultant and hymns, redolent of joy, are its appropriate expression: 'Hark the glad sound, the Saviour comes'; 'O happy day that fixed my choice'. His treatise *On the Rise and Progress of Religion in the Soul* (1745), which has been translated into nine languages including Tamil and Syriac, was a much used guide to evangelical spirituality, not least in the Church of England, where his communion hymn, 'My God and is thy table spread?' has been greatly loved. The book traces the progress of the Christian life from conversion to the honouring of God in death. Doddridge set great store by the 'ordinances', particularly the Lord's Supper, but it is a spirituality which, though it leads him to the table in reverence and rapture, makes him free to honour this as but one means of grace. He writes indeed of the 'absence' of Christ in the sacrament, for 'he is not here; he is Risen' and the Supper is not the heavenly feast. That he lived constantly in the presence of the one whom he always wrote as GOD (an Anglo-Catholic custom too) is beyond dispute. 'When I awake in the morning, which is always before it is light, I address myself to him, and converse with him, speak to him while I am lighting my candle and putting on my clothes, and have often more delight before I come out of my chamber, though it hardly be a quarter of an hour after my awaking than I have enjoyed for whole days, perhaps weeks of my life. He meets me, in my study, in secret, in family devotions.' This rapture was not diminished by his sorrows – five of his nine children died in infancy. He was one of the leading educationists and philanthropists of his age, as well as a pioneer of missions overseas.

G. F. Nuttall (ed), *Philip Doddridge 1702–51. His Contribution to English Religion*, 1951.

EDITOR

Dominican Spirituality, Dominicans

Founded in 1216 by St Dominic Guzman (*c.* 1170–1221), the Dominican Order grew out of the preaching campaign against heresy in the south of France and its objective was, from the outset, apostolic. Its spirituality is characterized by a concern 'to be useful to the souls of our neighbours'. Humbert of Romans (Master of the Order 1254–1263, d. 1277) insists that those who have a 'grace of preaching' ought to prefer preaching to all other spiritual exercises, even prayer. Domenico Cavalca (d. 1342), St Catherine of Siena (d. 1380) and Bl. John Dominic (d. 1419) make usefulness to others the criterion of validity of a spiritual life. The Order took over many traditional monastic practices, but subordinated them to the apostolate by extending widely the use of dispensations. It wanted its laws and customs to be adaptable to new demands and new situations. St Dominic adopted rigorous mendicant poverty, but this was ancillary to the preaching and was subsequently modified; in 1475 Sixtus IV authorized the Order to own properties in addition to its convents and furnishings.

The Order is united by its members' profession of obedience to the Master of the Order. Generosity of self-giving is the keynote of Dominican obedience, rather than meticulous observance of rules or conformism to a detailed programme of life. The Dominicans were the first Order to declare that their laws are not binding in conscience, and this is explained as safe-guarding the spontaneity of the individual's service. The traditional monastic concern to protect people from their own frailty is replaced by trust in the individual and trust in God's providence. The risk involved in the preachers' unprotected life is accepted explicitly by Humbert, and justified on the grounds that the meritoriousness of their good works outweighs the 'sins that will unavoidably occur' in their active life.

Throughout the history of the Order there has been a certain tension between the demands of conventual, contemplative life and the demands of the apostolate. In response to the marked decline in religious fervour which followed the Black Death, a succession of reform movements attempted to restore fidelity to regular observance, but these were often marred by fanaticism (especially that associated with Savonarola [1452–1498]) and exaggeration (Bl. John Dominic abandoned the principle of Dominican law not binding in conscience, Savonarola refused the permission to accept properties and revenues, and some Spanish reformers largely abandoned study and the apostolate). In the twentieth century there has been controversy as to whether preaching or contemplation was the primary goal of the Order, but it is now more generally accepted that the goal of the Order is preaching, with contemplation as an integral part of the preaching life.

The Order's apostolate was intended to be doctrinal, and so theological study was insisted on from the time of St Dominic. Since 1259 philosophy too has been officially part of the Order's study. Intellectual work replaced the traditional monastic manual labour. Dominican spirituality is generally strongly intellectualist rather than affective (*see* **Thomas Aquinas**), and Dominicans have rejected the notion that higher spiritual states are incompatible with the normal operation of the mind (e.g. Pedro de S. Maria Ulloa, who was accused by the Carmelities in 1688 of attacking their doctrine). 'Contemplation' in Dominican texts often means 'study'; Francisco de Victoria (d. 1546) maintains polemically that 'true contemplation means studying the scriptures', and Cajetan (1469–1534) and Tommaso Campanella (1568–1639) use the word to mean scientific investigation.

Dominican theologians have generally espoused a simple, practical doctrine of prayer. They repeat the monastic recommendation of frequent, brief prayer. They have opposed both quantitative and methodical approaches to private prayer (Savonarola, Luis of Granada [1504–1588] warning against any attempt to force prayer). They also resisted the unduly spiritual notions of prayer proposed by the Alumbrados, Erasmians and, later, the followers of Molinos* (e.g. Augustín de Esbarroya [d. 1554], Juan de la Cruz OP [*Diálogo sombre la Necesidad de la Oración Vocal*, 1555], Bl. Francisco Posadas [d. 1713]). Typically only two 'grades of prayer' are recognized: the prayer of the person not in a state of grace, and the prayer of the person in a state of grace (Bartolomé Carranza [1558–1576], Noel Alexandre [d. 1724]).

Dominicans also resisted the tendency which appeared in the sixteenth century to make prowess in prayer the criterion of spiritual progress (e.g. Juan de la Cruz, OP), insisting on charity as the only true criterion. Even Dominicans engaged in more conventional mystical theology (Arintero [d. 1928], Garrigou-Lagrange [d. 1964]) stress that Christian perfection depends on charity, not on para-normal experiences and phenomena.

Various devotions have been associated with the Order. In the thirteenth century Dominicans propagated devotion to the Holy Name. Bl. Alvaro of Cordoba (d. *c.* 1430) introduced into Europe the Way of the Cross, which developed into the Stations of the Cross. In particular, since the late fifteenth century, the Rosary* has been the typical Dominican devotional practice.

In addition to the friars, St Dominic founded several enclosed monasteries of women (the 'Second Order'), to provide a more rigorous monastic life than was generally available at the time. In 1285 a Dominican Order of Penance was founded, from which grew the active Dominican sisters (of whom there are now many Congregations throughout the world, engaged in a variety of works, chiefly teaching), cloistered Third Order nuns, and the Dominican laity. There is also a Dominican Secular Institute.

See also **Catherine of Siena, St; Eckhart; Suso; Tauler.**

W. Hinnebusch, *Dominican Spirituality*, 1965; S. Tugwell, *The Way of the Preacher*, 1979; (ed), *Early Dominicans: Selected Writings* (Classics of Western Spirituality), 1983; V. Walgrave, *Dominican Self-appraisal in the Light of the Council*, 1968.

SIMON TUGWELL, OP

Donne, John

Donne (1571/2–1631), a Roman Catholic in his youth, took Anglican Orders in 1615 and was Dean of St Paul's from 1621 until his death.

He was a 'metaphysical poet' in every sense, learned and allusive in 'strong lines' which were harsh, difficult and employed the 'discordia concors' of witty writing. His poetry united both the ecstatically physical and the intensely spiritual; the incarnation was therefore for him the 'wittiest' form of theology, the incomprehensible union of nature with supernature, the human with the divine, man's weakness with the omnipotence of God. It is still confounding to some modern readers that there is no final distinction in method or content between Donne's secular poetry and the *Divine Poems*. 'Mark but this flea' is an unlikely opening to a love poem, yet it proceeds from the observation that the flea has sucked the blood of both lovers to the conclusion that its little body is their 'marriage bed and marriage temple'; moreover, from this triple union of the flea and the two lovers, to kill it is 'sacrilege, three sins in killing three'.

This reference to the Holy Trinity and its material analogues is more seriously pursued in the sonnet 'Batter my heart, three-personed God', where the exhortation to God to subdue the poet's will proceeds in triple images: 'knock, breathe, shine', 'break, blow, burn', until the poem concludes with the paradox that the poet,

Except you enthral me, never shall be free,
Nor ever chaste except you ravish me.

This witty spirituality is seen at its most intense in 'A Hymn to God the Father'. Fearing death, the poet asks that his part in the Fall of Man be forgiven and redeemed:

Wilt thou forgive that sin where I begun,
Which was my sin though it were done before?

and then begs that his own personal sins be wiped out:

Wilt thou forgive that sin through which I run
And do run still, though still I do deplore?

Already in the first couplet the pun on his own name has been lightly stressed, linking John Donne to the fallen Adam; now the pun is made more complex:

When thou hast done, thou hast not done,
For I have more.

in which even divine redemption is not complete ('done') until he 'has done', has finished and held Donne in the divine grasp.

If this witty 'metaphysical' spirituality unites the sacred and secular poetry—indeed demands their union to establish Donne's incarnationalist theology – it comes to an equal fruition in the prose works. The best-known extension of this wit is that of *Meditation XVII* which concludes with the characteristic natural analogy for the condition of man: 'No man is an island entire of itself . . . Any man's death diminishes me, because I am involved in mankind, and therefore never send to know for whom the bell tolls; it tolls for thee.'

But probably the finest of these extended metaphors concludes the sermon, 'Death's Duel', delivered not many days before he himself died: 'There we leave you in that blessed dependency, to hang upon Him that hangs upon the Cross . . .' Here the punning reverberation, 'dependency – hang – hangs', is the issue of devotion, oratory and a witty intelligence; Izaak Walton justly spoke of Donne's 'commanding judgment'.

MOELWYN MERCHANT

Drugs

The use of psycho-active drugs for spiritual ends is very ancient. One-tenth of the Rig Veda refers to a drug called *soma*, often identified with the mushroom *amanita muscaria*, though some scholars believe that it was cannabis. Cannabis is certainly mentioned in a religious context in many ancient documents. The *amanita* mushroom has been seen as the basis of a wide range of cults. Allegro even associates it with the beginnings of Christianity, though this has attracted little support. The ritual and sacramental use of drugs other than alcohol is more common outside the Jewish and Christian traditions, though the Native American Church has used peyote for many years.

The possible value of certain drugs in raising the level of consciousness and enhancing religious awareness was discussed by William James in 1902, when he ascribed 'metaphysical significance' to his experiences under nitrous oxide. Later Aldous Huxley discussed the same questions in relation to mescalin. In the early 1960s Leary and his colleagues at Harvard experimented with psilocybin. But it was the increased use in the 1960s of lysergic acid diethylamide (LSD-25) which led to widespread debate in the west about the role of these substances in spiritual development. The term 'psychedelic' (mind-expanding) had first been used of these drugs by Humphrey Osmond in 1957, and it spread into common usage in the mid-60s. The principal effects of LSD were: the intensifying of experience; the illumination (or altered perception) of reality; and the temporary dissolution of the boundaries of the ego. It was therefore claimed (e.g. by Leary, Watts and others) that this and similar drugs were of considerable value in aiding spiritual growth. Parallels have been made between the experiences under such drugs and those described by mystical writers: the most detailed work in this area is that by Pahnke.

However, since the 1960s there has been a marked tendency to devalue regular drug use. Many spiritual teachers have warned against reliance on chemicals as a route to God. Some claim that the main value of these drugs was to enable some people within a materialistic and chemically oriented culture to experience a breakthrough to neglected or suppressed areas of consciousness. But continued reliance on them was more likely to lead to spiritual decline. Hence the interest shifted away from drugs towards non-chemical approaches to spirituality. However, the possible contribution of certain drugs as aids to spiritual perception should not be ruled out.

The comparison of religion itself to an intoxicant or an opiate, often associated with Marx, in fact goes back to the eighteenth century. As psychopharmacology has developed, the study of what Huxley termed 'the chemical conditions of transcendence' has become more sophisticated. The connection between the use of chemicals and religion (including its pathological forms) has come to be seen as more complex than earlier mechanistic and deterministic writers were able to see. The use of drugs in a religious context raises wider issues such as the relation between chemical changes and personality, between body and spirit, questions which are basic to all incarnational religion.

J. M. Allegro, *The Sacred Mushroom and the Cross*, 1970; William Braden, *The Private Sea: LSD and the Search for God*, 1968; W. H. Clark, *Chemical Ecstasy: Psychedelic Drugs and Religion*, 1969; Aldous Huxley, *Heaven and Hell*, 1956; William James, *The Varieties of Religious Experience*, 1902; Timothy Leary et al, *The Psychedelic Experience*, 1966; Kenneth Leech, *Youthquake*, 1973; R. E. L. Masters and J. Houston, *The Varieties of Psychedelic Experience*, 1966; R. E. Schultes and A. Hofmann, *Plants of the Gods: Origins of Hallucinogenic Use*, 1979; R. G. Wasson, *Soma: Divine Mushroom of Immortality*, 1971; Brian Wells, *Psychedelic Drugs*, 1973; R. C. Zaehner, *Drugs, Mysticism and Make-Believe*, 1972.

KENNETH LEECH

Ecclesiology and Spirituality

The relation of spiritual pioneers, men and women of religious genius, those whom we may loosely call mystics, to the institutional church is ambivalent. There is a sense that the institution quenches the spirit; there is an element of protest in all religious insight and a desire to break free of the tyranny of ecclesiastical systems, and storm the heights of holiness from which established churches and hierarchies pull one back. Karl Rahner has seen it as inevitable that there should be uneasiness and that the church should often recognize sanctity only in retrospect. George Fox * denounced all religious buildings as 'steeple-houses', and condemned the whole of church history as 'the Apostasy since the Apostles' days'. The Carmelites * suffered much from their co-religionists and were threatened at times by the Inquisition as well as ill-treated by those who had been their partners in reform. Dom David Knowles, the church historian and interpreter of mysticism *, severed himself in the end from the Downside community and wrote of obedience merely as a means which 'as soon as it leads from and not towards its end becomes preposterous'. 'In the last resort the mind can only obey Truth . . . St Benedict * presupposes the cadres of the monastic life beyond which the abbot cannot move. Beyond and above both is true, spiritual obedience, which can only be given to one more enlightened than myself.'

Nor does the pioneer necessarily flourish

in an atmosphere of lavishly decorated churches and elaborate ceremonial. External aids, like supernatural phenomena, locutions, levitations, miracles, ecstasies belong to the lower stages of spirituality, as does the whole religion of experience and of feelings.

Yet the spiritual leader, or loan venturer, whom in the end the multitudes follow, is nurtured by the institution and grows out of it. And very often the result of his work is to institutionalize further. 'By the end of his life, Fox had moulded his Society into a regularly and efficiently organized body, the further reformation of which was as abhorrent to him as his own Quakerism had been to the Puritans' (G. F. Nuttall). Methodism * brought freedom to many, lack of inhibition in worship and deliverance from the tyranny of evil habits, but it became a rigid centralized organization, and in the nineteenth century, there were appalling and inglorious schisms, in order to attempt to return to its 'primitive' evangelicalism and also to assert democratic rights.

The institution may confine if not crush, but without it there might be no spiritual life at all, and it is necessary to those forces which may overthrow it. Unrestrained enthusiasm may be divisive and destructive. It needs some structure of orthodoxy to contain it just as Caribbean Methodism, for instance, was saved from hysteria and excess by Wesley's hymns and the Prayer Book liturgy. The Charismatic Movement * may have been more beneficial to the Catholic than the Protestant Churches – it has enlivened the devotion while not being able to wreck forms of worship and church government so adamantine. 'The form,' wrote Charles Smyth in 1937, 'is valueless without the spirit' . . . but 'the spirit without the form may be equally . . . disastrous' . . . there is a good deal to think about in Mr Eliot's * classic paradox: 'the spirit killeth but the letter giveth life'.

And in the end even the religious genius needs a home. 'Lord, I am a daughter of the Church,' cried Teresa of Avila * with relief and joy when she had received the last sacraments; while spiritual leadership may be restrained from arrogance by learning with Augustine's friend not to be ashamed of 'the sacraments of the humility of God's word'.

———

V. A. Demant (ed), *Prospect for Christendom*, 1945; T. S. Eliot, *The Idea of a Christ-*ian *Society*, 1939; Ronald Knox, *Enthusiasm*, 1950; G. F. Nuttall, *The Holy Spirit in Puritan Faith and Experience*, 1946.

EDITOR

Eckhart, Meister

Meister Eckhart, Dominican mystic and prophet, was born in Hocheim near Erfurt, Germany, in 1260. He died in a place unknown in 1329 after a papal trial but before the actual condemnation of seventeen propositions ascribed to him. Scholars today agree he was unjustly condemned and the Dominican Order in 1980 formally requested Rome to lift all censures. He supported the lay women's movement of his day called the Beguines and told the peasants in their own vernacular that they were all 'aristocrats' because God had made them all so beautiful. He criticized the 'merchant mentality' of Cologne, the trade centre for Eastern and Western Europe in his day. With his condemnation his thought went underground where it influenced Luther via John Tauler *, the radical Protestant movements, John of the Cross *, Julian of Norwich *, Nicolas of Cusa * and George Fox *. Basically, however, his effort to develop a holistic spirituality that combined deep cosmic mysticism with prophetic consciousness was lost in mainstream Christianity. Instead, his influence has been more deeply felt outside Christianity: Karl Marx, Carl Jung, Martin Heidegger, Erich Fromm owe him a great debt and Dr Suzuki considers him the greatest Western Zen thinker.

Eckhart was the greatest spokesman of the creation-centred spiritual tradition *. Steeped in biblical thought of wisdom literature and the prophets, he wrote sermons like the Gospel writers wrote the Gospels – out of an unconscious immersion in creation-centred themes of blessing, cosmos, creation, compassion, beauty, healing, darkness, emptiness, creativity, celebration, justice, humour. He was strongly influenced by the Celtic tradition along the Rhine – as was his predecessor Francis of Assisi * – and by women mystics like Hildegarde of Bingen and especially Mechthild of Magdeburg from whom he derived an immense amount of his powerful imagery. A graduate of the University of Paris and a professor there and at Cologne, still his major conversion happened on ministering with Beguines in Strasbourg and in Cologne.

Eckhart's was a spirituality-in-the-world, a politically conscious spirituality which culminates in social justice – 'the person who understands what I say about justice understands everything I have to say' he declared. At the same time he understood profoundly that spiritual living concerns a psychological journey.

Eckhart rejected Neoplatonism's* three-fold path of purgation, illumination and union in favour of the following four-fold path:

1. Via Positiva: Creation. 'Isness is God', declared Eckhart – we are to take delight and joy in creation for creation gives 'joy and rapture' to God. Eckhart had a well-developed theology of pleasure and therefore of gratitude and praise. 'If the only prayer you say in your whole life is Thank You, that would suffice.' Every creature is a word of God. The word of God is a creative energy that is constantly making things new and beautiful. 'God is a great underground river that no one can damn up and no one can stop.' All things are continually 'in the process of beginning to be created'. The human person is the image of God and Christ came more to 'remind us' of this than to redeem us because true redemption is found in reminding us of our kinship to God and even to the Godhead.

2. Via Negativa: Letting Go and Letting Be. God is not only the God of Creation but also the 'not-God, not-person, not-thing, the denial of all names, the nameless no-thingness and superessential darkness'. How do we experience this God? By letting go and letting be (*Abgeschiedenheit* and *Gelassenheit*) and by sinking into God. 'We sink eternally from letting go to letting go into God.' There is no authentic via negativa without a true via positiva for Eckhart who had no patience with ascetic mortifications which, he said, reveal a great ego instead of child-like spontaneity. We let go of things not because things are bad – they are in fact divine – but because we want to cling to them. 'There, where clinging ends is where God begins to be.' We sink into our depths which are dark – 'the ground of the soul is dark' and befriend the darkness and even nothingness. Our nothingness is not psychological but metaphysical – nothingness is the origin of all things: Before I was I was nothing. Instead of mortification of passion he recommended 'a bridle of love' that will steer passions of anger and of desire in the direction we need to travel.

3. Via Creativa: Birthing. All creation and all creativity is 'ex nihilo' and from nothing. Our union with God is a fruitful union, not a contemplative gazing at but an act of mutual generation and birthing. Here is revealed our divinity – where we give birth. To touch our own creativity is to touch our divinity, for God is essentially a birther: 'What does God do all day long? God gives birth.' We need to develop our art and disciplines of extrovert meditation, i.e., centring by way of giving birth, for this is the prophetic spirituality. Trusting one's images is the key to empowering others in an adult spirituality: 'Whatever can be truly expressed in its proper meaning cannot come from outside to inside of a person, but must emerge from within.' We birth God and the Son of God when we birth. In birthing 'you will discover all blessing'. But 'neglect the birth and you neglect all blessing'.

4. Via Transformativa: Building the New Creation by way of Compassion and Social Justice. Creativity is not for its own sake but needs to be channelled towards a fuller goal – that which Jesus describes in Luke 6.36 as compassion. Compassion is first about a consciousness of interdependence, the end of subject/object dualisms. 'All things are interdependent', Eckhart stated simply. Furthermore, 'Relation is the essence of everything that exists.' Next, compassion is about acting out of this interdependence. One does this by acts of healing and especially of justice-making, since injustice is the basic rupture in the cosmos and in all human relationships. Justice is more than ethics: It touches our very being. 'For the just person as such, to act justly is to live; indeed, justice is his life, his being alive, his being.' Since truly creative work comes from our being, if our being is just our works will be. The third dimension to compassion is celebration. Compassion is our origins – 'whatever God does the first outburst is always compassion' – and since God is compassion, all creatures celebrate in the divine, cosmic, womb which is the fetal waters of compassion. Until God works compassion through us we do not yet have soul. We are not yet spiritually born.

In path 1 is Eckhart's theology of creation and incarnation. In path 2 is his theology of the cross. In path 3 is his theology of the resurrection. In path 4 is his theology of the Holy Spirit for the Spirit is 'the Spirit of Transformation'.

Four volumes of his Latin works and four of his German works are now available in critical editions. One more volume of each remains to be finished.

E. Benz, J. Koch et al (eds), *Meister Eckhart: Die lateinischen Werke*, I–IV, 1938–1975; J. Quint (ed), *Meister Eckhart: Die deutschen Werke*, I, II, III, V, 1958–1976; M. Fox, *Breakthrough: Meister Eckhart's Creation Spirituality in New Translation*, 1980; *Meditations with Meister Eckhart*, 1982; A. Mauer, *Master Eckhart: Parisian Questions and Prologues*, 1974; R. Schürmann, *Meister Eckhart: Mystic and Philosopher*, 1978.

MATTHEW FOX, OP

Ecstasy

A sense of being taken out of oneself, caught up, like Paul, into the third heaven, and united with some higher power. The word is often used to describe the raptures of sexual intercourse, which, as in Donne's* poem 'The Ecstasy', is not simply a 'transport of delight', but enables the lovers to penetrate the mystery of love itself. Such union is the climax of contemplation more than of physical or mental activity and provides an analogy of the type of mystical experience, which Plotinus* e.g. describes, though, unlike Donne, the Neoplatonist* finds ecstasy in deliverance from the body, rather than in psycho-somatic harmony. Ecstasy is not always of God or of joy. English literature knows of an ecstasy of terror and anxiety. Philo distinguishes four types, and the fourth is not mystical union but prophetic inspiration. The Divine Spirit 'evicts' the mind and the result is inspired frenzy. This is not a perpetual state, but transient, for a purpose. When the ecstasy passes, the prophet becomes a normal, rational being, with no supernatural knowledge.

Some Christian teachers, mystical and otherwise, are suspicious of ecstasy. Paul sets greater store by his 'thorn in the flesh' than by his mystical rapture (II Cor. 12), and warns the Corinthians against mistaking elation for grace. For Gregory of Nyssa, ecstasy is non-attainment rather than attainment. 'This truly is the vision of God;

never to be satisfied in the desire to see him' (*Life of Moses* 239).

Augustine* finds in ecstatic experience a fleeting glimpse on earth of the joys of heaven, but he also writes of ecstasy as that flash of the divine light and beauty, which arouses our longings and is, in fact, the beginning of the quest. Luther* knew of moments of an ecstasy in which 'through faith a man is raised above himself that he may behold good things in the future' (*WA* 4,237). For the Cambridge Platonists* contemplation is not the goal. Ecstasy inspires to action; it must have moral consequences. Henry More, using a much-employed metaphor, speaks of the soul 'inebriated as it were, with the delicious sense of the divine life', but this is a state, more sober than sobriety, which restores man to rationality and virtue. There is a Puritan 'devotion of rapture' found in the lyrical passages of many sermons and prayers and linking the seventeenth and eighteenth centuries. The age of reason was also the age of rapture. Joseph Butler can soar as high as the loftiest flights of contemplative devotion. Wesley*, like Addison, can be 'lost in wonder, love and praise', while for Doddridge, 'delight is not calm, it is rapture, transport, even ecstasy' (G. F. Nuttall).

Denys the Areopagite* is not afraid of erotic language to describe the ecstasy which he finds in Paul's words: 'I live, yet not I, but Christ lives in me.' But he also dares to speak of the ecstasy of God himself. It is no illegitimate extension of his thought to say that creation, providence, incarnation are all of the divine ecstasy, of God himself inspired, taken out of himself, made man so as never to be unmade more, united with us for ever by his own initiative of love, which antedates the worlds.

Anne Freemantle (ed), *The Protestant Mystics*, 1964; Marghanita Laski, *Ecstasy*, 1961; Andrew Louth, *The Origins of the Christian Mystical Tradition*, 1981; Gordon Rupp, 'A Devotion of Rapture in English Puritanism', in *Reformation, Conformity and Dissent*, ed R. Buick Knox, 1977; R. C. Zaehner, *Mysticism, Sacred and Profane*, 1957.

EDITOR

Ecumenical Spirituality

Ecumenical spirituality expresses the common life shared by Christians in spite of the separation of their churches. It is the recognition that in virtue of their baptism and commitment to Christ, Christians are brought into membership of the church. This common Christian life has to be manifested by the followers of Jesus if his gospel of reconciliation and unity is to have relevance and credibility for non-Christians. The rediscovery by many Christians of their obligation to live together in the spirit of the gospel has inspired the modern ecumenical movement. The very soul of that movement is spiritual ecumenism. As Christians meet and interact there develops an atmosphere of acceptance and friendship. They become aware of the need to eliminate words, judgments and actions which do not correspond with the truth and fairness demanded by the actual conditions of each other's belief and practice.

Ecumenical spirituality focuses on the life of prayer and worship, especially prayer for unity. The prayer of Jesus recorded in John 17 has become a very special prayer within the ecumenical movement. In it Jesus asks his Father to keep the disciples united 'that the world may believe'. The Week of Prayer for Christian Unity has become a feature of the movement among mainstream churches. Christians pray together for the unity Christ wills and by the means he chooses. In this way the prayer intention is more closely associated with the mind of Christ and the movement of the Holy Spirit.

Recognition must be given to the continuing activity of the Holy Spirit over long periods of separation among churches. Such recognition leads to a mutual evaluation and appreciation of particular spiritual gifts and practices found in various churches and Christian communities. Such traditions are acknowledged as gifts preserved or bestowed by the Spirit. As various Christian churches sought to reform and renew themselves in fidelity to the gospel, the Holy Spirit granted certain valid insights and spiritual gifts proper to authentic Christian life. Subject to spiritual discernment, such gifts and insights may well be intended for the future life of a visibly united church. Spiritual ecumenism respects the work of the Spirit uniting God's people in a diversity of gifts and ministries.

Ecumenical spirituality entails some sort of conversion or change of heart towards Christians of other churches. This takes the form of a commitment to pray and work for the renewal of one's own church or community in order to let essential elements of church life surface and prepare the way for Christian unity. It is a search through prayer to rediscover what is essential to faith and to what truly expresses Christian belief and life. Such a discovery ought to express a rich variety in Christian life that does not exclude a richer deeper visible unity of faith. The spiritual approach to ecumenism is more than simple piety. Its expression of unity in diversity exhibits the catholic mission of the church to the world (Matt. 28.19–20). It is the renewed search for an integral lived experience of being one with Christ as members of his body, the church.

Ecumenical spirituality is a spirituality of hope. Its dynamism and effectiveness is based on a joyful trust that the reconciling power of God is at work already in the heart of the world in Jesus Christ 'through whom we have now received our reconciliation' (Rom. 5.11). The unity of the church is prophetic of the unity of mankind in Christ. Jesus inaugurates the life that characterizes God's kingdom. In him the reign of God has begun in a definite way (Luke 17.21). Those united with him as his disciples and members of his church manifest the life of the kingdom. Such unity has to be more than institutional cohesion and loyalty. It has to demonstrate the power and effectiveness of Christ's reconciling love. Unity is for love. Jesus formulated this as his own commandment. His precept of charity is the sign of true discipleship (John 15.12, 17). In the short history of the ecumenical movement a particular form of this charity is Christian friendship; friendship has proved itself an indispensable element in the process of Christian unity. The hope engendered by the practice of reconciling love is universal in scope and reaches out to all men. What is said of mutual relationships, behaviour and attitudes among Christians must be extended with appropriate terms of reference to the Jewish community and to people of other faiths. Our roots are in the religion and faith of Israel. Our quest for communion with God makes us fellow seekers and pilgrims with those of other faiths.

Spiritual renewal is important for the development of ecumenical spirituality. Renewal is an honest willingness to examine one's own life and one's own church in order to discern Christ's will for both. It holds up to the mirror of the gospel personal and ecclesial life. Christian unity and Christian holiness enjoy a special relationship, for the latter releases the attractive power of Christ, converting the mediocre and speaking directly to the heart of mankind as the fulfilment of its truest and deepest aspirations. Common study of the Bible is a major influence in this area of Christian life. Scripture enables us to tap the roots of our shared faith and life in Christ. It provides a common idiom with which to share, express and communicate the one faith. In a special way it reflects the basic constituents of ecumenical spirituality. These are the notions of *covenant, reconciliation, unity in Christ, the unity and diversity created by the Spirit, renewal.*

Jesus took over the OT notion of covenant*. This was a solemn undertaking by divine initiative to establish a close relationship between God and his people. Their part of the agreement was to carry out God's will and purpose among the nations (Ex. 19, 24; Matt. 26.26–28; Mark 14,22–24; Heb. 9.15). Today churches often enter into closer working, living relationships at local, national, regional levels. These may be called covenants by analogy with this biblical notion. Under such covenants churches undertake together specific lines of action which they hope will lead to a deeper ecclesial relationship and ultimately to full communion according to the will of Christ for his church. Underlying the action a spiritual relationship of love and intercession is established between churches.

Reconciliation follows the covenant concept. While God is utterly faithful, his people break faith with him and among themselves. Covenants need to be renewed. God's people need to be reconciled if unity is to be of God and truly in Christ. Reconciliation is a basic notion of Christian life (Matt. 5.23–24) and much stressed in the Pauline corpus (II Cor. 5.16–21; Col. 1.20) God is the agent of reconciliation; Christ is the means. Because of God's action through Christ there is the possibility of persons, Jews and Gentiles, overcoming their state of estrangement and hostility (Eph. 2.14–16).

Unity in Christ is essential in understanding the church. In the New Testament this is expressed under various images, e.g. the vine and branches of John 15. It is more formally theologically expressed in the Pauline corpus with the recurring notion of 'being in Christ', having a new existence in him, a newness of life from him, e.g. Rom. 6; Gal. 3. The church is portrayed as the body of Christ with a splendid diversity of members which build up one another in mutual service. Through an exchange of gifts and ministries the manifold riches of Christ's grace for the life of the world find an outlet for witness and mission. The life of charity in the Christian community is perfected (I Cor. 12–13; I Peter 3.8; 4.8–10; Eph. 4.1–16).

The renewal factor springs from the promise of God and Jesus to do a new thing, to lead us towards the fullness of truth, and make all things new (Isa. 43.18–21; John 14.26–27; 16.13; I Peter 2.9–10; Rev. 2.7; 21.5). God heals the sinful condition imposed by our division and separation and simultaneously renews our mutual relationship in Christ (Gal. 6.15). Thus the church is able to be renewed in every age and circumstance by the power of God's Spirit introducing a new order of life to the church for its service to the world. It is an order of reconciliation and unity.

Consequently, the development of ecumenical spirituality, far from being esoteric or specialized, is an imperative for the whole church and manifests the most common and essential elements of our life in Christ (I Cor. 1.10–13).

Peter Brooks (ed), *Christian Spirituality*, 1975; Geoffrey Curtis, *Paul Couturier and Unity in Christ*, 1964; Matthew Fox (ed), *Western Spirituality: Historical Roots, Ecumenical Routes*, 1981; Michael Marx (ed), *Protestants and Catholics on the Spiritual Life*, 1965; Evelyn Underhill, *Worship*, 1936; Gordon Wakefield, *The Life of the Spirit in the World of Today*, 1969.

EMMANUEL SULLIVAN, SA

Edwards, Jonathan

Jonathan Edwards (1703–1758), Congregational pastor and one of America's greatest theologians, produced, among other things, a theology of Christian spirituality for his age that incorporated elements of a Lockean psychology with a theology that conformed to the Calvinism* of the Synod of Dort (1618–19). Throughout his pastoral career, but especially during the Great Awakening, Edwards was preoccupied with the central question of Puritan Protestants: how shall the presence of the Divine Spirit be discerned? Edwards not only asserted against the opponents of revivalism that true religion consisted in 'holy affectations', but he also provided, against those enthusiasts who had reduced religion to a false emotionalism, criteria for testing true religious affections. Although 'affections' included emotions, passions and the will, they were more essentially that which moved a person to accept the divine majesty. Love was the chief affection and the foundation of all other affections, internal as well as external.

Although Edwards admitted that there were no infallible signs that could publicly test the fruits of the Divine Spirit, nevertheless he discerned some signs that were helpful to the individual as guides in discovering the presence of saving grace. Spirituality was certainly an inward experience, but inexorably it became outward in practice and therefore was somewhat public and verifiable. In his *Religious Affections* (1746), Edwards described twelve signs he discovered in scripture and reason that could help the individual discern the presence of the Divine Spirit. Some signs pointed to the cause of affections, others to affections themselves and still others to their consequences. Affections are truly holy if, among other things, they are spiritual (i.e., born of the Spirit, who produces a new spiritual sense – a 'new foundation laid in the nature of the soul'); manifest a genuine love to God that has no other intention than the transcendently excellent nature of the divine glory; arise from enlightened minds that have a taste for and commitment to the divine beauty; are accompanied with a positive conviction of divine reality and with an evangelical humility; transform human nature by turning it from sin to holiness; beget meekness, quietness, forgiveness and mercy; produce fear and joy in symmetry and proportion; increase the spiritual appetite creating a longing of the soul after spiritual attainments; and persistently and perseveringly produce fruits of Christian practice in which behaviour in the world is conformed to and directed by the Christian vision of reality. Christian practice, of course, was not just the realization of faith, but an essential and inherent part of the inner religious experience of the Holy Spirit. Christian action, in fact, was the paramount sign, but not the cause, of true spirituality and activity in the world. The affections themselves were always signs of something more ultimate – God and the Spirit.

Prayer and fasting were indispensable signs of practical Christian living in this world. Edwards, therefore, encouraged prayer and fasting in secret, in small groups and in public worship as the chief and principal means of manifesting and renewing the holy affections. Prayer and fasting, ordered by Jesus Christ, received the assistance of the Holy Spirit, warmed the heart, increased devotions, revealed the glory of God and the weakness of man, renewed and strengthened the covenant of God, and besought the fullness of the Spirit in advancing Christ's kingdom in the world. For Edwards, the regeneration of the world, like the renewal of the Christian life, was the result of the new outpouring of God's Spirit.

S. E. Dwight (ed), *Works of President Edwards*, 10 vols, 1829–1830; P. Miller and J. E. Smith (eds), *Works of Jonathan Edwards*, 6 vols, 1957ff.; C. Cherry, *The Theology of Jonathan Edwards: A Reappraisal*, 1966; *Nature and Religious Imagination: From Edwards to Bushnell*, 1980; P. Miller, *Jonathan Edwards*, 1949.

PATRICK W. CAREY

Egypt

Egypt has had a powerful influence on the development of Christian spirituality and devotion, first through the formative Alexandrian tradition of theological thought in the early centuries, and then through the monastic and eremitical traditions of the Desert Fathers* and their successors. The main Christian tradition of Egypt is expressed in the Coptic Church, which is 'Monophysite' in christology and belongs to the Oriental Orthodox communion (*see* **Coptic Spirituality**). Other traditions of spirituality in contemporary Egypt are represented by the Catholic Church (both Eastern Uniate and Latin) and the Greek Orthodox Patriarchate of Alexandria and, of more recent origin, small communities of Anglicans and Protestants. All, however, exist within a predominantly Moslem culture, though there are some parts of the country where Coptic Christians are a very significant section of the population.

GEOFFREY ROWELL

Eliot, T. S.

Thomas Stearns Eliot (1888–1965) was born in St Louis, Missouri and educated at Harvard, the Sorbonne and Oxford. His spiritual explorations were conducted intensively in criticism, editing and in poetry and drama; in 1922 he founded *The Criterion*, in which some of his weightiest literary/theological essays were published, and in which *The Waste Land* first appeared. In 1927 he became an Anglican and also took British citizenship.

There is a special value in a spirituality, hard-won, which has faced desolation. *The Waste Land* is its completest expression, beginning with a landscape of desolation and reaching a conclusion with an ending to an Upanishad equivalent to 'the peace that passeth understanding'. This epic journey into a strenuous spirituality remarkably echoes Ezra Pound's description of the aim of his *Cantos* 'to write an epic which begins "In the Dark Forest", crosses the Purgatory of human error, and ends in light'. This goal was not to be reached by Eliot until *Ash Wednesday*, published in 1930, and he had meanwhile to explore 'death's other kingdom' in *The Hollow Men*. The scarecrow/guys ('shape without form, shade without colour') are those who attempt to pray but 'form prayers to broken stone', while their stumbling utterance of the doxology to the Lord's Prayer leads only to anticlimax and despair. After this it is significant that the Christian resolution of *Ash Wednesday*, Eliot's plunge into faith, should be expressed in muted forms and tones out of the tension of this mortal life.

Murder in the Cathedral (1935), a celebration of martyrdom, comes to a more complete resolution. Becket's cry to his monks as he faces his killers, 'I am not in any danger, only near to death,' carries the spiritual paradox of the crucifixion and the martyrdom of St Stephen. In *Family Reunion* (1939), an overtly 'secular' play, a similar pilgrimage towards martyrdom, expresses the Christian transcendence of suffering but in the tones and allusions of Greek tragedy.

But the fine fruit of Eliot's spiritual search is found in *Four Quartets* (1944); here three preoccupations recur from his earlier work:

the sacramental significance of time and place (the four poems centre upon three places in England and Cape Ann in Massachusetts); the relation of the word incarnate to human articulacy; and the life-long quest for holiness. It was natural for a poet and critic to be concerned with precision of speech – the satirical *Sweeney Agonistes* had said wryly, 'I gotta use words when I talk to you' – and through each of the *Quartets* is 'a raid on the inarticulate', a protest against 'imprecision of meaning', the ultimate spiritual insight is the knowledge that words can penetrate the silence of a universe which may seem empty and void. And 'Little Gidding' is the summit, reached in that silence, a place where the seeker can become 'renewed, transfigured in another pattern'. For the house and chapel at Little Gidding, the community which Nicholas Ferrar * established, was not only a place of meditation, where George Herbert * was able to gather himself; it was also a sanctuary, a turning point in history, where the fugitive King Charles found a moment's rest. In this poem, Eliot's search, the dereliction, the vision of glory, the poetic imagery, are all resolved.

Complete Poems and Plays, 1969.

MOELWYN MERCHANT

English Mystics, The

The title is given to a remarkable group of fourteenth century writers: Richard Rolle *, the anonymous author of *The Cloud of Unknowing *, Walter Hilton and Julian of Norwich *, with whom one or two others are associated, notably Margery Kempe, who was born in 1373 and lived on into the 1430s. It may be said without fear of disclaimer that their influence has never been greater than in the twentieth century and that they speak very much to the condition of those in our world, uncloistered, who seek the way of contemplative prayer. This may be because there are parallels between their time and ours, though to draw them too closely results in slipshod and superficial historiography. But the fourteenth century was an age of great technological achievement, accompanied by a flight from metaphysics and much insecurity due to plague, social discontent, disorder, poverty and war. It was also in contrast the period when national self-consciousness was rising, the great decades of Middle English were at hand, and Gothic cathedrals soared. But the English mystics represent personal religion, not without benefit of clergy, or disloyal to holy church, yet not hidebound by unimaginative and rigorous schemes, open to God's love and willing to let our loving desires have free course as they seek to penetrate the clouds which surround the Divine Being. Two of them are women, Julian, the anchoress, never moving from her cell, a theologian if not of the schools; Margery, mother of fourteen, always wandering about the world, even going to Rome and Jerusalem, and with many of the symptoms of hysteria, so that she aroused much suspicion. So attractive are they in style, and so manifest is the reward they have received, that it is tempting to think that their way is open to all and to forget the asceticism which undergirds it. Their dark night is not the fashionable doubt and wandering mind of the worldly intellectual and their revelations are not the nice feelings which result from a study of mystical eloquence or the beauty of their most elevated passages.

They were contemplatives, which may be a better way of describing them than to call them 'mystics', though probably both terms are equally bedevilled and confusing. But like the Victorines*, their word for mysticism was contemplation*, which refers to a state of love for God and knowledge of him utterly different from anything previously experienced, profounder than what may be achieved by the processes of rational thought, and ultimately incommunicable. Though it may crown a life of disciplined prayer, not without suffering, it is never 'something attempted, something won'. It is entirely the gift of God. The English mystics would agree with John of the Cross*, (whom the author of The Cloud in many ways anticipates), when he says 'Pure contemplation consists in receiving'. In the end, prayer is made 'in' us rather than 'by' us.

There were three sources of their life and teaching, though Hilton was the only one who could claim academic stature, and their theology for the most part was in the air they breathed and the ideas they inhaled from the spirituality around them and the writings they sometimes read, or more often heard. But they owed much to Augustinianism as formalized by the Victorines for whom contemplation was 'a half-intellectual, half-devotional, grace-enlightened penetration of Christian truth, the normal if somewhat uncommon result of long ascetic and mental preparation. Beyond this was the fully mystical, transient, ascetic experience' (David Knowles). This was very evident in Hilton. There was, secondly, the influence of Denys the Areopagite* and Neoplatonism*, mediated by German Dominicans. This meant the via negativa and a journey through darkness rather than light. This is obviously the principal influence on The Cloud. Basic to all this is, in the third place, the long tradition of disciplined prayer, first made articulate in the teaching of the Desert Fathers*.

The passion of Christ is the focus of the English mystics' devotion, as was inevitable in an age when pieta were everywhere, and the Mass overshadowed worship. Julian wished to share the sufferings of Christ except for death, and her 'showings' are of his torn and bleeding body. In Jerusalem, Margery Kempe, who knew Julian and had been guided by her, was in a paroxysm of grief and lamentation, as she went in pilgrimage along the way of the cross. Then began her manner of shouting, which, uncontrollable, embarrassed her and enfeebled her body and alarmed onlookers for many years. 'And sometimes, when she saw a crucifix, or if she saw a man, or it might be an animal, wounded, or if a man beat a child in front of her or struck a horse or another animal with a whip, if she saw or heard this it seemed to her that she saw our Lord beaten or wounded as were the men or the animals whom she could see.' For Hilton, devotion to the passion is the door to contemplation, and anyone who does not enter by it, but seeks some other way than by knowing the bitterness Christ knew and the compassion he showed in his humanity, is but a thief and a robber. Such sentiments from what is almost certainly Hilton's translation with his glosses of Stimulus Amoris the work of James, a Milan friar, are somewhat deprecated in The Cloud, where meditations on the passion are included among the distractions to be given up if the soul is to be emptied for contemplation. The author has to correct this by admitting that such meditation is an essential preliminary, but this would seem to be more of a concession to conventional counsels than a matter of conviction. Thought about the passion of Christ with all other activities of the mind must pass under the cloud of oblivion if the cloud of unknowing is ever to be pierced.

It is here that many will demur. Clarendon, in the seventeenth century, so loyal a member of the English church, was aware of other mystics if not the English, and, as vehemently as any Calvinist, deplored the fact that vigorous spirits might be 'mortified and moped by the absurd documents of contemplation before they have anything to contemplate on'. This would make them incapable of being revived 'out of that dull and lazy lethargy, to be applied to any magnanimous activity'. It cannot be too strongly stated in reply that *The Cloud* is not written for bookshop browsers. It is dealing with an advanced stage of a particular vocation of prayer. But perhaps contemplative 'emptiness' is not so far removed from the evangelical 'Nothing in my hand I bring/Simply to thy cross I cling'.

Yet apparently one must not cling forever to the cross. Here is a further difficulty. Is it not a misunderstanding of the gospel to presume that we are to advance beyond the sacred humanity and the passion, that there is a realm of beatitude where Christ and his cross are to be viewed simply as the ladder by which we have ascended so far, but shall not need again? This is disturbing. Yet it could mean that we are not forever to be obsessed by the physical horrors and sufferings of Christ which so grieved poor demented Margery. 'Do not cling to me for I am not yet ascended to my Father. But go to my brethen and say to them that I ascend . . .' So Jesus to the distraught Magdalene, a Margery in her day. We follow Christ to his glory and, as with Julian, there is a transition from the 'bodily sight' to the understanding and thence to inexpressible contemplation. But Julian is the least 'contemplative' of the mystics, thoroughly christocentric and superbly trinitarian. We cannot be quite so positive about *The Cloud*; yet it is suffused with the Johannine belief that God is love.

In spite of the preoccupation with the sufferings of Jesus in four of the English mystics, they are redolent of what has been called the 'optimism of grace'. This, of course, was the other side to the dolours of Western mediaeval Christianity. It was an age of troubadours as well as of elegant wit, to say nothing of rough humour. Margery Kempe could be rumbustuously cheerful amid her tears; there is an earthy, public-house humour about her, which appeals to many. Rolle may be too absorbed in the raptures attendant on the physical phenomena and on visions of angels, in language not unlike that of the hymn of Frances Jane Van Alstyne (1820–1915), an American Methodist, 'Blessed Assurance'. Walter Hilton says rather that 'this song of the angels is not the soul's greatest joy' but a secondary delight. The soul's true joy is in the love of God himself.

Eric Colledge (ed), *The Mediaeval Myths of England*, 1962; David Knowles, *The English Mystical Tradition*, 1961. Also see bibliographies to individual entries

EDITOR

English Spirituality

Geography – and topography – are important factors. 'The offshore island' – or that part of it which is England – has been much affected by the world beyond yet has made what it has received peculiarly its own – e.g. the Bible of 1611, the Book of Common Prayer. It may also be significant that some of the fourteenth-century mystics lived in the rather flat terrain of the East Midlands or East Anglia (*see* **English Mystics**), Puritans similarly in East Anglia, or in the concealing Chilterns where conventicles could survive. 'As sure as God is in Gloucestershire' referred to the vast number of splendid churches in which reposed the sacrament, evidence perhaps more of human wealth than divine glory. Wesleyan Methodism flourished in London, Newcastle, Bristol and Cornwall, Primitive Methodism along the Trent. Economic, physical and human geography are here all bound up. A modern, though highly-personal, illustration is found in W. H. Auden's 'In Praise of Limestone' and 'Amor Loci', both celebrating limestone landscape and deriving an awareness of God from its very solitude and desolation.

In his fine study of *English Spirituality* (1963), Martin Thornton has discerned a 'submerged continuity', in spite of periods of disintegration, from the fourteenth century and earlier to William Temple*, but his scheme is too tidy and really covers a certain type of Anglican spirituality, not the whole of the English interpretation of the Christian life. We may single out seven characteristics of this.

1. *Devotion to the Passion of Christ.* 'Rood' is a word from Anglo-Saxon, the so-called *The Dream of the Rood* (*c.* eighth century) being the oldest English Christian poem. Christ is depicted as the young warrior, who mounts the cross to suffer in triumph. By the twelfth century, there had taken place what J. A. W. Bennett called 'one of the greatest revolutions of feeling that Europe has ever witnessed' and devotion was concentrated on the agonized Saviour, the unexampled afflictions of the Crucified, his head bowed with grief, his wounds bleeding, his arms outstretched in dying love. This is evidenced throughout the Middle Ages, notably in Julian of Norwich *, and continues through the seventeenth-century to the Evangelical Revival. Isaac Watts' * communion hymn, 'When I survey the wondrous Cross' is its epitome. The communion service of the 1552/1662 Prayer Book, though it is free of any visual preoccupations, is concentrated on the atoning sacrifice. There is another, more rationalist tradition represented by Thomas Browne *, John Milton, the Cambridge Platonists * and on into the eighteenth-century, while the Oxford Movement * led much more to a spirituality of the Risen Glory and, later, of the incarnation.

2. *Tenderness, affective, or 'affectionate' piety.* Some Calvinist theologians from the low countries have castigated the Puritans as 'the English mystics' and deprecated their spirituality as 'the cultivation of a soft-life of feeling' in contrast to Calvinist rigour. Richard Baxter * wrote of George Herbert's * 'heart-work'. In Bunyan's * words, 'the water' often stood in the Englishman's eyes, until the public school tradition contemned it. In the Middle Ages 'tears were accounted a grace rather than a disgrace' (J. A. W. Bennett). Later Donne * would weep before the cross, and Andrewes' * *Preces Privatae* were 'slubbered all over with his pious hands and watered with his penitential tears'.

3. *Homeliness.* From the sixteenth century family religion was central, 'breathing household laws' (Wordsworth). Bunyan's pilgrims visit houses not churches or cathedrals. English spirituality is neither baroque not decorated; nor is it confined to schools or clergy, or the 'establishment'. It owes as much to Margery Kempe, the uncouth and 'full homely' woman of Lynn, to Bunyan, the mechanic, who makes the mystic flame into a rickyard bonfire, to the Quakers *, and to the Methodist travelling preachers, some of whom, in another tradition, would be called contemplatives.

4. *A sacramental sense.* The English were reproached by Bede * for being infrequent at the altar and, until the Oxford and even more the Liturgical Movement, many members of the English church confined themselves to three or four times a year, while the Puritan and Methodist traditions, which in origin had sought greater regularity, were frightened into the supremacy of the Word by some lay reluctance and the Romeward tendencies of Anglo-Catholicism. But the Real Presence has often been discovered in the world around, 'the traffic of Jacob's ladder pitched between heaven and Charing Cross' (Francis Thompson, d. 1907), while Baxter believed that we might learn 'to have a fuller taste of Christ and heaven in every bit of bread that we eat and every draught of beer that we drink than most men have in the use of the Sacrament'.

5. *Intellectual integrity and ethical concern.* 'Jesus confirm my heart's desire/to work and speak and *think* for thee' (Charles Wesley *). Julian showed ability to question her revelations, to distinguish between fantasy and truth even when she was ill, and to spend the rest of her life in seeking to understand what her experiences should mean. There is a philosophic streak from Anselm * to the Cambridge Platonists and the Hanoverian and Victorian moralists. Joseph Butler (1692–1752) and William Wilberforce (1759–1833) are notable instances, the moral theologian and the philanthropist, who wrote a famous treatise on a practical view of the contrast between formal religion and real Christianity.

6. *Scriptural roots.* Cranmer's revision of the offices makes them services of the Word, and daily hearing and reading of the Bible has been the Protestant ideal. Reverence for scripture, for which lives were laid down, has not been incompatible with a sober biblical scholarship, which has availed itself of critical methods in the belief that honest exegesis should not undermine faith. Fundamentalism is an American, revivalist

importation, not genuinely in the English tradition.

7. *An 'optimism of grace'*, never better expressed than in Julian's words 'And all shall be well, and all shall be well and all manner of thing shall be well.' This is repeated in many forms, in the Cambridge Platonists, in the gentle, austere Anglicanism of the Victorian Dean R. W. Church, in the whole of Methodist spirituality* with its lyricism and social concern, and in the immense influence of the poet Robert Browning (1809–1889) which continued until the second war.

The first war did much to destroy the complacent spirituality of Imperialism, though it is still sometimes apparent. It revived devotion to the passion as in G. A. Studdert-Kennedy's rhymes railing at the notion of the divine impassibility. Calvary was seen again in the sufferings and horrors of the front, as indeed in atrocities since. David Jones, son of a Welsh father and Kentish mother, whose prose poems *In Parenthesis* and *Anathemata* are kaleidoscopes of the whole of Western culture in the light of the creed and the Mass, returns to the theme of Christ the soldier rather than the helpless victim, and war is seen as a macabre liturgy.

In the new English society, races and religions mingle as never before and Christianity has not its ancient power. There is now no common translation of the Bible and new liturgies and hymns are replacing the old. The Charismatic Movement* and a powerful biblical fundamentalism as well as a new stress on personal experience mean that the traditions are less understood or prized. Yet Julian is a best seller in some circles and 'Rock of Ages' (A. M. Toplady, 1740–1778) is a favourite hymn among Christians of mixed races in the 'inner city'.

J. A. W. Bennett, *Poetry of the Passion,* 1982; Gordon Huelin, *The Cross in English Life and Devotion*, 1972; David Newsome, *Two Classes of Men*, 1974; E. G. Rupp, *Six Makers of English Religion*, 1957; C. J. Stranks, *Anglican Spirituality*, 1961; G. S. Wakefield, *Puritan Devotion*, 1957.

                                        EDITOR

Enthusiasm

The derivation of the word (nowhere found in NT Greek) is from relatively late classical Greek *entheos* and the corresponding verb *entheazein* – to be God-possessed – to be caught up in a psychic excitement transcending the limits to the rational. Enthusiasm as a quickening and release of emotions is a usual accompaniment of lively faith. In the history of religion the phenomenon of the uncontrolled flow of emotional energy is commonplace. Christian spirituality from NT times has always been concerned with the need to discern the object of emotional fervency and to place controls on this drive when it threatens the balance of the person or the group.

Enthusiasm is also the term used specifically in spirituality for a perennial tendency (usually though not always ending in a sect) to claim additional revelation of an ecstatic nature. Early examples are the Book of Revelation, the Shepherd of Hermas, and surprisingly, Ignatius of Antioch (Ephesians 20, Philadelphians 7).

In the second century of the Christian era Montanism presented the great church with a challenge to its institutions and rational theology by its appeal to high moral separation from the world and reliance on the word of prophecy. As a result of the prolonged struggle which ensued, there began a long period of discouragement of hyper-emotional states by the Christian church which lasts until this day. Enthusiasts, in this specific sense, were usually preoccupied either with detailed visionary schemes of the end of the world (Joachim of Fiore*, twelfth century) or with vision of judgments on social injustices (Thomas Münzer, d. 1525) or with an insistence on separation from Christians who did not accept contemporary revelation (Joseph Smith and the Latter Day Saints).

New forms of enthusiastic indigenous Christianity are proliferating in Africa at a rate which causes problems to the old missionary churches, and an excessive attention to religious experience of the paranormal in some charismatic movements has given rise to similar anxiety in the main-line churches of Europe and America. Once again the phenomenon of enthusiasm in both its general and specific sense is becoming, as it was in the second century, a central concern of twentieth-century Christianity.

Spirituality in the Bible, in the writings of the Fathers, and the great tradition of the mystics has consistently maintained the need for the union of mind and heart, reflection and experience, spirit and truth. There is, therefore, a strict correlation between objective faith and subjective 'heart-work'. The latter gives rise to a warm, usually strongly felt emotion of adhesion and attachment which has reasons the mind knows nothing of. God in himself as revealed in the person of Christ is the centre and focus of all such attachment and fervency. The source of the fervency is the Holy Spirit of God. Especially by such folly of love in Christ he leads us to love God with all our heart as well as with all our mind. When such fervency and heart-felt devotion engages another object, e.g. a point of doctrine, a particular church, or the following of a religious leader, or a particular vision they are in danger of becoming obsessive to the point of irrational idolatry and cease to have the marks of the Holy Spirit. This state of affairs belongs to the realm of religious pathology, and it is usually accompanied by an arrogance, and a self-opinionated attitude wholly insubordinate to the Body, and causing divisions within it. The sad history of Enthusiasts illustrates both the dangers of unchecked fervency not centred on the revelation of Jesus Christ, and also the inadequacy of merely institutional or rational authority, or repression to deal with it. The faith is endangered when Christians have to choose between this uncontrolled fervency and dessicated, authoritative, uninspired orthodoxies of Protestantism or Catholicism.

The Spirit of God is the Spirit of love and community, the Spirit of reflection and control. Apart from the Spirit of God religious enthusiasm is merely an operation of fleshly man's religious capacities leading to the cancer of apparent liveliness and growth, independent of and finally destructive of the Body. This can lead ultimately to such catastrophies of despair as the Jones mass suicide in Guyana. In most Christian churches affected by the charismatic movement * there has developed in the last decade or so an awareness of the need to discern the spirits whether they be of God – at the local group level, or at the level of parish and diocese, and in some churches by the issuing of directives of encouragement and caution for the whole of Christians in their care.

A growing number of Christians are finding help from the unbroken monastic tradition of Eastern Orthodoxy which has been at pains to spell out the difference between natural and supernatural enthusiasm. In this tradition, undisciplined enthusiasm arises more from psychic and disturbed emotional sources than from single-minded devotion to love of God and our neighbours. The more enthusiasm has religion as its object the more the insidious danger of the passions of fallen man asserting themselves. These passions hate repentance and self-knowledge; they foment consciousness and the dismissal of views and people not in agreement with ourselves, ending in anger, pride, and often in sitting loose to the truth. The only fires that can be trusted are those of love of God and our fellow men, and the cleansing fire of repentance. These alone are the fires of the Holy Spirit. For this tradition martyrdom is the ultimate limit of the true spiritual enthusiasm of self-giving love.

Ignatius Branchaninov, *Arena*, 1970; R. A. Knox, *Enthusiasm*, 1951; G. R. Stratton, *The Psychology of Religious Life*, 1911; Leon-Joseph Suenens, *Ecumenism and Charismatic Renewal*, 1971.

ROLAND WALLS

Ephrem Syrus

Born in or near Nisibis, *c.* 306, died 9 June 373 at Edessa (SE Turkey), St Ephrem is best known as a religious poet of outstanding originality. His writings (all in Syriac) consist of some biblical commentaries and polemic treatises against heresies in prose, a few works in artistic prose, and, above all, a series of extended hymn cycles (over 400 hymns in all). Many of the works in Greek and Latin attributed to Ephrem are not by him.

Ephrem is the most important representative of Syriac Christianity in its most semitic form (*see* **Syrian Spirituality**), his whole approach being barely touched by Greek thought patterns and philosophical presuppositions; yet at the same time, even though his language and the structure of his thought are so very far removed from those of his Cappadocian contemporaries, at a profound level Ephrem's theological insights are remarkably similar to theirs, albeit expressed entirely differently.

Ephrem's soteriology can most succinctly be expressed by means of the clothing imagery which abounds in his poetry. At the

Fall Adam and Eve lost the 'robe of glory/ praise' with which they had originally been clothed; to remedy this situation God the Word 'put on the body of Adam/humanity', at his baptism depositing in the Jordan the 'robe of glory' for humanity to put on again, in Christian baptism. Baptism is thus the potential re-entry into paradise; the eschatological paradise, however, is to prove far more glorious than the primordial, since Adam/humanity will there attain to divinity. For Ephrem the aim of the Christian life is accordingly to realize in this life the baptismal gift of the 'robe of glory', thus anticipating the resurrection life of the eschatological paradise. Such a life will have as its prime characteristic an attitude of praise and wonder, and out of this response to the paradoxical consequences of divine love all human action should stem.

It was divine love which led God to bridge the ontological gap between Creator and created by revealing himself, not only at one focal moment in time, the incarnation, but also continuously through his 'two witnesses', scripture and nature. Each of these is infused with 'symbols' (*lit.* 'mysteries') and types, linking this world with the heavenly, the OT with the NT, and the NT with the sacramental life of the church. By becoming aware of these symbols the eye of faith is enabled to make connections between the innumerable places in which God has in some way revealed himself and his ultimate hiddenness and unknowability. These 'symbols', far from being empty, actually contain within themselves some measure of the higher reality to which they point; the value of the material world, thus infused with them, is consequently greatly enhanced.

True perception of the created world and its inherent significance has been lost through misuse of free will; the means, whereby this perception can be regained, are provided by the incarnation, and the model of the restored relationship between creation and Creator is continuously present in the eucharist. For Ephrem the Christian life is to be lived out in accordance with this vision of the material world transfigured.

S. P. Brock, *The Harp of the Spirit: Eighteen Poems of St Ephrem*, 1983; R. Murray, *Symbols of Church and Kingdom*, 1975.

SEBASTIAN BROCK

Eriugena, John Scotus
see Celtic Spirituality

Eschatology

Modern theology has rediscovered the eschatological dimension of the gospel and the faith. Complaints that a vogue word has been overstretched may stem from a failure to notice the full range of the substantial question. Although the term eschatology is only a nineteenth-century coinage, earlier Western theology had included a tractate on 'the last things', understood as death and judgment, heaven and hell. Twentieth-century scholarship has underlined the centrality of the kingdom of God in the preaching and ministry of Jesus, and eschatological has become a convenient adjective corresponding to that decisive and definitive reality of God's rule and realm whose effects are not limited to the end in a merely chronological sense.

Exegetes differ about the extent and mode of the realization of God's kingdom according to the perception of Jesus and the perhaps varied understandings current in the church after Easter and Pentecost. Schweitzer saw in Jesus an apocalyptist whose hopes for the imminent irruption of God's kingdom from beyond were dashed, and all Schweitzer could salvage from this 'consistent eschatology' was a 'reverence for life'. Dodd stressed the arrival of the kingdom during the ministry of Jesus, and his own interpretative framework was a platonic eternism, though 'realized eschatology' could also lead to the presentist existentialism of Bultmann's 'In every moment slumbers the possibility of being the eschatological moment: you must awaken it.' Fuller considered the kingdom to have arrived with the cross and resurrection of Christ; this may allow ecclesiological interests to equate the kingdom with the historic church. In their various ways, Cullmann, Kümmel and Jeremias opted for an 'inaugurated eschatology' whereby Jesus had fulfilled the earlier promises of salvation but their final consummation still tarried. The most traditional view, which is not without exegetical support, is in fact that the end is present only by an anticipation granted in the Spirit of the risen Lord, and that the final parousia of Christ for the consummation of God's kingdom may still be expected according to the promise of Jesus and the hope of the apostolic church. What does this mean now?

Corresponding to the hermeneutical question of the interpretation of eschatological sayings is the practical problem of accommodating an eschatological lifestyle to the fact that the old world is a long time in passing. In the earliest centuries of Christianity, recurrent persecution kept alive the hope of an imminent parousia; but with the peace of the church the question of a new world became chronic. With the conversion of the Empire came civic responsibilities for the church, bringing both the opportunities and the dangers of a more established relationship with a world under the threat of judgment and the offer of salvation.

The gifts and demands of God's kingdom have always been radical in respect of both praying and living. The Lord teaches his disciples to pray 'Thy will be done on earth as it is in heaven', and the apostle enjoins believers to 'do everything, in word and deed, in the name of the Lord Jesus, giving thanks to God the Father through him' (Col. 3.17) and to 'pray without ceasing, giving thanks in all circumstances' (I Thess. 5.17f.; cf. Luke 18.1). The Lord's injunction to be perfect (Matt. 5.48) is recognized by the apostle as his goal, for which others also are to strive (Phil. 3.12–21). How is this life in constant communion with God to be achieved?

Is the eschatological tension to be marked by compromise or by sacrament? Some, like the hermits, the 'sleepless ones' and the pillar-saints, refused all compromise; but it has more generally been held that the prayerful lifting of holy hands calls for sustained shoulder-rubbing and elbow-jostling with the neighbour; there is 'no holiness but social holiness' (Wesley). Others have rationalized a compromise by distinguishing between evangelical precepts, which are incumbent on all, and counsels of perfection, which are for the chosen few; but such an implied division into classes of Christians is unacceptably gnostic, even if it is mitigated by talk of stages on the way. Better is a sacramental perspective in which the part, from the beginning, stands and calls for the whole. Even the monastic round of prayer and work is only a provisional representation of a finally uninterrupted fusion of

orare and *laborare*. As a seal unto the day of redemption (Eph. 4.30), baptism sets the pattern for a daily dying to sin and a continued walking in newness of life, which will be consummated in a final resurrection to eternal life (Rom. 6). Eucharistic food is the viaticum of a pilgrim people, a foretaste of the heavenly banquet. The tangible reality of the sacraments makes clear that what is now done 'in the body' is definitive of us in eternity (cf. II Cor. 5.10). From time to time a martyrdom, in which rite, reality and reward are wonderfully concentrated, comes to assure us that the sacramental game is a serious one: baptism in water is consummated by baptism in blood, and the good confessor and faithful servant is at once taken from the eucharist into the feast of the master's joy.

Although Christians must heed the Marxist critique against a hope of heaven which would divert attention from earthly injustice, yet they would be cheating the poor yet again if they failed to proclaim a kingdom beyond death, in which every tear will be wiped dry and people from every time and place will share together in the joyful feast. In the sense that every man is his own Adam, death and the end of one's world coincide. But in the sense that the human race has a history and is part of a universal process, the social and cosmic dimensions of eschatology are inescapable. The Christian answer lies in the communion of the saints which embraces time and space. But even the saints in heaven are waiting and, it is traditionally believed, assisting us with their prayers (cf. Luke 23.43; Phil. 1.23; Rev. 6.9–11): the salvation of none is complete until all are saved; none is perfect until all are perfect. The kingdom of God will (have) come only when each and all of its beneficiaries have been irreversibly transformed into the moral and spiritual likeness of God. The whole creation shares in our groaning until we have received the redemption of our bodies (cf. Rom. 8.18–25).

The sacraments, the martyrs and the saints alike point us to the combination of activity and passivity which avoids either the heaven-storming pursuit of the millennium or the quietistic waiting for Godot. The key eschatological attitudes are vigilance and hope, the key processes judgment and renewal. It is time for us 'to wake from sleep, for salvation is nearer to us than when we first believed' (Rom. 13.11). To 'cast off the works of darkness and put on the armour of light' (13.12) is a polemical way of describing that 'repatterning' whereby even in this age we may be so renewed in mind as to prove (know and do!) what is the good and acceptable and perfect will of God, presenting our bodies to God as a living sacrifice, which is our spiritual worship (Rom. 12.1f.). By the power of the Holy Spirit, the God of hope enables us to abound in hope (Rom. 15.13). Our heart is set on heavenly treasure (Matt. 6.19–21, 24–34) yet not so as to despise the earthen vessels (II Cor. 4.7). The relative liberty of Christians towards earthly existence (the 'as if not' of I Cor. 7) derives from the fact that the world is qualified by the threat of judgment and the offer of salvation in the new creation of God's kingdom.

R. E. Brown, *New Testament Essays*, 1968, ch 12; E. Jüngel, *Death*, 1975; H. Küng, *Ewiges Leben?*, 1982; B. McGinn (ed), *Apocalyptic Spirituality*, 1979; H. R. Niebuhr, *Christ and Culture*, 1951; W. Pannenberg, *Theology and the Kingdom of God*, 1969; G. Rowell, *The Liturgy of Christian Burial*, 1977; G. Wainwright, *Eucharist and Eschatology*, [2] 1981.

GEOFFREY WAINWRIGHT

Eucharist

The spirituality of the Catholic and Orthodox Churches is dominated by the eucharist, though in very different forms. The Orthodox emphasis is much more on the assembled people being brought within sight and sound of the heavenly altar, while in the West sacramental devotion is more personal, though the liturgical movement has sought to recover the primitive aspect of the fellowship meal. For a certain type of devout Roman Catholic the eucharist has been the supreme opportunity of contemplation*, whether in the movement of the post-Tridentine Mass with its secrets and its silence and its vertical dimension, the prayers of the people lifted up to heaven through the consecrating priest, his back towards them that he may not only present their offering, but be the means whereby Christ descends; or in private devotions before the reserved sacrament when, as the Breton peasant said, 'I look at him; he looks at me.'

In the Protestant churches, it would not be true to say with an Anglo-Catholic priest 'Christianity *is* the Blessed Sacrament.' But in spite of the eucharist being the sign of priestly power, the badge of clericalism, and of the need of wider pledges of loyalty, the Reformers did not repudiate it. Calvin and some of the English separatists wanted holy communion every Lord's Day, and where, as in the Church of Scotland, communion seasons were twice-yearly, there was an intensive preparation and most solemn observance. The Methodist was a sacramental revival and Wesley believed that the Lord's Supper was a 'converting' as well as a 'confirming ordinance'. The disciples were hardly converted when they first received it in the upper room, and Article XXV asserts that the Sacraments are for the 'quickening' as well as 'strengthening' of faith.

The eucharist has a 'drawing loveliness', an allure, which has produced volumes of devotion, some written on paper and others in the lives and prayers of humble Christians. It has provided a rich store of meditation, a harvest field of inexhaustible gleanings and a mead of poetry. It has been loved for its own sake and for him who gave it, to whom it is believed to unite the adoring believer. 'These mysteries do as nails fasten us to this very Cross, that by them we draw out as touching efficacy, force and virtue, even the blood of his gored side ... why should any cogitation possess the mind of a faithful communicant but this, *O my God thou art true, O my soul thou art happy*' (Richard Hooker).

Remembrance and thanksgiving are the essentials of eucharistic spirituality. John Donne*, citing Plato who placed all learning in the memory, places all religion in the memory too; while E. M. Forster remarked that the title of Proust's masterpiece was not 'Things Past' but '*Remembrance* of Things Past'. So the eucharist is constant 'recall' and reconsideration of what Christians believe are the saving events of the crucifixion and resurrection of Christ. And this prompts praise. The remembrance of Christ before God is itself an anaphora, a sacrifice of thanksgiving, while to eat and drink is simultaneously to receive the gifts of his grace, to be infused with his life, to have part with him in his finished and continuing work, and to have a foretaste of the heavenly feast.

See also **Liturgical Spirituality.**

Gregory Dix, *The Shape of the Liturgy*, 1945; Philip Martin, *Earnest Pennies*, 1973; N. Micklem (ed), *Christian Worship*, 1936; J. E. Rattenbury, *The Eucharist Hymns of John and Charles Wesley*, 1948; A. Schmemann, *The World a Sacrament*, 1966; Massey H. Shepherd (ed), *Holy Communion*, 1960; Geoffrey Wainwright, *Eucharist and Eschatology*, [2]1981; *Doxology*, 1980.

EDITOR

Eudes, St John *see* **Sacred Heart**

Evagrius, Ponticus
see **Accidie;** *Apatheia; Apophthegmata;* **Asceticism; Cappadocian Fathers; Cassian, John; Deification;** *Fuga Mundi;* **Syrian Spirituality**

Evangelical Spirituality

The main ingredients of evangelical spirituality have always been early rising, prayer and Bible study. Wilberforce spent two hours each day before breakfast, praying and studying the Bible, and rebuked himself when the time became shortened. He writes in his diary: 'I have been keeping too late hours, and hence I have had but a hurried half hour in the morning to myself. Surely the experience of all good men, that without a due measure of private devotions the soul will grow lean.' Evangelicals kept a diary, not as a means of recording events, but of self-examination of the recent past and adjustment to the future; it was the evangelical equivalent of the confessional. Wilberforce and Simeon fasted on occasion, but only when their work was not hindered by so doing. Simeon writes of a fast day in 1807: 'I have always judged it inexpedient for a minister to fast, because he is thereby in danger of unfitting himself for his work; but my neglect of it on other occasions laid a ten-fold obligation on me to consecrate this day to God in fasting as well as in prayer.'

Evangelical books on prayer were few. Simeon's new edition of Benjamin Jenks, *Evangelical Meditations* (1702), was popular, Hannah More's *Spirit of Prayer* (1836) went into ten editions and Edward Bickersteth's *A Treatise on Prayer* (1826) was for many years considered the most helpful guide to prayer by an evangelical author. It includes an introduction to the theology of prayer, the relationship of public prayer and private worship and discusses problems caused by distraction and lack of feeling. There is a chapter on family worship and another on forms of worship to be used privately and in the home. These two chapters were expanded into a separate volume of *Family Prayers*.

Family prayers were expected to take place in every evangelical household, the head of the household calling his family and servants together every morning and evening and reading a portion of scripture before the prayers. Another book of Family Prayers was compiled by Henry Thornton, which proved to be even more popular and widely read than Bickersteth's, but gradually these forms of prayer were supplanted by extempore prayer.

Prayer meetings* also formed a part of Anglican evangelicalism. 'I look upon prayer meetings,' writes John Newton, 'as the most profitable exercise in which Christians can engage: they have a direct tendency to kill a worldly trifling spirit, to draw down a divine blessing on all our concerns, compose differences and enkindle the flame of divine love amongst brethren.'

Sunday observance was considered an essential part of evangelical spirituality. On Sunday afternoons Wilberforce, carrying Baxter's *Works* or some other spiritual classic, would leave his guests to themselves. 'Often on my visits to Holwood,' he wrote in old age, 'when I heard of this man's place or that man's peerage, I felt a rising inclination to pursue the same objects, but a Sunday in solitude never failed to restore me to myself.' Unfortunately what Sunday did for Wilberforce he thought should be done for the rest of the community, and with others he formed a Society for the Better Observance of Sunday. In 1809 Spencer Perceval, who was Prime Minister and an evangelical, stopped Monday sessions of Parliament so that members should not have to travel on Sundays. *The Record* in letters and leading articles protested against the Sunday opening of parks, the zoological gardens and museums. Children complained that Sunday was 'a heavy day', since on Saturday evening they had to put away all their toys and books, leaving only a box of letters to make a verse from scripture, and picturebooks with Bible scenes!

Where the boundary was between Christians and the world was not always easy to define, and parents were divided on the issue of whether their children should be taught dancing, many considering dancing to be one of 'the vanities of this world'. Most of the Victorian generation of evangelicals did not dance, though one correspondent commented in *The Record*: 'There may be vanity in a Bible Society, as well as humility in a ballroom.' *The Record* deplored hunting and dancing clergy and sometimes took names of those attending hunts and balls. Novel-reading, too, also earned disapproval. John Venn and Wilberforce enjoyed the Waverley novels but they were condemned by the next generation as 'in the highest degree injurious'. Temperance was disliked because of its apparent emphasis on good works. In the 1860s Dean Close made the case for total abstinence.

The Keswick Convention (1875) resulted in a movement for personal holiness. Some evangelicals came to believe in sinless perfection, others in a Christian life in two stages of conversion and consecration; victory over known sin being possible. Frances Ridley Havergal (1836–1879) in her hymns and Bishop Handley Moule (1842–1920) in his devotional writings, interpreted the movement.

From Keswick onwards the conservative wing of evangelicalism became even more 'world-denying'. Christians were expected to give themselves entirely to the gospel, which meant frequently answering the call to serve as a missionary overseas. To become a politician or a painter or an actor was to succumb to worldliness and to earn the disapproval of the elect. It was even said by one in the Keswick tradition in the twentieth century that Wilberforce should not have spent his time abolishing the slave trade but in converting people.

By the twentieth century there had emerged a movement of liberal evangelicals eventually known as the Anglican Evangelical Group Movement. It was centred on the annual Cromer Convention. It affirmed all that Keswick denies and denied Keswick's biblical fundamentalism. At the Cromer Convention in 1928 a book of prayers and meditations for private and public use was drawn up and given the title, *The Splendour of God*.

The pattern of evangelical spirituality has remained what it had been from the begin-

ning – early rising for prayer and Bible study. In a parish, usually a conservative evangelical parish, there is Bible study and a prayer meeting mid-week. The prayer at the beginning may include a collect, but the season of open prayer which follows the Bible study is extempore. The Bible exposition is usually from a fundamentalist outlook, and much of the interpretation is allegorical. Pentecostal evangelical Anglicans follow the same pattern though their meetings tend to go on longer. They have another focus for their devotion in the healing service.

In anglo-catholic parishes it is sometimes said that the mainstay of the parish consists of those who come to mid-week communions; in an evangelical parish it consists of those who are regular attenders at the mid-week Bible study and prayer meeting. Evangelicals have been very ready to learn from anglo-catholics in the matter of retreats, quiet days and three hour services. Some also took a full part in the *Parish and People* movement with its stress on the centrality of the parish communion. In the debate on the revised services some evangelicals have come to use the Alternative Service Book, though others prefer the 1662 service.

In 1946 W. A. Kelk edited a number of books by evangelical Anglicans; they were mainly on doctrinal subjects but they did include Frank Chadwick's *The Inner Life*. Max Warren contributed a book on holy communion entitled *Strange Victory* which is partly devotional and partly doctrinal. He makes great use of the evangelical heritage, drawing particularly on Edward Bickersteth's *Treatise on the Lord's Supper*. All who wrote for the St Paul's Library were members of the Evangelical Fellowship for Theological Literature, a community of evangelical scholars of all outlooks. Among these were Frank Colquhoun, whose *Parish Prayers* and its successors are widely used.

In the early seventies a revolution occurred in the conservative evangelical camp. Under the leadership of John Stott, conservative evangelicals began to abandon their world-denying attitude as taught by Keswick. Many evangelicals have become world-affirming; politics and social concern are no longer seen as a distraction from the gospel, but as part of Christian concern. Culture and the arts are now approached with enthusiasm and a good conscience.

Ian Bradley, *The Call to Seriousness*, 1976; Reginald Coupland, *Wilberforce*, 1945; Michael Hennell, *Sons of the Prophets*, 1979; *John Venn and the Clapham Sect*, 1958; George W. E. Russell, *The Household of Faith*, 1906; *Seeing and Hearing*, 1907.

MICHAEL HENNELL

Everard, John

A mysterious and fascinating personality, Everard (1575–*c*. 1650) belongs in part to the spiritual underworld of the seventeenth century. Influenced by the Familists*, though by no means wholly, he translated Hermes Trismegitus (the 'Thrice-Greatest'), a corpus of writings from *c*. 50 to 290, which fuse Neoplatonic, Stoic, Egyptian and Eastern religious ideas, and describe the ascent of the soul to God through the seven spheres of the planets. He also translated Denys the Areopagite* and the *Theologia Germanica*. He was imprisoned so often that James I punningly called him 'Dr Never-out'. He is constantly contrasting 'the dead and killing letter' with the holy and life-giving Spirit. At times he reveals a violent anti-historicism and could almost be charged with denying that the things recorded in scripture actually happened. He contends that we need 'a dayly doing all scriptures over again'. All the events of Christ's life must have their counterpart within us from the miraculous conception to the cross. 'It was not that Christ the Virgin Mary carried in her womb that did save her, but that Christ she carried in her heart.' 'You are deceived if you think the Passion of Christ was past when he suffered under Pontius Pilate.' Apocalyptic describes spiritual rebirth. Not that Everard would destroy the letter. It is the vehicle of the Spirit and once we have that Divine seal we can no more throw away the letter than a man can kill the wife he loves. Scripture is a bottomless sea: all of it should enter our experience. But these 'literal black letters' cannot possibly contain the Mighty Eternal Majesty of the Word of God, which is Christ. Everard's theology is christocentric and trinitarian and for him as for Augustine*, the Holy Spirit is the act of love, or the bond of love between the Father and the Son. He preferred preaching to humble folk and was critical of 'the Protestant ethic'. Some Puritans,

like Thomas Brooks, approved of him, and his sermons on the Divine love, and the reality of union with Christ here and now are powerful still. 'Glory is grace begun and Glory is grace perfected: For he that is united and made one with Jesus Christ by faith hath a true and real glimpse of those ravishing glories and delights which he shall forever enjoy.'

Rufus M. Jones, *Spiritual Reformers in the Sixteenth and Seventeenth Centuries*, 1914, p. 239ff.

EDITOR

Exercises, Spiritual
see Spiritual Exercises

Exorcism

Exorcism has been practised by the Christian church in baptismal rites and pastoral care from the beginning, and of course by all pagan cults which accept the idea of a cosmic struggle between good and evil. In the Protestant churches it fell into disuse to some extent with the rise of Rationalism, and the later optimistic theologies based on the belief that, the victory having been won, there could be no more conflict. The decline of nineteenth-century optimism has seen a recovery of interest in this particular ministry, but within the context of the total ministry of healing, therefore taking its place in the general disciplines of healing such as psychiatry and medicine. It is understood to be the work of Christ, acting through his church, and in no way the action of a person with magical powers.

Whatever model or mythology is used, e.g. the biblical picture of Satan and the demonic powers, or a modern psychological picture of being overwhelmed by the 'shadow'; whatever theological language is used, e.g. of a personification of evil or of cosmic negative forces, matters little for the pastoral care of those who are afflicted. In addition to the Laying on of Hands with prayer and the Anointing with Oil, the ministry of healing also includes confession and absolution, and the 'binding and loosing'. Exorcism is that which calls upon the healing power of the Risen Lord to give freedom to those who are in bondage. It is neither prolonged pastoral counselling, nor psychotherapy, but a command in the name of Christ that that which holds in bondage should release. It is important to note that exorcism is only the first step in pastoral care of someone who has (usually through persistent self-will) given away his God-given freedom. By far the more important part of pastoral care is the subsequent building up into the Body of Christ in Christian fellowship.

Because of the resemblance of certain mental disorders to the generally understood signs of possession, exorcism should be strictly controlled and practised only by trained persons working in close co-operation with those trained in the diseases of the mind, and with a supportive prayer group. Preferably the exorcist should work with the psychiatrist, both examining the person's symptoms and noting those which are not germain to their own particular discipline. Practitioners relying on subjective 'feelings' or 'discernment' as opposed to psychiatric opinion have been proved wrong in many cases, and have caused tragedies in others, although sixteenth-century instructions to Exorcists warned them to take medical and social opinion before becoming involved.

In brief, exorcism consists of three parts: a statement that the exorcism is carried out 'in the Name of Jesus Christ'; an instruction to the binding power to depart, harming no one and nothing and not returning; and the order to go. The actual rite may be formal or informal as far as ritual is concerned, and may vary according to the churchmanship and circumstances of those concerned.

It is important to differentiate between the greater and lesser exorcism; the former consisting of the full rite and being administered under strict control and only in established cases of possession; the latter, which is really a simple prayer of intercession such as the ancient Compline Prayer, 'Visit we beseech Thee, O Lord, this place, and drive from it all the snares of the enemy ...'

With the ministry to places, again it is important that the exorcism is not used in conditions for which it is not intended. Poltergeist phenomena and place memories, being purely psychic and not spiritual, are not in themselves caused by demonic influence and are not therefore occasions on which exorcism would be the appropriate pastoral response.

ALAN HARRISON

Experience

If the world is a vale of soul-making, there is a sense in which all experience is religiously significant, if not actually experience of God. The significance, however, is plain only to the eye of faith, and faith itself is often prompted by experiences which are more explicitly 'religious' – experiences of a *mysterium tremendum et fascinans* or of personal encounter with God or of regeneration. On the other hand, not all believers can point to a vivid moment of 'conversion': they have been aware of God as long as they remember and, as much as any 'convert', they claim to enjoy communion with him. Yet the accounts given of the nature of that communion vary considerably, not just between the 'once born' and the 'twice born' (to use William James's not entirely satisfactory terminology) but within each group.

All these and a host of related issues have long been debated by theologians, psychologists and philosophers of religion. Their relevance to spirituality, however, is rarely systematically explored and therefore remains largely a matter of inference. Note, first, the contrast between faith and experience in both Protestant and Catholic Christianity. Faith, after all, is not knowledge and involves a willingness to venture where we cannot prove – in that sense, to go beyond experience. But faith has been variously understood, sometimes as assent to biblically or ecclesiastically guaranteed propositions, sometimes as trust generated by the gospel message. Both positions have suffered since both biblical and ecclesiastical authority came under attack. But throughout Christian history a third position has always had its representatives, holding that God is his own authority and that every believer can speak of him on the basis of personal acquaintance. On this view, there is plainly no justification for a simple contrast between faith and experience.

Groups otherwise widely separated, chronologically and in other ways – Montanists, Catholic Mystics, Quakers and Pietists, for example – are united by this conviction. For all of them, the place of the biblical revelation in the Christian life is a key issue. Are 'revelation' and 'experience' different ways of speaking about the same reality, one stressing the divine pole and the other the human? If so, how do the experiences of contemporary Christians relate to those recorded in scripture? If not, what is the relationship between faith and experience, in the Bible and today? In either case, can contemporary experience ever do more than confirm scripture? Such questions clamour for refinement and elucidation but they point to a crucial issue for Christian faith and practice, past and present.

The question has been complicated by the debate about 'secularization'. In the 1960s, it was repeatedly asserted that modern man could not have experience of God but that he could still live by faith, by commitment to the way of Jesus in a world where God is 'hidden', if not 'dead'. At the time, such claims seemed sweeping, and they have been challenged by the upsurge of interest in mysticism*, Eastern and Western, and the burgeoning of Pentecostalism* and the Charismatic Movement*. The former has coincided with developments in the study of religious language to produce an understanding of religion as spirituality, i.e. a technique for spiritual development which need not presuppose the existence of a being called 'God'; the latter has popularized a questionable two-stage analysis of Christian discipleship: faith is followed by baptism in the Holy Spirit, itself evidenced by speaking in tongues. Perhaps the most important result, however, has been a growing appreciation of the effect of the social setting upon the whole of life, including the life of faith.

Further difficulties centre upon the place of Jesus Christ in the Christian revelation. In what sense can a historical figure be the object of contemporary experience? When the Gospels were viewed as biographies of a striking personality, the problem was not acute: it was possible to check the 'experienced' Christ against the historical Jesus – indeed, C. E. Raven (1885–1964), among others, seems to have tried to do just that. But now that there is constant debate about how much can be known about Jesus, claims, e.g. to share his present 'friendship' become problematical. Yet we cannot ignore testimonies like that of Evelyn Underhill*: 'I went to the Baron (Baron von Hügel*) . . . he said I wasn't much better than a Unitarian. Somehow by his prayers or something he compelled me to experience Christ.'

After experience of the Holy Spirit and of Christ, what of God, the Father? So-called 'encounter' theology, which made much use of Buber's I–Thou terminology, has been widely influential. It has also come under fire from linguistic philosophy and theology, on two main grounds: that, since there are no independent checks of God's existence, such experience can be delusory; and that God is not just another person over against us but a transcendent reality. Even if these criticisms are not decisive, they highlight the fact that experience is not a simple datum which we report but the result of interpreting something given in the light of a conceptual scheme. The validity of experience is thus bound up with the adequacy of the concepts employed, and the sense in which we 'learn from experience' is seen to need careful analysis.

Two conceptual schemes for understanding the spiritual life, the mystic's Ladder of Perfection and the evangelical's Plan of Salvation, are studied and valued today but applied with caution. For the aim of spiritual direction is to help the individual to find his own way forward, not to deduce instructions from a predetermined directory. Moreover, in the process of spiritual maturation, the habitual experience of worship is valued as highly as moments of mystical awareness, since in this context the stress must inevitably be upon what lies within our power. At the same time, there is evidence of a desire to affirm God's presence in his world, enriching life's routine activities: see, for example, Martin Thornton: *My God: a re-appraisal of normal religious experience*, 1974.

John Baillie, *Our Knowledge of God*, 1939; F. W. Dillistone, *Religious Experience and Christian Faith*, 1981; Peter Donovan, *Interpreting Religious Experience*, 1979; Alister Hardy, *The Spiritual Nature of Man*, 1979; W. R. Inge, *Christian Mysticism*, 1899; William James, *The Varieties of Religious Experience*, 1902; A. J. Krailsheimer, *Conversion*, 1980; Olive Wyon: *Desire for God: a Study of Three Spiritual Classics*, 1966.

GRAHAM SLATER

Extra-Sensory Perception

The most common, misleadingly positive expression employed to label certain alleged or actual phenomena which we are at this time entitled to describe only in an almost wholly negative way. The same phenomena or alleged phenomena are sometimes spoken of in a more technical fashion as $\psi\gamma$ (read, *psi gamma*), and taken to constitute the best evidenced sub-class of ψ phenomena in general – the *psi* being derived from psychic as the *gamma* is derived from (the Greek word for) knowledge. Nor have the older terms 'telepathy' and 'clairvoyance' ceased to be used.

If we are to be unprejudicial and properly cautious then ESP or $\psi\gamma$ has to be defined, in a rather long-winded and awkward way, in terms of people being caused to have beliefs which are, as it turns out, true; but being caused to have those beliefs in certain peculiar and negatively specified circumstances. That the facts are what the subjects come to believe them to be has to be a causally necessary condition of those subjects coming to have these beliefs; if it is by chance alone, however improbable that chance, that these beliefs happen to correspond to the facts to which they do correspond, then we do not have, by definition, a case of ESP or $\psi\gamma$, whether telepathic or clairvoyant. This is one thing which counts in favour of classifying $\psi\gamma$ as a kind of perception. For it would certainly be wrong to assert that someone had perceived something where the parallel causal requirement was not satisfied.

In addition to this positive stipulation, there are the negatively specified essential circumstances. If it really is to be a case of genuine ESP, then the true beliefs which the subjects are thus caused to have must not have been acquired by any familiar, normal means; neither by any sort of inference from information already available to those subjects; nor by any use of the recognized five senses. (It is not clear whether the 'extra' in ESP is to be construed as 'additional' or as 'outwith'. In the latter interpretation the whole phrase would appear to be self-contradictory: it is like speaking of non-male husbands or non-tauroid bulls. Yet the former runs up against two other objections: that no one can point to any sense organ in which this supposed additional sense is localized; and that no one even claims to enjoy in this connection any further form of sensory experience as different from visual, tactual, gustatory and olfactory as each of these is from every other.)

ESP or $\psi\gamma$, as thus defined, may be distinguished into two kinds. If the causally necessary condition of the subjects coming to have the beliefs in question is the possession of the relevant information by some other conscious being or beings, then the ESP is telepathic: it is traditional to speak of mind to mind information transfers. If the causally necessary condition is the presence of the relevant information only in the inanimate and non-conscious world, then the ESP is clairvoyant: the corresponding tradition speaks now of object-reading or of a matter-to mind effect.

The possible relevance of such phenomena to spirituality is two-fold. 1. It is often assumed, although much more rarely argued, that ESP faculties could be attributed only to minds or souls or spirits, conceived as essentially incorporeal and nonphysical substances. 2. It certainly would appear that such beings could communicate with one another, or be understood by creatures of flesh and blood, only through the mediation of some such meansless means.

C. E. Hansel, *ESP and Parapsychology: A Critical Revaluation*, 1980.

ANTONY FLEW

Faber, F. W.

Father Faber (1814–1863) was the first superior of the London Oratory and a popular writer of hymns and devotional works. An Evangelical in his early youth, he came under the influence of the Tractarians as an Oxford undergraduate. In 1839 he was ordained priest in the Church of England and in 1843 became Rector of Elton in Huntingdonshire. Such was his persuasiveness that he succeeded in introducing to Elton many of the devotions and practices of continental Catholicism. In 1845 Faber followed Newman* into the Catholic Church, taking with him thirteen of his own disciples. At first Faber thought of founding a new religious order, but in 1848 joined Newman's newly-established Oratory near Birmingham, bringing his disciples with him. The following year Newman sent him to London to start a new Oratory. The success of the venture in an assembly room in King William Street led in 1853 to the purchase of land at Brompton for the construction of a house and church. Under Faber's enthusiastic though somewhat autocratic rule the London Oratory flourished. No further Oratories were founded in England, however, chiefly because of an unfortunate quarrel between Newman and Faber on the correct relationship between the two houses.

Faber sought to bring a spiritual life to ordinary people living in Victorian London. Although not a profound thinker like Newman, he knew how to adapt the classic ascetic teaching of the church to modern urban life. His eight devotional books, written between 1853 and 1860 during bouts of illness, have been criticized for their emotionalism, Italianate style and occasional banality. Yet they also reveal a wide reading of the spiritual authors, particularly Teresa of Avila* and Francis de Sales*, a knowledge of human psychology, and a deep understanding of the consequences of the incarnation for the union of the faithful with Christ. Moreover, Faber was open to everything that was positive in secular culture. He revelled in the beauties of nature and welcomed the advances of science as partial revelations of God. God, whilst infinitely transcendent, dwells intimately among us. For through the incarnation he has 'mingled Himself' with our world, and in the sacraments has 'rendered the blessings of his incarnation omnipresent and everlasting', so that the world is continually being transformed by divine love. Both the strengths and the weaknesses of Faber arise out of his intense desire to remove all obstacles to the experience of the love of God. Prayer is easy if only we would try it. God's love is ready to flood over us if only we would let it. Yet the necessity of ascetic effort is also stressed and the insidious way in which our comforts and routines can blind us to God is well analysed.

Faber, in a truly Philippine way, presents a lay spirituality with an emphasis on the sacraments and the love of God. Some purple passages may not be to the modern taste, but much that he has written is shrewd and persuasive. His works which have best stood the test of time are *Growth in Holiness* (1854, reprinted 1960) and *The Creator and the Creature* (1858, reprinted 1961).

See also **Oratorians**.

R. Addington, *Faber, Poet and Priest*, 1974; Ronald Chapman, *Father Faber*, 1961; Louis Cognet, *DS*, V, cols 1–13.

NORMAN RUSSELL

Faith

Faith in the context of spirituality involves at least four aspects of human experience.

1. 'The faith' to which a response is made, the core of beliefs that form the basis of describing what a person believes. For the Christian this core is drawn from the biblical witness to the revelation of God in Christ and finds expression in the credal statements of faith and in the teaching of the church. The Letter of Jude, for example, exhorts its readers to struggle 'in defence of the faith' (Jude 3). It is chiefly with the mind and the intellect that 'the faith' is accepted as a statement of truth. Intellectual questioning and doubt sometimes feature as part of the response to 'the faith'.

2. The personal response in trust that is the mark of the person who has faith. Faith *that* is transformed into faith *in*. On this level faith is a response of the whole personality, heart and mind, to the God who calls men and women to himself. It is deeply personal and is experienced as a response to God. Paul's Letter to the Romans explores this faith in some depth. 'Everyone who has faith in God will be saved' (Rom. 10.11ff.). The believer has peace with God through his faith which is itself drawn out by the grace of God working within him (Rom. 5–8). The episode in the Gospel of John (20.24–29) exploring the faith response of Thomas the Apostle to the risen Christ shows how faith *in* and faith *that* are closely linked. Faith *in* Jesus as 'my Lord and my God' implies a faith *that* Jesus is Lord and God, though the converse is not necessarily the case. In Christian spirituality an association with the general faith of the church can act as an anchor in times of personal doubt and the lack of a sense of the presence of God.

3. Faith that is recognized in and expressed through action. The Letter of James in particular within the New Testament explores this aspect of faith. 'If faith is not seen in actions it is dead' (James 2.17). There has been much debate about the apparent divergence of view between the Letter of James with its emphasis on the works of faith and the Letters of Paul with their stress on a person being at peace with God through personal faith. Paul also, however, is aware of the importance of 'faith active in

love' (Gal. 5.6). In Christian spirituality personal faith has a public aspect which is seen in the activities, words and relationships of the believer (cf. also I John 4.20f.).

4. The consequences for the character of the believer. Living with a particular system of faith, trusting in an object of faith and acting according to that system and in the light of personal experience gained through it leaves its mark. Faith here becomes faithfulness and in Christian spirituality a person of faith who seeks to continue steadfast in faith is enjoying one of the fruits of the Spirit of God at work within him (Gal. 5.22). The other fruits of the Spirit are also marks of the Christian character.

These four aspects of faith form a unity. Christian faith involves an assertion of the truth of what is believed (the faith), a personal experience of that truth (trust in God), a kind of loving that flows from it (faith in action) and a constancy of approach (faithfulness).

Some significant modern writings on faith and the faith from different traditions include: John Austin Baker, *The Foolishness of God*, 1970; Karl Barth, *Dogmatics in Outline*, 1949; Leonard Hodgson, *For Faith and Freedom*, 1968; Hans Küng, *On Being A Christian*, 1977; Wolfhart Pannenberg, *The Apostles' Creed*, 1972; Karl Rahner, *Foundations of Christian Faith*, 1978; the report of the Church of England Doctrine Commission, *Christian Believing*, 1976; the so-called 'Dutch Catechism', *The New Catechism*, 1967.

REX CHAPMAN

Faithfulness *see* Fruit of the Spirit

Familists

They were founded by Henry Nicholas, (Hendrik Niclaes) *c.* 1501–*c.* 1580, a Westphalian of a devout Roman Catholic family, who was yet one more precociously religious child visionary, but grieved because the redeeming death of Christ had not yet conquered the world's sin. It was not, however, until he was almost forty that he received the Divine communications telling him to found a new sect, the 'Family of Love'. This he did at Emden and organized it more on the basis of the Roman Catholic hierarchy than on any Protestant model. His teaching was anabaptist and preached inward re-

ligion, not dissimilar from John Everard* and George Fox* later, but there was also a tinge of mystical pantheism. Like the Quakers*, the Familists had no faith in outward ordinances. They were much reviled and charged with antinomianism, but there is no evidence of immorality of life, though some of them may have claimed perfection or infallibility by a combination of the desire to take Christ seriously, and crankiness. They renounced war and violence both in private and public behaviour. They appeared in England as early as 1552 and attracted much suspicion for more than a century. They formed an inchoate underground movement of humble folk, lower artisans and the like, and were anti-clerical and anti-trinitarian. They were not of the stuff of martyrs* and tended to recant under questioning without changing their beliefs, and thus, unheroically, survived. Cromwell allowed them liberty of publication but by the end of the seventeenth century they had gravitated towards Quakerism and other sects.

Christopher Hill, *Milton and the English Revolution*, 1977; Gertrude Huehns, *Antinomianism in English History with special reference to 1640–60*, 1952; Rufus M. Jones, *Studies in Mystical Religion*, 1909.

EDITOR

Family of Love *see* Familists

Family Spirituality

'For every householder's house ought to be a school of godliness, for as much as every householder ought to be a bishop in his own house, and so oversee his family that nothing reign in it but virtue, godliness and honesty.' Thomas Becon in his *Catechism set forth dialogue-wise between the father and the son* was addressing a boy not yet six years old. He was fulfilling the ideal set out by Thomas Cromwell in his *Injunctions to the Clergy* of 1536 which described fathers as 'rulers of their own family', a concept which provided the firm foundation for the household piety of the sixteenth and seventeenth centuries. 'To have children and servants is thy blessing, O Lord, but not to order them according to Thy work deserveth Thy dreadful curse.' This prayer for householders from the primer of 1553 assumes that children and servants come under the same authority, a most important aspect of contemporary thought. In *A Priest to the Temple*, George Herbert* said that a priest should take equal pride in his children and his servants for he would find 'as much joy in a straight-growing child or servant as a gardener in a choice tree'.

With such high expectation placed upon him as head of the household and ruler of his family, it is hardly surprising that the father sought practical help and advice in the conduct of those household prayers which were so central to his rule. Special devotional books, many of Puritan origin, poured from the presses and were an extremely popular form of literature. It is interesting to see how the church, having specifically repudiated the monastic way of life, in trying to organize morning and evening prayer within a domestic framework in fact turned to much of the traditional material that lay to hand. St Augustine and the *Imitation*, even if purified or 'corrected' by the editor, would be used together with the psalter and primer, and the psalms in fact enjoyed greater popularity than ever before. Many of the elements common to most devout households were deepened and extended by Nicholas Ferrar* in that remarkable and unique experience of the Little Gidding community. But an average family would probably follow something like the pattern of prayer laid down by Jeremy Taylor: sentence; confession; absolution; Lord's prayer; doxology; psalms; creed; collects. A typical phrase from a prayer for children is revealing: 'Give them grace to obey their parents, that doing the duty they may receive the promise.'

Grace was always said before and after meals, and catechizing based on the forty or fifty competing domestic catechisms was widespread, the method being simply that of learning by rote, in Lancelot Andrewes'* words, 'to goe over the same matter, as the knife doth the whetstone'.

The disappearance of the regular practice of family prayers after the Civil War was much regretted by contemporaries. The Bishop of Coventry lamented in 1725: 'Formerly a man's house was a little oratory, where the master prayed with all the family . . . it went far towards keeping up the face of virtue and piety, and preventing much wickedness.' Yet by the later eighteenth century, family prayers had again become common. The evangelical revival made the home central. The authority of the parents was emphasized, together with the vital role of the family as a training ground. This involved family prayers twice a day; much reading of holy books; a return to catechizing; and the widespread use of Isaac Watts' *Divine Songs*, simple didactic verses whose main concern was to inculcate the virtues of obedience, above all to parents.

While some heads of families enjoyed extempore prayer, many preferred printed manuals, of which Henry Thornton's *Family Prayers*, published in 1834 and running into thirty editions in the following twenty years, was typical. The strengthening of Christian family life continued steadily throughout the nineteenth century. Bible reading, prayers and early instruction in the catechism set the common pattern. Sundays were regarded as the bastion of a godly nation and toys and secular books were replaced by edifying moral tales, popular religious journals or missionary magazines. It was constantly emphasized that the will of the parent was the will of God, and the lengths to which some went to fulfil this sense of divine mission often led to such practices as exposing small children to death-bed scenes and corpses to drive home the message of death and judgment. Yet when Wilberforce showed concern that his children should not associate prayer with gloom or be 'overdosed with religion and that of an offensive kind when young' he probably provides a necessary corrective to gain a balanced view of Victorian family spirituality.

E. E. Kellett, *Religion and Life in the Early Victorian Era*, 1938; P. Sangster, *Pity my Simplicity. The Evangelical Revival and the Religious Education of Children*, 1963.

ESTHER DE WAAL

Farrer, Austin Marsden

In the remarkable range of his writings, Austin Farrer (1904–1968) reflects a vision of Christian theism which is at once traditional and innovative, and which bridges the gulf between ascetic and speculative or academic theory. Scripture and metaphysics, as he puts it in his Bampton Lectures (*The Glass of Vision*, 1948), were equally his study, and these seemingly disparate interests have a common grounding in the same spirituality evident in his devotional works and in some 150 published sermons. Farrer's philosophical theology takes its bearings from high scholasticism's view of God as creator and from modern linguistic analysis, but also from the paradoxical experience of being a self-creating creature, of which the most luminous instance is 'willing the will of God' in prayer. Thus the 'proof' of God's existence in his masterly *Finite and Infinite* (1943) takes the form of a Bonaventurean ascent of the mind to God through a step-wise refinement of natural, finite analogies that approximate but never reach their infinite goal. A similar emphasis on converging images appears in Farrer's exegetical studies, less well known and at times notoriously quixotic. He explains the abrupt conclusion of the Gospel of Mark by interpreting Jesus' healings as signs that the inspired imagination of the evangelist has arranged so as to point beyond themselves towards a reality that cannot be imagined – the resurrection of Christ. 'The use of the many healing miracles is to exhibit the richness and diversity of the one saving act, much as the many creatures exhibit the multiform fecundity of the one creative power' (*A Study in St Mark*, 1951). In this way the N T and the created universe become complementary parables, mirrors that dimly but truly reflect the divine.

Raised a Baptist, Farrer entered the Church of England as an undergraduate. He was considered one of the ablest preachers of his time, and his homiletical style retains evangelical fervour within a catholic spirituality. While the emphasis of nearly all the sermons is personal and practical, they are built on a doctrinal foundation that gives them the timeless quality that has often been noted. In works such as *The Triple Victory* (1965) and *Lord, I Believe* (1958), it is impossible to draw a line between scholarly exposition and devotional advice. The first of these books shows how Farrer's exegesis of Christ's temptation according to Matthew complements meditational reading of the Gospel narrative. The second, which develops the thesis that 'no dogma deserves its place unless it is prayable, and no Christian deserves his dogmas who does not pray them', concludes with an adaptation of the use of the rosary combining imaginative participation in the events of the Gospels with the traditional Jesus prayer.

Austin Farrer, *Reflective Faith* ed Charles

C. Conti, 1972, includes a chronological list of published writings: see also Jeffrey C. Eaton, *The Logic of Theism: An Analysis of the Thought of Austin Farrer,* 1980; Charles C. Hefling, *Jacob's Ladder: Theology and Spirituality in the Thought of Austin Farrer*, 1979.

CHARLES C. HEFLING

Fasting

Abstinence, for religious reasons, from nourishment in varying degrees, especially at sacred seasons, by religious groups (church, nation, order, congregation) and individuals. In some Christian traditions and in Israel and Islam (Ramadan), abstinence from matrimonial relations is included – compare the Christian custom of deferring weddings until after penitential seasons. As a specifically *religious* act, fasting is to be distinguished from dieting; as a practice to clarify the mind and direct the will, it may be associated, even in a secular setting, with spiritual intentions.

Fasting is attested in ancient Egyptian, Persian, Greek and Roman religion, in Shinto, Taoism, Confucianism, Hinduism and Islam, and was inherited from Judaism by Christianity. It is probably universal and instinctive in all cultures. For Christians, the practice has the authority of Jesus' own example and teaching. In older Christian traditions, it is an established usage. The Reformation churches, having denied its meritorious character, retained it in legislation but allowed it to fall into neglect until it was revived by renewal movements, evangelical, sacramental, pietistic and charismatic.

In Judaism fasting was associated with particular occasions. Some examples are: mourning (I Sam. 31.13; II Sam. 1.2; I Chron. 10.12; II Sam. 12.21ff.); after humiliation in battle (I Sam. 7.6); in time of danger (Judges 20.21); in commemoration of past dangers and deliverences (Esther 4.16; Zech. 7–8); at times of repentance (Joel 1.14; Jonah 3.5; Jer. 36.9); before great undertakings (Ezra 8.21); for intercession (Neh. 1, 4). Such occasions may be institutionally prescribed (e.g. Day of Atonement, as in Lev. 23, 24–32); or customary (e.g. the fast of the firstborn on eve of Passover); or voluntary, like the Pharisee in Luke 18.12 who fasted twice in the week – Jesus assumed his disciples would retain such voluntary fasts (Matt. 6.16).

Fasting typified the spirituality of Pharisaism and John the Baptist (Mark 2.18ff. and parallels), devoted to the penitent renewal of the people in preparation for the Messiah. The time of fulfilment and of Christ's coming was better typified by festival, but Jesus' disciples were also to know times of fasting. The NT refers explicitly only to fasting in times of intense prayer, specifically before commencement of a new mission (Acts 13.2–3); but Mark 2.18ff. seems to imply that the fast immediately before Easter (the Paschal Fast) is a primitive observance. The forty-day fast before Lent*, as a period of penitence and anticipation, was in the Western mediaeval church paralleled by similar seasons before Christmas and Pentecost, and shorter fasts were added before some saints' days, and before baptism and ordination. 'Days of Public Fasting and Humiliation', 'Buss-und-Bet-Tage', whether annual or occasional, have had some place in all Christian traditions. Twice-weekly 'stational' fasts on Wednesday and Friday (day of crucifixion), a deliberate adaptation of Jewish usage, are attested as early as the *Didache* (*c*. AD 100?).

At all seasons, Christians of most traditions have fasted as an act of reverent and penitent expectation before communion (in the RC church, for example, from the preceding midnight, or since Vatican II for one hour before Mass), before baptism, and before and in some cases after ordination.

For shorter fasts (maximum 72 hours) fasting may be total, only water being permitted. For longer fasts, those fasting take only one meal, and perhaps also a slight repast ('collation') each day. The Western church especially has had complex and varying legislation on fasting, now much simplified. The very old and young, the sick, expectant mothers, travellers and those with demanding work are exempt from the exercise.

Intention and interpretation are essential to Christian fasting, as one element in the offering of the living sacrifice of oneself in a rational service (Rom. 12.1). It is a praying with the body, affirming the wholeness of the person in spiritual action; it gives emphasis and intensity to prayer; specifically it expresses hunger for God and his will; it asserts the goodness of creation by means of

the temporary surrender of enjoyment of some of its benefits and therefore always includes an element of thanksgiving; it is a training in Christian discipline and specifically against the sin of gluttony; it expresses penitence for the rejection and crucifixion of Christ by the human race; it is a following of Jesus on his way of fasting; it is one element in mortification; the acceptance of the death of self in the death of Christ, and thereby an act of faith in the resurrection.

Fasting has deep psychological roots as a purity ritual, and has therefore a natural aptness for acts of prayer, but needs protection against implications of magic, masochism, the search for exaggerated self-denial and formalism (cf. Isa. 58.3–12). Association of fasting with almsgiving (certainly since Tertullian*) has been an attempt to prevent the usage from being self-regarding. The fasting of Jesus has served as a model for this discipline confronting the disciple with the temptations of the human condition (physical exhaustion, euphoria, depression: Luke 4.1–13) and of specifically religious vocation (self-display, testing God, compromise with evil: Matt. 4.1–11) and as a reassurance that where temptations are, there the saviour has already been and is.

———

Augustine, *Sermons* (205–211) on Lent; Leo the Great, *Sermons* (39–50) on Lent, (12–20) on the Fast of the Tenth Month, (88ff.) on the Fast of the Seventh Month; Tertullian, *On Fasting*; A. J. Maclean, 'Fasting and Abstinence', in *Liturgy and Worship*, ed W. K. L. Clarke, 1932, pp. 243–56; R. Nelson, *A Companion to the Fasts of the Church of England*, London, 1703.

DAVID TRIPP

Feminine Spirituality

Human spirituality in the Christian mode is the response of a woman or man to the mystery of Christ, primarily to the mystery of the death–resurrection of Jesus the Christ. This mystery recapitulates and gives meaning to all the Christian mysteries such as creation, incarnation, spirit.

This response to Christ, however, is both conditioned and structured by one's historical situatedness and one's sexuality. Thus, the feminine experience of God is distinct but not separate from the masculine experience. The two experiences are complementary. Each states and calls forth in the other essential elements of response to Christ. So, the qualities of a feminine spirituality are not the exclusive domain of the female sex although they are initiated by a uniquely female experience of life.

The bodily experience of a woman is intrinsic to understanding her response to the divine. Biologically, a woman is determined by her role as bearer and deliverer of life. Thus, her entire life is a preparation for the birthing experience and the subsequent nurturing of the life to which she has given birth. There is no woman, whether she has actually given biological birth or not, whose psyche, soul and spirit remains outside the influence of these bodily imperatives.

One must, however, avoid the pitfall of identifying the specifically feminine attitudes, affects and responses that devolve from such biology with the mechanics of biology. To do so would be to allow the particularity of a material phenomenon to take precedence over the transcendent to which the material should point. This would lead to a type of spiritual positivism based on an extroverted understanding of materiality rather than one based on meaning achieved by interiority. It would deny the intersubjectivity of human experience by limiting experience to a particular, discrete occasion, experienced by a specific person at a particular time. The feminine response to God in Christianity, if appropriated symbolically, however, is freed from its biological base and made available to all women and men. Consequently, such qualities of symbolically understood feminine spirituality can be described as transtemporal rather than spatial; generic rather than specific; existential rather than extrinsic. The telos of the concrete experience of women is transcendence in which all can participate.

On this view, one can say that feminine spirituality as appropriated by both male and female is characterized by receptivity, affective response, waiting or attentiveness and the acceptance of pain as intrinsic to the bringing forth of life. Further, there is a natural propensity for intimacy derived both from connectedness with bodily processes and the rhythms of life as well as the need of the other to fulfil one's destiny to give birth.

All of these characteristics are ideally suited to contemplative prayer, which is an experience of union with God occasioned by one's receptivity to the divine initiative. Although such receptivity has been traditionally described as passive, it is not to be equated with the passivity of inertia. It is a creative passivity that responds in an ever-increasing degree to the movements of grace. It is creative in that the divinely initiated coming to awareness of one's gracefulness results in new ways of viewing and interpreting everyday realities. One's horizon is broadened to include possibilities of living never before considered. The writings of both Teresa of Avila* and Catherine of Siena* describe such prayer. Although they describe what a contemporary person might name extraordinary spiritual experience, this must not divert one from recognizing the basic dynamic of the prayer they describe: response to the initiative of God which leads to union, a union frequently described in sexual imagery.

Such receptivity to God issues in bringing forth new life in oneself and others. This inevitably involves one in the pain of giving up a former mode of life, a less appropriate response to God, and allowing the new to be delivered. This is a feminine response to the mystery of life out of death, the meaning attributed to the death–resurrection of Jesus the Christ. Thus, the creativity of birthing and the risk such a process involves in the face of the unknown is directed to and authenticated by the central mystery of Christianity. Retrospectively, the daily nurturing of new life is sustained by this same knowledge that the old cannot contain the new; it must be relinquished.

This receptivity to the other, the birth process, and nurturing is rooted in cyclic images more than in linear ones. Archetypal symbols often used to portray this cyclic aspect of feminine spirituality are the vessel, the circle, the moon and the ocean. These symbols are more apt to initiate one into the Mystery of God's eternal creativity than into an episodic understanding of salvation history. Throughout church history, these symbols have been metaphorically identified with Mary, the Mother of Jesus, who remains, perhaps, the pre-eminent symbol of feminine spirituality.

In her book *God and the Rhetoric of Sexuality* (1978), Phyllis Trible has indicated the feminine images of God contained in the Jewish scriptures, images frequently overlooked by a male-dominated culture which has shaped the linguistic consciousness of the Christian. If, though, one acknowledges the presence of these images which arose from the experience of the various authors' responses to God, and one also holds the doctrine of the *imago dei*, then it can be stated that the development of both the feminine and the masculine in Christian spirituality is essential if the church is to respond in an appropriate manner to God in Christ.

Nor Hall, *The Moon and the Virgin. Reflection on the Archetypal Feminine*, 1980; Mary Esther Harding, *The Way of all Women*, 1975; Helen Luke, *Woman, Earth and Spirit: The Feminine in Symbol and Myth*, 1981.

NANCY C. RING

Fénelon, François de Salignac de Lamothe

Fénelon (*c*. 1651–1715) studied in Cahors and in Paris and was ordained in 1675, showing already the instinctive, spontaneous, mystical tendencies that complemented the rational, common-sense emphasis of seventeenth-century classicism and were eventually to detach themselves from it in conscious opposition. He soon distinguished himself in the work of preaching, spiritual direction and education. In 1688, his meeting with Madame Guyon*, of whom he had previously been suspicious, led to a crisis: entering fully into her teaching on the prayer of quiet and the union of pure love, he came to regard it as fundamentally traditional, though inadequately or misleadingly expressed. Until 1695, when he was made Archbishop of Cambrai, his influence continued to grow in court circles. But in 1695 began the period of controversy that opened with the condemnation of Madame Guyon's teaching by a court of enquiry led by Bossuet*. The book, *Explication des Maximes des Saints sur la Vie Intérieure (1697)*, in which he sought to defend as truly Catholic the spirituality of which he thought her an authentic representative, was condemned by Rome in 1699 as equivocal and dangerous. The participants in this controversy saw Fénelon's book as a summing-up of the Quietist presentation of the doctrine of grace (*see* Quietism). Fénelon argued that the love of God moves eventually into a state in which God is loved for himself alone, without any admixture of hope for salvation or

personal reward. One is now so filled with the desire to please God in all things that one would abandon all hope of eternity if such were indeed the will of God. The soul is entirely passive in the hands of God, in a state of perfect quiet, unaware of itself and its own acts. (*See* **Disinterested Love.**)

The depreciation of the value of human response to God's grace implied by this teaching could be taken to render outward acts of mortification or of charity superfluous and even led to the suggestion that sinful acts could be committed without personal sin; the judgment of Pope Innocent XI on this score against Molinos* in 1687 lay behind the adverse reactions in Paris and Rome.

Fénelon at once accepted the Roman decision and for the rest of his life remained in his diocese, to which he had been restricted by Louis XIV. His pastoral teaching directed itself against Jansenism* and against the new generation of free-thinkers, with a method and a poetic style that anticipated Rousseau and Chateaubriand.

In his later years, the attraction of his personality and of his writing won for Fénelon, with Madame Guyon, wide influence in Britain, particularly through the translations and writings of A. M. Ramsay, which persisted throughout the eighteenth century. Their desire to foster the spiritual life, with its emphasis on the disinterested love of God, won appreciation and respect for them among High Churchmen, Methodists and Quakers. Alexander Knox declared that 'no Catholic was more popular in Protestant countries than Fénelon'.

Oeuvres et Correspondance, 35 vols, 1820–1830; *Correspondance*, ed Jean Orcibal, to comprise 15 vols, 1972–: an edition which will make possible a reappraisal of the Querelle du Quiétisme; Fénelon 1651–1951: a special number of the review *XVIIe Siècle*, 12–14, 1951–1952; L., Cognet, *Crépuscule des Mystiques. Bossuet, Fénelon*, 1958; M. Raymond, *Fénelon*, 1967.

MICHAEL RICHARDS

Ferrar, Nicholas

A brilliant Cambridge scholar, Ferrar (1592–1637) travelled widely on the continent for health reasons in his youth, and on his return had a meteoric six years in the Virginia company which opened a career in politics. From this he turned aside rather as his friend George Herbert* left the court, and withdrew from the world to dedicate himself entirely to God. For this purpose, he acquired the deserted manor of Little Gidding in Huntingdonshire, and was ordained deacon by William Laud (then absentee Bishop of St David's) in 1626. He never became a priest. Into retirement at Little Gidding he took with him his mother, his brother and his brother-in-law with their families – about thirty people in all. Puritan traducers damned the place as 'the Arminian nunnery', but the rule cannot be called monastic. On weekdays there were offices every hour, the whole of the Psalter was recited each day and the Gospels were read through each month. Rather than take the latter in succession Nicholas Ferrar directed the production of a 'harmony' so that they would provide a continuous account of Christ's life – a method which would horrify a NT scholar of the late twentieth century. On Sunday mornings there would be Matins, and, after an interval, Ante-Communion. Holy Communion was celebated only on the first Sunday in the month and on major festivals.

There was much other activity. Gruel and milk were dispensed to the poor, children were taught, books were bound, the estate was organized and farmed. Every night there was a vigil from 9 pm to 1 am shared by two members of the community, a man and a woman, though with no one doing duty more than once a week. Ferrar himself always rose at 1 am and spent the time until the first office of the morning in his own prayers. He was not only a man of a serene, methodical, completely unexciteable devotion, but a skilled spiritual director. The community was not free from the personal difficulties, quarrels and bad relations endemic to such ventures but it attracted royal attention as well as Protestant obloquy. King Charles I paid at least two visits. Ferrar's health gave out in 1637. The community survived him into the turbulent years of the Civil Wars, but was ransacked and dispersed in 1646, lingering on in haunting and nostalgic memory for high Church Anglicanism, sensitively described in J. H. Shorthouse's remarkable and incredibly plagiaristic novel *John Inglesant* (1881), and immortalized in the last of T. S. Eliot's* *Four Quartets*.

A. L. Maycock, *Nicholas Ferrar of Little Gidding*, ²1963.

EDITOR

Fire

A universal feature of human life and one of the four ancient elements constituting the universe. It is a natural symbol, paradoxically signifying purification and life. In primitive cultures fire is usually sacred; in fact, it is an element particularly associated with the divine. Fire is common to the rituals of the religions of the world. At Rome the Vestal Virgins guard the holy fire. Fire is also a frequent symbol in ancient mythology. From its ashes the phoenix arises to new life. Prometheus gives fire, stolen from heaven, to mortals. (For a modern spiritual re-telling of this myth, see Thomas Merton, 'Prometheus: A Meditation' in *Raids on the Unspeakable*, 1966.) Fire is a complex symbol with multiple significations, e.g., divine love, divine presence, transcendence and holiness of God, transformation through purification, punishment, human love and passion: in fact, fire signifies whatever is intense.

Fire has a prominent place in the OT where it is especially a sign of God's presence. Thus the Lord goes before his people in the wilderness 'by night in a pillar of fire to give them light' (Ex. 13.21). Fire is also a usual element in the theophanies of the Old Testament: to Abraham (Gen. 15.17–18); to Moses at the burning bush (Ex. 3.2–3); to Moses at the top of Sinai (Ex. 19.18–19). But God is not in the fire of the theophany to Elijah at Horeb (I Kings 19.12). Fire has a place in the call of Isaiah (Isa. 6.6–8) and Ezekiel (Ezek. 1.27). 'The fire of the Lord' consumes the burnt offering of Elijah (I Kings 18.38). The prophet Elijah is also taken up into heaven in a chariot of fire and horses of fire (II Kings 2.11). The servant of Elisha sees a mountain full of horses and chariots of fire (II Kings 6.17). A perpetual fire burns on the altar of holocaust (Lev. 6.12–13) and symbolizes a continual prayer to the Lord on behalf of the Hebrews. Isaiah speaks of 'the Lord whose fire is in Zion, and whose furnace is in Jerusalem' (Isa. 31.9).

In the New Testament John the Baptist says that Jesus 'will baptize you with the Holy Spirit and with fire' (Luke 3.16).

Tongues of fire symbolize the coming of the Holy Spirit at Pentecost (Acts 2.3–4). Judgment by fire is a theme in the literature of the New Testament (II Thess. 1.8; II Peter 3.7; Rev. 15.2; I Cor. 3.12–15; 13.3) Fire is also an image for divine chastisement. The Lord 'rained on Sodom and Gomorrah brimstone and fire' (Gen. 19.24). The seventh plague includes lightening (fire) as a punishment upon the Egyptians (Ex. 9.23–24). Jesus rebukes James and John when they ask if he wants them to bid fire come down upon a village of the Samaritans who would not welcome Jesus (Luke 9.51–56). Fire appears often in apocalyptic literature. Gehenna is described as a place of fire (Matt. 5.22; 18.9; James 3.6). In the Christian tradition fire is the imagery for the punishment of purgatory and hell.

Fire is a constant image among the spiritual writers of Christianity. John Cassian* uses fire to describe the highest form of contemplative prayer (*Conferences* 9 and 10). In the 'Canticle of the Sun' Francis of Assisi* praises the Lord 'for Brother Fire, by whom Thou lightest the night; He is lovely and pleasant, mighty, and strong'. The most sublime imagery of fire appears in John of the Cross* whose poem and its commentary, 'The Living Flame of Love', speaks of the flame of love as the Holy Spirit who transforms and 'bathes the soul in glory and refreshes it with the quality of divine life' (*Commentary* 1, 3). For John fire is also human desire, tribulation, purification, and an inflaming of love. Christianity does not use fire as matter in any of its seven sacraments as it does water, but fire is frequently used in its rituals, e.g., the new fire of Holy Saturday, the burning of incense, candles for services.

Fire is a basic symbol of the poets who offer Christian spirituality an immense reservoir for imaging the dynamics of the relationship of the divine with the human. Influenced by Dante, T. S. Eliot* sees the paradox of suffering and love resolved in the heavenly contemplation of God when 'the fire and the rose are one'. Christian spirituality has yet to assimilate the meaning of the modern Jewish Holocaust which usually is thought of only in ethical terms.

J. Gaillard, 'Feu', *DS*, V, cols 247–73.

KEITH J. EGAN

Flagellants

The practice of flagellation (Latin: *flagellum*, a whip or scourge, *flagellare*, to scourge) went back to the early church and was understood both as a form of penance and as sharing in the Passion of Christ. It was not, however, until the thirteenth century that a widespread flagellant movement occurred. Contemporary sources agree that it started in Perugia, sparked off according to legend by the Lenten preaching of a Franciscan, Raniero Fasani, in 1260. Citizens began to process through the city scourging themselves and singing penitential psalms and hymns. At the height of the movement the whole population took to the streets in long processions of half-naked men. The movement spread south as far as Rome and north into Tuscany and Lombardy. By the end of 1260 it was dying down in Italy but had crossed the Alps into France, Germany, Austria and even Poland. Leaving aside local variations, certain common characteristics emerge: it was essentially an urban movement; it involved men of all classes (women were encouraged to do their penances privately); although not officially inspired by the church, it was not, as a rule, anti-clerical and the local clergy often participated; it was focused on penitential devotions but – although not politically revolutionary – it often issued in attempts to reconcile factions, free captives and make peace between cities. The backcloth to this upsurge of religious emotion was seen as the impending Day of Judgment. The contemporary hymn, *Dies irae, dies illa*, catches the mood powerfully. Contemporary writers found this eruption mysterious and puzzling. There was local famine and plague in 1258–1259 and Italy was torn by Guelf/Ghibelline conflict, but these factors do not explain the movement north of the Alps. Attempts have been made to connect it with Joachimism, since 1260 was a crucial date in the Joachimist programme, but there is little else in common. Joachim's disciples, however, contributed to a general mood of apocalyptic expectation out of which, it seems, the flagellant movement was born (*see* **Joachim of Fiore**). The only permanent result was the formation of confraternities typical of late mediaeval Italian cities, especially the companies of *laudesi* whose main function was to sing lauds in the vernacular to patron saints and the Virgin Mary. There were sporadic local outbursts in 1296, 1334, 1340, but the next widespread movement was in 1348–1349 at the time of the Black Death, starting with processions in Hungary and spreading westward as far as the Low Countries and Picardy. Although emotions ran high, the oath taken by flagellants imposed a strict discipline and ritual. Nevertheless extravagances and anti-clerical acts did occur in these later movements. Hence in 1349 Clement VI condemned the movement, though there were later outbursts, notably in Thuringia, associated with the mysterious Conrad Schmidt (1369).

J. Henderson, 'The flagellant movement and flagellant confaternities in central Italy 1260–1400', *Religious Motivation: Biographical and Sociological Problems for the Church Historian* ed D. Baker, [15]1978; G. Leff, *Heresy in the Later Middle Ages,* 1967, II, pp. 485–93.

                                        MARJORIE REEVES

Focolare

Focolare (the name means 'little fire') is a movement of spiritual renewal which began within the Catholic Church in Italy at the end of the Second World War and spread throughout the world and into all branches of the Christian church. Its proper name is *Opera di Maria,* 'the works of Mary'. Its founder, Chiara Lubich, was born in Trent, Italy, on 22 January 1920. At the age of nineteen, she had a profound experience in Loreto and returned home to commit herself to live a consecrated life as part of God's family in the world. A few years later, during the bombing of Trent, she gathered a group of girls and young women in the air-raid shelters to read NT and try to live by its teaching. They committed themselves to one another and went out together to serve the poor. When her family left Trent she remained in the bombed city to be with her spiritual family. From this simple beginning, the movement grew, always concentrating upon the family community.

At first it was a cohort of virgins devoted to the Virgin Mary, their religious life centred on the eucharist, completely obedient to the church. With the entry of Igino Giordani into the movement, it became possible for married members to be equally committed. Men had already come into

membership and communities of men and of women were formed. Some lived in community homes and continued their ordinary work in the world, sharing their worldly goods. Others, although married, belonged to communities whose meetings they attended; husband and wife would each be assigned a separate community. Yet others were volunteers, with spiritual commitment. The biblical basis of spirituality remains now the movement has become world-wide and highly organized to penetrate every aspect of life. Each month, a quotation from the Bible is selected as the 'word of life' for that month. Every member is expected to live by that word during the month, keeping it constantly in mind and testing life by it day by day. Commentaries on these 'words of life' are carefully prepared and circulated through the organ of the movement which appears in many different languages, usually with the title, *New City.*

From the beginning of the movement members have met during the summer to comfort and strengthen one another. These meetings are called *Mariapoli,* 'cities of Mary'. The strong sense of fellowship and commitment is brought out in talks, discussions, the sharing of experiences and 'testimonies' to what Jesus has meant to them since they followed the 'Ideal', which is God. The promise of Jesus that 'where two or three are gathered together in my name, there am I in the midst of them' is frequently quoted. Focolare speak of 'putting Jesus in the midst' when they meet.

The secret of the Focolare Movement is in the simple experience of 'the girl from Trent'. Chiara is the inspiration of the movement. Although many more experienced and better educated people have joined the movement in the course of the years and it has become of international importance, its entire spirituality can be traced to the experience of Chiara. In an early letter, Chiara writes with wonder to her friend: 'Think, Elena, with this little heart we can love God.' She saw from the beginning that the movement must be one of unity and love. She has persistently striven to keep the approval of the church. Within the Catholic Church she has taken the movement to priests, parishes, theological students, religious orders, universities and educational institutions. All this has been organized on a world-wide basis with a centre at Rocca di Papa. In journeying and in building new communities she has made ecumenical contacts of great importance in Orthodoxy, the Lutheran Church, the Church of England, and more recently outside the Christian community, particularly among Buddhists of Japan. In all this, the spirituality has remained central to the Catholic tradition; the eucharist, Mary, the Bible, hierarchy.

Edwin Robertson, *Chiara*, 1978.

EDWIN ROBERTSON

Fosdick, Harry Emerson

For decades, Fosdick (1878–1969) was the most prominent voice of the American pulpit. His ministry was distinguished in several ways. In times of national crisis he provided prophetic moral leadership. In a warlike century he spoke as a champion of peaceful approaches to human and national problems. In a time of great social upheaval he helped guide the changes in channels concerned with human values. In a time of conflict between religion and science he found a common ground where the truth of each could supplement the other. In a time of human stress he put his pastoral counselling ministry first. When millions of people were struggling for goals in life he made a Christ-centred ministry relevant and appealing.

As a scholar Fosdick wrote important interpretations of the Bible. As a pastoral psychologist he wrote the books that set the course for a pastoral ministry that survived the fads of the day. As a seminary teacher he helped several generations of young preachers to understand person-centred preaching. As a person he set standards of courage, integrity and selflessness that buttressed his message.

Underlying his ministry was a spirituality that manifested itself in prayer, faith and service. His books on these subjects became guides in the spiritual quest for decades in the early part of this century. A dozen books of sermons became the yardstick by which preaching was measured for many years. Characterized by brief but sharp illustrations, these sermons asked the basic questions people were asking and addressed them from the perspective of high purpose and Christian standards for living. Biography was important to Fosdick in sermon content, and studies of Jesus, Luther, Paul and Rufus Jones were explorations of human motivation to which he added the open clarity of his autobiography. Theological studies include a book on immortality, Christianity and progress, a modern perspective on religion, and what is vital to Christianity. Books on pastoral care speak to tension, personality development, personal relations and social living.

After the First World War a tide of reaction in religion and social processes swept across America with waves of anti-social anti-intellectualism, racial conflict and a rejection of science, with fundamentalist interpretation of the scriptures and retreat to the theological perspectives of times past. In the midst of this reaction Fosdick stood firm as a voice of reason, patience, Christian tolerance and personal courage. As a part of this time of conflict Fosdick was forced out of First Presbyterian Church in New York. This action tended to bring the atmosphere of conflict into focus and every word and act of his was given great importance. Acceptance or rejection of his views became a matter of vicious contention and yet his spirit was not contaminated and he never allowed himself to be brought into the mood of meanness that prevailed. He used the opportunity of his prominence to educate, guide and inspire a new and more adequate perspective in American Protestantism. Called to a new and beautiful church built to facilitate his concept of ministry, he served there from 1930 until his retirement in 1946.

In another time of reaction and anti-intellectualism, Fosdick's reasoned utterance may still merit a hearing in protest at once against low moral standards and a repudiation of the social gospel, questioning not only conservative evangelicalism but also some of the more superficial influences of oriental mysticism and anti-institutional faddism. He speaks of the redemptive and worshipping community which undergirds social life with purpose and human sensitivity. He verifies the role a preacher can play in the lives of millions of people. In a time when the medium is often misused for small and selfish purposes, he stands out as a teacher who refused to abuse the medium or abridge the message.

The Manhood of the Master, 1913; *The*

Meaning of Prayer, 1915; *The Modern Use of the Bible*, 1924; *Successful Christian Living*, 1937; *Living under Tension*, 1941; *A Faith for Tough Times*, 1952; *Living of These Days* (autobiography), 1956; *Riverside Sermons* (a collection issued in honour of his 80th birthday), 1958.

EDGAR N. JACKSON

Foucauld, Charles de

Charles Eugène de Foucauld (1858–1916) was born an aristocrat and was inordinately rich. He served as a cavalry officer in Africa, which gave him a passion for the Sahara. After some daring explorations, particularly in Morocco, the influence of Abbé Huvelin * brought him back to the Catholic faith and he went on pilgrimage to the Holy Land. In 1890 he joined the Trappist Monastery of Nôtre Dame des Neiges, but desiring greater solitude than it could provide he joined the Poor Clares in Nazareth and then in Jerusalem. He returned to France in 1900 and was ordained priest a year later. He was concerned to identify himself with the really poor and had already discovered that the most austere monastery, because of its security, could not help him to do this. So he went to Algeria to live the life of a hermit: first, from 1901 to 1905, at Beni Abbès; then from 1905 in the even more remote oasis of Tamanrasset in the heart of the Sahara, among the Tuareg Moslems. All that concerned the Tuareg became his concern: family life, agriculture, health, hygiene, education, culture. He studied the language, compiled a Tuareg dictionary and translated into Tuareg. As a hermit among them he spent his time in 'prayer, penance and works of charity'. He won the admiration of the French soldiers and of the Moslems but never converted any. He was assassinated in the Sahara by a Tuareg in 1916.

Charles de Foucauld saw all men as children of God, brothers of Christ, destined to be happy in the same heaven by grace of the redemption. It troubled him that in a universal church the Latin liturgy should be unintelligible to vast numbers of Arabs, Turks and Armenians. He wanted to see priests and religious men participating in the lives of those around them. He believed that the laity should play a greater role in the spread of the gospel. His vision was of men and women spreading Christianity, not by

words or ceremonies, but by sheer goodness, warmth of heart, generosity; not necessarily mentioning religion or God, but 'being patient as God is patient, loving as God is loving', eschewing all bitterness or condescension. He could look beyond his own church to other Christians and also to Jews and Moslems. Christ had come to all men without exception; but there must be no question of preaching to Moslems. That would alienate them. When the aunt of Mousa, the Tuareg chieftain, was dying, they sent for Charles de Foucauld, whom they called the 'Christian Marabout', to comfort her. There was no confusion in the mind of either. Each respected the other: they met on common ground, in that each believed in God.

Before he was assassinated, de Foucauld compiled rules for communities of what he called 'Little Brothers' and 'Little Sisters', but no one joined him.

After de Foucauld's death, Fr René Voillaume and some of his friends attempted to follow these rules at El Abiodh Sidi Cheikh. They were scattered by the Second World War, but returned in 1945, and the community soon grew, spreading throughout the world. There was a deeply contemplative element in these communities of 'Little Brothers of Jesus', who according to the rule laid down by de Foucauld conformed to local economies and milieu, wearing working clothes like the rest, whether factory hand, farmer or fisherman. René Voillaume explained to the Little Brothers how their name should mould their attitude: 'Little we are before the task we have to accomplish. Little we shall be in the eyes of men also. All our lives we shall remain unprofitable servants, and we must wish so to be dealt with.' In the same year (1933) as René Voillaume had founded the Little Brothers of Jesus in the Sahara, the Little Sisters of the Sacred Heart was founded in Montpelier in France. In 1939 the Little Sisters of Jesus was formed in Touggourt. This was followed by the Little Sisters and the Little Brothers of the Gospel in 1958 and 1965 respectively.

It soon became evident that these brothers and sisters of solitude had to adapt Charles de Foucauld's original rules in order to fit more easily into the environment of Europe's dechristianized proletariat and subsequently the Third World. A section of the 'Sisters' had already started evolving in this way as early as 1939, meeting in this new form with rapid success.

De Foucauld's idea of realizing the message of Jesus entirely through the example of his own life, without any physical protection in the midst of a Moslem world, was seen by his followers to be a prophecy of the condition of Christian life in the future – despite or because of the fact that he died in absolute solitude.

Elizabeth Hamilton, *The Desert My Dwelling Place*, 1968.

EDWIN ROBERTSON

Fox, George

Founder of the Society of Friends (Quakers*), George Fox (1624–1691) was born at Fenny Drayton in Leicestershire, son of a Puritan weaver, and on his mother's side 'of the stock of the martyrs'. In 1643 he experienced a profound disillusion with the forms of religion he saw around him, and with those who professed them. 'Young people go together into vanity and old people into the earth.' After a time of 'sorrows and troubles', during which he abandoned corporate worship 'walking solitary abroad', he was released by a sense of God's 'light, spirit and power', uniting him to Christ. 'Now was I come up in spirit through the flaming sword into the paradise of God. All things were new, and all the creation gave another smell unto me than before, beyond what words can utter. I knew nothing but pureness, and innocency, and righteousness, being renewed up into the image of God by Christ Jesus, so that I say I was come up to the state of Adam which he was in before he fell . . . even into a state in Christ Jesus, that should never fall.' He moved into Nottinghamshire, preaching the indwelling Christ and the falsehood of 'customary worships': frequently imprisoned and sometimes savagely beaten, he remained utterly uncompromising. His mission took fire in 1652 in north-west England. He based himself at Swarthmoor, near Ulverstone, the house of Judge William Fell, who protected the young movement though he never joined it. At the Restoration the 'Quaker' movement might have died. Fox quelled its more extravagant manifestations of individualism and gave it the structure which, substantially, it still retains. He married Fell's widow in 1669. The remainder of his life

was spent in tireless missionary journeys (Ireland, West Indies, North America, Holland). He died in 1691, and his journal, one of the most remarkable documents of the seventeenth century, dictated to Thomas Ellwood, was published in 1694.

Fox was 'an original, being no man's copy'; his religion was one of immediacy, the possession of the inner light which was Christ, and which placed the believer above all external authorities, however sacred. 'You will say, Christ saith this, and the apostles say this; but what canst thou say?' Many in his time claimed such an inner light, and justified thereby fanaticism and antinomianism. Fox's insistence on the believer's present possession of righteousness, purity, truth and tenderness (a favourite word), his singleminded devotion to the light, preserved him. 'Do not look at the temptations, confusions, corruptions, but at the light which discovers them, that makes them manifest', he told Cromwell's daughter, Lady Claypole, 'and with the same light you will feel over them, to receive power to stand against them.' Loathing hypocrisy and injustice, compassionate to the poor, he found much to enrage him in seventeenth-century England, and made many enemies by his outspokenness. But his nature was 'tender' too – beaten senseless at Ulverstone, he stood up 'in the eternal power of God' and 'was in the love of God to them all that had persecuted me'.

His teaching, which everywhere bears his personal stamp, nevertheless drew on many sources. The Civil War threw up much that was by modern standards bizarre, and his message is indebted to Behmenism, the Hermetic tradition, the strain of mysticism found in puritans like Richard Sibbes, but above all to the Bible, read with a wholly unconventional eye. 'I saw plainly that none could read Moses aright without Moses' spirit.' The language he uses to describe his profoundest experiences, like much that is a product of the Civil War period, is often dualistic, reflecting a conflict between light and dark, the seed of God and the seed of the devil; he applies even the historical sections of the Bible to the inner life of man, but underlying all is an earthy wisdom and salt entirely his own, and an insistence on the love and light of Christ which is centrally Christian.

He aroused fierce loyalty and devotion in

those close to him, high and low. The husbandman, Robert Widders, wrote to him from prison that 'when I think on thee, the power rises and warms my heart'. After Fox's death the courtier William Penn* wrote: 'Many sons have done virtuously in this day, but dear George thou excellest them all.'

Best edition of the *Journal* is by J. L. Nickalls, 1952, with introductory essay by G. F. Nuttall and Preface by Penn; see also H. J. Cadbury, *George Fox's Book of Miracles*, 1948.

EAMON DUFFY

Francis of Assisi, St

Francis of Assisi (1181/2–1226) was the founder of the Franciscan Order of Friars, the Poor Clares and an Order of Penance for laypeople, called today the Secular Franciscan Order. His father, Pietro Bernadone, was a wealthy cloth merchant. At about the age of twenty-three, after a dissipated youth, he underwent a radical conversion of life. It was connected with a number of mystical experiences among which a leper and the crucifix at San Damiano had crucial significance.

On hearing the text of Matt. 10.7ff. at Mass on the feast of St Matthias 1209, he embraced a life of total poverty in literal obedience to Christ's words. From that moment the gospel became an absolute in his life, and his life unfolded as a kind of exegesis of the gospel. He founded an evangelical movement whose inspiration was not only the Synoptic Gospels but the good news contained in the NT as a whole. As a reform movement his observance of Christ's teaching was coupled with a deep love of the church, for it was in and through the church that he had come to know the gospel. His writings, and especially the prayers he composed, are full of adoration of the Triune God and a burning love of Christ our Brother. He writes 'How glorious . . . it is to have a Father in heaven . . . How holy and beloved . . . it is to have a Brother like this who laid down his life for his sheep.'

His radical poverty was not primarily ascetical; it was evangelical and christological. Christ's freely-chosen poverty was for him a revelation of the humility of God. Hence he loved Jesus above all in the crib, on the cross and in the eucharist as manifestations of God's powerlessness, vulnerability and littleness. His first biographer, Thomas of Celano, says of him 'he was always thinking about Jesus; Jesus was in his mouth, in his ears, in his eyes, in his hands; Jesus was in his whole being'.

His evangelical movement was committed to brotherhood and poverty and pledged to preaching peace. After some hesitation Pope Innocent III gave oral approval to his way of life. Later in the *Rule of 1223* St Francis identified the rule and life of his friars with observing the gospel.

Poverty and brotherhood are dominant themes in his writings, especially the non-approved *Rule of 1221* and the *Admonitions*. To live a life of freely-chosen material poverty coupled with humility, its spiritual counterpart, involves a mystical death to self in order to be made alive again through the gifts of God's Spirit. Without possessions it is not necessary to have weapons to defend them and so by poverty we become instruments of God's peace. To be a brother is to be related in Christ to all creatures and to observe meekness towards them all. He called every creature his brother or sister, even death was his sister. This was no mere nature mysticism, but an expression of belief in the fatherhood of God the Creator and in the gift of unity in Christ.

In September 1224 while at prayer on Mt La Verna the marks of Christ's stigmata appeared on his body, which he bore until death. It was the final configuration of his life, prior to death, to Jesus Christ. According to St Francis the destination of the soul's journey to God is total conformity to Christ by following in his footsteps a life of poverty, humility and meekness, whereby the disciple becomes a living symbol of the master.

See also **Franciscan Spirituality, Franciscans**

Regis Armstrong, OFM Cap and Ignatius Brady, OFM (eds) *Francis and Clare: The Complete Works*, 1982; Auspicius van Corstanje, OFM *The Covenant with God's Poor*, 1966; *Francis' Bible of the Poor*, 1977; Eric Doyle, OFM, *St Francis and the Song of Brotherhood*, 1980; Omer Englebert, OFM, *St Francis of Assisi*, 1965, including extensive research bibliography by Raphael Brown; David Flood, OFM and Thadée Matura, OFM, *The Birth of a Movement: A*

Study of the First Rule of St Francis, 1975;
Marion A. Habig, OFM, *St Francis of
Assisi. Writings and Early Biographies. English Omnibus of the Sources*, 1972.

ERIC DOYLE, OFM

Francis de Sales, St

A native of the high Savoy, Francis (1567–1622) renounced his rights as eldest son to become a priest. His conversion as a very young man was a consequence of his realizing the full horrors of Augustine's* teaching on predestination, which he received by way of Aquinas* and which was the central article of the prevailing Calvinist 'heresy'. Aware of his likely damnation, he lived for some weeks in an agony of 'disinterested love'*, determined to love and serve God all his life since this would be impossible for him in eternity. One day, kneeling before the statue of the Black Virgin in the Parisian Church of St Etienne-des-Grès, he heard a celestial voice overriding the Eternal Decrees. 'I do not call myself the Damning One, my name is Jesus'. The first period of his ministry was spent as a missionary to the Catholics of the Chablais on the southern shores of Lake Geneva. Appointed co-adjutor to the Bishop of Geneva then in exile at Annecy, he was sent to Paris in 1602 and came under the influence of Bérulle* and others who were anxious to renew the religious life of France in the aftermath of the Reformation and in the 'brave new world' of exploration and discovery. Here Francis emerged as a preacher and man of exceptional spiritual gifts. He succeeded his bishop in the difficult see of Calvinist dominated Geneva and spent his last two decades writing the two devotional classics for which he is famed, preaching and directing souls, often by letter, and founding a new religious order for women, the Visitation, in which he was chiefly associated with the widow Jane Frances Fremyot de Chantal (1572–1641). Their relations are a notable instance of the spirituality of friendship (cf. Aelred of Rievaulx*).

Francis's two works are *Introduction to a Devout Life* (1608) and *Treatise on the Love of God* (1616). The former is important because along with the *Spiritual Exercises*, and even more influential in the lives of ordinary people, it asserts that holiness is possible to those whose lives are entirely in the world, in towns, households, at court

and in ordinary circumstances. It does not claim to be more than an elementary manual. It teaches a method of meditation not unlike the Ignatian, albeit gentler, more conscious of the goodness of the human soul, less dominated by the thought of the awesome warfare against demonic powers. There is attentive apprehension of God, and invocation at the beginning, the 'setting forth of the mystery' which may include the use of the imagination and 'composition of place', the 'consideration' or meditation proper resulting in stimulus to love, resolution to act, thanksgiving and offering. And then the spiritual 'bouquet' or 'nosegay', as though the whole act had been a walk through a garden from which we have culled a few particularly beautiful flowers to refresh and delight us by their sight and smell. It may seem at first a little too bland, pleasant, even effeminate; yet it demands a total dedication of the self to Christ, as of the most heroic sanctity. It has been pointed out that although supposedly so elementary, it asks a good deal in 'remote preparation' i.e. a life given over to good reading, holy thoughts and refined observation, which provide material for meditation. Camus, Bishop of Belley, Francis's friend, cannot have been unmindful that his trenchant criticism of clogging methodology which prevents the childlike, ordinary soul from rising to the heights he could attain by a simple instinct of love, applied to the *Introduction*.

The *Treatise* is Francis's greater, though no more significant work. We may think that it was proleptic in the youth kneeling before the Virgin's statue, but it was fulfilled through his years of friendship with Mme de Chantal. He called it 'our book', and she, his 'penitent', is its model. The heart of love for Francis is mutuality and *eros* and *agāpē* cannot be disjoined. God in his perfection needs our poverty. 'He courts our love with infinite esteem' (Traherne). The union of God and man in Christ is not only the remedy for sin: it is the purpose of creation. 'All things are created for prayer', says Francis, but not for prayer as a pious escape from living, sign of a dualism between our Godward and earthbound inclinations, or a desire for spiritual experience. Prayer is the life of Christ, his communion with the Father, the perfect expression of his love, and its price is the cross. 'Mount Calvary is the Academy of Love.'

would no doubt soon find congregation becoming more responsive; and the teacher can learn much about the art of teaching itself simply by watching Peter Brooks undertaking the task in this book. Most important of all, underlying all that he writes is a theological understanding which is made accessible through the penetrating profundity of the way he uses story and parable and image in communicating truth.

For me the only boring part of the book was its most practical one — the last chapter dealing with the nuts and bolts of the electronic media themselves and the design for their development in the future. But then I suppose even Tortelier would tell us that we need to know how instruments are constructed if we are to play them effectively, and certainly the technical developments in all mass communication media are going to make it all the more imperative that we learn how to master them. So this book is in more senses than one compelling reading for anyone who has a conviction to communicate.

Pauline Webb

WAKEFIELD, Gordon (ed.), *A Dictionary of Christian Spirituality* (SCM 1983 £15.00) pp. 400

'SPIRITUALITY' is an 'in' word of our time, a catholic word turned ecumenical, and perhaps the eighteenth century had better words in their conjunction of 'inward religion' with 'practical theology'. But this is an important and timely volume at a time when there is growing recognition of the need to recover a dimension of 'depth', in some relief from a too strident activism. Great credit must be given to the Editor of this attractive and valuable compilation. No less than sixty articles are from his pen, and it would be needlessly cynical to suppose that he wrote in default of other contributors. But his articles are all lucid, readable and scholarly and as they range the centuries and the churches, he expresses a quite admirable catholicity. His old teacher, Dr Newton Flew, would have rejoiced to see this volume and to know that it was edited by a Methodist.

There is an enormous range in a volume which begins with 'Abandon' and ends with 'Zen'. A galaxy of learned and generally percipient authors from many communions have been co-opted though they have different measures of success with this compressed and tricky art form.

'Prayer' is the centre of a fine constellation of articles which will be much quoted. Other religions are well catered for and there are the desirable 'insights' from East and West. Some of the modern movements seem to be concessions to the modern cult of relevance, and those middle-aged, unexamined clichés of the 1960s which now appear as the mind of the church, will no doubt be eventually seen to be the most dated. There are scores of fine biographical studies and generally the book lists are admirable.

One may have one's grouses and bouquets. Ten bonus points for an article on Péguy (the book list should include Roman Rolland's volumes with the photographs, and the lovely recent poem by Geoffrey Hill). I do not think that that splendid man Leslie Weatherhead should have been included, while those of much more significant depth and influence such as W. R. Maltby (and A. E. Whitham) are omitted. And I can see no justification whatever for the inclusion of Norman Vincent Peale who seems no more relevant to the real purpose of this volume than Pocahontas. I cannot excuse the omission of separate articles on Hildegarde of Bingen and Thomas Ken. The article on Scottish Spirituality is too Presbyterian and omits the great mystics of the North East, Scougal, the Garden brothers, the Chevalier Ramsay.

One wonders if evangelical religion has justice done to it, in the light of a thin article on 'Conversion' which makes too much of Erik Erikson. It is not an English failing to solemnize about the subject of humour but I find the article on 'Humour' rather horrifying and would have rather entrusted it to Frankie Howerd than a learned French Benedictine. In private duty bound, we may draw attention to very good pieces by Ben Drewery, David Tripp and Robert Gribben. 'Inward religion' is indeed practical theology and this work is a tool and a work of reference from which a great many sermons, meditations and prayers will derive in coming years. It is also a book to be dipped into for pleasure and profit. It may join Peake's commentary, The Oxford Dictionary of the Christian Church, and *Alice in Wonderland* among the short list of indispensables in every parson's study.

Gordon Rupp

BONINO, José Miguez, *Toward a Christian Political Ethics* (SCM 1983 £5.50) pp. 126

How can we develop a Christian political ethics? To some, this might seem a strange question to find in the work of a leading theologian from Latin America. We have become familiar with the political dimension of the life of the Christian church in Latin America, and familiar too with Latin American theologians' sharp criticism of the wordy theological theorizing found in so many of our own church debates. It is therefore interesting to find a leading figure in the liberation theology movement insisting on the necessity of theory, and explicit theory at that, as an integral part of the struggle for Christian liberation.

In this book José Miguez Bonino sketches a theoretical framework for a Christian political ethics. The author is already well-known for his work in liberation theology. He admits that many of his friends and colleagues in that movement will be impatient with this book, seeing it as a step back from reality; others will be impatient with it because it spends more time discussing the history of Latin America than the Bible; yet others will be impatient because it does not provide neat definitions of basic terms. However anyone interested in the relationship between Christian faith and political action will profit from reading the book.

The book begins with a clear statement of the need for a Christian political ethics in a world in which so many decisions have a political dimension. Then there is a brief sketch of some Christian responses to this need, ranging from Martin Luther to John Yoder via the World Council of Churches and Roman Catholic 'social doctrine'. A tantalizingly brief chapter introduces some models, which are then used to analyse part of the history of Latin America

In spite of this, the spirituality of Francis de Sales is in contrast to the austere and sombre discipline of more militant schools. He wished to place souls in their inmost depths 'in an attitude of suavity'. Bremond* says that he sweetened all and attenuated nothing. Herein lies his originality.

Henri Bremond, *A Literary History of Religious Thought in France*, Vols I & II, 1928, 1930; John Burnaby, *Amor Dei*, 1938, pp. 277–86; K. E. Kirk, *The Vision of God*, 1931, pp. 404–13; Elisabeth Stopp (trs and ed), *St Francis de Sales: A Testimony by St Chantal*, 1967; *Selected Letters*, 1965.

EDITOR

Franciscan Spirituality, Franciscans

St Francis of Assisi did not found a school of spirituality, nor is there a systematic Franciscan spirituality. He was keenly aware of the uniqueness of each individual's call to union with God, as his *Letter to Brother Leo* shows. Franciscan spirituality covers a wide spectrum of approaches to the Christian mystery. It has been called christocentric, evangelical, existential, tender, devotional and practical. All these descriptions are justified from its origins in the faith and holiness of St Francis.

He had a profound sense of God as transcendent mystery and holy love. Out of that sprang his passionate love of the Saviour. He was filled with awe that God, exalted in his majesty, should come among us in humility. His one desire was to follow 'the teaching and the footsteps of our Lord Jesus Christ'. Everything centred on Christ, the poor, humble, obedient, suffering Servant who died and rose for us. Scripture and the liturgy were his sole guides on the journey to God, and he sought to observe the gospel literally. That was no form of fundamentalism or legalistic literalism. Literal observance meant a total commitment to the spiritual values the gospel proclaims.

This simple and direct approach influenced and shaped Franciscan theology and piety. St Bonaventure* teaches that Christ is our metaphysics and logic, holding the central position in everything, because he is mediator between God and humanity. All intellectual activity has to begin at that centre (*medium*) in order to arrive at wisdom, not just knowledge. Reason has its

place in the soul's journey into God, but it remains subject to faith. There comes a point where reason reaches its limits and then the will passes over into God. St Bonaventure presents his master, St Francis, as the perfect exemplar of Christian action and contemplation, and of the latter especially in his configuration to the Crucified on La Verna. Theology according to St Bonaventure is primarily the study of scripture, which led him to consider human beings, not in the abstract, but in their historical condition as fallen and redeemed.

The place of Christ is taken a step further by Duns Scotus in the doctrine of the absolute predestination of Christ, which became a distinguishing feature of Franciscan spirituality and theology. It was resumed later by the great Capuchin Doctor of the Church, St Lawrence of Brindisi, who demonstrates its scriptural origin. Christ is first in the plan of God, the incarnation is not decreed because of sin. God's love alone is the reason because 'God is formally love' and sovereignly free. Redemption is the way his love overcomes the powers of evil. This teaching is taken directly from scripture (cf. e.g. Col., Eph.) and it has seminal expression in the writings of St Francis. The incarnation is decreed because God wills to have co-lovers in his love.

Love of the incarnate Lord found form in a variety of devotions. St Francis' crib at Greccio may have influenced crib-building at Christmastide. In any case, devotion to the Child Jesus is a theme found in most Franciscan spiritual writers. St Clare wrote to Bl. Agnes of Prague that she should meditate daily on the King of angels lying in a manger. St Bonaventure* composed a beautiful little treatise *On the Five Feasts of the Child Jesus* which explains how the Child is spiritually conceived, born, named, sought and adored with the Magi and presented in the Temple, by the devout soul. St Francis' devotion to the passion and his *Office of the Passion of the Lord* inspired a wealth of literature on the sufferings of Christ. The devotion greatly influenced the practice of the Way of the Cross whose most ardent advocate, in the form we now have it, was the Franciscan, St Leonard of Port Maurice. St Francis' love of the Risen Lord present in the littleness and silence of the eucharist, made eucharistic devotion a pillar of Franciscan spirituality. He also revered the names of God and cherished above all the holy name of Jesus. Devotion to the name of Jesus was encouraged by Franciscans in the thirteenth and fourteenth centuries, but its most staunch defender was the Franciscan Observant, St Bernadine of Siena, in the fifteenth century. He preached the name of Jesus as the summary of the gospel of salvation (cf. Acts. 8.12). Love of the humanity of Jesus in the Franciscan tradition also encouraged devotion to the Sacred Heart*. It is the theme of a number of St Bonaventure's mystical writings.

St Francis had a tender devotion to the mother of Jesus which never degenerated into sentimentality. His biographer, Celano, writes: 'Towards the Mother of Jesus he was filled with inexpressible love, because it was she who made the Lord of Majesty our brother.' He seems to have been the first to have called Mary 'spouse of the Holy Spirit'. She is presented as model of the spiritual life: 'we are mothers to (our Lord Jesus Christ) when we enthrone him in our hearts and souls by love with a pure and sincere conscience and give birth to him by doing good'. Spiritual motherhood and the tenderness which accompanies it should be a mark of every Christian disciple. Maturity in the spiritual life for St Francis requires one to arrive at a balance of the feminine and masculine elements in human nature. The Franciscan Order held to the doctrine of the Immaculate Conception for centuries before it was officially defined. Duns Scotus received the title Marian Doctor for his defence of the doctrine which must always be understood in the light of his teaching on the absolute predestination of Christ. Mary's redemption took place through the foreseen merits of Christ. On the devotional side the Order introduced the feasts of the Visitation and Espousals of the Virgin Mary. The crown rosary in honour of the seven joys of Mary became established in the Order in the early fifteenth century.

St Francis looked on all creatures as brothers and sisters united in the vast friary of the universe: he called even the stars his sisters. He gave mystical expression to this vision in *The Canticle of Brother Sun*. So far from being distractions, all creatures are revelations of the infinite richness of God. There is therefore a definite ecological element in his spirituality. This attitude to creatures took theological form in St Bonaventure's doctrine of exemplarism, according to which all creation is seen as God's sacrament.

The Franciscan Order has been described as contemplative-active. It is an accurate description not only in the sense that apostolic works should flow from and lead back to prayer, but also because St Francis made provision for the eremitical life in the Order. He wrote a short *Rule for Hermitages* which marks a new development in the history of this form of life. Those who feel called to it must live in small hermitages, numbering not more than four friars. Two of them are to be 'mothers' whose duty it is to take care of their 'sons', that is, those who are given completely to prayer. Thus, in his notion of the eremitical life St Francis combines fraternity and prayer. He inspired St Clare and her sisters to lead an enclosed life of contemplative prayer after the model of the hidden life of Jesus at Nazareth. St Francis also founded a successful lay movement which was called the Order of Penance. The members pledged themselves to do penance and lead simple lives. The movement had important social consequences. The brothers and sisters undertook every kind of charitable work and they set up a common fund to help brethren who were in need. They did not take up arms, nor would they hold public office. St Francis wrote a Rule for this order. No copy of it survives but the shorter text of his *Letter to the Faithful* may well be a version of it. It contains a genuine lay spirituality.

The virtues cultivated in Franciscan spirituality are wisdom, poverty, humility and love. Wisdom, which is surrender to the truth as personal, is mentioned first by St Francis in his *Praises of the Virtues*, and it is, as has been said, the aim of all theological study and spiritual endeavour. To embrace poverty is the highest wisdom because it demands a self-emptying which conforms one to Christ and allows the mind and heart to be filled with divine gifts. 'Lady Poverty', as St Francis called the virtue, has been the topic of heated and often acrimonious arguments in the history of the Order and, ironically, the cause of division. It is of course multi-faceted, and while Franciscan spirituality has had to accommodate itself over the centuries to influences and developments which make the observance of St Francis' radical poverty well-nigh impossible, it has always insisted on detachment, powerlessness and sharing, without which mere material poverty becomes an idol or a tyrant. Humility is, as it were, the inner side of material poverty. It is basically recognition of the truth, as St Francis writes 'What a man is before God, that he is and no more'. In that truth St Francis discovered that we are all brothers and sisters in Christ, little brothers and sisters. Our first duty is to love in Christ the most high God and one another, and love is a free act of the will. Franciscan spirituality has always taught the primacy of the will and the primacy of love, and nothing could summarize it better.

See also **Francis of Assisi, St.**

Ewart Cousins (ed), *Bonaventure: The Souls's Journey into God. The Tree of Life. The Life of St Francis*, 1978; Christian Duquoc and Casiano Floristán (eds), 'Francis of Assisi Today', *Concilium* 149, November 1981, whole issue; Kajetan Esser, O F M, *Repair My House*, 1963; *Rule and Testament of St Francis. Conferences to Modern Followers of St Francis*, 1977; Kajetan Esser, O F M and Engelbert Grau, O F M, *Love's Reply*, 1963; Agostino Gemelli, O F M, *The Franciscan Message to the World*, 1934; Zachary Hayes, O F M, *The Hidden Center: Spirituality and Speculative Christology in St Bonaventure*, 1981; Duane V. Lapsanski, *The First Franciscans and the Gospel*, 1976; Damian McElrath (ed), *Franciscan Christology*, 1980.

ERIC DOYLE, OFM

Francke, August H. *see* **Pietism**

French Spirituality

To the historian of spirituality, few nations, if any, present a more rich and varied experience of spirituality than Christian France. Indeed this very richness poses a significant challenge to the historian who would propose to capture the spirituality of France in summary form.

1. *The Early Christian Period.* Relatively little is known regarding the first four centuries in France. As Christianity moved westward, Christian life struggled to supplant other indigenous religious traditions. As the church established itself in the major trade and military sites across Europe, the central location of France placed the country in a position to exert a great influence elsewhere in the now Christian Empire.

By the fourth century the impact of Eastern spirituality took root in French soil. The ascetical tradition of the Eastern Desert Fathers* in particular found adherents in France. Martin of Tours, who had laid down his arms as a soldier, saw the ascetical life as a call to Christians to take up the spiritual combat as the *militia Christi*, the army of Christ. By the fifth century asceticism took on a more careful, methodical, though no less severe, form in the setting of monastic life.

During this period early monastic forms of life exercised the most powerful influence in shaping Christian spirituality in France. At the monastery of Lérins the monastic rule was adapted to be more accessible to lay persons. Thus the evolving spirituality took on a more pastoral expression. Bishops formed in the monastic tradition transferred this monastic spirituality to the lives of a poorly trained clergy. Many of these clergy came to adopt life in community as the foundation for their pastoral efforts. The spiritual discipline of Lent*, for example, is evidence of the lasting impact of monasticism on the spiritual life of the entire church.

2. *The Middle Ages.* During the age of Charlemagne, the influence of St Columbanus* and other Irish monks brought a distinctive penitential tone to monastic life in France. In addition, the social chaos attendant upon the barbarian influx demanded that the monastic life assume a greater pastoral responsibility. Hence French monastic spirituality continued to exhibit a strong pastoral thrust. Devotion to Mary and to the eucharist added two important elements to this common spirituality.

The period of decline which followed Charlemagne saw the decay of feudalism begin and lay princes gain increasing control of the church. Paradoxically, this period of societal breakdown called forth the reform of Cluny. This monastic reform reintegrated the ecclesial dimension into Christian life thanks to Cluny's close ties with the church of Rome. The liturgical life was enriched and the life of prayer structured to be available to the laity. Piety and learning were joined as Cluny left its mark on the life of Christians in France and beyond.

From another point of view, the institution of chivalry provided the metaphors of military life to describe the life of the Christian as a combat against the powers of evil. As often happens with metaphors, the spirituality so described came in time to be acted out by means of the crusades, where Christian knights enacted their spiritual quests by travelling to distant lands to conquer the 'infidel'. Spirituality, whether for knight, peasant or prince, demanded the faithful enactment of the duties accorded to one's state in life.

Monastic reform again gave birth to innovative directions in spirituality in France. Bernard of Clairvaux * lyrically expounded a christological piety which became the touchstone for most authors through the twelfth century. Though of a mystical bent, Bernard was nonetheless pastoral. His insistence that the development of the inner life was necessary for fruitful pastoral care gave direction to the lives of countless clergy.

By the twelfth century, the transformation of cathedral schools into the famous universities was well underway. Paris became a centre of intellectual endeavour and drew the learned from many parts of Europe. Scholastic theology strove to give greater intellectual order and coherence to the Christian life. Paris and other centres of learning were in time to receive the formative influence of the mendicant Orders, especially the Order of Preachers (*see* **Dominican Spirituality, Dominicans**).

One cannot recount the spirituality of the late Middle Ages without acknowledging the rise of the mendicant Orders. Amid political tensions and religious upheaval, Francis of Assisi * led his band of simple brothers, and later sisters as well, along the precarious path to spiritual renewal of the evangelical roots of the church. Dominic Guzman and his followers banded together to counter the heretical movements in France and elsewhere. The contribution of other Dominicans such as Thomas Aquinas * and Albert the Great, both lecturers at Paris, has been inestimable in the history of Christian theology and spirituality. In time the Carmelites, Croisers and other religious communities added their distinctive spiritual heritages to the spirituality of the time. In addition to the strong focus on the humanity of Christ,

the mendicants brought a solid Marian devotion and a profound mysticism to the spiritual landscape of France.

Following the Hundred Years War, the mendicants and the Benedictines led the religious renewal in France. The university at Paris assumed major importance, as within its halls a theologian and spiritual director of the stature of Jean Gerson * developed his theory of mysticism which was to have a great impact on the theological understanding of mysticism.

3. *The Reformation and the Catholic Renewal.* The impact of the humanism of Erasmus and others in the sixteenth century was felt in France also. Reacting against a now sterile scholasticism, these thinkers developed a practical, affective theology well suited to the new, less institutionalized Christian life arising in Europe. Later, Ignatius Loyola * and his Jesuit * followers, proponents of the same humanistic tradition, formed the basic spiritual foundations for their work of inner reform and renewal of outer structures. The Roman Catholic response to the Reformation focused both on the inner life and on basic sacramental practice. Although the Council of Trent afforded the opportunity, real structural change in the Roman Church was not characteristic of this period. In France the impetus for renewal came largely from Italy and Spain. Again the religious Orders assumed leadership, since their close contact with Rome insured that the reform decrees of the Council of Trent would be followed. The spiritual renewal proposed for the laity stressed the basic practices, such as confession, the eucharist and prayer. Unfortunately the fierce religious wars which broke out towards the end of the sixteenth century between Roman Catholics and French Calvinists wiped out much of this fledgling spiritual reform.

4. *The Seventeeth Century: Highpoint of French Spirituality.* It may well be true that the seedbed for the spiritual genius of seventeenth-century France was found neither in the lecture halls nor in the monasteries, but in the parlour of Madame Acarie, later to become the Carmelite Mary of the Incarnation. In this setting, a group of Christians gathered regularly which included some of the best known spiritual writers of the era: Dom Richard Beaucousin, Benedict of Canfeld, Jesuit Pierre Couton, the young

Pierre de Bérulle* and others. Embued with the spirit of Denys the Areopagite* by means of the Rheno-Flemish mystics, this circle of gifted people inaugurated one of the greatest eras of Christian mysticism.

Canfeld's *Exercise of the Will of God* presented holiness as accessible to everyone. What was necessary for holiness, according to Canfeld, was adherence to the will of God as discovered in one's life. As Jesus Christ had to come to his passion and death to follow the will of the Father, so must the Christian be reduced to 'nothingness' to move towards union with the will of God. This so-called mysticism of 'nothingness' (*anéantissement*) became one of the major themes adopted by many of the great writers on mysticism in the seventeenth century.

Cardinal Pierre Bérulle's writings reflected numerous influences; in addition to the 'circle' at Madame Acarie's, he was in touch with the Carmelite nuns of the reform of Teresa of Avila* from Spain as well as with the Jesuits. His writings, notably *Les Grandeurs de Jésus*, were characterized by both a strong, original christological dimension and a great reverence for the hierarchical priesthood. Bérulle later founded the Oratory, a community for diocesan priests, which reflected his rich spirituality. The influence of Bérulle was profound in French spirituality, as witnessed by the creativity of his later followers, men such as Charles de Condren, Jean Jacques Olier and Jean Eudes.

Another great figure of the early third of the seventeenth century was Francis de Sales*. His *Introduction to the Devout Life* remains a classic to this day among Christians of many faith communities. A pastoral man, de Sales' approach was more focused on the pursuit of holiness in everyday life than on mysticism. Through his contact with Jeanne de Chantal, the Foundress of the Visitation Sisters, the influence of de Sales' spiritual direction was to be lasting in French spirituality.

The early Jansenism* centred in the monastery of Port Royal in the mid-seventeenth century was one of the most complex and controversial spiritual movements of the century. Men and women such as the Abbé of Saint-Cyran, Mère Angélique Arnauld and Blaise Pascal* were enmeshed in a situation which involved political, economic as well as theological issues of

great moment. The moralism and spiritual excesses later associated with Jansenism have coloured the real significance of the movement in the mid-seventeenth century.

The suppression of the movement at Port Royal in the 1660s signalled the anti-mysticism which characterized the latter part of the seventeenth century. The condemnation of the so-called Quietism* of Madame Guyon*, the controversy surrounding Jacques Bossuet* and Francis de Fénelon* and the debate between the Jesuit J.-J. Surin and the Carmelite Jean Chéron all pointed to a profound tension between mysticism on the one side and traditional theology and established political and social order on the other. The net result of this period of conflict was to impose a subtle restraint on open discussion of the interior life, an attitude which endured until well into the twentieth century.

5. *The Eighteenth and Nineteenth Centuries*. The eighteenth century in France might be characterized as a period of borrowed lustre. No authors of the stature of those in the seventeenth century appeared on the scene. Instead the spiritual lives of Christians were nourished by some reissues of the works of de Sales, Fénelon and others. Nevertheless, a certain caution regarding the life of the spirit prevailed. This is not to suggest that the practice of the spiritual life itself was in decline. Rather, spirituality during this epoch was expressed more forcefully through deed than through books.

Indeed the vitality of Christianity in France during this era was richly evidenced in the new structures by which the laity especially expressed their piety and compassion for others. Confraternities became more numerous and provided a setting and guidance for those seeking a deeper spiritual experience. New religious orders, such as the Sisters of the Sacred Heart and the Sisters of St Joseph of Cluny, arose to minister to the population. The followers of Vincent de Paul and other similar societies tried to respond to the many needs of the poor. Certainly the period of the French Revolution can be regarded as a low point in the life of the church as an institution. Yet the era saw a courageous spiritual resistance against the destructive forces present in the Revolution. As the older orders were suppressed, often enough new ones arose to respond to the situation. This spiritual resistance was exercised at times at the cost of the lives of many Christians.

The tendencies in spirituality in the nineteenth century need to be discussed in the context of the socio-cultural milieu of the time. The scepticism generated by the atheistic tone of segments of the French Enlightenment created an areligious, even anti-clerical atmosphere in French intellectual and academic circles. Among the working class religious practice gradually eroded due to the religious indifference of the time. In this climate creativity in the realm of spirituality was meagre during the first half of the nineteenth century.

Three major themes dominated R C piety in France during the latter part of this century. The christological was the most visible, bringing forth numerous religious congregations dedicated to eucharistic adoration or to the devotion to the Sacred Heart of Jesus*, for example. One strain of this christological piety focused on the life of Jesus as model for Christian life. The life of Charles de Foucauld* and the Little Sisters and Brothers of Jesus was especially noteworthy in this regard.

The nineteenth century in France has come to be called the 'century of Mary'. The apparitions of Mary at LaSalette in 1846 and at Lourdes in 1858 (see **Bernadette of Lourdes, St**) provided occasions for an intense, popular devotional response expressed through prayer and pilgrimages, a piety which lasted into the twentieth century.

The liturgical life of the Catholic community received a great impetus during the period in question thanks to the work of Dom Guéranger and the Benedictines of the Abbey of Solesmes. The renewed interest in Gregorian chant and the rediscovery of a devotional life centered on the liturgical year were major contributions of this movement.

On the popular level, men such as Léon Hormel, Léo Dehon and others developed a spirituality suited to action, to the works of charity and the Christianization of the working world. The life and holiness of the humble Curé d' Ars * were to be publicly acknowledged by the entire Catholic Church in the twentieth century. Similarly, this spirituality geared for active ministry brought into existence new religious communities such as the Congregation of the Holy Cross and the Little Sisters of the Poor, to name just two.

6. *The Twentieth Century*. The renewal of Catholic life and spirituality inaugurated during the last part of the nineteenth century carried over into the earlier part of the twentieth. Thinkers such as Maurice Blondel, Louis Duschesne and later Jacques and Raïssa Maritain brought credibility to a restored Christian life in French intellectual circles. The theological seeds implanted by such men and women were to blossom in the mid-twentieth century into a spiritual renewal in France which had an impact on the entire R C Church.

Chief among these creative spirits was the scientist and mystic Pierre Teilhard de Chardin*. Embued with the christological piety of his Jesuit heritage, Teilhard attempted to connect the world of evolutionary science with traditional Christian spirituality. The air of suspicion in official Catholic circles towards modern science made Teilhard's work often controversial. A prolific writer, he presented his vision of spirituality in original ways, but his *Le Milieu Divin* has become a classic in contemporary spirituality in many translations. Indeed, though he died in 1955 in relative obscurity, the impact of Teilhard's profound Christian humanism was powerful and decisive on the deliberations of the Second Vatican Council* (1961–1965).

The political and cultural crises which resulted from the two world wars left France physically and spiritually devastated. Yet this situation served to call forth the spiritual gifts of a Cardinal Suhard in Paris, Dominican theologians M. D. Chenu and Yves Congar, the enigmatic laywoman Simone Weil*, and Jesuit scholars Henri de Lubac, Henri Bouillard and Jean Daniélou. The insights of such men and women launched a renewal in which the best of biblical, patristic and scholastic thought was brought to bear on twentieth-century Christian life.

The post-Second World War period saw a church intent upon bringing the Christian life to new vigour on a popular level. One venture, the so-called Priest–Worker movement, strove to bring a Christian presence to the working class. Despite setbacks, the era between 1945 and 1960 witnessed a significant Catholic revival. The Young Christian Worker and Young Christian Student movements effectively prepared a generation of lay readers (*see also* **Jocists**). The parish of St Sulpice in Paris exerted on-going leadership in the restoration of the liturgical life in the parish.

The mid-twentieth century also called forth an interest in mysticism. French spiritual writers and historians of spirituality naturally looked to the seventeenth century and hence to the mysticism of Denys the Areopagite. Historian Jean Orcibal's studies of Jansenism shed new light on that controversial episode in the history of French spirituality. Louis Cognet, using the richness of the seventeenth century, opened new avenues of approach for contemporary spirituality in his writings and lectures.

In an age of ecumenism, the monastic community of Taizé* quietly pioneered in the practice of and reflection upon a contemporary ecumenical spirituality. Gathered from many nations and faith communities, the monks' witness both in France and many other countries to the vitality of Christian life amid the varied traditions linked in honest dialogue and the spirit of love.

7. *Summary*. The diversity of spiritual visions evidenced in France across these many centuries speaks eloquently of the complexity and genius of the French personality. Formed into a nation at the confluence of European society, the French have survived wars, plagues and profound cultural upheavals continually to provide Christianity with the most original spiritual movements. At the risk of rendering a complex tableau overly simple, one might distinguish three major characteristics which seem to mark French spirituality through the centuries.

1. The contemplative life, especially in its monastic form, appears with amazing regularity and fruitfulness from Martin of Tours through to Taizé.

2. The explicit focus in French spirituality on the person of Christ stands out even for the casual observer. Indeed names like Bernard of Clairvaux, Cardinal Bérulle, Marguerite-Marie Alocoque and Pierre Teilhard de Chardin hold a privileged place in the annals of christological piety of the entire Roman Catholic Church.

3. Lastly, French Christianity has never ignored the reality of pastoral life. No matter how erudite the theological speculation, the need to offer concrete spiritual nourishment and challenge to the laity has been recognized in every century. The concern of the monks of Cluny to make their spiritual life available to the peasants is reflected in the life of a nineteenth-century Curé d' Ars as well as in the contemporary *Prayers* for everyday life of a Michael Quoist.

Selected works of many of the spiritual masters mentioned in this article may be found in English translation.

DANIEL DIDOMIZIO

Friendship

1. *The classical background.* Greek and Roman views of friendship were extremely influential in the Christian spiritual tradition, especially through the influence of three writers. Plato, in the *Lysis* and *Symposium*, argued that physical attraction for a friend was only a first step in the discovery of the true meaning of love (*eros*). We should grow to love the soul more than the body, and the soul only in so far as it reflected the ultimate good. From this doctrine there developed the famous idea of 'Platonic friendship' in which friends are united in a purely spiritual love. (Though strictly, in Plato himself, physical attraction is secondary rather than irrelevant to friendship.) The second writer was Aristotle, who devoted two books of the *Nicomachean Ethics* to a discussion of friendship (*philia*), and laid down some distinctions which became classic. Friendships differ in kind according to whether they are for the sake of pleasure, as is common among the young; or profit, as among the old; or the good. True friendship must be for the good, and the love must be reciprocated. On the issue of whether true friendship is for our own good, (given our need of friends for the full life), or for the good of the friend, he adopted a middle position. A true friend is 'another self', so that although we should love him for his own sake, in loving him one is also inevitably loving the highest part of oneself. The third writer was Cicero, whose *De amicitia* follows Aristotle closely, but adds the useful distinction between an advantage to us that is the *result* of true friendship, and an advantage that is the source or motive of (a lesser) friendship (VIII, 26).

2. *Friendship in the Bible.* Examples of friendship in the Bible provided another source for Christian reflection. Of particular importance were the examples of David and Jonathan (I. Sam. 18–II Sam. 1), and the

friendships of Jesus, such as those for John and Lazarus and Mary of Magdala. These encouraged many Christian writers to claim that the command to love all men did not rule out a special relationship with a few.

3. *Friendship in the Christian tradition.* From these sources it is easy to see how the main stress in Christian accounts of friendship, at least until recent times, has been on a spiritual friendship between members of the same sex, who share a common faith, and support each other in the search for the Good; that is for God. Sometimes 'spiritual friendship' has been a technical term for a relationship that involved little or no physical contact, as between two monks who exchanged letters. In this context the term could include the relationship of man and woman, as in the famous example of Francis of Assisi and Clare. But friendship between man and woman, even within marriage, had little emphasis in the spiritual tradition until the seventeenth century, when writers such as Jeremy Taylor introduced a more positive approach to sexuality, a change which has been widely accepted. (In his *Discourse* on friendship Taylor says 'marriage is the queen of friendship'.)

Despite the technical sense of 'spiritual friendship' Christian writers have seen all true friendship as spiritual. This is most evident in Aelred *, Abbot of Rievaulx from 1147–1167, whose *Spiritual Friendship* is one of the spiritual classics. In form this book follows Cicero closely, but it is filled with a deeply Christian understanding of the role of love and friendship, both of which are founded on the love of God; an understanding that the contemporary accounts show to have been exemplified in Aelred's own life. In contrast with some writers we find in Aelred's writings a continuity between man's love for his friends and the love of God, while at the same time he is fully aware of false examples of love, when cupidity replaces genuine love. This continuity even leads him to declare that 'God is friendship (*amicitia*)'. It is this continuity which helps the Christian to affirm that we can be *friends* with God, or with Jesus. Friendship with Jesus, which is at the heart of the spiritual life, is mirrored and foreshadowed in our human friendships. (In this century compare Leslie D. Weatherhead's *The Transforming Friendship.*) Another emphasis in Aelred is on the role of will and reason and affection,

which can collaborate in true friendship, although the main stress is on the will (*Speculum caritatis* III, 20). He also reiterates that while we are commanded to love all men, it is proper to have a few friends 'to whom we can fearlessly entrust our hearts'.

Aelred had a profound influence but not all have followed him on the propriety of special friendships, except with Jesus. For example Francis de Sales * and Vincent de Paul forbade them altogether within the cloister. (Some have seen this as a reaction to the danger of cliques within a small community, whereas Aelred ruled over a community of hundreds.) Others have drawn a gulf between human friendships, even at their best, and the love of God for us or the love that we are meant to have for God (for example, A. Nygren in his *Agape and Eros*). On this issue most spiritual writers side with Aelred, accepting the view that friendship at its highest is a reflection of the love of God, and has God as its source, however little this may be realized. God's love is infinitely greater than ours, but through his grace all men can reflect it to some degree within their friendships.

In the light of the tradition an important question that arises concerns the possibility of true friendship between a Christian and one who does not share his faith, or with someone who cannot be said to represent the good (except in so far as all men cannot but reflect their maker). While a certain spiritual intimacy may be impossible in such cases the traditional Christian writers on friendship seem largely to have overlooked the undoubted depth of many such friendships. They do not fit into any of Aristotle's categories, for they are not necessarily for pleasure or profit or the good. But when the friend is loved for himself this too must surely be a variety of spiritual friendship.

Aristotle, *Nicomachean Ethics*, VIII and IX: Aelred, *Spiritual Friendship*; Cicero, *De amicitia*; C. S. Lewis, *The Four Loves*, 1960; G. Vansteenberghe, *Amitié*, in *DS*, I, cols. 500–529.

M. J. LANGFORD

Fruit of the Spirit

This phrase is drawn from Gal. 5.22–3 and is elaborated or defined in terms of the ninefold list which follows – 'love, joy, peace, patience, kindness, goodness, faithfulness, gentleness, self-control' – to which the Vulgate text adds 'modesty, continence, chastity'.

Love* (*agapē*) in the NT usually means divine love, as manifested in Christ, as experienced by believers and as overflowing in their love to others (e.g. Rom. 5.5; 8.38–9; II Cor. 5.14; Gal. 5.13–14). It is not simply an emotional experience, nor simply a social activism (I Cor. 13.1,3), but includes something of both – a depth of emotional surrender and commitment which sustains both devotion to God and concern for neighbour (I Cor. 13.4–7).

For Paul, joy is something shared, particularly the great delight and pleasure he had in the company of his fellow believers and in news about his converts (Rom. 15.32; II Cor. 1.15; 2.3; Phil. 1.4; 2.29; 4.1; I Thess. 2.19–20), something which affliction and persecution could not quench (II Cor. 7.4; I Thess. 1.6). Peace*, as its OT background makes particularly clear, is not merely the absence of strife, but a positive beneficial relationship between God and man and between man and man making for spiritual and social well-being (Rom. 5.1; 14.17,19; I Cor. 7.15; Eph. 2.14, 17).

Patience means 'persistence, steadfastness' in the face of adverse circumstances, or 'forbearance, endurance' of wrong directed against oneself, without anger or seeking vengeance (Eph. 4.2; Col. 1.11; II Tim. 3.10). The Greek words translated 'kindness' and 'goodness' have the same general breadth of reference as the English equivalents used here (Col. 3.12; II Thess. 1.11).

Faithfulness is preferable to the technically possible alternative 'faith', and denotes fidelity in what one has committed oneself to and been entrusted with – hence 'trustworthiness', 'reliability' in mutual relations (cf. Rom. 3.3; Tit. 2.10). Gentleness denotes recognition and concern for others in contrast to the arrogant and self-assertive character – hence 'considerateness' (II Cor. 10.1; Gal. 6.1; Tit. 3.2). Self-control, that is, mastery over one's desires and appetites (cf. I Cor. 7.9; 9.25), is only possible in the strength of God through the believer's constant vigilance (cf. Rom. 6.12; 7.5–6; 13.11–14).

The contrast between 'works of the flesh' (Gal. 5.19) and 'fruit of the Spirit' is clearly deliberate. The characteristics listed are not something the believer does or produces. They are outgrowths from his possession of the Spirit*, that is, from the active relation between God and the believer established and sustained by God's power. This does not mean that the believer is wholly passive in the process, for presumably the implied metaphor of growth includes the thought of the believer's active co-operation with and response to the promptings and enablings of grace (cf. self-control). The element of selfless spontaneity and immediacy is also highlighted by the double contrast with 'works of the flesh' and 'law' (5.23) – fruit cannot be legislated or ritualized, it can only grow.

Also significant is the singular 'fruit' (not fruits). In contrast to 'the works of the flesh' which can be activated individually and independently, 'the fruit of the Spirit' is a single growth, the initiative and response of the same Spirit-imbued character in different relationships and situations. 'The fruit of the Spirit' describes the quality of the person who is ever conscious of his vulnerability before the selfish grasping of his sinful nature and who therefore lives all the more out of his dependence on God.

W. Barclay, *Flesh and Spirit*, 1962.

JAMES D. G. DUNN

Fuga Mundi

A spirituality which posits both affective and actual flight from the world as the prerequisites for living a life of Christian perfection.

In this regard, it gives evidence of stronger antecendents in Platonic and Neoplatonic philosophy than in the documents of the New Testament. Until 313 Christians, although only sporadically and capriciously subjected to actual persecution, were always under the threat of such persecution. As such a minority, they disdained integration into the mainstream of society and thus affective flight from society's values became the norm for Christian perfection. Martyrdom was considered the ultimate witness to the distinction between Christian values and those of the prevailing society.

With the Edict of Milan in 313, which granted official status to the Christian religion, the situation of the Christian in the world was dramatically changed, and the Christian was faced with developing a new stance towards society. Many seeking perfection substituted actual flight from the centres of population into desert and less-populated areas. Here, they imposed upon themselves the 'white martyrdom' of virginity, asceticism and prayer. The first hermits became their own persecutors and, in solitude, struggled with the demons of their own evil in order to achieve sanctity without martyrdom.

The Life of Saint Antony (355), attributed to Saint Athanasius*, portrays this life-style to an eminent degree. Evagrius Ponticus (346–399) provides us with the most reflective contemporaneous study of the evolution of this *fuga mundi* spirituality.

Eventually, those who lived solitary lives began to group themselves into cenobitic communities. This institutionalized the *fuga mundi* spirituality which remained a dominant characteristic of the monastic mentality until the mid-twentieth century.

Zoltan Alszeghy, 'Fuite du monde', *DS*, V, cols 1575–1604; L. Bouyer, *The Spirituality of the New Testament and The Fathers*, 1963.

NANCY C. RING

Fulbert of Chartres

Fulbert of Chartres (*c.* 970–1028) made perhaps the most significant contribution to the development of the cult of the Virgin Mary and to the custom of celebrating the Feast of her nativity after Odo of Cluny (d. 942) and before the prayers of Anselm of Canterbury* and the sermons of Bernard of Clairvaux* in the late eleventh and early twelfth century enriched the tradition.

Little is known of his early life. His two short autobiographical poems tell us only that Fulbert was 'a child of poor parents' and rose to be bishop 'without the help of birth or riches'. He was probably born in northern France and is likely to have been a pupil of Gerbert of Aurillac (later Pope Sylvester II), the great master of dialectic and mathematics, in the last decade of the tenth century. There is no evidence that he was ever a monk, but as master of the school at Chartres he was outstandingly successful, bringing the cathedral school to a prominence it was not to enjoy again until the twelfth century. His teaching seems mostly to have been in grammar and the literary aspects of the arts of language, although he

was up-to-date in his knowledge of the latest work on Boethius' logical writings. In 1006 he was appointed to the bishopric. The years of his episcopate before the 1020s remain obscure, largely because of the disappearance of much of his letter-collection for this period. In September 1020 the cathedral was destroyed by fire and Fulbert set about a rebuilding which was not completed in his lifetime. In late 1022 he went on a pilgrimage to Rome – his only known journey of any length. He seems to have been a conscientious churchman in an age when much of a bishop's work consisted of the administration of ecclesiastical offices and revenues, but he was not a reformer.

He was rated a learned man by his contemporaries, but his surviving works suggest that he was a pastoral and devotional writer at heart rather than a scholar. His letters show us the pastoral side of the bishop full of concern for the souls in his charge, exhorting them to repentance, as well as the administrator. His *Contra Judaeos*, too, contains much that reflects his strong spirituality.

His sense of the towering divinity of the Godhead and of the presence of Christ complements the emphasis of his Mariology upon the holiness and dignity of the Virgin (the *Summi Auctoris et Creatoris Genetrix*, the *Genetrix Domini*), her glory as the Bride (*sponsa sine exemplo Deo coniuncta*), and above all her role as intercessor.

F. Behrends (ed), *Letters and Poems of Fulbert of Chartres*, 1976; L. C. Mackinney, *Bishop Fulbert and Education at the School of Chartres*, 1957; P. Viard, 'Fulbert de Chartres', *DS*, V, cols 1605–11.

GILLIAN EVANS

Fuller, Thomas
see **Caroline Divines, The**

Gandhi, Mohandas Karamchand

Gandhi (1869–1948), known as the Mahatma, literally 'great souled', because of his social, political and religious activity, was born into an orthodox Hindu family of the Bania caste, broadly within the Vaishya or merchant group. His father was an administrator of distinction, Prime Minister of Rajkot and later Vankaner. His mother, his father's fourth wife, was a woman of saintly character and religious commitment, regular in worship and often fasting. The family were in close touch with Jaina monks, ascetic, vegetarian, abstainers from alcohol, practitioners of *ahimsa* or non-harming.

At thirteen Mohandas, an earnest boy, was married to Kasturbai. Three years later his father died, during an interval when Gandhi left his side to be with his wife. This intensified the sense of guilt with which Gandhi associated sex. He came to regard celibacy as a precondition of spiritual growth and after 24 years of marriage himself took a vow of celibacy. In later life he would sleep with naked girls as a demonstration of his continence and the power of spirit over flesh.

In 1888, against his family's wishes, he came to England to study law. Despite contrary advice he continued to abstain from meat and alcohol. In England he read two books which were seminal of his life and thought, the Bhagavad Gītā*, a story of war, which he allegorized, and the Bible, in which the Sermon on the Mount spoke directly to his understanding.

From 1893 to 1914 Gandhi was mainly in South Africa. Here he was exposed to two other seminal books. One was Tolstoy's *The Kingdom of God is Within You*, pacifist and anarchist; he spoke of its 'independent thinking, profound morality, and . . . truthfulness'. The other was Ruskin's *Unto This Last* from which he gained the insights that the good of the individual is contained in the good of all, that all work is equally of value, and that the life of farmer or craftsman is the life really worth living. Now he began his practical experiments in communal living, later furthered in Indian ashrams*. Now too he began working out the methods of non-violent resistance to injustice which he called *satyagraha*, love-force or truth-force.

This pattern of life, community living, encouragement of work at the spinning-wheel, non-violent campaigns for the oppressed (including the 'untouchables'), fasting and imprisonment, prayer and devotion, continued for more than thirty years after his return to India. He guided India through to independence, and was horrified by the communal violence. He was assassinated by a Hindu fanatic on 30 January 1948. His last words were 'Ram, Ram' ('God, God').

Gandhi believed that the physical was inferior to the spiritual. He used the disciplines of prayer and fasting as an essential part of his actions. His lasting achievement lies in the practical spirituality of *satyagraha*, bringing together Indian *ahimsa* and Christian love.

The Selected Works of Mahatma Gandhi, ed S. Narayan, 6 vols, 1968; see also Peter D. Bishop, *A Technique for Loving*, 1981; R. Iyer, *The Moral and Political Thought of Mahatma Gandhi*, 1973; V. Mehta, *Mahatma Gandhi and his Apostles*, 1977.

JOHN FERGUSON

Garden of the Soul
see **Challoner, Richard**

Gentleness *see* **Fruit of the Spirit**

German Spirituality

There are problems in writing about German spirituality when one remembers that spiritual and religious life has to be seen in much wider contexts and that there are many different influences on it, just as it may exert influence in its turn. However, there is no denying the fact that every people gives a particular stamp to its own spirituality by virtue of its patterns of thought and its cultural history. Hegel's pupil Karl Rosenkranz may have been thinking of this when in the nineteenth century he coined the phrase 'German mysticism'. By this he understood 'the mystical speculation of Meister Eckhart* and his circle as the initial stage in the development of the "German spirit" . . .'

Eckhart is a first high-point in this kind of spirituality. Before we come to him, however, it must be remembered that strong stimuli towards Christian mysticism emanated from a number of German convents. Mention should first be made of the deeply spiritual and generally versatile Benedictine nun Hildegard of Bingen (d. 1179). She already draws on a rich tradition of inner experience, but also herself had visions which were based on spiritual experience that began early in her youth. Hildegard was able to give practical expression to her inner knowledge in ways which extended to the spheres of medicine and pharmacy.

From the second half of the twelfth century we have the 'St Trudberter Hohe Lied', a mystical poem in which – along the lines of the Song of Solomon – Christ in the form of the bridegroom meets Mary in spiritual love and carries on intimate conversations with the human soul. Mechthild of Magdeburg towers above the great host of mystical nuns (she died about 1300). In her work 'The Flowing Light of the Godhead' ('Das fliessende Licht der Gottheit'), which she composed in Low German in 1250, with the help of the Dominican Heinrich of Halle, a deep experiential love of God is given lyric and poetical form.

The birth of God in the soul is the great theme of the German mysticism of the Middle Ages. It is represented above all by members of the Dominican Order, led by Meister Eckhart (c. 1260–1328), who was followed by his most famous pupils, Johannes Tauler* and Heinrich Suso* (Seuse). Eckhart taught partly in Paris and partly in Cologne, and preached in Dominican convents to the nuns there: in a boldly speculative way he considers the mystery of the nearness of the human soul to God. The German sermons and tractates which have been preserved as well as his Latin writings soon drew the attention of the church's Inquisition to this most important representative of German mysticism. The sermons of Tauler express more the masculine element of mystical piety, with emphasis on the will, whereas from Suso there emanates a feeling of pious devotion.

It should be noted that this early German mysticism extended far beyond the bounds of what is now Germany, above all into Switzerland, where e.g. Suso and representatives of the 'Friends of God', in the fifteenth century Nicolas of Flüe (Brother Klaus), were active. During the period in question Holland, too, came into the sphere of German mysticism. Here Jan van Ruysbroeck* (Ruusbroec) wrote his book 'The Adornment of the Spiritual Marriage' (*Die Zierde der geistlichen Hochzeit*). At the end of the fourteenth century a community was founded in the Netherlands and Low Germany with the characteristics of an Order, the so-called *Devotio Moderna** ('modern piety'). It took the form of the 'Brothers of the Common Life'. The *Imitation of Christ*, circulated under the name of Thomas à Kempis* (Kempen, on the lower Rhine) is one of the most widely read books of devotion. Hardly less significant is an anonymous mystical writing from the pen of a Teutonic priest from Frankfurt; it was held in high esteem by no less a person than Martin Luther* (1483–1546) and became widely known through repeated publication (1516 and 1518). This was the *Theologia Deutsch*, which is sometimes also known as *Der Frankfurter* or *Theologia Germanica**. Luther's verdict on it is: 'Alongside the Bible and St Augustine I would not place a book from which I have learnt more . . . I thank God that I can hear and find my God in the German tongue' (Vorrede zu 'Theologia Deutsch' (1516–1518)). In particular it was the young Luther who found his way into Tauler's mysticism and the *Theologia Deutsch* and passed on his discoveries with commendations to groups of his friends.

One of those who were set alight by the spirit of this mysticism in the Reformation period is Thomas Müntzer (d. 1525), who later became Luther's opponent. It should be stressed that Müntzer is not just to be seen as one of the leaders in the German Peasants' War of 1524–1525. His writings, and in particular his famous 'Sermon to the Princes', make it clear that the ultimate stimulus to his action came from mysticism, for he was concerned that the Christian should perceive the 'inner word' in the outward word of Holy Scripture and 'receive the revelation of God in the abyss of the soul'.

Now German spirituality in the sixteenth and seventeenth centuries is not just to be limited to the sphere of an inner piety. Contemporary views of nature, astrology and alchemy cannot be judged by the standard of modern science. Rather, they constantly express the spiritual dimension of reality. At the latest after Renaissance philosophy (Marsilio Ficino, Pico della Mirandola, etc.) nature is included as a field within the quest for religious knowledge. One of those involved in the quest, who made a name for himself not only as a doctor and pharmacist but also as a *homo religiosus*, was Paracelsus (d. 1541). According to the ancient Hermetic conception of the interrelationship of 'above and below', man as microcosm goes with the world as macrocosm. The 'light of nature' shines on him when he succeeds in penetrating the mysterious depths of creation and discovering its saving powers. This is not to ignore the 'light of grace', the gift of the spirit from 'above'.

Valentin Weigel (1533–1588) draws on Lutheran theology, Paracelsus' view of nature, and mystical piety (*Theologia Deutsch*). During his lifetime he refrained from expressing his thought in public so as not to become a victim of post-Reformation orthodoxy. However, after his death his writings were printed (from 1608) and circulated widely.

It is possible to trace lines of thought to Jakob Boehme* (1575–1624) not only from Paracelsus and Weigel but also from alchemist and cabbalistic authors. This simple Silesian cobbler is known as 'philosophus Teutonicus' because of his numerous mystical and theosophical writings. More than anyone else, for centuries he nourished the spiritual and religious life of Europe. First of all comes his famous 'Aurora or the Breaking of the Dawn' (1612). Here and in the rest of his work he unfolds a picture of God, the world and man which is full of obscurities and sudden flashes of light. Hegel calls him 'truly German'; Schelling judged that he had a 'theogonous nature'. His vision and speculations had a great effect in the Netherlands, where it was first possible for all the writings of Boehme to be published (after 1682). In England, his books were translated by John Sparrow and William Law. Among the first followers of Boehme were the so-called 'Philadelphians', with John Pordage (1607–1681) and Jane Leade (1623–1704). The Pilgrim Fathers brought Boehme's writings to the New World. John Milton and William Blake took up his ideas in their poetry and art.

In France, Boehme found a zealous translator and advocate in Louis Claude de Saint-Martin (1743–1803), and interest in him can be traced down into eighteenth- and nineteenth-century Tsarist Russia.

Johann Scheffler, the Silesian baroque poet, known as Angelus Silesius, wrote his *Cherubinischer Wandersmann* (1657), a poetical and mystical *Vade mecum* which has enjoyed increasing popularity down to the present day. Meanwhile, in the eighteenth and nineteenth centuries, Boehme again won wide recognition in his home country. The Swabian theologian and pietist Friedrich Christoph Oetinger (1702–1782) managed to combined Christian theosophy, alchemistic practice and cabbalistic mysticism into an impressive overall view. The theme of his programme was: 'Corporeality is the end (i.e. goal) of the works of God.' Alongside the Lutheran theologian we have

the Bavarian Catholic philosopher Franz Xaver von Baader (1765–1841), the chief of the Munich Romantics along with the early Schelling. The late influence of Boehme on the German Romantics, including Ludwig Tieck and above all Friedrich von Hardenberg-Novalis (1772–1801), calls for special mention. Finally, extended influence reaches right down to the present: to the Russian philosophers Solovyev and Berdyaev; to the Marxist wing up to and including Ernst Bloch; through Goethe to the anthroposophy of Rudolf Steiner; in psychotherapy and depth-psychology down to C. G. Jung.

Another hardly less fruitful trend in German spirituality is represented by the Rosicrucians. The young Swabian Johann Valentin Andreae, a younger contemporary of Boehme, produced his three manifestos *Fama*, *Confessio* and *Chymische Hochzeit Christiani Rosenkreuz*, anonymously, between 1614 and 1616. They arise out of a spiritual attitude which can be described as pansophy (all-wisdom). To a mystical movement inwards (introversion; self-knowledge) is added a chemical movement outwards (extraversion; knowledge of the world). At the heart of this spirituality lies the mystery of man's transformation and spiritual renewal. This process is reduced to a short formula in Andreae's Rosicrucian Mantra:

> *Ex deo nascimur* – From God we are born;
> *In Jesu morimur* – In Christ we die;
> *Per spiritum reviviscimus* – By the Holy Spirit we are reborn.

These notions were taken up in a series of more or less secret societies, including mystical Freemasonry; they were often changed and reshaped depending on particular needs. All in all, German mysticism, alchemy, Boehme's theosophy and the Rosicrucians represent developments of an esoteric Christianity, i.e. one grounded on inner experience.

Now it cannot be denied that this esoteric approach, concerned for spiritual vision, spiritual experience and the transformation of the inward man, has continually been forced aside over the course of centuries. Protestant orthodoxy and rationalism continually drove the representatives of this spirituality underground. To over-simplify, this process of repression extends from the days of Martin Luther to Karl Barth and his school of dialectical theology which once coined the polemical formula: 'Either mysticism or the Word of God' (Brunner). The particular political situation of the church in Germany after 1933 and after 1945 meant that theologians like Paul Tillich, who once started from Boehme's admirer Schelling, hardly had a chance there. Mystical spirituality was taboo.

It is for future historians of the churches to judge whether in the meantime – i.e. after Barth, Bultmann and Bonhoeffer*–a change has come about. At all events, some observations are worth making. Religious experience, once condemned so harshly by the Karl Barth of *The Epistle to the Romans*, has now gained new respect. Many people have found that meditation in its many forms is a way towards the inner life without necessarily leading to neglect of the great theme of change, which has to take the form of an emphatically political theology. 'Anxiety about having religion,' as Dorothee Sölle put it, has not disappeared altogether, but it has been made the subject of serious reflection. Some people, above all in the younger generation, have discovered – perhaps via drugs or a trip to India – that there are a great many possible ways of becoming involved in the mystical tradition. Hence we can understand the increasing interest in the testimony to religious experiences. Places for adult church education (the Protestant and Catholic Academies in Germany) offer courses and lectures on Christian mysticism which attract a large audience. Long forgotten figures like Jakob Boehme and F. C. Oetinger are rediscovered – not least because *Collected Works* of both these men have been recently published. Of course there is no cause for euphoric assessments of these and similar developments. But the signs of the time are unmistakable. They include renewed reflection on the great traditions of Christian spirituality in history and in the present. And in view of the great challenges which face mankind, our slogan needs to be, 'Change begins within'.

See bibliographies for individual entries: also Emil Brunner, *Die Mystik und das Wort*, 1924; Gordon Rupp, *Patterns of Reformation*, 1969; Dorothee Sölle, *The Inward Road and the Way Back*: *texts and reflections on religious experience*, ET 1978; Gerhard Wehr, *Deutsche Mystik*, 1980;

Martin Luther, 1983; *Rudolf Steiner*, 1982; (ed), Angelus Silesius, *Der Cherubinische Wandersmann*, 1977; Frances A. Yates, *The Rosicrucian Enlightenment*, 1972.

GERHARD WEHR

Gerson, Jean

Born Jean Charlier on 14 December 1363, at Gerson-lez-Barby near Rethel, Jean Gerson became one of the most prominent figures in French ecclesiastical life at the end of the fourteenth and the beginning of the fifteenth century. He studied at Paris from 1377 to 1392, succeeding Pierre d'Ailly in 1395 as chancellor of the university. He retained this title until his death at Lyons on 12 July 1429, though his involvement in the quarrel between the Armagnacs and the Burgundians made it impossible for him to return to Paris after the Council of Constance.

Gerson was a member of the delegation sent in 1408 to Avignon and Rome to confer with the two rival claimants to the papal throne and to urge upon them a voluntary resolution of the Great Schism. Though he did not attend the Council of Pisa, he defended its legitimacy. At the Council of Constance he led the French delegation and sided with those theologians who argued for the superiority of a council over a pope.

Although Gerson did not write the *Imitation of Christ* once attributed to him, he did compose more than sixty-six works on the spiritual life, drawing inspiration from Bonaventure*, Hugh and Richard of St Victor (*see* **Victorines**), Augustine*, Bernard of Clairvaux* and Denys the Areopagite*. Mystical theology for Gerson is an experiential knowledge of God which takes place through the unitive power of love. Speculative theology resides in the intellectual powers whose object is the true, while mystical theology resides in the affective powers whose object is the good. Mystical theology is not rationalistic in the sense that it does not proceed by a process of deductive reasoning to a theoretical conclusion, and yet it is also not irrational in the sense that it does not dissolve the rational structures of the mind but elevates the mind's highest powers so that the mind attains the wisdom which transcends theoretical understanding. Mystical theology is concerned with union with God through the ecstasy of love. The ecstatic soul does not lose its being in the

Being of God as a drop of water is dissolved in a cask of strong wine, but retains its identity at the very moment it becomes one spirit with God through conformity of will. On this point Gerson decisively separated himself from the views of Jan van Ruysbroeck*, whose *De ornatu spiritualium nuptiarum* he criticized.

Gerson's attitude towards the spiritual life and his distaste for theological questions which were divorced from practical and pastoral concerns influenced his vision of university reform. In his treatise *Contra curiositatem studentium* (1402) he warned against the recurrence in his own day of a vain curiosity which led theologians to speculate about matters which lay beyond reason's competence to judge. Moreover, he expressed mystification at the apparent willingness of the Franciscans to abandon what he regarded as the wholesome teaching of St Bonaventure for the arid and unprofitable trinitarian speculations of the Parisian Scotists. Gerson's prominence as a theologican, educator, mystic and conciliar theorist conspired to make him one of the most popular and frequently cited authorities on the spiritual life in late mediaeval Europe.

Jean Gerson, *Oeuvres complètes*, ed P. Glorieux, 1960–1973; A. Combes, *La theologie mystique de Gerson*, 1963–1964; J. L. Connolly, *John Gerson: Reformer and Mystic*, 1928.

DAVID C. STEINMETZ

Gifts of the Spirit

'Gifts of the Spirit' is one rendering of the Greek word *charismata*, frequently transliterated as 'charisms'. Its presence in Christian vocabulary is almost entirely due to Paul, whose usage therefore becomes largely determinative of its meaning. Fundamental is the fact that *charisma* is derived from *charis* (grace). A *charisma* (charism) can be simply defined therefore as anything which brings grace to concrete expression, whatever embodies and manifests the generous giving of God. As such it can be used to sum up the gift of salvation and eternal life (Rom. 5.15–16, 6.23), but usually the thought is of particular interventions and enablings of God's grace (as in I Cor. 7.7; II Cor. 1.11). The plural form with which we are here concerned (gifts of the Spirit) usually has in view the sort of charisms mentioned in Rom. 12.4–8 and I Cor. 12.4–11, 28–31. These lists are clearly not intended to be definitive, far less exhaustive, but presumably itemize gifts either in regular manifestation or of particular relevance (particularly to the Corinthians).

1. They include gifts of *revelation* – 'knowledge' and 'wisdom' being probably insights into God's will or plan whether overall or in particular situations (cf. I Cor. 8; 13.2; 14.6; II Cor. 1.20–25; 2.6–11; 6.5). Here could be included also the kind of visionary and ecstatic experiences of which Paul speaks in II Cor. 5.13 and 12.1–7, or the more mundane experience of being led by the Spirit (Rom. 8.14; Gal. 5.18) or being given discernment to make difficult choices or ethical judgments (as in Rom. 12.2; 14.22; Phil. 1.10).

2. They include gifts of *healing*. As grace is the operation of God's power, so *charisma* is the effective output of that divine energy (1 Cor. 12.6) in particular instances (12.9, 28, 30). 'Faith' with which Paul links this gift (12.9) is probably to be understood as a particular trusting in specific cases, the confidence that God will minister the desired healing (cf. Acts 3.6–7; 14.9–10). Paul may well mean that the two go together, effective release of healing power being somehow dependent on the gift of such faith (cf. Rom. 12.3; 14.23). 'Miracles' which Paul also mentions here (I Cor. 12.10, 28–29) presumably include more than healings, but are otherwise unspecified.

3. The most frequently mentioned gifts are those of *inspired speech* – proclamation of the gospel (I Cor. 2.4–5; 1 Thess. 1.5–6), teaching (1 Cor. 14.6, 26), exhortation (Rom. 12.8), singing (I Cor. 14.15; Eph. 5.19; Col. 3.16) and prayer (Rom. 8.15–16, 26–27; I Cor. 14.14–17; Eph. 6.18). Most important of all for Paul is prophecy (Rom. 12.6; I Cor. 12.10; 14.1; I Thess. 5.19–20), words given by the Spirit to provide needed insight, to encourage and console, to build up the community of faith (I Cor. 14.3, 6, 24–26, 30–31). All the more valuable, it is all the more dangerous as being open to manipulation and abuse – hence Paul mentions also the accompanying gift of 'discerning spirits' (I Cor. 12.10) and insists that every prophetic utterance must be evaluated by prophets or people (I Cor. 14.29; I Thess. 5.19–22). Even more open to abuse, because it by-passes the mind, is the gift of (other)

tongues (I Cor. 12.10, 28, 30). Paul is in no doubt as to its benefit to the individual who exercises it (14.2–5, 18), but he discourages its use in the congregation unless accompanied by the gift of interpretation, which presumably puts into the vernacular the substance of the unknown tongue (14.3, 5–19, 23, 27–28).

4. Although interest usually focuses chiefly on the foregoing gifts it is important to note that Paul thinks of acts of service also as charisms (Rom. 12.7; cf. I Peter 4.11). These will include the 'sharing' and 'giving' at the end of Rom. 12.8, which sandwich a word which could mean either 'ruling' or more probably in the context 'caring for'; also the 'helpful deeds' and 'giving direction' mentioned in I Cor. 12.28.

For Paul charismata are gifts for the body, given through individuals as means of grace to the congregation as a whole (I Cor. 12.7). They are not given for personal enjoyment or aggrandisement; they are characterized as acts of service (12.5). Hence the relative disparagement of such gifts where love is not evident (I Cor. 13.1–3) and the emphasis on benefiting others which makes prophecy so much more valuable than tongues in I Cor. 14. Paul can even describe them as the 'functions' of the body (Rom. 12.4), the point being that each member has his function, which may be exercised regularly or infrequently, may carry a great weight of responsibility or relatively little, but all of which are indispensable to the health of the whole (I Cor. 12.12–31). Paul certainly sees the importance of regular ministries (most frequently mentioned are apostles, prophets and teachers – Rom. 12.6–7; I Cor. 12.28; Eph. 4.11), but the thought of ministry being confined to them, or of a sharp distinction (marked by ordination or whatever) between them and the more episodic ministries of all the other members would be a contradiction in terms for Paul. In the proper sense of the word all members of the body of Christ are 'charismatics'. And since charisms as phenomena are not distinctively Christian (cf. I Cor. 12.2–3), Paul emphasizes the need for charismatic contributions to accord with the character of grace as revealed in Christ, marked by power in weakness and love for the neighbour (I Cor. 13; II Cor. 12.1–10).

In the post-biblical period charismata are spoken of with decreasing frequency, usually with reference to the more striking gifts (1–3), as in Irenaeus*, Haer. 2.32.4 and Tertullian*, Marc. 5.8. But the tendency is to regard such charisms as belonging to the apostolic age, and the phrase 'gifts of the Spirit' comes in traditional theology to denote the anointing of the seven-fold Spirit of Isa. 11.2 (foreshadowed in Justin, Dial. 39). On the other hand there is considerable evidence particularly of healings, prophecy and ecstatic manifestations at various periods in church history, the latter more among millenarian and enthusiastic movements (cf. N. Cohn, The Pursuit of the Millenium, 1957; R. A. Knox, Enthusiasm, 1950) or within Christian mysticism (cf. H. Thurston, The Physical Phenomena of Mysticism, 1952).

In this century the emergence of Pentecostalism, and from the 1960s onwards of the charismatic renewal in the older churches, has brought the Pauline teaching once again to the fore. The Corinthian overemphasis on tongues has been strengthened by classic Pentecostalism's identification of tongues as the sign of the desired second experience of 'baptism in the Spirit', and many have found 'speaking in tongues' to be a very edifying personal experience of worship, with praise liberated from the confines of rational articulation. Healing too became a 'big-time' business with successful healers able to establish themselves as free-lancers. In the charismatic renewal, however, the chief emphasis has increasingly focused on the concept and practice of charismatic community and on charisma as service within the congregation.

A. Bittlinger, Gifts and Graces, 1967; J. D. G. Dunn, Jesus and the Spirit, 1975; J. Koenig, Charismata: God's Gifts for God's People, 1978; M. T. Kelsey, Healing and Christianity, 1973; K. McDonnell, Charismatic Renewal and the Churches, 1976; S. Tugwell, Did You Receive the Spirit?, 1972.

JAMES D. G. DUNN

Gilbert of Sempringham

Gilbert (c. 1083–1189) was born in Lincolnshire, the son of a Norman knight and an Anglo-Saxon woman. As a young man he studied in Paris and on his return his father gave him, though he was still not a priest, the churches of West Torrington and Sempringham, where he provided rudimentary education for the children of the neighbourhood and soon gained a reputation for piety. About 1122 he became a clerk of the Bishop of Lincoln, who persuaded him to become a priest. Refusing the offer of an archdeaconry, Gilbert returned to Sempringham c. 1130 where he soon became adviser to a group of anchoresses, whom he enclosed in a cloister adjoining the parish church. On the advice of his friend William, Abbot of Rievaulx, he established a small lay sister- and brotherhood to provide for the community's temporal needs.

There is considerable evidence to suggest that Gilbert never intended this group to expand further, but being unable to prevent recruits or grants of land being made to him, he travelled to the General Chapter at Cîteaux in 1147 hoping that the Cistercians might take over his priories and allow his retirement. Instead St Bernard, encouraged by Pope Eugenius III, helped Gilbert to draw up the rules of a new Order. These provided for double houses, contained within one precinct, of nuns and canons and the provisions made for their government were unusual in allowing almost total control of individual priories to the prioresses. The rule itself was eclectic: the nuns followed the Benedictine rule, the canons that of St Augustine while that of the lay brothers and sisters was based, with modifications, on that of Cîteaux.

On Gilbert's return to England a number of new priories were founded, and by the time of his death at a very advanced age there were said to be thirteen priories containing 1,500 nuns and 700 canons. Gilbert was canonized in 1202.

Virtually none of Gilbert's writings survive. His *De Constructione Monasteriorum* is now lost but presumably embodied at least part of the Gilbertine rule. A letter addressed to the canons of Malton priory and written between 1186 and his death is his sole work to have been preserved. In it he expresses his sorrow that he is too infirm to visit them and urges them to maintain the provisions of his rule and to live at peace with one another. Knowledge of Gilbert's character and teachings must, therefore, be gained from other sources, notably the *Vita* written shortly after his death and the collection of miracle stories, some of which preserve traditions and accounts of his later life. They reveal a man never wholly at ease in

the Order he reluctantly created and one who found most satisfaction in living the life of a lay brother, helping in building work or in the scriptorium, fasting frequently, dressing humbly and never sleeping outside the dorter. Nevertheless the successful growth of his Order (though it never spread outside England) within his lifetime demonstrates the appeal of his teaching, particularly to women, and it is within the context of the considerable development of the role of women in spiritual life in the twelfth century that his greatest achievement lies.

B. Golding, 'St Bernard and St Gilbert' in Benedicta Ward (ed), *The Influence of St Bernard*, 1976; R. Graham, *S. Gilbert of Sempringham and the Gilbertines*, 1903.

BRIAN GOLDING

Glory

The Hebrew and Greek words translated 'glory' are frequently used by the writers in the OT and NT to tell of the revealed character of God and of the response of his people in worship and in action. No words indeed are more suggestive of the range and character of Christian spirituality than the words glory and glorify. The Hebrew word *kabod* comes from a root meaning 'weight', and it is used of the power or riches of a man. Applied to God, it tells of his power and character, not least his majesty, transcendence and sovereignty. Besides the idea of weight the idea of light is sometimes linked with the word, and it tells thus of God's dazzling radiance in himself and in his manifestation in the world. The word had also a distinctive use for the divine presence in the cloud seen by the Israelites in the tabernacle in the wilderness. It seems significant that the word used for God himself in his transcendental aspects is also used for a particular sign of his presence amongst the people. It is part of the theme of glory that the glory of God evokes the human response both of acts of worship and praise and of living in accord with God's purpose. In both these ways God's people are called to 'glorify' him or to 'give glory' to him.

When Hebrew religion came to be involved with Greek culture and language the Greek word *doxa* was used to translate the *kabod* of God. The word in normal Greek usage meant opinion (what I think) or distinction (what people think of me);

and the use of the word to express the glory of the deity involved indeed a revolution in language. The contrast is thus apparent between the ideas of divine glory and human glory. One passage in the Gospel of John suggests this contrast vividly: 'How can you believe who received glory one of another and do not seek the glory which comes from the only God?' (John 5.44).

In the NT the words glory and glorify express the OT concepts now deepened and fulfilled by the revelation of God in Jesus Christ. The Pauline Epistles frequently tell of the glory of God now made known in Jesus and specially in his resurrection, and the imagery of light is apparent no less than the theme of sovereignty. The response of the Christians is to give glory to God, and the Epistles contain some outbursts of praise with glory as the theme. But the response is also by human lives in every aspect, for *all* must be done to the glory of God.

It is in the Fourth Gospel that the concept of glory is specially linked with the person of Jesus. The evangelist shows that the divine glory is visible in the life, teaching and signs of Jesus. Throughout his mission on earth Jesus glorifies the Father and the Father glorifies him, and there is thus revealed the eternal glory of the Father and the Son as the glory of self-giving love. Thus revealed, glory has its climax in the crucifixion of Jesus which the evangelist describes not as a defeat but as the victory of self-giving love. On the night before the crucifixion Jesus prays (John 17) that in his death the Father may glorify him and he may glorify the Father, and that the glory may be given to the disciples as a gift. Receiving the glory in their lives, they will one day come to the vision of it in heaven. All this is the theme of the prayer of Jesus. In the discourse at the Last Supper Jesus has prayed that the Holy Spirit will glorify Jesus in the disciples. It is fair to say that in the Fourth Gospel Christianity is presented as having two chapters. The first chapter is the revelation of glory in Jesus, and the second chapter is the bringing of this glory into the lives of the believers as they make the glory their own.

Not surprisingly, the word glory has come to have a large place in the imagery of Christian spirituality, telling as it does of the majesty and the self-giving of God and of man's response to God in adoration and in fellowship, in worship and in life. It is the Christian belief that man exists in order to glorify God with the glory of heaven as his goal. This response includes both adoration, with its awe and dependence, and participation as men and women come to share in the glory and are thereby glorified. The participation, however, never blurs the line of distinction between adorer and Adored, redeemed and Redeemer, creature and Creator.

The two-fold character of the Christian concept of glory is illuminated by Hebrew scholarship in the study of the verbal roots. *Kabod* is one of the 'bivocal' Hebrew words which combine active and passive nuances: God in being glorified vindicates his own glory. But the theme is far more than a linguistic one. It belongs to the experience of Christian saints through the ages, and of the Christian saints nothing is more characteristic than a growing Christlikeness which owes nothing to self and all to God, and the quest of a goal in which Godlikeness and the adoring vision of God are one.

G. B. Caird, *The Language and Imagery of the Bible*, 1980; A. M. Ramsey, *The Glory of God and the Transfiguration of Christ*, London, [2]1968.

A. MICHAEL RAMSEY

Glossolalia

Speaking in tongues, or glossolalia, is a feature of pentecostal and charismatic devotional life. It is practised by Christians who believe themselves to be filled with the Holy Spirit, but it is not exclusive to Christianity. E. Schweizer, when writing about Christians in Corinth, says that 'supernatural phenomena like speaking in tongues or other ecstatic experiences occurred also in the former lives of the people in heathen cults' (*The Church as the Body of Christ*, 1965). Pentecostal Christians would say that speaking in tongues, when inspired by the Holy Spirit, glorifies Christ and helps build up his church, but they would point also to a counterfeit phenomenon which could be evil (Satanically inspired) or of the flesh (psychologically induced).

Some Christians who claim a pentecostal experience and speak in tongues say that the first utterance of glossolalia occurs when they are filled by or baptized in the Holy Spirit. Others say that speaking in tongues

GORDON S WAKEFIELD: Modern theology

"SPIRITUALITY", that vogue – term, is often regarded, whether as the attempt to reach contact with an impersonal Ultimate Reality or as Pauline "Life in the Spirit", as deliverance from intellectual wrestling and escape from worldly concerns.

This splendid collection of essays, **Spirituality and Social Embodiment**, edited by L Gregory Jones and James J Buckley (£14.99), the first volume in Blackwell's "Directions in Modern Theology" series, challenges this and shows that Christian spirituality is incarnational and concerned with the totality of human relationships body and soul. This is illustrated by excerpts from Bernard of Clairvaux (in contrast to the modern American Thomas Moore), Thomas Aquinas, Julian of Norwich, Martin Luther and African American spirituality.

There is an essay by Rowan Williams which shows that the so-called "interior" life, largely inaccessible, cannot, in Christianity, be divorced from actions in the body. "Christian ethics is relentlessly

political." Nicholas Lash, in a piece rather different from the rest, is concerned with "The Church in the state we're in" where, as in Will Hutton's title, "state" is a double entendre. Lash does not think that liberalism will save us from the crisis of contemporary culture for which, in the United Kingdom, the Thatcher years must bear some, though not all, responsibility. His hope is that the Church, "in collaboration with other such traditions as in Judaism and Islam", will rediscover what Newman saw "as its identity as a kind of school, within a wider culture, in which identity can be recognised and subjected to critique and in which the word of life that is the wisdom of God's peace may once again be heard, enfleshed, considered and prophetically displayed".

The essays are long and detailed and many readers will not find them easy, but they get near to the heart of authentic Christian spirituality.

● **The Rev Dr Gordon S Wakefield is a former principal of Queen's College, Birmingham.**

crown commended. AA QQQQ selected. Tel. 01524 51240.

(4)19-3/3-9-4/01

BLACKPOOL, LOCHNIVAR CHRISTIAN guest house. Join John and Mollie McArdle for a happy holiday with good food and warm Christian fellowship. Central heating, tea/coffee facilities in all rooms, most rooms en suite. Senior citizens special, May 9-23 and August 22-29. The Easter People conference booking now. Send for brochure or ring 01253 351761. 14, Chatsworth Avenue, Norbreck, FY2 9AN.

(6)5-3/9-4/01

BLISLAND, CORNWALL. Riverside cottage, bed and breakfast. Close Bodmin Moor, 30 minutes coast, beside camel trail, ideal cycling/walking. Also self-catering cottage. Telephone 01208 850138.

(19-4/01

BRECON BEACONS/ Black Mountains. Spacious B&B. Families welcome. Packed lunches. Flasks filled. Drying facilities. No smoking. £15 per night. 01874 622833.

(6)9-4/18-6(s)

BRIMHAM ROCKS Yorkshire Dales, early 1400 farmhouse, where John Wesley preached, offers guests warm welcome,

---

and Marian Walne for details or write for brochure. 15, Llanerch Road East, Rhos on Sea, North Wales, LL28 4DF. 01492 548333.

(3)12-3/3-9-4/01(s)

RHYL, CREST VILLA guest house. 2 minutes Sun Centre/ promenade. Televisions, tea-making, pensioners reductions, parking. 01745 334733.

(2)2-4/16-4/01(s)

YORK, STANLEY HOUSE. Genuine Yorkshire welcome. En suite rooms, car park, ETB 2 Crowns commended, non smoking. Telephone 01904 637111.

(18/6-11/2-7/01(s)

---

(6)19-3/14-5/03(s)

CHESHIRE VILLAGE, near Derbyshire Peaks, potteries. Converted barn. 4 keys, highly commended. Sleeps six. Ground floor bedroom. Non smoking.

(13)15-1/2-7/03(s)

CLITHEROE, LANCASHIRE. Cosy, well equipped cottage. Sleeps 4/5. Country outlook. Railway station, town centre, Methodist church nearby. Stairlift. Parking. Details telephone 01200 429833.

(13)5-3/28-5/03

DERBYSHIRE. Convenient for Derby, Matlock, Ashbourne and Peak District. Detached family home. Sleeps 5. All facilities. Garden. Non-smokers. Own linen. Tel/Fax 01773 822495.

(79-4/25-6/03(s)

NEW FOREST. Views from lovely first floor flat. Sleeps four. Non smokers. £200-£250 per week. 01703 282378.

(2)9-4/16-4/03

NORTH DEVON COAST. Superb house for families, babies and grannies. Sleeps

may come later than Spirit baptism and yet others do not speak in tongues at all. Those who do usually continue to practise the gift in subsequent devotional life.

Speaking in tongues is one of the spiritual gifts (charismata) mentioned in I Cor. 12.8–10, (*see* **Gifts of the Spirit**), but are such tongues those of known languages? More often than not the words used do not seem to indicate a known language, although a linguistic pattern and rhythm are frequently discernible. It is not just gibberish or the rolling of the tongue (*see* A. Bittinger, *Gifts and Graces*, 1967). J. D. G. Dunn concludes 'that Paul thought of glossolalia as speaking the language(s) of heaven' (*Jesus and the Spirit*, 1975). There are, however, those in pentecostal circles who claim to have heard people speaking in languages unknown to themselves but understood by another in the congregation.

On the Day of Pentecost it seems that the purpose of the gift was to communicate 'the mighty works of God' whether or not the miracle was one of hearing or speaking (Acts 2.6–11). Later in the life of the early church the gift appears as one of prayer and praise in the context of private or public devotion (I Cor. 14.14).

For pentecostals and charismatics the gift, then, has two main uses, one private and the other public. In the private use of tongues the gift is one which is said to edify the believer. With the mind focused on Jesus, the speaker utters prayer and praise to God in the language of the Spirit (I Cor. 14.2). In so doing he believes that the prayer he offers is God-inspired, even though the speaker may not comprehend its meaning. The gift is thought to be of particular value when a person is unclear about how to pray in a given situation: to pray in the language of the Spirit is to pray the correct prayer.

In public the gift is used only when followed by an interpretation which may be an utterance of praise or may be prophetic in nature. The interpretation is believed to be God's response to the prayer offered in tongues. Pentecostals distinguish sharply between interpretation and translation. Interpretation is sensed intuitively rather than understood rationally. Essentially, speaking in tongues is a medium of communication in ways similar to abstract painting or surrealist poetry or even music. The human spirit touched by the Divine Spirit finds expression in glossolalia in a way which transcends intelligible words. Gaston Deluz describes it as 'a kind of music' (*A Companion to I Corinthians*, 1963).

Christians who speak in tongues do not so speak in a trance-like condition. They are in full control of their faculties and can begin or cease to use the gift at will. Neither is their utterance necessarily ecstatic, though it may be. Many testify to the experience of speaking in tongues in a very unemotional manner.

A question often posed is why there should be public speaking in tongues with interpretation at all. Would it not be preferable to have the interpretation without the preceding tongue? In pentecostal or charismatic worship, whenever an utterance is given in an unknown tongue, there is a perceptible increase in attentiveness in the congregation gathered, so that there is greater receptivity to the interpretation when it is given.

There is, too, the phenomenon of singing in the Spirit (I Cor. 14.15), in which worshippers sing the words of unknown languages to equally unknown and unrehearsed tunes. The sound of such singing is usually beautiful, harmonious and inspiring. It begins softly, swells to a crescendo and finally subsides into absolute silence, a silence which pentecostals sometimes describe as one which is filled with the presence of God.

A number of Christians who speak in tongues have described their gift as a love language which they use when speaking to God. All pentecostals and charismatics would argue that their practice in using this spiritual gift is governed by the principles laid down by St Paul in I Cor. 14.

Perhaps speaking in tongues may be described best as a mystical experience of praise and prayer as practised by those Christians of the pentecostal pattern of spirituality.

See also **Charismatic Movement, The; Pentecostalism.**

In addition to the works cited in the text, see: J. Gunstone, *Greater Things Than These*, 1974; J. Sherrill, *They Speak with other Tongues*, 1965.

W. R. DAVIES

Gnosticism

Gnosticism is the name given (not by the gnostics themselves but by their opponents, especially the Church Fathers, though its generic use is later) to various movements which were especially prominent in the second century and constituted a serious threat to the infant church. Our sources of information about it include refutations by the Fathers (especially Irenaeus, Hippolytus and Tertullian), and also by pagan philosophers such as Celsus and Plotinus (who do not seem to distinguish them closely from the Christians), and also the fifth century library of Gnostic texts in Coptic discovered at Nag Hammadi in 1945. The writings of the *Corpus Hermeticum* might also be claimed as gnostic. The name derives from the Greek *gnosis* (knowledge) and refers to the Gnostics' claim to possess a secret knowledge in virtue of which they could escape from this evil cosmos and regain the realm of the true God who is unknown to this world. Gnosticism is thus characterized by a fundamental dualism between the universe and God: a dualism which is usually expressed by regarding the creator of the cosmos as an ignorant or malevolent lesser deity, who is mistakenly regarded as God by the Judaeo-Christian tradition, and indeed by the dominant philosophical systems of Hellenism. There is much dispute about the origins of Gnosticism: almost every religious and philosophical movement in the Middle East can be claimed to have contributed something. All these various traditions, however mediated, contribute to a bewildering variety of systems of heavenly beings and their relationships even more bewildering in their seemingly arbitrary detail. But since it was of the essence of the gnostic *gnosis* that it was secret and therefore not publicly available, what we have must be material for interpretation, the key to that interpretation being irrevocably lost. In relation to Christianity Gnosticism sought to detach the infant faith from its Jewish roots and present it as a religion of pure redemption; in relation to Hellenism Gnosticism challenged its fundamental optimism in regard to the cosmos (the very word in Greek suggesting something beautiful). The net result of this dual attack was to deepen the links that had already formed between the church and Hellenistic philoso-

phical culture. Sensitivity to the problem of evil has given Gnosticism a perennial attractiveness: it emerges in the history of the church as Manichaeism *, as Catharism *, and in occult movements in more recent centuries. But the Gnostic claim to a higher knowledge mediated by secret (and therefore unwritten) tradition has had through its attraction for Clement of Alexandria and Origen * a continuing influence on the Christian tradition. The term *gnosticos* is regularly used in the ascetic literature influenced by Origen's admirer, Evagrius, for one who knows the higher flights of contemplation, and in the stress within that tradition on personal initiation by one who is himself an adept we can perhaps detect an enduring influence of the gnostics' treasuring of secret tradition.

W. Foerster (ed), *Gnosis: A Selection of Gnostic Texts*, 2 vols, ET 1972, 1974; R. M. Grant, *Gnosticism and Early Christianity*, 1959; H. Jonas, *The Gnostic Religion*, [2]1963; S. R. C. Lilla, *Clement of Alexandria: A Study in Christian Platonism and Gnosticism*, 1971.

ANDREW LOUTH

Goodness *see* Fruit of the Spirit

Goodwin, Thomas

A nonconformist leader whose extensive writings provide a typical exposition of Puritan spirituality *, Thomas Goodwin (1600– c. 1679) believed that there is a 'natural light left even in corrupt nature' (VII, 44), but in order to create spiritual awareness 'the great hammer of the law' must be expounded 'that we may then . . . preach the gospel' (V, 6). We cannot expect 'by duties to get Christ and God's favour' (III, 472) but, once committed to Christ, good works are especially important as both an expression of new life and its confirmation. They are 'the daughters of faith' which 'nourish their mother, but not at first beget her' (IV, 13). Christianity is not simply 'Credenda' but also 'Agenda, things to be done and practised by us' (I, 132). Like Christ at his resurrection Christians are brought to life by the Holy Spirit (IV, 33) who also communicates assurance to the believer (VIII, 364; I, 231). Goodwin related the assurance theme to his understanding of the sacramental life of the church; at the Lord's Supper the Holy Spirit 'follows us to the sacrament, and in that glass shows us Christ's face smiling on us' (IV, 107–108; cf. VII, 312). Sanctification is God's work by which Satan is dethroned (I, 356) and a 'new disposition' is created within the soul (I, 359). Self-love is also deposed from that 'predominancy and regency . . . that is in all men's hearts' (I, 384). Sanctification, a gradual transformation (IV, 339), sometimes includes 'interruptions'. 'God may temporarily withdraw his grace from the souls of the elect.' Goodwin's intense pastoral concern is reflected in *A Child of Light Walking in Darkness* (III, 231–350). The believer may be 'filled with doubts whether God will ever be merciful to him' (III, 242) and even 'walk many days and years in that condition' (III, 237). Yet these 'withdrawals' may glorify God (e.g. Job, III, 288–289) and enable a Christian to utilize spiritual resources which 'would never see the light, if it were not for this darkness' (III, 303). Tested believers are driven to more earnest prayer (III, 306) and thereby become better equipped to help other people in similar trouble (III, 289). In desolation the Christian must renew his trust in God ('such a resolution can never go to hell with thee', III, 324), 'the mind quietly contenting itself till God doth come', expressing 'submission if he should not come' (III, 330). The means of grace are specially important for 'the devil endeavours nothing more than to keep such souls from the word, from good company, from the sacraments, from prayer, by objecting their unprofitableness unto them' (III, 331). After the Great Fire (1666) which destroyed most of his library, Goodwin wrote *Patience and its Perfect Work, under Sudden and Sore Trials*. Whatever a believer's loss, 'whilst God continues to be God' we 'have enough' (II, 441). In these experiences 'Prayer is the midwife by which faith, the mother, brings forth patience in the heart' (II, 464) and God gives 'a new special might for every new trial' (II, 466). Forged in times of intense hardship, Goodwin's spirituality was fashioned by immediate pastoral needs rather than mystical reflection.

Thomas Goodwin, *Works*, 12 vols, 1861–1866; William Haller, *The Rise of Puritanism*, 1938; Peter Lewis, *The Genius of Puritanism*, 1975.

RAYMOND BROWN

Grace

Greek *charis*, with basic sense of 'rejoicing'. Classical Greek uses *charis* objectively for 'charm', 'beauty'; subjectively for 'kindness', 'goodwill', 'gratitude'; concretely for 'favour', 'boon' and the corresponding 'gratification', 'delight'. In LXX *charis* translates *hēn*, 'favour', which one finds of God (with hints of an Oriental potentate). Philo distinguishes God's general *charis* (mainly plural, for natural endowments or facilities freely available to all) from his special *charites*, given only to the worthy. In the Hellenistic Greek of the *koiné*, *charis* becomes the imperial favour shown in gift or benefaction bestowed on a *polis* or an individual; the growth of the imperial cult was to give this a quasi-religious significance.

Charis is not found in the sayings of Jesus, and of the Synoptics only in Luke, and in him only in its secular sense. John's 'grace and truth', 'grace for grace' (only in Prologue) recalls the OT *hesed wā-hemeth*, where the 'truth' about God was his 'covenanted love' for Israel; but now the Word has become flesh, and God's grace is received at all points freely, not in return for obedience to the Law, but through the vision of its embodiment in the glory of the Son. This usage may hint at the transformation of *charis* by Paul as the technical term for the gospel – 'the grace of our Lord Jesus Christ'.

Paul's profound training in the OT above all in its master-concept of covenanted salvation flowing from the one God in whom 'righteousness', 'holiness', 'truth' are the complement (not, as in the Greek mind, the antithesis) of 'love', 'kindness', 'mercy', was confronted by its culmination and transcendence in Jesus Christ (Rom. 10.4), for whose person and work he recoined the word which its existing connotations made uniquely appropriate (*see* Rom. 3.24). In its *primary* sense grace for Paul 'signifies the generous love or gift of God by which in Christ salvation is bestowed on man and a new world of blessings opened' (W. Manson). Grace is God's act of self-giving (not a mere kindly or loving disposition), a decisive, final, 'eschatological' intervention in history, grounded exclusively in the person and above all the cross of Christ, 'abounding' and 'overflowing' (Rom.

5.17ff.), utterly independent of our wisdom (I Cor. 1.17ff.) and merit (I Cor. 15.10), translating into the present the conditions and perspectives of the promised era of salvation.

Grace has, however, for Paul a *derivative* sense, as it becomes effectual in men, received by and manifested through faith. It is the source of the new Christian status (Rom. 5.2) conferring special gifts (Rom. 12.6ff.), and inspiring to new callings and duties (Paul's apostleship Rom. 1.5, Rom. 12 *passim*, II Cor. 8.1 Macedonian 'generosity' for the Churches of Palestine). Such grace is not quantitative or even qualitative, but dynamic and always the fruit of God's self-giving. The effects of this grace in the life of the Christian – *charismata* ('grace-gifts') – are not so much the manifestations of an immanent, impersonal principle ('grace' in the abstract) as endowments of the Spirit (I Cor. 12.4 cf. Heb. 10.29, James 4.6). Grace is never detached from the *person* of Christ, and never acts impersonally on the believer.

T. F. Torrance has shown (with some exaggeration, especially in the case of Ignatius) the decline from the high Pauline doctrine in the 'Apostolic Fathers', when the gospel moved into the world of Judaistic legalism and Hellenistic humanism, and grace became something given by God to help the worthy to attain righteousness, the infusion into the soul of a mystical energy of which the church was the depository and sacramental dispenser. The Greek Fathers, especially Origen and Athanasius, developed the mystique of grace as an illumination of the mind and a reinforcement of the essential freedom of the will by the objective facts of providence, revelation, redemption. The Latin Fathers, following Tertullian, saw grace more practically as a divine quasi-physical energy working for righteousness and the reward of eternal life, leaving the status and contribution of human free-will to the later controversy between Pelagius and Augustine, the former regarding grace as the divine help which facilitates and perfects human potentiality, the latter, with his overwhelming conviction of human nature as a *massa peccati*, accrediting the total responsibility for conversion, the good life, ultimate salvation to *gratia gratis data*. The elaboration of his theme in response to the ethical challenge of

Pelagius led Augustine to formulate certain distinctions (grace prevenient/subsequent, co-operating/irresistible) which were later expanded, above all by Aquinas, into an exhaustive series (grace created/uncreated, external/internal, actual/habitual, sufficient/efficacious, natural/supernatural, justifying/sanctifying). These distinctions, while of the highest value in the delineation of Christian spirituality, are vulnerable to the attempted corrective of Luther* (who rejected the whole concept of 'infused' in favour of 'imputed' grace) and the modern rediscovery of biblical theology, with its return to the Pauline identification of grace with the *person* of Christ crucified and risen. 'If it is a matter of the grace of the *one* God and his *one* Christ, there can only be *one* grace for us' (K. Barth). In particular, it is to be hoped that the relatively modern un-scriptural distinction between 'covenanted' grace bestowed on certain churches and 'uncovenanted' on the rest, has been dissolved by the ecumenical movement and Vatican II. God's grace is 'covenanted' – wholly and all-sufficiently – in Jesus Christ, to all the churches and to the world.

J. Moffatt, *Grace in the New Testament*, 1932; J. Oman, *Grace and Personality*, 1931; T. F. Torrance, *Doctrine of Grace in the Apostolic Fathers*, 1948; W. T. Whitley (ed), *Doctrine of Grace*, 1932; N. P. Williams, *The Grace of God*, 1930.

BENJAMIN DREWERY

Greek Spirituality

Perhaps the most significant characteristic of Greek religion and the factor most decisive for its influence on all indebted to the Greeks was the realization that the divine is the beautiful. In its earliest stages Greek religion, like religion in general, saw the divine in the unpredictable, the unknown. The divine was an unknown power that threatened man and his endeavours; it turned to humanity a face that was essentially frightening. However, by the classical period, it is no longer as a grotesque inspiring terror that the gods are depicted, but as the beautiful. In particular they are depicted as beautiful human beings, indeed as naked human beings, not protected by power, but manifesting their power intrinsically in the perfect balance and perfect poise of their form. As such the divine does not primarily inspire terror, rather it attracts and compels attention: it becomes something to gaze upon, to contemplate. Such a conception of the divine inspired the art of Pheidias and Praxiteles.

To understand the history of Greek religion and its influence it is necessary to appreciate the split brought about in Greek consciousness by the criticism of religion and the myths by philosophers such as Xenophanes and Plato. Unlike the Hebrew prophets, the Greek philosophers did not demand the purification of religion; rather they consigned it to the realm of myth and fable and, while recognizing its practical value for the smooth running of society, denied to religion any relevance in the realm of truth. Religion became simply a matter of customary rites and practices; truth was the concern of philosophy. But it is equally important to see that this philosophical critique of religion was itself an expression of what we have suggested is the fundamental insight of Greek religion, namely the perception of the divine as the beautiful. If the perception that the divine is less the terrifying than the beautiful allowed the gods to be humanized and to appear in Homer and Hesiod in a form all too human, it was the perception of the divine as the beautiful that inspired the philosophical principle that nothing 'unfitting' be ascribed to the divine, and led to the philosophers' notion of God, manifesting in a pure and transcendent form the poise and symmetry of pure beauty, possessing a stillness beyond any possibility of disturbance. Truth, for the Greek philosophers, is that, the presence of which inspires awe. It is an object of contemplation: the philosopher is for Plato, as Walter Pater put it, 'a lover of the invisible, but still a lover . . . carrying into the world of intellectual vision, of *theoria*, all associations of the actual world of sight . . . Truth [will be], for Plato, to the last, something to *look* at.'

In the second century A D, when after his conversion Justin Martyr continued to wear his philosopher's robe and to teach Christianity as a philosophy, he healed, as it were, this split in Greek consciousness by claiming that the *religion*, Christianity (for it included rites that Justin was concerned to regard as authentic custom), was a philosophy, that is, a way of seeking and apprehending the truth. As the *true* religion, Christianity meant the rejection of false, 'pagan' religions, but equally, with its claim to truth, and therefore to the status of a philosophy, Christianity claimed to fulfil all that men had discovered in their age-long quest for the truth. Christianity, then, offered men the true object of contemplation; it could discern truly the lineaments of the beautiful that was the divine, and equally importantly Christianity showed men the way by which they could come to contemplation.

Greek philosophy was responding to the deepest inspiration of Greek religion in seeking God under the form of the beautiful. Its pursuit of truth under the form of the beautiful was then a religious quest. From at least the time of Parmenides accounts of the philosophical quest depict it in religious terms, seeing it as leading to revelation from the mouth of the gods themselves; and Plato, and following him many others, use the language of the mystery religions to express their account of the philosophical venture. Ritual purification, ascent from lower to higher mysteries: such religious themes are transposed into a philosophical key. Ritual purification becomes moral and intellectual purification, and both these notions are informed by the idea that it is as the beautiful that God manifests himself: for if God is to manifest himself as the beautiful then it will be to souls who have striven to realize in themselves such beauty as is theirs. Moral purification is then informed by aesthetic notions of poise and balance. Plato instructs the soul in the achievement of balance and order among its rational, passionate and desiring parts: the virtues of justice and prudence, courage and temperance bring the soul to a poised perfection. Aristotle sees moral virtue as a mean, a balance between extremes. The Stoics thought of the soul on the analogy of a lyre and saw virtue as bringing it into tune. Intellectual purification, for Plato especially, enables the soul to *understand* the principles of balance and symmetry which characterize the realm of truth and beauty. Such an aesthetic understanding of the soul's pursuit of virtue as the indispensable first step to the contemplation of truth is found throughout the Greek tradition: Plotinus, in a famous analogy, speaks of the soul's fashioning itself as a sculptor does a statue (*Enn.* I.6.9). The goal is the pure and beautiful soul's contemplation of peerless Beauty.

It was this that Christianity claimed to fulfil when it offered itself to men as the true philosophy. Here we find the legacy of the Greeks within Christian spirituality: it is an important tradition that we rarely lose sight of. It obviously inspires the whole mystical and contemplative tradition: the theme of the divine darkness is the way this tradition seeks to respond to the realization that the *Deus semper maior* of Christianity, while manifest as beautiful, must transcend and even contradict our conceptions of beauty. But the legacy of this tradition is found too in the poetic visions of such as Dante and St John of the Cross*, and in the attempts of such as Pascal*, Solovyev and Péguy* to explore more complex intuitions of beauty.

H. U. von Balthasar, *The Glory of the Lord*, ET 1983–; A.-J. Festugière, *Personal Religion among the Greeks*, 1954; W. K. C. Guthrie, *The Greeks and their Gods*, 1954.

ANDREW LOUTH

Gregory I, St

In spite of the outward turmoil which marked his pontificate (590–604) – plague, famine, floods and the Lombard invasion of Italy – and his own constant ill-health, Gregory the Great, born *c.* 540, the son of a Roman senator, not only extended the influence of the church by sending the mission under Augustine to England in 597, but also left behind him at his death a remarkable corpus of writings, in which he reveals himself as one of the great masters of the spiritual life.

Gregory's spirituality is marked by two important and interdependent characteristics: it is rooted in the Bible, and it is monastic. The prime source of his vast knowledge of the Bible and profoundly biblical outlook was no doubt the private *lectio divina*, which formed part of the monk's regular daily duties and which involved the use of the voice as well as the eyes. This habit of *legere et meditari*, which Gregory would have practised from his earliest years in St Andrew's, because it entailed vocal as well as visual activity, ensured that the meaning of the scriptures sank deeply into the reader's mind. Gregory's most important spiritual teaching is to be found in two works on the Bible, which were addressed to audiences of monks and *clerici*, with per-

haps a few devout laymen: these are the *Moralia in Hiob* and the *Homiliae in Ezechielem*. Gregory himself makes no secret of his preference for the contemplative life and of the personal conflicts to which this gave rise (e.g., *Dialogues* I, pref.); he believes it to be superior to the active life, but admits that both the *vita contemplativa* and the *vita activa* are valid ways of discipleship for Christian preachers (*Hom. in Ezech.* I.3.9). In the *Liber regulae pastoralis*, a handbook on the episcopal office, in which he displays considerable psychological acumen, he makes it clear that a man called to the office of bishop must not neglect his neighbours on account of his love of contemplation (I.6; II.1, 5).

Gregory's teaching on contemplation is closely linked with his teaching on compunction (see especially *Dialogues* III.34), which is derived from the Western tradition exemplified by Augustine* and Ambrose, on the one hand, and from the richer and fuller teaching of Basil, Evagrius Ponticus and John Chrysostom, on the other. This Eastern teaching seems to have been mediated to Gregory through the writings of Cassian* (e.g., *Collationes* IX.26, 28–29; *Institutiones* XII.18). Gregory, like Cassian, stresses the need for *purgatio*, before contemplation. He develops the teaching of Cassian further by listing the four modes of compunction and the four attitudes of compunction shown by the righteous man towards his sins (*Moralia* XXIII.41; cf. V.51).

Gregory's knowledge of Greek, though not non-existent, as has often been supposed, was certainly not sufficient to enable him to read Greek texts; yet his spirituality owes much to Eastern Christendom, including the writings of the Desert Fathers*. Some of his knowledge undoubtedly came through the writings of Cassian and through Latin translations of Eastern writers; but it is clear that in the late sixth century, though the linguistic division between East and West which had always existed was increasing, there was still a common body of theological and philosophical ideas.

E. C. Butler, *Western Mysticism*, [3]1967, J. H. Richards, *The Popes and the Papacy in the Early Middle Ages 476–752*, 1979; *Consul of God*, 1980.

JOAN PETERSEN

Gregory of Nazianzus, St
see **Cappadocian Fathers**

Gregory of Nyssa, St
see **Cappadocian Fathers**

Griffiths, Bede

Bede Griffiths was born 17 December 1906 and educated at Christ's Hospital and Magdalen College, Oxford, where he read English Literature. He was received into the Catholic Church in 1933 and became a Benedictine at Prinknash Abbey. In 1940 he was ordained priest; and became Prior of Farnborough Abbey. He went to India in 1955 to found a contemplative community; from 1958–1968 he was at Kurisumala ashram in Kerala; and from 1968 onwards at Sacchidananda ashram, Shantivanam, in Tamil Nadu, which had been founded in 1950 by two French Catholics as a pioneer attempt to be a Christian community following the pattern of a Hindu ashram, and adapting Christian worship and thought forms to the setting of Indian culture. (*See also* **Ashram**. The Christian ashram movement developed partly from a concern to preach and live a truly Indian Christianity compared with the style of earlier missionaries with their foreign associations, and also from a conviction that the insights of Hindu religious tradition could infuse and enrich Christian thinking and worship. Members of an ashram live a simple, community life with a spiritual leader, seeking the experience of God in the depths of each human soul.) Shantivanam is set in a forest, and consists of small, simple huts, a chapel, refectory and library containing books from many religious traditions. Its members' life is divided between prayer, study and physical work, including cultivation of the ashram's ten acres of land, and help to village neighbours through nursery schools and village industries. Members follow the style of Hindu ashrams in wearing saffron-coloured dress, going bare foot, sitting on the floor for prayers and meals, and eating vegetarian food. Griffiths himself exerts a wide spiritual influence, not just as leader of the ashram, but as a writer whose books are widely available in the West. The two most important in presenting his perception of the relationship of Hinduism and Christianity are *Return to the Centre* (1976) and *Marriage of East and West* (1982).

Bede Griffiths remains a Christian but reaches beyond the doctrinal formulations and specific revelations of particular religions towards a vision of the Mystery which is the source of all being and the truth to which all religions bear witness. He teaches that the Mystery is the ground of all being and of each individual's being, and can be apprehended by intuition and vision, not by rational thought. 'This is redemption, to be set free from the senses and the material world and to discover their Ground and Source in the Self, which is the Word of God within. The Fall of Man is the fall from this Ground, this Centre of freedom and immortality, into subjection to the senses and this material world' (*Return to the Centre*, p. 16). Obviously this owes much to the *advaita* teaching of Sankara within Hindu thought, that matter veils reality and is therefore in a sense illusory. Freedom from illusion and a glimpse of the Mystery is terrifying, for it means death to the self as understood and valued by the majority of people. Sin is refusal to recognize human nothingness and to act as though men's power is from themselves; and it leads man into isolation from the Ground of his Being and from others. Salvation in turn is not an individual matter but an organic, cosmic process, when all men come to realize their true being and hence their unity with each other. Despite the terror of the Mystery, and the reversal of values it demands, man is made for love and a sense of transcendent Reality, and only this will ultimately satisfy him. For Bede Griffiths the place of Christianity in a world of religions, its particular vision and glory, is the demonstration of these almost inexpressible truths in a human form in time. 'It is the revelation of the divine Mystery in the person of Christ. The one, eternal Truth, which cannot be uttered, which cannot be known, is "symbolized" in the life and death and resurrection of Jesus of Nazareth. At this point in history the veil is pierced, the Mystery shines through' (*Return to the Centre*, p. 73). This eclectic and embracing, rather than doctrinally exclusive, affirmation of faith, is accompanied in Shantivanam by a contemplative spirituality to enable inward movement of the soul in search of God and to encourage a trustful, intuitive response and a letting go of rational formulations. There is an hour of meditation in the morning and evening, and three daily times of communal prayer. In these much help is gained from Hindu meditative techniques and styles of worship; and the scriptures of the world's religions are all read to illuminate the worshipper with the particular insights each has into the nature of the Mystery to which they all tend. Bede Griffiths is not without critics, but he and Shantivanam have attracted many visitors, including foreigners as Western interest in India's religious heritage has developed. For many he has enabled a liberation from religious formulations which seem to deaden and constrict, and a new vision of a living God.

JUDITH M. BROWN

Groote, Geert *see Devotio Moderna*

Guyon, Jeanne-Marie Bouvier de la Motte

Married in 1664 to a rich husband much older than herself, Madame Guyon (1648–1717) was widowed in 1676 and felt called to devote her widowhood to making known the spiritual teaching she had acquired from her own reading and experience. In Geneva, where the bishop, at first favourable, soon became hostile, and in Savoy, her influence spread, and in 1685 she published her *Moyen court et très facile pour l'oraison*, written some years before. From 1686 onwards her activity was centred in Paris, where she moved with her director, a Barnabite priest, Père François Lacombe. The Archbishop of Paris, François de Harlay de Champvallon, frustrated in his attempt to marry his great-nephew to Madame Guyon's daughter, had them both imprisoned, Père Lacombe in 1687 and Madame Guyon in 1688, on suspicion of Quietism*. Released in the same year through the influence of Madame de Maintenon, Madame Guyon now found herself in a new circle in which she first met Fénelon*, on whose career she was to have such an influence.

Her desire to make available to everyone an easy way of prayer that would lead to the pure contemplation of God without formal object or distinctions, and her zealous conviction of her own mission and rightness of judgment, provoked the doubts, jealousies and opposition that came to a head in the condemnation of her teaching after the Conférences d'Issy in 1694–1695 (*see also* **Bossuet; Fénelon**) and by Rome in 1699. Madame Guyon was then imprisoned in the Bastille, which she did not leave until 1703. In her last years, her spiritual influence spread beyond the Catholics who continued to support her and to value her teaching to a wide circle of Protestants, who visited her in her retirement at Blois.

The sheer quantity and facility of her writing, which she practically never reread, and her impulsive, hypersensitive character, childish in certain ways, provoked adverse judgments, but should not be allowed to hide the real patience, resignation and charity which she showed throughout her life.

The core of her teaching situates her within the French seventeenth-century tradition derived from the Rheno-Flemish and Spanish mystics. A prayer of abstraction, laying little stress on imaginative or conceptual discursive meditation, even on attention to the humanity of Christ, and based on the divine omnipresence rather than on the historic revelation of God, it envisaged mystical union as a union of the human and divine wills such that the soul lost any capacity to distinguish between itself and God. Pure love, in Madame Guyon's teaching, meant the stripping away of all independence that might give rise to any kind of separation between the soul and God.

By the negative way, through a simplicity in prayer that was not devoid of the consoling experience of the presence of God, on which she laid great stress, the soul passed through the stages of a spiritual death, described in terms reminiscent of St John of the Cross* and Benedict Canfield. The final state of union is one of 'holy indifference' in which the soul wills nothing other than the will of God. Her explanations of this state left her vulnerable to unsympathetic interpretation.

Oeuvres, ed Poiret, 1712–1720; ed Dutrit, 1767–1791; Louis Cognet, 'La Spiritualité de Madame Guyon', *XVIIe Siècle*, 12-13-14, 1951–1952, 269–75; T. C. Upham, *Life*, 1848, 1894.

MICHAEL RICHARDS

Hadism *see Jewish Spirituality*

Hagiography

Hagiography consists of a literary and a critical tradition whose subject is the holy men and women (*hagioi*) of Christian history.

1. Literary hagiography. Literary hagiography has three genres. (i) The earliest hagiographical literature is the acts of the martyrs and liturgical lists of martyrs (martyrologies). The early acts, e.g. those of Polycarp (*c.* 155), Justin (*c.* 165), and the Scillitan martyrs (180), are simple narratives recounting the testimony and execution of the martyrs. Subsequent acts are embellished with dialogue, visions, and dramatized stories of suffering. (ii) A new literature, the lives of the saints, accompanied the rise of the ascetic movement. Athanasius' *Life of Antony* (357) and Sulpicius Severus' *Life of Martin* (397) are paradigmatic. This genre quickly spread beyond the ascetic movement, and developed certain conventions: signs of God's favour at birth, precocious holiness in childhood, renunciation of the world, struggle against the devil, fixed forms of asceticism, virtue, and miracles, a death foreknown and joyfully embraced. (iii) Stories of miracles attributed to the intervention of the saints in heaven comprise the third genre. An early example is Augustine's *City of God* XXII (426). These miracles occur through physical loci of divine power such as graves and relics, and are an important aspect of the mediaeval cult of the saints.

Beginning in the sixth century all three genres are used in hagiographical collections, most influentially by Gregory of Tours (d. 594) and Gregory the Great* (d. 604). Later mediaeval collections (legendaries) are organized according to the calendar of saints' feast days. The most famous mediaeval example is the *Golden Legend* of Jacob of Voragine (d. 1298).

Literary hagiography is a natural development within Christianity, in so far as Christianity is rooted in the manifestation of God through historical figures. The saints are the descendants of the patriarchs and prophets of the Hebrew scriptures, and of the apostles and disciples of the New Testament. Like the gospels, literary hagiography is not written as biography or history. Historical accuracy is subordinated to liturgical, catechetical, devotional, and polemical purposes.

The intent of literary hagiography is to build (*aedificare*) the faith of the church. To this end, the portrait of the martyr or saint has two related characteristics. (i) The saint is offered as a model of Christian holiness.

Consequently, literary hagiography has had a profound impact on the Christian understanding of moral and religious perfection. (ii) The perfection of the saint is both cause and consequence of a special relationship to God. Miracle stories, a preponderant feature of hagiographical literature, are reported as evidence of this relationship. The saint is therefore portrayed as a figure in whom God is encountered; the saints serve a sacramental function in the life of the church.

2. Critical hagiography. Critical hagiography is the study of literary hagiography using the methods of literary, historical, and theological criticism. While concern for the authenticity of the saints and their cults is found as early as the fourth century, critical hagiography was established by H. Rosweyde (d. 1629), J. van Bolland (d. 1665), and their successors in the Society of Bollandists. With the refinement of literary, historical, and theological methods since the mid-nineteenth century, work in critical hagiography has greatly increased. Important achievements include the editing of reliable hagiographical texts and the study of hagiographical literature for both historical information and theological content.

See also **Martyrs; Saints.**

Acta Sanctorum, 64 vols, 1643– ; D. Attwater and H. Thurston (eds), *Butler's Lives of the Saints*, 4 vols, 1956; D. Attwater, *The Penguin Dictionary of Saints*, 1965; *Bibliotheca Sanctorum*, 13 vols, 1961–1970; P. Brown, *The Cult of the Saints*, 1981; H. Delehaye, *The Legends of the Saints*, 1962; D. H. Farmer, *The Oxford Dictionary of Saints*, 1978; H. Musurillo, *The Acts of the Christian Martyrs*, 1972.

RICHARD M. PETERSON

Hall, Joseph

Joseph Hall (1574–1656) was born in Leicestershire and educated at Emmanuel College, Cambridge, becoming a Fellow in 1595. He gained an early reputation for literary and oratorical skills and has strong claims to be regarded as a pioneer in the 'naturalizing' of the classical genres of satire, epistle and the character. Hall was ordained in 1600 and held livings at Hawstead, and at Waltham Holy Cross; was domestic chaplain to Prince Henry, preached at the Synod of Dort, was consecrated Bishop of Exeter in 1627 and translated to Norwich in 1641.

He was swiftly victim to the anti-episcopal views of the Parliamentarians, was imprisoned and eventually evicted and dispossessed of his see in 1643. He lived in retirement at Higham, Norfolk until his death.

Hall was Calvinist in theology and a staunch defender of episcopacy, the sacraments and the liturgy. He thus earned both the suspicion of Laud and the scorn of Milton. Thomas Fuller's tribute, however, is still sound: 'not unhappy at *Controversies*, more happy at *Comments*, very good in his *Characters*, better in his *Sermons*, best of all in his *Meditations*' (*Worthies of England*).

The Arte of Divine Meditation (1606) consciously filled a gap in the devotional literature of the Church of England. A visit to the Low Countries in 1605 had stimulated Hall's interest and he drew on the rich resources of continental devotion particularly the writings of 'one obscure nameless monk which wrote some 112 years ago'. This is generally assumed to be J. Mauburnus whose *Rosetum* in turn drew on Gansfort. Hall also acknowledges a debt to Jean Gerson* (1363–1429), recently criticized by Bellarmine and thus acceptable as a model. *The Arte* had strong traditional roots but avoided any formal association with Jesuit practice. Hall's own tendency is to simplify. He does not separate prayer from meditation: they are as 'two loving turtles', for 'the heart must speak to God, that God may speak to it'. He discusses the preparation of the self by examination and the careful choice of place, time, posture and above all the subjects of meditation. These are principally God and his attributes, the life, death and glory of Christ, and the 'book of creatures', in which there is nothing so lovely, not even a worm underfoot as not to speak of the greatness of God. Meditation could be extemporal and outward or deliberative and inward. Man needs sense to behold the material world, reason to grasp the intelligible and faith to apprehend the spiritual. Hall formally analyses the stages of meditation but without regimenting the reader. The object is to move the affections to thanksgiving to God and to the enactment of his will.

Hall's earliest published meditations (*Meditations and Vowes*, 1605–1606) are aphoristic, practical and moral but his practice and writing became increasingly intense in spirit and more fluid in style. The richest collection is *Occasional Meditations* (1630). Many humble objects serve as starting points for meditation: a spider, a dormouse, street cries and more predictably a tolling bell or a death's head. But many of his meditations are more ecstatic in tone. Contemplation of the passion, Hall felt, had been neglected by the Reformers and his own response is warm and intense. It is evident in the aptly titled *An Holy Rapture or Patheticall Meditation on the Love of Christ* (1647). Hall published regularly in his retirement and his meditative works in particular earned him a wide readership, remarkably diverse in outlook.

Philip Wynter (ed), *The Works of the Right Revd Joseph Hall*, 10 vols, 1863; F. L. Huntley, *Bishop Joseph Hall*, 1979; R. A. McCabe, *Joseph Hall*, 1980.

ELUNED BROWN

Hammarskjøld, Dag

Dag Hammarskjøld (1905–1961), the Secretary-General of the United Nations, died in a plane crash in Zambia while trying to bring peace to the Congo. Although on his arrival at New York eight years before he had made a radio statement as far as he could about his faith, he appeared to be practically an agnostic humanist. So it came as an enormous surprise to find in his New York apartment after his death the manuscript of *Markings* (published 1964), what he himself called 'a sort of a White Book concerning my negotiations with myself – and with God'.

He was descended from soldiers and politicians on his father's side and from clergymen and scholars on his mother's. While a brilliant student at Uppsala university, he lost his faith. Then he went into business and government. He was elected to his post at the United Nations and served during some of the toughest years of its history.

His journey back to faith was long and slow. 'The longest journey,' he wrote, 'is the journey inwards.' He had a breakthrough, but so undramatic, that he could write: 'I don't know Who – or what – put the question. I don't know when it was put. I don't even remember answering. But at some moment I did answer *Yes* to Someone – or Something – and from that hour I was certain that existence is meaningful, and that, therefore, my life, in self-surrender, has a goal.'

He began, it seems, by reflecting on the mystics' firsthand experience of God, although he never became an expert in that field. He quotes Thomas à Kempis*, Eckhart* and St John of the Cross*. Then came his interest in Jesus' own fellowship with God – as the driving force of his life work. Later he turned again and again to the psalms with man's infinitely varied, profoundly rich experience of God. For himself he said: 'Faith is a state of the mind and the soul . . . The language of religion is a set of formulas which register a basic spiritual experience. It must not be regarded as describing, in terms to be defined by philosophy, the reality which is accessible to our senses and which we can analyse with the tools of logic.'

Nor did he participate in the corporate, liturgical or sacramental life of any church. He may have felt that publicly committing himself to a particular church would have labelled him as too much of a 'Westerner'. Anyway *Markings* shows no sign of wishing for such a commitment; indeed he quotes a cryptic saying: 'The lovers of God have no religion but God alone.'

But he had to do some hard theological thinking for himself. 'There is no formula to teach us how to arrive at maturity,' he said to some students, 'and there is no grammar for the language of the inner life.' He would not take over patterns of belief from others, however intellectual or however holy they might be. He wrote about 'my never abandoned effort frankly and squarely to build up a personal belief in the light of experience'. He maintained that it was honest thinking that finally led him round to the beliefs of his youth; in the end he recognized and 'endorsed unreservedly', he said, 'those very beliefs which were once handed down to me'.

It is now often said that a life of tranquillity is the most conducive to progress in the life of prayer. But on the contrary, what is very striking in *Markings* is just where Dag Hammarskjøld's great steps towards faith and prayer came. 'The years of his most rapid advance in faith and prayer were,' van Dusen says, 'precisely his years at the United Nations, years packed and overflowing with the problems and intricacies of world political affairs.' Dag Hammarskjøld himself wrote in *Markings*: 'For many of us in this

era the road to holiness necessarily passes through the world of action.'

This contemplation springing out of action is well illustrated by the fact that on his flight from Kennedy airport to the Congo he had with him, as always on his long flights, a pocket edition of Thomas à Kempis' *Imitation of Christ*, and as a bookmark in it a postcard, on which was typed his oath of office as Secretary-General of the United Nations.

G. Aulen, *Dag Hammarskjøld's White Book*, 1970; H. P. van Dusen, *Dag Hammarskjøld: a Biographical Interpretation*, 1967 (invaluable, as it puts the paragraphs of *Markings* in their chronological setting).
                                    MARK GIBBARD, SSJE

Harris, Howel

Howel, or Howell, Harris (1714–1773) was one of the leaders of the Methodist Revival in Wales. Born at Trefeca, or Trevecka, in the parish of Talgarth in Breconshire, the youngest son of a carpenter, he was educated at local schools and although given the opportunity of attending university at Oxford, due to the effect of his conversion on his life he was unable to stay there and returned home. Harris had expressed a desire to enter the ministry, but his conversion in the spring of 1735 led him to evangelize in the neighbourhood of Trefeca and as a result of his unusual activities the bishop refused his applications to be ordained on several occasions.

During the early years of the revival Harris met the other leaders of the Methodist movement in both England and Wales. A period of close co-operation followed, during which Harris displayed an unusual ability to organize the work. He gathered the leaders of the numerous Methodist societies to meetings known as 'associations' where general policies were discussed, various matters settled and discipline enforced when necessary. Towards the middle of the 1740s differences between Harris and Daniel Rowland became apparent, and these led to their final separation in 1750. Two years later Harris retired from his itinerant ministry and gathered together a number of his followers at Trefeca to live together as a Christian community under his rule and guidance. This community became known as the 'Trefeca Family' and survived well into the middle of the nineteenth century.

After a short period in the militia defending his Protestantism against the Catholic enemy, a reunion took place between Harris and Rowland in 1763. He found it difficult, however, to re-establish himself as a leader among the Methodists and was unable to make a similar contribution to that which he had made during his early years. Much of his time was spent in caring for the community at Trefeca, and when the Countess of Huntingdon opened her college there in 1768 Harris was deeply involved in the preparations preceding the event. His health deteriorated in 1772 and in July 1773 he died at the age of fifty-nine.

Harris was a profoundly spiritual man. He was very aware of the need to be near God at all times and therefore prayer was an essential part of his life. Nothing was too large or too small to be brought before God; he prayed as devoutly about the decor at Trefeca as he did about his own spiritual condition or the question of marriage. He believed in the immediate intervention of God as a result of prayer and not only in divine guidance but that some were gifted in an especial way to recognize and communicate the will of God. Throughout his lifetime Harris was a member of the Established Church, defended its articles and opposed any form of separation from it. In order to discipline himself and also to see the hand of God in his life, he kept a detailed diary from the time of his conversion until his death. In it he recorded his movements, sermons, prayers and thoughts and the collection, together with his letters, offers not only a detailed account of his day-to-day life but also an insight into the difficulties facing such a religious figure. As a gifted preacher and organizer Harris left the literary aspect of the revival to others, leaving only his private papers and a brief autobiography.

Richard Bennett, *The Early Life of Howell Harris*, 1962; Tom Beynon, *Howell Harris, Reformer and Soldier*, 1958; *Howell Harris's Visits to London*, 1960, *Howell Harris's Visits to Pembrokeshire*, 1966; Hugh J. Hughes, *Life of Howell Harris*, 1892; M. H. Jones, *The Trevecka Letters*, 1932; G. F. Nuttall, *Howel Harris, 1714–73. The Last Enthusiast*, 1965.

GERAINT TUDUR

Heart, Sacred *see* **Sacred Heart**

Heiler, Friedrich

Friedrich Heiler (1892–1967), originally a Roman Catholic, became a high-church Lutheran, and was Professor at Marburg, Germany. His main work in spirituality was his large book, *Das Gebet (Prayer)*, which classifies various types of prayer and illustrates them with quotations widely drawn from many religions. His main contribution lay in the distinction between mystical and prophetic piety. In the preface to the fifth edition he said that he had somewhat changed his view of mysticism under the influence of Friedrich von Hügel*, W. R. Inge*, and Evelyn Underhill*, and had freed himself entirely from the Ritschlian view which had made occasional appearances in the earlier editions of the book. But for technical reasons he could not alter the text, which was the same as that of the second edition, and his corrections were confined to an appendix. Even so the main text, even in the abbreviated form of the English translation, which most unfortunately omits the appendix, gives a fairly accurate impression of his view of mysticism, and it is unfortunate that some English writers, using rather isolated quotations, have viewed him as entirely hostile to mysticism, which was never his intention.

Mysticism, in his view, is fundamentally world-denying and ascetic. It is seldom carried to the extremes of identification with the Godhead, but that is its strict logical consequence. Its conception of God is static and negative; the idea of a revelation of God in history is quite foreign to it; it knows only a subjective inner revelation. Sin consists of delight in life and the world; salvation is a difficult ascent to union with God. It is individualistic; nothing matters but God and the soul; it is indifferent to cultural values; its ideal is the monk or the hermit. Its goal is the permanence of the ecstatic vision of and union with God, towards which it strives in this life. It is monist, devoid of contrast.

Yet all this is, so to speak, a theoretical construction. Though mysticism entered Christianity from without, it has there become intermingled with prophetic religion, which has quite different characteristics. It has been able to use the beautiful symbols of Christianity as a means to express itself; this has modified its conceptions of God and of salvation; but it has not thereby lost its purity; though it is wrong to regard it as the essence of Christianity, yet in Christianity it has assumed its finest and most beautiful form. Mystical prayer is therefore hard to describe, for it is generally found in close connection with popular religion or with prayer of the prophetic type. Thus a Christian mystic uses a biblical vocabulary and the devotional terminology of prophetic piety; but peculiarly mystical states of mind are combined with prophetic passion; a fine ear will always detect the mystical undertone. Mysticism and the religion of revelation are two opposite poles of the higher piety which ever avoid and yet ever attract each other.

See also **Mysticism; Prayer, Prophetic.**

***

Friedrich Heiler, *Prayer*, ET 1932.

A. RAYMOND GEORGE

Herbert, George

Born into a noble family, Herbert (1593–1633) had all the advantages of social security and the prospect of worldly advancement. He became Public Orator of Cambridge University in 1620, but was apt to neglect his duties for the interests and pleasures of the Court, and also perhaps because he was not a natural academic. He was always God-fearing and never dissolute but it was the deaths of two patrons and of King James I in 1625 which turned him to more serious thoughts which after much spiritual struggle led to his being ordained priest five years later. Nicholas Ferrar * was a great influence in this direction. For three years until his death, he exercised a parish ministry at Bemerton near Salisbury, then a small village. Brief as his ministry was, he has always been regarded as a model pastor. His famous account of the English clergyman, *A Priest to the Temple: or the Country Parson*, was not published until 1652: his poems appeared in the year of his death. They illustrate the lyrical gift which had been apparent from his musical youth, and several of them are much sung as hymns in our own time.

Herbert's spirituality is *par excellence* that of the Anglican middle way. Worship must be less gaudy than with Rome, yet 'colours and light' are valuable aids and may help simple people more than sermons. Preaching is important, but praying better and, as in a church he served in Huntingdonshire, the ambo for prayer must be as prominent as the pulpit. Outward gesture is the sign of inward grace and of body and soul in harmony, and to put on vestments is for Herbert a deeply spiritual act, a sign of his putting on Christ to cover his own unworthiness. He was no mystic. W. H. Auden has said that his poetry is representative of Anglicanism in that it is that of a gentleman, with the danger that it 'becomes merely genteel'. But his poem 'The Sacrifice' is full of Western mediaeval typology of the Passion with a hint of the Reproaches from the Good Friday Mass of the Pre-Sanctified. His poetic ejaculations have been compared to the Orthodox Jesus Prayer * and his poetry constantly evidences the intimacy of his dealings with God and his assurance that, alone in a vast universe, he is held safe by the Crucified. Richard Baxter * said of him '. . . (as *Seneca* takes with me above all his contemporaries, because he speaketh *Things* by *Words*, feelingly and *seriously*, like a man that is past jest, so) *Herbert* speaks to *God* like one that *really believeth a God* and whose business in this world is most *with God. Heart-work and Heaven-work* make up his Books'.

See also **Anglican Spirituality; Caroline Divines, The.**

***

Texts: *The English Works of George Herbert* ed G. H. Palmer, 3 vols, 1920; *George Herbert: The Country Parson, The Temple*, ed John N. Will (Classics of Western Spirituality), 1981; see also Margaret Bottrall, *George Herbert*, 1954.

EDITOR

Herman, Nicholas
see **Lawrence of the Resurrection**

Hesychasm

A term derived from *hesychia*, the Greek word for 'quiet', 'stillness', 'tranquillity'; hence 'hesychast', one who lives in stillness. The term can be understood in three main ways, the first broader, the second and the third more narrow.

1. In a general sense, hesychasm signifies the way of inner prayer, as taught and practised in the Christian East from the fourth

century onwards, especially in monastic circles:

(i) Sometimes *hesychia* is understood in an external and physical sense: the hesychast is a hermit or recluse, as contrasted with a monk living in community.

(ii) But more commonly the meaning of *hesychia* is inward: the hesychast is one who 'returns into himself', who seeks the 'kingdom within' (cf. Luke 17.21) and 'guards the heart with all watchfulness' (Prov. 4.23), closing not merely the outward door of his cell against visitors, but also the inward door of his heart against evil thoughts and distractions. Thus St John Climacus* defines the hesychast as 'one who strives to confine his incorporeal self within his bodily house, paradoxical though this may sound' (*Ladder* 27).

(iii) More specifically, *hesychia* often signifies prayer that is so far as possible free from images and concepts, that dispenses with the imagination and the discursive reason – the kind of 'pure prayer' that is commended by St Gregory of Nyssa, Evagrius, St Maximus the Confessor and St Isaac of Nineveh (none of these, however, can be styled a 'hesychast' in the two narrower senses given below). As Climacus puts it, '*Hesychia* is a laying aside of thoughts' (*Ladder* 27); the hesychast, says St Gregory of Sinai, is one who 'abstains from thoughts' (*PG* 150, 1333B).

2. In a narrower sense, hesychasm denotes the use of the Jesus Prayer (*see* **Jesus, Prayer to**), in particular when accompanied by the physical technique involving control of the breathing.

3. In a yet more restricted sense, hesychasm designates the theology of St Gregory Palamas*, developed during 1337–1347 in his dispute with Barlaam the Calabrian, Akindynos and Nicephorus Gregoras (the 'Hesychast Controversy'). Drawing on earlier Greek Fathers, Palamas believed that inward prayer, and especially the Jesus Prayer, leads to a vision of the divine light. This light he identified with the glory surrounding Christ at his transfiguration on Mount Tabor. Although seen by the saints through their physical eyes, it is not itself a material and created light but the uncreated energies of the Godhead, the splendour of the age to come. The divine energies, however, are distinguished by Palamas from the divine essence: man participates by grace in

God's energies, but God's essence remains always beyond all knowledge and participation, even in the age to come. (Contrast the mediaeval Western view, according to which man contemplates God's essence in the Beatific Vision.) Palamas, without attaching primary importance to the physical technique accompanying the Jesus Prayer, defended its legitimacy: the human being is a psychosomatic unity, and so the body as well as the soul participates actively in the work of prayer. Palamas' teaching was endorsed by three councils held at Constantinople in 1341, 1347 and 1351, and in this way has become an accepted part of Orthodox tradition. There has been a striking revival of Palamite theology in contemporary Orthodoxy.

The chief texts of the hesychast tradition, understanding the word in all three of the above senses, are included in the *Philokalia** of Macarius and Nicodemus.

To translate 'hesychasm' as 'quietism', while perhaps etymologically defensible, is historically and theologically misleading. The distinctive tenets of the seventeenth-century Western Quietists are not characteristic of Greek hesychasm.

P. Adnès in *DS*, VII, cols 381–99; M. Jugie in *DTC*, XI, cols 1735–1818, J. Meyendorff, *A Study of Gregory of Palamas*, 1964; *St Gregory Palamas and Orthodox Spirituality*, 1974; K. Ware in B. Pennington (ed), *One Yet Two: Monastic Tradition East and West* (Cistercian Studies 29), 1976.

KALLISTOS WARE

Hilary of Poitiers, St

St Hilary, probably born 310/20, was Bishop of Poitiers *c*. 350–367. He is usually remembered for his staunch opposition to Arianism and his championing of the Nicene faith, which led to his being exiled to Phrygia from 356–360. But his importance for the history of spirituality lies elsewhere: in his scriptural exegesis, his hymn writing, and his support and guidance for St Martin's monastic foundation of Ligugé. In all this Hilary's knowledge of Eastern developments, gained through his period of exile, was put to good use.

The opening chapters of Hilary's *Trinity* give an autobiographical account, albeit retrospective and stylized, of his search for a purpose in life: a search which ultimately led him to embrace Christianity. In some ways these chapters foreshadow Augustine's *Confessions*. Hilary, who came from a pagan background, soon saw the futility of pursuing wealth and leisure, and felt the inadequacy of the pagan philosophers' ethical precepts. Hilary longed to *know* God: 'My heart was inflamed with a passionate desire to discern him and to know him.' Dissatisfied with paganism in its many guises, he encountered various OT books whose portrayal of the mystery of the Godhead, 'I am that I am' (Ex. 3.14), rang true. Further reading of the OT increased his understanding of God, but he was apparently still unaware of the incarnation and of the Christian promise of eternal life until he encountered NT writings, especially John 1.1–14. This fulfilled and extended Hilary's previous understanding of God, and he was able to accept the incarnation in faith, measuring God's mighty powers 'not by my own abilities of perception, but by a boundless faith'. Hilary joyfully attained peace of mind, and was baptized.

When he became bishop, Hilary took seriously his role as teacher. All was based upon the Bible. Hilary believed that the Bible, inspired by the Holy Spirit, contained not only a surface (or literal) meaning, but also, if approached aright, bore witness to the central mysteries of Christianity. The faithful exegete, aided by the same Spirit as had inspired the original words, would be able to draw out this hidden, or spiritual, meaning. The Bible thus provides a ladder up which to ascend to the higher things of God (cf. *In ps.* 120, 4). And where human powers of comprehension fall short in fathoming such mysteries as the 'eternal birth' of Christ, study of the Bible can lift one to understanding (cf. *De Trin.* I, 34). Understanding and expounding scripture was thus primarily a religious exercise; and the OT as well as NT provided material which, interpreted in a spiritual sense, could be made to yield Christian insights. Hilary was the first Latin father systematically to expound biblical books in this way, and he did so even in his *Commentary on Matthew*, written before he encountered Origen's works during his exile. In his later *Commentary on the Psalms* he drew heavily, though never slavishly, upon Origen*. But, in comparison with Origen, he showed little interest in the contemplative life or mystical heights, and he

regarded the vision of God as unattainable in this life, even for ascetics (*In ps.* 118, 5–8). Instead, Hilary concentrated more on Christian teaching that was applicable to all. Though in subsequent centuries Hilary's commentaries were relatively little read, his methods and many of his interpretations were taken over by Ambrose and Augustine*, and thus helped to provide material for biblical reflexion through the Middle Ages.

Hilary was also the first to write hymns in Latin, intended for congregational singing. His three surviving hymns, centring upon Christ, show Hilary attempting to familiarize his congregation with the main themes of his theology.

———

Hilary, *On the Trinity*, in A Select Library of Nicene and post-Nicene Fathers, 2nd series, vol 9, 1899; C. F. A. Borchardt, *Hilary of Poitiers' role in the Arian Struggle*, 1966; *Hilaire et son temps:* Actes du Colloque de Poitiers 29 sept.–3 oct. 1968, introduction by E.-R. Labande, 1969; P. T. Wild, *The Divinization of Man according to Saint Hilary of Poitiers*, 1950.

C. E. STANCLIFFE

Hildegard of Bingen, St
see **German Spirituality**

Hilton, Walter
see **English Mystics, The**

Hinduism

Hinduism is a European name for the complex religions of most Indian peoples. Indians themselves often call their religion *sanatana dharma*, eternal law, right, truth or religion. It is that which governs all existence in ways of life and religious systems.

About 1500 BC Aryan invaders from central Asia overran the Indus Valley, destroying the buildings of an earlier literate culture whose religion must have continued among ordinary people, since after a thousand years or so the elements of it that seem to have been present originally reappeared amidst Aryan religion and became Hinduism. The religious beliefs and practices of the early Indian Aryans are preserved in the 1,028 hymns of the Rig Veda, passed on by great feats of memory for many centuries before being written down. These hymns were used in the sacrifices of the aristocratic Aryans, while two other Vedas, Sama and Yajur, were repetitive and liturgical. A fourth Veda, Atharva, consists of spells and incantations mingled with speculations and non-Aryan elements. Also included in the Vedic literature were ritual and religious treatises, Brahmanas and Aranyakas, and philosophical Upanishads*. The dating of these texts is hard to establish, but critical estimate puts them between 1500 and 500 BC.

The Vedic Aryans worshipped many gods (*devas*), the 'shining ones', mostly male and connected with the sky. Indra was a great warrior and storm god, Varuna the sky (Latin Uranus), Mitra a god of contracts (Persian Mithra), Agni a god of fire and intermediary with other gods (Latin ignis). In language and ideas the Indian Aryans were related to Iranians, Homeric Greeks, Roman and other European peoples. They were polytheist yet felt after an underlying unity, and a Vedic text says: 'They call it Indra, Mitra, Varuna, Fire, or it is the heavenly sun-bird; that which is One, the sages speak of in various terms.'

Sacrifice was central to Vedic cults, with fire and sacred drink, Soma, accompanying slaughter of animals. Priests conducted social rituals and heads of houses performed smaller sacrifices on domestic hearths. The gods were believed to come down, eat and drink with worshippers, and supply their needs.

A few texts (*mantras*) of the Vedas became more general religious utterances, but most were confined to priestly usage. They spoke of a mysterious power, *brahman*, sacred word, energy, magic. The priest became known as Brahmana (anglicized as Brahmin) and in time, especially in the Upanishads, brahman was the universal neuter divine power. Other holy men were silent magicians (*munis*), or non-Vedic priests of fertility cults, or ascetic world-renouncers who lived in 'penance-grounds' outside towns, or in the forest or on mountains. Here they practised forms of Yoga*, seeking quiet and calm, and often aiming at possession of supernatural powers.

The Upanishads were followed by masses of sacred literature in which Aryan, Indus Valley and other Indian beliefs and practices were merged to form Hinduism proper. Two great epic poems, Mahabharata and Ramayana, collections of 'ancient tales', Puranas, and books of Sacred Law, offered examples and precepts. The Vedas were *shruti*, 'heard' from the gods and restricted to high caste Indians, while much later literature was *smriti*, 'remembered' and available to women and other classes. Most people were and are illiterate, but texts were recited and plays performed from their stories.

Great gods appeared now. Vishnu who was only a minor deity in the Vedas became and remains the great and only God to many Vaishnavites, especially through his ten or more avatāras. Vishnu is believed to be the source and ruler of the universe, from whose body emerge the worlds in rounds of transmigration. His avatāras, descents or incarnations, include mythical animal figures: fish, tortoise, boar and man-lion, and legendary human characters: dwarf, Rāma with axe, prince Rāma of the Ramayana epic, Krishna of the Bhagavad Gītā and Purānas, Buddha either to delude or save devotees, and an eschatological Kalki, the next avatāra to come. Avatāras have often been compared with the Christian incarnation, but there is no evidence of influence one upon the other and Indian avatāras are plural and hardly historical. In popular devotion it is Krishna and Rāma, more than Vishnu, who are centres of devotions, cults and pilgrimages (*see* **Bhagavad Gītā**).

Parallel to Vishnu is Śiva, the only God to Śaivites. Unknown to the Vedas, though linked with a storm god Rudra and perhaps going back to Indus Valley religion, Śiva is both ascetic and god of fertility, haunting cemeteries as god of death or sitting in yogic meditation, or performing a world-shattering dance at the dissolution of the cosmos in which he is portrayed in many sculptures, bronzes and paintings. Although rarely said to have avatāras, Śiva is believed to appear to his followers in time of need and many think of him as kindly and moral. Worship of Śiva has been claimed as the purest Indian form of monotheism.

Vaishnavites and Śaivites have tolerated each other at times and persecuted at others. Efforts at harmony produced the notion of the Trimurti, the triple form of Vishnu, Śiva and a personal creator Brahma. But the latter has been little worshipped and attempts at comparison with the Trinity are forced. A greater third power in Indian religion is the Great Goddess, wife of Śiva, and known under various names as Mother, Shakti, Uma, Parvati, Durga or Kali. As the last she is a fierce black naked female warrior worshipped notably in Calcutta, Kali's ghat (steps) where blood sacrifices are still offered, to the horror of many other Hindus, such as Vaishnavites who worship with 'leaf of flower, fruit or water, given in loving devotion' (Gita 9, 26). (*See also* **Bhakti**.)

There are many other Hindu gods. The Vedic Indra, Varuna, Mitra and company have almost disappeared. The creating Brahma is said to have only one temple in the whole of modern India, but his wife Sarasvati is popular as patron of arts. Similarly Lakshmi, consort of Vishnu, is goddess of fortune who is invoked especially at the new year in the festival of lights, Divali. Ganesha or Ganapati is the popular elephant-headed son of Śiva and Parvati, perhaps an ancient forest deity, now patron of literature and luck.

Hindu philosophers, following the Upanishads, evolved elaborate systems. Shankara in the early ninth century A D taught a strict non-dualism (*a-dvaita*) or monism. Two centuries later Ramanuja proposed a 'qualified non-dualism' or 'difference nondifference' between divine and human, seeking to allow devotion to the neuter Brahman personalized as Vishnu. Later still Madhva taught a frank dualism (*dvaita*) of God and souls. The Sankhya (enumeration) philosophy early in the Christian era propounded a dualism of Spirit and Nature (Purusha and Prakriti) which came to merge with Yoga as theory for its practice. Salvation could be obtained by self-discipline but also by veneration of a Lord (*ishvara*) who was a divine example (*see* **Yoga**).

In popular Hindu religion there are many teachers, gurus, ten million in some estimates. A guru having himself attained insight instructs pupils and invests caste Hindus with the sacred thread in adolescence. The relationship of guru and disciple (*shishya* or *chela*) is one of veneration, even devotion. The first reference to bhakti, loving devotion, in the Upanishads says that the mystery of the scriptures should be given to 'one who has the highest devotion to God and to his guru even as to God'. The development of Bhakti Yoga, discipline of loving devotion, as one of the widest paths to salvation, emphasized surrender to both God and the guru.

Hindus of the three higher castes, 'twice-born' by initiation, follow patterns of personal devotion. The devout Hindu rises before dawn, utters the sacred syllable O M, repeating the name of his chosen God and remembers his Guru. He binds up the tuft of hair on his head and recites a favourite Vedic *mantra*: 'We meditate on the lovely light of Savitri (the sun), may he inspire our thoughts.' He goes to worship (*puja*) bare to the waist, with sacred thread diagonally across his body and marks of ash or paste on his forehead according to his sect. He sits cross-legged on a mat, eyes fixed, breath controlled, sipping and sprinkling water while repeating names of God. Parts of the body are touched to place the deity there, prayers and texts are uttered, and water or flowers are placed before an image, picture or symbol of the God. Images are dressed in fine clothes, cooled with water, offered fruit and incense and washed at annual rites. Geometrical designs are made with paste and powder for ritual use, and prayer beads help in repeating divine names.

A caste Hindu traditionally passed through three or four stages of spiritual life, called ashrams. The first was that of a student of Vedic scripture, followed by that of householder. When he had seen his children's children, and so ensured the continuity of ancestral rites, there came the stage of 'forest dwelling', leaving family to meditate, preferably with a wife or disciple to care for him. A fourth stage was that of Sannyasi, 'laying aside', complete renunciation of all cares. But the term Sannyasi is often applied to any religious ascetic or beggar and holy places are crowded with them, especially Benares (Varanasi, Kashi) where Sannyasis congregate to die in the holy city and hope to go direct from there to heaven.

An ashram * was also a hermitage, for retired saints and ascetics, and in modern times there are many such retreat houses founded by religious leaders, and also Christian ashrams.

Individual and family worship and sacraments of family life are usually performed at home. But great temples for which India is famous are places for priestly rituals and for public visitation and pilgrimage. Lay people may provide lamps for the shrine, pay for reading scriptures, receive blessings and sacred food, walk round the shrine or prostrate round the temple. Many temples have only small sanctuaries but large tanks for ritual washing and wide courtyards for recitations and plays.

Temple festivals are occasions for popular devotion. The chief images are carried round the temple and in procession through the streets to a river or sea for washing. They may be taken on elephants or on huge decorated temple carts, often drawn by pilgrims as at the Jagannatha (a title of Krishna Anglicized as Juggernaut) at Puri on the eastern coast where devotees used to throw themselves in front of the cart wheels. A popular festival is Holi in spring, a fertility ritual during which coloured water and powder are squirted on bystanders and effigies of demons are burnt. Similarly at Dasera in September–October the fight of the Avatar Rama against the demon Ravana is enacted with huge effigies of the contestants and culminates in the destruction of Ravana by fireworks.

There are many holy places associated with gods and holy men which receive constant visits. At Vrindaban (Brindabana) south of Delhi over a thousand temples and shrines are toured by pilgrims commemorating incidents in the life of Krishna. At Kataragama in Sri Lanka at a Śaivite shrine many Hindu ascetics are possessed and perform feats of endurance, and Buddhists, Muslims and Christians are attracted there.

Modern reform movements of Hinduism have been influenced by Christianity, the Brahmo Samaj tending to become a synthesis, but the Arya Samaj and the modern Hindu Mahasabha insisting on more traditional Hinduism. The Ramakrishna Mission insists on the unity of religions and in addition to its new shrines spreads its synthetic mission abroad.

A. L. Basham (ed), *A Cultural History of India*, 1975; Peter Brent, *Godmen of India*, 1972; Mariasusai Dhavamony, *Love of God according to Śaiva Siddhānta*, 1971; Klaus Klostermaier, *Hindu and Christian in Vrindaban*, 1969; Geoffrey Parrinder, *Avatar and Incarnation*, [2]1982; R. C. Zaehner, *Hinduism*, 1962; *Hindu Scriptures*, 1966.

GEOFFREY PARRINDER

Holiness

The holy lies at the heart of every religion and emanates from its heart. Lying at its heart, it has always an element of mystery and of the unknown, of the 'numinous', as Rudolf Otto calls it, in his great book, *The Idea of the Holy*, in which he draws attention to the fear, the wonder, the shock, and the amazement and astonishment which the holy may evoke. The holy is *mysterium tremendum et fascinans*. It knocks us back and draws us on. We recognize its transcendent value. It commands our respect. It may evoke from us our best works of art and strike us dumb.

In its most primitive form, the holy has little ethical content. You touch the holy and drop dead (II Sam. 6.1–8). But in the OT the ethical relation between man and the holy becomes increasingly important. Isaiah, for instance, sees the Lord, and is shattered with a sense of his own sinfulness and the sinfulness of his nation (Isa. 6). But the vision is not simply of the holy set apart, or of a holiness which fills only the temple, but of a holiness which ultimately fills all the earth as well as heaven. And the holy calls and empowers the prophet as a servant of the holy.

People – individuals and nations – places, times, things, are called into relation to the holy. They, like the holy, are set apart, consecrated (L. *consacrare*, *sacer*, sacred). This is the stuff of religion.

The history of Israel is the history of a holy people, a people set apart. But that history is also the history of the betrayal of holiness: of holiness presumed upon; holiness as merely enjoying religious practices; holiness as an automatic status. But the call of God to holiness is followed by the judgment of God upon its betrayal. Israel has to learn that the holy requires us 'to do justly, to love mercy, and to walk humbly before God' (Micah 6.6–8).

Holiness in the Bible reaches its climax in Jesus. He is the holy, 'fascinating', drawing all men to himself in his love and compassion; yet also the cause of wonder and astonishment, fear and trembling. The holy is revealed supremely in Jesus as self-giving love. He consecrates himself, and we 'behold his glory', in his coming amongst us as one who serves; in his washing his disciples' feet; and supremely in his laying down his life for his friends through the death on the cross.

The Christian church, the Israel of God, is God's holy people. The Holy Spirit reproduces in Christians the holiness which

Jesus revealed and embodied. The ancient phrase 'holy things for holy people' speaks of the eucharist as the vehicle of the renewal of the holiness of the Christian community. Baptism – holy baptism – the Word of God – the holy Bible, prayer, all have their indispensable part in our growth into holiness and into the Communion of Saints.

It is clear that the Christian idea of the holy has very little in common with a system of taboos. (*Taboo*: a Polynesian system of prohibitions connected with things considered holy.) In the Old Testament the holy is quite often forbidden ground, the God you must not look at; but the coming of Jesus radically altered that. He is the revelation of him whose 'new, best name is Love'; the revelation of the holy in a manger; a carpenter's son; crucified as a criminal. He was born and died not on days which were holy but on days which were made holy by the way he lived and died on them. He did not live in the 'the holy land' but in a land that was made holy by the way he spent his day-to-day life there. It was from the raw material of the everyday and ordinary that he fashioned his holiness. And for ever after, for the Christian, wherever we are, whoever we are, whatever the time and the day, that moment presents us in our decisions and responsibilities with the raw material out of which the holy has to be fashioned in response to God.

The holy for the Christian is therefore never simply the church, the chapel, the shrine, the sanctuary, the place set apart that a few can penetrate but which is taboo for others. It is never simply the holy day. (As George Herbert* wrote: 'Seven whole days, not one in seven, I will praise thee'.) It is never simply the holy man or woman – the 'sacred' ministry as distinct from everyone in their ministry. The place, time and person set apart have their function as resources for our holiness, lived primarily in the world; but they are rarely to be thought of as *the* place of holiness, and so on.

It follows that most people will have to work out their holiness through their marriage rather than through celibacy, through decisions at work as well as in the home – on boards of directors and in trades unions; in race relations and relations with the world's poor, hungry and unemployed; and with the people next door.

Holiness requires daily application. But if holiness requires us to 'work out your own salvation with fear and trembling', it requires us even more to remember and rely upon 'God who works in you, inspiring both the will and the deed . . .' (Phil. 2.12). The supreme witness to that is the holiness of Christ and of those whom we call his 'saints'. 'With the holy thou shalt be holy' (Ps. 18.25).

J. G. Davies, *Everyday God*, 1973; Donald Nicholl, *Holiness*, 1981; Rudolf Otto, *The Idea of the Holy*, 1923.

ERIC JAMES

Holy Name, Invocation of
see **Jesus, Prayer to**

Holy Spirit *see* **Spirit, Holy**

Hope

Hope as a universal human experience has two aspects that are relevant to spirituality. First there is hope that a person feels for the future. It is a personal experience, an attitude of mind, a way of approaching life in expectation of some future goal – a lover, for example, has high hopes of the relationship to be enjoyed when the beloved arrives. Secondly there is the nature of the hope itself, the goal or the object that is hoped for and awaited in confidence – the loving relationship that will ensue. Both emphases are very closely linked because expectant hope in the mind and the experience of a believer depends for its ultimate credibility on some confidence that the goal anticipated and for which hope is felt can in fact be achieved – just as anticipations that have been shared already of the coming relationship of love give grounds for confidence.

In Christian spirituality hope in the first sense as a hopeful attitude of a person to his life, to his own future and to that of the universe as a whole is a 'theological virtue' alongside faith and love – an essential mark of a Christian (I Cor. 13.13). Hope is very closely linked with faith* because the experience of trusting in God as the basis of faith gives grounds for confidence in the hope of final fulfilment. The New Testament Letters explore this idea in a number of places. Paul believed that faith in God's grace through Jesus Christ leads to the joyful hope of 'divine splendour' that is to come (Rom. 5.1f.). The author of the Letter to Hebrews began his portrayal of the faith of Old Testament figures with the assertion that 'faith gives substance to our hopes, and makes us certain of realities we do not see' (Heb. 11.1). Hope is also very closely linked with love * because God in his love involving himself in his world through his son gives grounds for hope in the possibilities of eternal life (John 3.16f.) and of a loving union with him.

The Christian hope, therefore, in the second sense as the goal of hopeful expectation is God himself, the God of love. This hope involves a number of strands that link the hope of an individual for himself in the eternal loving purposes of God (I Thess. 5.8–10) with hopes for the community of believers (I Cor. 1.1–9; Rom. 8.38f.), for the human race (John 12.32) and for the universe itself (Rom. 8.22–25). Although this hope is ultimately for future fulfilment in God it includes hope for the increasing manifestation of love, righteousness and justice on earth as signs of the eternal love and activity of God. The God of love who is the goal of Christian hope is encountered in part wherever love is expressed.

The hope of the Christian in God's eternal purposes is firmly grounded in the resurrection of Jesus Christ (I Peter 1.3). The resurrection as a fact of history vindicates the life and teaching of Jesus and gives credibility to the hope founded upon it that God is in Christ reconciling the world to himself. Following from this the resurrection as in some sense an experience by the believer in the risen Christ gives further assurance that the hopes placed in God are justifiable. The hope that is rooted in the gracious activity of God removes as a reason for hope either anxiety over the future or the anticipation of personal rewards.

Some significant modern writings include: Teilhard de Chardin, *The Future of Man*, 1968; John Macquarrie, *Christian Hope*, 1978; Jürgen Moltmann, *Theology of Hope*, 1967. The Book of Revelation in the New Testament concerns hope and an interesting comment is G. B. Caird, *The Revelation of St John*, 1966, especially pp. 289ff. On the so-called 'last things' see J. A. T. Robinson, *In The End, God*, 1968.

REX CHAPMAN

Hopkins, Gerard Manley

Reared as a member of the Church of England, Hopkins (1844–1889) converted to Rome in his final year at Oxford and became a member of the Society of Jesus *. He had a remarkable and original talent for poetry, though his work was not given to the world until long after his death when his friend Robert Seymour Bridges, by then Poet Laureate, who had preserved it, brought out a first edition. Obedient to his Order, his spirituality shaped by the Ignatian Exercises *, he reconciled his poetry and his obedience through his discovery of the schoolman Duns Scotus, whose teaching of the importance of individuality and personality made Hopkins believe that his vocation to serve the church might be fulfilled through the use of the gift which he and no one else in the same way possessed. He had amazing powers of finding new language, images and rhythms to describe the sights and sounds of nature. He was a Nature Mystic *, believing that 'the world is charged with the grandeur of God', the Blessed Virgin may be compared to the air we breathe and all is not dusty death at last. Through Christ's resurrection 'this Jack, joke, poor potsherd, patient, matchwood, immortal diamond,/is immortal diamond'.

His largest work was one of his first, *The Wreck of the Deutschland*, inspired by the brave death of five Franciscan nuns, exiles from German anti-Catholic laws, who were drowned when the *Deutschland* went down off Harwich in December 1875. This is no attempt to demean tragedy or insult the courage of faith by attempted philosophic explanation or theodicy. Disaster befalls, Christ was crucified, Francis himself bore the marks of the passion. If it were not for this there would be no joy, for the glory of nature and the horror of suffering and death are not to be separated. The Christ of the stigmata and the Sun of Righteousness are one. The poem breathes a Catholic hatred of Luther, much corrected by the Second Vatican Council, yet it is 'the finest expression in non-theological English of what Luther meant by "the Righteousness of God"' (E. G. Rupp).

EDITOR

Hours, The

'The Hours' or 'The Offices' are non-sacramental services celebrated at intervals during the day and night. They vary in number from the two hours of the Anglican book of Common Prayer (Matins and Evensong) to seven hours with the Night Office of the Roman Breviary. The history of the formation of the Hours is admirably treated in various places (see bibliography); only the spirituality implied is considered here.

The fundamental idea behind the formal meeting together of Christians for prayer is to hear together the Word of God in the scriptures and especially in the psalms and so to become more deeply established in the prayer of Christ to the Father for the salvation of the world. The use of the Psalter is the central element in the celebration of the Hours. The second element involved is the reading of other parts of the scriptures; and a third element is the offering of specific audible prayer to sum up the prayer of the Hour in either a collect or a litany. A result of this form of prayer at specific intervals of the day is the idea of the sanctification of time; by prayer at regular intervals this specific attention to the Word of God by the gathered people of God arises from and flows into the rest of time, giving it the dimensions of the kingdom.

The meeting of Christians for this form of prayer in the morning and evening is widely attested in the early church. In the monastic world of the fourth century, where prayer was the sole undertaking, underlying all other work, the continuous reading of the psalms and the rest of the scriptures became the central element in the monk's life. This gave formal meetings for prayer the character of private prayer practised in common as moments arising from a continual life of prayer. The monks therefore did not consider the use of Hours of Prayer as an exceptional activity but as part of the continual prayer of the monk, as a privilege belonging rather to the clergy than the monks, and indeed as a relaxation from the asceticism of prayer in the cell: 'The blessed Epiphanius, Bishop of Cyprus, was told this by the abbot of a monastery which he visited in Palestine: "By your prayers we do not neglect our appointed round of psalmody, but we are very careful to recite Terce, Sext and None." Then Epiphanius corrected them with the following comment: "It is clear that you do not trouble about the other

hours of the day, if you cease from prayer. The true monk should have prayer and psalmody continuously in his heart"' (*Sayings of the Desert Fathers, Epiphanius* 3).

The monastic approach to the Hours affected the use of the Hours throughout the Church, partly by making the continuous reading of the scriptures (as distinct from selecting appropriate portions) the norm; and also by making the monastic pattern of prayer at all hours of day and night the ideal for all Christians and especially the clergy. Throughout the Middle Ages, the celebration of the principal hours of the day, by morning and evening prayer (Lauds and Vespers), was supplemented by the observance of prayer at the third, sixth and ninth hours (Terce, Sext and None); and to these were added a short hour of prayer at the first hour of the day (Prime) and the bed-time prayer of the monks (Compline), as well as the Midnight Office (Vigils or Matins or Nocturnes). The desire of the laity to participate in these Hours of prayer led to the making of beautifully illustrated Books of Hours for their use. And popular piety associated each of the Hours with events in the Bible – for instance, Terce with the coming of the Holy Spirit at Pentecost; Sext with the crucifixion; None with the death and burial of Christ – traces of which can still be seen in certain parts of those Hours. The public performance of the Hours in parish churches, cathedrals and monasteries was elaborated with music and ceremonial, and the early tradition of the use of plain-chant for the Hours was overtaken by the use of polyphony. Such a high value was placed upon the celebration of the Hours by the faithful that at certain times and in some places (e.g. Cluny in the eleventh century) Hours were celebrated more or less continuously through the day, on a shift system, so that this form of monastic prayer could be seen by all to be offered publicly. Essentially a community act, this form of prayer became in the late Middle Ages a private devotion, and the Hours were arranged in single volumes (Breviaries) so that a monk or priest travelling alone could still recite the Hours. Recent reforms of the Breviary have tended to less elaboration both of content and structure for the Hours, though they still remain the official prayer of the church, in their various forms.

P. Bradshaw, *Daily Prayer in the Early Church*, 1981; J. D. Crichton, *Christian Celebration: The Prayer of the Church*, 1976; G. Dix, *The Shape of the Liturgy*, 1945; P. Salmon, *The Breviary through the Centuries*, 1962.

BENEDICTA WARD, SLG

Howe, John

John Howe (1630–1705) was a Presbyterian pastor and writer, widely recognized for his tolerance in time of ecclesiastical strife. In *Living Temple*, his largest work, he emphasized the importance of a distinctive Christian spirituality during a period when rationalistic scepticism was enlisting the service of able writers. Howe noted the possible connection between the popularity of atheistic ideas and the rancour of contemporary religious disagreement. He observed that no other century 'was ever more fruitful of religions, and barren of religion or true piety'. He maintained that the most effective argument for God's existence and his 'conversableness' with sinful man is that of the transformed life, 'a visible representation of an indwelling Deity, in effects and actions of life worthy of such a presence' making 'his enshrined glory transparent to the view and conviction of the irreligious and profane'. Howe's preaching expounds the view that sanctification, God's 'most friendly work', is cultivated by 'delighting in him' as 'a Lord to be obeyed, and a Portion to be enjoyed'. Meditation on the 'undiscovered wonders' of scripture, the beauty of God's truths, their 'lively sparkling lustre', and their purpose, 'what they drive at or lead to', is used not only to 'draw the soul into union with God' but to effect 'the transforming impression of his image'. The context of these sermons must not be forgotten; a faithful minister in time of persecution, he emphasized the importance of the life to come as an incentive to holiness. *The Blessedness of the Righteous* expounds the glories of heaven and our preparation for it. The nature of future blessedness is the beatific vision in 'assimilation to the character of God' and its consequent unparalleled satisfaction. Without heaven 'man is filled with desires which cannot be gratified, endowed with faculties which cannot be adequately employed, and capable of forming conceptions of a happiness which he is

destined never to realise' (*The Vanity of Man as Mortal*, cf. H. Rogers' biography of Howe, p. 406). The early 1680s were marked by occasionally fierce persecution of dissenters. Howe's pastoral concern is reflected in *Of Thoughtfulness for the Morrow* and its appendix *Concerning the Immoderate Desire of Foreknowing Things To Come*. In adversity believers will pray ('we have easy access daily'), not worry in advance about what might happen (Howe quotes an Arabian proverb, 'An affliction is but one to him that suffers it, but to him that with fear expects it, double') and think more of eternity: 'We are not the surer of heaven, if the sun shine out tomorrow; nor the less sure, if it shine not.' Howe's sermons on *Self-Dedication* and *Yield Yourselves to God* expound some of the central elements in his holiness teaching. Christians must recognize their evangelistic responsibility; all too often, in sharing the Christian message with unbelievers, 'Our words drop and die between us and them' (*The Redeemer's Tears Wept Over Lost Souls*). His ecumenical concern is reflected in *Concerning Union Among Protestants* in which he discusses 'what may most hopefully be attempted to allay animosities among protestants, that our divisions may not be our ruin'.

John Howe, *Works*, with memoir of his life by Edmund Calamy, 1832; R. F. Horton, *John Howe*, 1905; H. Rogers, *The Life and Character of John Howe*, 1863.

RAYMOND BROWN

Hügel, Friedrich von

Baron Friedrich von Hügel (1852–1925) was the son of an Austrian diplomat who was a Baron of the Holy Roman Empire, and a Scottish mother. His early life was spent in Tuscany and Belgium, till in 1867 the family settled in England. Educated privately by a variety of tutors he became one of the most learned men of his time. His culture was cosmopolitan and his religious affinities were ecumenical. His erudition embraced philosophy, history, theology, biblical criticism and geology. He combined this massive scholarship with a deep spiritual life and devotion to the Roman Catholic Church. For spiritual direction he was much indebted to Abbé Henri Huvelin*. Securely rooted in tradition he was also determined to reckon with new developments in the different sciences. 'When I cease to take in new ideas,' he said, 'I hope they will order in the undertaker.' The tensions involved in this openness he regarded as wholesome and salutary; they certainly were so in his case, and he was thus able to help many perplexed believers and searchers.

He played a leading part in the modernist movement of 1890 to 1910, though after its condemnation by the papacy he dissociated himself from what he considered to be the immanentism of many of his friends and collaborators. He never tired of bearing his witness to the transcendence of God. Religion, he said, is adoration, and religion without the adoration of God is like a triangle with one side left out. In his own church he was regarded with suspicion because of his association with modernism, and his influence there was restricted until the Second Vatican Council which in effect realized much for which he had hoped and worked.

His principal published work was *The Mystical Element of Religion* (1908) which is a magisterial exploration of religious experience with reference to St Catherine of Genoa *. Von Hügel distinguished between the mystical–emotional, the historical–institutional, and the intellectual–scientific elements in religion and maintained that they needed one another both as complements and as correctives. In particular he insisted on the importance of life within an organized church, while at the same time he confessed that the church was his hair-shirt! His other major works were *Eternal Life* (1912), *Essays and Addresses on the Philosophy of Religion* (1921 and 1926); and *The Reality of God and Religion and Agnosticism* (1931). The best introduction to his teaching about the spiritual life is his *Selected Letters* with a memoir by Bernard Holland (1927) and, above all, his *Letters to a Niece* (1928). His style of writing was unique and unforgettable: laboured and involved but also homely and lightened with flashes of colloquialism and telling illustration. He was handicapped by deafness during most of life and also by recurring ill-health, but this did not prevent him from meeting and corresponding at length with many scholars and seekers both in Britain and abroad.

M. de la Bedoyère, *The Life of Baron von Hügel*, 1951; P. F. Chambers, *Baron von Hügel, Man of God*, 1946; D. V. Steere (ed), *Spiritual Counsels and Letters of Baron Friedrich von Hügel*, 1961; Joseph Whelan, *The Spirituality of Friedrich von Hügel*, 1974.

A. R. VIDLER

Humanism

A word employed in various senses; quite often indeed with as near as makes little matter no sense at all. Its most useful and definite employment was perhaps its first job, as the trademark of a philosophical and literary movement originating in Italy in the second half of the fourteenth century. These Renaissance Humanists wanted to revive, and did in fact succeed in reviving, the study of the Graeco-Roman classics: to know Greek (as well as Latin) was a sufficient qualification for membership in this new class. The revival was intended to provide the basis for an education in *humanitas*, in humane letters; the classical 'Greats' school in the University of Oxford is still that of *Literae Humaniores* (Humaner Letters).

Under the guidance of their chosen ancient models these Renaissance Humanists were concerned: to promote toleration, especially in matters of religion; to bring out what all great religions, and indeed all reasonable people, were supposed to have in common; and to emphasize human welfare and human satisfaction, in this life, as opposed to any ascetic, purely theological, or other-worldly goods. Thus Desiderius Erasmus (1466–1536) campaigned for reform within an undivided Catholic Church, rather than Reformation and consequent religious wars. Again, the *Utopia* of St Thomas More (1478–1535) shows us a society based on the natural reason believed to be shared by all, without benefit of Revelation. And Lorenzo Valla (1407–1457), besides a masterpiece dialogue *On Freewill*, published a *de Voluptate*, which was in substance a neo-Epicurean treatise on pleasure.

Although such men were not themselves much interested in the advancement of natural science the revival of classical and especially Greek learning was one of the main reasons why the explosive development of modern science would occur in Western Europe rather than in China. For some of those who began again to study Plato heard in him echoes of the shadowy giant Pythagoras, and caught the seminal suggestion that – as Galileo was to put it –

'The Book of Nature is written in the language of mathematics.'

Those today who call themselves humanists, or scientific humanists, who subscribe to such journals as *The Humanist* (Buffalo) or *New Humanist* (London), and who identify with the American or the British Humanist Associations, are all or almost all avowedly atheist or at least agnostic; whereas the Renaissance Humanists were with equal unanimity theists, if not perhaps always fully Catholic Christians. Our contemporary humanists distinguish their approach to questions of fact as through and through naturalistic and scientific, while insisting that in matters of value we should give weight only to considerations of human welfare (and sometimes also of the welfare of other sentient creatures of flesh and blood). A favourite illustration is that of contraception; where this kind of humanist accuses traditionalist Roman Catholics of basing their repudiation of all (artificial) contraception upon the alleged wishes of their supposed God, rather than upon anything this worldly and genuinely real.

These are the two most clear, straightforward and legitimate uses of the term. But it has been and is claimed as a commendatory label for many other systems and collections of ideas. Thus F. C. S. Schiller before World War I claimed it for Pragmatism, adopting a slogan from Protagoras: 'Man is the measure of all things.' In the 1930s Jacques Maritain made the same claim for a Personalism insisting on our capacity to enter into relations with a transcendent reality. Immediately after World War II Jean-Paul Sartre entered a similar bid on behalf of his own atheist existentialism, in *L'Existentialisme est une humanisme* (1946). Most recently, and surely most preposterously, Sartre and many others have repeated it in favour of a system of ideas and institutions displaying in practice its total collectivist contempt for individual human beings. The intellectual grounds for the pretension are found in Karl Marx *The Economic and Philosophic Manuscripts of 1844*; where it is argued, at the highest possible level of abstraction, that Man (in the abstract) is alienated from his (or its) essence by private property in the means of production. It neither was nor is proposed, as good faith would require, to construct an alienation index, and to apply this to the workers first in private and then in state

owned mass-production plants, in order to determine how far this esoteric and supposedly dehumanizing disorder is in fact alleviated by socialization.

A. J. Ayer, *The Humanist Outlook*, 1968.

ANTONY FLEW

Humanity, Sacred
see **Sacred Humanity**

Humility

Humility as a Christian virtue is grounded in an understanding of the nature of God. The personal humility of Christ in facing rejection and death reflected his own teaching that the person who humbles himself will be exalted (Matt. 23.11f.) and is the basis for Christian meditation on humility as an attribute of God expressed in human form (being of the earth, Latin *humus*). Paul hinted at this idea in the imagery of the wealth and poverty of Christ (II Cor. 8.9) and explored it in his reflection that although Jesus was 'in the form of God' he 'emptied himself' in humility as a result of which he was exalted (Phil. 2.1–11). The great paradox of the incarnation, God in human form, is that the man in whom God uniquely dwells is the one who expresses his total dependence upon God (cf. Mark 14.36). A corollary of this is that the humility of God in human form is expressive of the humility of God in himself. It can be said that in allowing man and woman freedom in faith, to respond or not as they choose, he is treating them seriously as human beings and with the love and respect that is the mark of humility.

In Christian spirituality the search to fulfil the human vocation to be 'in the image of God' involves also a search to share Christ's humility of living in dependence upon God. The chief characteristic of Christian humility is this acknowledgment of total, absolute and utter dependence upon God as creator and redeemer, the beginning and the end of all life. It is a mature rather than immature dependence in that human beings remain free agents in acknowledging and expressing faith in God. This is sometimes described in terms of becoming God-centred rather than self-centred or other person-centred (e.g. Pss. 131; 146.1–3). It is at the heart of prayer. It is also seen by the church to be one of the chief virtues of Mary, the mother of Jesus, and the words of the Magnificat express the essence of biblical teaching on humility (Luke 1.46–55). For many Christians Mary is a sign both of personal humility before God – 'I am the Lord's servant; as you have spoken, so be it' (Luke 1.38) – and of the church's essential humility in being open to accept Christ within it.

Humility towards God as an attitude of mature dependence has at least two consequences both for human strengths and human weaknesses. The first is that all human strengths and achievements are seen to have their origin in the grace of God. This is succinctly expressed by Paul in reflecting upon his labours – 'not I indeed, but the grace of God' (I Cor. 15.10). The second is the acknowledgment in the face of human weaknesses that a lasting peace of mind stems from the strength God gives and from his forgiveness of follies and failures.

While humility is essentially an attitude towards God, it does also involve an attitude towards other people. It involves, for instance, an avoidance of ostentation (cf. Matt. 6.5f.; Luke 14.7–11), care in the claiming of high status for oneself (Luke 22.24–27) and above all being the willing servant of the needs of others (John 13.3–17). In no sense, however, does it necessitate personal feelings of inferiority (a so-called 'inferiority complex') and any measure of feeling 'lowlier than thou' may well be a form of inverted pride.

Humility is not so much an attitude towards oneself as an attitude towards God, a sense of mature dependence coupled with a knowledge of one's unique status before him as a recipient of his love. Derived from this is an attitude towards other people who being in the image of God are worthy of respect.

_____

A significant modern book that interprets the humility of God as the paradox of grace is D. M. Baillie, *God Was In Christ*, [2]1956. A review of the incarnation is J. A. T. Robinson, *The Human Face of God*, 1973. See also Lord Longford, *Humility*, 1969; John Macquarrie, *The Humility of God*, 1978. Personal expressions of humility in the tradition of prayer include St Benedict, *Rule for Monasteries*, ch. 7; Jean-Pierre de Caussade, *Self-Abandonment to Divine Providence*; Thomas à Kempis, *The Imitation of Christ*; William Law, *A Serious Call*.

REX CHAPMAN

Humour

The word has a long and complex history. It has been given many definitions which all go to show that the content of the word varies according to cultures and times. On the whole, however, humour has always retained something of its etymological meaning, connected with what is 'humid': it evokes a certain freshness of mind, a combination of the sense of wonder and discretion so that it is not always perceived identically by all. Humour is not hilarity: it supposes a wink of complicity and causes a smile rather than laughter.

It is a fact that this form of controlled yet natural playfulness, quite distinct from irony and satire, is to be found in the Christian spiritual tradition. Spiritual literature in all periods of history proves that authors and consequently their readers were often gifted with humour. Many an example could be quoted from iconography* and a variety of literary genres found in the writings of the Church Fathers, the Desert Fathers, the authors of the high and the low Middle Ages and more modern writers up to our own day. Humour is found also in works of art, images and illustrations of texts. Often enough the saints are the privileged witnesses to humour. We notice this in their writings or in texts written about them. However, like every other charism, humour is given to each one according to his capacity and is thus unequally shared out. The expressions of humour are as varied and diversified as the gifted persons.

The experience of humour has its roots in man's participation in divine transcendence and immanence: God is both present to the world and yet by reason of his quite-otherness he is distant. The same can be said of Christ, God made man, the Word who, without leaving the bosom of the Father, walked among us preaching and teaching, often with subtle oriental humour. All true Christians, his disciples, share in this divine distance – not to be confused with estrangement – from all that is not God or does not lead to him, and the divine attentive presence to every one of his creatures whom he loves and desires to draw to himself.

Fundamentally, then, humour stems from detachment. This is neither psychological indifference nor a sense of nothingness and absurdity but rather an experience of the relativity of all created things and the ability to discern what matters and what does not. In the first place this means stepping back from oneself, being serious, doing things seriously but never taking oneself seriously, never considering self as being of utmost and absolute importance. In other words, humour is a form of humility and one of its sweetest fruits. Humility helps us to see ourselves as sinners, justified and pardoned sinners, thus sinners living in joy and trusting in God: joyful in all circumstances, in spite of everything, smiling at the day to come even and especially amidst trial and difficulty: humour at its finest peeps out and winks just when everything seems to be going wrong and the situation is serious. Humour fosters the desire for God, an optimism founded on hope. It produces patience, perseverance and endurance when there is every reason to despair. Prayer is the best expression of humour: praise and contented consent to God's will in all circumstances; the confident appeal for help; thanksgiving, joy and peace. Such detachment blossoms in a constant availability and flowers in a gracious facility for sharing the divinely bestowed gifts in a humble disposition of service: humour begets charity.

Such joyful and committed detachment reveals itself in the different fields of spiritual activity: the life of prayer and the practice of the virtues in keeping with one's personal vocation. Humour is not natural. It is a grace which must be merited and once bestowed sometimes requires that we fight to keep it. Hence there is an ascesis of humour. There is also a diacony of humour: it is the duty of every Christian to propagate Christian joy by personal witness and it should be taught by every pastor and teacher. It is already the object of studies in comparative spirituality. Zen, Jewish and Sufi masters, for example, represent similar attitudes in their own religious traditions. Could not humour be a point of encounter?

Jesus, the entire Christian tradition and all inspired writers show that humour is an evergreen necessity. But it is particularly relevant in a time like ours characterized as it is by two major facts: a change of culture within the Christian tradition and the universal prevalence of fear. Stepping back from our own narrow outlook enables us to have a broader, world-wide and cosmic view

of things, thus setting our own little ideas in the total picture and seeing history from God's point of view, so to speak. At an age when things are not going too well – neither better nor worse than in preceding periods of history – but which is also an age of heightened sensitivity due mainly to the effect of modern means of communication which bring us into immediate touch with agonies and sufferings all over the world; at a time too of rapid evolution not always in keeping with every person's taste, it is imperious that the gospel of good humour be preached as a counter-balance to so much anxiety and discontent.

Andre Derville, 'Humour', *DS*, VII, i, cols 1188–91; Conrad Hyers (ed), *Holy Laughter*, 1969, pp. 150–207; Walter J. Ong, SJ, *The Barbarian Within*, 1962, pp. 88–130; J. Roi, *L'humour des saints*, 1980.

JEAN LECLERQ, OSB

Huvelin, Henri

Henri Huvelin (1838–1910), a saintly priest who might have acquired fame as a professor of theology or as an ecclesiastical historian, spent nearly the whole of his ministry in a subordinate position on the staff of a parish in Paris. Even as a student he was described as 'a walking dictionary'. Though unprepossessing in appearance, constantly suffering from physical infirmities, prone to near suicidal depression and always seeking obscurity, he became known as an exceptionally gifted spiritual director and confessor. He spent long hours in his confessional which was thronged by simple folk, but he was also consulted by, and he decisively influenced, some well-known men of his time, notably Emile Littré, Hyacinthe Loyson, Friedrich von Hügel*, Henri Bremond*, Maurice Blondel and Charles de Foucauld*. He had a rare capacity for understanding the needs of very different types of person and for meeting them where they were, even when they were repelled by the official church. Intellectual integrity and loyalty to conscience were signs in his view that the Spirit of God was at work in those who came to him: the task of a priest was to assist the work of God in souls. Much of his teaching was preserved in notes that were made by those who heard his addresses and lectures. His teaching about the spiritual life was quite unconventional and strangely refreshing; see e.g. the collection of his sayings that is reproduced in von Hügel's *Selected Letters*, pp. 58–63. A. Loisy who regarded Huvelin as both a saint and a sage prophesied, perhaps correctly, that he would never be canonized at Rome.

M. T. Louis-Lefebvre, *Abbé Huvelin, Apostle of Paris*, 1968; Lucienne Portier, *Un précurseur: l'Abbé Huvelin*, 1979.

A. R. VIDLER

Hymns

Text books of hymnology trace the early Christian use of hymn forms from the Psalms, the NT 'hymns' (Magnificat, Benedictus, Nunc Dimittis, Phil. 2.6–11, etc.) and the later hymnic styles like the Gloria, Te Deum and the 'Phos Hilarion'. In the christological controversies of the fourth century hymns were sung in popular style like rival football 'chants' of today. In the Middle Ages, East and West produced a great quantity of objective 'office' style hymns and 'sequences' for use at Mass as well as the more subjective style of the school of St Bernard of Clairvaux, St Francis and the heretical groups. It was at the period of the Reformation that hymns became truly part of the sung creed of the people, typified by the 'Ein feste Burg' of Martin Luther – the Marseillaise of the Reformation as Heine called it – and the metrical psalms of Geneva which got into the bloodstream of every Reformed Communion, of which the 'Old Hundredth' (word and tune marriage is important) is a classic example. In the church of England 'Sternhold and Hopkins' (1562) and 'Tate and Brady' (1696) – the 'old' and 'new' versions of the Psalms – supplemented the Book of Common Prayer for long before that major date in the history of English spirituality, the publication of *Hymns Ancient and Modern* in 1861.

The Reformation tradition produced bursts of hymnody in later Lutheranism (e.g. Rinkart, Gerhardt), Pietism and Moravianism, many examples of which came into Britain through the use of hymns in the Wesleyan revival (*see* **Wesley, Charles; Wesley, John**). These hymns stress that personal devotion to Jesus, especially the Jesus of Calvary, which forms a link between Bernard of Clairvaux * and the contemporary cult of the Sacred Heart * of Jesus. Both in Catholicism and Protestantism there is this deep popular stream of 'passion-piety'. In Britain there was a rich poetic spirituality typified by George Herbert * (1593–1633) – 'The God of love', 'Let all the world', 'King of glory', 'Teach me my God and king'; Richard Baxter * (1615–1691) – 'He wants not friends', 'Lord it belongs not to my care', 'Ye holy angels bright'; John Mason (1645–1694) – 'How shall I sing that majesty?'; and Samuel Crossman (1624–1683) – 'My song is love unknown', which were considered suitable for congregational use much later through the Wesleys and others.

Hymnody proper in England began with Isaac Watts * (1674–1748) who first used Psalms, then 'made David Christian' (e.g. 'Jesus shall reign' is Psalm 72; 'I'll praise my maker' is Psalm 148) and ended with his own hymn forms which included masterpieces like 'When I survey the wondrous Cross'. Philip Doddridge * (1702–1751) followed up this dissenting initiative with hymns written specifically for his own congregation in Northampton. Clearly it is in the dissenting tradition (including Methodism) that hymns have exercised a crucial role in spirituality. B. L. Manning spoke of hymns as the 'dissenting use'. They provide in Free Church worship the credal framework and articulate the height and depth of devotion in a way quite different from their often somewhat haphazard use in Anglican liturgy, where they are popular but not essential or even necessary. It is important to note here their use in private devotion. Certainly for Methodists they were the link between 'the secret place' and corporate worship.

The Oxford Movement * produced another rich crop of hymnody of varied styles, not least among them being the translations of John Mason Neale * (1818–1866) and the two 'hymns' of John Henry Newman * (1801–1890), 'Lead kindly light' and 'Praise to the holiest', neither of which were intended as hymns and which were never heard sung as such by Newman. In the American tradition in a quite different mode were the haunting songs of aspiration and liberation which the slaves of the cotton plantations sang and which have come to be called 'spirituals': 'Were you there when they crucified my Lord?' James Cone has recently shown the link between negro spirituals, black spirituality, black music and the theology of liberation. A 'white', more pietistic version of the spirituals is to be found in the type of hymn popularly called 'Sankeys' – it is significant that I. D. Sankey (1840–1908) was a musician and tune writer, not a hymn writer – which had a profound effect on popular Protestantism in the late Victorian age. Here was a spirituality of comfort, security and hope. It overworked individualistic sentiment and was feebler than the 'irresponsible ecstacies' of the eighteenth century. Yet if popular religion is to be taken seriously, this element in Christian hymnody is important.

Hymns became part of national and civic piety in Britain at the time of the strength of the British imperial tradition. In more recent years the movements of social protest have thrown up hymns and songs in profusion and the Charismatic Movement* in all the main stream churches (not least in the Church of Rome which has witnessed a popular renaissance of hymn singing) has provided short, effective scriptural 'choruses' which are now much used in formal worship as well as in small groups, where they play the role once played by Charles Wesley.

Each great epoch of hymnody carries with it equally characteristic music; the chorale, the psalm tunes of Geneva associated with Louis Bourgeois (1510–1561), the lilting floridity of the early Methodist tune, the chaste richness of Croft and Ravenscroft, the haunting melodies of Wales, the sturdiness of H. J. Gauntlett and John B. Dykes, the poignant refrains of the 'spirituals', the homespun melodies of Sankey, the gusto of the 'charismatic' chorus all provide essential musical undergirding to what is popular poetry and popular religious participation. Here indeed is the folk song of the church. While much of it may seem mawkish and sentimental to the purist, it is in its generation authentic popular religious culture and of crucial importance in the history of Christian spirituality.

J. Cone, *The Spirituals and the Blues*, 1972; N. P. Goldhawk, *On Hymns and Hymn Books*, 1979; C. P. M. Jones, G. Wainwright, E. J. Yarnold (eds), *The Study of Liturgy*, 1978, esp. pp. 454–64; C. Northcott, *Hymns in Christian Worship*, 1964; E. Routley, *A Panorama of Christian Hymnody*, 1979; G. Wainwright, *Doxology*, 1980, pp. 198–217.

J. MUNSEY TURNER

Iconography

The rise of Christian art may be seen as a natural consequence of the central Christian facts. The revelation of God in the visible form of the life and life-style of Jesus of Nazareth (including there the peculiar circumstances of his death and the mysterious post-lude of the Resurrection appearances) opened the way for the expression of the inner meaning of those facts through visual art. Despite certain reservations among the early Fathers, the instinct of the faithful in the first Christian centuries was that the OT prohibitions on images of God had been superseded by the incarnation. In any case, a more liberal Judaism, encouraged by late antique sensibility to see the human form and face as loci of religious experience, had produced a synagogue art whose aim was to encapsulate biblical revelation in narrative frescoes and which could serve as a model for the church. The origins of Christian iconography are popular and anonymous, although not for that reason outside the due influence of church authorities and individual teachers ('theologians'). The art of the church rose out of the prayer-life and sacramental experience of the common man, whose concerns largely dictated the themes early iconography would depict.

More sophisticated handling of motifs to produce greater interest, intensity and comprehensiveness in works of art (e.g. by the manipulation of 'types' and 'anti-types' for richer biblical allusiveness) soon developed, however, and over the course of the Christian centuries produced a densely symbolic art for whose decipherment considerable scriptural and hagiological expertise may be necessary. This is characteristic of any great artistic tradition, for such a tradition is essentially cumulative or, at the least, experimental within known conventions built up over time. Although individual Christian artists have made creative deviations of a personal kind from the tradition, these can be recognized as genuinely Christian and not merely religious only if they bear a relation of some fairly strong kind to the sources of Christian spirituality in the Bible as read in the church's tradition.

The stylistic specificities of Christian art in different periods (palaeo-Christian, Byzantine, Romanesque, Gothic, Renaissance, Baroque, Romantic, Modern) are partly determined by the artistic vocabulary available at the time in secular art. Equally important, however, is their expression of different dominant notes in the spirituality of their own epoch (e.g. the victorious Christ of the Romanesque tympana, the humiliated Christ of Gothic statuary). Each age makes its own contribution to the feeling mind's many-faceted grasp of the single Christian mystery. In this, images are not merely effects: they may also be seen as causes, shaping as well as reflecting the spirituality of those who contemplate them.

From time to time, an attempt is made to privilege one iconographic tradition (e.g. that of the Byzantine-Slav icon*) as alone of spiritual value, just as a given school of spirituality may make exclusive-sounding claims for its own wisdom. These attempts are contradicted by the inspirational power of images of many kinds in the life of prayer. In this respect, the history of Christian iconography is the history of the devotional mind of the Christian community as a whole.

'Art et spiritualité', *DS*, I, cols 899–934; 'Images', *DS*, VII, cols 1503–19; 'Images et imagerie de piété', *DS*, VII, cols 1519–35; A. Grabar, *Christian Iconography: a study of its origins*, 1969.

                                        AIDAN NICHOLS

Icons

Holy pictures of Christ, Mary and the saints, which are inseparable from Eastern Orthodox spirituality*, and are lavish adornments of churches and homes. The iconastasis or 'picture-stand' is a screen separating the altar (heaven) from the nave (earth) which seems to have developed in the Greek and Russian churches in the late fourteenth and early-fifteenth centuries. It is covered with icons.

They are pictures in a unique style which seeks to convey the heavenly as much as the earthly, and by Western standards they may appear somewhat stilted; they lack 'human interest'. They do not so much have numinous potency or *mana* as a sacramental efficacy. They represent the incarnation and are symbols of the truth that the whole creation is to be redeemed. They teach the faith, are the 'Bibles of the poor' (and of others too), and supreme 'visual-aids'. They are treated with greatest reverence and accorded the

utmost veneration. The faithful kneel before them, and burn candles, and they are censed in the liturgy and offices. But they are not worshipped; the devotion shown to them is directed not to wood, stone or paint, but to the one whom they represent. They have been described as 'dynamic manifestations of man's spiritual power to redeem creation through beauty and art ... part of the transfigured cosmos' (Nicholas Zernov). Their painting is as much an act of devotion as their contemplation.

V. Lasareff, *Russian Icons*, 1962; T. Ware, *The Orthodox Church*, 1963; N. Zernov, *The Russians and their Church*, 1945.

                                            EDITOR

Ignatius of Antioch, St

The seven surviving and probably authentic letters of Ignatius, Bishop of Antioch, were composed on his journey under guard to martyrdom in Rome (*c.* AD 107–110); they are addressed to some of the churches in Asia Minor which had offered him welcome or support, to Polycarp, bishop of Smyrna, and to the Roman church, and constitute a unique witness to the personal spirituality of a Christian of the second or third generation very little influenced by philosophical models of religious devotion. Naturally enough, martyrdom is the theme uppermost in his mind in much of his writing: he begs the Roman church not to interfere or intercede on his behalf, so that he may become 'an imitator of the passion of my God' (*Romans* VI.3; he refers elsewhere more than once to Jesus as *theos*). The enduring of martyrdom is the final conformation to Christ (*Romans* V.1) – and so to the full measure of humanity (*Romans* VI.2). It is the culmination of a discipleship in which the Christlike acceptance of insult and suffering (*Ephesians* X.1) is inseparable from humility, mutual reverence, and active love in the church (*Magnesians* VI, *Trallians* I and II) – and indeed, love and compassionate prayer for all humanity (*Ephesians* X.1). The repeated exhortations to obedience in the church and respect for the bishop must be read in this light: the bishop is the figure who guarantees the harmony of the church by gathering it around him to celebrate the eucharist, and this eucharistic harmony is the assurance and expression of a true harmony with the will of God, or the 'mind' of

God as embodied in Jesus (*Ephesians* III–V, *Smyrnaeans* VIII, *Philadelphians* I).

Martyrdom, self-oblation, is a gift to the church as a whole, uniting with the eucharistic self-giving of God in Christ: the martyr becomes, like Jesus and in Jesus, 'pure bread' (*Romans* IV). Those heretics who do not believe in the reality of Christ's sufferings (presumably gnostics of one sort or another) undermine the entire logic of Christian corporate life: if Christ did not really suffer and die, we might as well say that the martyr does not really suffer (*Smyrnaeans* IV). And if this free, redemptive, self-sharing suffering does not occur in the flesh, in history, there can be no communication through it of the 'immortal love' and stable or 'incorruptible' life by which believers live and hope (*Romans* VII.3; cf. *Ephesians* XX for the famous description of the eucharist as 'medicine of immortality'). So it is not surprising if heretics rupture the community of love and fail to show compassion for the destitute (*Smyrnaeans* VI). Their Christ is unreal, they have no communion with the reality of a God of crucified love, and so their own lives are phantasmal (*Smyrnaeans* II, *Trallians* X).

The Christian, in contrast, lives in the truth. Ignatius commends silence to the believer, because 'it is better to keep silence and to be than it is to speak and not to be' (*Ephesians* XV). The eloquent speech, the system-making, of the gnostic can never compensate for a fundamental illusoriness; but the Christian, even – or especially – the Christian leader, characterized by silence (*Ephesians* VI) allows God's truth and reality to speak in life and act. So it was in Jesus, whose whole life is 'worked in the silence of God' (*Ephesians* XIX): he communicates truth and life by silently witnessing to the love of God which is beyond containment in word or concept. His *life* is word and testimony; so must the Christian's be. Although the terms 'silence' (*sigē*) and 'repose' (*hēsychia*) are popular terms in gnosticism, it is clear that Ignatius has given them a distinctive and powerfully incarnational transformation; perhaps a deliberately polemical move.

The letters were well-known in the early church (Origen refers to *Romans*); and some of Ignatius' imagery is echoed in later Syrian writing (Ephrem, perhaps even the *Odes of Solomon*). But he is in no sense the founder of a 'school'. His importance is in marking out the ground for a eucharistic and incarnational devotion which could provide a bulwark against excessive spiritualization or de-historicizing of the gospel.

Ignatius' *Letters* in *Early Christian Writings* (Penguin Classics), 1968; H. U. von Balthasar, 'The Word and Silence', *Word and Revelation, Essays in Theology 1*, 1964; Rowan Williams, *The Wound of Knowledge*, 1979, ch 1.

ROWAN WILLIAMS

Ignatius Loyola, St

Ignatius Loyola was born, most probably in 1491, in the family castle of Loyola in the Basque province of Guipuzcoa. At baptism he was given the name Inigo de Oñaz y Loyola. Many years later he took the name Ignacio. Originally intended for a career in the church, he received a rudimentary education which was soon abandoned for a career at court and in the military. He underwent a profound change of life after being severely wounded while leading the defence of Pamplona in Navarre (20 May 1521). Long months of painful convalescence followed by almost a year at Montserrat and Manresa changed him into a man whose leader was Christ and whose heroes were Francis and Dominic. At Manresa he began writing the *Spiritual Exercises**. In late August 1523 he landed in the Holy Land in the hope of spending the rest of his life there. When he was refused permission to remain, he returned to Spain via Venice. At age 33 he joined schoolboys on their benches to begin his studies 'so as to be able to help souls'. He tried schools in Barcelona, Alcala and Salamanca, but it was at the University of Paris that he found the course of studies which fitted his needs. He remained there from 1528 to 1535 to complete his studies in philosophy and theology. During the Paris years a number of students gathered around Ignatius to share their lives and aspirations while studying at the university.

In 1535 Ignatius and his six companions went to Italy for the purpose of going on pilgrimage to the Holy Land. In 1537 Ignatius and some of his friends were ordained priests in Venice. War between Venice and the Ottoman Empire prevented their trip to the Holy Land. In November 1538 Ignatius and his companions placed themselves at the service of Paul III for whatever missions he might choose. In summer 1539 they petitioned the pope to permit them to form a new religious order. On 27 September 1540, Paul III issued the bull *Regimini Militantis Ecclesiae* which established the Society of Jesus. In spite of his strenuous objections, Ignatius was unanimously chosen the first superior general of the Jesuits. The last fifteen years of his life were spent in Rome as the head of the new order. These years were occupied with writing thousands of letters, his indefatigible efforts to secure support for his apostolic projects, and the writing of the Constitutions of the Society of Jesus. He dispatched men to missions through Europe and to Asia, Africa, and America. When he died, there were 1,000 members in the Society in various parts of the world. In the midst of his heavy burden of work and plagued by continuing ill health, his experience of mystical prayer grew and became a constant in his life. On 31 July 1556, he died quietly and unexpectedly in Rome. He was canonized a saint of the Roman Catholic Church by Gregory XV on 22 May 1622.

See also **Jesus, Society of.**

G. E. Ganss (ed), *The Constitutions of the Society of Jesus*, 1970; J. O'Callaghan (ed), *The Autobiography of St Ignatius Loyola*, 1974; H. Rahner (ed), *St Ignatius Loyola: Letters to Women*, 1960; W. J. Young (ed), *Letters of St Ignatius Loyola*, 1974; *The Spiritual Journal of St Ignatius Loyola*, 1958.

GERARD J. CAMPBELL, SJ

Imagery, Images

At least from the time when drawings were made in underground caves, humans have constructed representations of objects, animate or inanimate, in the external world. The original motivation leading to this exercise cannot be determined. The fact is, however, that innumerable images exist in the world today: painted, sculptured, modelled, photographed. These constitute the efforts of men and women to detach themselves from immediate experience and to hold before their imaginations significant phenomena in the world outside of and beyond themselves.

Edwyn Bevan used the term holy images to denote those expressing some apprehension of religious reality. Whenever there has been a perception of some manifestation

which appears to concern an individual or a community supremely and ultimately, the desire has arisen to hold it within the memory by expressing it in some outward form. This has been accomplished by hallowing natural objects (fire, water, rocks, bread and wine), by creating images (paintings, sculptures), and by reproducing sounds (words, music). Cultures have differed in the choice of which of these means shall have the ascendancy.

Hebrew culture, particularly in the prophetic tradition, repudiated images as improper means of representing divine realities and concentrated attention on words. The same has been true of Islam. In India and in Greece visual images played a major part in the life of religion. In the history of Christianity there has been a marked ambivalence: in Russian Orthodoxy images of great beauty have been honoured as links with transcendent realities, whereas in puritan Protestantism images have been denounced and frequently destroyed.

Broadly speaking four attitudes have appeared in Christendom.

1. Uncompromising iconoclasm supported by an appeal to the second commandment of the Decalogue.

2. Encouragement of image-worship, images being regarded as mediators of supernatural grace.

3. Defence of images as a valuable means of instructing the unlearned and stimulating their devotion.

4. Concentration on images of Christ himself as the unique 'image of the invisible God' (Col. 1.15).

These attitudes have influenced answers to the crucial question whether it is legitimate to construct external images of the Christ of the New Testament. Some have urged that it can be the noblest exercise of the human imagination to create an image of the human Christ: others have rejected any attempt to portray one who is essentially divine. The great majority have taken the view that because the Son of God was 'made in the likeness of man' (Phil 2.7) it is permissible to depict him as babe, as youth, as teacher, as crucified.

Whether any image can adequately represent him as resurrected, as ascending, as reigning depends largely on the view taken of the nature of matter and spirit and of their inter-relationship. The necessity of mental images in worship is unquestioned. Some find it helpful to contemplate images in external form: others fear that externalization can lead to fixation upon a single and limited representation. Such variations call for mutual respect.

Edwyn Bevan, *Holy Images,* 1940; A. C. Bridge, *Images of God,* 1960; Austin Farrer, *The Glass of Vision,* 1948; K. E. Kirk, *The Vision of God,* 1931.

F. W. DILLISTONE

Imitation of Christ

The idea of the imitation of Christ has an ambivalent status in the history of Christian spirituality. On the one hand it has been taken to be the classical and normative way of characterizing the Christian spiritual life and the role of Christ in it. On the other hand there are those, chiefly of the Reformed traditions, who have felt that the idea of the imitation of Christ matches ill with the Christian doctrine of grace and conceals a moral endeavour of a Pelagian kind.

Certainly there are difficulties in using the term 'imitation' about Christ, since it raises questions about the way in which he can be regarded as a model and how one can set about such imitation without suggesting some kind of literal mimicry. The imitation of Christ could not, in N T terms, be a matter of reproducing in some way facets of the historical life of Jesus of Nazareth. Paul of Tarsus certainly believed himself to be an imitator of Christ (I Cor. 11.1) and yet he says hardly anything about the historical life of Jesus. The life of Christ for the New Testament believer meant not only the past Jesus of Nazareth but the present Christ (of the eucharistic assembly) and the future Christ to come (of the parousia). There were therefore special features of the Christ-model. 'Christ' was a multiple term that denoted at one and the same time the historical figure of the past, a present reality, and an eschatological consummation. Christ as object of the Christian's imitation meant both the figure formed in the human imagination from meditation on the Gospel narratives and the Christ to be discerned in his followers, in so far as they exhibited the signs of Christ (gentleness, humility, love and obedience are the qualities picked out by St Paul). This is the checklist of the

qualities which indicate the same divine presence as was to be discerned in the historical Jesus of Nazareth. In this way Christians become, as Luther put it, a sort of Christ for one another and the marks of Christ are particularly to be discerned in the poor, the suffering and the underprivileged.

In virtue of the resurrection and the work of the Spirit, who takes of the things of Christ and reveals them in the lives of those who are his (John 16.14), there are therefore both subjective and objective dimensions to the imitation of Christ. There is an element of imitation in the form of concentrating on Christ and the Gospel stories in liturgy and meditation, but there is also the work of the Spirit, whose continuous activity in grace is to conform the lives of those made in the image of God in some likeness to him who is *the* image of God, Christ himself.

This polarity prevents the ideal of the imitation of Christ from degenerating into an antiquarian or romantic attempt to reproduce in some way the historical past. As H. J. Cadbury puts it: 'An imitation of Christ that imitates the first century ideas of history and nature is no more demanded than one that imitates a contemporary Galilean diet and clothing of Jesus.'

It was inevitable that in the history of spirituality these dimensions of the imitation of Christ should be lost sight of and the ideal be interpreted in an increasingly literalist way. This was particularly true of the Middle Ages. Bernard of Clairvaux * developed the practice of devotion to the 'sacred humanity'* of Christ by means of a point by point meditation on scenes from the life of Christ. Francis of Assisi* made a special point of reproducing as closely as possible the shape of the life of the Christ of the Gospels down to such details as the dress he wore and the arrangements which Francis made to be buried like Christ, naked in a tomb.

A significant turning point in the evolution of the ideal of the imitation of Christ was Martin Luther*. Not only did he demonstrate the absurdity of attempts literally to mimic Christ but he suspected that behind such strenuous endeavours after literalism lay concealed a doctrine of works and a denial of grace. Luther preferred a return to the Pauline concept of 'conformity' to Christ in preference to 'imitation' and epitomized his thinking on the difference between the two in his famous aphorism: 'it is not imitation which brings about our sonship of God but our sonship which makes possible imitation'. The imitation of Christ therefore was emphatically for Luther the fruit of grace.

A further significant stage was the advent of historical criticism as applied to the Gospels. Out of this came the conviction that the Gospels were not detailed biographies but portraits of Christ for the use of disciples. This reinforced the view that the NT Gospels themselves are early examples of the way the motif of the imitation of Christ worked in relation to the Christ story. The assumption that Christ takes shape in the lives of his followers may have exercised a conserving influence on the transmission of the NT material about Jesus of Nazareth and gives it a historical reference which distinguishes it from some modern Jesus-cults where the imitation of Christ becomes the pursuit of an anonymous vision of ideal humanity.

The imitation of Christ needs to be kept constantly in its eschatological setting. Growing into Christ ought not therefore to be conceived in terms of a constant looking back to a past model but a living process which attains its goal in the future. Christians can be confident that they are in the process, through the work of the Spirit, of being made like Christ, but full likeness is always, as with the fullness of Christ himself, something which is yet to be (I John 3.2). Christ is, in Gabriel Marcel's phrase, 'a memory of the future'.

The two aspects of imitation, the model and the growth into a similar likeness, are best seen in the sacramental union with Christ in baptism and in eucharist. This makes it clear that the imitation of Christ is not a simple moral endeavour but a conformation, through Christ, by the Spirit. This sacramental imitation of Christ is an expression of its corporate character: Christ taking shape in the community and the community becoming the body of Christ. Through this work of the Spirit Christ becomes both the subject and object of the process of Christian imitation.

Useful for the biblical and historical material are Edward Malatesta SJ (ed), *Jesus in Christian Devotion and Contemplation*, 1974; *Imitating Christ*, 1974. These are translations of articles in the *Dictionnaire de Spiritualité*; D. Bonhoeffer, *Ethics*, 1955, is a very stimulating development of Luther's teaching on conformation to Christ; E. J. Tinsley, *The Imitation of God in Christ*, 1960, studies the biblical background to the idea.

E. J. TINSLEY

Imitation of Christ, The
see **Thomas à Kempis**

Impassibility

There is an evident clash between traditional orthodox affirmations of the impassibility of God and the convictions about his nature which inspire many hymns and prayers and the spiritual experiences of many Christians down the centuries.

According to classical expositions, the doctrine of impassibility affirms God's freedom from 'passion' in the philosophical use of the word, i.e. of 'passivity' in regard to any external agent whatsoever. It is one aspect of the orthodox rejection of Modalism – that is of doctrines which asserted the unity of the Father and the Son in redemption. Many of the Fathers believed that such doctrines failed to affirm the immanent stability of God and therefore ultimately his absolute divinity. Patristic philosophical theology concluded that as pure act and as the source of all being God must be impassible.

In his well-known essay on 'Suffering and God', published in 1926, von Hügel* produced a modern defence of the doctrine. God in and for himself 'is pure joy, an ocean of it' with 'not one drop of sin or suffering or of the possibility of either'. He believed that this pure joy is 'utterly compassionate, utterly sympathetic' but that nevertheless 'religion itself requires the Transcendence of God in a form and a degree which exclude suffering in him'.

Classical statements of the doctrine go on to affirm that though the Son did indeed become passible as a result of taking human nature in the incarnation, this passibility pertained only to his human nature, and that since his resurrection the glorious Christ has become impassible in his humanity as well as in his divinity.

There is a profound contrast between such statements of the doctrine of impassibility and many modern theologians' understandings of the gospel of redemption in the New Testament, the language used by the writers of many classics of Christian spirituality and popular hymns and devotions such as that of the Sacred Heart * of Jesus. Critics of the doctrine who have influenced theological opinion in England in recent times include William Temple*, Jürgen Moltmann, David Jenkins and W. H. Vanstone.

William Temple described the problem in the following terms: 'We have to recognize that Aristotle's "apathetic God" was enthroned in men's minds, and no idol has been so hard to destroy ... There is a highly technical sense in which God, as Christ revealed him, is "without passions", for he is creator and supreme, and is never passive in the sense of having things happen to him without his consent; also he is constant and free from gusts of feeling carrying him this way and that ... But the term "impassible" really meant "incapable of suffering", and in this sense its predication of God is almost wholly false ... God does not leave the world to suffer while he remains at ease apart; all the suffering of the world is his' (*Christus Veritas*, 1924). Jürgen Moltmann wrote a book with the title *The Crucified God* (ET 1974), in which he affirmed that 'the most important progress in Christian theology today is being made in overcoming the "apathy axiom" ... To recognize God in the crucified Christ is to grasp the trinitarian history of God ... God is not dead. Death is in God. God suffers by us. He suffers with us. Suffering is in God.' W. H. Vanstone, reflecting on the experience of human love, concludes that the love of God must be infinitely more costly, more precarious and more exposed than it is commonly represented to be (*Love's Endeavour, Love's Expense,* 1977). And in *The Contradiction of Christianity* (1976) David Jenkins states the belief that God's 'transcendent way of being is not remote, tyrannical or self-preserving ... Above all he is present in the suffering of man's inhumanity to man.'

The congruity of these theological affirmations with many of the prayers, poems and hymns which articulate Christian spirituality is obvious. Mystics and devotional writers of many different centuries and traditions have expressed their conviction that suffering love lies at the very heart of the God who revealed himself in Jesus Christ.

Leonard Hodgson, *For Faith and Freedom,* 1968, II, pp. 78ff.; J. K. Mozley, *The Impassibility of God,* 1926; *Doctrine in the Church of England,* 1938, pp. 55ff.

FRANCIS H. HOUSE

Incarnation

The doctrine of the incarnation has had a profound effect on Christian spirituality. The belief that God has made known his love and reconciled men to himself by coming amongst them in the person of his Son and by making himself vulnerable, not only to the physical and mental conditions of human life, but also to hostility and a cruel death, was bound to shape, if not to determine, a specifically Christian approach to the knowledge of God and a specifically Christian way of life in the world. Christian spirituality and Christian ethics alike are elicited by the humanity of God in the incarnation.

That our knowledge of God is determined by the incarnation was already clear in the Johannine theology of the Word made flesh (John 1.14), so that he who has seen Jesus has seen the Father (14.9), and in the Pauline theology of Christian prayer and knowledge of God 'through Christ' and 'in Christ' (II Cor. 3.4; 5.17). Similarly it was Augustine's discovery that the point of mediation between God and man lay in the humility of God in the humanity of Christ that differentiated Christian spirituality from Platonism (*Confessions* VII.18). The same point represents the heart of the mystical theology of Bernard of Clairvaux*, for whom Christ became incarnate 'precisely in order to open a way of access to the unsearchable depths of God who otherwise would have remained entirely hidden from us' (E. Gilson). Thomas Aquinas*, too, held that because the human mind is weak, it must be led to knowledge and love of God through sensible objects, of which the chief are the humanity and passion of Christ (ST 2a2ae 82.3). The centrality of this theme in Western mysticism may be further illustrated by Julian of Norwich*, for whom Christ in his *body* bears us up to heaven (*Revelations of Divine Love* 55). If the emphasis in the Western tradition has tended to lie with the passion and cross of the incarnate Son, we have to remember, with Karl Rahner, that in the end it is Christ's *glorified* humanity that is 'for all eternity, the permanent openness of our finite being to the living God ...'

Stress on the permanence of the incarnation in the glorified humanity of the risen Christ as the vehicle of our knowledge of God can also be regarded as the hall-mark of Eastern Orthodox spirituality. The notion of man's salvation as 'deification', which may be traced back to Irenaeus*, Athanasius* and the Cappadocian Fathers*, is not to be interpreted as involving the loss of our creaturehood but rather the assimilation of our relation to God to that of Christ to the Father. It is in the sense that 'our Lord Jesus Christ, the Word of God, of his boundless love, became what we are that he might make us what he himself is' (Irenaeus, adv. Haer. 5). Admittedly, for the Orthodox tradition it is the Holy Spirit who unites us to the body of Christ and draws us into the divine life of the Trinity, but Christ's humanity remains the mediating focus of this process of sanctification. (See Deification.)

Christian theology has not always succeeded in sustaining these insights into the centrality of the incarnation for our knowledge of God. In one direction, certain strands of Christian mysticism, culminating perhaps in John of the Cross*, have tried to press beyond the mediation of Christ's humanity to an imageless void in which God is experienced directly. In the other direction, the union of man and God in the incarnation has been generalized in terms that seem to amount to pantheistic identity – an accusation brought against Eckart* and Boehme* as well as against the philosopher, G. W. F. Hegel.

An incarnational religion cannot easily or properly separate spirituality from ethics. The early monastic founder, Basil of Caesarea, wrote that 'humility is the imitation of Christ' (On Renouncing the World 211C). The pattern of Christ's self-emptying (Phil. 2.7), his life of service and the way of the cross have determined the characteristic shape of Christian life and action. But the idea of the imitation of Christ has not always found a properly balanced expression. In Thomas à Kempis'* The Imitation of Christ, there is perhaps too great a stress on internal consolation. A better insight into the consequences of incarnational belief is shown by those who stress the corporate nature of the humanity with which Christ identified himself by incarnation. 'There exists what can rightly be called a Christian

socialism by the very fact that the law of brotherhood is the law of Christ' (C. Gore). Similarly, the religion of the incarnation has been held to entail a high evaluation of the material creation (e.g. by John of Damascus) and a sacramental view of the universe (e.g. by Teilhard de Chardin*).

K. Barth, The Humanity of God, 1961; K. Leech, The Social God, 1981; E. Malatesta, SJ (ed), Jesus in Christian Devotion and Contemplation, 1974; E. L. Mascall, Christ, the Christian and the Church, 1946; P. A. Micklem, Values of the Incarnation, 1932.

BRIAN HEBBLETHWAITE

Indifference

A basic Christian stance concerning the proper use or non-use of creatures for reaching God, our final goal. Strictly speaking, it is a discreet, ordered, intelligent love of creatures with respect to serving God better. Although scripturally grounded, its real meaning has occasionally been perverted in the history of spirituality.

1. Scripture has no one word to designate the attitude of indifference. Abraham's willingness to sacrifice his son (Gen. 22), Job's blessing of the Lord during adversity (Job 1.21), Samuel's alertness to God's call (I Sam. 3.9), and the psalmist's cries of joy or lament, depending on how his current circumstances aid or hinder the praise of God are models of OT indifference. NT paradigms are: Mary's openness to the angelic message (Luke 1.38); Jesus' perfect receptivity to his Father's will (Luke 22.42; John 6.38), and the Father's 'indifference' towards the just and the unjust (Matt. 5.45). Because Christ freed us from the powers of this world (Col. 2.15) and revealed an all loving, providing God, the Christian can be indifferent to life's very necessities (Matt. 7.25f). Jesus' disclosure of the divine 'must' (dei) operative in history, the provisional nature of the schema of this world, and waiting for the day of the Lord (I Cor. 4.9f.) also ground Christian indifference. Its eschatalogical orientation allows Christians to use or not use the things of this world 'as though they had no dealings with it* (I Cor. 7.29f.).

2. The Stoics considered all passions evil. A passionless calm (apatheia)*, even in extreme adversity, became the ideal, even if attained by the total extinguishing of the use of the internal faculties (Plotinus). The

Eastern Fathers of the Church made *apatheia* a classic word in their spirituality, but humanized and Christianized the Stoic sense. The perfect Christian was a gnostic, indifferent to all created things by way of a perfect impassibility (*apatheia*), imperturbability (*ataraxia*), and insensibility (*eithetes*) which participated in God's and the risen Christ's impassibility.

By emphasizing the taming of the passions which results in spiritual rest, inner freedom, and charity, the Eastern Fathers shifted the eschatalogical dimensions of indifference. They saw *apatheia* as a kind of resurrection of the spirit before the body's. It elevated the heart above all creatures, rendered the senses totally obedient to reason, and established the soul in all virtues. Some distinguished between imperfect and perfect, or different levels, of *apatheia*. Cassian*, Evagrius, and Nilus linked it with perfect distractionless contemplation. Most Fathers forcefully rejected *apatheia* towards God's will and other persons. Even in perfect *apatheia*, moreover, human effort and the struggle against temptations continue. Some repudiated all material goods through mortification and designated even some personal goods (e.g., marriage) as indifferent and irrelevant for salvation (*adiaphora*). The Western Fathers of the Church, on the other hand, rarely emphasized *apatheia*, seeing it either as an unrealizable ideal, or as totally undesirable, or as heretical, Pelagian impeccability. Thomas Aquinas* stressed that the passions were not evil in themselves and could lead to virtue.

3. The *Spiritual Exercises** of St Ignatius of Loyola* (d. 1556) centre on freeing a person from 'inordinate attachments' so that he may be able to seek and find God's will for him. The person must, therefore, make himself indifferent, find himself indifferent, remain indifferent, or be indifferent (23, 157, 170, 179) in order to choose the correct means to the 'service and praise of God our Lord and the eternal salvation of my soul' (169). With a basis in Thomas Aquinas, Ignatius emphasizes the state of free will requisite for a correct choice ('Election'). He also limits the scope of indifference to those things 'left to the choice of our free will' and 'not forbidden' (23). Indifference to health, sickness, riches, poverty, a long or short life, is required so that in everything 'we should desire and choose only those things which will best help us to attain the end for which we are created' (23). Every single exercise prays to direct the person 'purely to the service and praise of His Divine Majesty' (46). To engender indifference, the exercitant must frequently pray for what goes counter to his own desires by seeking an Ignatian 'what I want and desire' (16, 48). The will must attain perfect equilibrium like the scales of a balance and be moved only by a love coming 'from above.'

Indifference may be acquired ascetically or mystically. Spiritual consolations may so inflame the person with the love of God that he can love creatures 'only in the Creator of all things' (316). In the *Exercises*, 'What ought I do for Christ?' (53), not being deaf to Christ's call (91), the desire to be placed under Christ's standard of poverty, humiliation, and suffering (98f.), the 'third class' of persons who accept or reject anything only 'as it shall seem better to them for the service and praise of His Divine Majesty' (155), and the four weeks of contemplations on the life, death and resurrection of Christ, underscore the christocentric and service dimensions of Ignatian indifference. It is the will's readiness to recognize and accept what is better in order 'to be with Christ to serve'. This total, absolute non-willing is also an act of liberty sensitive to the least movement of the divine liberty (G. Fessard). Ignatian indifference is always a means, never an end in itself, which must change into non-indifference once God manifests the means for his better service and praise.

4. In the Ignatian tradition the first commentators tended to limit the field of application of indifference to the Jesuit *Constitution*'s ideal of serving in any work, ministry, place, etc. Most distinguished the service role of indifference from both conformity to God's will and pure love of God. G. Fatio and J. J. Surin developed Ignatius' analogy of the will being in perfect equilibrium like the scales of a balance, indifferent to all but God's will and his better service. Others equated indifference with an inner resignation to one's natural and supernatural gifts, states of prayer, merits, etc.

5. The success of Ignatius' *Exercises* and the writings of St Francis de Sales* made the language of indifference in its ascetical and mystical connotations common in the seventeenth century. It often meant refusing

nothing and asking for nothing. Francis de Sales recommended a 'holy indifference', especially during periods of spiritual aridity, a 'forceful resignation' to serve God 'in roses and in thorns'. He spoke of 'indifference and liberty of spirit', 'abnegation or indifference of one's own will', and 'the spirit of holy liberty and indifference'. Less service orientated than Ignatius, he views the 'indifferent heart' as abandoning itself to receive what comes from divine Providence. He makes the important distinction between being *resigned* to God's signified will as known through the commandments, the laws and ordinances of the church, the rules of religious life, the commands of one's superiors, etc., and being *indifferent* to unforeseen events which occur through God's will of good pleasure. De Sales considered the entire Christian life a spirituality of the most holy indifference which loves nothing except in God.

6. Fénelon * systematized and made more explicit 'the state of holy indifference'. The will's perfect equilibrium accepts only God's counterweight. Although indifference is close to passivity, abandonment, conformity, contemplation and ecstatic, divine love, Fénelon expressly stated that we cannot be indifferent to God's will nor to any of the church's laws and precepts. Because of some infelicitous expressions and his often uncritical acceptance of Mme Guyon *, he has often been accused of holding the indifference of quietism *.

7. The quietism of fifth- and sixth-century Messalians, the twelfth-century Hesychasts, the thirteenth-century Béguines, perhaps Eckhart *, Mme Guyon and Miguel de Molinos * universalizes and interiorizes indifference to mean a total abandonment and absolutely disinterested love of God. It may claim a state of continual prayer which destroys the need for all human effort, regret for past sins, self-reflection, striving for virtue, repelling temptations and all inner activity. This state may even be consonant with objectively sinful behaviour. The person is thereby indifferent to his relationship with God, to holiness, to the virtues, to temptation, to sin, to heaven, to hell and to his own eternal salvation.

8. In the overall Christian tradition, indifference has tended towards indifference-*apatheia*, indifference-choice for service, in-

difference-conformity and indifference-pure love. Genuine Christian indifference, however, has nothing to do with a purely passive inwardness (quietism), world-flight, apathy, indifference towards good and evil, weary resignation, fatalism, or aloofness. It is essentially an alacrity, openness and alertness of spirit to a God who is lovingly committed to history. To be with Christ to serve God in the world means an inextricable dynamism between indifference and choice, freedom of spirit and active commitment, listening with the heart and responding lovingly and concretely. This inner openness to ever new ways to service follows God's lead in history's dynamics, no matter what the cost. Indifference is a spiritual disponibility and alacrity to respond to Christ's call to choose the proper means for the better service of him who is the historical incarnation of the Father's will who so loves the world.

G. Bardy, 'Apatheia', *DS*, I, cols 727–46; G. Bottereau and A. Rayez, 'Indifference', *DS*, VII, cols 1688–1708; E. Niermann, 'Indifference', *ET*, pp. 699–700.

HARVEY D. EGAN, SJ

Inge, W. R.

William Ralph Inge (1860–1954), Dean of St Paul's, one of the most effective Christian teachers and controversial ecclesiastics of his time, stressed the mystical element in the Christian religion in books, lectures and sermons, both scholarly and journalistic. His Bampton Lectures in 1899, *Christian Mysticism*, trace the core of religious experience, God glimpsed by men and women in different cultures through many centuries. Using the historical method and introducing English readers to then little known religious figures, such as Julian of Norwich *, he replied to current criticisms of the institutional churches and of the authority of the Bible by basing faith on experience. His great tribute to the contribution of Platonism to Christianity in his Gifford Lectures, *The Philosophy of Plotinus*, (delivered 1917–1918, third edition revised 1929), outlined a philosophy of value in which faith is belief in absolute value, all truths being shadows except the absolute which enables the good life to be its own reward. In his revealing preface, Inge described the 'riddle of the Sphinx' as how to preserve what is true and noble in the idea of evolutionary progress, without secularizing religion or positing a Deity vitally involved in the fortunes of his creatures, so indicating his debt to Platonism as distinct from orthodox dogmas and institutions. He was personally most at home at his desk, in a college chapel or a village church. His devotional books, especially *Personal Religion and the Life of Devotion*, led thoughtful people to a greater appreciation of religious experience, especially in connection with grief, seen as sharing the sufferings of Christ – Inge's finest thoughts were inspired by his daughter, Paula, who died as an infant and his son, Richard, killed in the Second World War. Preaching in St Paul's Cathedral at the age of 82, he said 'I came on a sentence in a French book the other day: "Souffrir passe; avoir souffert ne passe jamais."'

His veneration for the Fourth Gospel, of which he was one of the finest interpreters, led him to describe eternal life as the equivalent of the mystic's austere contemplation. As leader of the Modern Churchman's Union, arguing for a reasoned critique of the churches, he was suspicious of the Roman Catholic Church and of Anglican episcopal authority. He hesitated in accepting the mystical studies of his contemporaries, Baron von Hügel* and Evelyn Underhill*. He continued to lecture, preach and publish till the end of his life, attracting very large audiences to whom he expounded faith as the contemplation of absolute Truth, Beauty and Goodness. Depression and deafness did not dim his faith, though he found the common worship of the 'complacent' institutional churches of little value, and distrusted William Temple*, who urged that fidelity to Christ himself required changes in church and state, so that justice could be done to the 'have-nots' at home and abroad. His prophetic insights into the failure of shallow secular optimism were occasionally marred by narrow class prejudice.

Inge's gift of self-expression and mordant wit ('the gloomy Dean') ensured him a place amongst twentieth-century religious teachers of those on the fringes of the churches. Like St Paul, the subject of one of his most famous essays, for him the gospel was not a religion but religion itself, in its most universal significance. He saw himself as a Christian Platonist, a successor of the Cambridge Christian Platonists*, a third

school within the church, not less legitimate than Catholic or Protestant. In his 'Confessio Fidei', he wrote: 'Faith needs the help of imagination to make its affirmations real . . . The true religion for each of us is the most spiritual view of reality we are able to realize and live by.' At St Paul's, he was naturally drawn into constant comment (his dislike of taxation and trade unions was outspoken, and his advocacy of eugenics enthusiastic). Despite his philosophic idealism, he constantly returned to the incarnation and the person of Jesus in the New Testament. He held, with the Platonists, that at the core of our personality is a spark lit at the altar of God in heaven, an inner light which can illuminate our whole being; the 'evidence of the saints seems to me absolutely trustworthy, and the dimness of my own vision would be disquieting only if I felt I had deserved better. There is a considerable element of agnosticism in true Christianity.' To such themes he constantly returned as he endeavoured to reconcile Christianity, science and philosophy.

Adam Fox, *Dean Inge*, 1960.

ALAN WEBSTER

Intercession
see **Prayer (3) Intercession**

Invocation of the Holy Name
see **Jesus, Prayer to**

Irenaeus of Lyons, St

Although bishop of Lyons in Gaul, Irenaeus (*c*. 130–200) was born and brought up in Asia Minor, where he had known Ignatius' colleague, Polycarp of Smyrna. His major concern was with the defence of Catholic tradition against Gnosticism, and it is to this that his long treatise *Against the Heresies* (otherwise, *The Refutation and Overthrow of What is Falsely Called Knowledge*) is devoted. There is also a shorter work, rediscovered in this century, the *Epideixis* or *Demonstration of the Apostolic Preaching*.

Irenaeus is the first Christian writer to make the explicit point that the purpose of God's sharing of human life is that we might share the divine life (e.g. *Heresies* IV.52); if God is not fully incarnate in Jesus, we are not saved – i.e. our life is not transformed into the immortal and incorruptible life of

God. We are created to share – soul and body – in God's light and glory (*Heresies* II.47, IV.25, 34, V.27, etc.). Made in God's image, we must be transformed into his likeness: our potential for divine life (stability, love and freedom) must be realized, and our very flesh glorified. God deals with human beings by a process of gradual education, 'as if with children' (*Heresies* IV.62): in the Old Covenant, he brings them close to himself by enjoining righteousness, but in the New he actually shares his life with them. In Jesus – a human being, tempted as we are – he refashions human motivation, choice and action from within, 'recapitulating' and resolving the tragic history of Adam (*Heresies* VI and 10ff., *Epideixis* 33, etc.). Human liberty is thus restored to its true mode of operation, and its true Godward direction; we come to be free as God is free, but it is a freedom to yield ourselves to God's will (*Heresies* IV.24). By conforming ourselves to the *ordo* God creates, we come to share his glory (ibid. 64). So our 'deification' is our transformation into the image of the obedient Son, the primary image of God the Father (*Heresies* V.16); the pledge of it is that, in the Spirit, we may cry 'Abba, Father' to God (*Heresies* IV.8). The Pauline echoes are entirely characteristic of Irenaeus, to whom the language of Galatians, II Corinthians and (to some extent) Ephesians comes naturally.

His concern with the salvation of the flesh occasionally gives his writing a rather 'physicalist' flavour, heavy emphasis being laid on the communication of 'incorruption' to the material body by its union in the eucharist with the risen and glorified flesh of Jesus (*Heresies* II.44, 47, IV.31 – an important passage – V.2, 7, 8, *Epideixis* 31, etc.). However, this is qualified by the strong sense of flesh being transformed *by the Spirit*, almost transformed *into* spirit: there is 'nuptial' union between God's Spirit and fleshly human existence, such that the whole person is infused with the glory of God's love (*Heresies* V.9, 10). Glorification of the flesh, in other words, cannot be interpreted in a naively materialistic way – any more than it can in the case of Jesus' transfiguration (Irenaeus is the first Christian writer to use this as a foretype of the heavenly transformation of all believers, a theme very prominent in mediaeval Eastern writing; see *Heresies* V.13).

He has been called the first theologian of the 'negative way', chiefly because of his insistence that we never know God 'in his greatness' but only 'in his love' (*Heresies* IV.34); but the point of this seems rather to be an insistence that God is only known through his Son, and that therefore there can be no speculative or 'neutral' knowledge of God, as the gnostics implied (*Heresies* I.4, III.6, II, IV.11, 34, etc.) independently of the 'community of union' established between God and humanity through the incarnation and the work of the Spirit (*Epideixis* 6, 31). As in the Johannine tradition, living in the truth means participation in the divine life and light – 'seeing God and enjoying his generosity' (*Heresies* IV.34), living 'in newness by the Word, through faith in the Son of God and love' (*Epideixis* 89).

Vladimir Lossky, *The Vision of God*, 1963; G. Wingren, *Man and the Incarnation*, 1959.

ROWAN WILLIAMS

Irish Spirituality

Pagan Ireland lay outside the Roman empire. Yet it received with enthusiasm the new religion from Rome and Christianity there took on a completely Irish visage. A remarkable synthesis took place between the strong native oral tradition and the Christian Latin culture. In modern terms, a virtually complete inculturation was achieved.

More, St Patrick himself marvels in his *Confession* at the numbers of the new Christians who sought eagerly to be monks and virgins of Christ. These foreshadowed the multitudes who in the following century made the Irish church in life and structure overwhelmingly monastic. In a rural society divided into a hundred or more little states (*tuatha*) ruled each by its king the monasteries became centres of religious life and education. In the happy wedding of native and new there was a remarkable tolerance of the pagan inheritance, and that the monks and their successors preserved in writing, although for them the new book-learning was centrally scriptural. That understanding of the pagan no doubt helped them in their evangelization abroad. These monks too it was who left us the beautiful eremitical and nature poetry, so intensely clear and beautiful, even to modern eyes or ears and in translation.

In the guidance of souls, clerical or lay, great use was made of the *Penitentials* in the sacrament of penance. Suitable penances were laid down for the various offences. This system introduced by the Irish monks abroad soon replaced public penance. The oft-repeated principle was *contraria contrariis sanantur*, contraries are healed by their contraries, e.g. gluttony by fasting, etc. *Anamchairdeas* (soul-friendship), the guidance of the individual soul by the *anamchara* (soul-friend) was greatly esteemed and practised. Hence the proverb *colainn gan cheann duine gan anamchara* – a person without a soul-friend is a body without a head. This care for the individual accounted for a tolerance of diversity in monastic discipline, even in the same monastery.

The double fact of the compact civil community and the monastic one must have helped towards a ready appreciation of the church as the Body of Christ, so often mentioned or understood in the old literature. St Columbanus *, whom we may take as representative of Irish thought and spirituality in his time, shows in a famous passage in telling words his appreciation of the unity of peoples in the Body of Christ.

In the ancient state and monastery we have a double link with traditional Irish Christianity. God and Christ are still, as ever, addressed as *Rí* (king). In the ancient *tuath* the king was closely related to many of his subjects and lived in their midst, so *Rí* was no remote term but one of intimacy. In fact, God himself is addressed in an ancient poem as *mu chridecán* (my little heart). Add to that the word *muintir*, from *monasterium*, meaning originally the monastic family or *familia*. The word still lives, meaning people or family, and its derivatives, significantly, mean affection(ate), intimacy, neighbourliness.

This realization and feeling of solidarity shows through in many of the ancient *loricae* (breastplate) and litany-like prayers in verse, where one prays with or seeks the intercession of the various grades of the saints of the Old and the New Testament, of the heavenly and the earthly church. The church was also known by the biblical term, now once more in circulation, *Pobal Dé*, the People of God (still the common way of addressing the Sunday congregation). A desire for completeness of enumeration in prayer is still a feature of traditional prayer.

It is notable too that the modern prayers often oscillate between the singular and the plural.

The ancient spirituality was notably scriptural. The ninth-century Book of Kells and the ancient high crosses still bear witness to the high honour shown to the word of God and its living relevance for the Christian. The holy ones of the OT were honoured even liturgically. There is frequent reference to the three sacred languages, Hebrew, Greek and Latin. The psalms were' the prayer par excellence, the 'three fifties', which became a common form of enumeration. In a ninth-century poem we find fasting from the scriptures numbered among five fastings that are not pleasing to God. The great virtue of hospitality was referred to the famous passage in Matt. 25. The guest was always Christ. It is worth noting, among so many other things in St Patrick's life reproduced in his spiritual children, that the short writings of the saint abound in quotations and echoes from the scripture, notably from St Paul.

Intimacy is an abiding feature of Irish spirituality. In an eighth-century poem the poet asks our Lady to come to him that he may console her heart for the death of her beautiful Son. He ('their true heart'), says the poet, on returning to the people of heaven, bursts into tears! In a ninth-century poem St Íde fondles the divine Child and speaks to him as a mother would in loving diminutives – one of the verbs even is an utterly untranslatable diminutive! Later still, an eighteenth-century poet shows the apostles in heaven celebrating with a long dance the return to the fold of an erring friar. In olden times once more a charming intimacy even with the animal kingdom is shown.

Although life in the monasteries was severe, stress was laid firstly on love of God and the neighbour – on a tonsured heart, too, before a tonsured head. The body also, in genuflexions, prostrations and cross-vigils (arms extended cross-wise), had to share in penitential prayer. Final abandonment of all for love of Christ was perpetual exile and pilgrimage. *Rómh* (from 'Roma') became a common noun for a place of pilgrimage. In Ireland today there are over eighty places called *Diseart* (desert place), where anchorites of old sought solitude. Once again we are reminded of St Patrick praying, as he said, in all weathers, night and day, in wood and on mountain, and finally in permanent exile for the gospel. Significant, then, that the two ancient and living places of penitential pilgrimage should be ever associated with the saint – Cruach Phádraig and his Purgatory, Loch Dearg.

Ludwig Bieler, *The Life and Legend of St Patrick*, 1949; Nora K. Chadwick, *The Age of the Saints in the Early Celtic Church*, 1963; Robin Flower, *The Irish Tradition*, 1947; Françoise Henry, *Early Christian Irish Art*, 1963; Kathleen Hughes, *The Church in Early Irish Society*, 1966; Michael Maher (ed), *Irish Spirituality*, 1981; Charles Plummer, *Irish Litanies*, 1925; *Bethada Naém nÉrenn* (lives of the saints, with translation), 1922; *Vitae Sanctorum Hiberniae* (lives of the saints, with translation), 1910; John Ryan, *Irish Monasticism*, 1972; G. S. M. Walker, *Sancti Columbani Opera*, ²1970.

DIARMUID O'LAOGHAIRE, SJ

Islam

Islam is 'submission', surrender to the one God, and a believer is a Muslim or Moslem, from the same root. 'Religion in God's sight is Islam', says the Koran*, and 'I have surrendered myself to God' (3, 17f.). Proclaimed by the Prophet Muhammad in the seventh century A D in Arabia, true religion was traced back to Abraham who 'was not a Jew, nor a Christian, but he was a Muslim' (3, 60), an argument similar to Paul's claim that Abraham was the father of all believers.

Muslims reject descriptions of their religion as Muhammadanism since they do not worship the Prophet, yet he has a unique place in their religious life. The first of the Five Pillars of Religion is Testimony (*shahada*) or Confession of Faith (*iman*): 'I testify that there is no god but God. I testify that Muhammad is the Apostle of God.' This confession is repeated in all prayers, from every minaret and in every home. Muhammad has been maligned and denounced in the non-Islamic world, and his religious importance has been consistently under-estimated. But Constance Padwick, in her beautiful anthology of *Muslim Devotions* compiled from prayer-manuals used all over the Islamic world, wrote that 'no one can estimate the power of Islam as a religion who does not take into account the love at the heart of it for this figure'. Annemarie Schimmel also writes of 'the Prophet Muhammad as a centre of Muslim life and thought'. Blessings for Muhammad and his family are repeated daily by millions, resulting in 'a feeling that the Prophet is always close to a faithful Muslim who directs his love and trust towards him'.

The Five Pillars of Religion (*din*) are Faith, Prayer, Almsgiving, Fasting and Pilgrimage. Set prayer (*salat*) should be performed five times a day: at daybreak, noon, afternoon, evening and night. It is preceded by ritual washing of face, head, hands, forearms and feet. Prayer is made on a mat facing the direction of the Sacred Mosque in Mecca. At first the direction was towards Jerusalem like the Jews, but it was changed to the Sacred House (Ka'ba), said to have been built by Abraham and Ishmael. Since Muslims all over the world face in the prescribed direction they are like the hands of a clock pointing to the centre, in Europe roughly to the east but in India to the west, and so on.

The Muslim begins prayer with a silent intention (*niya*) of sincerity, repeats 'God is most great', recites the first chapter of the Koran, performs a series of prostrations, and may add recitation of other chapters and private prayers. Public worship follows the pattern of private prayer. Spontaneous prayer (*du'a*) may be uttered at any time and many Muslims use prayer beads to assist in reciting 99 Most Beautiful Names of God. Prayer beads probably originated in India, with Hinduism* and Buddhism*, were taken over by Islam and passed on to Christianity, traditionally through Dominicans* or Cistercians*, perhaps as one result of the Crusades.

Prayers may be said anywhere and Muslims unroll prayer mats by the wayside, on railway platforms, on board ship, in the mosque or at home. Islamic devotions may be private or congregational; for women they are always at home. The mosque (*masjid*, 'place of prostration') is a public building orientated to the direction (*qibla*) of Mecca and its sacred Ka'ba, the direction being indicated by a niche (*mihrab*) in the end wall. Mosques have no sculptures or paintings, for the religion is strongly iconoclastic, but fine lettering of Koranic verses adorns the walls. There is graceful architecture, and slender minarets outside mosques are towers used for calls to prayer. Friday is the day for congregational prayer at midday, though it is not a sabbath, and all males should then assemble for prayer led by a prayer leader (*imam*). The mosque may have a pulpit, often finely decorated, for sermons, and a wooden stand for reciting the Koran. Mosque floors are covered with mats for prayer. In addition to use for public prayer, mosques often serve as places of quiet devotion or teaching by lawyers. There is no priesthood in Islam but trained doctors interpret the law for daily life.

The Third Pillar is Almsgiving (*zakat*), obligatory charity to relatives, orphans, the poor and travellers. There is no collection of money in the mosque but at various times the alms tax has been levied on income and property, necessary in the absence of other social services. Freewill offerings (*sadaqa*) may be given at any time for special concerns.

The Fourth Pillar is Fasting (*saum*), obligatory on all adult Muslims during the daylight hours of the month of Ramadan. No food, drink, smoking or sexual intercourse are allowed on these days from first light to evening dark, which is especially trying in lands of long summer days since the Muslim year is lunar and gets earlier annually against solar movements. Exceptions from fasting are allowed for children, the sick, pregnant women and travellers, and in some states now these are extended for factory workers, soldiers and students. During Ramadan preachers tour towns with religious and social exhortations.

The Fifth Pillar is Pilgrimage (*hajj*) to Mecca, obligatory in every Muslim at least once in a lifetime. A Lesser Pilgrimage may be undertaken at any time, but the Pillar is the Greater Pilgrimage at the time of the new moon in the twelfth month of the Islamic year. About a million Muslims go to Mecca every year, by all means of transport, from foot to air. Pilgrims wear special dress, men two lengths of cloth and women are veiled head to feet; no non-Muslim may enter Mecca. Pilgrims go round the Ka'ba seven times anti-clockwise (reversing old pagan practice) and try to kiss the Black Stone, a meteorite, in its corner. There are processions to two hills, Safa and Marwa, and to Mount Arafat where the night is spent. On the tenth day there is communal confession of sins and slaughtering of animals for sharing and giving to the poor. All over the Islamic world on the same day there is general confession and animals are sacrificed and eaten in a Great Festival, Id al-Kabir or Bairam (festival). Many pilgrims go on to Medina some two hundred miles to the north to visit the tomb of the Prophet and those who can afford it may continue to Jerusalem, the third holy city of Islam which is believed to have been visited by the Prophet in a visionary ascent to heaven. Pilgrims take home holy water from the ancient Zamzam well in Mecca, associated with Hagar and Ishmael, and pieces of a great cloth which covers the Ka'ba and is renewed annually.

There are two major festivals in Islam, the Id al-Kabir during the pilgrimage month, and Id al-Fitr (breaking the fast) or Little Bairam, at the end of the month of Ramadan. In addition the birthday of the Prophet is popular in some countries. Many Islamic saints are celebrated in birthdays, with prayers and processions. Relics of the Prophet and other saints are treasured in mosques and other centres. Although Islam teaches a strict monotheism veneration is given to relics, tombs and places associated with saints, dervishes, mystics or founders of religious brotherhoods. Here people come to pray and present gifts, votive or otherwise. There are many shrines of holy people, mystics and 'friends of God', whose stories are recounted or legends adapted to need. Further, cemeteries are visited and prayers offered for the dead, usually of one's own family, Muhammad is believed to be the great intercessor for all Muslims on the day of judgment.

There are two major divisions of Islam. Probably over 80% are Sunnis, followers of the custom (*sunna*) of Islamic tradition, particularly Muhammad and his first successors, the Khalifas or Caliphs Abu Bakr, Omar, Othman and Ali. Then came a schism in which the followers (Shi'a) of Ali held he was the first true Caliph. The Shi'a further split into two major groups, the Twelvers who believe in twelve leaders (*imams*) from Ali, and the Seveners or Ismailis who hold to seven ending with Ismail. The last in these successions disappeared or went into hiding and will reappear as the Mahdi (guided one), an eschatological figure. In popular belief both the Messiah Jesus and the Mahdi will appear at the end of time. There are many other sub-divisions of Shi'a of which some of the best known are Khoja Ismailis who follow the Aga Khan, almost a divine figure. The Ayatollahs ('signs of God') of modern Iran are popular religious leaders, almost confined to that country, but not the highest doctrinal authority.

Shi'a worship follows much the same pattern as Sunni, but Shi'a prayer leaders stand in a small depression in the mosque, below the level of the congregation, as a sign of humility. In prayer Shi'a use tablets of clay from Karbala on which to place their foreheads, and although most Muslims refuse to have holy pictures there are many pictures of Ali and other saints in Shi'a lands.

In Shi'a tradition Ali, cousin and son-in-law of the Prophet, was succeeded as first Caliph by his sons Hasan and Husain. The latter was killed by the rival Sunni Caliph Yazid at Karbala in 680. To commemorate this martyrdom a great shrine was built at Karbala which remains almost as, or more important than, Mecca for many Shi'a and which is the focus of pilgrimages. Every year in Shi'a lands, notably in Iran and parts of neighbouring countries, there are great lamentations in Muharram, the first month of the year when Husain died. They culminate in long Passion Plays at which the story of Husain is told in some forty scenes, and at the end the archangel Gabriel gives the key of Paradise to Husain so that he may intercede and take thence all who honour him. The problem of righteous suffering is thus vividly portrayed in Shi'a Islam.

Islam teaches faith in God (Allah), his angels, his prophets, his book, judgment and the life to come. It seems simple but in fact it is complex, with many varieties of sect and patterns of devotion. Worship is public as well as private, as in Judaism and Christianity. There is a very strong sense of community in the House of Islam, with the application of Islamic law throughout society when the religion is dominant but causing difficulties for the faithful when it is in a minority.

Islam arose when Judaism and Christianity had been long in existence. The young Muhammad is said to have been recognized as a prophet by a Christian monk, Bahira, and his first wife's cousin, Waraqa, was a Christian who recognized Muhammad's vocation. But there seem to have been no organized Christian communities in either Mecca or Medina where Muhammad spent his life, and no translations of the Bible into the Arabic of the time. Islam expanded rapidly into much of the Eastern Christian world, affecting religious life, for example in iconoclastic controversies, and being affected in the development of its own mystical life.

See also **Sufism**.

Kenneth Cragg, *The Call of the Minaret*, 1956; Ahmad Kamal, *The Sacred Journey*, 1964; Constance Padwick, *Muslim Devotions*, 1961; Geoffrey Parrinder, *Worship in the World's Religions*, [2]1974; Annemarie Schimmel and Abdoldjavad Falaturi (eds), *We Believe in One God*, 1979.

GEOFFREY PARRINDER

Jansenism

This movement owes its name (originally awarded by its detractors) to Cornelius Otto Jansen (1585–1638), a leading theologian of Louvain, promoted Bishop of Ypres in 1636. His *Augustinus* (posthumously published in 1640), with its rigorist presentation of Augustine's* theology of grace, provoked immediate and violent hostility from Jesuits* and their allies in Paris. The case of Jansen was defended by Antoine Arnauld (1612–1694), a disciple of Jean Duvergier de Hauranne, Abbé de Saint-Cyran (1581–1643), Jansen's close associate. Arnauld had several relatives (including two abbesses) at the convent of Port-Royal, originally Cistercian but independent since 1627, which followed Saint-Cyran's spiritual teaching and much more than the theological technicalities of the *Augustinus* came to represent the focus of Jansenism. A community of male solitaries, bound by no vows, had grown up near the original site of Port-Royal (near Versailles) and through schools, retreats and religious writings disseminated Jansenist ideas to a wide public. The principal teachings are that grace is irresistible, that even the righteous may on occasion sin through insufficient grace, that in sacramental discipline strict standards should be observed (e.g. in confession the penitent should never be given the benefit of doubt through casuistry; abstaining from communion may be right or necessary if preparation is inadequate or simply as a means of mortification) and that the moral life of the Christian must make no concessions to self (e.g. the theatre and luxury are condemned, charitable works are demanded). Hostility to man-centred Jesuit theology polarized doctrine, ruthless persecution hardened attitudes. Arnauld was condemned in 1657, briefly rehabilitated, then forced into exile in 1679. At his death, the Oratorian P. Quesnel took over the leadership and was the primary target of the bull *Unigenitus* (1713), which provoked schism in Holland (perpetuated by the Old Catholics). Port-Royal suffered continual persecution until the community was finally dissolved in 1709, and the buildings razed next year. Jansenist self-righteousness and their partisan spirit were ultimately self-defeating, though the movement continued into the nineteenth century, but the issues they defended were fundamental and in no way trivial.

N. J. Abercrombie, *The Origins of Jansenism*, 1936; A. Adam, *Du mysticisme à la révolte*, 1968; L. Cognet, *Le Jansénisme*, 1961.

A. J. KRAILSHEIMER

Jerome, St

The priest Jerome (b. either in 331 or *c.* 345, d. 420) is one of the four doctors of the Latin church. A Latin speaker who learnt Greek, Hebrew and Syriac, and settled in the East, Jerome was well fitted to transmit Eastern achievements to the West, notably in the spheres of biblical scholarship and monasticism. His main original achievement was to retranslate most of the Bible, so giving us the Vulgate.

Jerome originated near Aquileia, but studied in Rome. He tried out the ascetic life with friends at Aquileia *c.* 370, then again as a hermit in the Syrian desert (*c.* 374–376), where he learnt Hebrew. He also spent time at Antioch and Constantinople, profiting from the biblical lectures of Apollinarius and of Gregory of Nazianzus. From 382–385 he was in Rome acting as Pope Damasus' secretary, and advocating an uncompromising asceticism *. Damasus asked him to revise the Latin translation of the Gospels, while the noble ladies in Rome who heeded his call to asceticism asked him to read and expound the Bible with them. These demands stimulated his subsequent labours. Forced by rumours of scandal and by his unpopularity to leave Rome in 385,

Jerome made a pilgrimage to Palestine and Egypt before settling at Bethlehem. Here he founded a monastery where he spent the rest of his life, largely engaged in biblical studies, but also maintaining a far-flung correspondence through which he continued to give ascetic counsel to many in Italy and Gaul.

Jerome's twin concerns, the fostering of the ascetic life and study of the Bible, were linked. To read the Bible with understanding was of cardinal importance; for in reading the Bible one is listening to God – just as in praying, one speaks to God. Reading and prayer thus belong together; one passes from one to the other, in a dialogue with God. The ascetic life exists to facilitate this dialogue; for a married person cannot 'pray without ceasing', as Paul had enjoined. Here Jerome may lose our sympathy as he depreciates marriage and exalts the life of chastity. However, he does see chastity, fasting, solitude and poverty as but means to an end: the dialogue of the soul with God, in prayerful seclusion. 'To live amongst these [books of the Bible], to meditate on them, to know nothing else, to seek nothing – does not this seem to you a corner of heaven already, on earth?' (Ep. 53, 10).

His dedication to biblical study eventually led him not just to revise the existing Latin translation of the Septuagint, but to re-translate the OT from the original Hebrew. In his many biblical commentaries he came to insist that the literal sense must be established first; from this he ventures out in quest of the spiritual sense, which is the heart of the matter (*medulla*). We must seek this through prayer, with our souls invigorated by asceticism, 'entering with Moses into the cloud'. Meditation on the Bible nourishes the ascetic's soul, and points him Godward.

Jerome propagated the ascetic ideal through hagiography, through translation of Pachomius' rule, and above all through his letters of exhortation and counsel. These mingle practical advice on dress, seclusion, reading, etc. with inspiring rhapsodies on the ascetic life and invectives against worldliness. Jerome adapts Egyptian monastic practices to the very different needs of household asceticism. He popularized in the West six regular monastic offices based on psalmody, the fundamental role within the monastic life of Bible reading and meditation (*lectio divina*), and a positive evaluation of manual work. Many of his letters circulated widely, in Gaul as well as Italy, winning a number of well-born (especially female) converts to asceticism; and they continued to serve as sources of inspiration long after Jerome's death.

English tr of *The Principal Works of St Jerome* by W. H. Fremantle in *A Select Library of Nicene and post-Nicene Fathers*, 2nd series, vol 6, 1893, repr 1954; D. Gorce, *La lectio divina des origines du cénobitisme*, vol I, *Saint Jérôme*, 1925 (important); P. Antin, *Essai sur Saint Jérôme*, 1951; *Recueil sur Saint Jérôme*, 1968; E. P. Burke, 'St Jerome as a Spiritual Director', in F. X. Murphy (ed), *A Monument to St Jerome*, 1952, pp. 145–69; P. Rousseau, *Ascetics, Authority, and the Church*, 1978.

C. E. STANCLIFFE

Jesuits *see* Jesus, Society of

Jesus, Experience of

Any form of *imitatio Christi* spirituality is bound to take seriously the subject of Jesus' own spirituality and experience of God. This point was given massive support by nineteenth-century liberal theology, typified by Schleiermacher's emphasis on Jesus' 'God-consciousness' and Herrmann's stress on 'the inner life of Jesus'. Twentieth-century scholarship in general has reacted against the views expressed in such phrases, and many would still take the position most forcibly expressed by Bultmann that it is neither possible as a matter of historical exegesis nor necessary on grounds of faith to uncover the inner life of Jesus.

The issue is complicated by the technical question of whether the Fourth Gospel provides a historical source for information about Jesus' own self-understanding and experience as Son of the Father. The most probable answer is that the extended dialogues and discourses are sermonic elaborations or meditations on aspects or themes of Jesus' ministry, or on particular sayings or events from his life. The degree of divergence and development between the Synoptic Gospels and the Fourth Gospel is so marked that few scholars would be prepared to conclude that the historical Jesus was conscious of having pre-existed with God or expressed his consciousness of relationship with God

in terms of the powerful 'I am' and 'mutual indwelling' sayings. For those who think John's Gospel does give straight historical information at these points the problem remains of how such a Jesus can be an exemplar for Christians to copy.

So far as the Synoptic Gospels are concerned it is most likely that the Bultmannian reaction against nineteenth-century Liberalism was too strong. We can in fact speak of Jesus' experience with a fair degree of confidence. To attempt to trace a development in Jesus' experience is probably over-ambitious. But at various points it is very likely that words, sayings and actions of Jesus bring to expression at least some aspects of Jesus' own experience and spirituality.

His piety so far as upbringing is concerned would almost certainly be that typical of most of first-century Palestinian Judaism. He would recite the *Shema* (Deut. 6.4) once or twice each day, and no doubt be familiar with the earlier forms of the *Tephilla* (the Eighteen Benedictions) and the *Kaddish* (with its striking parallels to the first two petitions of the Lord's Prayer). No doubt too he was instructed in the Torah, attended the Temple when possible and observed the great feasts. But whatever his earlier practice the period of his ministry at least is marked by several distinctive and striking features.

Luke emphasizes the importance of prayer for Jesus (Luke 3.21; 5.16; 6.12; 9.18, 28–9; 11.1; 22.41–45; 23.34, 46), and his picture is sufficiently reinforced by Mark to confirm that Jesus liked to pray in solitude, sometimes for lengthy periods, and particularly at crises and times of decision (Mark 1.35; 6.46; 14.32–42). His characteristic way of addressing God was 'Abba' (Father), a word expressive of intimate family relationship. Although there are a few parallels to Jesus' use of 'Abba' in the Judaism of the time, it was probably distinctive of Jesus as his characteristic usage. So it is fair to see in this idiom an expression of Jesus' experience of God: he experienced God in a distinctively intimate relation as his Father, and encouraged his disciples to share the experience (Luke 11.2). It would seem that only on the cross was he unable to say 'Abba' (Mark 15.34).

Jesus also expressed his experience in terms of the Spirit, particularly as the one in whom Isa. 61.1–2 had been fulfilled (Matt.

5.3–6; 11.2–6; Luke 4.18–19). For him evidently the Spirit was the power of God's final rule already active in and through him in healing (Mark 3.28–29; Matt. 12.28) and preaching. Hence his sense of prophetic commissioning (e.g. Luke 13.33; Matt. 10.40; 15.24), and the tremendous authority of his teaching with its distinctive 'Amen' and 'But I say to you' (e.g. Matt. 5.21–22; Mark 2.10; 13.31). On the basis of such passages it is quite justified to speak of Jesus' sense of climactic inspiration and unsurpassed authority, which can be linked explicitly with his sense of sonship as in Matt. 11.27. Its unschooled and charismatic quality of immediacy is noted in such comments as Mark 1.22 and Matt. 7.28–29, as also the depth of his concern for those needing help in such as Mark 1.41; 6.34; 10.21.

Jesus' anointing with the Spirit at Jordan is not presented by the Gospels as an experience of Jesus, but the narrative, however formed, probably reflects a determinative experience of Jesus in which consciousness of sonship and commissioning united in the fundamental conviction from which his whole mission sprang. That it was a visionary experience is implied. Other visions are indicated in Luke 10.18 and possibly Matt. 4.1–11. But Jesus can hardly be called a visionary, and there is no evidence that he sought mystical or ecstatic experiences. Though clearly self-disciplined in prayer, he neither encouraged nor practised the discipline of fasting, his ministry being marked rather by open handed celebration (Mark 2.17–19; Matt. 11.19; Luke 14.12–14). He did not seek to inflict suffering upon himself, but did not try to escape it when he saw it to be God's will (Luke 12.49–50; Mark 14.36).

There are only a few hints in the Epistles that Jesus' own experience was regarded as exemplary (e.g. Rom. 8.15; I Cor. 11.1; Phil. 2.5), though the Synoptic Gospels in the style of ancient biography use his words and deeds to show the sort of person he was, and the Fourth Gospel does present Jesus' relationship with the Father as a model for Christian spirituality (e.g. John 14.12; 15.10; 17.21). To that extent the later tradition of *imitatio Christi* is rooted in the NT.

See also **Imitation of Christ.**

J. D. G. Dunn, *Jesus and the Spirit*, 1975, chs 2–4; A. R. George, *Communion with God in the New Testament*, 1953, chs 2–4; J. Jeremias, *The Prayers of Jesus*, 1967; E. J. Tinsley, *The Imitation of God in Christ*, 1960.

JAMES D. G. DUNN

Jesus, Name of

From the time of the NT onwards, a close connection has been felt between the name and the person of Jesus, such that the name of Jesus is often regarded as a 'sacrament' and effective sign of the power and living presence of Jesus himself.

The origins of this attitude are to be found in the OT veneration for the name of God, which is viewed with awe as a source of power and protection (Ps. 8.1; Mic. 4.5), and also as a secret mystery (Gen. 32.29; Ex. 3.13–14; Judg. 13.17–18). In later Judaism from *c.* 300 BC, out of a sense of reverence the Tetragrammaton – the four-lettered name of God YHWH or JHVH – was usually not pronounced aloud, the title 'Adonai' ('Lord') being substituted in its place.

The name Jesus, announced by the angel to Mary (Luke 1.31; cf. Matt. 1.21), is a Greek transcription of the Hebrew *Jeshua*, which is in its turn a shortened form of the name *Jehoshua* (Joshua), meaning 'he whose salvation is Yahweh', 'salvation of Yahweh', or 'Yahweh is salvation'. In the first century AD it was a relatively common name.

Emphasis upon the name of Jesus is prominent throughout the NT; in most cases, however, it is not used on its own but with the titles 'Lord' or 'Christ'. In the name of Jesus Christ devils are cast out (Mark 9.38–39; Acts 16.18, 19.13), the sick are healed (Acts 3.6, 4.7, 4.30), and baptism is given (Acts 2.38, 8.16). Christ commands his disciples to pray 'in my name' (John 16.23–24); the apostles preach that salvation is to be found solely 'in the name of Jesus Christ of Nazareth' (Acts 4.10–12); according to Paul, Christians are 'justified in the name of the Lord Jesus' (I Cor. 6.11), which is to be honoured 'above every name' (Phil. 2.9). Thus the name is power and salvation.

Veneration for the name of Jesus continues in early Christian times. Hermas (second century) states, 'The name of the Son of God is great and boundless, and upholds the entire universe' (*Sim.* ix, 14). Origen ascribes to the name of Jesus the power to expel demons and to heal sickness (*Against Celsus* i, 67), and in his *Homilies on the Song of Songs* (i, 4) he applies the words

'Thy name is as ointment poured forth' to the name of Jesus; compare also his exegesis of 'Hallowed be thy name' in his work *On Prayer* 24. Among early Latin authors, devotion to the name of Jesus occurs in Ambrose, Augustine and more especially Peter Chrysologus (fifth century) (*PL* 52, 586 B C).

In the East from the fifth to sixth centuries onwards, and in the mediaeval West from the eleventh to twelfth centuries, devotion to the Holy Name has tended to take the more particular form of the repeated invocation of the name of Jesus (*see* **Jesus, Prayer to**).

H. Bietenhard in *TDNT*, V, pp. 242–81; W. Foerster in *TDNT*, III, pp. 284–93; I. Noye in *DS*, VIII, cols 1109–26.

KALLISTOS WARE

Jesus Prayer *see* Jesus, Prayer to

Jesus, Prayer to

A practice known also as the Invocation of the Holy Name.

1. *The Christian East*. In the Orthodox tradition Jesus is invoked primarily through the frequent repetition of the 'Jesus Prayer' or 'Prayer of Jesus'. In its standard form this runs, 'Lord Jesus Christ, Son of God, have mercy on me', sometimes with the words 'the sinner' added at the end; there are a number of minor variations in wording. Basically this is an adaptation of the prayer of the blind man outside Jericho (Luke 18.38); compare also the prayer of the publican (Luke 18.13). The practice of the Jesus Prayer is often described as hesychasm*, but this latter term can also bear a wider sense.

The origins of the Jesus Prayer are to be sought in fourth-century Egyptian spirituality. The Desert Fathers of Nitria and Scetis (*see* **Apophthegmata**) laid special emphasis upon *penthos*, inward mourning, and upon the need for God's mercy. They also recommended the use of monologic prayer – the employment of a short phrase, frequently repeated – as a method for maintaining the continual remembrance of God. But among the formulae that they employed the name of Jesus enjoys no particular prominence. More specific allusions to the 're-membrance' or 'invocation' of Jesus are first found in St Nilus of Ancrya (d. *c.* 430), and especially in St Diadochus of Photice (d.

before 486). Diadochus sees this 'remem-brance' as a way of controlling the imagination, unifying the memory, and so attaining the kind of prayer without images and thoughts that that is recommended by Evagrius. Thus, while being a prayer in words, the Jesus Prayer at the same time leads into silence.

The standard form of the Jesus Prayer, as given above, is first found in an Egyptian source, the *Life of Abba Philemon* (sixth to eighth centuries); without the words 'Son of God', it occurs in St Barsanuphius and St John of Gaza (early sixth century), and shortly after in St Dorotheus of Gaza, *The Life of Dositheus*. The invocation of Jesus is recommended by St John Climacus* (seventh century) and his followers St Hesychius and St Philotheus of Sinai (eighth to tenth centuries). It is just possible that Climacus and Hesychius envisage some co-ordination of the prayer with the rhythm of the breathing, but their language is not precise. References to the Jesus Prayer are also to be found in Coptic sources of the seventh to eighth centuries, above all in the Coptic Macarian cycle, where the invocation is explicitly linked with the breathing. There are, however, important representatives of Eastern spirituality, such as St Maximus the Confessor, St Isaac of Nineveh, St Theodore the Studite and St Symeon the New Theologian, who make no reference whatever to the Jesus Prayer.

Its use grew more widespread in the fourteenth century, when it is found above all on the Holy Mountain of Athos. A physical technique is suggested by St Nicephorus the Hesychast (late thirteenth century), St Gregory of Sinai, St Gregory Palamas*, and St Kallistos and Ignatius Xanthopoulos (fourteenth century): the head is bowed, the eyes (if open) are fixed on the place of the heart; the rhythm of the breathing is slowed down and co-ordinated with the words of the prayer; at the same time, the hesychast searches inwardly for the place of the heart, striving to descend with the intellect (*nous*) into the heart (*see* **Prayer of the Heart**). There are interesting parallels here with Yoga* and Sufism*. For the Orthodox tradition this technique is only an accessory, not an essential element of the Jesus Prayer. The use of the Jesus Prayer was popularized in the eighteenth-century Greek world by St Nicodemus of the Holy Mountain, editor of the *Philokalia**. Since at least the eighteenth century, and probably much earlier, a prayer-rope or rosary* (Greek *komvoschoinion*; Russian *tchotki*) is commonly used with the prayer.

The Jesus Prayer is found in Russia from the eleventh century onwards. It was taught by St Nil Sorskii (d. 1509), and was particularly popular in the nineteenth century, when it was commended by St Seraphim of Sarov, Bishops Ignatii Brianchaninov and Theophan the Recluse, and the anonymous author of *The Way of a Pilgrim*. A group of Russian monks on Athos, known as the *Imiaslavtsy* ('Glorifiers of the Name'), who were charged with advocating excessive devotion to the name of Jesus, incurred condemnation in 1913. In the past forty years, alike in Greece, Russia, Romania and the Orthodox diaspora, the practice of the Jesus Prayer has grown more and more extensive.

2. *The Mediaeval West*. Devotion to the Holy Name was greatly fostered by St Bernard of Clairvaux's* fifteenth homily on the Song of Songs. It was especially a feature of English spirituality: the *Jubilus* on the Name of Jesus, beginning *Dulcis, Jesu, memoria*, long attributed to Bernard, was probably written in England in the late twelfth century, and an ardent love of the Name marks the Yorkshire hermit Richard Rolle* (d. 1349). On the continent it was much commended by the Mendicant Orders, in particular by the Dominican Heinrich Suso* and the Franciscan St Bernardine of Siena.

Whereas the invocation of the name is seen in Orthodoxy primarily as a way of stilling the imagination and as a means of entry into imageless, contemplative prayer, in the mediaeval West it is more a prayer of the feelings and emotions, of affective, imaginative love, being closely linked with devotion to Christ's sacred humanity. It reflects in this regard the new spirit that entered Western spirituality in the eleventh to twelfth centuries with Anselm* and Bernard. In the West there is no standard formula corresponding to the Orthodox Jesus Prayer; while in Orthodoxy the name 'Jesus' is scarcely ever invoked on its own, in the Western Middle Ages this is common. In the West there is nothing equivalent to the physical technique of hesychasm.

The Jesus Prayer in its Orthodox form – but usually without the physical technique –

has become surprisingly popular in the West during the last twenty years.

P. Adnès in *DS*, VIII, cols 1126–50; I. Hausherr, *The Name of Jesus* (Cistercian Studies 44), 1978; K. Ware, *The Power of the Name*, 1974.

KALLISTOS WARE

Jesus, Society of

The spirituality of the members of the Society of Jesus (Jesuits) is a set of emphases, oriented towards service through love, which has sprung chiefly from the spiritual outlook or world view of their founder, St Ignatius of Loyola*. Since the Jesuits have always been aiming to apply his teachings and example, the surest way to understand their spirituality is to study Ignatius' personal religious experience and his inspirational world view into which it matured.

This somewhat worldly Basque nobleman had a profound experience of conversion which led him to become a mystic, saint, influential writer and founder of an apostolic order. Studies since 1935 by Hugo Rahner, Joseph de Guibert and others have greatly deepened our knowledge of his spiritual outlook, showing that it was formed largely through divinely infused contemplations which rank him among the great mystics of Christianity such as Augustine* or Teresa of Avila* – an aspect of his life not adequately treated in biographies before 1950. During six months of convalescence in 1521, he prayerfully read the Life of Christ by Ludolph of Saxony (d. 1378) and copied key passages from it. It was a long book, for its day profoundly biblical, patristic and theological, but written in the form of contemplations to foster devotion. Ignatius also read lives of the saints by Jacobus de Voragine, particularly those of Francis, Dominic and probably Augustine. All this stirred him to enthusiastic love of Christ. Thus when he left Loyola in 1522 to take up a new life totally dedicated to God, his outlook was already oriented, more deeply than he was aware, towards prayerfully intimate co-operation with Christ in achieving God's redemptive plan as it was slowly unfolding in the history of salvation. As a result, his spirituality was henceforth to be centred around the very core of the Christian gospel message.

Then during ten months of prayer at Manresa, Ignatius was flooded by God with illuminating contemplations, about the Trinity, creation of the world, humanity of Christ and the like. 'His understanding was opened,' he wrote, so that 'he understood many things ... of faith and learning ... with an enlightenment so great that everything seemed new to him' (*Autobiography*, 27–30). At Manresa, too, he wrote notes on his chief experiences likely to be helpful to others towards similar devotion. These writings slowly evolved into his *Spiritual Exercises**, published in 1548.

Under these warm perceptions of a mystic he gradually put an intellectual foundation, especially from 1528 to 1535 at the University of Paris, where he came to esteem Aquinas. Largely through his *Exercises* he formed the outlook of the nine companions with whom he founded the Society of Jesus. In 1537 at La Storta near Rome he had a vision of God the Father placing him into close association with his Son. This guided him in the formation of his Order, approved by Pope Paul III in 1540.

His matured spiritual outlook was one in which he saw all things as proceeding from the Trinity and becoming means by which one can make one's way to one's end, beatitude by glorifying God. 'Glorifying' here means praising and entails serving. Hence Ignatius' endeavour was to make all his activities result in praise to God greater than would have accrued to him without them. His norm for making decisions among options was: Which one is likely to lead to 'the greater glory of God'? – a phrase he used so often that it became a motto. To that supreme end he saw all else as means.

From this world-view sprang many other characteristics of his spirituality. It is biblical, theological, trinitarian, christocentric, contemplative, apostolic, ecclesiastical and as adaptable as the Christian faith itself; and it found expression in all that Ignatius said, did or wrote and thereby won many followers.

In his *Spiritual Exercises* he applied his world-view towards helping individual persons to discover God's will for themselves: How can they, by wise and prayerful decisions, fit themselves more co-operatively into his saving plan, in order to bring him greater glory from themselves and others? These

Exercises begin with an orienting principle which presents 1. the inspiring end, salvation through service; 2. the means to it, creatures wisely used; 3. an attitude of 'indifference' (suspended decision) before options until sound reasons for choice are prayerfully found; and 4. a norm for deciding: Which option is likely to be the better or best means to the end? Many of the topics and the gospel contemplations for the four 'weeks' are clearly selections from those in Ludolph's *Life of Christ*, and hence are focused on God's plan of salvation unfolding in history; but from Ignatius' originality comes their concatenation towards the end of his *Exercises*: to help an exercitant to order his life to God and fit himself here and now more co-operatively into his plan of salvation.

In his *Constitutions of the Society of Jesus* Ignatius applied his world-view to the founding and government of his apostolic religious order. With his characteristically sharp focus on ends and means, he started by stating its end: to aid its members to strive for their own and their fellow men's spiritual development (3); and this is ordered to the single higher end: to bring greater 'service and praise' to God (8, 133, 307). All else is means to this: for example, the three religious vows, and the vow of special obedience to the pope for a task anywhere on earth. These *Constitutions* are not merely a code of laws but also a spiritually inspiring manual of discernment to aid superiors and members towards choosing, among emerging options, the one likely to lead to greater glory of God.

Through his charismatic example, ministries and world-view, Ignatius in sixteen years from 1540 to his death in 1556 won over 1,000 recruits to his already worldwide order, and also shaped their spirituality and most important ministries, such as preaching, the sacraments, spiritual conversation, service of the sick and the Christian education of youth in a system which by 1710 numbered some 612 colleges, 15 universities and over 100 seminaries. Ignatius' *Constitutions* repeatedly stressed adaptation to persons, places and times, and also missionary activities. This led to Jesuits' preaching the gospel in India, Japan and the Americas, and to a stress on adaptation to native cultures by pioneers such as Xavier, Valignano, Di Nobili, Ricci and others.

The spirituality of the later Jesuits, 1556 until now, has included a constant effort at fidelity to the tradition inherited from Ignatius. Through these centuries all these members were trained by Ignatius' *Exercises* and governed by his *Constitutions*; and they were carrying out this spirit in all their activities. Their spirituality remained substantially the same as his, but its expressions were coloured by the thought-currents, controversies and cultural trends of successive eras.

This complex history can be divided thus into eras: 1. 1556–1580: the early generations, trained by Ignatius, lived out his doctrine and practice, but had as yet no published spiritual literature of their own except his *Exercises* and *Constitutions*, and were in danger of being pulled back into older spiritualities more contemplative than apostolic. 2. 1581–1616: Under Aquaviva a body of spiritual teachings took shape, such as the *Directory of the Spiritual Exercises* and works by Bellarmine, La Puente, Rodríguez and others. 3. 1617–1773: in the Old Society's Apogee publications proliferated, some devotional for Marian Congregations or parishes, some controversial on Jansenism*, Quietism* or Chinese Rites, some on Christ's heart as symbol of his love. 4. 1774–1814: during the near-suppression, the few able to remain in the Order, some 600 recruits, and the ex-Jesuits kept the tradition alive. 5. 1815–1899: the restored Society of the nineteenth century recovered the vitality of the old. Its first members had been trained in the old tradition and clung to its teachings. But they had to learn them chiefly from writings composed after 1600 and were impeded from adapting even these adequately to their vastly changed circumstances. 6. 1900 till now: a deepening insight into the primitive spirit or charism has been accelerating. Until 1894 most of the writings of the first Jesuits were extant only in handwritten manuscripts. But since then they have been published in the now 124 large volumes of the Historical Sources (*Monumenta*) of the Society of Jesus. Scholarly study of this material is producing voluminous treatises revealing the richness of this spiritual heritage.

These developments from 1521 onwards comprise a vast history of which even de Guibert's masterful 600 pages can be only a sketch. But they show clearly that Ignatius' charismatic world-view has constantly remained the life-giving core of Jesuit spirituality.

Ignatius of Loyola, *Autobiography, Spiritual Exercises, Spiritual Diary*, selected *Letters*; *The Constitutions of the Society of Jesus . . . with an Introduction and Commentary*, tr G. E. Ganss, 1970; H. O. Evennett, *The Spirit of the Counter-Reformation*, 1968; J. de Guibert, *The Jesuits: Their Spiritual Doctrine and Practice*, 1964.

GEORGE E. GANSS, SJ

Jewish Spirituality, Judaism

Though much of the content of Christian spirituality is paralleled in Judaism, 'spirituality' is not a term commonly used by Jews, nor is it given so much explicit treatment.

In Rabbinic Judaism holiness is achieved by the performance of God's will, as is indicated by the opening formula of Jewish blessings: 'Blessed are You Lord our God, King of the Universe, who makes us holy through the performance of His commandments, and who commands us to . . .' The commandments referred to are the 613 commandments derived from scripture and set out in the sixteenth-century *Sculchan Aruch* of Joseph Caro (1488–1575). It is indicative that this authoritative legal treatise was the work of a Kabbalist.

Other differences of emphasis between Jewish and Christian spirituality are:

1. Jewish writers are more sparing of intimate accounts of personal relationships with God.

2. Although the Zohar, the greatest work of Jewish mysticism, includes a commentary on the Song of Songs, fanciful quasi-erotic terminology is generally avoided.

3. Spirituality is treated under the heading of Law, Philosophy or Mysticism.

4. Apart from some mediaeval literature, spirit is not usually opposed to body, the same terms express both eros and agape, and there is little personification of evil – only 'the evil inclination'.

5. Jewish spirituality does not particularize states or degrees of feeling, such as the 'infused prayer' described by Teresa of Avila.

6. The aim of Jewish spirituality can never be union, for it rejects any possibility of incarnation. It therefore strives for *d'vekut*

– cleaving to God – as the highest state attainable.

7. A certain hesitation surrounds the subject. It is felt to be subjective and could lead to antinomian opposition to the Law rather than to its fulfilment.

The highway to spiritual refinement in Rabbinic Judaism is the study of the Law. Study must not be used as a 'crown for your own importance' nor as 'a spade to dig with'. This *lectio divina* is a duty for all and a spiritual enjoyment, and can be more important even than prayer. The devotion it requires is described in the Mishnah: 'This is the way of the Torah! A piece of bread with salt you will eat, a ration of water you will drink, upon the ground you will lie, a life of hardship you will lead, and you will labour in the Torah. If you do this, "happy shall you be" – in this world, "And it shall be well with you" – in the world to come.' The legal problems studied were ingenious and complex. Their importance often consisted in the devotion they awoke, not in their practical relevance.

This pious study was incumbent on everyone, and taken together with the obligatory three offices a day, the constant blessings, and observance of commandments, it gave Jewish life a spiritual underpinning not different from that of a religious order, though it was for all, and marriage was a duty.

In a Yeshivah (a Rabbinic Academy), this spirituality took its most concentrated form. The modern Hebrew poet Bialik, in his poem, *The Matmid* (the eternal student), describes such a life 'consecrated to the Law' and the sacrifices it entailed.

The forms and techniques of this democratic spirituality were varied. The phylacteries (prayer straps) were obligatory. With them rings were made around the fingers while the worshipper recited Hosea 2.21. Rituals in the home sanctified its occupants, making the dining room table an altar, and the householder and his wife a priest and priestess in piety. The presence of God in each room was marked by the Mezuzah (Deut. 6.9) on the doorposts. A wealth of short blessings sewed the life of this world to the life of eternity. Clothes as well as food had to be ritually fit, and the Mikveh (ritual bath) ensured ritual purity as well as cleanliness. These expressions of Rabbinic spirituality are current today.

Apart from this common or democratic

spirituality binding on all, schools of spirituality arose based on the Kabbalah, the Jewish mystical tradition. Until the eighteenth-century, when many mystical doctrines and practices were popularized by the Hasidic movement, these Kabbalistic groups were restricted to a learned élite, whose teachings were theosophic rather than personal. They pondered the problem of the creation, i.e. the root of good and evil in God, and the problem of the chariot (of Ezekiel), i.e. the ascent to God which is spirituality. Both the teachings and the methods derive from Neoplatonism, though the cited texts are scriptural or Rabbinic.

The chief work of the Kabbalah and its esoteric tradition is the Zohar. According to contemporary scholars it is the compilation of Moses de Leon (1250–1305), a Jew of Spain. Traditionally it derives from Rabbi Shimon bar Yochai. In it a theosophic system is elaborated, in which a hierarchy of emanations or Sephirot link God and his creation, the Infinite to the finite. Sparks of divinity subsist in the creation, and man, a creature, can redeem and uplift them to God. Elaborate systems of meditation and prayer help the worshipper to ascend the Sephirot or reunite the sparks. This high spirituality of Kavanah (intention) is best exemplified in the life and works of Rabbi Isaac Lauria (1534–1572). His grave in Safed in Israel is today the focus of pilgrimage.

The greatest movement of spirituality in modern Judaism was that of the Hasidim which began in the eighteenth-century in southern Poland. Although no direct connection with Christian movements of the time can be shewn, there are similarities to the Methodist revival of the Wesley brothers, and the Starets movement in the Orthodox church. Indeed the portrait of Father Zossima in *The Brothers Karamazov* is very close to that of a Hasidic 'rebbe'.

This movement of 'the pious' was started by the Baal Shem Tov (*c.* 1700–1760), the Master of the Good Name, a charismatic figure who preferred meditation in the solitudes of the Carpathian mountains to study in a Rabbinical Yeshivah. He wandered through the Jewish villages of southern Poland, inculcating a popular spirituality of the heart and addressing crowds, not in synagogues but in open fields. His teachings were condemned by the Rabbinic teacher Elijah of Vilna as pantheist, and only the intervention of the Tsarist authorities prevented excommunication.

Around him and his disciples clustered numerous legends, stories and sayings reminiscent of the Desert Fathers * or St Francis of Assisi *. Martin Buber * (1878–1965) has prepared and popularized them for contemporary reading, and presented their thinking systematically, stressing their love, laughter and piety. More recently, Gershom Scholem and his pupils have stressed their antinomian, Messianic, and Kabbalistic elements.

The teachings of the Baal Shem concerned the immanence and closeness of God. God was especially close to the simple and unlearned, and his voice spoke in the promptings of the heart. He was open to sinners and the repentant. Great waves of fervour accompanied these teachings, and prayers were transformed into songs and music in this Jewish revival.

As the Hasidic movement grew, many other masters arose known as 'righteous ones' or Tsadikkim. Their role was comparable to that of a guru, and by their merit the souls of their disciples could ascend, so close were they bound.

Two examples of the many important Hasidic Tsaddikim are Shneur Zalman of Lyady (1747–1813) and Nahman of Bratslav (1772–1811). The former reunited the charismatic qualities of early Hasidim to Rabbinic studies. The latter, in sharp contrast to the Baal Shem Tov, emphasized the distance separating God and man, the strength of evil, the importance of revelation and the Messianic coming. He expressed his theology and spirituality in tales and stories charged with deep symbolic meanings.

Today a number of Hasidic movements are active which inculcate orthodoxy, piety, and spirituality. Each has its own approach which derives from its founder and the dynasty of teachers which succeeded him. Some of the outstanding ones are:

1. The Lubavitcher, emphasizing piety. It evangelizes Jews, and welcomes the hitherto unobservant;

2. The Gerer, noted for its scholarship;

3. The Bratslaver, which is mystical, not so easy of access and somewhat apart from the others.

Many more exist, each with its own teacher (rebbe) and its own characteristic spirituality.

Outstanding modern teachers other than the Hasidic are Rav Kook (1865–1935) and Joshua Heschel (1907–1972). In the new revisions of the liturgy by the conservative, reform, and liberal movements in Judaism, personal prayer and meditation have been given greater emphasis. The Chavurah movement, especially in the USA, experiments with new forms of worship and religious organization. It plays a similar role to the house communion movement in Christianity.

Bahya Ben Joseph ibn Pakuda, *Duties of the Heart*, 1973; Nahman of Bratslav, *The Tales*, 1978; *Beggars and Prayers*, 1979; Shneur Zalman of Lyady, *Tanya*, 1981; *The Zohar* (tr H. Sperling and M. Simon), [2]1978; Martin Buber, *Tales of the Hasidim*, 2 vols, 1946, 1968; R. C. Musaph-Andriesse, *From Torah to Kabbalah*, ET 1981; Gershom Scholem, *Major Trends in Jewish Mysticism*, 1946.

LIONEL BLUE

Joachim of Fiore

Joachim of Fiore (*c.* 1130–1202), Abbot of the Cistercian house of Curazzo, Calabria, left his monastery to found his own congregation with a more contemplative emphasis at San Giovanni in Fiore in the Sila mountains. Later legends told of a mystical vision in youth when he received the gift of spiritual understanding; he himself recorded two later experiences – at Eastertide and Pentecost – when he was granted the divine illumination which he believed was the key to the meaning of history, interpreted as the three-fold work of the Trinity, embodied in the three *status* (stages) of Father, Son and Holy Spirit. The first, the rule of Law, had lasted until the end of the Old Testament; the second, the age of Grace, would shortly end after Joachim's day; the third, still to come, would be characterized by fuller spiritual illumination, by Liberty and Love. During the transition from second to third *status* the church would suffer the greatest tribulation of Antichrist. The third *status* would end in a brief revival of Antichrist before the winding up of history in the Second Advent and Last Judgment. Joachim established this 'pattern of threes' by a biblical exegesis based on typology. People and episodes in the Old Testament had their 'concord' in the New and by the *intellectus spiritualis* might be extrapolated into the third *status*. For example the twelve Patriarchs, twelve Apostles and twelve unknown leaders to come formed such a sequence. Again, the raven and dove despatched by Noah were types of Paul and Barnabas sent to the Gentiles and of two new orders of spiritual men who would lead the church into the Age of the Spirit. Joachim's main works – *Liber Concordie, Expositio in Apocalypsim* and *Psalterium decem chordarum* were published in Venice in the early sixteenth century. Although he associated separate Persons of the Trinity with each *status*, Joachim held that all three Persons operated together throughout history and – attacking Peter Lombard for 'quaternity' – sought to develop a mystical doctrine expressed as Three-are-One. The Fourth Lateran Council (1215) accepted the Lombard's doctrine and condemned Joachim's. To correct a common error, Joachim did not teach that in the third *status* Christ, the New Testament and the existing church would be superseded, but rather that, operating in a new mode, Christ's work would be fulfilled through spiritual understanding. Joachim was famed for his ecstatic devotion and deep spirituality: his disciple, Luke of Cosenza, recorded that when celebrating Mass his face, normally like a withered leaf, was suffused with divine light. In the thirteenth century he was widely hailed as the prophet of the Dominican * and Franciscan * Orders (raven and dove) and his theology of history was embraced by Franciscan Zealots and other groups believing themselves to be the 'new spiritual men', even as late as some Jesuits in the sixteenth century. Joachim's key concept of an Age of the Spirit still to come – though frequently distorted – has remained a powerful vision to the present day.

A. Crocco, *Gioacchino da Fiore e il Gioachimismo*, 1976; H. Grundmann, *Stüdien über Joachim von Floris*, 1927; H. de Lubac, *La Postérité spirituelle de Joachim de Fiore*, Vol I 1977, Vol II 1981; H. Mottu, *La manifestation de l'Esprit selon Joachim de Fiore*, 1977; M. Reeves, *The Influence of Prophecy in the Later Middle Ages. A Study in Joachimism*, 1969; M. Reeves and B. Hirsch-Reich, *The Figurae of Joachim of Fiore*, 1972; D. West (ed), *Joachim of Fiore in Christian Thought*, 1975.

H. Bett.   MARJORIE REEVES

Jocists

The name is based on an acronym of the French title of the movement (Jeunesse Ouvrière Chrétienne) of the Young Catholic Workers, which originated in Belgium. It was founded by Joseph Cardijn, who in 1924 attempted to spread Christianity among the largely alienated young factory workers. Its objective is to bring Christian moral principles to bear on modern industry and to keep the young of the working class within the RC Church. The First World War had increased hostility to the church among the industrial workers, a fact which was made evident to Pope Pius XI by the rise of Communism, so that he also gave support to the formation of Catholic Action, also the work of Cardijn, in 1925. The movement spread rapidly in France.

The idea of Catholic youth organizations was not a new one there. In the 1880s, Count Albert de Mun had founded the Association Catholique de la Jeunesse, given to large displays and mass meetings. It was led from outside and failed to generate a self-moving internal life. The essence of the JOC was that it sought to develop in young people personal thinking from which action should come. They were not told what to do but had to discover it.

The JOC is federated in regions, within which there are sections. Each section consists of up to forty young people. Their chosen formula is 'See, judge, act'. At a section meeting issues can be brought forward by any member; the agenda is like that of a trade union meeting or that of a caring church. Problems are freely discussed, and personal faith and reading the Gospels enable members to 'see' the problems in the light of Christian values.

A number of sections is gathered into local federations, and the federal system extends to the national level. However, the emphasis is always on the grass roots. The sections are each specialized: all members have the same employment. All treat as essential a living participation in the liturgy, gospel discussion, personal effort in society and in personal life. The leaders are known as militants. They have special meetings of their own and are more completely prepared than the rank and file to give everything. In the words of Cardijn, 'to bring all the young workers and all the world of labour to a realization of its divine origin and destiny'. The nature of the movement is thus three-fold: to educate the young worker, to serve him and to represent him.

It was not until the 1940s that the Young Christian Workers got under way in England, but the movement soon became a vital force throughout the Commonwealth and in the United States. This success was largely due to the energy of Patrick Keegan, which was recognized by his election in 1960 as President of the Mouvement International des Ouvriers Chrétiens.

Roger Aubert, *The Christian Centuries*, vol 5, *The Church in a Secularized Society*, ET 1978; Maisie Ward, *France Pagan?*, 1949.

EDWIN ROBERTSON

Johannine Spirituality

Discussion will be confined to the Fourth Gospel and the Johannine letters. The use of 'John' for the writer(s) of these documents is not intended to prejudge the issue of authorship. The quest for Johannine spirituality must take full account of the literary *genres* involved (a Gospel and three letters), within which John's insights about life in the Spirit may be discerned. To speak of 'Johannine spirituality', or (with Clement of Alexandria, *HE* 6.14.7) of John as a 'spiritual gospel', need not suggest that the Johannine tradition and its interpretation lacks historical basis.

1. *The context of John's spirituality*. All that John says about the gospel of Jesus Christ is ultimately concerned with salvation, for which his normal description is 'eternal life' (cf. John 3.16, 36; I John 1.2). This life is a gift of God (John 17.2; I John 5.11), mediated to the believer through Christ in his incarnation, death, resurrection and exaltation (John 3.14f.; cf. I John 4.14), and made possible in the Spirit (John 3.5, 8; I John 4.13).

John's theology of eternal life takes its particular character from his perception of the sacramental context in which God's saving activity has taken place. For the thought-patterns in the Johannine Gospel and letters are not only symbolic (cf. the 'light-darkness' motif; John 1.4; 8.12; I John 1.5–7); they are also sacramental. This means essentially that John views all Christian experience as deriving from a unique conjunction of the material and the spiritual

in the Word made flesh (John 1.14; cf. I John 1.1–3). Jesus is one in being with God (John 10.30; cf. I John 5.20); he is also 'flesh', and thus one with man (John 1.14; cf. I John 4.2; II John 7). From the decisive moment of the incarnation, therefore, history assumes a new meaning. As the seven 'signs' of the Fourth Gospel illustrate so tellingly, the temporal becomes the potential carrier of the eternal. Jesus made God known in a new way; now, in a new way, man can know God, and live in him and for him (John 1.18; 17.3; cf. 6.63; see also I John 4.12).

This christological focus is the basis of John's teaching about the work of Christ. Because Jesus participated fully in the two natures, human and divine, his death and exaltation (his 'glorification', John 17.5) became the means by which believers could pass from death to life (John 5.24; I John 3.14), enabling them to walk in the light and live as children of God (the twin themes of I John).

2. *The content of John's spirituality*. A leading category which John uses to interpret Christian experience is that of 'abiding'. The dynamic unity between God the Father and Jesus his Son (John 14.10) is the source of the believer's ongoing unity with God (John 17.21; I John 4.15f.), Christ (John 15.4f.; I John 2.24) and the Spirit (John 4.23f.; I John 4.2). It is also the basis of unity between the believer and other Christians (John 17.11). Equally, the spiritual life of the Christian is nourished by the abiding presence in the believer of God (John 14.23; I John 4.15f.), Christ (John 14.18–20; I John 3.24) and the Spirit (John 14.16; I John 4.13).

To express *in nuce* the infinite truth that regenerate humanity can share in the divine life of eternity (cf. John 3.5, 8), John uses the language of 'love' (John 14.21; I John 4.8f.). In his hands such language encapsulates the profound mystery of reciprocal abiding, both human and divine: 'God is love, and he who abides in love abides in God, and God abides in him' (I John 4.16). Evelyn Underhill* regards this as 'John's most characteristic contribution to the interpretation of the Christian life'. (*The Mystic Way*, p. 252). She goes on:

His was that piercing vision which discovered that the Spirit of Love is one with the Spirit of Truth, and that only those who love will ever understand. It was this which definitely established the essentially mystic character of Christian faith.

In the believer's experience of God, John regards three elements as fundamental.

(i) *Worship*. The *locus classicus* in the Fourth Gospel for a consideration of Christian worship is John 4.19–26, where Jesus speaks of the necessity of worshipping God 'in spirit and truth' (vv. 23f.). This does not refer to purely 'internal', as opposed to external, worship; for worship in the Johannine community, as in the NT church generally, included such 'external' activities as prayers and scriptural exposition (inherited from the Jewish synagogue), as well as the rites of baptism and the eucharist (Acts 2.42). Rather, the contrast between worship in Jerusalem or on Mount Gerizim, and worship in spirit (which includes the spirit of man, but primarily denotes the Spirit of God), recalls the familiar Johannine distinction between the dimensions of earth and heaven. Jesus is saying that the Spirit given by him inspires the worship which replaces the religious observances of the Temple (cf. John 2.13–22). The Father can be worshipped worthily through the regenerating Spirit (John 3.5), who is also the Spirit of truth (John 14.16f.; 15.26; I John 5.6).

John's teaching on prayer is closely related. In Johannine terms, the practice and results of prayer flow from the intimate relationship ('abiding') which the Christian shares with God through Jesus and by the Spirit. Proximity to the Father (John 16.23–27), the Son (16.16) and the Paraclete (14.17) results in the privilege of answered petition (16.23; cf. I John 3.21f.; 5.14f., where 'confidence' in this respect is an added thought). Such requests, asked and given in the name of Jesus (John 16.23f.), are concerned not only with the needs of daily living but also with the deepening of spirituality through the Paraclete (16.23a, 25). The prayer of consecration in John 17 (close to the Lord's prayer in the synoptic tradition), in which Jesus prays for himself and the church and the world, offers a model for all Christian intercession.

(ii) *Service*. Christian spirituality in John is not only devotional; it is also practical. The followers of Jesus are invited to serve, as well as worship. The paradigm of service in the Fourth Gospel is the occasion of the feet washing (John 13), in the course of which John reports that Jesus gave his followers an example of sacrificial humility. In that context the action of Jesus is inextricably related to his death and exaltation. In his spirit of self-offering, it is concluded, the disciples of Jesus are to respect others, and to demonstrate their mutual love empirically (13.34–35). On occasions this may even involve the ultimate sacrifice (15.12–13; I John 3.11–18; see also II John 5–6; III John 5–6). John demonstrates throughout that the means, as well as the supreme example, of such service can be found in Jesus himself, who came from God (John 13.3; 17.5, 8), and who promised the presence and power of the Spirit to his disciples before he returned to the Father (cf. John 14.16f.; 16.7; 17.11).

(iii) *Mission*. According to the Fourth Evangelist, the believer who worships God and serves the brotherhood is also sent out to bring the good news of life in Jesus to the world. John's special contribution to the theology of Christian mission is to show that the Father's sending of the Son provides both the model and basis for the Son's sending of the disciples (John 20.21; cf. 21.1–19). There is also a close connection in Johannine thought between the mission of the disciples and the gift of the empowering Spirit (John 20.22; cf. 15.26–27). Thus the mission and ministry of Christians, like that of Jesus himself, become salvific (John 6.39–40; cf. 20.31; see also I John 5. 11–13; III John 7).

Each of the three major aspects of Christian spirituality present in the teaching of John (worship, service and mission) derives from the intimate Christ-Christian relationship which is fundamental to his theology of salvation. (The spiritual life of the believer is made possible by the incarnation and glorification of Jesus, and sustained by 'abiding' in him as he abides in the Father.) The ministry of the Spirit (of God and of Jesus) is closely associated with the Christian's experience at all three points. This reminds us that John's soteriology is corporate, as well as individual; for the Spirit brings the believer into a dimension of new life shared by the whole church (John 3.1–8; 14.16f.; I John 3.24). Similarly, eternal life in John is present, as well as future (3.16–

21; 5.21–29; cf. I John 3.1–2); for Christian spirituality is initiated here, even if it is consummated hereafter.

C. K. Barrett, *The Gospel according to St John*, ²1978; R. E. Brown, *The Gospel according to John*, 2 vols, 1971; *The Community of the Beloved Disciple*, 1979; *The Johannine Epistles*, 1982; C. H. Dodd, *The Interpretation of the Fourth Gospel*, 1953; R. Law, *The Tests of Life: a Study of the First Epistle of St John*, 1909; E. Malatesta, *Interiority and Covenant: a study of* einai en *and* menein en *in the First Letter of Saint John*, 1978; S. S. Smalley, *John: Evangelist and Interpreter*, 1978; *1, 2, 3 John*, 1984; E. Underhill, *The Mystic Way: a Psychological Study in Christian Origins*, 1913; B. F. Westcott, *The Epistles of St John*, 1966.

S. S. SMALLEY

John of the Cross, St

Spanish saint and mystic, born 1542 in Fontiveros, Castille. He became a Carmelite *c.* 1564 and studied at the Carmelite College in Salamanca, one of Europe's foremost universities, where his thorough grounding in philosophy and scholastic theology was to be invaluable for his analysis of mystical experience.

His meeting with Teresa of Avila* in 1567, the year of his ordination, proved decisive. She enlisted him to promote her reform of the Order by returning to the rigorous primitive rule among the friars, and he founded fifteen such Discalced houses, the first at Duruelo (1568), where he became John of the Cross. Like Teresa, he spent the rest of his life in the service of the Reform, exercising wide responsibilities within it. The hostility of the unreformed, however, led to his arrest and solitary confinement in the Carmelite monastery at Toledo in December 1577. When he escaped, on a dark night eight months later, he brought with him a number of poems; more followed, with commentaries on the three most important, the *Spiritual Canticle**, the *Ascent of Mount Carmel* and the *Dark Night of the Soul* (in reality a single unfinished treatise), and the *Living Flame of Love*. He appears to have stopped writing in the mid-1580s, and died in 1591, after further disputes resulted in his banishment to a remote Andalusian monastery. He was widely read in mediaeval mystical literature, and his works, which he never

intended for publication (the first complete edition appearing only in 1630), make constant and searching use of the Bible. But the fame of his sanctity spread widely: he was beatified 1675, canonized 1726 and proclaimed a Doctor of the Church 1926.

His poems are among the supreme lyrical creations of Spanish literature, haunting, passionate and with an exuberance of imagery unequalled in his time. They are written in a cultured five-line stanza, the *lira*, though some of his lesser poems use traditional Spanish forms like the ballad and the *copla*. The *Canticle* and *Flame* commentaries follow the poetic text closely, while the *Ascent* and *Dark Night* is a more formal, systematic treatise on mystical prayer, loosely based on the poem 'On a dark night'.

This dark night* is the most famous of all St John's symbols, deriving ultimately from Denys the Areopagite, but extended and deepened. It comes to both senses and spirit, in an active and a passive form. The active nights deal with the soul's own preparation for contemplation and union, the corresponding passive nights with what God alone can work in the infusion of these gifts. The passive night of the spirit, in which the absence of God is most grievously experienced, becomes nonetheless the threshold of union, the darkest part of the night which precedes the dawn. The nights are not to be thought of sequentially, since aspects of them may be experienced together.

The twentieth century has witnessed a growing appreciation of St John's poetry, and his mystical treatises have come to exercise a commanding influence on Christian spirituality among Christians of many traditions and beyond Christianity itself.

The Complete Works of St John of the Cross tr E. Allison Peers, 3 vols, revd edn 1953; A Benedictine of Stanbrook Abbey, *The Mediaeval Mystical Tradition and St John of the Cross*, 1954; G. Brenan, *St John of the Cross: His Life and Poetry*, 1973; E. W. Trueman Dicken, *The Crucible of Love*, 1963; E. Allison Peers, *Spirit of Flame*, 1943.

COLIN P. THOMPSON

John XXIII

Born Angelo Giuseppe Roncalli at Bergamo

1542 – 1591.

on 25 November 1881 and baptized the same day. A pious boy, he was permitted to receive communion at the age of seven and was confirmed a year later. He carried with him throughout his advancement from child to priest, bishop to papal delegate, cardinal to Pope, a simple, old-fashioned piety. He was a child of the nineteenth-century revival of mediaeval piety, sometimes insipid and infantile, but closely centred upon the earthly Christ and his mother. His devotion to the Blessed Virgin Mary consistently accompanied his desire for purity.

He was ordained priest in 1904 and ten years later, he gives thanks to God in words that reveal his emerging spirituality: 'Ten years ago, when for the first time I celebrated the sacrifice of the Mass over the tomb of St Peter in Rome – oh blessed memory! – I had for the Pope and for the church one great thought, one fervent prayer. During these ten years that thought and that prayer have grown ever more insistent. "O Lord, in these days of storm and amidst the clash of nations, give your church liberty, unity and peace."'

A year later, he was called up and served in the Italian army. After his war service, which he called his 'Babylonian captivity', he was appointed spiritual director of the seminary in Bergamo. He developed his simple discipline of devotions into a lifelong attachment to the *Spiritual Exercises* * of St Ignatius *. His motto became 'obedience and peace'. He developed his passion for unity during his next appointment as Papal Representative in Bulgaria (1925–1934), resuming contact with the Orthodox Churches, a role which continued as his area changed to Turkey and Greece. With great appreciation he absorbed Eastern spirituality. His education was continued as papal nuncio in secularized Paris (1944–1953). Although not a progressive he learned there to appreciate the serious Christian intent of the radical Catholic priests. Finally, before becoming Pope in 1958 he was head of the Diocese of Venice.

Believing that evangelical simplicity was to be preferred to Byzantine subtlety, he delighted to make 'complicated things simple'. His habit was 'not to issue instructions straight off about how an affair was to be settled, but to wait for various proposals and estimates of their success before reaching a conclusion'. His papacy and particularly the Second Vatican Council * gave liberty to the church; his constant activities in Eastern countries and the larger vision during his Paris days led him to set the church on the reforming path in a pastoral direction with the hope of encouraging the reunion of the churches; when he realized he had only a short time to live, he determined part of the later deliberations of the Council he had called, but was not to see the end of, by issuing on 11 April 1963 the encyclical *Pacem in Terris*, which sounded a new note of potential harmony between East and West. He died on 3 June 1963.

___

John Paul XXIII, *Journal of a Soul*, ET 1965.

EDWIN ROBERTSON

Johnson, Samuel

Samuel Johnson (1709–1784) was born at Lichfield and moved to London in 1737 where he earned his living by writing. His works include a tragedy, poetry, literary criticism, essays and biography as well as the *Dictionary* and an edition of Shakespeare. Johnson experienced religious doubts in adolescence, but on reading Law's *Serious Call to a Devout and Holy Life* found Law an 'overmatch' for him and he continued afterwards to be profoundly interested in religion. He was staunchly Anglican, critical of Roman Catholicism and Dissent and suspicious of 'Enthusiasm', though not devoid of intense religious feeling himself.

Johnson defines spirituality as 'pure acts of the soul'. Towards the end of his life he collected copies of his prayers and meditations and gave them to the Revd G. Strahan, who published them in 1785. Johnson obviously thought of them as available for others' use, in spite of their origin in particular events of his own life. He formed the practice of composing prayers for New Year's Day, his own birthday, Good Friday, Easter Day and after his wife's death, for each anniversary. His prayers at the deathbeds of close friends and servants are among his most moving. Although Johnson's comments on his own spiritual life often make painful reading because he is so fearful of judgment and morbidly aware of his own failings, most of his prayers, with their measured phraseology reminiscent of the collects of the Book of Common Prayer, give stately expression to universal Christian aspirations. He regards prayer as 'a reposal of myself upon God and a resignation of all into his holy hand' (October 1765). Johnson is acutely aware of the need for mercy, often doubting his own worthiness, but he eventually expresses greater confidence though never complacency.

Johnson was well-read in the theologians and preachers of the sixteenth and seventeenth centuries, particularly admiring Hooker, Jeremy Taylor,* South (in spite of occasional verbal 'coarseness') and Samuel Clarke (in spite of his unorthodoxy). He composed forty or more sermons himself (not all extant), many of them for the Revd John Taylor who preached them at St Margaret's Westminster. Johnson was paid but made no claim to authorship. His sermons are clear, dignified and moral stressing primarily the necessity for repentance. His belief in the mercy of God is profound and he emphasizes that 'the mercy of God extends not only to those that have made his will, in some degree, the rule of their actions . . . but even to those that have polluted themselves with studied and premeditated wickedness' (*Sermons*). Several sermons stress the necessity of charity: 'It is sufficient that our brother is in want, by which way he brought his want upon him let us not too curiously enquire . . . no man is so bad as to lose his title to Christian kindness.' For all Johnson's fears, scruples and melancholy his sermon on holy communion affirms that 'Heaven itself will be accessible to many who have died in their struggles with sin.'

Johnson's prayers and sermons contain little relaxed joy, little serenity, but they document memorably both strongly felt unworthiness and strongly expressed faith.

The Yale Edition of the Works of Samuel Johnson, 1958–, esp vols I and XIV; W. J. Bate, *Samuel Johnson*, 1978; C. F. Chapin, *The Religious Thought of Samuel Johnson*, 1968; J. Gray, *Johnson's Sermons*, 1972; G. B. Hill (ed), *Boswell's Life of Johnson*, 6 vols, 1934–1950; M. J. Quinlan, *Samuel Johnson. Layman's Religion*, 1964.

ELUNED BROWN

Journal, Spiritual

Within the Judaeo-Christian tradition, the prototype for spiritual journal writing is sacred scripture. These writings reflect the soul-searching of a whole people: its fears, its doubts, its hopes, its struggles, its discoveries, its prayers, its most treasured experiences, its time-tested beliefs and traditions, its relationship to God and the world, its innermost sense of life's meaning and purpose. In brief, these writings reflect the story of a believing people's pilgrimage towards God. Some of these writings take an intimate and highly personal form, such as certain sections from the prophets and psalms, and many passages from the letters of Paul. Others take a more objective and even anonymous form, such as some of the historical and legal passages, and the Synoptic Gospels. However, all of them are recognized by the community of believers as authentic reflections of its corporate autobiography.

When sacred scripture is taken as the prototype, spiritual journal writing takes on a much broader scope than is customarily attributed to it. 1. Regardless of the form it takes, it is then seen basically to be an exercise in spiritual autobiography, an honest chronicling of the search for, and the discovery of, how God acts in human life. 2. It admits of a multiplicity of purposes, just as sacred scripture was written, sometimes to chronicle current events; sometimes to remember or reconstruct past experiences; sometimes to plumb the depths of the heart in prayer; sometimes to envision an unseen future; sometimes to edify, instruct, correct or inform others. 3. It admits of a multiplicity of literary forms, just as sacred scripture includes stories, prophecies, laws, proverbs, letters, songs, prayers, sermons, dreams, visions, and so forth. 4. It is capable of combining, in a symbiotic way, the secular and the sacred, as well as the personal and the communal, just as sacred scripture does. From these characteristics, it can be seen how important it is to keep the prototype of sacred scripture in mind, if we are to appreciate the full scope of journal writing as a spiritual discipline.

Among the Fathers of the Church, it is St Augustine* who best personifies the importance of journal writing as a discipline for spiritual growth. In his *Soliloquies*, Augustine tells how a voice prompted him to write down his innermost thoughts and discoveries so that he might become still more animated in his search for truth. When the voice finally asks what it is he wishes to know through all of his searching, Augustine replies, 'I desire to know God and the soul.' The 8,000 or so pages which remain of Augustine's writings over the next four decades of his life attest the depth of this desire and the seriousness of Augustine's response. The *Confessions* remain the most celebrated and the most influential fruit of Augustine's dedication to the discipline of spiritual journal writing, but they are by no means its only fruit. To the *Confessions* must certainly be added his early apologetic works, his highly personal commentaries on sacred scripture, his voluminous correspondence, his homilies and his *Retractions*, if not his *opera omnia* as a whole. The life and works of Augustine go hand in hand. For him, journal writing was not merely one among many literary forms. It was a privileged personal forum for spiritual growth and ministry.

Within the monastic tradition, journal writing frequently finds its place as a spiritual exercise which expresses the monk's attempts to internalize the sacred scriptures. It often takes the form of prayerful commentaries or sermons on a biblical text or of letters of spiritual direction. Some of the writings of St Bernard* (1153), William of Saint-Thierry* (1148), and St Bonaventure* (1274) exemplify this tradition.

Among the mystics, and within the Reformation tradition, the emphasis on personal religious experience gives journal writing a place of special prominence as a spiritual discipline. The journals of the Pilgrims and Quakers (especially George Fox*) give eloquent witness to this renewal as well as to the re-emergence of the Augustinian model of autobiography. It has even been claimed that the writing of a journal was the Puritan substitute for the confessional. While this claim may be exaggerated, the spiritual diary and the autobiographical meditation (e.g. Bunyan's *Grace Abounding*) remain distinctive marks of Puritanism*. Other examples would include the diaries, autobiographies, or spiritual treatises of Egeria (*c.* 384), Meister Eckhardt* (1327–1328), Julian of Norwich* (1416/23), St Ignatius of Loyola* (1556), St Teresa of Avila* (1582), Blaise Pascal* (1662), John Henry Newman* (1890) and Thérèse of Lisieux* (1897).

The soul-searching of the nineteenth and twentieth centuries and the emergence of psychoanalysis have served to highlight the importance of journal writing both as a channel for self-understanding and as a distinct literary form. Some find this modern form of journal writing to be too literary, too self-centred, and too secular to be considered spiritual. On the other hand, such writing can be seen to be foundational for the renaissance in journal writing as a spiritual discipline which is being experienced by the second half of the twentieth century. This renaissance is reflected in journals such as those of Anne Frank, Pope John XXIII*, and Dag Hammarskjøld*, personified in the writings of the late Trappist monk, Thomas Merton*, and mirrored in an increasing number of books and articles on the techniques of journal writing. Even more fundamentally, this renaissance shows promise of being perpetuated by the pioneering work Ira Progoff has done in developing a comprehensive methodology for journal writing as a discipline for spiritual growth.

A. Boland, 'Journal Spirituel', *DS*, VIII, cols 1434–43; H. Brinton, *Quaker Journals: Varieties of Religious Experience Among Friends*, 1972; I. Progoff, *At a Journal Workshop*, 1975; *The Practice of Process Meditation*, 1980; T. Rainer, *The New Diary: How to Use a Journal for Self-Guidance and Expanded Creativity*, 1979; F. Vernet, 'Autobiographies spirituelles', *DS*, I, cols 1141–1159.

FRANCIS DORFF, O PRAEM

Journey, Second

A midlife experience which can happen to people in their thirties, forties or even fifties. As such it is a natural phenomenon (exemplified classically by the midlife journeys of Aeneas and Ulysses), but it can be integrated into one's spiritual growth. We see that in the stories of Christians like Dante Alighieri, Dietrich Bonhoeffer*, Ignatius Loyola*, John Henry Newman* and John Wesley*.

The characteristic pattern of second journeys includes the following six features. 1. Something happens to break up the settled pattern of a person's existence. The catalyst can take such forms as exile, sickness, some major disappointment or simply boredom over successfully achieved goals. 2. An outer journey expresses and creates the context of the real, interior journey. 3. Loneliness marks second journeys. 4. Such journeys entail a profound crisis of feelings. 5. They involve a search for new meanings, fresh values and different goals. Those values which have so far supported life no longer satisfy the travellers – at least not in their present form. 6. Ideally the end of a second journey brings a self-knowledge and strength that lets people integrate their existence and reach out productively to enrich their world.

Such midlife pilgrimages will turn out to be an Aeneid or an Odyssey: leading either to a second career in a new setting or to a reaffirmation in a new way of one's original calling. In other words, journey's end will see the pilgrims moving like Abraham, Aeneas or Ignatius Loyola to their new place, or else going home like Moses, Ulysses or Kate Brown (in Doris Lessing's novel, *The Summer Before the Dark*).

In an unpublished 1973 Harvard University dissertation in English literature, Bridget Puzon created the term 'second' or 'midlife journey' and identified a number of its characteristics in works of John Bunyan, Joseph Conrad and Tobias George Smollett.

Occasionally in the writings of St Basil and other Church Fathers the term 'second voyage' (*deuteros plous*) occurs – as a proverb applied to those who fail in their first project and shift to another. Such a 'second voyage' would then take the form of an *Aeneid* or movement to a different place and project.

'Second *conversion*' is a theme which goes back through Louis Lallemant (1587–1635) to Clement of Alexandria (c. 150–215). In the case of those like Bonhoeffer, Newman and Wesley, a second journey coincided with their second conversion. In their teens or twenties they had undergone a first conversion. Then a fresh call, experienced in midlife, led them to a fresh and powerful dedication. However, the case of Ignatius Loyola illustrates how a second journey need not take the form of a second conversion. What happened to him in these middle years did *not* come after some earlier, decisive episode of commitment which we would call his first conversion.

H. Pinard de la Boullaye, 'Conversion, secondes conversions', *DS*, II–2, cols 2259–65; G. O'Collins, *The Second Journey*, 1978.
GERALD O'COLLINS, SJ

Certainly it!
fits Wesley.

Journey, Spiritual
see **Catharsis; Creation-Centred Spirituality; Pilgrimage; Unitive Way**

Joy *see* **Fruit of the Spirit**

Julian of Norwich

Julian of Norwich c. 1342–1420, the most popular of English mystics, lived as an anchorite beside St Julian's church in Norwich, from which she probably took her name. The original church, destroyed by bombing in 1942, has been restored as a place of prayer by the Anglican Sisters of All Hallows, Ditchingham. Little is known about Julian's life, though she is mentioned in bequests and by her contemporary, Margery Kempe of Lynn. In the later Middle Ages many people found an answer to their religious needs by becoming recluses rather than by joining the regular religious orders. This was particularly marked in East Anglia, and in Flanders, with which Norwich had commercial links. From the thirteenth century to the Reformation fifty hermits and anchorites are recorded for Norwich and about thirteen for Lynn, which compared well with London, where there were about twenty. Norwich is the only English city known to have contained informal sisterhoods, or beguinages. Julian experienced the first of her visions on 8 May 1373, and her reflective interpretation in the *Revelations of Divine Love* took many years to complete. She is now remembered on 8 May in the Anglican Calendar, and Julian Groups drawn from many churches use her Meditations as a springboard for silent prayer.

The *Revelations of Divine Love* in two versions, longer and shorter, entitle Julian to be regarded as the first English woman of letters, and one of the greatest woman church teachers. Taken seriously ill, she prayed for a bodily sign of Christ's passion. Subsequently she received her sixteen Revelations. Despite her conventional disclaimer 'I am a woman, unlettered, feeble and frail', her book is in vigorous English prose combining French and Anglo-Saxon culture in a style very much her own. She had been well trained in biblical thought, especially St Paul and St John, and she had some knowledge of patristic theology and of the writing of Denys the Areopagite *. Her lively images – the hazel nut, the clothes blown in the wind, the vision of the sea bed – suggest that as she reflected on life around her in East Anglia, she saw God at work in his world; this approach inspires those who unite theological and ecological insights. She described the drops of blood from Christ's head as 'round like a herring's scales'.

Julian bases theology on mystical experience, the primacy of love in the relationship with God and with each other, the importance of being able to pray to God the Father and to Jesus Christ, and to our mother as well as to our father and our Lord. She wrote of the homeliness and courtesy of God. These insights have made her work a handbook of patience, to which many Christians fully committed in secular professions scurry for encouragement, using it not as a systematic treatise but as a source of hope in their Mother God, their courteous Lord. Julian heard the words, 'I am the foundation of your praying.' After fifteen years reflection she concluded that the Lord was saying to her 'You would know our Lord's meaning in this thing, know it well. Love was his meaning ... Hold on to this and you will know and understand love more and more, but you will not know or learn anything else – ever!'

She sees that the attributes of God are life, love and light. The nature of the Holy Trinity as revealed by Christ to Julian is always creative, redemptive and enabling. His is an unprotected love, never coercive or destructive. The essential pre-condition of all love is humility. (This is something the *magisterium* of the church has always failed to understand, but of course Julian does not say this!) She believed that though sin was inevitable, we are given an imperishable godly will by which we can assent to and respond to the essential rightness of things. God is loving and forgiving. She was delivered from shallow optimism by her own experience of suffering in the anxious days in which she lived, the Black Death, social unrest in East Anglia and the Wyclif-ite challenge. In his redemptive act, Christ is at one with the suffering of all men and indeed all nature and his salvation is planned for all creation. She says: 'For in mankind that shall be saved is comprehended all that is made and the maker of all: for in man is God and so in men is all.' Her story of the servant, the cosmic but anonymous Christ, is her recognition of the human dilemma.

But she concludes that 'All shall be well and all shall be well, and all manner of thing shall be well.' She is a joyous mystic, stressing the homely love of God which has been poured upon this planet and mankind from all eternity.

See also **English Mystics, The.**

Revelations of Divine Love, tr Clifton Wolters, 1966; *Julian of Norwich Showings*, tr Edmund College and James Walsh, 1978; Frank Sayer (ed), *Julian and her Norwich*, 1973; Alan Webster (ed), *A Light in the Darkness*, 1980.

ALAN WEBSTER

Kabbalah
see **Jewish Spirituality, Judaism**

Keble, John
Poet, priest and one of the progenitors of the Oxford Movement*, John Keble (1792–1866) came from a High Anglican, Tory background. Formed by the spirituality of the Caroline Divines*, the Nonjurors* and Bishop Butler, Keble gained high honours at Oxford, becoming a Fellow of Oriel College and subsequently for a time Professor of Poetry in the University. The greater part of his life was spent as parish priest of Hursley near Winchester in Hampshire where, like his seventeenth-century counterpart, George Herbert*, he was an outstanding example of pastoral care. He edited the works of Richard Hooker, and Thomas Wilson, the eighteenth-century Bishop of Sodor and Man, whom he revered as an outstanding example of pastoral episcopacy.

As a Fellow of Oriel, imbued with a high pastoral ideal of the tutorial office, Keble had a marked influence on John Henry Newman*, Isaac Williams, and Robert Isaac Wilberforce, who revered him as an example of saintly life. Through his collection of poems, *The Christian Year* (1827), which was based on the Sundays, Festivals and services of the Prayer Book, Keble's influence spread more widely. In these poems, and in his other writings, the sacramental character of Christian spirituality was stressed and a renewed interest was kindled in the typological interpretation of scripture. Although influenced by contemporary Romantic interest in image and symbol, Keble looked primarily to the Fathers and the Caroline Divines for his inspiration, and he defended the patristic understanding of scripture in his tract, *On the Mysticism attributed to the Fathers of the Church*. In his tract of 1857, *On Eucharistic Adoration*, Keble maintained the doctrine of the Real Presence of Christ in the eucharistic elements and the legitimacy of worship being given to that Presence: 'wherever Christ is, there he is to be adored'.

With his brother Thomas, Keble stressed the discipline of the daily office and encouraged its revival, as well as more frequent celebrations of the eucharist, even though his own liturgical practice remained very restrained in comparison with the later Ritualists. He urged the importance of sacramental confession as a normal part of the Christian life, and was himself much used as a confessor, notably by Pusey * (*see* **Penitence**). Together with Newman * and Pusey, Keble shared an emphasis, derived from the Greek Fathers, on the Christian life as a discipline and devotion through which God imparted his grace in order that Christians might share in his own divine life.

G. Battiscombe, *John Keble: a Study in Limitations*, 1963; W. J. A. M. Beek, *John Keble's Literary and Religious Contribution to the Oxford Movement*, 1959; B. W. Martin, *John Keble, Priest, Professor and Poet*, 1976; S. Prickett, *Romanticism and Religion: the Tradition of Coleridge and Wordsworth in the Victorian Church*, 1976; G. Rowell, *The Vision Glorious*, 1983.

GEOFFREY ROWELL

Kempe, Marjorie
see **English Mystics, The**

Kenosis

The concept of *kenosis* is as important for spirituality as it is for christology. Paul of Tarsus in Phil. 2 pictures the incarnation as a process of self-emptying, self-giving in love and probably bases his picture on the act of pouring out in the libations of sacrificial procedure. It is interesting that the imitation of Christ * in Paul is referred for its model not to the historical life of Christ, but to the dimensions of divine humility and self-sacrifice discerned in the process of incarnation * as such. Behind Phil. 2 there is probably some reference to the historical course of the life of Jesus as a basis for this presentation of Christ as the new Adam who unlike the old Adam 'did not think it something to be snatched at to be equal to God but emptied himself'.

Kenosis has been used as a category for interpreting the doctrine of the incarnation in Jesus of Nazareth and particularly for emphasizing that the end product of that process was a veritable human being. In Russian Orthodox theology it has been used also as a way of interpreting the creation of God and the creativity of man: the creation of God being seen as a case of God limiting himself by making the realities of finite time and space real to himself and endowing humanity with a genuine freedom. In Russian thought *kenosis* is a most appropriate term for elucidating human creativity because of the kind of self-giving involved in the work of the artist. 'In his creative work the artist forgets about himself, about his own personality, and renounces himself' (N. Berdyaev).

This *kenosis*, or self-givingness, on the part of God in creation and incarnation has been taken up in modern theology notably in the work of Dietrich Bonhoeffer *, who in a famous sentence said, 'God allows himself to be edged out of the world and on to the cross, and the God who makes us live in this world without using him as a working hypothesis is the God before whom we are ever standing.' *Kenosis* is also an important category in the theology and spirituality of Teilhard de Chardin * who speaks of the historical incarnation as 'kenosis into matter' and thinks of the eucharist as the symbol of this.

Progressive de-selfing by means of gradual detachment from egotism and self-regard has always been one of the features of Christian spirituality and it is interesting to compare this emphasis with the importance attached in both Hinduism and Buddhism to the disciplining of egotistical desires prompted by the false self and the progressive attachment to the self-giving and self-denial necessary in order to enable the true self to come into being.

The Christian life in grace can be seen as a *kenosis* of the Holy Spirit and the historical Jesus of Nazareth appears in one way as the Spirit moulding human nature after the image of the eternal Son. Christian life therefore is in its inconceivable variety the

Holy Spirit's kenotic way of moulding fresh individual versions of the inexhaustible image of Christ.

D. Bonhoeffer, *Letters and Papers from Prison*, ³1971, has some seminal thoughts on *kenosis* in doctrine and practice; N. Berdyaev, *Destiny of Man*, 1937, illustrates Russian Orthodox thought on *kenosis* and human creativity; Teilhard de Chardin's ideas on the incarnation as '*kenosis* into matter' are to be found in the chapter 'My Universe' in *Science and Christ*, 1965.

E. J. TINSLEY

Kierkegaard, Søren

Søren Kierkegaard (1813–1855) described himself as a poet in the service of Christianity. But instead of poems in the usual sense he wrote an extremely varied 'literature' which included psychology (*The Concept of Anxiety, The Sickness Unto Death*), literary criticism (*Either/Or*, Vol I, *Two Ages*), social criticism (*Two Ages*), ethical discourse (*Either/Or*, Vol II), philosophical polemics (*Philosophical Fragments, Concluding Unscientific Postscript*), and Bible exposition (*Works of Love, Christian Discourses, Practice in Christianity*). He wrote a number of works under various pseudonyms such as the Watchman of Copenhagen, John the Climber, and Hilarius Bookbinder. But there was, he contended, a single purpose running through it all, and that was to 're-introduce Christianity to Christendom'.

Until recently Kierkegaard was widely regarded as 'the father of existentialism', and interpreted with the help of concepts deriving from philosophers like Martin Heidegger and Jean-Paul Sartre. However, more recent scholarship has appreciated points of fundamental contrast between him and the existentialists, and has sought to interpret him more in the way he interpreted himself – as a Christian writer whose concerns were primarily spiritual.

Kierkegaard was not a systematic theologian or philosopher, nor a scientific interpreter of the Bible; much less did he contrive a new theology which would be acceptable to modern man. He saw his Christian task as that of *correcting* certain spiritual misdirections in Christendom. To people who thought of themselves primarily as members of a race or a nation or an age, rather than as individuals responsible to God, the con-

cepts of sin and grace had become opaque. With people who had managed to turn all of knowledge, including that of ethics and Christianity, into ammunition for lectures and philosophical systems and other intellectual curiosities, it had become next to impossible to communicate spiritual things directly. As Kierkegaard put it, people had 'forgotten what it means to exist' [as a human being]; they had lost the sense of being spiritual creatures.

Consequently many of his writings – ethical, psychological, literary-critical, philosophical, biblical – are aimed at 'awakening' people to their human nature as beings who are made for a relationship with God and whose existence is therefore a momentous matter. If people understand better the urgencies of their own existence, thinks Kierkegaard, they will be more fit to understand the Christian message – for that message addresses serious spiritual concerns.

On this task of 'awakening' the individuals of his age to themselves, Kierkegaard expended his enormous poetical and intellectual powers. He was never content merely to present a theory of human nature – that could too easily be assimilated to the spiritual degeneracies of his age. He always sought to present his ideas so that they would make the deepest impression possible on the reader. To this end he employed irony and humour, embedded spiritual truths in fascinating aesthetic contexts, used exaggeration and understatement, metaphor and parable, and spoke indirectly through the mouths of his pseudonyms.

Kierkegaard also wrote correctively in a more theological manner. Through the philosophy of Hegel a number of the central concepts of Christianity had been distorted. In particular the concepts of sin and salvation and therefore of Jesus as the saviour had been so altered that the outlook of anyone who tried to live his life by them could hardly resemble the Christian outlook. Kierkegaard's book *Philosophical Fragments*, in which he elaborates the contrast between Christ and the Socratic (that is, Idealist) concept of a teacher, is perhaps the clearest example of this more theological sort of correction in the service of Christianity.

But all of Kierkegaard's major writings, whether more 'theological' or more 'awakening', are carefully wrought for their effect on the reader, and the effect sought is the conformity of the mind and heart to the upward call of God in Christ.

ROBERT C. ROBERTS

Kindness *see* **Fruit of the Spirit**

King, Edward

Edward King (1829–1910) was a convinced high churchman in the authentic Tractarian tradition of Oriel College, Oxford. He acknowledged his debt to Charles Marriott (1811–1858), Fellow of Oriel and Newman's disciple, as 'the most Gospel-like man I have ever met'. The Tractarian amalgam of scholarship, pastoral care, concern for the poor, and disciplined devotion, flowered in King's ministry at Cuddesdon College as chaplain (1858) and principal (1863), and equally as professor of pastoral theology at Oxford (1873–1885). He left Oxford for Lincoln to become 'a big curate' (i.e. bishop) in the diocese, where he spent his last twenty-five years. On his consecration he rejoiced that 'it is John Wesley's diocese. I shall try to be the Bishop of the Poor.'

The key to King's character lies in his profound catholicity, which had none of the puritanical severity which sometimes disfigured Tractarianism. His thoroughly English spirituality sets him in the tradition of Aelred of Rievaulx*, Julian of Norwich*, George Herbert*, and Nicholas Ferrar*. This tradition, so warmly pastoral in its blend of doctrine and devotion, homeliness and holiness, comes alive in King's life and teaching: 'I do value so highly a natural growth in holiness, a humble grateful acceptance of the circumstances God has provided for each of us, and I dread the unnatural, forced, cramped ecclesiastical holiness, which is so much more quickly produced, but is so human and so poor' (*Spiritual Letters*). King's character impressed others by its 'rounded normality' in which 'Grace had so intimately mingled with his nature that it was all of one piece. Grace itself had become natural' (H. Scott Holland).

As nature and grace were integrated in him, so were his Englishness and his catholicity. The universal was focused in the particular. He drew on the Bible, Fathers, Schoolmen, Caroline Divines*, Tractarians; but also on nineteenth-century Roman Catholicism – Lacordaire, Dupanloup,

Döllinger, Sailer. Sailer was his special mentor in moral and pastoral theology. He knew Wesley and the Free Church tradition. For confessors he recommended pre-eminently the Bible and good novels.

He longed to heal the breach between churchmen and nonconformists; sympathized with the Methodists particularly; and confessed 'the want of spiritual life in the Church and brotherly love which led them to separate'. His evangelical preaching led Lincolnshire Methodists to say, 'He's nowt but an owd Methody.' Yet his sturdy Catholic Anglicanism embraced eucharistic devotion, confession, vows, the renewal of the religious life.

King's joy and goodness irradiated his face. His sympathy and gentleness betokened not weakness but restrained strength. Widely recognized as a saint in his lifetime, on 24 May 1935 he was formally acknowledged as one. Archbishop Lang preached in Lincoln cathedral at a solemn eucharist on 'Edward King, Bishop and Saint.' Collect, epistle, and gospel, specially prepared for his commemoration, have been used in the diocese ever since on 8 March, the day of his death.

Lord Elton, *Edward King and Our Times*, 1958; Eric Graham (ed), *Pastoral Lectures of Bishop Edward King*, 1932; John A. Newton, *Search for a Saint: Edward King*, 1977; B. W. Randolph (ed), *Spiritual Letters of Edward King DD*, 1910.

JOHN A. NEWTON

Koinōnia

1. *History*. *Koinōnia* has always been important for Christian spirituality, and is especially so today. It has too many connotations to be captured in a single translation: fellowship, communion, participation, sharing. The root's fundamental meaning is 'sharing in something (genitive) with someone (dative).' Both the Hebrew and Greek Old Testament avoid words for communion to relate God and humans. Paul's synthesis does use OT 'corporate personality' notions.

Paul had the most distinctive and influential usage in the Bible. Pauline *koinōnia* was christocentric, not just companionship or community, nor a synonym for church or local congregation. It meant the union of believers with Christ (esp. I Cor 1.9, 10.16–22 [eucharist], Phil 3.10), in the Spirit (II

Cor 13.13, Phil. 2.1), and hence among one another (Gal. 2.9, cf. Rom. 11.17). The Jerusalem collection embodied this *koinōnia* (II Cor 8.14. Rom 15. 26–27).

I John 1.13 was first to apply *koinōnia* to union with God through Christ. Acts 2.42–47 and other summaries spotlighted the Pentecost community's common life. Thus Acts 4.32–33 (with Heb. 13.16 and Psalm 133.1) became a major text for monastic sharing of goods and common life centered on God through prayer and eucharist. Before the monks, the fathers viewed salvation as *koinōnia* with God, and stressed communion with other churches, especially in the eucharist. The fifth-century Apostles' Creed described the fellowship of all united to Christ by 'communion of saints'. Mediaeval Western Christianity emphasized intercession of saints in heaven and help for those dead not yet perfected. Reformers opposed these approaches.

Post-Reformation schisms eventually occasioned the Ecumenical Movement's search for renewed *koinōnia* among churches. *Koinōnia* today has renewed liturgy and taken such new or diverse forms as social action teams, charismatic and base communities, communities of vowed religious, communes and *kibbutzim*.

2. *Theology*. Already Isocrates (3, 40) had treated the *koinōnia* of one's whole life in marriage as the most comprehensive kind. But the eighteenth-century individualist and twentieth-century collectivist movements have broken down intermediary communities between family and state, impaired family *koinōnia*, and made life today anonymous. Consequent hunger for community has made some people vulnerable to domination by groups. To avoid abuses of *koinōnia* (as through 'total environment' control in brainwashing cults), community must centre on God, not human personalities or causes. It must balance common good with personal dignity, authority with shared responsibility. Communion with leaders of the larger church is a major safeguard.

In scripture, humans are saved not as isolated individuals but as members of God's people (NT, in Christ). Communion with God and others actualizes the human person. Spiritual sharing often leads to material sharing. To serve God's plan, communion may even express itself in common political action (e.g., in Poland and Latin America).

Individuals often find *koinōnia* in genuine community a source of profound conversion. They experience being the Father's adopted children along with others called to God's love. The self-sacrifice and forgiveness needed to preserve *koinōnia* counteract the self-promoting individualism of current culture, and narcissistic introspection in some spiritualities. Mutual accountability and correction protect against spiritual deception, and aid towards Christian maturity, union with God, and service of others.

F. Hauck, '*Koinōnos*', *TDNT*, III, 789–809; L. T. Johnson, *Sharing Possessions: Mandate and Symbol of Faith*, 1981; G. Paniculam, *Koinōnia in the New Testament: A Dynamic Expression of Christian Life*, 1979; H. Seesemann, *Der Begriff Koinōnia im Neuen Testament*, 1933; H. J. Sieben et al., '*Koinōnia*', *DS*, VIII, cols 1743–69.

WILLIAM S. KURZ, SJ

Koran

Al-Qur'ān, the sacred book of Islam*, is regarded by Muslims as the very word of God, its verses being quoted with the phrase 'God said'. The root of the name seems to be 'reading' or 'recitation', and divine instruction to the Prophet Muhammad at his vocation appears in the Koranic verse, 'Recite, in the name of thy Lord who created' (96). The Koran is believed to have been 'sent down' to Muhammad from God directly or through the archangel Gabriel on 'the night of power' (97), traditionally held to have been during the fasting month of Ramadan, and its revelation is celebrated at that time.

Muslims believe that Muhammad was illiterate, that he recited the divine word which was later collected together by scribes from scraps of parchment, bones, pots, leaves and the hearts of men. Some Western scholars consider that the Koran was actually written by Muhammad himself, which would be an unequalled feat in writing the scripture of a world religion. The Koran itself refers to the Jewish and Christian scriptures, Torah and Gospel (Injil) given by God to their communities, and now the divine word comes to the Arab peoples in their own language: 'We have made it an Arabic Koran, and lo, it is in the Mother of the Book in our presence' (43, 2). This may suggest that there is a heavenly source or archetype from which all true scriptures come. Muslims consider that Jews and Christians received the word of God, but misunderstood or distorted it where they disagreed with the Koran.

The Koran is arranged in 114 chapters (*suras*) and after the first short prayer they have been arranged in order of length, the longest first. Yet the later short, often staccato, chapters of judgment are thought to have been composed or revealed first at Mecca and they resemble some biblical prophecies of faith and judgment. The longer chapters reflect more of the Prophet's situation in ruling a growing community at Medina in the closing years of his life, with social and moral as well as religious directions. Every chapter but one opens with the ascription (Bismillah or Basmala) 'In the name of God, the Merciful, the Compassionate'. God is Al-lah, *the* God, properly rendered into English in the singular and with the capital as in Jewish and Christian usage.

The first chapter of the Koran is the Opening, praising God as merciful, compassionate, Lord of the day of judgment, and praying for guidance on the Straight Path. Later in the Koran there are favourite chapters and verses which stand out of mixed contexts. The Throne verse declares, 'Allah, there is no god but He, the living, the eternal . . . His throne extends over heaven and earth' (2, 256). The Light verse has been interpreted, in the West, as suggested by the light of a monastery in the desert: 'God is the light of the heavens and the earth; his light is like a niche in which is a lamp . . . In houses which God has permitted to be raised, and his name remembered therein, glorifying him in the mornings and evenings' (24, 35f.).

The Koran sees true piety not in turning to east or west, but in belief in God, the last day, the Book, angels and prophets, prayer, and giving alms to kinsmen, orphans, travellers, beggars, the needy and ransoming slaves (2, 172). The differences of religion are seen as in the mysterious will of God, but men must rival one another in good works and the truth will be told them at the resurrection (5, 53).

The Koran has some personal references to the life of Muhammad but it is in no sense a biography. The bereaved childhood of the Prophet is given as an example: 'Did he not find thee an orphan and give thee shelter . . . So for the orphan do not oppress him' (93, 6f.). There are sketches of early visions: 'He stood straight on the high horizon, then he drew near . . . He saw him too at a second descent . . . one of the greatest signs of his Lord' (53, 6f.). Muhammad is called 'the Messenger of God and the Seal of the Prophets' (33, 40), perhaps in the sense that he confirmed and sealed the former prophets, though it has been taken that he closed the revelation and was the last and greatest prophet.

'Every nation has its messenger', and the Koran also lists eighteen biblical prophets, from Adam to Jesus, always treating them with respect as also in later Islamic tradition. Moses, David and Jesus are singled out as bringing books. Jesus receives the most honourable titles, being mentioned in fifteen suras and ninety-three verses. His mother Mary is the only woman given her proper name in the Koran. The Virgin Birth is mentioned twice, miracles and teachings are referred to. But the crucifixion is denied in the Koran, perhaps under Docetic influence or with the intention of defending Jesus as Messiah against Jewish critics: 'they did not kill him and did not crucify him . . . God raised him to himself' (4, 156). This statement has caused problems for some modern historically-minded Muslims, and Kamel Hussein in *City of Wrong* (1959) suggests that at least Jesus was crucified in intention but raised to God when the cloud of darkness descended on Calvary. In popular Islamic belief Jesus will return to earth and reign as a just king.

The Koran gives religious teaching and moral instruction, with few prayers. It is the primary authority for faith and life, though traditions and commentary also have a part. But in Muslim devotion the Koran is both lectionary and psalter. Muslim spiritual writings are full of Koranic texts, often used for protective virtues, and its style dominates them. There are many prayer manuals of Koranic verses with some connections of subject arranged for devotional use. Some have been collected and analysed in Constance Padwick's *Muslim Devotions* (1961).

———————————

Arthur J. Arberry, *The Koran Interpreted*,

1964; Geoffrey Parrinder, *Jesus in the Qur'ān*, 1965; W. Montgomery Watt, *Bell's Introduction to the Qur'ān*, 1970.

GEOFFREY PARRINDER

Ladder, Spiritual

The ladder has been a persistent theme in world religions and especially in Christian spirituality. In the latter it has been a figure for progress towards union with God. A pluri-form image, it has been a ladder of virtues, or love, or of contemplation. At times the ladder has been the Virgin Mary, the cross, or often Jesus Christ. The Christian image of the ladder derives principally from the dream of Jacob in which a ladder reached from the ground to the heavens with angels going up and coming down the ladder (Gen. 28.12). This dream affirms a connectedness between earth and heaven, the human and the divine. Later Jesus associated himself with the ladder from Jacob's dream (John 1.51). Commentaries on Genesis have elaborated this theme and numerous treatises have taken it up, often to articulate the steps or stages of the journey to God. Origen * under the influence of Philo first introduced the ladder to post-biblical Christian literature. In the East the best known treatise is *The Ladder of Divine Ascent* of St John Climacus * (d. 649); in the West it is *The Ladder of the Monks* by Guigo II (d. 1188), whose steps of the monastic ascent to God are reading, meditation, prayer, and contemplation. A widely-known text in English is *The Scale of Perfection* of Walter Hilton (d. 1396). In Protestant literature, Luther * and Calvin * among others have used the ladder. Modern criticism of the appropriateness of the ladder as an image for growth in one's relationship with God stems from a literalist, spatial, and individualistic understanding of the ladder. Admittedly, there has been a one-sided emphasis on the ladder as ascent with too little attention paid to the aspect of descent. Thus the ladder has become for some exclusively associated with the apophatic (unknowing) character of the journey to God to the neglect of its cataphatic character (the descending revelation and self-communication of God in creation and the incarnation). The theme of the ladder has had its limitations; yet, it is a rich, symbolic theme that imparts the developmental and progressive qualities of the mystery of God's way to humanity and the human journey to God. At its best, the ladder is an introduction into the mystery of this downward and upward movement which keeps in mind the wisdom of Hericlitus that the way up and the way down are the same way, a truth realized by St John of the Cross * (*Dark Night*, II, 18–20) and T. S. Eliot * in the *Four Quartets* (Prefatory lines).

E. Bertaud and A. Rayez, 'Échelle spirituelle', *DS*, IV–1, cols 62–86; K. J. Egan, 'Guigo II: the Theology of the Contemplative Life', *The Spirituality of Western Christendom* ed E. Rozanne Elder, 1976, pp. 106–115, 200–201.

KEITH J. EGAN

Law, William *see* Nonjurors

Lawrence of the Resurrection

Lawrence of the Resurrection (Nicholas Herman) was a Discalced Carmelite laybrother and mystic. He was born in Hérimesnil, Lorraine, France, in 1611; and he died in Paris on 12 February 1691. After having served in the army for eighteen years and for a time in the service of William de Fruibert, treasurer to the King of France, he entered the Parisian monastery of the Carmelites where he served for thirty years as the community's cook until blindness made this impossible. Surrounded by his Carmelite brethren, he died when he was about eighty years old.

Abbé Joseph de Beaufort, the vicar general of Cardinal de Noailles, collected Lawrence's writing, including sixteen letters, spiritual notes and maxims found in his cell. In addition to this collection, de Beaufort added accounts of the conversations that Lawrence had with him. Four of these discussions are noted beginning with the first on 3 August 1666, and ending with the last on 25 November 1667. In 1691 he published these along with many of Lawrence's sayings.

A study of Lawrence's teaching reveals his thought as informed by the tradition of French spirituality that is found more developed in the writings of the Abbé François de Salignac de la Mothe Fénelon * and the Jesuit Jean-Pierre de Caussade *; yet the humble Carmelite is unsurpassed by these authors. It is obvious that his own experience of the sacred enabled him to explain in simple words profound truths of the interior life.

His concern is that the meaning of life should be grasped; and he stresses the importance of the opportunities of daily life for deepening an awareness of God and the consequent freedom from anxieties that this brings.

Lawrence's doctrine is marked by an insistence on the ability of the self to attain through grace a high state of prayer. Although he avoids the more developed statements of some other mystics, his direct and practical reaching illustrates the ways leading to an awareness of God's presence. It is obvious that he is sharing his own experiences both in pointing out the dangers encountered in distractions and the benefits achieved through a deepening consciousness of God.

In a letter to a priest religious, Lawrence describes his approach to God: 'My most frequent method is simple attentiveness and a loving gaze upon God, to whom I often feel united with more happiness and gratification than that of a baby at its mother's breast. Indeed, such is the inexpressible happiness I have experienced that I would willing call this state "the breasts of God".'

In his letters his teaching is adapted to the problems of daily life, both of those living in the cloister and those in secular society. Three of the extant letters are addressed to lay people while the other thirteen are written to religious. All are informed by the same spirit that stresses the possibility of achieving union with God through the constant practice of prayer.

Nicholas Herman, *The Practice of the Presence of God* tr D. Attwater, 1962.

ADRIAN JAMES COONEY

Lay Spirituality

The greatest lay influence upon the Christian church has been Monasticism*, which it must never be forgotten was a lay movement, though under clerical authority. Relations between the Orders and the hierarchy have never been easy, and the former have often been less rigid and more ecumenical than the secular clergy and the episcopate. But with this commanding exception, it may be asserted that since the time of Jesus and his disciples, who were laymen in his day, the Christian life has been under clerical

control. This may well have been the only way in which the church could advance in the world, maintain the holy tradition and be free from destructive chaos, wild heresy or immovable conservatism, but it has affected spirituality. Would the eucharist* have held its dominant position, or developed as it did in East and West if it had not been a clerical preserve? And have people sometimes been discouraged from attaining their proper spiritual freedom because of a paternalistic, if not jealous, clerisy? The sad, smothered movements of the Middle Ages and the Reformation were predominantly lay, and heterodox, but they are most remarkable because they were an upsurge of the piety and longing of the poor. The greatest iniquity of church history has been the lay–clerical alliance of the rich and powerful. Methodism* has used lay persons to preach and care for the society members, though the Wesleyan Conference until 1932 was controlled by the 'legal hundred' who were all itinerant preachers, not lay. And as with the Quakers*, lay movements soon become 'establishments' and as resistant to change as any others, eager to keep the power that they have won.

Once a person becomes a full-time religious, even if he be a George Fox* – especially if he be a George Fox – he ceases to be, in the true sense of the common usage, lay. The best fruits of lay spirituality in our time, have been the writings of Simone Weil*, and Dag Hammarskjøld's* *Markings*, or the testimonies of the martyrs either of Nazi or Soviet or South African tyranny. But all these were either highly educated and articulate or in circumstances demanding exceptional heroism. Lay spirituality will not often be heard in the streets or the media. It will be written not in books but in souls. And if the influence of mothers, especially those of priests and ministers, be reckoned, it may be claimed that lay spirituality has been paramount in the church after all. Its epitaph and its immortality will be in those ill-carved words of the fourth century from Asia Minor, which Gregory Dix quotes: 'Here sleeps the blessed Chione who has found Jerusalem for she prayed much' (*The Shape of the Liturgy*, 1945).

EDITOR

Leighton, Robert

Of Scottish extraction, Robert Leighton was

born in London in 1611, the son of Alexander Leighton who had graduated at the University of St Andrews in 1587, a Presbyterian minister and a practising physician. Little is known of Robert Leighton's childhood, but in his seventeenth year he entered the University of Edinburgh where he graduated in 1631, academically qualified for the ministry of the Reformed Church. After graduation he spent ten years travelling in England and on the continent where he was influenced by Jansenism* and Port Royal.

Leighton's personal faith was the accepted Calvinism* of his time, with a liberal tendency which made him hospitable to catholic faith and worship. Characterized by Hume Brown as 'rather a Christianized philosopher than a Christian theologian', he was of utilitarian and humanitarian outlook, himself writing that 'religion is not only highly conducive to all that is most desirable in human life, but is also, at the same time, most pleasant and delightful'.

Presented by the Earl of Lothian to the parish of Newbattle in 1641, he was ordained and admitted to the ministry of the Church of Scotland. Often absent on wider church duties, he was respected for his scholarship and piety, although often criticized for his apparent supineness in matters of church polity.

Episcopacy was restored in the (Reformed) Church of Scotland in 1610, and the presbyterian–episcopalian debate and conflict culminated in the National Covenant of 1638. Leighton continued to regard rival systems of church government as largely irrelevant to the work of the Evangel, regarding the pastoral office as preeminent in inculcating prayerfulness and Christian gentleness.

In the deep divisions and bitter controversies of the Covenanting movement, Robert Leighton was only too ready to resign his charge to serve as Principal of the University of Edinburgh from 1658 to 1662, commending his own other-worldly piety to the student body.

Following the Restoration of King Charles II and the re-imposition of episcopacy in the Church of Scotland, Robert Leighton became Bishop of Dunblane appointed in 1661: he was persuaded to accept this office as it was the smallest and most poorly paid of the Scottish sees, for he shrank from anything which savoured of prelacy. His episcopal consecration after re-ordination at Anglican hands in London implied for Leighton no judgment upon Church of Scotland 'orders', but was rather his Erastian acquiescence in the State's ordering of the church in those matters which did not affect a faith concerned with heaven. In the same spirit he accepted appointment in 1672 as Archbishop of Glasgow where he was little in residence before retiring to England, where he remained until his sudden death in London on 25 June 1684.

Leighton's spirituality was that of a gentle peacemaker for Jesus' sake, who regarded the *Imitation of Christ* of Thomas à Kempis* as the best book outside holy scripture. His Christian gentleness modified his understanding of the doctrine of Election, and he shied off any harsh emphasis on Assurance: 'I would have Christians called off from a perplexed over-pressing of this point of their particular assurance.' In an age of intolerance he pled for gentle toleration seeking for routes of escape from the narrowness and bigotry of the times.

Although Leighton regarded church government as of little importance in the realm of the Spirit, yet as bishop he endeavoured to promote an accommodation between the presbyterian and episcopalian systems, clearly valuing the government of presbyteries and synods, while attracted to bishops as permanent moderators, the bishop to be the chief presbyter in ordination. As peacemaker he advocated this compromise for the well-being of the Scottish Church, still viewing polity as very much secondary to faith and worship, devotion and piety. Through his loving and friendly spirit, by his prayerful and devout personal faith, and from his predilection for reverent worship of a catholic sort, Robert Leighton has remained the symbol of possible ecumenical reconciliation between the Church of Scotland and the Episcopal Church in Scotland. His spiritual significance and influence stem from a gentle pastoral emphasis in the understanding of all ministry, and from an ecumenical dimension which he required for the embodiment of the gospel of reconciliation. 'A purer, humbler, holier spirit never tabernacled in Scottish clay' (Robert Flint, 1834–1910). S. T. Coleridge said he was the most inspired writer outside the canonical scriptures. On the tombstone erected in 1857 over his place of burial in Horsted Keynes it is inscribed that 'in an age of utmost strife he adorned the doctrine of God his Saviour by a holy life and by the meek and loving spirit which breathes through his writings'.

Sermons, 1692; Select Works, 1746; E. A. Knox, Robert Leighton, Archbishop of Glasgow, 1930.

R. STUART LOUDEN

Lent

A forty-day season of penitential exercises in preparation for Easter, known (from its length) as Tessarakoste in the Greek Church, Quadragesima in the Latin Church.

1. Origin and Development. A twenty-four hour fast immediately before the celebration of the Christian Passover ('the Paschal Fast') is attested from the earliest times; its proper dating was the subject of the 'Paschal' or 'Quartodeciman Controversy' of the late second century, the underlying issue being the relationship of the Christian community to its Jewish parent body. The forty-day fast, certainly established by the fourth century, is more than a development of the Paschal Fast, but the latter must have provided a precedent for ordering a penitential and preparatory season to a triumphal culmination in the Easter liturgy. The forty-day period is clearly modelled on the fast of Jesus after his baptism, and the association of baptism and its preparation with the Easter festival and its theme of burial with Christ is attested as early as Tertullian (de baptismo) in early third-century Africa. The forty days formed the demanding climax of the early Christian catechumenate. Also from the third century comes evidence of devotional observance of the forty-day preparation season by the baptized members of the church, as an act of intercessory fellowship with their future fellow members. Both the Christian commitment to humility and growth in holiness and the effects of the church's acceptance by civil authority (and apparent compromise with the world) in the fourth century assisted the process by which this sympathetic custom developed into an institutionalized exercise of penitential spiritual renewal for the whole body of believers.

Independently of the growth of Lent, the Paschal Fast developed into the observance of Holy Week. Lent and Holy Week are differently related in East and West. After a complex development, the situation emerged thus: in the East, Lenten fasting claims forty days without Saturdays (Sabbaths) and Sundays before Holy Week; in the West, Lent includes Holy Week and Saturdays are fast days. Hence the shorter Western Lent (although the memory of a longer season was preserved by the name of Septuagesima, the start of the Lent of the clergy). Of the Reformation churches, Lutheranism and Anglicanism kept Lent, but denied meritorious quality to its observance. More radical Reformers questioned its validity altogether. 'Enlightenment' liberalism undermined its traditional status among Protestants generally. The Liturgical Movement brought it back into prominence as a common Christian heirloom, both liturgical and spiritual.

2. Observance. The development of the catechumenate introduced 'scrutinies', days of exorcism, etc., for the baptismal candidates. Of more general concern was the scheme of Sunday readings. The revised Roman lectionary restores a pattern once common to several of the liturgical families: Lent 1, the Temptation; Lent 2, the Transfiguration; Lent 3, the Barren Fig Tree; Lent 4, the Prodigal Son; Lent 5, the Woman taken in Adultery. Lent, liturgically regarded, is a rehearsal of the life of Jesus as the model and source of Christ's life as lived by his disciples, the climax of both being in sacrifice and resurrection. It is quite probable that the four Gospels themselves in their final form are based on this schema, and were designed for preparation for the Christian Passover.

Within the liturgical framework of the life of the congregation, corporate and individual observances of Lent have three elements; fasting* or some other form of renunciation: prayer; and acts of Christian service (almsgiving, etc.). 'Prayer, compassion, fasting – these three are one, and they give each other life. For fasting is the soul of prayer, compassion is the life of fasting. Let no one tear them apart, for they cannot be separated' (St Peter Chrysologus, Sermon 43).

The classical summary of the themes for meditation and for the formation of the soul during Lent is provided by St Leo the Great (*Sermons* 39–50). It is a time of spiritual combat, of exercises in self-control and mastery over temptation and self. It is characterized by confidence in spiritual victory through grace. It is a resolute donning of the Christian's armour. Not only the temptations of the flesh but also the more subtle temptations of the mind, such as wrath and pride, are identified and combatted. It will be a time of struggle, for the tempter will seek to re-possess what he has lost. It represents an opportunity for personal growth, but this personal growth will be reflected in outward goodness and good effects upon others. Lent calls Christians to be better spouses, parents and children, to find a new harmony in their family life. There is a new purity in thought and personal relationships. The special temptations such as self-righteousness and hypocrisy which are attendant upon religious practice will be seen for what they are and confronted. Lent will be an exercise in truly rational living, in the adaptation of oneself to the needs and duties of changing circumstances. Above all, it is a time of reconciliation. Not only are public penitents restored to the church's communion, but all Christians rejoice in the blessing of forgiveness, and are spiritually endowed with forgiving charity. The joy of the redemption celebrated at Easter and imparted in baptism is anticipated and renewed in this season.

R. Buckler, *The Perfection of Man by Charity*, 1953; Leo the Great, *Sermons* 39–50; Lorenzo Scupoli, *The Spiritual Combat*; H. Thurston, *Lent and Holy Week*, 1904.

DAVID TRIPP

Levitation *see* **Abnormal and Psycho-Physical Phenomena**

Liberation, Spirituality of

A mode of living the Christian gospel which both underlies and grows from the theology of liberation, which had its origins in Latin America after the close of Vatican Council II* in 1965.

That Council, in its Pastoral Constitution on 'The Church in the Modern World', linked Christians with the griefs and anxieties of the people of this age, 'especially those who are poor or in any way afflicted'.

For the Roman Catholic Church in Latin America, the attempt to bring into practice this special concern for the poor and afflicted had to move beyond rhetoric. To cite but one example: what does it mean to proclaim the Good News to the poor on a continent at least nominally Christian where the majority of the people are literally poor, hence illiterate, politically powerless, and, in many nations, subject to repressive military dictatorships?

This effort to read the scriptures through the prisms of the poor led bishops, priests, and theologians to see in this existential situation of poverty and oppression the root of both a spirituality and theology of liberation. The OT shows Yahweh as freeing the Israelites from bondage and forging them into a nation. It also shows that poverty and oppression are not 'God's will' but are evils to be removed by the joint actions of Yahweh and his people. The NT sees Jesus as Christ, the Liberator, who brings life (John 10.10), preaches love (I John 4.20), and proclaims freedom (John 8.32).

Yet Latin America, the only 'Roman Catholic continent', gives the lie to the scriptures. God's people by the millions suffer poverty and oppression. Death, hatred and repression are more obvious than the life, love and freedom of which the gospel speaks.

As Vatican Council II profoundly influenced the Roman Catholic Church in Latin America, that church in turn profoundly influenced the entire church. The Latin American bishops were very influential at the Synod of Bishops meeting in Rome in 1971 to discuss the topic 'Justice in the World'. From that Synod came the following strong, keystone statement: 'Action on behalf of justice and participation in the transformation of the world fully appear to us as a constitutive dimension of the preaching of the gospel, or, in other words, of the church's mission for the redemption of the human race and its liberation from every oppressive situation.' But to 'act on behalf of justice' and share in the liberation of the human family demands *metanoia*, conversion. The understanding of this conversion is distinctively Latin America. In the words of Gustavo Gutierrez, 'To be converted means to commit oneself to the process of the liberation of the poor and the oppressed, to commit oneself clearly, realistically and concretely.'

A major result of such 'realistic and concrete' commitment on the part of millions in Latin America has been the phenomenon of the Basic Christian Communities. Distinguishing marks of these communities (over 80,000 in Brazil alone) are that most of their members are abjectly poor, whether in farming villages, working-class neighbourhoods or urban slums. These people gather regularly to read the scriptures and reflect on them in the context of their own almost sub-human lives. The leadership of these communities is not clerical but lay, and the leader is not appointed, but emerges from and is chosen by the group. These communities usually move, as a result of their scriptural reflections, to socio-political awareness and begin to demand reforms.

Significantly, these Basic Christian Communities are strongest and most numerous in those countries like Brazil, Chile, Uruguay and Bolivia, where military regimes oppose the church because bishops, priests and nuns have sided with the poor, who remain poor precisely because of the economic policies of the repressive regimes.

In Latin America, a spirituality of liberation is based on the conviction that the option for the poor is at the heart of the scriptures. If that be so, obviously such a spirituality is applicable to Christians everywhere, for poverty and oppression scar almost every nation on the planet. Thus, a spirituality of liberation envisions contemplatives committed to social reforms, political saints, who pray, 'Thy kingdom come – now, Thy will be done – here.'

See also **Radical Spirituality.**

Leonardo Boff, *Way of the Cross – Way of Justice*, 1980; Segundo Galilea, *Following Jesus*, 1981; Gustavo Gutierrez, *A Theology of Liberation*, 1973.

PHILIP SCHARPER

Liturgical Spirituality

This is focused on the corporate acts of Christian worship in the assembly or congregation, the ordinances that have been handed down for generations and are believed to go back to the very beginning, if not to Christ himself. In *Das Gebet* (*Prayer*), Friedrich Heiler* divided prayer into two kinds – prophetic and mystical. A. M. Ramsey maintains that his thesis suffers 'from the fact that he never discusses the

connection between Christ's prayer and Christ's redemption, and that he treats our Lord solely as a man of prayer and a teacher about prayer without reference to His place as the redeemer who sums up the prayers of those who come before him and who is the centre and focus of the prayers of those who now approach God through Him . . . If . . . the Lord's prayer and the phrase "through Jesus Christ" be interpreted in the light of the NT, then clearly Christian prayer is neither mystical nor prophetic in its essence, but *liturgical*. It is the sharing by men in the action of Christ, through their dying to their own egotisms as they are joined in one Body with his death and resurrection.'

This frees proper Christian individualism from being pietistic either in a Catholic or a Protestant sense. I shall not 'pray at the Mass' but 'pray the Mass' (Gregory Dix). The deplorable expression 'making my communion' will be outlawed. My private prayers will be the extension of the eucharist into my seven weekly attempts at living (Neville Ward). My personal devotion to God in Christ will be in his Body, the church, which is not simply a mystical ontological reality but the fellowship of believers.

Liturgical prayer is the prayer of the church 'throughout all ages world without end'. It is not something devised by a committee, either of the local church or of liturgiologists compiling new service books. It is my entry into the continuing worship of Christ's people on earth and in heaven. It is grounded in the actions of God and both antedates my response and is independent of my feelings. It may indeed lift me and my fellow worshippers into the empyrean 'with angels and archangels and all the company of heaven', but 'the solid fact of what God has done is always "the perch" (so to speak) from which Christian prayer takes its flight and to which it returns' (C. F. D. Moule).

Liturgical prayer may be the means by which we can come to terms with the unspeakable horrors and sufferings of humanity. This does not mean that they are a mere ritual any more than that Christ on the cross was acting out some liturgical drama. There may have been a liturgical pattern in wars of the past. War may be 'a sacrament of religious infidelity, a sign effecting what it signifies' (Thomas Dilworth). The Christian liturgy implies that the only response to human tragedy is prayer – not attempted philosophies or even credal formulation – but prayer in which we seek to share in the fellowship of Christ's sufferings through which evil is defeated and the grisliest failure and death do not cancel out the possibility of eternal life and infinite love.

Liturgical spirituality, however, is not confined to the liturgy of the eucharist. The daily office is an age-old accompaniment of the sacrament, and whereas the latter helps us to view our lives *sub specie aeternitatis*, the former is the liturgy of time, which hallows the hours of the proceeding day, particularly morning and evening. This has value in that it is *officium* (duty), and its simple basic structure supports us in our 'dry seasons' when extempore inspiration fails. It may also be offered as an act of sheer love to God when there is no ostensible reward or consolation to be obtained; and like the eucharist it is objective. It is very much felt by some modern teachers that the office has become too much assimilated to the monastic pattern with psalms recited in course. Some would seek a return to what has been distinguished as the older 'Cathedral Office', less stereotyped and 'stinted', perhaps more congruous with evangelical Christianity and more redolent of praise. The Prayer Book Offices of Morning and Evening Prayer, though a matchless combination of Matins and Lauds, and Vespers and Compline respectively, are with their long lections services of the word, and their decline in the Church of England in the interests of the all-encroaching parish communion, impoverishes a rounded liturgical spirituality, and together with the new eucharistic orders diminishes meditation. There will, however, continue to be debate as to the extent to which 'edification' should be a legitimate aim of the office, and whether since the Reformation a didactic strain in worship has not become too prominent. Some Anglican Catholics in particular would feel that the pedagogic may be in danger of ousting the kerygmatic, and that liturgy should primarily be participation in the mystery of Christ, rather than 'praise with understanding'. To devise a programme for the whole Christian congregation on a Sunday morning called 'Partners in Learning' would seem unlikely to foster liturgical spirituality;

though God is to be loved with our minds.

J. H. Newman* preached an Anglican sermon on 'Religious Worship, the Remedy for Excitements'. It is anti-enthusiastic and doubtless anti-Methodist; but in a period of turmoil and irrationalism, when religious hysteria may be a danger, it may speak to those immersed in secular anxieties, and those seeking religious thrills alike, in its advocacy of the daily offices of the church as a calming, recollecting influence whereby we may gain comfort to our souls and bring Christ's presence home to our very hearts and perform 'the highest and most glorious service for the world': 'Is any among you afflicted? let him pray. Is any merry? let him sing psalms' (James 5.13).

See also **Ecclesiology and Spirituality**; **Eucharist**.

P. F. Bradshaw, *Daily Prayers in the Early Church*, 1981; Thomas Dilworth, *The Liturgical Parenthesis of David Jones*, 1979; R. C. D. Jasper (ed), *The Daily Office*, revd edn 1978; Nathaniel Micklem, *Prayers and Praises*, ³1975; A. M. Ramsey, *The Gospel and the Catholic Church*, ²1956; Ulrich E. Simon, *A Theology of Auschwitz*, ²1978.

                                                    EDITOR

Lord's Prayer, The

Jesus is reported to have given this in response to the disciples' request that he teach them to pray (Luke 11.1–4). Their reason was that John the Baptist was giving his disciples some instruction in prayer. Presumably they did not want to feel at a disadvantage compared with John's followers. The incident may also imply that Jesus had a characteristic way of praying, or even an unusual prayer of his own, and the disciples wished to be instructed in this. The prayer has always been taken by Christians as a model for prayer according to the mind of Jesus and, as coming from Jesus himself, of the greatest importance. In early days Christians regarded it with great pride and awe. The two forms of it (Matt. 6.9–13, Luke 11.2–4) probably owe their differences to the fact that they come from different parts of the church between AD 65 and 80. Each is thought to have different features that point more clearly to the Aramaic original. The prayer was probably given without the concluding sentence of praise 'For thine is the kingdom . . .'; but doxologies and Amens were often added to prayers, and the familiar addition to the Lord's Prayer will not have taken long to become general.

As the prayer is an example of the way in which Jesus thought God could be meaningfully addressed, the kingdom of God, the will of God, the daily bread of human beings, their forgiveness and deliverance (whatever these terms meant to him) are clearly the matters about which he thought it worth while approaching God in prayer. They were not unfamiliar to the people he was instructing. The phrases of the prayer were part of their religious tradition. What was new in it was its brevity and directness and the warm affection and trust of its attitude to God.

This affection and trust are established at the outset. Jesus normally addressed God with the word 'abba' ('dear Father' is the nearest English equivalent) and he would have used the word to begin the prayer. It is in this atmosphere of love and trust that our dealings with God, with human beings, with life itself are to be conducted. The faith of Jesus is the way to that and the truth of it. The words 'who art in heaven' provide the due element of mystery and awe. God is not only Father, he is also God, that is to say, never more than partly understood, the one whose thoughts are immeasurably far from ours, so that inevitably we use the word 'father' of him in both love and perplexity.

God's 'name' does not refer to anything like the word or words that a person is called, that we use when we call him and wish to attract his attention. God's 'name' is his being, his universal reality and purpose. Jesus believed that God's purpose is to bring to the world his 'kingdom', that condition of things in which he will be the first love and reality of all hearts and the direction and inspiration of everything that exists. To pray that God's name be 'hallowed' is to pray for that time beyond time when his purpose will be completed, and also that meanwhile, here and now, men and women may increasingly come to know God in faith and acknowledge him as the holy centre and meaning of life.

'Thy kingdom come, thy will be done . . .' virtually repeats the prayer for the hallowing of the name and carries the same range of ideas. The coming of the final kingdom will be God's work. Jesus knew nothing of the developmental utopianism that inspired some nineteenth-century idealism and in places still survives. The fulfilment of life is not something that human beings achieve; but it was Jesus' faith that God will certainly achieve it, and he longed for this and prayed for it. To long and pray for it involve a kind of living here and now that is consistent with such desire and vision and is a visible anticipation of the glory that will be its reward. Such living is summed up in the doing of God's will. The life and teaching of Jesus are the spelling-out of what Christians think the doing of God's will entails.

In 'give us this day our daily bread', the most obscure of the prayer's clauses, the unsatisfactory English translation tends to conceal the eschatological character of the Our Father. The word translated 'daily' means 'of the coming day', and 'of the coming day' must refer to the unique final 'day' of God's consummated purpose, the coming kingdom. The bread of the kingdom is an image of God's presence in the heavenly feast, in the love and satisfaction which the people of God will enjoy in the great fulfilment. The prayer asks for an anticipatory sense of that presence and joy now, this very day. So it is essentially the longing for God himself in this our life. To read into the petition other meanings suggested by the word 'bread' may have a place in devotional use as long as their subsidiary and adventitious character is acknowledged and the eschatological thrust of the clause is maintained.

The request for forgiveness must have had a special meaning for Jesus in that it is the one clause to which he added some expository comment (Matt. 6.14; cf. Mark 11.25). The comment is of the greatest interest in that it is not related to any aspect of penitence, as might have been expected, but to the sinner's forgiveness of others. In Jesus' view God's forgiveness of us is inextricably tied to, may indeed even be verified by, our forgiveness of others and our dispersal of the resentments and hostilities which the injuries we have received from them have provoked. To say the Lord's Prayer is to take into oneself Jesus' personal faith and inevitably thereby to commit oneself to a deep and costing knowledge of the place of forgiveness in life's meaning and reconciliation.

In the spiritual tradition in which Jesus learned what faith is it was believed that before God's kingdom finally and fully came there would be one last attempt on the part of evil to frustrate his purpose. That final struggle, with its sufferings and tests of Israel's faith, was referred to as 'the Temptation'. There was no doubt about its coming. Therefore 'lead us not into' is otiose if the words signify their surface meaning. It has been shown, however, that in the original they would mean rather 'let us not succumb in'. It is accordingly a prayer that the believer will be given grace to come through the last great struggle and be delivered from its essential evil, which is to deny the true God and renounce one's faith in the Father whose providence embraces everything that happens and can happen.

J. Jeremias, *The Prayers of Jesus*, 1967; E. Lohmeyer, *The Lord's Prayer*, 1965.

J. NEVILLE WARD

Love

The supreme Christian virtue because it is the being and activity of God himself. 'God is love' (I John 4.8). 'God so loved the world that he gave his only begotten son, that whosoever believeth in him should not perish but have eternal life' (John 3.16). God's love precedes and creates ours; we love in return for his love and the sign of our love for him is that we love our fellow-members of the Christian family who are his surrogates. That is the Johannine tradition; in the Synoptic Gospels Jesus does not say, 'Love one another as I have loved you,' but repeats the precept of Leviticus, 'Love your neighbour as yourself,' a somewhat wider commandment. He also says 'Love your enemies,' 'the singular glory of our religion' (Isaac Watts). But the NT nowhere bids us 'Love all men,' which would make love too general to be particular, immediate, practical.

The NT uses a fairly uncommon Greek word for love, *agape*, which suggests that love as Christianity understands it is *sui generis* and the more conventional terms are inadequate. It is love for the undeserving. The question to what extent *eros*, or human love, often related to desire and sometimes sexual, is a true analogy of Christian love has proved difficult. The OT certainly compares God's love with that of husband for wife, even faithless mistress, and it also extols friendships as passionate as that between David and Jonathan. *Philia*, the love of a friend, is also a Johannine concept. 'It differs both from Eros and from Agape in being a mutual relation, a bond which links two centres of consciousness in one; and the Bible knows it not only as a human relationship which binds together a David and a Jonathan. Behind the Law of Moses stands the Covenant which makes Israel God's people and Jehovah their God; beyond the Body broken on the Cross is the love wherewith the Father loved the Son before the foundation of the world, the unity into which all the friends of the Crucified are to be made perfect: that they may be one, even as we are one . . . that the love wherewith thou lovedst me may be in them and I in them' (John Burnaby).

Anders Nygren in *Agape and Eros* regards *eros* as entirely of human search, striving and ardour, of 'works religion', the tormented longing to attain God by effort and self-torture, and inimical of true Christianity. Nor does the Johannine teaching meet with his approval, for here is a metaphysic which is the beginning of the contamination of the gospel and which in its insistence that we love our friends opens the door to *eros* and the love of those to whom we are attracted. Nygren maintains that Augustine's *caritas* (charity) is a synthesis of *agape* and *eros* on which the Middle Ages unevangelically lived until Luther's 'Copernican revolution' recovered the full implication of the truth that 'while we were yet sinners Christ died for us'.

Powerful and inspiring as Nygren's work is, and necessary in its emphasis on a great truth of the gospel, it is arbitrary in the extreme and untrue to Christian as well as human experience. Better to say with Origen * that *agape* is used in the NT because there is a distinctive quality in Christian love and *eros* may lead to misunderstanding in that it can refer to love which is lustful, sensual and salacious. Natural love certainly needs to be purified – it may be solely the desire for self-satisfaction and for power over another person. But Augustine * and Bernard of Clairvaux * imply that *eros* itself is the creation of *agape*.

Much of Christian spiritual writing is concerned with the analysis of love, and contains profound psychology. Must we not love ourselves (self-hatred is self-destructive) if we are to love at all? What are the stages by which our love grows and advances towards perfection? How may we love God and his creatures without conflict? To what extent must we renounce earthly love if we are to love God without distraction? Did not Jesus, the prophet of love, also call on those who follow him to hate their dearest, a hard saying, which if it is removed from the crisis of his ministry and his demand for supreme loyalty then even at cost to others, must mean that we love those whom God has given us 'in him'? This alone saves family love from becoming a wider selfishness and places our kindred and friends in those hands where they are secure from change and death.

The love of God has dominated much modern Christian thought. A poet such as Robert Browning took for granted the divine omnipotence. In poems such as 'Saul', or 'A Death in the Desert' he proclaims the discovery that almighty power is also infinite love. God empties himself of his power in Christ ('tis the weakness in strength that I sigh for; my flesh that I seek in the Godhead') so that in Christ there is nothing but love. And then the love resumes the power. More recent theology may regard the divine omnipotence as an eschatological concept, revealed only at the end. What we see of God in this long span of history is Christ crucified, whose only power is of love. He is neither Old Testament king, nor Greek impassible, condescending, manipulating, cajoling in order to claim his rights. He is rather 'whelmed under weight of the wicked, the weak, the dead' (Bonhoeffer). By clinging to traditional ideas of God, we may make him less loving than ourselves. The ruthless dichotomy between *agape* and *eros*, by destroying human love as the analogy of the Divine, may leave us with an intolerable doctrine of God and a failure to take seriously the declaration 'God is love'. To pursue the analogy to the end makes us accept the cross as the heart of Christianity and understand how near to tragedy the gospel is. It brings us to the realization that suffering is the Christian's métier and that the world will not be saved unless we learn love and how to live by it even to death.

See also **Fruit of the Spirit.**

John Burnaby, *Amor Dei*, 1938; M. C.

D'Arcy, *The Mind and Heart of Love*, 1945; Julian of Norwich, *Revelations of Divine Love*; Anders Nygren, *Agape and Eros*, ET 1953; W. H. Vanstone, *Love's Endeavour, Love's Expense*, 1977; D. D. Williams, *The Spirit and Forms of Love*, 1968.

EDITOR

Love-Feast

A fellowship meal, also known in some contexts as agape (from the Greek *agapē* = love).

1. Early Christian fellowship meals for devotional and charitable purposes are attested by Tertullian (N. Africa) and Clement of Alexandria (Egypt), and perhaps by Methodius Olympus, in the third century. They were occasions of sharing and specifically of sharing with the poor, in the life of the church as Christ's Body. They were also probably reinforcements of solidarity in times of unpopularity (cf. the Langar in Sikhism). As with the cult meals of pagan sodalities, they were accompanied by choral singing and spontaneous offerings of instruction and prayer. They influenced the early history of the evening office, but their place in the Apostolic church and particularly their relationship with the eucharist, are very uncertain. See Acts 2.42–47, 4.32, 6.1–6, I Cor 11.17–34, Jude 12.

2. The Renewed Moravian Church instituted fellowship meals to foster unity and mutual spiritual support, e.g. the Cup of Covenant before new missionaries set out. Largely under this influence, the British Evangelical Revival developed Love-Feasts, with shared cake and water drunk from special loving-cups, as occasions for Christians to share their progressive awareness of God's forgiving love, guidance and protection: young believers were to be thus encouraged and protected, more mature believers to check their moral and devotional growth in mutual fraternal care. The fissiparous tendencies of revival experience were to be combatted by this sense of responsibility for the Body, and individual gifts fostered by and harnessed to the mutual dependence of its members. (Cf. Charles Wesley's* hymn 'All praise to our redeeming Lord' with its celebration of unity, shared gifts and 'perfect harmony' in the name of Jesus). The usage was felt to be at once a renewal of Apostolic practice and an

anticipation of the Messianic banquet (an ancient eucharistic theme, which had been largely lost from eucharistic worship itself).

3. Ecumenism, especially since the Roman Catholic Church's involvement, has found the problem of intercommunion virtually intractable. In this setting, the agape has been experimented with, sometimes as a substitute for eucharistic fellowship, sometimes (more prudently) as an affirmation of an increasingly shared life which cannot yet find eucharistic expression and as a shared admission before God that such eucharistic fellowship, while not yet attainable, is essential to the goal for which Christians pray. The table-fellowship of the disciples with the risen Christ (Luke 24.28–35, 28.40–49; John 21.1–14) is sometimes taken as the model; in any event, careful distinction between such observances and the eucharist is found to be advisable. The gatherings are variously structured, but usually the participating bodies share the leadership of them, each offering Bible reading and interpretation, hymns etc. typical of each, and prayers for unity in life, mission and spiritual growth. Couturier's insistence that the quest for unity is a quest for holiness proves to be an effective guide in this setting.

F. Baker, *Methodism and the Love-Feast*, 1957; P. Batiffol, 'Agapés', *DTC*, I, pp. 551–6; R. L. Cole, *Love-Feasts. A History of the Christian Agape*, 1916; H. Leclerq: 'Agapé', *DACL*, I/1, pp. 775–848; A. J. Maclean, 'Agape', *ERE*, I, pp. 166–75.

DAVID TRIPP

Luther, Martin, Lutheran Spirituality

An Augustinian Eremite friar and theology professor at Wittenberg, who emerged as the principal guide and spokesman of the Protestant Reformation, giving his name to the strongest wing of that movement, Martin Luther (1483–1546) is predominantly regarded as a church leader, reformer and innovator. Since, however, the most urgent questions of doctrine underlying his reforming measures concern the very basis of the spiritual life, he is best judged as an exponent of spiritual theology. His markedly existential approach, not surprising in a man whose religious experience was so tumultuous, treats theology as a pastoral discipline; this must be remembered when the tempta-

tion is to dismiss his theology as merely subjective or egocentric.

The end and meaning of life is to worship God, 'to have no other god but' the One. But this God is not accessible to the human spirit: 'Verily thou art a God that hidest thyself' (Isa. 45.15) is a note running all through Luther's thought. There can be no unmediated contemplation of the divine nature (*theologia gloriae*), both because of the limitations of the creature and the lasting effects of human disobedience, but also because of the transcendent nature of deity. Yet the nature of deity is such that knowledge of Godhead is offered to the human creature – but only on the terms chosen by the divine will. It is only as the human creature yields up its self-assertive will and allows God to be his divine self in undeserved love to the human soul that God can be known.

What faith is for Luther can be appreciated only as Luther's presentation of the church and the life of faith; but here it must be insisted that faith is not an emotional state, not even one particular spiritual stance among the various possibilities of human personality – it is a gift from God, miraculously made available to the human person by the incarnation of God the Son.

For Luther, Christ is 'the proper man, Whom God himself hath chosen' to be the mediator. His coming in the flesh is in itself the act of divine grace that both reveals and is God's love to us. Luther revives the early Christian imagery of Christ as our champion. Hence the paschal theme of Luther's theology, summed up perhaps best in his Easter hymn 'Christ Jesus lay in death's strong bands' (ET Massie).

Only at this stage can the believer see that even his sense of God's condemnation was part of the work of Christ the Word – his *opus alienum* or 'strange work' – as part of the strategy of grace to bring him to peace.

The life of faith begins, not in a vacuum, either social or historical. The individual begins the Christian life in a world already containing the church, sent by the risen triumphant Christ to bear his word to all. This church, however corrupt, can be renewed by its Lord's grace – particularly in a restored obedience to scripture – and its commission never fails: to hold out the offer of grace in Word and sacrament, to guide its children through law into the light of the gospel, to foster this faith and to express and support their faith in the fulfilment of their calling.

Each Christian has a calling, first to be God's child in living faith, secondarily to be a priest offering grateful service to God. This may be within the orders of the church, but every morally acceptable station in life is a fulfilment of the Christian calling and a form of the common priesthood.

The church's sacraments are acts of God evoking faith and meeting the requests of faith by God's own presence. Baptism (and its renewed realization in penance*) speak unambiguously of divine love given and promised. Like Luther himself, a believer assaulted by doubt has a right to defy his fears on the grounds of God's pledged love: 'I have been baptized!' The Mass also, as the Lord's Testament, is not a memory of an absent figure: 'This *is* my Body', says the present Christ, giving himself in grace as a revelation of forgiveness and as the one who unites those who seek him with his own faith – union with the Father.

The church's catechetical responsibility is dictated by the gospel, and by the human need revealed and met by the gospel. Thus, the small catechism, the very foundation-stone of Lutheran spirituality, has three parts in a purposive order: 1. the Commandments – God's law, in the fulfilment of which we fail, and before the demands of which we learn humility; 2. the Creed, and the sacraments – the gospel in words and effectual signs, setting the believing life on the foundation of God's unmerited gift; 3. the Our Father – the believing life as the communion of the Father and the forgiven child, sharing their joys and desires and their care for the world around.

The church rejoices in the triumph of the cross. Martyrdom* is natural to its life, for Christ loved it into existence by suffering.

In some degree, the way to faith assumes the fear of God. 'In his nature and majesty God is our foe; he makes demands in the law; he threatens transgressors with death. But when he makes himself partaker of our weakness, takes our nature upon him – and also our sins and our evils, then he is not our foe . . . he gives himself to us as the true God, he is made our priest and our Saviour' (W A 39/1, 370). The true fear of God may terrify, but it opens the eyes to the extent of the divine mercy.

The sense of need which opens the way to faith is the knowledge that one is a sinner (*cognitio peccati*).

The sense of oneself as sinner is counterbalanced by awareness of Christ as Saviour. 'Christ dwells only in sinners. On this account he descended from heaven, where he dwelt among the righteous, to dwell among sinners' (W A 1, 33–6).

Faith is both totally positive and totally passive – totally passive because it can only receive, as the sovereign love of God is omnipotent giving; but also totally active, for it is a bold seizing on Christ: 'Christ is truly and properly yours, with his life, his works, his death, his resurrection, to the extent that everything he is, everything he has, everything he can do – all that is yours' (W A 40/1, 291).

There takes place a miraculous exchange with Christ, 'by an intimate, indescribable transformation of our sin into his righteousness' (W A 5, 311). This has been the subject of controversy. If, by a mere legal fiction, Christ is listed among the sinners and we are 'credited' with his goodness, where is God's own moral integrity? Much discussion of this has overlooked the fact that Luther's christology is a doctrine of *God*: it is God himself who loves us undeservedly, and takes the burden of our fault upon himself: hence Luther's use of 'nuptial theology' language.

This new relationship of grace is daily renewed: The church is then the hostelry (cf. the Good Samaritan) where we are cared for daily and healed.

The believer knows liberty. In earthly relationships, this has the effect of revolutionizing worldly standards of power and privilege: 'A Christian is no-one's servant, subject to none; and he is every-one's servant, subject to all' (*The Liberty of a Christian Man* 1).

Christians must expect always to be pilgrims, growing (and needing to grow) spiritually; but they have the right to live confidently, defying the opposition both of the outside world and of their own inner troubles: 'The City of God remaineth'.

Luther's guidelines on prayer are found in the little book written at the request of his barber Peter in 1535. The remote preparation (ordering of the day, choice of priorities, discipline of the will) follow standard ascetical principles. The immediate

preparation is the rehearsal of Commandments, Creed, Our Father – law, gospel,
acted faith. The mental prayer takes one or
more of the texts and makes of it 'a garland
of four twisted strands. That is, I take each
commandment, First, as a teaching, which
is what it actually is, and reflect on what our
Lord God so earnestly requires of me here;
Secondly, I make of it a Thanksgiving;
Thirdly, a Confession; Fourthly, a
Prayer . . .'

Lutheranism since Luther has been
dominated by the heritage of its eponymous
hero more than any other major Protestant
denomination. Lutheran spirituality has
tended simply to adorn the schema which
he left. Seventeenth-century orthodoxy
tended to diminish faith to a disciplined
mental assent (largely as a defence against
the fanaticism of sects and Roman Catholic
charges of subjectivism). Johann Arndt
(1555–1621), whose *Four Books on True
Christianity* (1606–1610) was the first Lutheran work of popular devotion, restored the
balance: his appeal to the emotions, his expectation of practical holiness, were criticized by more conservative Lutherans, but
had a marked effect on hymn-writing,
prayer composition, and the whole Pietist *
movement. The hymns of Paul Gerhardt
(1607–1676) gave lasting lyrical expression
to the Lutheran confidence of faith, especially in the midst of disaster and oppression
(Thirty Years War), and gave it the added
dimension of delight in nature. Eighteenth-
century Pietism, centred in Halle, enabled
Lutheran devotion to meet an age of major
social change: emphasis on personal apprehension rescued Lutheranism from excessive identification with one stable culture.
A balancing 'Catholic' revival, led by Wilhelm Löhe among others, with a rediscovery
of liturgical resources of prayer, came in the
next century. The critical theology of the
late nineteenth and twentieth centuries has
not failed to enrich Lutheran spirituality.
One example is Adolf von Harnack's *Vom
inwendigen Leben* (1931, ET *A Scholar's Testament*), with its closing prayer: '. . . I thank
thee that thou hast given me the desire for
truth and knowledge, and the longing for
moral integrity. I thank thee most of all, for
the gift of the Lord Christ, and for my
neighbour, to whom I may be a Christ too.
In all these things I find not merely Thy
gifts by Thyself . . .' Another example is

Paul Tillich's attempt to create a spiritual
theology, with something like a Dionysian
God at the depth of our being, but a truly
Lutheran 'dynamics of faith' – cleaving to
the one who is our ultimate concern, embracing the reality of our own uncertainty,
and being prepared to undergo any shaking
of our personal foundations in the confidence that God can, in love, make the believer a new being.

Perhaps even more striking is the testimony of two further Lutheran spiritual
writers for whom the support of a surrounding Christian culture seemed to have
vanished: Søren Kierkegaard * (1813–1855),
for whom, left unnourished by an apostate
church, the individual must be ready to
trust God through the facing of the un-
thinkable about himself as an individual;
and Dietrich Bonhoeffer * (1906–1945),
for whom the most elementary contacts
between the gospel message and modern
thought had ceased to be reliable, and for
whom the only way was to rediscover,
as a total novelty, the simple unqualified
following of Jesus, to the point of martyrdom.

W A = *Dr Martin Luthers Werke*, 1883
onwards; ET = *Works of Martin Luther*,
1955 and going on; see also *Martin Luther*,
ed E. G. Rupp and B. Drewery in series
Documents of Modern History, 1970; C. C.
Eastwood, *The Priesthood of All Believers*,
1960, ch 1; W. Herrmann, *The Communion
of the Christian with God, Described on the
Basis of Luther's Statements*. ET [2] 1906
reissued 1972; A. Nygren, *Agape and
Eros*, ET 1957, ch 6; E. G. Rupp, *The
Righteousness of God*, 1953; P. S. Watson,
The State as Servant of God, 1946; *Let God
be God!*, 1947; J. Wicks, 'Luther, Martin,
doctrine spirituelle' in *DS*, IX, cols 1218–42;
G. Wingren, *Luther's Doctrine of Vocation*,
ET 1955. On Lutheran Spirituality see
G. Casalis, J.-L. Klein, 'Luthériennes (Spiri-
tualités)' in *DS*, IX, cols 1243–59; R.
Prenter, 'The Lutheran Tradition' in M.
Chavchavadze (ed), *Man's Concern with
Holiness*, 1969, pp. 123–44.

DAVID TRIPP

Macarius the Egyptian

Several different but interrelated collections
of homilies on the spiritual life are attributed
to 'Macarius the Egyptian' or 'M. the Alex-

andrian'. It is now recognized that these homilies originate from Syria or N. Mesopotamia, and not from Egypt; they probably belong to the late fourth or early fifth century.

The total corpus consists of about one hundred texts: the 'Great Letter', two other letters, some twenty dialogues, fifty homilies and thirty short collections of sayings. The mediaeval Greek manuscripts provide four different collections: I (64 texts; no. 1 is the 'Great Letter', ed Jaeger; nos. 2–64, ed Berthold. There are literary links between the 'Great Letter' and the *de instituto christiano* attributed to Gregory of Nyssa; it now appears that the Great Letter is the earlier work). II (50 texts; the best known collection, printed in *PG* 34; critical edition by Dörries, Klostermann and Kröger. Seven extra texts, found in two manuscripts, were edited by Marriott). III (43 texts; those missing, or different, from homilies in collection II were edited by Klostermann and Berthold). IV (26 texts; variants of this recension, the oldest in Greek, are given in the edition of I). The early versions represent yet different combinations of the materials.

The discovery that the homilies contain some verbal agreements with texts of the Messalian Asceticon, quoted and condemned by John of Damascus, has led some scholars to suppose that the homilies are of Messalian origin, or even represent their Asceticon; as a consequence they are sometimes attributed to the Messalian Symeon of Mesopotamia (mentioned by Theodoret). Although the Homilies exhibit some of the tendencies for which the Messalians were later condemned, they do not (e.g.) share the Messalian rejection of the sacraments. It is thus perhaps preferable to see the Homilies as originating in circles out of which Messalianism grew.

The Homilies are the chief representative in Greek of an experiential tradition of spirituality, far removed from the intellectual approaches of Evagrius and the Dionysian corpus. They offer no systematic teaching, but certain themes are recurrent, notably the interiorization of the spiritual life (often described in terms of the Exodus from Egypt), and the great emphasis laid on the importance of assiduous prayer and the activity of the Holy Spirit. The spiritual life is a struggle of cosmic dimensions, between 'the two kingdoms, of darkness and of light'. Baptism does not itself eradicate evil from the heart, but it provides the possibility for this to take place; free will must continually discern between good and evil, and choose to co-operate with grace. Prayer is essentially the place for discernment, and the basic criterion in all discernment is the love of God and of the brethren. Given the co-operation of human effort, the grace of the Holy Spirit will manifest itself in the form of various charisms, culminating in the granting of 'true prayer', an experience identified as baptism in fire and the Spirit.

The Homilies have always proved popular reading, and during the sixteenth–eighteenth centuries they were translated into many different languages, including English (first printed 1721), Dutch and German.

I. V. Desprez, *Ps. Macaire, Oeuvres spirituelles* I (SC 275), 1980, and (with M. Canevet) in *DS*, X, cols 20–43; H. Dörries, *Die Theologie des Makarios/Symeon*, 1978; G. A. Maloney, *Intoxicated with God: the Fifty Spiritual Homilies of Macarius*, 1978; A. J. Mason, *Fifty Spiritual Homilies of St Macarius the Egyptian*, 1921.

SEBASTIAN BROCK

Mahayana see **Buddhism**

Manichaeism

A religious movement that arose in Persia in the third century after Christ. In essence, Manichaeism – a species of Gnosticism – was a dualistic religion that offered salvation through the knowledge of revealed religious truths. Its fundamental principle was ontological dualism. It had the structures and institutions of an organized church.

Manichaeism is named after its founder, Mani (or Manes), who was born in 216 in southern Babylonia (now Iraq). Mani's father was deeply concerned with religion, and during Mani's infancy converted to the sect of the Elkhasites, a Judaizing Christian group that practiced rigorous asceticism and daily ablutions. Mani thus came under Christian influence. At the age of twenty-four, in 240, he publicly broke with the Elkhasites as a result of a revelation and proclaimed his new religion. Mani believed himself to be the last of a series of heavenly prophets, among whom were Adam, Zoroaster, Buddha and Jesus. For a while he was allowed to preach his religion openly in the Persian Empire. But representatives of the official Zoroastrian religion succeeded in having him arrested and tortured to death, an event that became known as Mani's 'crucifixion'. He died between 274 and 277. Mani recorded his revelations in writing, but his writings are lost.

Manichaeism had as its point of departure the anguish of the human condition. Man feels threatened, even overwhelmed, by evil, but also superior to the body, the world, and time. He comes to see an affinity between his true self and God, who is Truth and Goodness. God cannot have willed evil; hence evil must have come from another, evil principle. Salvation consists in escaping from the evils of the body, the world, and time, and returning to God.

Basing his religion on this perception, Mani developed an elaborate mythological explanation for the conflict between Good and Evil. He described the two eternal principles, Good and Evil, as Light and Darkness, Spirit and Matter, Truth and Error. Originally, the two principles existed separately. But at some moment, Darkness tried to invade the Kingdom of Light. The Father of Greatness responded by evoking from himself a son, Primal Man, through the mediation of the Mother of Life. Primal Man, accompanied by five sons of his own, went down into the infernal abyss. But the five sons were devoured there, and particles of Light were thus mixed in with Darkness. The particles of Light strive to return to the Kingdom of Light. The human race, which is a mixture of Darkness and Light, is the offspring of two demons. By asceticism – abstention from fornication, procreation, killing, farming, eating meat, and drinking wine – man is enabled to free his true self (which is Light) from Darkness, the body, and matter, and at death return to the Paradise of Light. Otherwise, he is condemned to successive reincarnations.

The Manichaean church was highly organized, with teachers, bishops and priests, an elaborate liturgy, fast days, a cultic meal (the Bema Feast) that commemorated Mani's 'passion' and 'ascension', and – perhaps – a baptismal rite. Manichaeism did not demand rigid asceticism of all its members. Besides the 'elect', who lived the full ascetical regimen, there were 'hearers', who supported the elect financially and hoped for eventual salvation.

Mani considered his religion a true ecumenical movement: it transcended and could absorb all other religions. Manichaeans were enthusiastic preachers and missionaries, and adapted the externals of Manichaeism to the religious beliefs and practices of each area that they evangelized.

Manichaeism was especially strong in the Western Roman Empire in the fourth century. There St Augustine of Hippo was a member of the sect, as a 'hearer', for nine years, and later wrote more than a dozen works in refutation of Manichaeism. Manichaeism was also strong in Iran, and in the seventh century reached China. Manichaeism may also have been at the root of three Christian sects: the Paulicians (in Armenia in the seventh century), the Bogomils (in Bulgaria in the tenth century), and the Cathari or Albigensians (in France in the twelfth century), but the connection is far from certain.

C. R. C. Allberry (ed), *A Manichaean Psalmbook*, 1938; J. P. Asmussen (ed), *Manichaean Literature: Representative Texts Chiefly from Middle Persian and Parthian Writings*, 1975; F. C. Burkitt, *The Religion of the Manichees*, 1925; L. J. R. Ort, *Mani: A Religio-Historical Description of His Personality*, 1967; J. J. Rickaby, *The Manichees as Saint Augustine Saw Them*, 1925; S. Runciman, *The Medieval Manichee: A Study of the Christian Dualist Heresy*, 1947; G. Widengren, *Mani and Manichaeism*, 1965.

JOSEPH T. LIENHARD

Marian Devotion

Cultic devotion to Mary the virgin mother of Jesus can be observed in Christian piety beginning in the second century. A sizeable amount of the Christian pseudepigraphical writings concern the life and death of the Virgin. This literature may have been inspired by interest and belief in the sacred powers of Mary; it certainly added to her profile in Christian worship. By filling in New Testament silence about Mary's life on a principle of congruence with the life of Jesus, the marian pseudepigrapha invested Mary with a sacred and special birth and death, setting her apart from the human realm.

The two most influential of the non-canonical writings about the Virgin are the

'Protevangelium of James' and the dormition cycle, classically represented by the text known as the 'Pseudo-Melito'. The former, which claims to have been written by James, a step-son of Mary, describes the conception and birth of the Virgin, replete with visitations of angels and promises of a special redemptive role for the sanctified child. The latter gives nearly as fanciful an account of Mary's death, after which she was taken up body and soul to be reunited in incorrupt eternity with her son.

These stories are closely related to the liturgical and cultic development of the most ancient marian feasts, the Nativity of the Virgin (8 September) and the Assumption (15 August). Devotees of Mary celebrated these feasts enthusiastically, in spite of the unwillingness of many church leaders to recognize them as divinely ordained or even doctrinally sound. From the piety surrounding the Nativity of the Virgin developed the idea that Mary was specially conceived as well, sanctified in her mother's womb in preparation for her role as the Theotokos, the God-bearer. The institutionalization of these customs came slowly; the Immaculate Conception of Mary was declared dogma (uncontestable teaching of the church) in 1854; the Assumption achieved like status in 1950.

The most ancient devotion to Mary may have been influenced by Hellenistic goddess cults. The Virgin is often portrayed, visually and verbally, in the trappings of Isis, Queen of Heaven, and in the city of Ephesus, devotion to Diana of the Ephesians was translated into a strong local cult of Mary, visible by the fourth century. The Arian controversy of the same century, in which the mainstream of Christianity insisted on the total divinity of Christ, further escalated the position of the Virgin in Christian devotional life.

By the Middle Ages, the major aspects of the cult of the Virgin were well in place. Hymns and prayers to Mary were widely used in both Eastern and Western Christianity, and belief in Mary's intercessory powers was widespread. The rosary*, a set of beads used to count off prayers to Mary, was in use as early as the ninth century, and was greatly popularized by fifteenth-century Dominican priests, especially Alanus de Lupe (d. 1475). The repeated prayer of the rosary, the Hail Mary, is a composite of the words of the angel Gabriel at the Annunciation (Luke 1.32–33) and the exclamation of Mary's cousin Elizabeth at the Visitation (Luke 1.42). (*See* **Ave Maria**.) Perhaps the most widespread and enduring hymn to the Virgin, the eleventh-century 'Salve Regina', combines the maternal and majestic aspects of the figure of Mary, and clearly portrays her as a heavenly mediator for human needs and aspirations.

Besides investing Mary with the significant power to intercede in heaven for the earthly sins of her followers, the cult of the Virgin also portrays the mother of Jesus with the power to work miracles. Cycles of legends of the wondrous acts of the Virgin flourished through the fifteenth century, and are found in Latin, Greek, Coptic and other languages. Relics of the Virgin, such as the veil given to the cathedral of Chartres by the Carolingian monarch Charles the Bald, are thought to have special powers. In 911, this relic put an invading Norman army to flight. After the cathedral was burned to the ground in 1194, discovery of the undamaged relic led to the building of a new structure especially to house it; this was the first of the soaring gothic cathedrals dedicated to the Virgin, still a major pilgrimage site.

Since the sixteenth century, the liveliest form of devotion to Mary can be seen in the apparitional cults formed around sites where the Virgin has appeared to individuals. The recipients of these visions are characteristically the most humble members of the Christian community, children and the poor. The message of the Virgin is similar in all apparitions: she calls for repentance, turning away from the violence and materialism of the modern world, devotion to the hierarchy of the church, and the prayer of the rosary. In spite of the conservatism of this message, the church has traditionally been careful, even slow, in recognizing the authenticity of Marian apparitions. The unshakable devotions of pilgrims to Guadalupe (Mexico), Lourdes (French Pyrenees), and Fatima (Portugal), the most famous apparitional shrines, has forced official sanction of these cults. But many other claims for Mary's appearance, including those in Necedah, Wisconsin, Bayshore, Long Island, and La Talaudiere remain unofficial despite the enthusiastic and often well-organized response of devotees.

The phenomenon of modern marian devotion shows that the need for a female, specifically maternal, figure in Christian spirituality is an enduring part of the tradition. The history of devotion to the Virgin shows the consistent pressure of popular belief on hierarchical definitions.

In Catholic and Orthodox Christianity, where devotion to Mary has been long, if cautiously, institutionalized, this pattern of veneration shows every sign of continuing into the twenty-first century, adapting itself (as it has always done) to the needs of each place and century. Protestant Christianity, which basically rejected marian devotion in the Reformation re-evaluation of faith and belief, has shown increasing interest in understanding this phenomenon, and may ultimately accept some aspects of marian devotion as important vehicles for asserting the feminine principle of God and the symbolic role of the church in the ecumenical enterprise.

Juniper B. Carol, *Mariology*, 2 vols, 1954; Hilda Graef, *Mary: A History of Doctrine and Devotion*, 2 vols, 1964; Edgar Hennecke and Wilhelm Schneemelcher, *New Testament Apocrypha*, vol I, *Gospels and Related Writings*, 1963; Michael O'Carroll (ed), *Theotokos: A Theological Encyclopaedia of the BVM*, 1982; Montague Rhodes James, *The Apocryphal New Testament*, 1926; Rosemary Radford Ruether, *Mary – The Feminine Face of the Church*, 1977; Victor and Edith Turner, *Image and Pilgrimage in Christian Culture*, 1978; Marina Warner, *Alone of All Her Sex: The Myth and the Cult of the Virgin Mary*, 1976.

E. ANN MATTER

Marriage, Spiritual

The term is generally used to describe the highest degree of contemplative prayer experienced by the mystic. This usage was established by St Teresa of Avila* and St John of the Cross* in the sixteenth century, but it is a term which has a much longer history. The use of the image of marriage to describe the union of the soul with God is found in pre-Christian sources, both Jewish and Platonic. Philo of Alexandria, for instance, sees the union of the soul with God in nuptial terms (*De Cherubim*, 42–52) and Gnostic writings describe the return of the soul to unity with the divine in terms of the marriage of Sophia with the Lord. It is,

however, in the OT that the image is most clearly used, in describing the relationship of God to Israel. This theme is reinterpreted in the NT in terms of the union of Christ with the Church, the New Israel (II Cor. 11.2; Gal. 2.20; Eph. 5.25). Concerned in the first instance with the union of God and his people, the image is also extended to refer to the union of Christ with each individual soul. The particular case of the monk who by his celibacy participates in this mystery in a direct and obvious way is an extension and not a change in the use of this symbol. It is by baptism that the soul enters into this nuptial relationship which is established already between Christ and the church by the death of Christ on the cross; as St Thomas Aquinas* says, when discussing the sacrament of marriage, 'from the side of Christ sleeping on the cross flowed the sacraments, that is the blood and water, by which the church is established' (ST, 1a, 93.3) and by extension of this image, the Christian becomes part of this 'marriage' through the sacrament of baptism.

The tradition of applying the imagery of marriage more specifically to the individual soul in its relationship of prayer to Christ has received formulation from commentators on the Song of Songs*, beginning with Origen* and Gregory of Nyssa, and continuing through St Bernard* to St John of the Cross. It is, however, in the *Interior Castle* of St Teresa that the mystical analysis of spiritual marriage is fully formulated. This degree of union between the soul and God is reserved for the seventh and last mansion, the culmination of the life of prayer. St Teresa does not regard this stage as a passing experience but as the habitual state of union between the soul and the three persons of the Trinity, in which the person concerned acts from that centre henceforward in peace and certainty.

The description of spiritual marriage (or spiritual betrothal) is also found and indeed explored further by St John of the Cross in the *Spiritual Canticle*★ and the *Living Flame of Love*. He makes a distinction between the union of the soul with God by grace and the direct communication of God with the soul in mutual love which he calls 'spiritual marriage'. This union is for St John of the Cross as for St Teresa a matter of reality and not of emotional experience; he speaks of it thus; 'the sweet and living knowledge ... is mystical theology, that secret knowledge of God which spiritual persons call contemplation ... Love is the master of this knowledge and that which makes it wholly agreeable ... it is a knowledge belonging to the intellect and it pertains to the will' (*Spiritual Canticle*, St 27.5). Moreover, it is a relationship of the soul with God which continues after death, but it is not in itself the vision of God appropriate to heaven: he says, 'a reciprocal love is thus actually formed between God and the soul like the marriage union and surrender in which the goods of both (the divine essence which each possesses freely by reason of the voluntary surrender between them) are possessed together by both ... In the next life this will continue unintermittently in perfect fruition, but in this state of union it occurs, although not as perfectly as in the next, when God produces in the soul this act of transformation' (*Living Flame of Love*, St 3.79). Both St Teresa and St John of the Cross are profoundly scriptural and theological in their understanding of prayer, and the imagery of spiritual marriage is used in a severely ascetic sense by both.

Other spiritual writings, and in particular some of the accounts of visionary 'betrothals' in later literature, have obscured the firm theological basis of this doctrine in the Spanish mystics and have brought the concept under suspicion as being emotional and perhaps neurotic. It remains, however, one of the fundamental scriptural images for the work of redemption and sanctification which is carried out in the souls of men; it is a flexible concept and relies upon an image basic to the Christian understanding of the relationship between Christ and the church.

St Bernard of Clairvaux, *On the Song of Songs*, ET Kilian Walsh, 1979–1980; St John of the Cross, *The Spiritual Canticle* and *The Living Flame of Love*, ET E. Allison Peers, 1977, 1978; St Teresa of Avila, *The Interior Castle*, ET E. Allison Peers, ²1974; E. W. Trueman Dicken, *The Crucible of Love*, 1963; Marie-Eugène of the Child Jesus, *I am a Daughter of the Church*, 1951.
BENEDICTA WARD, SLG

Martyrdom, Martyrs

Those who have laid down their lives for the Christian faith have always received especial honour in the church, in the succession of

Jesus Christ himself who is called 'the Amen, the faithful and true witness (martyr)' in Rev. 3.14, and 'King of Martyrs' in a rare stained glass widow in a Shropshire church. 'The ink of the scholar is of more worth than the blood of the martyr' is an Arab proverb without Christian parallel. Martyrdom of the unbaptized was a baptism of blood as efficacious as baptism of water. The cult of the martyrs arose early and had great influence in liturgy. Altars and shrines arose over martyrs' tombs and they were honoured in worship on the days of their deaths, their spiritual birthdays, long before there was any commemoration of the apostles or cult of the saints, which latter came into vogue after the Constantine peace when there were no more martyrs. The murder of Archbishop Thomas Becket in 1170 revived the cult of both martyrs and saints and released a flood of popular devotion which created an industry.

The sixteenth-century Reformation had its martyrs on both sides, and their histories did much to perpetuate fear and bitterness. John Foxe's *Acts and monuments of matters happening in the Church*, (Foxe's Book of Martyrs, 1563) was one of the most popular and powerful pieces of Protestant mythology for centuries. There is some point in the distinction that the Catholic martyrs were agents of a subversive power and were killed more for political than religious reasons, while the Protestant reformers were burnt for the doctrine of justification by faith. But religion and politics were as confused in those days as ideology and politics are now, and it is best in the spirit of ecumenism to honour the courage and sacrifice of all who died for their sincerely held beliefs, and not inevitably to deny spiritual sanctity to those who perished in what we may deem doctrinal error. Martyrdom is an important part of Lutheran understanding of discipleship (*see* **Lutheran Spirituality**).

The twentieth century has produced more martyrs than any preceding age, in the concentration camps of the Nazis, the Soviet religious persecutions and assassinations all over the world. In May 1982, on the visit of Pope John Paul II to Canterbury Cathedral, seven representative church people placed lighted candles in the Chapel of Saints and Martyrs of Our Own Time and named a group transcending denominations – Maximilian Kolbe, Dietrich Bonhoeffer*, Janani

Luwum, Maria Skobtsova, Martin Luther King, Oscar Romero, and those unknown. Apart from the records themselves, the most signal modern contribution to the spirituality of martyrdom has been T. S. Eliot's* *Murder in the Cathedral* (1935).

See also **Saints, Sanctify.**

Peter Brown, *The Cult of the Saints*, 1980; Johannes-Baptist Metz, Edward Schillebeeckx (ed), 'Martyrdom Today', *Concilium*, March 1983; J. F. Mozley, *John Foxe and his Book*, 1940; E. G. Rupp, *Studies in the Making of the English Protestant Tradition*, 1947.

EDITOR

Mecca see **Islam**

Mechthild of Magdeburg, St
see **German Spirituality**

Meditation, Mental Prayer

Christian tradition is familiar with the word and the concept of meditation. In recent centuries spiritual writers have introduced the notion of mental prayer as distinct from vocal prayer. Strictly speaking, as Augustine Baker* wrote in the seventeenth century, 'this division is improper' (*Holy Wisdom*). All authentic vocal prayer should involve the mind, as St Benedict* clearly stated in the sixth century when speaking of the Divine Office. 'Let us take part in the psalmody in such a way that our mind may be in harmony with our voice' (*Rule*, 19.7). However, in certain forms of prayer the recital or singing of words takes up the greater part of the time. We may then rightly speak of silent prayer as 'mental prayer', private and personal. Traditionally this coincides with meditation, which has always been understood as one of the exercises of the spiritual life of prayer, as distinct from the ascetic life of virtuous living and corporal asceticism manifested in charitable works of mercy towards our fellow beings.

The word meditation has always been used in Christianity for defining an activity of the mind, stemming from two closely-related traditions: the Bible and graeco-latin antiquity. According to the Bible and the rabbinic schools of thought, meditation is an exercising of the memory based on the repetition of words and phrases pronounced aloud. In the Latin tradition more stress was laid on the cognitive faculties. Three stages marked this historical evolution.

1. *Non-methodical meditation.* Up to the eleventh century, meditation was closely linked with *lectio divina*, holy reading, reading about God. The mind applies itself to the word of God as transmitted by the holy scriptures and by the writings of those who commented on them in one way or another. The attention is sustained and stimulated by the sacred text. Such meditation gives rise to prayer, *oratio*. Though the three activities, *lectio, meditatio, oratio* may be distinguished for the sake of logical clarity, in practical reality they are one and each activity leads quite naturally into the other. They combine in that active spiritual attitude called *contemplatio*. This form of prayer is never regulated by a fixed time-limit nor can it be cultivated by any determined method. It is an essentially free activity. The joy engendered by familiarity with God's self-revelation in the reading of the scriptures, the easy, natural and loving reaction to his divine presence make meditation something agreeable and delightful. However, since human nature inclines in general to less arduous activities, perseverance in such prayer requires a certain asceticism. At the cost of this effort and with the help of divine grace, meditation leads to union with God and bears fruits of joy and peace. It requires, too, a certain dogged tenacity and repetition. For this reason it is often described in terms suggesting that the text is chewed over and ruminated in order to get out of it the whole savour, the whole taste of the sweetness of God.

2. *Meditation as a text of prayer.* Certain texts in scripture, for example the psalms, or the hymns of the New Testament, tell us something about God in prayerful terms. In later writings such as the *Confessions* of St Augustine*, a man of God set down his own meditation, fruit of a spiritual experience and which he wishes to share with his readers who are invited to identify with it. From the seventh and eighth centuries onwards, formulas for private prayer became increasingly more numerous and elaborate. They were diffused by the Irish books of prayer and the prayerbooks of the Carolingian period. In the second half of the eleventh century, John, abbot of the monastery of Fécamp, composed three successive redactions of a 'theological confession' which was

a long contemplative prayer known to many generations as the Meditations of St Augustine. At the beginning of the twelfth century, St Anselm * wrote a complete anthology of meditation and prayer of the same order. This was followed by the meditative prayers of William of Saint-Thierry * and similar texts coming mainly from the Franciscan school of spirituality. The Benedictine reformer, Louis Barbo, wrote a *Forma orationis et meditationis*. From that time on, such literature was continually produced and used. In this way meditation and prayer came to be founded no longer directly on scripture or a patristic commentary of the scriptures, but on the writings of an author who shared with his readers his own spiritual experience, his own prayer and meditation.

3. *Methodical meditation.* From the twelfth century onwards, with Hugh of Saint-Victor (d. 1141) and especially the Carthusian Guigues Du Pont (d. 1297), there began to be developed methods of prayer intended to organize meditation and make it easier. Clear distinction was made between its different phases and its various objects: pictures, ideas, affections. In the fourteenth century Gerard Groote composed a systematic treatise, 'On the Four Kinds of Things to be Meditated', *De quattuor generibus meditabilium*. From the fifteenth century onwards, the trends of the two preceding stages fused together in writings which were either texts for meditation or increasingly more precise, and sometimes more complicated methods and fore-composed 'meditations'. This resulted in a very vast and often beautiful literature rich in content coming from the pens of the greatest spiritual masters of the times: Ignatius of Loyola *, Francis de Sales *, Dom Augustine Baker *, the Anglican and Puritan Divines such as, in the seventeenth century, Andrewes *, Donne *, Dent, Hall *, Baxter *, Bunyan *, and in the eighteenth Wesley *, Butler, Law.

Today and throughout the last few decades there has been a noticeable return to the simplicity of bibilical meditation based on the reading of the scriptures, with less stress being laid on those methods which have been developed since the twelfth century. There is a return, too, to scriptural commentaries of the Fathers of the church, for every true reading of the scriptures must conform with the interpretation given by

tradition, a living and dynamic process begun in the past and continued even today. Such exegetical and theological works help us to penetrate the word of God and offer further food for meditation, prayerful and contemplative reading. It is this return to biblical simplicity in prayer which accounts for the abundant use of the traditional expression *lectio divina* as a title to a series of biblical studies (coll. *Lectio divina*, du Cerf, Paris, 103 volumes published up to date), and in other contexts.

Meditation is not without its difficulties for those who practise it today, and these can only be overcome by meditating in loving faith and faithful love. The main hindrances relate to the balance between modern scientific exegesis and prayerful reading; the need to maintain a simplicity of heart in the midst of the increasing complexity of contemporary culture and psychological analysis; the unification of personal prayer rooted in the Bible and the liturgy with participation in public worship offering a rediscovery of traditional prayer with its moments of meditative reading of the scriptures in common. A last but no less important difficulty is the correct use of non-Christian methods of meditation, especially those coming from Hinduism * and Buddhism *, without however letting go of the specific identity of Christian prayer animated by the Holy Spirit and based on the revelation of God in Jesus Christ.

JEAN LECLERCQ, OSB

Meditation, Poetry of

Samuel Johnson *, in his coinage of the phrase 'metaphysical poetry' to characterize the school of Donne *, appeared to have achieved a satisfactory summary of their methods and aims. The witty toughness, the learning sunk in the lines, appeared to answer to the turmoil of an age which explored new relations between theology and natural science, between rival systems of law, between warring systems of government, a struggle which cost Charles I his throne and his life. But underlying this strenuous poetry in its reflection of social upheaval was a conscious pursuit of a particular quality of spirituality based on well-founded systems of meditation.

Probably first in their impact on the European practice of meditation, and still potent today, were the *Spiritual Exercises* * of St Ignatius Loyola* which appeared between 1521 and 1541. The Salesian system of meditation became known in England early in the next century and in 1606 Joseph Hall* published the popular *Art of Divine Meditation*. (The flood of earlier devout manuals has been charted by Helen White's *Tudor Books of Private Devotion*, 1951.) The quality of this practice of meditation may be seen at its highest and most deeply spiritual in Donne's *Devotions upon Emergent Occasions* (1624) in which the title page gives a sufficient summary of the method and its progress at any one day's period of meditation:

1. Meditation upon our Human Condition

2. Expostulations and Debatements with God

3. Prayers, upon the several occasions, to Him

Our increasing knowledge of this kind of spirituality led to a remarkable reappraisal of metaphysical poetry and the title of the seminal work of criticism, Louis Martz, *The Poetry of Meditation* (1954) provided a new critical term for this relationship between the practice of meditation and the writing of poetry; crudely it might be said: Ignatian or Salesian meditation issued in prayer; the poet's employment of the meditative method issued in a poem.

George Herbert* and Henry Vaughan* demonstrate this relationship very clearly and on occasion declare precisely in the poem's title and biblical reference the scriptural topic which initiated both meditation and poem. Herbert's 'The Pearl: Matt.13.45' sends the reader back to the concept of the kingdom of heaven as a goodly pearl for which all other wealth must be renounced. But the poem, after the title, makes no mention of the pearl but only of the alternatives which must be renounced ('I know the ways of Learning . . . of Honour . . . of Pleasure'); he knows 'at what rate and price I have thy love' and in conclusion determines 'To climb to Thee'.

In 'Easter-wings' Herbert's meditation on the resurrection takes actual visible form on the page, the outline of the stanzas forming a double pair of wings to 'advance the flight in me'. The most complex and ambiguous instance, however, is the intensely dramatic 'The Collar'. Here the initial scriptural passage is not so easily determined. The opening lines suggest the Prodigal Son:

I struck the board and cry'd, No more.
I will abroad.

And yet the conjunction 'board, 'wine', 'corn', 'blood', 'thorn' suggest the eucharist and its source in the passion and the Last Supper. But the poem again turns upon itself and after rebellious 'raving',

Me thoughts I heard one calling, *Child!*
And I replied, *My Lord*

and we return to the tone of the parable of the Prodigal.

Henry Vaughan regularly identifies the scriptural source of the meditation but the process of composition is given a more personal twist. In an untitled poem he speaks of the morning period set aside for his meditation:

I walked the other day (to spend my hour)
Into a field . . .

The technical turn of phrase, 'spend my hour', is qualified not by the solitude of chapel or study but by the 'field' where the scriptural contrast of natural creatures ('masques and shadows') and divine revelation ('that day which breaks from thee') is thought upon by way of the 'death' of winter and the bursting of spring growth. There are moments in other poems where the union of natural and biblical revelation issues in near-effrontery:

I saw Eternity the other night
Like a great Ring of pure and endless light.

But the most startling 'Composition of Place', the starting-point of a scriptural meditation, is to be found in 'The Dawning'. Here the subject is the Coming of the Bridegroom, as the parable of Judgment Day. When and where will it come? The poet is again in open country and wonders whether the angels will descend at that last day on the hill before his home, Pen-y-Van. This thought grows in the poem into the bold pun:

And with thy angels in the *Van*
Descend to judge poor careless man.

'Vanguard angels on Pen-y-Van' is indeed greatly to extend the implications – and territory – of the poetry of meditation.

MOELWYN MERCHANT

Meditation, Transcendental

A technique for achieving deep relaxation.

It has been practised in the East for thousands of years, mainly by Hindu devotees who use it as a way of reaching a state of oneness with the Absolute.

At the end of 1957 the Maharishi Mahesh Yogi, a Hindu monk, a disciple of Sankara and pupil of Swami Saraswati, began to teach transcendental meditation (TM) in the United States of America in an enthusiastic and systematic way. TM became so popular, especially among young people and those disillusioned with Western religion and culture, that it acquired a cult status for a few years. The method has survived the initial controversies surrounding its introduction and it is still widely practised in many countries. Trained teachers pass the technique on to their pupils in carefully designed sessions of personal instruction for which payment is expected on a sliding fee basis. Bursaries are sometimes available.

Beginners are encouraged to meditate twice a day, usually for periods of twenty minutes at a time. They are taught to focus their attention on to an internally heard Sanskrit syllable in a way which allows them to become so relaxed that they go beyond ordinary consciousness to reach a state of mental and bodily stillness which is an intermediate stage between consciousness and unconsciousness. The experience is hard for a meditator to describe since a resting brain does not interpret its experience consciously.

A large number of scientific observations have been made on volunteers during meditation. These have demonstrated definite physiological changes during meditation such as decreased respiration and pulse rates, a fall in blood lactic acid and brain wave (EEG) changes indicative of deep relaxation which differs from wakeful resting or sleep. Meditators themselves are unaware of these bodily changes but they experience post-meditation effects such as an overall feeling of well-being, increased energy and a sense of harmony with their environment and their neighbours. Once they have established a regular meditation routine many people change their life-styles in order to continue to experience the benefits of meditation on their health.

The Maharishi Mahesh Yogi has always insisted that TM is not a religion. It can be practised by members of any faith or none with a good conscience. Nevertheless his teachers undertake a ritual preparation, clearly based on Hindu spirituality*, which their pupils are expected to witness. Many people cannot accept this and many different modifications of the technique have become popular.

Many Christians have recognized the affinity between transcendental meditation and the practical teachings of the mystics such as the author of *The Cloud of Unknowing**, about the prayer of simplicity. These Christians are willing to use TM as a way of relaxation and preparation for prayer but never as a substitute for it.

Used sensibly and in moderation TM is not harmful in itself, but it is wise to consult a good teacher and an experienced spiritual guide when beginning to meditate.

Una Kroll, *TM – A Signpost for the World*, 1974; Maharishi Mahesh Yogi, *On the Bhagavad Gītā*, 1969; *The Science of Being and the Art of Living*, 1963.

UNA KROLL

Merton, Thomas

Thomas Merton was born on 31 January 1915 at Prades, France. He had a difficult and often unhappy childhood. His mother, Ruth, died when he was six. His father, Owen, an artist, moved him from place to place, often left him alone as he pursued his art, and died when Merton was fifteen. Through his teens and early twenties Merton led a sensual, confused, but searching life. In his mid-twenties he experienced a religious conversion, joining the Catholic Church while a student at Columbia University. He entered Gethsemani Abbey in Kentucky at the age of twenty-six and continued the search as a Trappist* monk until his death on 10 December 1968 at the age of fifty-three.

In 1946 Merton published *The Seven Storey Mountain*, an autobiography which spoke so tellingly to the spiritual condition of the times that it became a world-wide literary success. This book alone would have earned Merton a lasting reputation as the first American writer to make a significant statement about monastic spirituality. But many more books were to follow – the quantity and quality of which have secured Merton's place as a leading contemplative and prophetic voice of the twentieth-century church.

The range and depth of Merton's search is indicated by the diverse categories into which his writings fall. There are personal journals (e.g., *The Sign of Jonas*); devotional mediations (e.g., *New Seeds of Contemplation*); theological essays (e.g., *The Ascent to Truth*); social criticism and commentary (e.g., *Seeds of Destruction*); explorations in Eastern spirituality (e.g., *Zen and the Birds of Appetite*); biblical studies (e.g., *Bread in the Wilderness*); poetry (e.g., *Emblems of a Season of Fury*); and collections of essays and reviews (e.g. *Raids on the Unspeakable*). The general movement of Merton's writing over the years reflects his own spiritual growth – from the enthusiastic but constricted Catholicism of the young convert, to the radical openness of the mature Merton, reaching out to other spiritual traditions and to the world beyond the monastery walls.

No matter how widely Merton reached in his spiritual search, he remained grounded in the personal experience of God in Christ. For Merton, the spiritual search is deeply inwards, towards the Christ in each of us who is also our True Self. We meet this Christ in solitude and contemplation. But such a life is not the special prerogative of the monk; every Christian is called to it. It was Merton's genius to articulate monastic spirituality for people 'in the world', and to remind monks that they are in the world too. Not only are we all in the world; the world is in us. Within ourselves we meet all the problems and possibilities of the world, even as we meet the Christ who is about the work of redemption in us and in our world. Merton's life and thought speak so powerfully to so many precisely because he overcame our false and crippling separations between self and God, church and world, prayer and politics.

Merton's accidental and premature death at an international conference of monks in Bangkok was an immense loss to all seekers. But that trip, and his death itself, symbolize the call implicit in all of his writing: To become pilgrims, to journey into the gaps where God is found, and in the finding to bridge those great divides that alienate us from each other and from ourselves.

Monica Furlong, *Merton: A Biography*, 1980.

PARKER J. PALMER

Methodist Spirituality

The young men of the 'Holy Club' at Oxford in the early 1730s gained the nickname 'Methodist' because of their earnest approach to the practice of their religion, and the name remained with the societies (later the church) founded by their leaders John* and Charles Wesley*.

Their earliest rules required frequent attendance at the holy communion, meetings for the study of the Bible and other religious texts, the encouragement of each other in ethical conduct, regular visits to the prison and service to the poor. This balanced and 'methodical' spirituality is characteristic of the movement. The *Large Minutes*, a tract summarizing rules and practices during John Wesley's lifetime, carefully enumerates the 'Means of Grace'. Those described as 'Instituted' were 1. Prayer: private, family, public; 2. Searching the scriptures by reading, meditating – for which the methods of Bishop Hall* and Richard Baxter* were commended elsewhere – and hearing; 3. the Lord's Supper – 'at every opportunity'; 4. Fasting – on Fridays; 5. 'Christian Conference' – i.e. conversation with fellow Christians. In pursuance of these means, the Methodists attended the Church of England services on Sundays and also their own preaching service at 5 a.m. Further prayer meetings occurred during the week. The head of a household would both pray alone and pray regularly with his family. Wesley published forms for each type of prayer, though extempore prayer was a familiar mode.

In addition were 'Prudential Means', consisting chiefly of occasions for Methodist fellowship. Every Methodist belonged to a class, and the more earnest to the smaller band. These provided opportunity for prayer, learning, sharing and testing the spiritual life. Matters spoken 'in band' were confidential. An early Methodist needed no confessional: on joining a band, the question was asked: 'Do you desire to be told of all your faults, and that plain and home?' Wesley also provided forms for self-examination as a regular penitential discipline. The original purpose of the classes was to create groups from which monies could be collected for the work of the movement. Those members with further responsibilities as leaders, helpers, Preachers or Assistants (later Superintendents) saw these meetings as means of grace.

There were also other opportunities for growth in faith. A variety of occasions for corporate prayer provided rich soil: the periodic Love-Feasts* were chiefly meetings for testimony, at which biscuits or cake and water were shared; the annual Covenant Service, when believers solemnly renewed their relationship with God. Watchnights were further times of prayer and witness, late into the night, and modelled by Wesley on the vigils of feasts in the primitive church. The frequent hearing, reading and discussion of sermons was a mark of evangelical piety, and Methodism is notable for including sermons (forty-four of John Wesley's) as part of its official doctrinal standards.

The hymns provide the most enduring of influences on private prayer and public worship. The 1780 *Collection of Hymns*, compiled by John Wesley and composed mainly by his brother Charles, was described as 'a little body of experimental and practical divinity'. Its index reads like a creed: there are hymns 'for Believers rejoicing/fighting/praying/watching/working/suffering/groaning for full redemption/brought to the Birth/saved/interceding for the world'. Hymns were provided to describe 'the Pleasantness of Religion' and 'the Goodness of God', as well as judgment and its consequences. 'Backsliders' found verses for their encouragement. A section supplied the needs of societies and classes when they met. Another important collection was *Hymns for the Lord's Supper* (1745) with 166 items. Through the hymns the Methodists learned their doctrine and found a pattern for their lives. They not only sang them, but meditated on and prayed them. They would recall their words, as well as those of scripture, on their deathbed.

A great deal of this pattern continued to characterize Methodism after the death of John Wesley (1791), but his personal supervision of the life of the societies and their leaders was lost. Several new bodies grew up, owing a debt to Wesley but independent of the continuing church (as it became after 1795), closer to Dissent in structure and spirituality, and usually with a strong Revivalist flavour. This 'enthusiasm' marked, e.g., the Primitive Methodists. At their open-air Camp Meetings, preaching was directed to obtaining conversions and was accompanied by fervent prayer. After their Sunday evening service, devout members remained for a prayer meeting consisting of extempore prayer and hymn-singing.

It is clear that a great deal of excitement accompanied these manifestations of faith, yet it would be wrong to conclude that Methodism was mere emotionalism. The Methodists (of all varieties) sought to bring people to Christ for the forgiveness of their sins and the salvation of their souls. These benefits were *felt*, and a proper aspect of sanctification (being made holy) was an experience, bringing a sense of release, of peace of mind, or a vision of Christ. It produced changed characters, but it was not in fact normally marked by excessive emotional states. Nevertheless, the settled state of a Methodist was one of cheerfulness and of simplicity of life.

Methodism no doubt gives some credence to the thesis of some social historians that a new movement with its attendant initial enthusiasm eventually becomes a denomination duly ordered and in proper relation to similar bodies. Yet something of the original character remains to the present day. The preaching services, the observance of the Lord's Supper and the Covenant Service, the singing of hymns and the use of extempore prayer continue in British Methodism; Love-Feasts, watchnights and class meetings are only occasionally found or revived. Fasting, when it occurs, is more an identification with the world's hungry than a spiritual discipline. Family prayers and small prayer meetings have diminished. Methodism has been influenced for good and ill by twentieth-century ecumenical, theological and liturgical movements. Yet contact with other traditions has encouraged many Methodists to seek the roots of their own, not through fear or nostalgia, but to reveal an inheritance to be shared with the *oikumene*.

See also **Hymns**.

R. Davies and E. G. Rupp (eds), *History of the Methodist Church in Great Britain*, vol 1 1965; with A. R. George (ed), vol 2 (1978), vol 3 1983; R. Davies, *Methodism*, 1976; G. S. Wakefield, *Methodist Devotion*, 1966.

R. W. GRIBBEN

Molinos, Miguel de

Born near Saragossa in Spain, Molinos

(1640–1697) was sent to Rome in 1663 once his theological education was complete. He soon became a fashionable director, with friends in high places. In 1675 he published his famous book: *The Spiritual Guide which leads the Soul to the Fruition of Inward Peace*. The teaching is not unlike that of many mystics in the tradition of the Neoplatonists* and Denys the Areopagite*, and raises no sharper questions than those of e.g. *The Cloud of Unknowing*. Is the negative way of divesting the self of all images of God compatible with Christianity? What about Christ? Molinos told nuns to banish all religious paintings and statues and to cease systematic meditation on the Gospels as well as excessive services in church. Yet they were to receive holy communion almost every day (presumably because this is a bare, and in many ways unrealistic, sign). All he was saying was that God is beyond our knowledge and thought; in his own words, 'He who loves God in the way that reason argues or the intellect understands, does not love the true God.' But he emphasized the importance of silence – words, ideas, devotional exercises distract, intention is all. And if this is towards God, nothing else matters. Evil thoughts may invade, temptations assail; they should be ignored rather than fought, for this conscious resistance recognizes and honours the devil and he soon takes possession. Even sin may not be sin if it is due to irresistible forces of nature and does not have the consent of the will. 'Job cursed God but did not sin with his lips. This happened because the devil worked in him forcibly.' It follows that the practise of confession and acts of penance may encourage the evil they are designed to counteract. This is subtle teaching and dangerous. Molinos was a man who inspired great personal affection. His servants adored him and women were strongly attracted. He might be better understood in the psychological climate of the twentieth century than of his own. He allowed two of his women penitents some consoling physical intimacy, though without fornication. And he believed that the devil's work may tend to God's glory if it forces the soul back in utter dependence on God. So sin may not always disrupt the union, but make it more close.

It is hard to think that Molinos was anything other than imprudent, with a touch of complacency and over-confidence in his own spiritual wisdom. He was tried by the Inquisition – the proceedings were protracted – and had to endure some mob hysteria. He had bitter and vindictive enemies, but the trial seems to have been fair and on the genuine, if confused and elusive, evidence. He bore his condemnation with a dignified and impassive mien which goes some way to validate his spirituality. He was imprisoned for life, though in civilized conditions. He was influential among German Protestants and Pietists*.

Owen Chadwick, 'Indifference and Morality' in Peter Brooks (ed), *Christian Spirituality*, 1975, pp. 206–30. For contrasted accounts, one sympathetic, the other hostile, see J. H. Shorthouse, *John Inglesant*, 1881, p. 268 onwards and R. A. Knox, *Enthusiasm*, 1950, pp. 295–318.

EDITOR

Monastic Spirituality, Monasticism

Monasticism, a term derived from *monos*, alone, single, is used to describe a type of ascetic life followed in various religions by men and women either for a limited period or for life. It is *monos* both in the sense that it is followed outside the normal bonds of society and also in the sense that it is undertaken in celibacy, without a partner.

Christian monks have found examples of ascetic life in both the OT and NT, especially in the lives of Christ and the Virgin Mary; they have also seen the lives of consecrated virgins, widows and the apostles as part of their tradition. It was not until the fourth century, however, that the monastic way of life was fully established in the Christian church. The earliest records relate to Egypt, Syria and Palestine and to the households of certain bishops (*see* **Augustine of Hippo, St; Cappadocian Fathers**). In Egypt, three main forms of monastic life emerged: cenobitic houses for men and women; small groups of solitaries living near together for mutual support; and hermits living entirely alone. In Syria, the more extreme examples of individual asceticism were linked to a concept of the monastic life as the ideal of Christian living, which was to affect later monastic theology. The monasteries of Palestine, while following the essential ascetic traditions of Egypt, also produced some of the main literature of monasticism, in the work of Jerome*, Rufinus and John Cassian*.

In some of the households of bishops in the fourth century, the ascetic ideals of the desert were combined with a pattern of liturgical prayer and practical service of those in need, a form of monasticism necessarily more articulate and closer to society. Such centres drew their inspiration from the desert and also from the descriptions of the apostolic band in Acts (cf. Acts 2.42). The ascetic life was articulated in such centres, especially by the most influential of all monastic writings, the *Life of St Antony the Great*, by St Athanasius of Alexandria*.

The ideals and practices of early monasticism were known in the West through the writings of monastic apologists such as John Cassian and also through the eye-witness accounts of visitors to Egypt, such as Palladius and Rufinus. In the sixth century, St Benedict of Nursia* compiled his *Rule* for monks at Monte Cassino in Italy, a document based on the ideals of early monasticism and making extensive use of earlier documents, especially the *Rule of the Master*. The *Rule of St Benedict* provided a brief, practical and spiritually uncompromising guide for the monks of the West and by the end of the ninth century it had become virtually the only Rule for monastic houses to the north of the Mediterranean. The peculiar genius of Celtic monasticism alone stands outside this pattern (*see* **Celtic Spirituality**).

From the actual practices of the early monks, certain writers constructed an apologia for Christian monasticism, notably Evagrius and John Cassian. They described the monks as pursuing the fundamental baptismal vocation of the Christian to follow Christ according to the gospel, in a dialectic of losing in order to find, according to the pattern of the death and resurrection of Christ (*see* **Desert Fathers**). It is here that monastic spirituality finds its clearest expression. For the monk, the whole of his life is orientated towards the kingdom of God and the establishment of the life of Christ in the soul. This is not an idealism but a practical and living tradition, which has led monks to structure their lives according to certain practices characteristic of monasticism: fasting, silence, solitude, meditation, poverty of goods, simplicity of

life-style. The central activity of this life of prayer is the continual meditation of the scriptures, both alone and in a liturgical setting, and this has in turn given monasticism a special concern with a certain kind of learning, based upon the discovery of the Word of God within the written texts of the Bible. In order to protect their way of life and ensure their freedom to continue in this life of total conversion until death, the monks have made vows relating to a life-commitment to God, through celibacy, poverty, obedience and stability. From this concept of a life of conversion through the work of prayer and asceticism, the monks have been distinguished by a desire for the service of others, whether in prayer, study, teaching and preaching, or in the active charity of visible care for the brothers themselves, for visitors, or for the needy.

Monastic spirituality produces a kind of life which is recognizable in any age or country and it cannot be separated from the practical and detailed following of that life. It has, however, taken on different forms according to the kind of society from which its members are drawn and to which they are related. The dangers of such a way of life have always been exclusivism and perfectionism, the creation of a little church for the perfect within the church, based on a dualistic view of the world and a contempt for the sacramental understanding of creation exercised by those outside its ranks. Monastic renunciation, which is the basis of its spirituality, is not, however, meant to be a rejection of the created order. More specifically, it is not a rejection of human fulfilment normally realized through marriage, the use of possessions, and work that is service, but rather a thorough-going undertaking of an alternative interpretation of the loss of self in order to grow in the reality of relationships in the love of Christ. It is an anticipation by the power of the Spirit of the salvation obtained by the resurrection of Christ from the dead: 'for our conversation is in heaven' (Phil. 3.20).

L. Bouyer, *The Meaning of the Monastic Life*, 1955; D. Chitty, *The Desert a City*, 1966; C. Marmion, *Christ the Life of the Monk*, 1926; Thomas Merton, *The Climate of Monastic Prayer*, 1969; *Contemplation in a World of Action*, 1971; J. Peifer, *Monastic Spirituality*, 1966; D. Rees (ed), *Consider*

Your Call. A Theology of the Monastic Life Today, 1978.

BENEDICTA WARD, SLG

Moravian Spirituality

The Moravian Church exists today and has organized adherents in Europe, Britain and North and South America. Its English branch whole-heartedly supported the Covenanting for Unity proposals of 1982.

By the third decade of the eighteenth century, the Moravians were able to offer a spirituality which many people found overwhelmingly attractive. They seemed to have everything that the Catholic Christian needed; a devotion at once ordered and free, intimate, warm and tender, in contrast to the terrors of the church, the severe God of Calvinism and the Deistic tendencies and conformist laxities of some Anglicans.

They were the successors of the Bohemian Brethren, the *Unitas Fratrum*, founded in 1467 as a breakaway from the Utraquists, a sect which contended that communion should be given in both kinds (sub utraque species). They followed the teachings of a Czech, Peter Chelcicky (d. 1460), who, like so many pre-Reformation reformers, felt that the church had lost the simplicities of Jesus and was unmindful of the Sermon on the Mount. Later they sought to make common cause with the Lutherans to whom they have always been close; but they continued a separate path, sometimes persecuted, sometimes prospering, producing at least one outstanding leader, the educationalist Johannes Amos Comenius (1592–1670), until they were revived at Herrnhut by Count Nicholas Ludwig von Zinzendorf (1700–1760), who made a home for their Austrian emigrants on his estates, and received Moravian episcopal consecration. Under his fervent and evangelical leadership their mission spread far and wide out of all proportion to their numbers; and not least in England. Their appeal rests on five qualities:

1. A clear, definite and disciplined church order. They maintain the threefold ministry of bishops, priests and deacons and hold that their pedigree is apostolic. Their discipline is firm, their worship liturgical. They believe that Christian faith is professed in worship, not in verbal formulations. Their doctrinal symbol is the 'Easter Litany' – the Apostles' Creed with scriptural expansion which they recite in worship on Easter morning. There is drama in their customs, such as the blowing of trumpets in cemeteries at dawn on Easter Day.

2. Close fellowship. They hold lovefeasts*, practise foot-washing, and form settlements such as Herrnhut, where life in community is realized without the unnatural features of monasticism. They have some 'single-sister' houses and undoubtedly restore for many souls what has been lacking since the dissolution of the monasteries. Their membership is divided into smaller societies and 'bands', and in this the Moravian church anticipated and directly influenced Methodism. In true Lutheran fashion, hymn-singing is important in their worship and common life.

3. Missionary zeal. They carried the gospel into the Americas and from Greenland to South Africa. They made converts; and they underwent the ardours of missionary journeys with a calm and courage which impressed John Wesley* in the storms of his voyage to Georgia in 1735, and made him feel that they had a faith and an assurance which he lacked.

4. Devotion to the person and passion of Christ. They celebrate the tenderness of the Redeemer and are in the succession of those who had adored his Sacred Humanity* and found refuge in his wounds. They preach the compassion of a bleeding Saviour rather than hell-fire. 'Jesus thy blood and righteousness/my beauty are, my glorious dress' is a much-loved hymn of Zinzendorf's which was often quoted in the sermons of Pastor Martin Niemoller during his resistance to the Nazis.

5. Simplicity. Childlike innocence and total dependence on Christ are the hallmarks of the Christian. We go to him just as we are, in our 'poorsinnership', not attempting to make anything of ourselves, or struggling for assurance.

It will at once be seen that one of the Moravian dangers was Quietism*, though recent scholarship limits the use of the term to a seventeenth century group, but through Pietist* influence they were disciples – direct or indirect – of Molinos*. Some of the very early Methodists found the peacefulness of their life and activity a welcome and refreshing contrast to the noise and excitement of their own people. But John Wesley himself who had been so impressed in America and owed much to the Moravian Peter Bohler, and his evangelical conversion of 24 May 1738 to his unwilling visit to a 'little society' in Aldersgate Street, suspected 'stillness' and indifference to the 'means of grace'. After a visit to Herrnhut in search of the Christians, he became disillusioned on this score, and felt also that the Count was given too prominent a place as a spiritual guide.

The Moravian spirituality of the wounds could be repellent to some and the whole too sensuous and, in a favourite pejorative of Wesley's, 'namby-pambical', with sentimental diminutives like 'brotherkin', 'lambkin' and the almost blasphemous vulgarity of talk of 'the side-hole' of Christ. This goes with excessive gentleness. An Anglican evangelical, Richard Cecil, wrote that Moravians 'seem very nearly to have hit on Christianity. They appear to have found out what sort of a thing it is – its quietness – meekness – patience – spirituality – heavenliness – and order. But they want fire.'

J. E. Hutton, *A History of the Moravian Church*, 1909; 'The Moravian Contribution to the Evangelical Revival in England 1742–1745' in T. F. Tout and J. Tait (eds), *Historical Essays*, ²1907, pp. 427–8; Edward Langton, *History of the Moravian Church*, 1956; C. W. Towlson, *Moravian and Methodist*, 1957; John Walsh, 'The Cambridge Methodists' in Peter Brooks (ed), *Christian Spirituality*, 1975, pp. 263–7.

EDITOR

Mortification

The word 'mortification' (from Latin *'mortificare'*), appears in the OT and NT, and means literally 'dying', i.e. the activity of dying to one's compulsive pursuit of lesser goods in order to pursue with undiluted energy and affection relationship to God, the ultimate good of the whole human being. Mortification is one of the most constantly insisted upon features of spiritual life, not only in historical and contemporary Christianity, but also in the spirituality of other religions. In the Christian tradition, historic authors from the desert ammas and abbas of the fourth century, mediaeval monastic authors, and fourteenth-century mystics like Meister Eckhart*, Lady Julian*, and Richard Rolle* agree with the twentieth-century monk, Thomas Merton*: 'Spiritual joy depends upon the cross. Unless we deny ourselves, we will find ourselves in everything, and that is misery.' Ascetic practices that integrate the body in spiritual discipline assume that the condition of the body affects the state of the soul, and that physical disciplines that effectively strip the soul of its habitual defensiveness are indispensable to the spiritual well-being of the whole human being. Ascetic theology, which often uses the distinction of body and soul to describe the need for bodily disciplines as access to the soul, actually assumes the mutual interaction of these experientially distinguishable aspects of human being. The model of Christian asceticism, then, is not the hostile struggle of one part of human being against the other, but the unified intentional direction of the whole human being towards its greatest good.

Methods and goals of practices of mortification differ widely through the history of Christianity and occupy a spectrum from the harsh disciplines of Heinrich Suso*, Angela of Foligno, and St Francis of Assisi* to the gentle and often temporary ascetic practices that aim at removing the habituations and addictions of ordinary life. This wide spectrum of methods and goals has in common – if it is to be recognized as Christian asceticism* – motivation in love for God and commitment to purification and clarification for purposes of love and service. Both the conditioning of ordinary socialization and the habits of everyday life deaden one's capacity to receive, to experience, and to convey to others the new life of Christian faith. Mortification is the systematic 'dying to' this conditioning to the habitual compulsive pursuit of sex, power and possessions. Indispensable to effective mortification is discernment, either by self-knowledge or by a spiritual director, of the personal patterns of compulsive attachment to habits and objects and the prescription of ascetic practices designed to confront and eliminate this anxiety-ridden orientation. It is important to emphasize that the object of mortification is neither deprivation, the rejection of objects, or the refusal of pleasure and delight, but rather the identification of attachments that prevent delight in God and the loving service that flows spontaneously from this delight.

David A. Fleming, *The Fire and the Cloud:
An Anthology of Christian Spirituality*, 1978;
Margaret R. Miles, *Fullness of Life: Histori-
cal Foundations for a New Ascetism,* 1981;
'Mortification', *DS*, X, cols 1791–9; Donald
Nicholl, *Holiness*, 1981; Henri J. M.
Nouwen, *With Open Hands*, 1972; Daniel
Rees, *Consider Your Call: A Theology of
Monastic Life Today*, 1978.

MARGARET R. MILES

Muhammad *see* Islam

Music and Spirituality

Music has been the accompaniment of worship from time immemorial, and although
in certain Reformed churches some kinds of
music and musical instruments were condemned as improper, the Christian tradition
has from the beginning produced its own
hymns, 'spiritual songs' and musical settings
of the eucharist. Groups of Christians in
particularly difficult situations have also
sought to express and alleviate their sufferings through music, the most notable
corpus of compositions being the negro
spirituals sung by the black slaves of the
American south.

However, since the Renaissance Christianity has also inspired works which by the
grandeur of their conception, their length
and the demands on their performers stand
outside the life of the churches and form
part of the repertory of Western classical
music: Bach's *St Matthew Passion* and *B
Minor Mass*, Handel's *Messiah*, Verdi's
Requiem and Elgar's *Dream of Gerontius* are
just a few obvious examples. There is no
doubt that performances of these works are
an element in modern spirituality, and can
be profound spiritual experiences for those
who hear or attend them.

Moreover, precisely because the classical
repertoire cannot be neatly compartment-
alized into genres, it can also be argued that
similarly deep experiences are prompted not
only by works which are specifically religious in inspiration and content and contain words which identify them with the
Christian tradition, but also by 'absolute'
music, like symphonies, and by operas and
other settings of words which have no direct
religious content. Karl Barth is not the only
listener to whom Mozart's music has seemed
to come from God and speak of God; others

have found a similar transcendent dimension in the music of, say, Beethoven, Wagner
or Bruckner.

This raises important questions for the
place of music in spirituality. That *de facto*
it has a place may be hard to dispute; to
define that place more closely verges on the
impossible, not least because of the vague-
ness of the word music. Even if one limits
the question to 'On what basis might one
claim that some music can bring about an
encounter with the divine or the transcendent?', the problems are formidable. Certainly there is an imposing body of testimony by composers, e.g. from Beethoven to
Tippett, couched in what can only be called
religious terms, to the effect that in writing
music they are responding to and drawing
on a spiritual world beyond themselves, so
that when the resultant musical works are
performed the listener may be drawn into
that response as well. Messiaen goes even
further in relating music to the religious tradition in a creative way. But it can be argued
compellingly, particularly by those who
have a professional involvement in making
music and thus know it more thoroughly
than often dilettante outsiders, that whatever some composers may think that they
may be doing, music is – music; and nothing
more. It is therefore illegitimate to impose
on music a content and a significance which
is extraneous to its strictly musical content.

This difference of viewpoint is likely to
remain for a considerable time, simply because there is so little vocabulary or concep-
tuality for discussing what Hans Keller once
called 'the metaphysical problem' of music.
When it comes to talking about the meaning
of music which goes beyond musicological
analysis, the professional is as tongue-tied
as the amateur. To say that, for example,
Mahler's Ninth Symphony has no meaning
other than what can be said in strictly musical terms, is surely nonsense; to try to put a
meaning into words is literally to be confronted with the impossibility of expressing the verbally inexpressible. It *is* music and
says what it does say in that medium.

Perhaps the most constructive approach
in this connection is that which sees Western
tonal music, at least (and that has the closest
connections with the Christian tradition of
spirituality), as being above all an expression
of emotions. In particular the tonal relationships between the different notes of the

scale, relationships with various degrees of tension about them, serve to induce a wide and complex range of emotions focusing on the two basic categories of pleasure and pain. Developing phrases incorporating different intervals which over the centuries have proved to have particular emotional associations, composers can create works which make it possible to experience the fundamental impulses which move mankind without the need of ideas and images, words or pictures.

If this approach were accepted, then one could argue, as does its proponent, Deryck Cooke, that spiritual or mystical intuitions could be expressed through the emotional terms of musical language just as, say, the writings of St John of the Cross * express his mystical experience in the emotional terms of spoken language. The case is far from being demonstrated, and reactions to it will depend on the picture of the modes of the divine-human encounter which a person has built up in other contexts. But there will always be those who will quite confidently include Schubert's *An die Musik* among the world's great prayers of thanksgiving.

Deryck Cooke, *The Language of Music*, 1959; *Vindications*, 1982; Wilfred Mellers, *Bach and the Dance of God*, 1980; *Beethoven and the Voice of God*, 1983; L. A. Reid, *Meaning in the Arts*, 1969; Michael Tippett, *Music of the Angels*, 1980.

JOHN BOWDEN

Mysticism

Behind the word 'mysticism' lies the Greek root 'mu-', suggesting something closed, and a group of words built out of it – *mystikon, mysterion, mystes* – which were used in connection with the Greek mystery religions. This is, however, less informative than one might hope, as the use of such language as little more than a stylistic device to highlight the idea that truth is hard of access, less something discovered than something disclosed, goes back to Parmenides and is found in Plato. To discover the Christian use of such terminology it is necessary to look at the meaning of the word, *mysterion*, mystery, in Christian vocabulary, as it is this to which reference is being made when the word, *mystikos*, mystic, is found on the lips of Greek Patristic writers.

Mysterion means a secret, but in its use in the NT it has a very specific reference – to the mystery of God's love for us revealed in Christ – and is a secret, or a mystery, not because it is kept secret, on the contrary it is something to be proclaimed and made known, but because since it is a matter of the revealing of *God's* love for us, it is the revelation of something that remains hidden in its revealing, inexhaustible and inaccessible in the very event of its being made known and accessible to us in the life, death and resurrection of Christ. In Christian vocabulary *mystikos* means something that refers to this mystery of God's love for us in Christ and makes it accessible to us. Thus it has three ranges of meaning: 1. A reference to a 'mystic' meaning of scripture; 2. A reference to the 'mystic' significance of the Christian sacraments or mysteries; 3. 'Mystical theology', knowing God as revealed in Christ, belonging to the 'fellowship of the mystery' (Eph. 3.9), living the mystery into which we are incorporated in baptism and which comes to fruition in us through the sacramental life and growth in faith, hope and charity. In the writings of the Fathers 'mystic' perhaps most commonly refers to the hidden, spiritual meaning of scripture, by which is meant not some arbitrary 'allegorical' sense, but an understanding of the scriptures in which we grasp, or rather are grasped by, the mystery of Christ. Origen *, who in this is followed by most of the Fathers, sees the 'mystic' meaning of scripture as something not so much discovered by man's reason, as disclosed to one who in prayer and love approaches the scriptures with a desire to hear the Word of God speaking to him. Understanding the scriptures is not a simply academic matter for the Fathers; rather it is something for which one prepares by prayer and purification, by humility and love, so that through attention to the scriptures one may come to engagement with God, an engagement in which by the power of the Holy Spirit one is conformed to the Image of God, the Son, and so enabled to contemplate the Father. This is the 'mysticism' of the Fathers, and it is thus a mistake to try and drive a wedge between 'spiritual interpretation' of scripture and 'mysticism' or 'mystical theology', as some have done. So too in relation to the sacraments, to speak of their 'mystic' meaning is to speak of the reality in which the sacraments enable us to participate: the mystery of Christ, the paschal mystery of his death and resurrection. In relation to the individual then the 'mystical' life is that life 'hid with Christ in God' (Col. 3.3.), a life implanted in us in baptism, and brought to fruition as the union with God effected in baptism is made manifest in a life which participates in the death of Christ and shows the signs of his risen life.

All this is summed up by Denys the Areopagite* whose writings gather up the patristic mystical heritage and were vastly influential on posterity. With him the word *mystikos* has the three ranges of meaning we have outlined: the deeper meaning of scripture in which God reveals the mystery of his love, the significance of the sacraments through which Christians participate in this mystery, and then 'mystical theology' which is not something different, but looks less to the means than to the end, where the soul surrenders to God and, passing into the meaning of the signs and concepts it uses to grasp the mystery of love, is itself grasped and transfigured into that love. With Denys too we find the regular use of the 'three ways' of purification, illumination and union, a triad which has its roots in the Greek mystery religions but which now refers to the three 'moments' of engagement with God: purification from the sin and ignorance which is man's lot as a result of the Fall, illumination as man is restored to the life of grace, and union in which man regains the life of Paradise. The notion of the mystical life as a foretaste of the recovery of Paradise also makes sense of some of the phenomena associated with it: friendship with the wild beasts, ability to read the thoughts of men, perhaps even some of the physical phenomena associated with mysticism.

The influence of Denys, at least in the West, was partial and this is manifest in a change of emphasis to be discerned in mediaeval mysticism, which reaches a climax in the writings of St Teresa of Avila*: a change from the objective participation in the mystery of Christ, with no particular interest in subjective phenomena, which we find in the Fathers, to an attention to the subjective mystical experience which is the preserve of the mystic. Such a change would seem to be part of a general cultural shift in the West towards an interest in the individual and his feelings in which his indi-

viduality is most manifest. The change as far as the mystical tradition is concerned can be characterized by saying that the growing influence of Denys in the West from the twelfth century onwards is the influence above all of his *Mystical Theology*, taken out of relation to the rest of his work, and seen as an account of the soul's movement beyond symbols and concepts into the darkness where God is known in an ecstasy of love. Crucial figures in this shift of emphasis are St Bernard of Clairvaux* (who seems relatively untouched by Denys) and the Victorines*, and it is manifest in a concern with inwardness and the modalities of the experience of such an inward and individual piety (sometimes, it almost seems, to the exclusion of the sacraments and the life of the church). There is manifest sometimes a certain anti-intellectualism and thus an incipient split between theology and spirituality. There is also a considerable openness to visionary experiences in such affective mysticism, especially in the writings of female mystics such as Bridget of Sweden, Catherine of Siena* and Julian of Norwich*: the quality of engagement in the mystery of Christ's death and victory evinced especially by the *Showings* of the Lady Julian makes it impossible to dismiss these, as some have done, as 'unmystical'.

What this change of emphasis amounts to can be seen from the writings of St Teresa of Avila, for in her writings we find an attempt to distinguish different levels of prayer – prayer of recollection, prayer of quiet, prayer of union – by reference to the psychological characteristics of such states. There are parallels to this in the patristic period, in Evagrius for example, but there it is a matter of different states of the soul assessed according to how far it has advanced along the path of virtue, from a state of disordered desires and passions to *apatheia** and love*, where the soul regains its original state as intended by God and becomes free to commune with him in pure prayer. It is less a matter of subjective experience, more of objective state. And the ruling concern of such analysis is with tracing how one can attain the freedom to surrender to God's own action within the soul. Teresa knows this but confuses her account by identifying the effects of God's action with certain states psychologically defined. With St John of the Cross* we find a much more rigorously defined understanding of how the soul responds to God by purifying itself (active purification) and submitting to God's purifying action (passive purification) in the two stages of the Dark Night*: the night of the senses and the night of the spirit. St John's analysis is controlled by his theological understanding of what the soul is undergoing as it opens itself to the action of God and ultimately union with God, a God whose action, because it is *his* action, is beyond our comprehension.

St Teresa was still concerned with the heart of the mystical life – a union with God in love – but her use of the notion of analysing states of prayer in accordance with their psychological characteristics opened up a development of which she would hardly have approved. For once mysticism is thought of as a matter of certain psychological states; it becomes part of the study of man as a religious animal, and, because of the attractiveness of the writings of many of the mystics, a very congenial study. With the growing stress on the authenticating value of experience in the thought of the Enlightenment and thereafter, the study of mystical experience presents itself as a way of establishing or assessing religious claims. A further factor enters: for if mystical experience is defined not in terms of the mystery of faith being worked out in the soul but in terms of phenomenologically observed psychological states, then there is the possibility of cross-cultural comparison between mystics (as they are now called) of all faiths and none. With this we have what is generally meant by 'mysticism' in the twentieth century: a study of the supposed essence of religion, or God-consciousness, that prescinds from any particular dogmatic framework. So Evelyn Underhill* spoke of the mystics' 'impassioned love of the Absolute . . . which transcends the dogmatic language in which it is clothed and becomes applicable to mystics of every race and creed'. And even R. C. Zaehner, who was critical of such claims, believed that 'comparisons between the mystical writings of quite divergent religions is at least comparison between like and like'. More recent work has tended to question such assumptions, drawing attention to the crucial bearing of the dogmatic framework of individual 'mystics' on the kind of experiences they claim. But whatever may be the results of

such study, which is still in its infancy, it is so far from the objective 'mystical theology' of the Fathers, whence the term mysticism derives, that one may wonder whether it is the same subject.

Ruth Burrows, *Guidelines for Mystical Prayer*, 1976; Cuthbert Butler, *Western Mysticism*, [2] 1927; John Chapman, *Spiritual Letters*, 1935, and art on 'Mysticism (Christian, Roman Catholic)' in *ERE*; Friedrich von Hügel, *The Mystical Element of Religion*, [2] 1923; Steven T. Katz (ed), *Mysticism and Philosophical Analysis*, 1978; K. E. Kirk, *The Vision of God*, 1931; David Knowles, *What is Mysticism?*, 1967; Vladimir Lossky, *The Mystical Theology of the Eastern Church*, 1957; *The Vision of God*, 1963; A. Plé et al, *Mystery and Mysticism*, 1956; Anselm Stolz, *Théologie de la mystique*, 1939; Evelyn Underhill, *Mysticism*, 1911; R. C. Zaehner, *Mysticism: Sacred and Profane*, 1957; *Hindu and Muslim Mysticism*, 1960.

ANDREW LOUTH

Mysticism, Nature

Against those who have denied the reality or goodness of the world, Gnostics or Manichaeans (*see* **Gnosticism; Manichaeism**), the Christian tradition has consistently reaffirmed the creation as the handiwork of God, shot through with his loving and creative wisdom, his Logos. 'And God saw everything that he had made and behold it was very good' (Gen. 1.31).

Christian mystics have continually found this truth pressing in on their own experience. In mystic conversion there is regularly an ecstatic awareness of the abounding life of the world; the light, love and sheer vitality of creation trigger off an experience overwhelmingly real and joyful.

But in Christian mysticism this has been seen as a beginning, not an end. R. C. Zaehner has emphasized that the Christian mystic is drawn out of self, through a translucent creation, into a relationship of love with the transcendent creator. Such a relationship with the divine demands discipline, but its fruits are fresh illumination in nature, and a renewed joy. Yet this is a costly, tragic joy. St Francis of Assisi*, whose 'Canticle of the Creatures' represents a real high-point of insight into the natural order, also received the stigmata as he entered into the sufferings of the crucified Christ.

Baron von Hügel*, reviving ideas shared with the Greek Fathers, characterized this Christian nature mysticism as properly 'panentheistic'; the Christian nature mystic is a 'panentheist', seeing in all created things God's 'energies', yet moving also towards the Transcendent 'essence'.

Such an appreciation differs from the broadly 'panenhenic', monistic experience of Buddhist or Hindu, where the soul is oned with nature but moves no further, for God and the soul are one. The contrast is not, however, complete, for some Christian mystics have tended in such a direction, among them Meister Eckhart*. But the tradition as a whole speaks against such figures.

Another contrast, this time with the 'mysticism' induced by drugs, points back to the central feature of Christian mysticism. Huxley's *Doors of Perception* suggested that mescalin might induce a state similar to that experienced by Christian nature mystics. Yet he speaks there regularly of 'escape', equating mysticism with escapism. Loving engagement with God and his creation is at the heart of the Christian experience.

But to many the loving wisdom of God has appeared absent from nature. For Tennyson nature seemed 'red in tooth and claw', and after the death of his brother at sea, Wordsworth turned from natural to revealed and institutional religion.

Others, however, have seen the sufferings of man in nature as an entry into the sufferings of Christ. Gerard Manley Hopkins* saw in the death at sea of five Franciscan nuns aboard the Deutschland in 1875 a sharing in Christ's (and St Francis') tragic joy:

Joy fall to thee father Francis
Drawn to the life that died;
With the gnarls of the nails in thee,
   niche of the lance, his,
Lovescape Crucified
And seal of his seraph – arrival! And
   these thy daughters
And five livèd and leavèd favour and
   pride,
Are sisterly sealed in wild waters
To bathe in his fall-gold mercies, to
   breathe in his all-fire glances.

———
E. Underhill, *Mysticism*, 1911; R. C. Zaeh-

ner, *Mysticism Sacred and Profane*, 1957.
                                        JOHN H. DAVIES

Mystics, English
see **English Mystics, The**

Name, Invocation of the Holy
see **Jesus, Prayer to**

Nature Mysticism
see **Mysticism, Nature**

Neale, John Mason
Educated at Trinity College, Cambridge, Neale (1818–1866) was instrumental in founding the Cambridge Camden Society (later the Ecclesiological Society), whose advocacy of Gothic architecture and mediaeval liturgical symbolism had a marked influence on Anglican church building and worship in the nineteenth century. For most of his ministry, from 1846 until his death, he served as Warden of Sackville College, East Grinstead, Sussex, an ancient almshouse and religious foundation, which gave him the freedom to pursue his scholarly interests in liturgy, hymnody and the history of Eastern Christianity. His liturgical practice, which seems from 1859 to have included Benediction*(the earliest Anglican use of this service), attracted episcopal displeasure. His founding of the Society of St Margaret likewise drew some of the fire that such sisterhoods commonly did at the time.

Although there was an undoubtedly Romantic side to Neale, his solid contribution to Anglican spirituality is through his many translations of ancient Greek and Latin hymns, which have permanently enriched English worship. In the *English Hymnal* more than one tenth of the hymns are Neale's translations.

From his acquaintance with the history and liturgical inheritance of the Eastern Church Neale gained a strong sense of the Easter victory of Christ; of the Christian life as transfiguration; and of the glory of heaven. Deeply learned and widely read in the mediaeval commentaries on scripture, Neale in his preaching could press allegorical and typological interpretations of scripture to extremes. But alongside fanciful numerological exegesis there is a deep resonance with the great images of scripture, and a strong awareness of the importance of icon and symbol in prayer and worship. When he wrote, as one of the first Anglicans to do so, of the Iconoclastic controversy, he condemned the Iconoclasts as an instance of 'secret, creeping Manichaeism'. His published volumes of sermons, many preached to the East Grinstead sisters, witness to his strong *via affirmativa* spirituality. His symbolic interpretations of the ecclesiastical art and architecture of the Gothic Revival contributed to the transformation of Anglican worship and gave wider currency to the sacramental ideals of the Oxford Movement*.

A. M. Allchin, *The Silent Rebellion*, 1958; A. G. Lough, *The Influence of John Mason Neale*, 1962; G. Rowell, *The Vision Glorious*, 1983; J. F. White, *The Cambridge Movement*, 1962.

GEOFFREY ROWELL

Neoplatonism

Neoplatonism usually refers to the philosopher Plotinus* (205–270) and those individuals who fundamentally adhered to his teachings. Other important Neoplatonists are Porphyry (233–306), Proclus* (412–484), Denys the Areopagite* (*c.* 500), and Boethius (*c.* 480–524), whose Neoplatonism is strongly modified by Aristotelian influences. Neoplatonism is the last great philosophical tradition in the ancient world; it plays a decisive role in the formation of mediaeval thought.

What follows is a brief summary of some significant Neoplatonic teachings. The totality of beings exists as a hierarchy ordered to the One (Good), which some Neoplatonists also regard as God. The One brings forth all beings through emanation, like the sun emits its rays or an inexhaustible spring gushes forth out of itself. The first realm to be produced is the intelligible cosmos comprising pure intellects and intelligibles. The soul emerges out of this realm and then generates the material cosmos out of itself. (The elegant economy of Plotinus' world – the distinct hypostases of the One, Intellect, and Soul – is transformed by the later Neoplatonists into a multiplicity of finely distinguished grades of being.) The universal structure of causation is abiding (*monē*), procession (*prodoos*), and reversion (*epistrophē*). That is a cause, especially an immaterial cause, abides undiminished in itself and produces its effects by differentiating them out of itself (procession). The effects achieve existence by turning back or reverting to the cause, that is, by attaining

a likeness to the cause. Since all things emerge out of a single cause all things, according to a favourite Neoplatonic maxim, are in all things in a manner appropriate to each.

The soul, and thus individual human souls, traverse the whole range of reality. In its highest part the soul is pure intellect and, beyond that, mystically united with the One. In its lowest part the soul is enmeshed in the material order. While the Neoplatonists generally do not regard the material order as inherently evil (although Plotinus at times seems to offer such a suggestion), they follow the Platonic deprecation of the material world. Thus the soul's quest for authentic existence lies in gaining freedom from attachments to the material realm in order to be united with intellect and the One. Union with the One is achieved through mystical contemplation. Such contemplation must be distinguished from any intellectual or noetic contemplation, for it is not a super-intellectual cognition but a trans-intellectual experience of the One in which the 'eye of the intellect' is closed and self-consciousness, consciousness of differentiation from the One, ceases.

Neoplatonic teachings about the One or Good are important in themselves and for their historical influences. The conception of the One is based largely on interpretation of Plato's *Parmenides*, Hypothesis I and other aspects of the Platonic dialogues. The One, the undifferentiated, unlimited power which brings forth all beings, is both beginning and end of beings, for beings are beings in virtue of unity. Further, no determinate characteristics apply to it. For example, Plotinus denies that being or thinking pertain to the One; he even denies that it can be called one or good. Later Neoplatonists such as Denys the Areopagite who are influenced by the Christian tradition will attribute infinite being to the One. Nevertheless the One cannot be viewed as a being, not even an infinite being. Yet, on the other hand, since the One brings forth all beings, is present to them and can be comprehended in them, it is all beings. The apparently paradoxical status of the One is expressed by saying that the One itself 'is' nothing, yet it is all beings.

Neoplatonism is frequently accused of being pantheistic, of abolishing a proper difference between the One and beings.

However the Neoplatonists all insist on a difference between the One and beings but deny that that difference can be understood in entitative terms. Thus Neoplatonism is neither properly a theism, if this means that the One subsists as a being independently of other beings; nor is it a pantheism, if this means that there is an entitative or substantial identification of the one with beings.

Neoplatonism permeates mediaeval thought and subsequent traditions, especially speculative mysticism. Neoplatonic teachings are transmitted to the mediaeval period through the writings of Denys the Areopagite, Boethius, the tract *Liber de Causis*, and St Augustine (who is not properly a Neoplatonist). While exerting a profound influence on mediaeval Christian thought, e.g. on Aquinas and Dante, Neoplatonism has never been easily compatible with more orthodox Christianity. Indeed those persons influenced by the more radical tendencies of Neoplatonism, for example John Scotus Eriugena and Meister Eckhart*, have frequently been regarded as heterodox or heretical. Orthodox Christianity is suspicious of Neoplatonism for its apparent pantheistic tendencies, the abolition of difference between the soul and God in mystical union, and the denial of divine freedom in creation.

There has been a contemporary revival of interest in Neoplatonism which coincides with the increased general interest in spirituality. For example, various scholars such as D. T. Suzuki regard the more radical forms of Neoplatonism as providing the closest Western counterparts of Zen Buddhism*. Also the established connection between Heidegger and Eckhart has led to various attempts both to show that Neoplatonism escapes some of the criticism that Heidegger levels against Western metaphysics and to explore the relation between mystical experience and Heidegger's own conception of thinking as releasement.

A. H. Armstrong (ed), *The Cambridge History of Later Greek and Early Mediaeval Philosophy*, 1959; Boethius, *Theological Tractates* and *Consolation of Philosophy* (Loeb), 1918; Denys the Areopagite, *The Divine Names and Mystical Theology*, ET 1980; Plotinus, *Enneads*, ET ² 1957; Proclus, *The Elements of Theology*, ET 1933.

JOHN D. JONES

Neri, St Philip

St Philip Neri (1515–1595) was one of the leading figures of the sixteenth-century Catholic spiritual revival. Born in Florence, he came to Rome as a young man and for many years led a simple life of prayer and asceticism. At the church of the Florentines, San Girolamo della Carità, he met Persiano Rosa, who became his confessor. With Philip's help Persiano formed a confraternity of the Trinity to assist poor pilgrims, which did great work in the Holy Year of 1550. In 1551 Philip was ordained at Persiano's bidding and went to live at San Girolamo. He soon gathered round him his own disciples who met daily for prayer and spiritual reading. When some of these were ordained in 1564, the Congregation of the Oratory came into being. By then Philip was well known for his spiritual direction and his lenten pilgrimages to the Seven Basilicas. The rapid growth of the Oratory led to its transfer in 1575 to the church of Santa Maria in Vallicella. In 1593 Philip resigned as superior but continued to exercise enormous influence until his death.

Among the writings which shaped Philip's spirituality were the *Laudi* of Jacopone da Todi, the Life of Blessed John Colombini, and the Lives of the Desert Fathers*, whom he once called 'old men like me'. As he never published anything himself, his teaching is to be found in the depositions of witnesses in the process for his canonization. Although he sent many to the religious orders, his main endeavour was to help people lead spiritual lives without changing their outward circumstances. Frequent confession and communion was the means by which this was to be achieved. As a confessor he was sought out for his gentleness, his joyful optimism, and his supernatural gift of reading hearts. Spiritual mortification was much more important to him than physical austerity. His famous eccentric behaviour in the 'fools for Christ's sake' tradition was precisely mortification of this kind for the attainment of humility and detachment. Unusually for the time he celebrated Mass every day and with intense devotion.

Philip made prayer attractive and accessible to people from all walks of life. There were no special techniques or exercises. One of his favourite maxims was 'Be humble and obedient and the Holy Spirit will teach you how to pray.' As a preparation for prayer he recommended meditation, particularly on the Four Last Things and on the Passion. We know that he taught a child to pray by saying the Our Father and meditating on it phrase by phrase. Others were encouraged to use short ejaculatory prayers repeated many times in the fashion of a rosary*. In times of dryness he advised going from saint to saint asking spiritual alms of them. Through Philip's work family prayers were introduced into many homes in Rome. But the love of God had also to be expressed in action. Philip frequently sent his penitents to care for the sick in the hospitals. By the time he died his influence had been so profound that he was called 'the Apostle of Rome'.

See also **Oratorians.**

Louis Bouyer, *The Roman Socrates*, ET 1958; Louis Ponnelle and Louis Bordet, *St Philip Neri and the Roman Society of his Times*, ET ² 1979; Meriol Trevor, *Apostle of Rome*, 1966.

                                   NORMAN RUSSELL

Newman, John Henry

The development of the spirituality of John Henry Newman (1801–1890) shows a consistent theme, despite the movement of his views on doctrine and ecclesiology. As the young Evangelical, as the Tractarian from 1833–1844, and as the most scholarly and intellectually gifted of English Roman Catholics from 1845 until his death, Newman's spirituality was based upon the principle that religious faith is of the heart as well as the mind. The biographies of Newman relate how disciplined a man he was, as scholar, teacher and priest. The *Parochial and Plain Sermons* of his late Anglican days, preached while he was Vicar of the University Church in Oxford during the 1830s, speak in a very practical way to the spiritual problems of ordinary people. They speak of prayer not as a duty but as a privilege, beginning in a sense of personal dependence on God. He placed the growth of the spiritual life within the context of the church's seasonal worship, emphasizing the opportunities in the liturgical year for versatility and richness in the corporate and personal lives of Christians. The Christian life is conceived as an exciting mystery and adventure, a quest for 'holiness

rather than peace', as Newman described it in his *Apologia Pro Vita Sua* (1864). His sermons convey a strong sense of the social character of prayer, that intercessory prayer bridges the gap between self and others: in coming to understand his role in the body corporate of the church, the Christian becomes aware of his personal moral responsibilities.

Newman's spirituality owes much to the Anglican Caroline Divines* of the seventeenth century, and through them he reached back to the Fathers of antiquity. The theology of St Athanasius of Alexandria* had a particularly strong influence on him. Newman's preaching a doctrine of learning to pray always, rooted in a profound sense of the divine indwelling, the living of Jesus in the heart of every Christian, links his spirituality with that of Eastern Orthodoxy. Similarly, his emphasis on the eucharist as the focus of theology and the spiritual life in corporate prayer, and his sensitivity to the hiddenness of God's providence, discerned only through prayer, exhibit a definite patristic character. The Christian deep in prayer is aware of the mystery of his relationship with and in God. 'Prayer is to the spiritual life what the beating of the pulse and the drawing of the breath are to the life of the body' (*Parochial and Plain Sermons* VII, 1842–1843, p. 209). Newman's analogy of the growth of body and soul is strongly reminiscent of what the Eastern Fathers called the 'prayer of the heart'.

Newman's writing on prayer was always more practical than theoretical: he shied away from systems of prayer. And he was cautious about the real effectiveness of prayer: 'let no one rashly pray for [the] scriptural life', he wrote, 'lest before he wish it, he gain his prayer' (*Sermons on Subjects of the Day*, 1843, p. 48). Newman's spirituality emphasizes a practical quest for holiness, nourished in the disciplines of formal prayer, particularly eucharistic (an example of which can be seen in *The Greek Prayers of Lancelot Andrewes*, which Newman translated into English in 1843), and in a highly developed sense of personal moral communion with God. His choice of the phrase of St Francis de Sales*, *Cor ad Cor Loquitur* ('heart speaks to heart'), for his motto as cardinal, crystallizes the character of Newman's spirituality.

See also **Oxford Movement, The.**

Owen Chadwick, *Newman*, 1983; R. W. Church, *The Oxford Movement 1833–1845*, 1892; C. S. Dessain, *John Henry Newman*, 1980; *Newman's Spiritual Themes*, 1977; Hilda Graef, *God and Myself*, 1967; W. Ward, *Life of Cardinal Newman*, 2 vols, 1913. *I. Kerr JHNewman. 1988.*

R. D. TOWNSEND

Nicholas of Cusa

Born in 1401 into a middle-class home at Cues (Cusa) in the Moselle valley, Nicholas, whose family name was Krypffs, or Krebs, began his distinguished ecclesiastical career with studies at Heidelberg (1416) and then at Padua (1417–1423) where he received the doctorate in canon law. Later studies at Cologne introduced him to Herymeric de Campo, Albertus Magnus, Denys the Areopagite* and Raymond Lull and these gave his theology a bent that was both mystical and dynamic. Bonaventure's* *Itinerarium mentis in Deum* and Gerson's* *De mystica theologia* were also among the earliest influences on him. The writings of Meister Eckhart* have likewise left their demonstrable imprint upon his early works. Oft-repeated assertions that the youthful Nicholas attended school at Deventer and there came under the direct spiritual influence of the Brothers of the Common Life and the *Devotio Moderna** cannot be substantiated and have been plausibly criticized.

In his early programmatic and most well-known work, *De docta ignorantia* (1440), Nicholas outlined his view of the world as an 'unfolding' of all which in God is 'enfolded'. As the Absolute Maximum, God is the *complicatio* of all creation which is related to its creator as human artifacts are related to the human mind which originates them out of its own inherent fecundity. Because of the immediacy and continuing nature of the relationship between the Absolute Maximum and the reality unfolding from it, Nicholas' spiritual vision places a positive valuation upon the world and upon human activity; their relational status, however, denies them any ultimate value but urges the mind to ascend even higher in its search for the purest Unity-Equality-Connection (the undivided divine Trinity) which it somehow 'knows' by experience. The knowledge of God is thus intuitive rather than discursive but Nicholas insists that the mystical ascent to God cannot be merely affective or intellectually blind. It is a knowledge which 'knows' the object of its quest is unknowable, which 'sees' the darkness – a knowledge which realizes the necessity of the impossible. This coincidence of opposites, which reason and logic abhor, is the 'wall' beyond which the soul finds God. Such knowledge is 'learned ignorance' and it is accessible to the unlettered lay person for it is not to be found in books or through scholastic disputations.

Christ himself mirrors the coincidence of opposites because he is at once divine and human, the *Maximum Contractum*. He is the person in whom human nature and indeed all nature reaches its maximum. Through this divine Word made visible and audible in our world those minds which receive its nourishment come to live by faith and union with him. It is they who will reach final glory.

Nicholas' experience of God's immediacy and presence found expression in his treatise *De visione dei* in which he likens God's presence to the eyes of a picture which 'see' all simultaneously and without moving. This 'seeing' is God's creative power and love which, in the person of Jesus, brings truth itself to the human intellect. Nicholas' spirituality is thus markedly intellectual as was, of course, his own life.

Nicolai de Cusa Opera Omnia, vol I, *De docta ignorantia*, ed E. Hoffmann and R. Klibansky, 1932; Nicholas of Cusa, *The Vision of God*, ET 1960; R. Haubst, *Die Christologie des Nikolaus von Kues*, 1956; E. Vansteenberghe, *Le Cardinal Nicolas de Cues (1401–1464) – L'Action – La Pensée*, 1920. *H. Bett.*

JAMES E. BIECHLER

Nietzsche, Friedrich
see **Death of God**

Nirvana see **Buddhism**

Nonjurors

The original Nonjurors, the bishops and clergy who refused the oath to William of Orange in 1689, and, being deprived of their benefices, were forced to set up their own ecclesiastical organization, which they regarded as the legitimate Church of Eng-

land, included among their number many of
the 'Caroline Divines'*, and they and their
successors during the eighteenth century
continued the Laudian and Caroline tradition, in spirituality as in other things, while
it all but disappeared within the establishment. Nonjuring spirituality in general,
therefore, exhibits but little difference from
that of Anglican high churchmen of the
seventeenth century, although the more 'extreme' high churchmen among the Nonjurors went well beyond what was in their time
a recognizably Anglican position in, e.g.
their sacramental theology, liturgy and devotion.

The best known of the later Nonjurors is
undoubtedly William Law (1686–1761),
and that precisely on account of his ascetical
and mystical writings, although it should be
emphasized that in a number of ways Law
was far from being a typical Nonjuror, and
indeed was decidedly unpopular with many
of his brethren. Law stands out, even among
the Nonjurors, who by definition were
people unwilling to compromise, and ready
to pay the inevitable price, for his firm, uncompromising and even rigid teaching on
the manner of life required of the Christian.
This is already evident in his 'Rules for my
Future Conduct' which he formulated
before he went up to Emmanuel College,
Cambridge, in 1705. Ordained deacon and
elected a fellow of the college in 1711, he
refused the oaths on the accession of George
I, was deprived of his fellowship, and joined
the Nonjuring Church, in which he took
priest's orders in 1728. The same year saw
the publication of his best known and most
influential work, A Serious Call to a Devout
and Holy Life.

This book is well described in ODCC as
'a forceful exhortation to embrace the
Christian life in its moral and ascetical fullness. The author recommends the exercise
of the moral virtues and meditation and
ascetical practices; corporate worship, however, finds little place. He insists especially
on the virtues practised in everyday life,
temperance, humility and self-denial, all
animated by the intention to glorify God, to
which every human activity should be
directed.' Spiritual classic though it be,
however, the Serious Call is marred by Law's
rigidity: for Law the proportion of human
activity which can be directed to the glory of
God is exceedingly limited – there are no

innocent amusements or relaxations, learning is suspect, and almost everything that
comes under the heading of culture is dangerous. Austin Warren, in his introduction
to the most recent edition of the book, sums
it up: 'The bow must always be taut, never
relaxed.'

In 1740 Law retired to his family home at
King's Cliffe, Northamptonshire, where he
lived for the remainder of his life in a sort of
religious community with a Mrs Hutcheson,
a widow, and Miss Hester Gibbon, sister of
the historian's father to whom he had been
tutor between 1727 and 1737. Previously
influenced in particular by Tauler*, Ruysbroeck* and Thomas à Kempis*, by this
time he had fallen under the spell of the
writings of Jakob Boehme*, of whose
idiosyncratic mystical teaching he became a
fanatical adherent, going so far as to speak
of 'the mystery of all things opened by God
in his chosen instrument Jakob Boehme'.
Law's own spiritual teaching became less
and less concerned with the moral and ascetical values so prominent in the Serious Call,
and more and more marked by a high-flown
mysticism and an adventurous theological
speculation which is neither entirely orthodox nor entirely sane. It is not surprising
that many who had greatly valued the
Serious Call – John Wesley* and Samuel
Johnson* among them – reacted very differently to the products of Law's later years, of
which The Spirit of Prayer (published in two
parts in 1749 and 1750) and The Spirit of
Love (similarly published in 1752 and 1754)
are the most notable.

A Serious Call to a Devout and Holy Life
and The Spirit of Love (Classics of Western
Spirituality), 1979; S. H. Hobhouse, Selected
Mystical Writings of William Law, 1938;
J. H. Overton, The Nonjurors: their Lives,
Principles and Writings, 1902; A. K. Walker,
William Law: His Life and Thought, 1973.

W. JARDINE GRISBROOKE

Oratorians

The first Oratorians were a group of laymen
who gathered round St Philip Neri* at the
Roman church of San Girolamo della
Carità. They met every afternoon in the
attics above the church for two hours or so
of reading, discussion, discourses, hymns
and prayers. The venue, a place of prayer
without an altar, gave the name 'Oratory' to

these informal spiritual exercises. The Congregation of the Oratory came into being unofficially when some of Philip's disciples were ordained in 1564 to help him with his work, but was not formally erected until 1575, when the Congregation was given the church of Santa Maria in Vallicella. The idea of the Oratory, a Congregation of secular priests and clerics without vows, was quite new and spread rapidly, many Oratories being founded in the seventeenth and eighteenth centuries, particularly in Italy, Spain and Latin America. France developed her own form of the Oratory under Cardinal de Bérulle * in 1611. The most significant foundations in the nineteenth century were made in England, in Birmingham (1848) and London (1849), by J. H. Newman *. In the twentieth century the Oratory has spread to Germany and the United States.

The keynote of Oratorian life is its family character. Numbers are small, each house is independent, and though there are no vows there is an almost Benedictine commitment to stability. Each father keeps his own possessions, but there is a common table and a common period of prayer each day. In spite of a rich liturgical tradition in which music has always been important, the Office is not said in common. This is because St Philip wished to safeguard the availability of the fathers to the laity. In their work the fathers give priority to preaching, hearing confessions and spiritual direction. A gentle, easy and lay-orientated spirituality has always been characteristic of the Oratory. St Philip wanted his sons to be free, to be 'at home' in the Congregation, and to exercise their ministry through personal influence, while at the same time submitting willingly to the ascetic discipline of community life. 'Our perfection is in community', as Newman said.

When Newman settled on the Oratory of St Philip in 1847 for himself and his converts, he found a Congregation well suited to mature and well-educated men accustomed to a collegiate life. Even in Philip's time the Oratory had been for 'formed men' not youths, and community duties left the fathers with much time to give to prayer and intellectual or cultural pursuits. The most notable Oratorian scholars have been C. Baronius, O. Raynaldus and A. Theiner. The Oratory in England was specifically entrusted by Pius IX with an apostolate to the educated classes, and Newman and Faber * both exercised a wide influence through their writings. Nothing is undertaken, however, which is incompatible with community life.

The Oratorian path to God lies in the personal influence exercised by holy men, in an unobtrusive asceticism, and in freedom with regard to the practice of prayer. Four Oratorians have been beatified, Anthony Grassi of Fermo (1592–1671), Sebastian Valfré of Turin (1629–1710), Joseph Vaz of Goa (1651–1711) and Luigi Scrosoppi of Friuli (1804–1884).

Raleigh Addington, *The Idea of the Oratory*, 1966; A. Cistellini; *DS*, IX, cols 853–76; Placid Murray, *Newman the Oratorian*, ²1980.

NORMAN RUSSELL

Origen

Origen (*c*. 185–254) reflects in his spirituality, as in all else, his attempted domestication of scriptural revelation within current Hellenistic culture, especially the eclectic Stoicized Middle-Platonism which he could use objectively – turning impartially the arguments of one school against another in line with his theological purposes – but which he would often presuppose without question. These processes served in some ways to darken, in others to illuminate, his Christian insights, as well as to imperil the systematic consistency of doctrine and ethics in his vast literary output.

1. Although Origen distinguishes the Christian doctrine of providence from the subtly materialized and impersonal Stoic conception, he accepts implicitly both Stoic 'natural law' and its 'universal intuitions' of the human conscience. Christian ethics *is* natural morality, but activated by an inbred longing for the true God. This is the point of departure.

2. Origen assumes the Platonic distinction between the visible and the intelligible or spiritual world, with its unsolved problem of the relationship between them ('imitation' or 'participation'?) and the consequent uncertainty of the *status* of the former. Sometimes life in this world is a mere congeries of symbols or veils of eternal reality, with echoes of the Platonic 'wherefore we ought to fly away from earth to heaven as quickly as we can, and to fly away is to become as

far as possible like God' (*Theaet.* 176) – and a resultant enfeebling of Origen's sense of history. At other times the centrality of the incarnation suggests that this world is the setting of a genuine moral drama involving the supreme will of God and the free will of the creature. All this is in line with Origen's inconsistent valuation of the literal interpretation of scripture ('the flesh').

3. Origen assumes the Platonic definitions of God as transcendent, immutable, impassible, in need of nothing although creating the world by his overflowing goodness. In imitation of these ideals the Christian is called to a life of asceticism * – vigils, fasting, daily study of scripture, (preferably) abstention from marriage, detachment from worldly responsibilities – and *apatheia* * (passionlessness, invulnerability). This latter the Stoics had elevated to the master-theme of the ethics of Graeco-Roman culture. The notorious story (true or false) of Origen's self-mutilation, and the whole picture of his mode of life given by Eusebius (*HE* VI) is in line with the dominant asceticism of his whole life.

4. Origen adopts the normal patristic distinction between the 'image' and 'likeness' of Gen. 1.26: man received the dignity of the 'image' (i.e. the possibility of attaining perfection) at his creation, while the latter could be acquired in the end, when he will become 'as like God as possible', through the grace of God and his own merits. Here Origen, in the Platonic tradition of the 'intellectual aristocracy', distinguishes 'simple faith' from 'faith in its fullness', the ordinary Christian from the 'gnostic', 'spiritual' or 'perfect'. For the latter the pathway to God is the mystical ascent, in which there is a constant but in the end victorious dialectic between inward afflictions from the allurements of the devil and his demons, and the consolation of ever higher and purer visions of the glory of Christ. The Pauline 'discernment of spirits' remains essential, because the demon of sin may well disguise himself as an angel of light. In such trials lies the imitation of Christ *, who was likewise 'tempted' – above all at the cross – but through our ascetic discipline we steadily climb the Mount of Transfiguration until the unveiled light of Christ shines on us and the voice of the Father is heard. This theme is brought to a climax in Origen's *Commentary on the Song of Songs*, where the mystical ascent is symbolized by the marriage of the Christ-Logos with the soul. The ultimate ideal is the mystical union with God, which Origen (again in line with patristic tradition) formulates in terms of deification * – 'You too must become a god in Christ Jesus'.

5. The above elements of Origen's spirituality may all be traced in his two 'practical' treatises – *On Prayer* and *Exhortation to Martyrdom*. The latter, written for two friends at the outset of the persecution of Maximinus A D 235), insists on martyrdom * (taking upon ourselves the cross with Christ) as the duty of every true Christian, because all who love God wish to be united with him; the reward will be greater in proportion to the worldly goods left behind. Martyrdom is the repayment to God for his blessings, and procures not only eternal bliss for the martyr but forgiveness for others. The blood of the martyrs can become a means of redemption. The treatise *On Prayer* traces the 'mystical ascent' through the phases of prayer * itself: petition, adoration, supplication, thanksgiving. Prayer culminates in vision, and overflows into intercession for our brothers. It should not be directed to Christ, but through him to God: one cannot pray to someone who prays himself, and Christ insists that only God the Father may be called 'good' and as such adored. Still less should prayer be directed to 'the saints'.

The interior preparation of the soul for prayer, which Origen carefully delineates, does not obscure the overriding truth that prayer is a gift of the Holy Spirit, who prays in us and leads us to prayer.

The basic source is W. Völker, *Das Vollkommenheitsideal des Origen,* 1931; in recent years the French school has been preeminent: von Balthasar, *Parole et Mystère chez Origène,* 1956; F. Bertrand, *Mystique de Jésus chez Origène,* 1951; V. H. Crouzel, *Théologie de l'Image de Dieu chez Origène,* 1956; M. Harl, *Origène et la Fonction Révélatrice du Verbe Incarné,* 1958. See also L. Bouyer, *The Spirituality of the New Testament and the Fathers,* 1960, pp. 276ff. Translations, etc. of *Origen's Treatise on Prayer* by E. G. Jay, 1954, and *Martyrdom* by J. J. O'Meara, 1954; also by Oulton and Chadwick in *Alexandrian Christianity* (LCC II), 1954.

BENJAMIN DREWERY

Orthodox Spirituality

The essentials of Orthodox spirituality are summed up in the words which introduce the Lord's Prayer at the Divine Liturgy, 'And count us worthy, Master, with boldness and uncondemned to dare to call upon you, the heavenly God, as Father and to say: 'Our father . . .'' Man is a creature, a fallen and sinful creature; God is utterly transcendent, absolutely holy and 'dwells in unapproachable light' (I Tim. 6.16), and yet he calls man to be one with him, to become a 'sharer in the divine nature' (II Peter 1.4), to become his son by adoption (cf. Rom. 8.15; Gal. 4.5). The radical separation between God and man has been abolished by the Incarnate Word, for, in the words of St Irenaeus *, 'if the Word has been made man, it is so that men may be made gods', and man the redeemed sinner may henceforth approach the infinite majesty of God with the 'freedom of speech', the boldness, 'the intimate communion' or, in Greek, the *parrhesia* of beloved sons. Orthodox spirituality, then, is the spirituality of the Lord's Prayer, a spirituality of praise and penitence, of love and trust, of fellowship with the Holy Trinity in union with all the Father's children, both those who have gone before and those who here and now share, through baptism and the eucharist, the common life of the Spirit in the Body of Christ. Somewhat schematically we might say that the notes or marks of Orthodox spirituality are that it is biblical, theological, ascetic, sacramental, liturgical and ecclesial.

1. *Biblical*. The Bible, and supremely the Gospel, is at the heart of the Orthodox spiritual life. This is expressed symbolically by the reverence accorded to the actual book of the Gospels, which always lies upon the altar and is venerated as an icon of the living Word in the midst of the people. At the liturgy it is carried solemnly into the congregation as the Beatitudes are sung, which summarize the evangelical life. This outward reverence to the Gospel book is not mere picturesque symbolism but springs from the profoundly biblical conviction that the divine economy both in the creation and in the incarnation and redemption involves the whole of creation, both spiritual and material. If the Creed proclaims the belief of Christians in '*one* God, maker of heaven and earth', it is because Christianity has always rejected all forms of Gnosticism, Manicheanism and dualism. It is the whole man, both body and soul, who is called to be transfigured into the glory, into the image and likeness of God, and with him the cosmos. 'The entire universe is called to enter within the Church, to become the Church of Christ, that it may be transformed after the consummation of the ages into the eternal Kingdom of God' (V. Lossky).

With the exception of the book of Revelation, which took longer to establish its place in the Canon in the East than in the West, the whole of the N T is read each year at the Divine Liturgy, the year being divided into the four periods of the four Evangelists, starting with St John on Easter Day and ending with St Mark in Lent.

Next to the Gospel the Psalter is the most used and best loved book of the Bible. Certain Psalms, such as Ps. 51 (in the West, Ps. 50, since the Psalter has a slightly different numeration in the two traditions) and the six psalms which always begin Matins, and Ps. 119 (118) which is read at funerals and daily in the full office, have entered deeply into the soul of the Orthodox people. If the O T is only read extensively in Lent, its language, images and symbolism are so inextricably woven into the hymns and prayers of the church that the whole prayer life of the Orthodox Christian is, even if sometimes unconsciously, profoundly biblical. Moreover the typological use of the O T in the hymns means that the O T lives as part of contemporary Christian experience.

2. *Theological*. Orthodox spirituality is strongly theological, strongly trinitarian and christological. This is not mere intellectualism, but the result of the Orthodox belief that the understanding of the scriptures which the Spirit gives to the church in the holy tradition of the Ecumenical Councils and the Fathers concerns the inner life of the Christian and should direct his actions and his thoughts. If the Word became man 'for us and for our salvation', then theology is not a purely academic exercise but affects the way we live and act. As Evagrius says, 'If you are a theologian, you will pray truly. And if you pray truly, you are a theologian' (*On Prayer* 61, cf. *The Philokalia*, vol 1, E T 1979, p. 62).

God has revealed himself to man as Trinity, as a Unity of Godhead in a Trinity of persons, and this self-disclosure of God is at the heart of Christian prayer. The God whom the Christian worships is the God who manifests himself as Father, Son and Spirit, not the God of philosophers and academics, and so the standard doxologies of Orthodox worship, which end nearly every prayer and hymn, are trinitarian. But since God has also revealed himself to man as man, the mystery of the incarnation also holds a central place in Orthodox spirituality, particularly in the devotion and veneration given to the Virgin Mary. For the Orthodox, Mary is always understood in relation to the economy of her Son, and the greatest of her titles, Theotokos, 'Mother of God', marks the christological assertion that the human child whom she bore was none other than the Divine Word Himself. The central place then given to Mary in the spirituality of the Orthodox is a constant reminder to them of the central truth of the faith: that God himself so loved fallen man that he was ready to empty himself and become man, to die on a cross, to bring man to him. Orthodox spirituality is one of amazement and gratitude at the love of God for man (*philanthropia*).

3. *Ascetic*. The life and prayer of the Orthodox has been and continues to be deeply influenced by the ascetic and monastic tradition. Since the fourth century, monasticism has flourished in the Eastern churches and the spiritual tradition has been largely formed under monastic influence. The service books of the church are monastic and the laws of fasting are monastic also. Monastic life is a life of repentance, a life of turning from sin and return to the Father; it is an icon of the life of fallen man. Orthodox spirituality is full of this spirit of repentance, the figures of David, Manasseh, the prodigal, the publican, the sinful woman and Peter forming a gallery of repentant sinners who meet the Orthodox Christian as he confesses his sins, as he prepares to receive holy communion and as he advances during the long weeks of Lent to the brightness of the resurrection. This concentration on sin and repentance is not a question of morbid sentiment but a realistic acknowledgment of a factual situation. God alone is without sin, God alone is holy and the more the Christian becomes aware of God's holiness the more he becomes aware of his own distance from God, becomes aware of his sin, which

is why the Jesus Prayer* is a prayer for mercy. But asceticism is not an end in itself; it is the necessary training, the necessary preparation for the life of prayer, leading to the life of union with God. And this is not something for specialists, monks and nuns; in the words of the translators of *The Philokalia*, 'the distinction between the monastic life and life in the world is but relative: every human being, by virtue of the fact that he or she is created in the image of God, is summoned to be perfect, is summoned to love God with all his or her heart, soul and mind' (*The Philokalia*, p. 16). Asceticism too is seen as a sharing in the suffering of Christ and the martyrs. Every Christian is called to the arena of the conflict with the powers of darkness and he enters it in the full assurance that Christ himself has gone down there before him and has won the victory, in which the Christian is to share.

4. *Sacramental*. For St Simeon the New Theologian the realities of the new age of which the mystic receives a foretaste in ecstasy and eventually in constant communion with God are already present in every Christian, for they are none other than the grace of baptism. Every Christian by his baptism has died and been raised with Christ, every Christian by communion becomes a partaker in the life of God, is made one with him. Hence there can be no separation of the mystical and contemplative life from the ordinary sacramental life of the whole church. There is a profound significance in the tradition whereby all the monks of a monastery return to the monastery for Holy Week and Easter. The way to deification, to union with God, is to take part in the sacramental life of the church. 'If a man asks "How can I become god?" the answer is very simple: go to church, receive the sacraments regularly, pray to God "in spirit and in truth", read the Gospels, follow the commandments' (Kallistos Ware).

In addition to baptism and the eucharist, the sacrament of confession has an important place in Orthodox, particularly Russian, spirituality, and is linked to the importance given in Orthodoxy to the Spiritual Father, in Greek *geronta*, in Russian *starets* or 'old man', although the Spiritual Father, or Mother, is sometimes not a priest, in which case he will send his spiritual child to a priest to receive sacramental absolution. The sins of the individual affect not only the sinner but the whole body of which he is a member and so the church publicly receives back the penitent who has publicly acknowledged that his sin has offended not only God but also his brethren, which is why Orthodox confessions are frequently heard in the open church with both priest and penitent in full view of other worshippers.

5. *Liturgical.* The spirituality of Orthodoxy is essentially liturgical and ecclesial, for though private prayer is frequent and encouraged, the main source of strength comes from the public worship of the church and the majority of prayers in the manuals of private devotion are in fact taken from the official service books. Private prayer is nourished by the formal prayer of the church, and the Orthodox Christian learns day by day, year by year, to enter more deeply into the mysteries of his faith by using the words of scripture and the Fathers. 'It is a strange thought that Christ did not teach his disciples to pray. St John did. In exasperation and perhaps impatiently they had to drag it out of him, and whatever the "Our Father" is – compared with the desert nights when "he drew apart" they got a formal answer' (Mother Maria of Normandy). If there is no tradition of formal meditation in Orthodox spirituality this is because the great richness of the texts of the offices and the large amount of repetition they contain, both of whole prayers and hymns and of particular images and expressions, render it unnecessary. 'Its place is taken in the Orthodox church by corporate liturgical worship. As the Orthodox Christian stands in church, hour by hour, during the vigil for some great feast or at the services on an ordinary day, he has the same necessary and saving truths continually underlined, now in one way, now in another . . . The words that are read or sung in church are by themselves sufficient to provide him with abundant nourishment for his life in Christ' (Kallistos Ware).

6. *Ecclesial.* Finally, Orthodox spirituality is not individualistic, since the Christian by his baptism has become a member of the body of Christ and it is as a member of that body that he advances on the road to deification. 'No one is saved alone, he is saved in the Church, as a member of it and in union with all its other members' (A. Khomiakov), and this includes all those who have gone before and those to come. Orthodox Christians are vividly aware of the communion of the saints. They have a particular devotion to their patron saint and to their guardian angel and they believe that they are linked with all who have gone before them in the faith, with those 'who have been pleasing to God' from Adam and Eve through the patriarchs, prophets and kings, including even Manesseh and Ahaz, of the old convenant, all of whom are celebrated liturgically as saints, down through the Forerunner and Baptist John, the apostles and the martyrs and the Fathers, to their own families and friends, both those who are alive and those who 'sleep with Christ' for, as St John of Damascus says, 'We do not speak of the departed Christian as dead but sleeping.' The departed sleep in Christ as they wait for the final resurrection of which they have the full assurance of faith since Christ himself the first-fruits 'has risen from the dead, trampling down death by death and on those in tombs bestowing life.'

An excellent introduction to the subject is *Orthodox Spirituality*, by A Monk of the Eastern Church, [2] 1978; other useful books are Kallistos Ware, *The Orthodox Way*, 1979; V. Lossky, *The Mystical Theology of the Eastern Church*, 1957; Sister Thekla, *Mother Maria. Her Life in Letters*, 1979.

SYMEON LASH

Oxford Movement, The

The name given to the movement of religious revival within the High Anglican tradition which began in 1833. Traditionally dated from the Assize Sermon on National Apostasy preached by John Keble* in the July of that year, its Oxford period ended with the secession of John Henry Newman* to the Church of Rome in 1845, and its influence thereafter became more significant outside Oxford.

In part a defensive reaction against the institutional and constitutional changes affecting the relation of church and state and the character of the Church of England, as a movement of religious revival it was far more than this. Stressing the identity of the church as a divine society, with an apostolic ministry continued through the historic episcopate, and sacramental worship as the means of grace, Keble, Newman and Pusey*, as the leaders of the Movement, endeavoured to resist the encroachments of latitudinarian rationalism and Protestant individualism. They all had a deep sense of the mystery of the Christian gospel and of the holiness of God, transcending human language and demanding a rich use of image and symbol as the way God had used in his self-revelation. Keble's poetry and Newman's sermons at the University Church in Oxford were powerful ways in which these themes and this call to holiness was expressed, but it was the series of *Tracts for the Times* through which the Movement had its initial impact, and from which its adherents gained the name Tractarians. The series came to an end with *Tract 90* in 1841, in which Newman attempted to show that the Thirty-Nine Articles of Religion were patient of a Catholic interpretation.

The spirituality of the Oxford Movement owed much both to the Fathers, as embodying the theology and devotion of the undivided church, and the seventeenth-century Caroline Divines*. They stood firmly for the doctrines of baptismal regeneration; the Real Presence of Christ in the eucharist; the apostolic succession and the necessity of episcopacy; and the communion of saints. The pursuit of intellectual truth was to be subordinated to the quest for moral excellence, the holiness without which no man could see God. The influence of the Greek Fathers is particularly striking, with their theme of salvation as a participation in the divine nature.

The reaction of the Tractarians against the rationalist theology of the eighteenth century was in part an instance of the wider movement of Romanticism, but their return to the Fathers indicates more than this. As a result of their teaching and writing Anglican worship underwent a remarkable transformation. The eucharist was restored to an increasingly central place; there was a renewed appreciation of liturgy and a demand for both richer forms and more ceremonial expression. The pattern of prayer in the daily office grew to be widely observed among the clergy. There was a revival of sacramental confession and of the religious life. With the increased interest in traditional forms of worship went a new openness to Roman Catholicism and, to some extent, Eastern Orthodoxy, which led to a growing search for unity with these churches. On the 'branch theory' of the church espoused by the Tractarians and their successors, these churches, together with Anglicans, comprised the Catholic Church.

In the later Ritualist movement there was a greater willingness to adopt Roman Catholic practice than had been the case with the Tractarians themselves, who, apart from certain adaptations of the Roman Breviary for private use, were staunch defenders of the Book of Common Prayer, believing it to be an essentially catholic form of worship. Although Tractarians and Evangelicals were often opposed in the religious polemics of the nineteenth century, the two movements shared in common a concern for the religion of the heart, and many of the Tractarian leaders were men who had been formed by the Evangelical Revival (*see* **Evangelical Spirituality**). The innovations in worship by the successors of the Tractarians led directly to the first attempt to revise the Prayer Book in 1927–1928. The Anglo-Catholic congresses of the inter-war years witness to the growth and strength of the tradition stemming from the Oxford Movement in the theology and spirituality of Anglicanism.

Y. Brilioth, *The Anglican Revival*, 1933; O. Chadwick, *The Victorian Church*, I, 1970; *The Mind of the Oxford Movement*, 1960; R. W. Church, *The Oxford Movement, 1833–45*, 1892; E. R. Fairweather, *The Oxford Movement*, 1964; A. Härdelin, *The Tractarian Understanding of the Eucharist*, 1965; G. Rowell, *The Vision Glorious*, 1983.

GEOFFREY ROWELL

Palamas, St Gregory

One of the most important theologians of the Greek Church, though he is not of the three – John the Divine, Gregory Nazianzen and Symeon – who alone have received the title. Palamas (*c.* 1296–1359) was the chief exponent of *Hesychasm**, which he learned from Mount Athos. He became Archbishop of Thessalonica in 1347, but had many vicissitudes both before and after, through the advance of the Turkish armies, and a theological controversy with Barlaam, a Greek monk from Calabria, who had been influenced by Western scholasticism.

Palamas taught that human nature is a psychosomatic unity. Hence the importance and legitimacy of the physical exercises practised by the Hesychasts in prayer. He believed that the Divine Light could be seen with bodily eyes as at the Transfiguration, because it is Light which communicates the energies of God, and in these we may participate and become partakers of the Divine nature. He distinguished between the Divine essence and energies. In his essence, God is totally inaccessible; but through his energy we become deified, i.e. in his light we see light. This is an antinomy like the doctrine of the Trinity itself. God is one, yet three. He is also 'both exclusive of, and in some sense open to participation'. Barlaam challenged this rather as a Western theologian might, insisting on God's complete Otherness, Kierkegaard's 'infinite qualitative distance'. Some modern Protestant theologians have felt that Palamas makes God too abstract and fails to take seriously the humanity of the risen Lord, who crosses the gulf and makes possible a unity between God and us which is best described as *communion* rather than in the phraseology of the mid-second century tract, with its halfdigested Hellenism, which is the latest work in the NT (II Peter).

But Eastern theology – and some Western Catholic – has sided with Gregory, who was canonized in 1368.

B. Drewery in P. Brooks (ed) *Christian Spirituality*, 1975, pp. 35–62; Vladimir Lossky, *The Mystical Theology of the Eastern Church*, 1957; E. L. Mascall, *The Openness of Being*, 1971, esp. Appendix 3, pp. 217ff.; John Meyendorff (ed), *Gregory Palamas: The Triads*, 1983.

                                                        EDITOR

Pascal, Blaise

Blaise Pascal (1623–1662) had already made a name for himself as an outstanding scientist and mathematician when in 1654 he underwent a conversion experience, recorded on a scrap of paper found accidentally after his death. Already in 1646 he and his family had been converted by Jansenist* laymen, and as far as doctrine and practice went his second conversion probably taught him nothing new. Unlike the first, however, he felt it to be a direct, personal contact with Christ, for whose suffering he acknowledged his share of responsibility but whose love freely forgave

him. This experience is the foundation of Pascal's spirituality, an outstanding example of which is to be seen in the *Mystery of Jesus*, a private meditation not intended for publication (*Pensées* 919).

The immediate consequence of his conversion was a retreat at Port Royal, and submission to spiritual direction from there, but it is misleading to label him a Jansenist in any narrow sense. Next year his publication of the *Provincial Letters* (1656–1657) was undertaken in support of the Jansenist leader Antoine Arnauld, but far from seeing this as a challenge to legitimate authority, Pascal and his friends regarded themselves as defending ancient truths against the assaults of unscrupulous innovators who had tricked even the pope. The polemical and satirical content of the letters stresses the alleged cynicism and frivolity, amounting to blasphemy, of Jesuit casuists, but tends to obscure the positive side of Pascal's case. This he realized even before the last letter appeared, and to make up for it he planned his *Apology for the Christian Religion*, the unfinished elements of which are preserved in the posthumously published *Pensées* (1670).

The apology is specifically aimed at the intelligent, worldly sceptic of Pascal's own class and skilfully appeals both to the intellect and the emotions. The argument starts from the fact of corrupt human nature, but instead of beginning with revelation and the Fall, Pascal begins with nature. He opens with an analysis of the human condition, not in terms of sin, but in terms of insecurity, inconstancy and anxiety. He speaks not of guilt, but of vertigo provoked by the vastness of the firmament above and the equally vast universe of the infinitesimal revealed by the microscope. He contrasts the outward pomp and dignity of the great with their human frailty, the rational certainties of the philosopher with his discomfiture by a buzzing fly. He shows how trivial are the diversions with which men dispel feelings of grief or anxiety. In short he gives a psychological analysis of a nature in which glaring defects combine with lofty aspirations, in which the individual is terrifyingly isolated, in which mankind rushes heedlessly over an unknown abyss. This condition he characterizes as 'wretchedness of man without God', and his anticipation of so many modern reactions to a hostile cosmos and an alienating society no doubt accounts in part for his continuing great popularity.

To explain man's paradoxical state Pascal offers the hypothesis of a fall, but since Christianity links the Fall and the Redemption inseparably, he proceeds in his second part to expound the faith in a rigorously christocentric way. One of his most characteristic arguments concerns the phenomenon of the 'hidden God': if, as Christians maintain, revelation is so certain, why do so many, including Jews, fail to recognize the truth? Because, he replies, they look for it in the wrong 'order', that is the Jews looked for an earthly king (in the 'carnal order'), while the true Messiah came in the 'order of charity' to deliver them from sin, not from political oppressors, just as philosophers insist on rationally watertight proofs in the 'order of mind' while living their daily lives quite happily by instinct and approximation. The truth of scripture is there for those who approach the 'figures' (typology) correctly, Christ will be found by those who listen to their 'heart' (associated with the 'order of charity') above the presumptuous demands of reason, which they ignore when they fall in love but set up as paramount when the stake is eternal life.

Pascal's fundamentalist approach to scripture, particularly his unhistorical interpretation of prophecy, is typical of his age, but does not seriously detract from the value of his argument, which he describes as always convergent, tending always back to Christ. He has often been criticized for exaggerating the dark side of human nature and for a typically Augustinian pessimism, but he also makes much of the joys awaiting those who seek, even in anguish, and the concrete ways in which Christian commitment can improve one's neighbour's lot here and now. It must finally be said that membership of the Roman Church was for Pascal an integral part of following Christ, and he was no less opposed to indifferentism than to deism, which he condemned as no better than atheism.

Pascal, *Œuvres complètes*, ed L. Lafuma, 1963; *Pensées and Provincial Letters*, tr A. J. Krailsheimer, 1966, 1967; J. H. Broome, *Pascal*, 1965; J. Mesnard, *Pascal, His Life and Works*, ET 1952.

A. J. KRAILSHEIMER

Patience *see* **Fruit of the Spirit**

Patrick, St

A British Christian c. 390–460, educated for the ministry in Britain and sent as a bishop by the British church. The text of two works which he wrote in Latin survives, his *Letter to Coroticus* and his *Confession* which he wrote at the end of his life to render thanks to God and to vindicate his own name and career. The latter is a little-known masterpiece of self-revelation and incidentally of spirituality. One of its main purposes is to recount the occasions when Patrick received special guidance in a message (his word is *responsum*) from God or underwent unusual interior experiences in prayer and meditation. God, he says, warned him when in captivity in Ireland to leave his master, saying to him in a dream 'You are right to fast because you will soon go to your own native country' (*Conf.* 17.2, 3) and a little later 'Look, your ship is ready' (17.4, 5). Some years later at home among his kinsfolk in Britain he had another dream in which he saw a man called Victoricus bringing him letters from Ireland and heard the 'people of the wood of Voclut' (where no doubt he had spent his captivity) calling him to return to them (*Conf.* 23). Once when during his ministry as a bishop in Ireland he had been imprisoned he received a message predicting exactly how long his detention would last (*Conf.* 21). At a moment when he was threatened with disgrace owing to the treachery of a false friend in Britain he was cheered by a vision assuring him that God was on his side (*Conf.* 29). On his journey back to Britain after escaping from captivity he had a strange experience when he woke as the sun was rising and found himself invoking *Heliam, Heliam* (*Elias* = Elijah, *Helios* = the sun; *Conf.* 20). And on two other occasions he had an experience startlingly reminiscent of the 'Prayer of the Holy Spirit in the Christian' in the Orthodox tradition, one accompanied by the words 'He who gave his life for you, he it is who gave himself for you' (*Conf.* 24), and again when he saw and heard the Spirit praying and groaning in him (*Conf.* 25). Patrick's accounts of his messages and visions are remarkably convincing for they have the inconsequentiality and surrealist atmosphere of dreams and do not all suggest conventional hagiographic material. They share the quality of directness, spontaneity and freshness which breathes through all his writing.

Patrick's own faith is deeply evangelical in the non-sectarian sense of the word. He does not expect God to rescue him from trouble; he rather hopes for martyrdom (*Conf.* 59). He has a profound, almost obsessional sense of his own insufficiency, especially in education; he calls himself 'very uneducated' three times, even when excommunicating Coroticus and his men (*Conf.* 12.1; 62.3; *Letter* 1.1). But he is full of joy and gratitude and confidence and trust. He gives us the first, almost the sole, picture of the spirituality of the ancient British church, a very favourable one. His faith is nourished on scripture, which he quotes continually, relevantly or otherwise, especially the Psalms in the OT and Romans in the NT. He instituted monks and nuns (probably individual ascetics not communities) in Ireland (*Conf.* 41; 42; 49.3; *Letter* 12.8; 19.4). He may himself have taken a vow of asceticism of some sort while he was in Britain. He admired the monastic institutions of Gaul, some of which he had probably visited (*Conf.* 32.4, 5; 43.3–5). The well-known hymn 'St Patrick's Breastplate' is not his composition.

R. P. C. Hanson, *St Patrick: his Origins and Career*, 1968; *The Life and Writings of the Historical St Patrick* (ET with commentary), 1983; A. B. E. Hood, *St Patrick*, 1978.

R. P. C. HANSON

Pauline Spirituality

For Paul the Christian, spirituality began with his Damascus road experience and was thereafter oriented completely by reference to Christ. Previously he had been an admirably devout Jew in the tradition of the Pharisees (Gal. 1.14; Phil. 3.5–6). But outside Damascus he saw Jesus, Christ appeared to him risen from the dead (I Cor. 9.1; 15.8), and this 'revelation of Jesus Christ' (Gal. 1.12) totally transformed his faith and the values on which his life was based. What had been of value to him up till then he now counted as loss 'because of the surpassing worth of knowing Christ Jesus my Lord' (Phil. 3.8). Thereafter to be 'in Christ' summed up both the starting point and the goal of all his endeavour (Phil. 3.8–14) – as the frequency of the phrase itself

('in Christ') and of other closely related phrases ('in the Lord', 'through Christ', etc.') in the Pauline corpus (about 150 times) bears witness.

Out of this initial experience grew all the chief features of Pauline spirituality.

For him the gospel is about the God who calls into being what is not, who accepts the sinner and acquits the guilty (Rom. 4.5, 17). Whereas human folly and corruption stem directly from man's desire to be independent of God, wise in his own right, salvation starts from the recognition that man can never be independent in reality, for if not dependent on God then dependent on things (Rom. 1.21–23). Faith then consists of acknowledging one's total need as creature of the Creator's kindness and strength (2.4–5). Part of the message of the cross is that it crucifies all attempts to estimate one's own worth and to live on the basis of such a self-evaluation (Gal. 6.14–15). If *Christ* was crucified, if God offers salvation through the degradation of crucifixion, if life only comes through death, then that means the end of any attempt to show oneself worthy of God's favour. The creature can only submit to the Creator who made him thus. The sinner will always be sinner, as dependent on the grace of God till the end of his Christian pilgrimage as he was at its beginning. For those who despaired because of their weakness and failures or who have felt imprisoned by traditions which tie salvation to a particular discipline or which confine salvation to a particular nation or race or group (or church) Paul's gospel is as liberating as it was for Paul himself and for Luther.

Christ's resurrection is the beginning of the final resurrection (Rom. 1.4; I Cor. 15.20–23). Those who have identified themselves with Christ in his death through baptism have taken a decisive step (Rom. 6.1–11) – they have recognized that life is no longer to be lived as though all those desires and values which will end anyway with death are the primary determinants of how their lives are to be lived now (Rom. 6.12–23). But though one with Christ in his death, so long as this life lasts they cannot be completely one with Christ in his resurrection (Rom. 6.5, 8; 8.11). They have *already* begun to experience the power of the risen Christ, of his life from beyond death, but they are *not yet* wholly free from 'this body of death'

(Rom. 7). Consequently spiritual growth consists of sharing in Christ's sufferings, becoming like Christ in his death, as well as of experiencing the power of his resurrection (Rom. 8.17; Phil. 3.8–11) – consists of learning ever anew the truth that grace comes to its fullest expression in weakness (II Cor. 4.7–12; 12.7–10). Consequently too the life of faith is also life in the flesh (Gal. 2.20), and so is a life of tension between the enabling from the risen Christ to live 'in Christ' and the appetites and weaknesses of this bodily existence (Rom. 6–8).

This eschatological tension comes to sharpest expression in the warfare which the believer experiences within himself between Spirit and flesh (Rom. 8.12–14; Gal. 5.13–26). Life 'in the Spirit' is as basic for the Christian as life 'in Christ', because these are synonymous ways of describing a life lived out of the grace of God – to have the Spirit is to belong to Christ, a Christian without the Spirit is a contradiction in terms for Paul (Rom. 8.9). But the gift of the Spirit, this opening up of an effective flow of grace ('Spirit' and 'grace' are almost equivalent for Paul), is only the *beginning* of the Christian life (Rom. 8.23; Gal. 3.3), the first instalment and guarantee of God's purpose of salvation and redemption (II Cor. 1.21–22; Eph. 1.13–14). To live 'in Christ', 'in the Spirit', the process of being saved, should ideally be a steady maturing towards perfection, a process of becoming like Christ (II Cor. 3.18; Col. 3.10). But that means becoming like Christ in his death, for only when the dying of Christ is fully mirrored in this mortal body will the living again of Christ come to complete expression in the body of the Spirit (Rom. 8.10–11, 18–23; I Cor. 15.44–50; Phil. 3.21). That process is inevitably painful, given the weakness of the flesh and man's continuing capacity for self-deception; if Rom. 7 is any guide it will not exempt the believer from frustration and failure. However, in this age, so long as the believer is in any sense 'in the flesh', it cannot be otherwise. Spiritual warfare not continuous victory, frustration not perfection, is the mark of spiritual life so long as this age lasts. Hence prayer, which for Paul is characteristically 'through Christ' and 'in the Spirit' (e.g. Col. 3.17; Eph. 6.18), is characterized in particular by the 'Abba' cry of Jesus' own earthly life (Rom. 8.15–16; Gal. 4.6) and is if anything most effective when our weak inarticulateness allows the Spirit to intercede through us according to the will of God (Rom. 8.26–27).

The already/not yet of the believer's existence, suspended as it were between the death and resurrection of Christ and his own, also comes to expression as an ethical tension. In Paul's understanding sin uses both the fixity of the law and the weakness of the flesh in its endeavour to prevent the believer from becoming like Christ (Rom. 6.14; 7.7–11; 8.3). The power of sin can be defeated only by the power of the Spirit (Rom. 7.6; 8.2–4). The believer must therefore live his life 'according to the Spirit' and neither 'according to the flesh' nor as determined by a written code (Rom. 7.6; 8.4–13; Gal. 5). Such inner liberty which avoids the outward extremes of both legalism and license is the mark of all spirituality and ministry for Paul (Rom. 2.28–29; II Cor. 3.6–17; Phil. 3.3) and looks to Christ's own spirituality as its model (Rom. 6.17; I Cor. 2.16; Gal. 5.14; Phil. 2.5; Col. 2.6).

To be 'in Christ' also means being a member of the body of Christ (I Cor. 12.13). Paul warns against self-indulgent flights of spirituality (I Cor. 14; II Cor. 12.1–10). As a member of the body the believer is both dependent on the grace (*charismata*) which is ministered through the different members of the body, and responsible to be a means of grace to the other members – the believer can exist as a believer neither by himself nor for himself (I Cor. 12). As the unity of the body derives from their common participation in the Spirit (*koinōnia*)* and comes to expression in their common sharing of the one loaf (I Cor. 10.16–17), so it grows through the ministries and manifestations of grace. Not surprisingly the measure of corporate (as well as individual) maturity is again Christ (Eph. 4.11–16).

M. Bouttier, *Christianity according to Paul*, 1966; A. Deissmann, *Paul*, 1957; C. H. Dodd, *The Meaning of Paul for Today*, 1920; J. D. G. Dunn, *Jesus and the Spirit*, 1975, chs 8–10; C. F. D. Moule, *The Phenomenon of the New Testament*, 1967, ch 2; A. Wikenhauser, *Pauline Mysticism*, 1960.

JAMES D. G. DUNN

Peace

The dominant meaning of the word in common parlance is freedom from war, 'that condition of a nation or community in which it is not at war with another'(*Shorter Oxford English Dictionary*). When used of individuals it has the equivalent meaning of freedom from disturbance or dissension. And in spirituality it has tended similarly to denote cessation of divine wrath, freedom from the disturbing sense of guilt or from inner turmoil and conflict.

This somewhat negative idea of peace is part of our classical heritage. For particularly in Greek, peace means primarily the opposite of war, the state without which there can be no prosperity, classically expressed in the absence of internal strife within the Empire during the reign of Augustus, the golden age of the *pax Romana*.

In Hebrew thought, however, peace was a much more positive concept. It embraced the idea of absence of war (as in Deut. 20.12; Judg. 4.17; I Sam. 7.14; I Kings 2.5; Isa. 36.16), or indeed, victory in war (Judg. 8.9; I Chron. 22.18; Jer. 43.12; Mic. 5.5). But its basic meaning was something like 'well-being'. For the ancient Israelite, *šālôm* (peace) was all that makes for wholeness and prosperity (e.g. Deut. 23.6; Ps. 72.3,7; 147.14; Isa. 48.18; 55.12; Zech. 8.12).

Two aspects are worthy of particular note. 1. *Šālôm* did not refer simply to a 'spiritual' condition. 'Peace is growth and expansion, fertility in husbandry and family, health and strength throughout life' (J. Pedersen). This did not make it any the less a gift of God (e.g. Num. 6.26; Judg. 6.24; Ps. 29.11; Isa. 66.12; Jer. 29.11). On the contrary, it was precisely the correlation of 'spiritual' and 'material' which was in view in the wholeness of peace (Ps. 85). Not just war, not just private sins, but injustice and oppression destroy peace (Isa. 59.8; Jer. 6.14; Zech. 8.16).

2. In Hebrew thought peace was primarily a relational, a social concept. Thus it could be used of a relationship of friendly co-operation and mutual benefit (as in I Kings 5.12; Zech. 6.13), whereas there is no obvious text where it denotes an individual's sense of inner peace (G. von Rad). Peace was something visible and usually included the idea of a productively harmonious relationship between people (family, covenant partners, nations).

This richer concept is carried over into the earliest Christian vocabulary – peace as spiritual and physical wholeness (Luke 7.50; 8.48), peace characterized by unselfish, active concern for one's neighbour, both within the community of faith (Rom. 14.17,19; I Cor. 14.33; Eph. 4.3) and beyond (I Cor. 7.15). To develop and maintain such positively beneficial relationships is a duty urged on the first Christians by several authors (Rom. 12.18; II Tim. 2.22; Heb. 12.14; I Peter 3.11). The 'peacemaker' whom Jesus called 'blessed' (Matt. 5.9), therefore, does not simply prevent or stop conflict; rather he seeks to promote those spiritual and social relationships which remove the causes of conflict (James 3.18).

For the first Christians it was particularly important that the good news they proclaimed was the gospel of peace (Luke 2.14; 10.5–6; Acts 10.36; Eph. 6.15). Through their faith in Christ they had found a breaking down of barriers both between God and man (Rom. 5.1; Col. 1.20) and between man and man (Eph. 2.14, 17). Hence the characteristic greeting of the risen Christ was 'Peace to you' (Luke 24.36; John 20.19, 21, 26), and Paul especially used the same word again and again to sum up all his most heartfelt hopes for his readers, both in his opening salutation and in his parting blessing. (*See also* **Fruit of the Spirit**.)

More distinctive among the first Christians was peace in the sense of inward spiritual calm, the serenity of a secure relationship with God which is sustained by grace through all kinds of tribulation and pressures (John 14.27; 16.33; Rom. 15.13; Gal. 5.22; Phil. 4.7; Col. 3.15). It was presumably this sense of being a recipient of God's peace which inspired and sustained the first Christians in their proclamation of the gospel of peace and in their peace-making between Jew and Gentile (cf. Rom. 8.6).

In the history of the church, thought about peace has tended to fall into two strands – a political concern for matters of war and peace, focused classically in the doctrine of the just war, and a spiritual, often mystical or pietistic concern for the individual's peace of soul. If the biblical concept is to guide our thought, however, spiritual should never be divorced from social (including political), nor the individual's peace from the well-being of the wider community. Only so can the Christian truly 'live in peace' and the Christian blessing retain its richness: 'May the Lord of peace himself give you peace at all times in all ways' (II Thess. 3.16).

R. H. Bainton, *Christian Attitudes toward War and Peace*, 1960; J. I. Durham, '*Šālôm* and the Presence of God', in J. I. Durham and J. R. Porter (eds), *Proclamation and Presence: Old Testament Essays in Honour of G. H. Davies*, 1970, pp. 272–92; J. Pedersen, *Israel: its Life and Culture* I–II, 1926, pp. 263–335; G. von Rad and W. Foerster, '*eirēnē*', *TDNT*, II pp. 400–420.

JAMES D. G. DUNN

Peale, Norman Vincent

Norman Vincent Peale (b. 1898) has had a long and distinguished ministry in New York City. Graduating from Ohio Wesleyan and Boston University School of Theology he served briefly in a Methodist church in Brooklyn. Then he was called to the large Marble Collegiate church, the largest Dutch Reformed parish in the city. Here he has preached to overflow congregations for decades. Also he has been effective in disseminating his message by publication and hundreds of thousands receive his sermons every week by mail. In addition to this he has written several books that have been widely read. These include *The Power of Positive Thinking* (1952), *A Guide to Confident Living* (1948), *Faith is the Answer* (1974), *The Art of Real Happiness* (1966), and *Enthusiasm Makes the Difference* (1967). Peale also has an active radio and television ministry which has been going on for more than forty years.

Peale's preaching and writing is directed towards personal fulfilment with success measured in terms of a conservative value system. He consistently avoids controversial or prophetic utterances. Rather he encourages people to overcome hazards in life and press on courageously towards the goals of personal achievement. His message is essentially repressive-inspirational in content. He urges his audience to accentuate the positive and eliminate the negative from life. His homilies are filled with stories of persistence and success in adversity, with a constant emphasis on inspirational themes. He has a devoted following among people who depend on his encouragement to keep them going week after week. He provides simple formulas for facing each day. Chapter headings in *The Power of Positive Thinking* indicate his approach to life and ministry. They are 'Believe in yourself', 'A Peaceful Mind Generates Power', 'How to Get Constant Energy', 'Try Prayer Power', 'Expect the Best and Get it', 'Power to Solve Personal Problems', 'Inflow of New Thoughts Can Remake You', and 'Relax for Easy Power'. This message is neither strenuous nor complicated and it speaks with a strong appeal to a day of constant stress and pressure. Peale closes his most successful book with these words: 'I wrote this book out of a desire to help you. It will give me great happiness to know that this book has helped you. I have absolute confidence and belief in the principles and methods outlined in this volume. They have been tested in the laboratory of spiritual experience and practical demonstration. They work when worked. We may never meet in person, but in this book we have met. We are spiritual friends. I pray for you. God will help you – so believe and live successfully.'

Peale is much in demand as an inspirational speaker at conventions of business organizations. His message directed towards sales persons and affluent business people is guaranteed to be free of embarrassing challenges or social responsibilities. So also his theology is positive and God is viewed as a personal resource ready and waiting to fulfil the highest hopes of those who think the right thoughts and adhere to the basic demands of an upper-middle-class society. He supports a clinic in his parish where disturbed people can gain counselling aid or psychiatric intervention. Those who suffer acute dismay are provided with the care and benefits of clinical support with the idea that success in life may still be achieved. Peale in his own life illustrates the validity of his perception for he is still carrying on an active ministry as he moves into his eighties. Perhaps no one in the American pulpit has been so single-minded or as constant in his emphasis through so many years.

EDGAR N. JACKSON

Péguy, Charles

Charles Péguy was born in Orléans on 7 January 1873 and died on 5 September 1914, killed in the Battle of the Marne. Of humble origins, he acquired a solid classical and literary education in Orléans and Paris, and the Greek and Latin writers, Pascal*, Corneille and Hugo were lifelong sources of inspiration. His early and lasting preoccupation with suffering and salvation led him to reject the Catholic doctrine of Hell, and he left the church, became a Socialist, and married into a Republican anti-clerical family.

As a socialist he fought for Dreyfus, but subsequently left the party in disgust at the way the leaders used the Dreyfus Case to further their own ends. In 1900 he founded the *Cahiers de la Quinzaine*, which he controlled until his death. The two mottoes of the *Cahiers*, 'Nothing but the truth', and 'The social revolution will be moral or nothing', sum up its aim and spirit. He brought together a group of able young contributors to attack the evils of the day, especially intolerance, clerical and anticlerical. All Péguy's own works published in his lifetime appeared in the *Cahiers*.

He was a patriot as well as a socialist. In 1905 he published *Notre Patrie*, which foresaw the inevitability of war between Germany and France. However about this time he experienced a growth of the inner life and the emergence of the spiritual insights that shaped all his future literary output. 'I have found my faith again, I am a Catholic,' he told a friend in 1908. The salvation the young socialist had sought in solidarity, he now found in the Redemption and the communion of saints. But this recovery of faith led to great tensions in his personal life. His wife continued to be fiercely anti-Catholic, his marriage was never validated and his children remained unbaptized. The fact that he was excommunicate is central to a grasp of the depth and power of his spirituality. Few have written about the sacraments with more insight and respect, and yet he distrusted contemporary French clericalism, and extolled the lay married state. Far from being torn apart by his almost impossible position of a 'half rebellious and entirely docile son of the church', it made him into a man of prayer and a poet of hope and trust in God, in abandonment to the Divine Will.

The first literary fruit of his new found faith was *Clio*, a work not published until 1955. It contains most of the philosophical and religious themes he was to develop in his best-known works, and at the heart of it is a meditation on the Agony in the Garden

which can stand comparison with More and Pascal. The remaining years of his life saw the publication of a number of important spiritual writings: the three *Mysteries*, the *Tapestries of Our Lady*, *Saint Genevieve*, *Joan of Arc*, and finally the great poem *Eve* which appeared shortly before his death.

In the first of the Mysteries, the *Mystery of the Charity of Joan of Arc*, Péguy speaks through Joan's mouth, as he had done in an early drama of 1897, of his anguish about war, poverty and damnation. But here he answers the cry in the person of a Franciscan nun who points to the mystery of Christ crucified and the passion Our Lady had to undergo. The second and third mysteries, the *Porch to the Mystery of the Second Virtue*, and the *Mystery of the Holy Innocents*, together make a hymn to hope. Their poetic beauty, inseparable from their spirituality, lies in their liturgical quality. The many repetitions with variations and the recurrent invocations are like litanies. Péguy loved the liturgy of the church, which he called 'relaxed theology', and his poems should be read aloud, just as the Office needs to be said or sung. In the light of this affection, it is fitting that eleven texts of Péguy were included in the French breviary (1973). These works are full of theology expressed in images and symbols: the great fleet of prayers, the child going to sleep, the people of France likened to good gardeners, Saint Louis and Joinville, the saint and the 'good sinner' (as Péguy used to describe himself), Luke's three parables of hope, and greatest of all perhaps, God's invocation to his daughter Night, which alone justifies the claim that Péguy is a mystical poet.

His last poems are written in regular rhymed verse. The *Tapestries* reveal his ever-growing devotion to the saints of France, and especially to Our Lady of Chartres. *Eve*, over 2,000 quatrains long, is best approached with the help of the poet's own commentary, the *Durel*. But his spirituality was always rooted in the needs of the present, and to the last he deplored the siege mentality of the church of his day. His very last work, *Note conjointe*, which he left unfinished at the outbreak of war, is a spirited defence of his philosophical master Bergson, whose three major works had just been put on the Index.

Péguy was only forty-one when he was killed, and his spiritual journey was brief in years. At the time of writing the *Porch* (1911), he was in the depths of despair, but the poem nevertheless conveys a trust and hope in God that he was to display more and more fully in his own life. A passage in the poem describes a man at work in the wintry forest, reflecting as he cuts wood on how he had entrusted his sick children to the care of Our Lady. When he wrote these words Péguy did not foresee that a year later he would do the same for his son Pierre, and then make a pilgrimage to Chartres in thanksgiving. There is something mediaeval in the simplicity of his faith and spirituality, and there is something mediaeval about at least one aspect of his influence: every Whitsuntide for over thirty years people in their hundreds, mainly students, have made a pilgrimage on foot from Paris to Our Lady of Chartres, where a plaque in the cathedral commemorates her faithful servant Charles Péguy.

Charles Péguy, *Oeuvres en Prose*, 2 vols 1959, 1968; *Oeuvres poétiques complètes*, 1975; *Men and Saints* ET 1947; *The Mystery of the Charity of Joan of Arc*, ET 1950; *The Portico of the mystery of the second virtue*, ET 1970; *The Holy Innocents and other poems*, ET 1956; Alan Ecclestone, *A Staircase for Silence*, 1977; Daniel Halévy, *Péguy and the Cahiers de la Quinzaine*, 1946; Bernard Guyon, *Péguy*, 1973; Yvonne Servais, *Charles Péguy, the pursuit of salvation*, 1953.

ANNIE BARNES

Penance *see* **Penitence**

Penitence

In the OT man is shown as a creature who keeps turning his back on his creator. He continues to go his own way, with all the consequent havoc in both personal and political life, despite God's undeviating goodwill towards him. Hence throughout the OT the necessity of repentance is stressed, that is, a recognition of the true state of affairs, sorrow for it and a turning back to God with a new resolve to do his will. This pattern, of God continuing to reach out to an unresponsive mankind, came to its climax and fulfilment in Jesus. 'The time is fulfilled, and the kingdom of God is at hand; repent, and believe in the gospel' (Mark 1.14). Jesus accepted the OT but emphasized

particularly the inner dimension of sin (Mark 7.15); the unconditional nature of the moral claims upon us (Matt. 5.48) and the likelihood that those who pride themselves on their religion or morals will miss the heart of the matter (Luke 18.10–14, Luke 15.11–32).

Whilst the apostolic teaching on the necessity of repentance was directed at those outside the church, the problem of those who had sinned after becoming a Christian soon arose. By the third century a system of public penance had emerged. This was regarded as a 'second baptism' and was extremely severe in its requirements of prayer, fasting and almsgiving. The sinner had to join an order of penitents and he was not allowed to marry or be a soldier for the rest of his life. These requirements were later waived as a result of the influence of the penitential books of certain Celtic and Anglo-Saxon missionaries, but the penance remained long and arduous. At the Fourth Lateran Council (1215) private penance, which had been practised from the fifth century, received its charter and every Christian was required to confess his sins in penance at least once a year.

The Protestant Reformers objected to the sacrament of penance because of the abuses that had become associated with it, though Luther and Melanchthon commended it and the Anglican church made provision for it. The result was that the Reformed church tended to emphasize the place of penitence in private prayer and public worship, though there is more Reformed and Puritan counsel on the subject than is popularly supposed; the Methodist band and class-meeting were confessionals and modern Protestants such as H. E. Fosdick * and Leslie Weatherhead * have taught the value of a private confession. As Kierkegaard wrote, 'the abolition of confession was the joint action of priest and people . . . it made religion all too real'. Bonhoeffer* encouraged his students to confess to God before a brother Christian and there is evidence that this practice is growing in some evangelical circles. Recent years have seen great changes in RC practice. The *ordo Poenitentiae* which appeared in 1973 contains three different rites for reconciliation. These have a new emphasis on the corporate dimension of sin and reconciliation and on the work of the Holy Spirit in renewing the life of the penitent.

Since the nineteenth century the Christian stress on an attitude of penitence has been attacked, explicitly or implicitly, by such diverse writers as Marx, Nietzsche and Camus. Alternative self-images of man as assertive, rebellious, self-sufficient, beholden to no one, responsible for shaping mankind and himself, and with a sense of his own God-like dignity, have been offered. These challenges have often been sustained by moral passion. But the Christian, whilst not denying some of the truth in these attacks, presents an alternative moral vision in which penitence is an indispensible precondition for the communion with God for which man is destined. Psychoanalysis has both confused and enriched Christian teaching on penitence. On the one hand Christians have been forced to question sometimes simplistic views of good and right and wrong. On the other hand they have often been led, particularly with the help of a wise counsellor, to a deeper understanding of the springs of behaviour.

Dietrich Bonhoeffer, *Life Together*, 1954, ch 5; Richard Harries, *Turning to Prayer*, 1978, ch 4; Eric James, *The Double Cure*, 1957; Kenneth Leech, *Soul Friend*, 1977, pp. 194–225; Kenneth Ross, *Hearing Confessions*, 1974; Max Thurian, *Confession*, 1958.

RICHARD HARRIES

Penn, William

Eldest son of Admiral Sir William Penn, Penn (1644–1718) was sent down from Christ Church, Oxford in 1661 for nonconformity. After a period of travel from which he returned according to Pepys with 'too much . . . of the French garb and affected manner of speech and gait', he joined a military expedition to Cork, where he was converted by the preaching of Thomas Loe, a Quaker tradesman. He became a preacher and writer in defence of Friends. His tract *The Sandy Foundation Shaken* (1668) attacking current teaching on the Trinity, incarnation and justification led to his imprisonment in the Tower. While there he wrote the first version of *No Cross, No Crown* (1669) his most enduring writing, though the form in which it is known is the second edition of 1682, hardly recognizable as the same book. His trial at the Old Bailey in 1670 gave rise to a classic test case for the freedom of Juries. Penn turned to planning a colony in America which would practice freedom of conscience: in 1682 he founded Pennsylvania. He returned to England in 1684 and became a close friend and apologist of James II, because of the latter's interest in toleration. After the Revolution he was suspect as a Jacobite, and in 1692 was deprived of the governorship of Pennsylvania. In 1693 he published *Fruits of Solitude*, an aphoristic work which drew on fashionable literary models. In 1696 he argued in *Primitive Christianity* that Quaker principles are identical with those of the early church. He died at Ruscombe near Twyford.

Penn's conversion and writings symbolized a new phase in Quaker history. The periwigged man of fashion contrasted strongly with the 'first publishers of truth' – he continued to wear a sword for some time, with Fox's permission. His cast of mind is altogether cooler, and more rational than Fox's. His appeals for a hearing for Quakers are based on a general principle of toleration rather than a monolithic certainty of the possession of truth. He can show some of Fox's fire when dealing with old Quaker enemies – 'I had rather be Socrates on the Day of Judgment than Richard Baxter', but one cannot imagine Fox conceding, as Penn did in 1678, that Quakers were 'of the same belief as to the most fundamental positive article of her creed' as the established church. The inner light in Penn is more like conscience than the indwelling Christ, the power of God. *No Cross, No Crown* is a powerful work of exhortation to a suffering discipleship, but only once, in defending Quaker refusal of hat-honour, does it rise to the sort of mystical tone which everywhere pervades Fox's *Journal* (ch IX, sect 5), and it is notable that here he is describing the historic Quaker experience. The Bible for Penn is not, as it was for Fox, a chart of the struggle of light and dark within the soul of man, it is a storehouse of exemplars for imitation or avoidance. Nor can one conceive any of Fox's generation of Friends endorsing any argument by appeal to the great moral figures from pagan antiquity, from Agasicles to Xenophon, as Penn in the second part of *No Cross, No Crown*. Penn is an Augustan writer, as the tone of *Fruits of Solitude* makes clear 'We must needs disorder ourselves if we only look at our losses. But if we consider how little we deserve what is left, our passion will cool, and our murmurs will turn into thankfulness'.

Nevertheless, even in a periwig much of the power of the Quaker message lives through Penn's life and writing, and *No Cross, No Crown* deserves its place as a classic of persecution literature. Penn's fundamental faithfulness to the Quaker way is reflected in his great love for Fox, and perhaps more significantly in Fox's tenderness for him. The Preface Penn contributed to the first edition of the *Journal* has never been surpassed as a picture of the essential Fox, or as an analysis of the spirit of early Quakerism.

See also **Fox, George; Quaker Spirituality.**

No Cross, No Crown ed N. Penney, 1930; selections of his works in F. B. Tolles and E. G. Alderfer, *The Witness of William Penn*, 1957, and in H. Barbour and A. O. Roberts, *Early Quaker Writings*, 1973; see also M. R. Brailsford, *William Penn*, 1930; M. M. Dunn, *William Penn; Politics and Conscience*, 1967.

EAMON DUFFY

Pentecostalism

Pentecostal spirituality is the experience of a rapidly growing number of Christians both within and outside the historic churches. Alongside Catholicism and Protestantism Pentecostalism may be regarded as a third major force in christendom. It is an attempt to rediscover the spirituality of the early church, and Pentecostals would claim that both their belief and practice originated in the NT church.

Whilst the history of the movement could be traced from the early Christian centuries to the present day, twentieth-century Pentecostalism has its more immediate links with the Wesleyan revival of the eighteenth century, the Irvingites of the nineteenth century and the holiness movements of the latter half of the nineteenth century.

As F. D. Bruner has pointed out, the second experience of sanctification following Christian conversion foreshadowed the subsequent experience of baptism in the spirit which assumed importance in later Pentecostalism. G. Strachan, on the other hand, sees Edward Irving 'as a John the Baptist' of the Pentecostal movement, 'the

forerunner of all those who believe in Christ as the Baptizer with the Holy Spirit'.

This twentieth-century phenomenon may be divided conveniently into two phases: Pentecostalism, referring to a movement dating from the beginning of the twentieth century and Neo-Pentecostalism, or the Charismatic Movement*, referring to the manifestation of the chief characteristics of Pentecostalism within all the historic churches of christendom. The earlier phase may be described also as classical Pentecostalism.

Classical Pentecostalism had baptism in the Spirit as its central doctrine. Following Christian conversion, believers could be baptized in the Spirit and such a baptism was accompanied by speaking in tongues. If speaking in tongues was seen as the initial evidence of Spirit baptism, it is true to say that in addition one or more of the other spiritual gifts experienced by the early church (for example as described in I Cor. 12.8–10) was also to be expected in the lives of Spirit-baptized believers.

Originating in the United States of America during the early decades of the twentieth century, classical Pentecostalism spread into Europe and other parts of the world giving rise to churches like the Assemblies of God, the Elim Church and the Apostolic Church.

Neo-Pentecostalism, or the Charismatic Movement, took root in America in the 1950s involving Episcopalians, Roman Catholics, Lutherans, Presbyterians, Baptists and Methodists, and this, too, spread into Europe and beyond, affecting in varying degrees most of the historic churches. Although to a large extent it was contained within these churches, the House Church movement developed apart, and now threatens to become another denomination despite the fact that its adherents would oppose such a claim.

Amongst Neo-Pentecostals the central experience of the Spirit is viewed in different ways. Some, like the classical Pentecostals, believe that baptism in the Spirit is a second experience or blessing subsequent to conversion. Others believe baptism in the Spirit to be conversion with the experience following better described as fullness of the Spirit. A third view has emerged in which it is argued that both conversion and what follows in terms of fullness may be called properly baptism in the Spirit: theologically both experiences belong to Spirit baptism. Such experiences may occur concurrently or consecutively, but theologically speaking both refer to one work of the Holy Spirit, as do any other blessings of the Spirit one may experience, however many. The reality of the experience would be confirmed by any of the Spirit's gifts or fruit, but most would agree that the true criterion is love.

Efforts have been made by different denominations to interpret the experience in terms of traditional theology. In this respect, perhaps J. Rodman Williams reaches the heart of things when he writes: 'The turn we need to make, I am convinced, is towards an action of the Holy Spirit which fits no category, but one that does make much of our traditional theology operational.'

How is baptism or fullness of the Spirit to be described in experience? There is no ready answer. Those who experience Spirit baptism or fullness claim that their whole being is pervaded by the Spirit of God. Jesus becomes more real in experience. Testimony is given to a heart filled with praise or love or peace or joy or all these things. To express oneself in other tongues is not an uncommon feature. For most, the Bible becomes alive in that it begins to speak to everyday needs in a new and living way. It may be said that whilst not all Neo-Pentecostals are fundamentalist, most are fairly conservative in their view of scripture. Some Neo-Pentecostals, like their classical predecessors, would regard speaking in tongues (*see* **Glossolalia**) as the sign that the Spirit had come, but most would see this as just one sign amongst many: others would be equally valid.

Within Pentecostal worship and prayer, freedom, spontaneity, exuberance and joy are the hall marks. Alongside more traditional expressions of worship such as kneeling and clasped hands, there is clapping, dancing and the raising of hands in praise. Tongues, interpretations, prophecy, visions, words of wisdom and knowledge and healings all find their place with a centrality being given to the Bible as the sword of the Spirit.

In some churches this kind of worship takes place within the framework of the normal liturgy whilst in others no such framework is in evidence, and the only guidelines followed are those described in I Cor. 14.26–33.

A feature of Neo-Pentecostalism is the plethora of spiritual songs it has produced, many of which are simply words of scripture set to music.

The Pentecostal movement may be seen as a reaction against the arid rationalism of the twentieth century. Others may view it as a movement which counters the prevailing secular and materialistic spirit of the age. It could be seen as an expression of man's longing for the 'otherness', the 'transcendent', some would say the 'supernatural'. Pentecostals see it as a gift from God to renew and restore his church.

F. D. Bruner, *A Theology of the Holy Spirit*, 1971; J. D. G. Dunn, *Baptism in the Holy Spirit*, 1970; J. Gunstone, *A People for His Praise*, 1978; W. J. Hollenweger, *The Pentecostals*, 1972; T. A. Smail, *Reflected Glory*, 1975; G. Strachan, *The Pentecostal Theology of Edward Irving*, 1973; E. Sullivan, *The Pentecostal Movement and its Relation to the Ecumenical Movement*, 1972; S. Tugwell, *Did You Receive the Spirit?*, 1972; J. R. Williams, *The Era of the Spirit*, 1971.

W. R. DAVIES

Perfection

'Ye therefore shall be perfect as your heavenly Father is perfect' (Matt. 5.48; RV 1880). Just as the Orthodox tradition has not allowed the promise that Christians may become 'partakers of the divine nature' to be buried in a late peripheral NT writing – II Peter 1.4 (*see* **Deification**), so Catholic spirituality has been dominated by the thought of holiness and has set no limits to what God's grace may do in the lives of his saints, even though these have been rare examples of supernatural spiritual heroism, eagles among the sparrows. Perfectionism, belief that sinless perfection is possible in this life, has been a characteristic of the sects, partly in protest against the compromises of conformity and the low standards of majority religion, partly because the promise gave hope to the submerged and suffering whom the establishments despised and persecuted. There was danger of excess and blasphemy, but in the religious underworld of the Middle Ages, of the Parliamentarian armies and of revivalist movements, the 'future imperative' of the gospel has been kept alive and has been part of the secret of vitality and power.

A great deal depends on what is meant by perfection and to what extent it is believed to be obtainable in this life. The canonized saint has achieved it here below. Protestant teachers have tended to be more cautious. Richard Greenham, Vicar of Dry Drayton in the reign of Elizabeth I, was convinced that there could be no absolute unspottedness in this life. 'Albeit to that perfection which the Scripture taketh for soundness, truth and sincerity of heart, which is void of careless remissness we may come ... Let us not seek to be more righteous than we can be. But let us comfort ourselves in the truth of our hearts and singleness of our desires to serve God, because he is God; and so shall we be accepted of God.' William Perkins, the most eminent Puritan theologian of the Elizabethan period, like Bernard of Clairvaux*, distinguishes four degrees of God's love – 'an effectual calling' which unites the repentant sinner with Christ's mystical body; justification, sanctification, 'whereby such as believe, being delivered from the tyranny of sin, are little by little renewed in holiness and righteousness'; glorification, which begins at death, 'but is not accomplished and made perfect before the last day of judgement'. John Preston, 'Prince Charles's Puritan Chaplain', is a theologian of the divine love and argues from the Geneva Bible version of the command to Abraham in Gen. 17.1, that perfection is integrity of heart and can co-exist with those infirmities which are an inevitable part of our humanity. Otherwise the second Adam would be less powerful to instill grace than the first to communicate sin, and the work of God in the new creation would come short of that in the beginning, when the Lord looked on everything that he had made and behold it was very good. Christ implants in the heart a perfect seed, which wants only growth to become a perfect flower. Its growth will be menaced by the hazards of climate and many pests, but it will be strong enough to resist them all, unless we are to make nonsense of our claims for divine grace. The perfect man is cleansing and purifying himself throughout his whole life and repents radically from each lapse, whereas the one in whom evil reigns wallows in his sin 'as a swine in the mire'.

The main difference is between those Puritans who are cautiously realistic and dread even the semblance of human presumptuousness, and those so possessed with the love of God that their longing for him and his goodness breaks all bounds and they will set limits neither to their desire nor his redemption. The whole issue is that of love in Puritan theology. Of course, not all who have been on fire with the love of God have shown that concern and compassion for their fellow-man which, according to St John, is its essential principle of verification, while in theory – and this is Luther's doctrine – a change of status through faith in God is the only possible source of good works and the boldness of faith itself should free us from any inhibitions in the quest for perfection. But it was in 1628 that John Earle wrote of the 'precise hypocrite ... so taken up with faith she has no room for charity', and so sympathetic a scholar as G. F. Nuttall admits that the criticism has force against Puritan piety as a whole.

John Wesley* regarded the promise of perfection as the raison d'être of his whole movement. He safeguarded his teaching with great care. Christian perfection is 'the establishment of a state of holy penitence, which does not exclude the probability of involuntary sin but feels secure against the threat of any sin that would separate from Christ'. 'By perfection, I mean the humble, patient, gentle love of God and our neighbour ruling our tempers, words and actions' (Plain Account of Christian Perfection, 1765). On this William Telfer comments, 'Such a state may in fact represent very closely the indefectibility of the baptized as it was actually looked for in the Church of NT days' (The Forgiveness of Sins, 1959, p. 140). Unfortunately, Wesley was over-anxious for evidence that his followers were manifesting perfection within the limits of mortal life, and his almost 'social science' approach in the collection of cases cannot have been to the spiritual advantage of those whom he sought to identify, even though he insisted that love of God and neighbour and freedom from resentments, hatreds, jealousies and bitterness was the only test, and warned repeatedly that 'a gracious soul may fall from grace'. In the nineteenth century arose the notion of a 'second blessing' whereby a person might enter into the state of entire sanctity with the suddenness of a revivalist first conversion.

Modern Reformed theologians have not wanted to define perfection in terms of sinlessness. P. T. Forsyth (1848–1921), a notable British Congregationalist, in *Christian Perfection* (1899), distinguished between 'sin as the principle of a soul and sin as an incident, sin which stays and sin which visits. Visitation of sin may cleave indefinitely to the new life.' He states his doctrine in vigorous epigrams: 'Communion with God is possible along with the cleaving sin.' 'Love, not sinlessness is the maturity of faith.' 'Perfection is not sanctity but faith.' 'It is better to trust in God in humiliated repentance than to revel in the sense of sinlessness' (op. cit., pp. 36, 13, 16, 84, 135).

Modern spirituality, too, hesitates to talk of sinless perfection, due to psychology's awareness of the subconscious, and also to the realization that sin is to be understood, not as a poisoned part of us which may be removed as a rotten tooth, nor as a series of evil deeds which, though always repented, may come to an end, but rather as the deformity of our whole being. Even more, it is doubtful whether a perfect person is possible without a perfect society. The perfection of each depends on the perfection of all and demands the eschaton. The opportunity to be virtuous may depend on a freedom bought by the exploitation of others, or the readiness to use destructive weapons which cannot by any moral standards be tolerable. Yet the idea of perfection will not go away, but remain in the Christian *depositum* to be a cure for complacency, and rouse restlessness and discontent with our spiritually unambitious earthbound lives. Is the gospel fully contained in the proclamation that God became incarnate to disclose his mercy and change our relationship to him, our status in grace, or must we not also say that Christ's work is unfinished until we are altogether as he is, our personalities transformed into his perfect love? Some twentieth-century writers have come to see perfection, after the Cappadocian Fathers*, not as a moral state which cannot be improved, but as a life of constant growth in disciplined love to God and man. Paul is near it when he says, 'Not as though I had already attained, nor were already made perfect; but I press on . . .' (Phil. 3.12). A Methodist scholar, W. F. Lofthouse (d. 1965), put it paradoxically: 'Perfection is an attitude of mind; and if so (as every saint

and lover really knows), attainment and non-attainment imply each other; they are one and the same thing.'

See also **Cappadocian Fathers; Deification; Vision of God.**

Marina Charcharadze, *Man's Concern with Holiness*, 1970; R. N. Flew, *The Idea of Perfection in Christian Theology*, 1934; William Law, *A Treatise on Christian Perfection*, 1726.

EDITOR

Petition *see* **Prayer (3) Petition**

Philokalia

A Greek term, meaning literally 'love for what is beautiful or good', and used as a title for anthologies. It is applied in particular to two Greek works:

1. The *Philokalia* of Origen*: extracts from his writings, selected by St Basil the Great and St Gregory of Nazianzus during 358–359, dealing especially with the interpretation of scripture, and also with providence and free will.

2. The *Philokalia* of St Macarius of Corinth (1731–1805) and St Nicodemus of the Holy Mountain (1749–1809), two leading members of the group known as the 'Kollyvades', a movement for spiritual renewal in the eighteenth-century Greek Church (from *kollyva*, boiled wheat eaten at memorial services for the dead). Originally published in 1782, this is a far longer work than (1), running to more than 1200 folio pages in double column, and containing for the most part not merely extracts but complete works, by some thirty different writers extending from the fourth to the fifteenth century. Among those included are Evagrius (fourth century), Diadochus of Photice (fifth century), Maximus the Confessor (seventh century), Symeon the New Theologian (eleventh century), Peter of Damascus (twelfth century), Gregory of Sinai, Gregory Palamas*, and Kallistos and Ignatius Xanthopoulos (fourteenth century). The original selection of texts was made by Macarius, and the material was then revised by Nicodemus, who added a general introduction, together with introductory notes on each author.

Covering all aspects of ascetic and mystical theology, the *Philokalia* constitutes the primary source-book for the spiritual tradition known in Orthodoxy as hesychasm*. It deals at length with the eight evil 'thoughts' and the virtues, the passions and *apatheia**; with the interpretation of scripture and the contemplation of the natural creation; with prayer of the heart* and in particular the Jesus Prayer (*see* **Jesus, Prayer to**), along with the physical technique involving control of the breathing.

The *Philokalia* has exercised a notable influence on modern Orthodox spirituality*, not least in the last twenty-five years. An abbreviated Slavonic version entitled *Dobrotolubiye* appeared in 1793, edited by Blessed Paisii Velichkovskii, while Russian translations were made by Bishop Ignatii Brianchaninov (1857) and Bishop Theophan the Recluse (5 vols, 1877). Its impact on Russian nineteenth-century piety is strikingly exemplified by *The Way of a Pilgrim*, the work of an anonymous Russian peasant who carried the *Dobrotolubiye* in his knapsack. A Romanian edition, running to ten volumes and with valuable notes by Fr Dumitru Staniloae, appeared in 1947–1981. Since the Second World War translations have also been made into English, French and German.

Texts: (Greek) *The Philokalia of Origen* ed J. Armitage Robinson, 1893; *Philokalia ton Ieron Neptikon*, reissued in 5 vols 1957–1963; (English) E. Kadloubovsky and G. E. H. Palmer, *Writings from the Philokalia on Prayer of the Heart*, 1951; *Early Fathers from the Philokalia*, 1954; G. E. H. Palmer, P. Sherrard and K. Ware, *The Philokalia: The Complete Text*, vols I, II, 1979–1981 (3 vols forthcoming); *The Way of a Pilgrim*, ET 1954.

KALLISTOS WARE

Pietism

The classical German pietism, as it was expressed by its two main representatives, P. J. Spener (1635–1705) and A. H. Francke (1663–1727), is to be understood as a reaction against the Lutheran-orthodox interpretation of justification as a forensic act. Sin was condemned, the sinner was acquitted, but sin remained, so that the believer was justified and yet a sinner still. Pietism claims that it is not only possible to be free from the guilt of sin but also from its power. This has to be the central point in its spirituality because salvation is understood as restoration of *Imago Dei* in man, i.e. salva-

tion is conquest of sin: participation in *Imago Dei* is participation in the power which makes man able to do what is good.

It is in re-birth that man gets this sin-conquering power, and therefore we find the notion of re-birth at the very heart of pietistic theology and spirituality. It is God's ordinance that only those who are converted shall taste his grace and salvation. Penitence has therefore to come before man can grasp saving and sin-conquering faith. When man – disturbed by God's call – awakes from his sleeping in sin he decides to change but only to discover that sin has become too powerful to get rid of. And simultaneously he is longing for forgiveness. In this condition he can hear the gospel: 'I will cure you.' He experiences the *power* of the gospel. This is the moment of grace, the moment of re-birth. He has been delievered from the state of nature and has reached the state of grace. Thus misuse of God's love and perversion of the doctrine of justification by faith are alike prevented. The notion of re-birth expresses a total change. The result is participation in divine nature (II Peter I.3f., one of the pietists' favourite Bible passages). The idea of participation in divine nature is to be understood more in ethical than in mystical terms. The experience of re-birth, of participation in divine nature, is an experience of God's merciful action to save the world – and now me. Participation in divine nature means therefore participation in God's activities, in his act of salvation where he takes upon himself the world's need.

Although re-birth means that man has got a new nature and that the power of sin is broken, it does not mean that man now has gone over to a state of sinlessness. Just because the power of sin is broken, the fight against the actual sins can start. The sinner has now got power – the power of the gospel and the faith. Now the growth can and must begin. He has been re-born. Now he must grow up. And growth is understood mainly in relationship to fighting and defeating actual, concrete sins. Ultimate salvation depends on this fight. The ultimate salvation can be lost through evil deeds but is not deserved through good deeds.

A form of Christianity where the fight against sin and sanctification play such a role as in pietism (and in its English sister movement Methodism*) is bound to be rather pedagogically orientated. It has even been maintained that pietism as one of its consequences brought an increase of didacticism into Christianity. The pietists were convinced not only that man was able to grow spiritually (because he through the rebirth had got a new nature) and that they had an aim for the growth (defeating sin, and sanctification) but also that they had the necessary means:

The basic means in the fight against sin is prayer. However, prayer is meaningful only if one loves God and one's neighbour. Love – a work of the Holy Spirit – is in itself a continual prayer.

Besides prayer comes the training of man's will as the most efficient means in the fight against sin. Man's *Eigen-Wille* has to be broken to enable him to do what God wants. It is of course not a question of breaking man's will as such because the will plays a decisive role in the fight. One needs a strong will to break the *Eigen-Wille*. Concrete obedience is considered the best means.

Most important in the fight against sin is the test of oneself. When salvation is the defeating of sin and therefore sanctification plays a most important part in the spiritual life it follows that the state of grace becomes something visible. There are signs. For example, when you are not sure whether a particular course of action will involve you in sin or not, you should choose – as a matter of precaution – what is against your natural inclination. The more particular signs are faith, love, humility, patience, renunciation of the *Eigen-Wille*, joy, prayer and to be satisfied with one's material situation. Faith and grace release a power which will be seen, indeed measured, in practice. And the testing becomes mutual, which had important ecclesiological consequences. On the left wing of the pietistic movement these were drawn quite deliberately: The true church became visible.

Within the main stream of the pietistic movement arose the *conventicle* – small groups of believers who had passed the test. Prudence became a key-word. One had to be careful in one's relation to the 'world' in order to be sure to remain in the state of grace without obvious sins. Nature and grace were seen in sharp contrast, not as co-operators. This resulted principally in a negative attitude to culture. Originally the withdrawal to the conventicle was a tactical

manoeuvre in order to provide a complete alternative to the 'world', a universal reform, a conquest of all corruption and misery in the world. This was not for man to realize. This could be achieved only through God's grace. The hindrance was man's actual sin and it could be defeated through the power of grace materialized in the new man, the re-born man, and through the fellowship of re-born men, a fellowship in experience which crossed national and denominational borders and therefore made pietism the first ecumenical movement within protestantism.

The principal works are in German, notably M. Schmidt and W. Jannasch (eds), *Das Zeitalter des Pietismus*, 1965 (texts); M. Schmidt, *Pietismus*, 1972.

TROND ENGER

Pilgrimage

In all the higher religions the custom of going on pilgrimage to a holy place has been an important aspect of spirituality. Hindus have journeyed to various shrines, Muslims to Mecca, and Jews, Muslims and Christians to Jerusalem, and the last to the tombs of the saints and martyrs, such as St Thomas Becket martyred in Canterbury Cathedral in 1170. Fundamental is the belief that certain sites have an especial spiritual power because of what happened there as revelations of the Divine presence and activity, either in manifestation of the holy or in events which by heroism or suffering demonstrated God's nature and entry into the cataclysms of human experience. The expedition itself should involve hardship and demand discipline. Sometimes pilgrims have themselves created difficulties like a Hindu moving to a distant shrine in perpetual prostration. Often a lifetime's savings have been expended. The pilgrimage may be solitary or in company. It could degenerate into tourism and be capable of abuse, becoming indulgent holiday travel, though that has given us Chaucer's *Canterbury Tales*. It has often been of value to those left behind because of the reports brought back of adventures and disclosures. Egeria's travels to fourth-century Jerusalem, just after the holy places had been discovered, are of the greatest interest for what they describe of the liturgy of the Jerusalem church and the origins of Holy Week. They resulted in attempts of far-off churches in south-western Europe to copy the Jerusalem customs. Often a pilgrimage has been undertaken not simply as a discipline to strengthen faith, or in fulfilment of a vow, but to achieve some good, like a cure at Lourdes. And there has been psychological benefit if not a miracle of bodily healing. It is vital for spirituality to have a goal, to travel hopefully towards some object of numinous transcendent power to which distance undoubtedly lends enchantment. The place or object becomes a sign of heaven 'afar beyond the stars'.

Inevitably pilgrimage has been seen as an allegory of the Christian life, from Abraham going out by faith, the wilderness wanderings of old Israel, the return from Babylonian captivity, through Bonaventure's* *Itinerarium mentis in Deum* to Bunyan's* *Pilgrim's Progress*. It has seemed to be entirely scriptural – the people of God seeking a country, Jesus himself in John's Gospel the spiritual dragoman going ahead to prepare a mansion of his Father's house for his disciples, himself also 'the Way' as was his religion itself in early days, according to the Acts of the Apostles. And the Letter to the Hebrews in particular is aware of the transience of mortal life. We have no abiding city here, but are strangers and pilgrims (lit. sojourners) on the earth; therefore we must not linger unduly or invest in temporal goods which pass away. The language betokens a revision of early eschatology. We no longer wait for the imminent coming of the Lord but venture out in quest of his holy city or kingdom which is always over the horizon, even though we are already its citizens and stand proleptically before its gates. In a world where journeys are made swift by transport, which brings not simply the other hemisphere but the moon within reach, the old image may seem outdated and distance to have lost its mystery. But holy places remain even though they may be as often as not tourist attractions, or in danger of obliteration by the weapons of modern warfare. The connection between pilgrims and explorers has been traced by T. S. Eliot*, who in well-known passages from his *Four Quartets* declares that in the end we find ourselves back at home where we started, and know the place for the first time.

Peter Brown, *The Cult of the Saints*, 1981; A. Kendal, *Mediaeval Pilgrims*, 1970; Jonathan Sumption, *Pilgrimage, an image of mediaeval religion*, 1975.

EDITOR

Platonism

The influence of Plato and his successors has been evident in Christian spirituality from the earliest times, in particular where there has been an interest in the transcendent or an emphasis on the self-subsistent existence of metaphysical entities apart from human awareness of them, and a willingness to combine spiritual effort with rational thinking or to imagine the spiritual life in terms of contemplation and knowledge. Christian terminology, especially of the soul, owes much to Platonism.

Plato (c. 429–347 BC) wrote between twenty and thirty dialogues in which his master Socrates is portrayed talking with his Athenian friends. Their doctrine differs from most earlier Greek philosophy (the Pre-Socratics) in giving a spiritual account of the nature of the world. Every thing we see is the shadow of an ideal archetype, its Form. We learn by recollection of these Forms, by making our latent awareness of them conscious. Of special importance is the Form of the Good, which is in some sense beyond being, and is to the world of Ideas as the sun is to the physical world. In the *Republic* it is compared to a bright light at the mouth of a cave; men inside should turn to the light rather than watch the shadows on the walls. The *Symposium* shows how love, desire to procreate upon the beautiful, can proceed from enjoyment of the material to contemplation of higher beauty. It is unclear how far the thought of the dialogues is Plato's and how far Socrates'; the dramatic art is certainly Plato's.

After Plato's death his doctrine continued to develop in the Academy he founded and in the wider world, where it mixed with subsequent traditions, particularly those of Plato's pupil Aristotle (384–322 BC) and of the Stoics, who evolved the idea of the *logos* as the force which holds all things together. The influence of Platonism on Judaism may be seen in the Wisdom literature of the OT and in Philo. By the time of Christ it provided the language in which men of education around the Mediterranean considered metaphysical matters. It was, then, only natural that intelligent Christians such as Justin Martyr, Clement of Alexandria and Origen* should try to explain their new faith to themselves and to their contemporaries in terms of the current philosophy nowadays known as Middle Platonism.

In the third century Plotinus* composed a new variation on the Platonic theme. A 'golden chain' of non-Christian pupils handed this philosophy, known today as Neoplatonism*, down to Proclus* in the fifth century and beyond. Christians who shared ideas with Plotinus included the Cappadocians*.

The most dramatic and sustained influence of Neoplatonism on Christians was in the Latin West a century after Plotinus' death, on thinkers like Augustine* and Ambrose. It was through Augustine, and through Boethius and Denys the Areopagite*, who both also knew the works of Proclus, that Platonism reached the early Middle Ages. Until the twelfth century only part of one work of Plato was available in Latin, but the thinking of learned men in Western Europe, notably of John Scotus Eriugena in the ninth century and of the schools of Chartres and St Victor (*see* **Victorines**) in the twelfth century, was often motivated by a spirituality both Platonist and Christian. Platonic presuppositions persisted throughout the Middle Ages, despite the rediscovery of Aristotle by scholars in the twelfth and thirteenth centuries.

In the Byzantine world Platonic influence was even more diffused. In a general way Platonic language might be detected whenever an adept of the Inner Learning speaks of God as light, or of the icons as windows on to eternity. Plato himself, however, was read rather by secular students of the Outer Learning, such as M. Psellus, J. Italus and G. G. Pletho, who all fell foul of the church authorities for their views.

In the Renaissance, humanists, tired of the grinding dialectic of the Schools, were inspired by Plato to consider natural religion. M. Ficino (1433–1499), head of a new Academy in Florence, translated all Plato and some Neoplatonic works into Latin; in his own writings he showed the harmony between the natural wisdom of the ancients and the Christian revelation. His admirers included John Colet, Dean of St Paul's, Erasmus and Thomas More.

In the sixteenth and seventeenth centuries Platonic ideas inspired a number of English poets and spiritual writers; they include Spenser, Sidney, Henry Vaughan, Marvell, Traherne and Sir Thomas Browne* ('this visible world is but a picture of the invisible'). In the mid-seventeenth century a group of scholars known as the Cambridge Platonists* reacted against the acrid polemics of their Puritan contemporaries and the materialism represented by Thomas Hobbes towards a positive appreciation of the 'instinctive reasonableness of divine truth'.

Plato has continued to exercise a varied influence ever since. The Romantics liked him because he took seriously the affections of the soul; Shelley translated some of Plato into English. Victorians as different as F. D. Maurice and B. Jowett appreciated his positive estimate of human capabilities. The influential Absolute Idealism of late-nineteenth-century Oxford, initiated by the non-Christian F. H. Bradley, and formative to minds as different as W. R. Inge*, Dean of St Paul's and writer on mysticism, and William Temple*, Archbishop of Canterbury, had a Platonic as well as a Hegelian character. Literary figures, such as Walter Pater and C. S. Lewis and the poets W. B. Yeats and Kathleen Raine, have also come in different ways under the Platonic spell. Recent critics have included those who find Plato's political philosophy authoritarian, those who think metaphysics arises only from mistakes in the use of language, and those who believe Christianity should be seen as a religion of semitic rather than of classical origin.

Among the many texts of Plato available are the editions in the Oxford Classical Texts, ed J. Burnett (5 vols), and in the Loeb Classical Library (with translation, several editors, 12 vols). B. Jowett translated all the dialogues (4 vols, 1871), often reprinted; many are also available in Penguin Classics. Introductions to Plato include A. E. Taylor, *Plato: The Man and His Work*, [3]1929; F. M. Cornford, *Before and After Socrates*, 1932. Aspects of later Platonism are covered by J. Burnaby, *Amor Dei: A Study of the Religion of St Augustine*, 1938; H. Chadwick, *Early Christian Thought and the Classical Tradition*, 1966; M.-D. Chenu, *Nature, Man and Society in the Twelfth Century*, 1968; J.

Dillon, *The Middle Platonists*, 1977; A. Louth, *The Origins of the Christian Mystical Tradition*, 1981; F. J. Powicke, *The Cambridge Platonists*, 1926. Surveys containing relevant matter include W. R. Inge, *Christian Mysticism*, [7]1933; K. Kirk, *The Vision of God: The Christian Doctrine of the Summum Bonum*, 1931; P. Shorey, *Platonism Ancient and Modern*, Sather Classical Lectures 14, 1938.

OLIVER NICHOLSON

Platonists, The Cambridge
see **Cambridge Platonists, The**

Plotinus

Plotinus (205–270), first of the philosophers now called Neoplatonists*, wrote, as one of his pupils put it, 'for the man who considers what he is, whence he came and whither he ought to tend'. He did not mean to alter the public religion which it was the duty of every member of the community to acknowledge, but rather to enlighten those who had decided to devote themselves to the philosophic life. His influence was, however, extensive; his teaching passed down through his pupils to Proclus* and was eventually incorporated in mediaeval Islamic philosophy. Greek Christians who were aware of him included the Cappadocians*; through Augustine* and Boethius, Neoplatonism came to dominate thought in the early mediaeval West.

All we have of Plotinus is the mature thought of his last fifteen years, expounded in fifty-four tractates, each written fast and without revision and edited after his death as the *Enneads* by his pupil Porphyry. It is therefore not possible to follow in detail the mental formation which produced his mature metaphysical convictions. There is some tantalizing information in his biography by Porphyry. Plotinus was a Greek from Egypt. In his late twenties he was converted to philosophy and scoured Alexandria for a master. He eventually found Ammonius Saccas, a thinker who wrote nothing but passed on his ideas only to his pupils, and stayed with him eleven years. Then, after a brief interval, when he went with the Emperor Gordian to Persia in order to investigate Eastern religious traditions, he made his home at Rome. Here he was favoured by the court and was active in phi-

lanthropic works; he was much in demand as a guardian for orphans and as an arbitrator. Plotinus taught at regular seminars where senators, doctors and poets as well as philosophers would gather to hear him lecture, 'his intellect visibly illuminating his face'. Discussion was rigorous; objections from his associates as well as the writings of other philosophers helped to form Plotinus' philosophy.

Plotinus' metaphysics and his mysticism are inextricably associated. We come to understand the world because our minds participate in the ideas which shape things and bring them into being: 'in perfect knowing subject and object are identical'. Things are brought into being by the operation of intellect on matter; matter denotes the dark formless raw material on which intellect sets to work. It is not actively evil; it exists only in potentiality. So soon as it is touched at all by intellect it ceases to be merely matter; all the things we can identify are a 'compound of matter and shaping principle'.

There are higher and lower levels of things; their status is determined by the degree to which intellect in them has mastered matter. The lower levels are more complex and darker, but they are not positively evil. Unlike the Gnostics against whom he wrote, Plotinus made no sharp distinction between material and spiritual levels; all flows continuously down from the One: 'to despise this sphere and the Gods within it, or anything else that is lovely, is not the way to goodness' (*Enn.* 2. 9. 16).

Most people do not rise above perceiving the action of intellect on material things. There is, however, a higher principle of Soul which unites all souls, including the soul of the entire universe. This principle is able constantly to shape things out of matter because it is permanently in contemplation of the Intellectual-Principle or *Nous*, which holds in itself all the Ideas or Forms (a concept derived ultimately from the Platonic Forms). This Soul-Principle is the agent through which the wisdom of *Nous* is actualized: 'it is the forthgoing heat of a fire which also has heat inherent in its essence' (*Enn.* 5. 1. 3). Above both these principles, infinite and utterly transcendent, is the One, also referred to as the Good. Nothing can be predicated of it; the One can be said to exist only in the sense that it does not not exist. Though it is the source of everything, it does not consciously create; the universe over-flows from it, like a fountain spilling over.

Nothing in Plotinus' universe is static. Things pour down from the One; at the same time philosophers try to return upwards to it. They are like the heroes in Homer wanting to go home: 'Let us flee then to the beloved fatherland' (*Iliad* 2. 140 = *Enn.* 1. 6. 8.). Their first step is to remove what holds them down, just as one might strip off clothes before celebrating holy mysteries. Once the soul is unencumbered it will become light enough to see and understand the ideas in *Nous*, and maybe to be united through vision to the One, an ecstasy accorded to Plotinus four times in the six years Porphyry knew him. 'In this seeing we neither hold an object nor trace distinction; there is no two ... the man is merged with the Supreme, sunken into it, one with it, centre coincides with centre' (*Enn.* 6. 9. 10).

Christian Neoplatonists have found it easy to assimilate Plotinus' supreme triad of One, Intellectual-Principle and Soul-Principle to the Christian God. Among Latin thinkers, Plotinus was discovered about a century after his death. Ambrose preaching before a congregation of imperial courtiers in Milan larded his sermons with gobbets of the fashionable philosopher. Augustine was among his listeners; on him Neoplatonic influence was deeper and more subtle. The vision he had at Ostia, after his conversion to Christianity was, as it is described in the *Confessions*, like a Neoplatonic ascent, though it culminated not in union with Plotinus' One, but in the companionship of the Good Shepherd in the pastures of paradise.

The Western Middle Ages knew Neoplatonism through such Christian mediators. Plotinus himself was discovered once more at the Renaissance, when M. Ficino put the *Enneads* into Latin. He has been periodically rediscovered since, notably by Thomas Taylor, the Platonist friend of William Blake, by the literary lions of Edwardian Dublin, among them W. B. Yeats, S. MacKenna and the young E. R. Dodds, and by W. R. Inge*, Dean of St Paul's, who found in the *Enneads* a source of comfort during the First World War.

Editio major of the *Enneads* by P. Henry and H.-R. Schwyzer, 3 vols, 1951–73; text with translation, as yet incomplete, ed A. H. Armstrong in the Loeb Classical Library, 3 vols so far, 1966–. Classic translation by S. Mackenna, *Plotinus: The Enneads*, 1917–30, [4]1969. Studies include A. H. Armstrong, *Plotinus*, 1953; P. Hadot, *Plotin ou la simplicité du regard*, [2]1973; J. Trouillard, *La purification plotinienne*, 1955; J. M. Rist, *Plotinus: The Road to Reality*, 1967; E. R. Dodds, 'Tradition and Personal Achievement in the Philosophy of Plotinus', *JRS* 50, 1960, p. 1–7.

OLIVER NICHOLSON

Poverty

1. *As endured deprivation.* Poverty is a deprivation, a deficiency in what a being can be. It is absolute when a being is permanently incapable of acquiring a more-than-being (e.g. when deprived of movement, or of power to reflect, or of achieving divinity). It is relative when a being is currently incapable of acquiring a better-being (for instance, through being physically or mentally handicapped, or in slavery, or otherwise underprivileged).

Living beings instinctively refuse poverty, which is experienced as a threat and a handicap. They struggle for life by adapting themselves and surpassing themselves. That is why the refusal of poverty can be considered as a basic biological urge which governs the evolution of living beings. Negatively, poverty prevents them from realizing their total fulfilment, and positively, it obliges them to go beyond themselves, to adapt themselves in order to ensure their own survival and that of their species.

Each living species is more or less fit to defend itself, to invent and forge weapons for survival. Each establishes itself within a given order, a hierarchy based on the survival of the fittest. Each tends to evolve, perfect itself and multiply, first by passing on its strengths to the members of its group to ensure its own security, and then by subjecting and eliminating everything which threatens its own life and that of its kin. Superior categories eliminate inferior categories which do not possess adequate defences. The history of humanity is the struggle of individuals (who may be grouped together by race, or class or caste) who forge for themselves means of expression and action (language or customs) which are suited to combat their own deficiences and ensure their own survival at the expense of weaker beings. In this way they acquire a more-than-being or better-being. From this vital instinct stems the injustice which brings suffering, and revolt or submission, to the weaker ones. This basic desire for more-than-life, together with the dangers that threaten survival, results in a more and more complex society – deeper interdependence, a greater plundering of the earth's resources, a faster arms race – and all to the detriment of those least fit to defend themselves. The weaker ones sustain the logical consequences of this evolution, and are subjugated by the stronger elements who, the more their security is threatened, the more they build up their defences to guarantee their supremacy. Thus, having reached the summit of its evolution, humanity reaches a breaking-point. To satisfy its need for better-life or more-than-life, it puts itself in the position where it can provoke its own total annihilation.

2. *As spiritual value.* All religions have made of poverty a virtue which transcends human life. Either poverty is accepted in others and refused for oneself – riches being the proof of God's blessing (Gen. 49.25; Deut. 28.3–8), although the rich man has an obligation to share or to give alms – or it is sought for oneself as a liberation from material constraints. This search for voluntary poverty (as undertaken, for example, by Buddhists* and Cathari*) is meant to indicate that the value of a person is not to be measured by what he possesses but by what he becomes. Freely-chosen poverty demands respect for and solidarity with the poor and underprivileged. It counter-balances the instinct for power which, pushed to extremes, threatens the survival of the planet. Love is the motive for voluntary poverty, both love of self leading to perfect self-fulfilment, and love of others, those who by enduring imposed poverty are deprived of the possibilities of fulfilment and are obliged to turn to the substitutes of drugs and delinquencies in order to survive. Acceptance of voluntary poverty enables one to share the poverty of those who are forced to endure it, and to help them towards fulfilment themselves. Only in this state are they able to choose poverty freely.

3. *As basic gospel condition.* By becoming man, God radically reverses the meaning of endured poverty and gives to voluntary poverty the fullness of its meaning. The incarnation of the Son of God brings a radical change to the law of evolution, giving it its full meaning and leading it to its total fulfilment.

In becoming man, the Son of God renounces his divine privileges (Phil. 2.6–8). To free human beings from the entanglement into which they have let themselves be drawn by the law of evolution, God chooses to become poor (II Cor. 8.9). He identifies himself with the underprivileged on whom the rich build up their wealth, with those who are obliged to endure the suffering which every man tries to reject (Isa. 53.1–6). He chooses the poverty which oppresses (and which the prophets denounce: Isa. 1.10–16; 10.2; Hos. 6.6; Jer. 22.13; Amos 5.24; 8.4–6) in order to make of the poor the 'blessed in spirit'. Through him they attain the kingdom as the ones chosen by God, with whom he has identified himself. The poor are the first ones to be called (Matt. 11.2ff.), together with children, whom Jesus contrasts with the proud and powerful (Luke 2.8; Matt. 11.25; 18.3; Luke 1.52). This is why the poor are not the drop-outs of society; in their nakedness, they are the centre of the world, because they are both the reflection of the human poverty which each being carries within himself, and also, since the Son of God identifies himself with them, they are the means of attaining the ultimate purpose of humanity: union with God, reconciled in Christ. God's presence in the world is symbolized by the scrap of bread and drop of wine which we use in our eucharists, humble objects which identify him with the poor.

4. *The theological basis of poverty.* The poverty of the Son of God, revealed in his incarnation, is based on the radical poverty of each of the persons of the Trinity. God the Father is absolute Gift. He retains nothing for himself, but totally dispossesses himself for his Son. The ecstasy of the Son in the face of this gift provokes an absolute gift in return. The communication, or the breath, between them is the Spirit. It is therefore a radical poverty, a total divestment, which characterizes each of the three persons of the Trinity in relationship to the other two, and which allows them to co-exist in one God. The total gift, which results in total poverty, shows forth perfect love. Christ is at once the Son of God, who gives

himself to the Father in the Spirit, and the Son of Man, who identifies himself with the most poor (Matt. 25.40) to communicate divine love to them. The community of the people of God, the body of Christ which assembles round him, takes up itself the attitudes which were in Christ Jesus (Phil. 2.1–5). That is why the church's first mission must be to teach people to live in the way of Christ Jesus. They share what they have, and what they are, with the underprivileged, and lead mankind to total fulfilment in union with God.

Conrad Boerma, *Rich Man, Poor Man – and the Bible*, 1979; Benoit Charlemagne, *A Camel in the Needle's Eye*, 1981, esp ch. 11.

BENOIT CHARLEMAGNE

Praise *see* **Prayer (5) Thanksgiving**

Prayer

1. *Adoration*. Adoration is a form of prayer which lies at the very heart of religion. The word which seems to characterize adoration most aptly is 'absolute'. On the one hand, there is the sense of the absolute claim of God. It is indeed this claim which initiates and calls forth the prayer of adoration. God is unique in his absoluteness, and so he is different from everything created and finite. That is why adoration may be offered to God alone. Christians may and do venerate the saints and invoke their prayers, but even the deepest veneration is relative and is called forth in any case by the presence of God in his saints. To adore any finite being would be to mistake that being for the absolute, and this would be idolatry. Thus the church has distinguished between adoration (*latreia*) which is offered to God alone and veneration (*duleia*) accorded to the saints. Because of her unique place among the saints, the Virgin Mary receives a high degree of veneration (*hyperduleia*), but excesses of devotion to the Virgin have been discouraged from the early centuries down to Vatican II, which makes it clear that the veneration of Mary is relative to the Incarnate Son.

It is important not to think of adoration as a kind of homage such as might be paid to an earthly ruler. That again would be to overlook the uniqueness of God's absolute being and the unique character of adoration. Homage is a bad analogy. We do not adore God for his power or even for his goodness but as the limit which surpasses everything that is admirable in our finite experience. God is the supremely Holy One, and the adjective 'holy', as Otto showed, not only includes the perfection of power and goodness and mercy and so on, but the mystery of the 'numinous' which surpasses all our powers of comprehension. Mystical writers have declared God to be more than power, more than goodness, more than beauty, and this is their way of saying that although these qualities do point us to God, when they are raised to the absolute they transcend our understanding. The vision of God infinitely surpasses the most beautiful and most impressive sights upon earth. But perhaps this analogy with aesthetic experience is a more fitting clue to the nature of adoration than the bad analogy of homage which we have already rejected. The sublime is not far from the holy. Kant defined the sublime as 'that which is beyond all comparison great'. This may help to explain the long connection between religion and art, and the fact that today many people who say they have no religion seek the sublime in art. The human being has a need to adore, to relate to that which is incomparable and absolute.

Because he who is adored stands at the very limit of being and eludes our full comprehension, the language of adoration comes eventually to an end. The prayer of adoration may often therefore be silent, though this is the silence that lies on the other side of speech, the silence of a fullness which words are inadequate to express. But when words fail, other forms of language come into play. Adoration finds expression in typical gestures – bowing, kneeling, genuflection, even prostration. These acts recognize the absolute claim of the adorable. Although the New Testament is reticent in speaking directly of the deity of Jesus Christ, C. F. D. Moule points out that it records gestures of adoration offered to him, such as the disciples' falling down and worshipping (*proskunein*) in Matt. 28.17.

We turn now to the other side of adoration – the absolute self-surrender of the one who adores. Before the absoluteness of God, only an absolute response is appropriate. The human being becomes aware of his own 'absolute dependence', as Schleiermacher expressed it. No doubt this goes against the grain for the modern man who has been taught to pride himself on his autonomy. Yet it is surely apparent that any human being in isolation is a mere fragment, and we are all dependent on persons and things beyond ourselves. But what would we mean by an absolute dependence? Again, let it be said that this is not homage or in any sense oppressive. It is a question of relating to an absolute which for the first time lets us be truly ourselves. Addison caught the meaning of adoration when he wrote: 'Transported with the view I'm lost in wonder, love and praise.' Intense adoration brings a kind of ecstasy in which the person who adores is taken out of himself and set in the context of a reality which so transcends his own in love and beauty and every perfection that he is filled with wonder and thanksgiving. Alongside the words of Addison may be set a testimony from Teilhard de Chardin: 'To adore . . . that means to lose oneself in the unfathomable, to plunge into the inexhaustible, to find peace in the incorruptible, to be absorbed in the immeasurable, to offer oneself to the fire and the transparency, to annihilate oneself as one becomes more deliberately conscious of oneself, and to give of one's deepest to that whose depth has no end.' It is worth noting that although he speaks of absorption, this does not mean the disappearance of the self but its purification and strengthening. It is the NT paradox that one must lose oneself to find oneself. The person who loses himself in the wondering contemplation of God begins to reflect something of the divine glory so that the image of God in which he was made becomes more manifest in his being.

That last point is important, because it emphasizes the connection between adoration and growth in the Christian life. It is exposure to the absolute in adoration that helps to draw human beings out of their own pettiness, stretching them to a fuller stature in which they will be fit to live in communion with God and in true community with one another.

K. E. Kirk, *The Vision of God*, 1931; P. Teilhard de Chardin, *Le Milieu Divin*, 1960.

JOHN MACQUARRIE

2. *Confession.* If ever there is childlike innocence, society destroys it by inculcating guilt, often out of love and care since fear will save from danger and 'Thou shalt not' prohibits to protect. But the child soon learns that wilfully or no he or she is in a state of disobedience and this grows because self-consciousness becomes what the *Theologia Germanica** condemns as 'the I, me, mine and the like', and instincts inflame to self-indulgence and power over others. The sensitive soul in horror at the cruelties of history realizes that there is a universal guilt, that much of the world's ills are due to my sins writ large, and that I enjoy the benefits and privileges of my 'decent', educated poverty, because my brother or sister of another race or time has dust to eat. Not to feel sin is inhuman, let alone unchristian. 'When a Christian man declares that the four times repeated response in the Litany of the English Church – "Have mercy upon us miserable sinners" – has no meaning for him, he proclaims that he has as yet no understanding of the Christian religion or that he has apostasized from it' (Edwyn C. Hoskyns).

Yet if I am forever hag-ridden by guilt, I shall be tormented into the grave, and shall be useless as a human being. What is more, I may sink into even worse sin, for it is often the person already overwhelmed by a sense of guilt who commits the crime. And if I seek to conquer sin by perpetual self-examination, I may not only become self-absorbed, but fascinated and half in love with my sins.

The Christian believes that all sin is ultimately against God, for it overthrows his purpose in creation and breaks the union of love with him which is our destiny. Yet 'if we confess our sins he is faithful and just to forgive us our sins and cleanse us from all unrighteousness'. This he does not by the fiat of his almighty and arbitrary power, but because in the life and death of Christ, cosmic evil has been overcome, though neither the war nor the suffering is over, and a new humanity is being created into which the whole activity of prayer seeks to make our incorporation sure.

Confession is the acknowledgment of our sins, the honest recognition that we fail and fail and fail again. It brings sin out into the open instead of burying it in our deep minds and is intended to save us from despair. There is forgiveness, new life and eternal hope.

Confession may be made direct to God

and in private. There are those who feel that other agencies bar the way, that confession to a priest, or pleas for the help of Mary and the saints are like being referred from one civil servant to another and never meeting the Lord. And some cannot receive sacramental assurance. None of the elaborate procedures of the church evolved from the skill of centuries will avail unless somehow there is the word of Christ himself spoken directly to the heart. This accounts for the spiritual struggles and depressions of a Luther* or a Bunyan*. For them, though they sometimes read damnation, the Bible in private brought faith and peace.

Many people need human help. 'Confess your faults one to another', says James. And the Methodist class-meeting encouraged this therapeutic honesty, though it became too severe for some, and degenerated into wearisome repetition of testimonies for others. Bonhoeffer* maintained that he who is alone with his sin is utterly alone and that the Christian fellowship is the company of those who are not trying to pretend that they have no faults but who dare to be sinners, for God loves sinners, though he hates sin. This does not mean that confession must always be a group activity, and most people may welcome the help of one other person, whatever his order in the church, who will be a 'soul friend'. Confession should help us to understand our faults, to know ourselves better and discern where our danger lies, as well as to know God and the meaning of his forgiveness.

In the public service of the church, confession should not be omitted, because there will always be someone in especial need of absolution, and all of us must shake the dust from our feet before we go into God's presence. (Cf. Charles Péguy's* poem in *The Mystery of the Holy Innocents*.) It is fashionable to complain that the Book of Common Prayer is overweighted with penitence and psychologically injurious. Not that other and newer offices fail to give those who use them opportunities of confession several times a day; but the penitential introductions to Morning and Evening Prayer, first introduced in 1552, even though the opening exhortation sets Confession of Sin in the full context of worship and of the everlasting mercy, are excessive, and like the shorter modern acts, may become formal and perfunctory. When one considers that the classical Church of England Sunday Service was Morning Prayer, Litany and Communion, though admittedly it usually ended with the Prayer for the Church, since the eucharist was celebrated infrequently before the evangelical and tractarian revivals, and that this full diet would include a further confession in preparation for the sacrament, the effect is oppressive, at least for the liturgist in his study. The church seems somehow to have survived! It can be argued that, after the opening confession which is an act of politeness as God's guests and assurance of the welcome of our forgiving Lord, we may need to confess further in response to the Word of God, which has brought a new awareness of sin's nature and calamity. And the cry 'Lord have mercy', constantly repeated in the Jesus Prayer* of Orthodox spirituality as well as in liturgy, is not the cry of the condemned begging to be saved from death. It is a prayer for all that God has to give; for his mercy is his perfection (Matt. 5.48; cf. Luke 6.36) and to have it lighten upon us is to be received into his eternal joy.

———

Dietrich Bonhoeffer, *Life Together*, 1954; Edwyn C. Hoskyns, *Cambridge Sermons*, 1938, 1970; William Telfer, *The Forgiveness of Sins*, 1959.

EDITOR

3. *Intercession.* Intercession is prayer with, for and on behalf of another person, group of people or even the world, which is undertaken by an individual or group. For true intercession, the intercessor must be in solidarity with God, that is trying to live out faith faithfully. In NT terms, the intercessor lives in solidarity with Jesus Christ: 'For there is one God and there is one mediator between God and men, the man Christ Jesus, who gave himself as a ransom for all' (1 Tim. 2.5). Intercession is therefore first an act and way of life in which the intercessor in solidarity with Christ through baptism and a life of faith enters Jesus' life of reconciliation. Jesus' intercession begins with incarnation (John 1.14), immerses him in the world's sin in the Jordan (Matt. 3.13), and brings him through desolation in death (Matt. 27) and resurrection (Mark 16) and intercedes for us (Rom. 8.34).

At another level, intercession is simply seen as praying for someone (sick, in trouble, without faith) or some object (peace in some part of the world, a solution to a dispute, justice in a particular country). Here, modern thought queries what is being attempted. Is it changing God's will, or reminding him of his 'duty'? Normally, the answer is that as Christ enters the world in reconciliation, so the intercessor is part of God's plan, God's economy of salvation. Jesus said: 'Ask and it will be given you' (Matt. 7.7), not explaining how, simply stating the fatherhood of God.

Intercession is work for others. It is an act of faith in God, his caring, his goodness. It is involved in the mystery of God and the freedom of man. We intercede for others because of what we believe about God as loving Father, who works directly, but also through men and women, using their co-operation. Intercession depends on the life of faith, not on words. We intercede with our whole being, opening a door for God, becoming channels, bringing people to God as Aaron did (Ex. 28.29). We can do this by name in a list, on request, because we are aware of need. We can cover all persons and subjects. Results are only sometimes known, and all intercession implies: 'Not my will, but thine, be done' (Luke 22.42).

Intercession has a long history, beginning in the OT. Examples are Abraham pleading for Sodom (Gen. 18.22–23), Moses frequently interceding and mediating (Ex., Lev., Num. and Deut.), Elijah (I Kings). Jesus interceded for Peter (Luke 22.32), for his disciples' sanctification (John 17), for unity (John 17.20–23), and for forgiveness of his executioners (Luke 23.34). After Pentecost, the church prays for the imprisoned Peter (Acts 12. 5), Paul prays for the Ephesians (Eph. 1.16) and James tells the people what to do when anyone is sick (James 5.13–17). In Jesus' life, individuals intercede with him; the centurion for his servant (Luke 7.1–10), the sisters for their brother Lazarus (John 11.1–4).

The mediaeval church prayed not only directly through Christ, but also invoked the angels, the blessed Virgin Mary and the saints to intercede for them. This was strongly repudiated by Calvin, Luther and other reformers who insisted that it was sacrilegious to address a prayer to anyone other than God or Christ. Even more radically, some believe any kind of intercession is unnecessary, since all has been achieved by Christ, and God knows all we want before we ask (Matt. 6.8).

The other view, much emphasized by Roman Catholics, is that there is a communion of saints, that we can all intercede for each other, and that, while not detracting from the sole mediator Jesus Christ, nevertheless we can and should all of us call upon the angels and saints to back up our prayer from their position of joy in the presence of God. The practice of prayer to the Virgin Mary and the saints was manifest for centuries in shrines and places of pilgrimage, where people prayed for themselves and for others.

One of the most common types of intercession was for the dead. Earliest examples are found on the walls of the catacombs. The practice was upheld by Cyprian, Tertullian and others, while in the fourth century, Arius was condemned for refuting the efficacy of such prayers. In England there were many 'chantry chapels' within churches set aside for prayer for the founders and benefactors and their families. These were suppressed at the Reformation. But in RC circles praying and having Mass said for the dead has continued to this day, especially at the time of death and during November.

Vicarious offering is another facet of intercession – the offering of oneself for another. This is marked especially in contemplative religious orders, among missionaries, those committed to living with the poor, lepers, prisoners. St Thérèse of Lisieux * offered each painful step during her last illness for missionaries; Fr Kolbe took the place of another prisoner to die in the gas chamber; Fr Damien, giving himself for lepers, became a leper.

The growth of the Charismatic Movement * across the denominations has led to more group intercessory prayer, in general, in particular, and especially for the sick with the laying on of hands, and widespread prayer for healing.

The Church of England has always retained the possibility of intercession. Examples are in the Book of Common Prayer – the Litany and Prayers of Thanksgiving, and for the Queen. There have been divergent views between the evangelical and the catholic wings of opinion, but both in their own way have continued to use some form of intercessory prayer. In the Church of England, among the Methodists and in the Church of Rome the revision of the eucharistic rite has included more scope for intercessory prayers, with greater freedom of intention.

Maurice Nédoncelle, *The Nature and Use of Prayer*, 1964.

MICHAEL HOLLINGS

4. *Petition*. Petition is the prayer of asking. It is often regarded as a 'low level' of prayer like the mewing of a cat for milk, and it may be selfish. Some spiritual writers feel that we should grow out of petition and not expect answers, that if we do we may become frantic with disappointment and torture ourselves with guilt like the prophets of Baal cutting themselves with knives to call down fire from heaven. We have to learn that prayer is communion with God, perhaps even a support for him in his cause against evil, rather than a demand for ourselves and the satisfaction of our wants.

Those who take this view are embarrassed by the teaching of Jesus – 'Ask and it shall be given you, Seek and you shall find; Knock and it shall be opened unto you' (Luke 11.9). The Lord's Prayer is petitionary and Jesus holds before his hearers human importunity, persistent and discourteous, as an example of prayer (Luke 11.5ff.; 18.1–8).

Petition means that we recognize our entire dependence on God and that the earth is his and we should ask his permission before we take anything, even a crust of bread. It demands the recognition that we are not lone individuals but members of a family and that my request may have to be denied for the sake of others. It is the prayer of faith and may not be the simplest and easiest stage of prayer, but one which requires great spiritual maturity. Fundamental is the belief that God waits for us to ask not only to try our faith, but because he wants the whole of our life to be in relation to him, every need, hope and fear binding us to himself. We must not become absorbed in our own needs but in God and his unbounded mercy, love and generosity.

Jesus promised that God would do for us all that we ask in Christ's name. This means more than adding 'through Jesus Christ' at the end of each prayer. It means praying as Christ himself would pray, asking only for the things for which he would pray. In John 15 Jesus puts it in another way: 'If you abide in me and I in you, ask what you will and it shall be done unto you.' This is an even stiffer condition, if we allow him to pray in us in our name. Yet with our asking there is the assurance that God is always more ready to hear than we to pray, and that he gives more than we deserve or desire. It is easy enough to believe that God gives more than we deserve; we perhaps find it more difficult to believe that he gives more than we desire. Jesus assured us that God our Father is more generous than human parents: 'If you then who are evil know how to give good gifts to your children, how much more will your Father in heaven give good things to those who ask him?' (Matt. 7.11). Luke in his version in 11.13 has 'How much more will the heavenly Father give the Holy Spirit to those who ask him?' Our greatest need, perhaps our ultimate need, is as Luke suggests, God; so our fundamental prayer should be, 'O God, give us Yourself.' Thomas Aquinas*, meditating before the crucifix, heard a voice saying to him, 'You have written well of me. What reward would you like to have?' His reply was, 'No reward, but you yourself, Lord.' Not God's gifts but the giver should be our desire and prayer.

Gifts and giver seem inseparable in Isa. 11.2: 'And the Spirit of the Lord shall rest upon him, the Spirit of wisdom and understanding, the Spirit of counsel and might, the Spirit of knowledge and the fear of the Lord,' a text much used in confirmation rites. Christians might also pray for the virtues mentioned in Gal. 5.22–3: 'love, joy, peace, patience, kindness, goodness, faithfulness, gentleness, self-control', which Paul thinks of as the fruit of the Spirit's indwelling (*see* **Fruit of the Spirit**).

James in 1.5 urges us to pray like Solomon for wisdom: 'If any of you lack wisdom, let him ask God who gives to all men generously . . . and it will be given him.'

The distinction between petition and intercession – which is petition for others – is not always easy to draw. But the two should be kept separate. Petition concerns our straight course to God; intercession our placing of ourselves between him and the world.

GEORGE APPLETON

5. *Thanksgiving*. Thanksgiving and praise are closely related in Christian spirituality. It is sometimes said that Christians praise

God for what he is and thank him for what he has done. But those concepts interpenetrate, for it is hard to separate gratitude for what God has done from joy that he is what he is. In the Old Testament praise is directed towards the Name of God which means his revealed character which is ever the same. But as it is in his acts in history that his name is made known, the praise of his name is mingled with thanksgiving for his acts. Nowhere is this seen more vividly than in the last six psalms in the Psalter.

The themes of praise and thanksgiving are carried from the Old Testament into the New, with thanksgiving for the blessings brought by the gospel of Jesus Christ and praise of the God who is there revealed with new realization of his sovereignty and his fatherhood. The earliest Christian writer to tell of thanksgiving in the Christian life is St Paul. His letters frequently begin with outbursts of thanksgiving (I Thess. 1.2; II Thess. 1.13; I Cor. 1.4; Rom. 1.8; Phil. 1.3; Col. 1.3) and it is in that context that he passes on to make requests in prayer. He 'gives thanks praying'. The thanksgiving is made for the events of the gospel, the blessings given to St Paul and to the churches to whom he writes, and sometimes include recent happenings which evoke special gratitude. In Colossians and Ephesians the thanksgivings are set out in paragraphs of a rhythmical kind not unlike liturgical forms. Thanksgiving, St Paul insists, is a recurring characteristic of the Christian life. It should be happening at all times and for all things (I Thess. 5.16; II Thess. 2.13, Phil. 4.6; Col. 3.8; Eph. 5.26). Thanksgiving to God separates true religion from false for it is the mark of paganism to neglect thanksgiving to God (Rom. 1.26). While the word 'thanksgiving' tells of the Christians' relation to God in the most practical way the word 'glorify' tells of the deep theological meaning of this gratitude, and all things should be done for the glory of God.

The Synoptic Gospels tell of the outbursts of praise to God evoked from time to time by the works of Jesus in his ministry. These outbursts are most prominent in Luke's Gospel and continue in the narratives of the Acts of the Apostles, after the Gospel has ended with the disciples in the Temple continually praising and blessing God (Luke 24.23). Matthew and Luke record in different contexts the outbursts of thanksgiving when Jesus says 'I thank thee Father, Lord of heaven and earth, for revealing these things to babes' (Matt. 11.25; Luke 10.21). Here the word translated 'thank' is the verb meaning rather to 'confess' or 'acknowledge', used for acknowledging sins as well as acknowledging blessings. In the Fourth Gospel the theme of thanksgiving seems to be drawn into the theme of giving glory, as Jesus lives and dies to the glory of the Father, a glory to be reproduced in the believers by the Holy Spirit.

For Christianity through the ages no act of thanksgiving is more significant than the thansgiving of Jesus in connection with the loaf and the cup of wine at the Last Supper. The thanksgivings spoken by him with the loaf and the cup were no doubt familiar Jewish thanksgivings, either those of the Passover meal or those of the evening before the Passover. To these familiar thanksgivings Jesus added the words identifying the loaf and the cup of wine with his body and his blood, creating thereby the rite in which both the disciples and the future believers would feed upon his death. In this new rite the Christians give thanks for the saving events of the gospel, commemorate the death of Jesus which is recalled into the here and now, feed upon him as their spiritual food and offer themselves as a thank-offering in union with Jesus. The word eucharist, thanksgiving, came at an early date to be one of the titles describing the sacramental rite.

Thus prominent is thanksgiving in the prayer and life and common worship of Christians. The prominence of thanksgiving in Christian prayer is linked with the essential character of such prayer. The pattern prayer for Christians, the *Our Father* given by Jesus to the disciples, begins in the version of Matthew's Gospel with the words 'Our Father who art in heaven, Hallowed be thy name, Thy kingdom come'. Here is the recollection of God's fatherhood and heavenly transcendence and sovereign purpose, and that recollection inherently involves thanksgiving before the praying Christian passes on to petition. Indeed all prayer which is addressed to the God who is king and father implies the approach of thankful trust before petitions follow. Thanksgiving is an integral part of the Christian's response to the God and Father of Jesus.

Through the centuries thanksgiving has been prominent in eucharistic liturgies, in the worship of all Christian churches and in the personal prayer of Christians. In each of these spheres thanksgiving for particular blessings is linked with the praise of God for his acts as creator and saviour. Like all prayer, thanksgiving is offered to the Father through Jesus Christ in the power of the Holy Spirit. As he prays 'Abba, Father', within the Christians the Holy Spirit is stirring them to thanksgiving no less than petition. Thanksgiving is properly expressed in silence as well as in words and the silence needs emphasis inasmuch as thanksgiving includes awe and wonder no less than happiness and joy.

A. MICHAEL RAMSEY

Prayer, The Apostleship of

The Apostleship of Prayer as known today is primarily an association and movement of apostolic prayer and evangelization.

The association originated in the theologate of the Society of Jesus* in the small town of Vals (France) in 1844. It was there that Fr Francis Xavier Gautrelet, the then spiritual director of the seminary, proposed to the young Jesuits not yet able to engage in a direct apostolate, a programme of prayer and offering of their whole life as a way of apostolate and continual intercession for active apostles.

This simple idea soon passed beyond the walls of the seminary to spread among Christian people in general.

Successor of Fr Gautrelet in directing the work was Fr Henri Ramière who in 1844 has been one of the young professors of theology in the Vals seminary. With Ramière the AP became worldwide. Before forty years had passed the work counted 35,000 centres and more than 13 million associates in every part of the world. To Ramière we owe also the origin of the *Messenger of the Sacred Heart*, a review that would propagate the AP spirituality from its first publication in Toulouse in June 1861. The *Messenger* aimed at lived devotion to the Sacred Heart of Christ united with active dedication to the interests of the church. Fr Ramière had thus linked up AP spirituality with cult and devotion to the Sacred Heart of Jesus*.

From its earliest stages the AP suggested concrete practices to its members: daily offering of the whole day to the Heart of Christ, recital of a part of the rosary* and monthly communion of reparation. Practices that were vitalized by a strong, dynamic evangelical spirit: the Christian apostolic dimension was to be lived through the interests of the Heart of Christ and an outstanding devotion to Mary. Such interests were regularly made concrete in the Toulouse *Messenger* as 'the monthly intention'. This aspect drew Christians of various parts of the world to pass beyond personal interests and unite in prayer for the general intention thus giving AP spirituality a profoundly ecclesial and universal value.

From the outset the popes were interested in the work and on five different occasions approved the AP statutes; every year since 1887 they have proposed the intentions of prayer for the great needs of the church and the world to the members directly.

This spirituality reached its peak in 1968 when the Holy See approved the latest statues brought in line with Vatican II. They stressed the essential aspects of the original work in the light of the universal priesthood of the faithful, liturgical renewal and the action of the holy Spirit.

At present across the world some twenty-nine reviews entitled *Messenger* or some such name are published as official AP organs in each country. In addition there are the fourteen reviews of the youth section entitled EYM (*Eucharistic Youth Movement*) and formerly known as the *Eucharistic Crusade*. Leaflets and sheets with the monthly intentions are published in approximately thirty-nine languages. Diffusion also takes place on a world level through innumerable calendars, ecclesiastical bulletins, posters and various popular publications of Christian spirituality. Each month Vatican Radio broadcasts commentaries on the pontifical intentions in different languages, not to mention those transmitted through other channels.

According to the statutes the Superior General of the Society of Jesus is the general director of the AP. From 1927 the general secretariat office has been in Rome. Its official bulletin is entitled *Prayer and Service* and is published in English, French and Spanish.

Joseph Hogan, SJ, *This Way Up*, 1964;
Henry Ramière, SJ, *The Apostleship of
Prayer*, 1864.

MARIANO BALLESTER, SJ

Prayer for the Dead

In view of the church's confidence in the
face of death and its awareness of the
unity of all Christ's people, living and
departed, one would expect the Christian
community to have commemorated its dead
from the first. This does not seem to have
been the case. The NT is virtually silent on
the subject and the first century as a whole
offers little evidence of the practice. Its
silence is the more remarkable when seen
against the backcloth of Judaism where the
custom of praying for the dead was not uncommon (II Mac. 12.43f.) and was certainly
sanctioned in pharisaic circles; but is, at
least in part, a natural concomitant of
the church's expectation of Christ's imminent return. Only as more and more
believers 'fell asleep' and the sense of
living in the last hours of a dying age began
to fade, did the church begin the slow process of articulating a theology of the
departed.

As the numerous inscriptions and prayers
for peace and refreshment which cover the
catacombs reveal, prayer for the dead
emerged in the general heart of the church
as ordinary Christians coped with bereavement. These early prayers for 'rest' are not
so much concerned with the repose of the
soul after death (as was to become the case)
as with the hope of sabbath rest and festivity. Prayer was positive and confident: a
celebration of the departed's possession of
the kingdom. The *Martyrdom of Polycarp*
(155/6) provides evidence for the *natalicia*
of martyrs, a celebration of their 'birthday'
through the gateway of death, with the
holding of an anniversary agape or com-
memorative eucharist.

North Africa was probably the first place
where prayers and offerings for the dead in
general found a recognized place in the
public life of the church. Tertullian* (160–
220), for example, states that a Christian
widow should 'pray for her husband's soul,
and meanwhile beg refreshment for him and
a share in the first resurrection and yearly
offer sacrifice for him on the anniversary of
the day on which he fell asleep' (*De Mono-*

gamia 10). And there can be no doubt from
the writings of the early Fathers (Clement,
Origen*, Cyprian*), and from the frequent
commemorations of the dead in the early
liturgies (*Didascalia*, *Sacramentary of Serapion*, Cyril of Jerusalem) that the practice
was established and widespread. Indeed, one
of the counts against the heretic Arius was
precisely that he denied the efficacy of praying for the departed.

Augustine's* description of his mother's
death provides us with a unique insight into
the mind of the fourth century church. 'Now
that my heart is healed of that wound . . . I
pour forth to thee O God, tears of a very
different sort for thy handmaid . . . for
though she had been made alive in Christ
. . . I dare not say that from the moment of
her regeneration in baptism no word issued
from her mouth contrary to thy command'
(*Confessions* 9, 13). Tertullian had already
mentioned the possibility of some sort of
remedial discipline which the righteous (or
some of them) might incur after death; and
Clement of Alexandria had spoken of a
purifying fire (*Stromateis* 7, 6). In this way,
prayers for the dead were coming to include
petitions for cleansing, forgiveness and
sanctification. This, combined with an
understanding of the eucharistic sacrifice as
propitiatory, legalistic notions of merit, and
a developing penitential system, formed the
seed-bed of the Western doctrine of Purgatory.

The Western church, with its more systematic approach, had for some time found
it an embarrassment to pray for saints and
martyrs. The East, on the other hand, which
was never to articulate a doctrine of Purgatory, also declined to 'grade' the departed
into those for whom it might be deemed
theologically appropriate to pray, and those,
who by divine favour, are considered worthy
to be entreated. Western mediaeval liturgy,
with its sombre mood and its preoccupation
with punishment in the after-life, requires
no comment. It was inevitable that the Reformers in their rejection of the doctrine of
Purgatory as unscriptural, and in their reaction against the multiplication of masses for
the dead and other 'abuses', should also
rebuff prayer for the dead. It had become
an integral part of an unacceptable web of
theology and spirituality. In England, with
the exception of the Prayer Book of 1549,
explicit prayer for the dead was to be largely

absent until recent times. In fact, it was not until the First World War, with its tragic loss of life, that prayer for the dead became not only acceptable but also pastorally necessary. Once again, its roots were in the anguish of bereavement. Since then, with the exception of a minority of evangelical churchmen, prayer for the departed both at funeral services and in the context of eucharistic worship has become normative. The reforms of Roman Catholic liturgy indicate a growing convergence of opinion and practice, with a recovery of the spirituality of the early church.

See also **Martyrdom, Martyrs; Saints, Sanctity.**

Prayer and the Departed: A Report of the Archbishop's Commission on Christian Doctrine, 1971; Dom Gregory Dix, _The Shape of the Liturgy_, 1945; J. A. Jungmann, _The Early Liturgy_, 1960; Michael Perham, _The Communion of Saints_, 1980; Geoffrey Rowell, _The Liturgy of Christian Burial_, 1977.

ROBERT ATWELL

Prayer of the Heart

In early Greek spirituality, prayer is regarded sometimes as an activity primarily of the mind or intellect (_dianoia, nous_), and sometimes as an activity of the heart (_kardia_). Typical of the first tendency, during the fourth century, are Evagrius and St Gregory of Nyssa. Viewing the human person in Platonist terms, Evagrius defines prayer as 'the converse of the intellect with God' (_On Prayer_ 3); by intellect (_nous_), however, he means not only the discursive reason but also, and more fundamentally, man's direct, intuitive understanding of spiritual truth. For Gregory man is constituted in the image of God by virtue of his mind (_dianoia_): it is by this that he communicates with his Creator, whereas the heart links him to the body and is involved with the passions (_On the Creation of Man_ 5, 8, 12).

But other writers of the fourth and fifth centuries, such as the author of the Macarian Homilies (collection H, xv, 20, 32–33; xliii, 7; _see also_ **Macarius the Egyptian**) and St Diadochus of Photice, see prayer as _par excellence_ an activity of the heart. They understand by 'heart' not primarily the emotions and feelings but – as in scripture –

the moral and spiritual centre of the human person, the seat of wisdom and intelligence, the place where the individual becomes most truly personal, and at the same time closest to God. In such authors prayer of the heart denotes, not just affective prayer of the feelings, but prayer of the whole human person. The same sense is found in St John Climacus * and his disciple Hesychius of Sinai. 'I cried with my whole heart,' writes Climacus, 'that is, with my body and soul and spirit' (_Ladder_ 28).

The heart is particularly emphasized by Hesychast authors of the thirteenth and fourteenth centuries (_see_ **Hesychasm**). In prayer, so they teach, we should strive 'to descend with the intellect (_nous_) into the heart', so that our prayer is not merely 'prayer of the mind/intellect', but 'prayer of the heart' or, more exactly, 'of the intellect in the heart'. The invocation of the name of Jesus (_see_ **Jesus, Prayer to**) assists in this, especially when accompanied by the physical technique. As in the Macarian Homilies, the heart is here understood in a biblical sense as the unifying centre of the human person as a whole; according to Gregory Palamas *, it is 'the treasury of the intelligence ... the throne of grace, where the intellect and all the thoughts of the soul reside ... the primary organ' (_Triads_ I, ii, 3; II, ii, 28). Thus to 'descend into the heart' signifies reintegration, the recovery of primal integrity; prayer of the heart means prayer of the united person, prayer in which the one who prays is totally identified with the act of prayer. Moreover, since the heart is not only the centre of the human person but also the dwelling-place of God – the frontier and point of encounter between the created and the Uncreated – prayer of the heart means prayer in which God is as much active as man, and may thus include what the West terms 'infused contemplation'.

See bibliographies for **Hesychasm**; **Jesus, Prayer to.**

KALLISTOS WARE

Prayer Meeting

A gathering for spontaneous worship, most typically in a Christian tradition derived from the Evangelical Revival of the eighteenth century. Any assembly for worship is in a sense a 'prayer meeting', so the place of assembly is 'a place of prayer' – cf. _euche_

(Acts 16.13) for the Jewish synagogue outside the walls of Philippi. Spontaneous worship, as expressive of the living presence of the Holy Spirit, had a place in the chief corporate liturgy of the early church, which created a need for order and guidance: 'When you come together, each one has a hymn, a lesson, a revelation, a tongue, or an interpretation ... Let all things be done decently and in order' (I Cor. 14.26, 40). With the increasing formality of public worship, spontaneous devotion in fellowship became the preserve of ascetics, either in their own communities or as an adjunct to the public liturgy – cf. the voluntary recitation of the psalter before the 'cathedral office' in Jerusalem described in the *Pilgrimage of Egeria* – wittingly or unwittingly an adaptation of Jewish Hasidic practice.

Gatherings for devotion with free, open prayer originate particularly with the Pietist movement and the evangelical revival. Where mission preachers went, their hearers began to meet in small groups to support the mission by intercession, to strengthen the spiritual growth of converts in their new experience of faith, to support those seeking an experience of conversion. People seeking knowledge of God sometimes came 'cold' into these gatherings, and found there their first experience of Christian worship. Such gatherings sprang up in areas not yet visited by the revival preachers, and were in some cases centres of revival before public preaching began. Prayer-meetings survived as more or less vital institutions in the Free Churches after the revival, and have come back into their own in all the renewal movements. They have proved to be valuable as ecumenical worship, in connection with evangelical missions and local inter-church projects; in their charismatic form, they have become integral to the life of RC and Anglican parishes.

A prayer meeting may be no more than, quite literally, prayer offered freely (aloud or silently) by those present as they believe the Spirit wills. Where the prayer meeting is, or is becoming, an institutionalized event, members may read scripture passages, sing or lead the singing of hymns, give addresses; the introduction of an element of instruction inevitably creates the need for and the tendency to liturgical structure, however flexible. The needs of group dynamics indicate the importance of a recognized leader, to steer the proceedings, to decide who shall speak, to restrain ill-advised, uninstructed or un-Christian utterance, to care for the more vulnerable members. In charismatic phases of the history of the prayer meeting, phenomena judged to be demonic have been known.

The prayer meeting will be for some an early stage of pilgrimage, with its appropriate uncertainties and temptations: 'the devil hates prayer meetings; and why? because he well knows that beginning to attend them is the open declaration of renouncing his service and enrolling under the banner of Christ' (*Wesleyan-Methodist Magazine*, May 1877). It is in this sympathetic setting that personal commitment to Christ may occur and that commitment grow by the exercise of faith and hope and charity as expressed through prayer. Participants in the prayer meeting are encouraged to love as compassionate and courageous members of the Body of Christ, and in this disciplined fellowship the gifts of the Spirit to the individual may be fostered and their application guided. One major criterion of the welfare of the prayer meeting is the humble mutual openness of the members.

For some parishes or congregations, the prayer meeting is simply one more feature of the church's varied life, while elsewhere the prayer meeting is natural only to a few. Pastoral wisdom is taxed by the danger that in the latter case a divisive pietist faction may emerge. If held within the organic unity of the church, the prayer meeting may be a major addition to its weekly cycle of worship (in this case formal leadership, and Bible study or other exposition or teaching will probably be prominent), or an adjunct to public worship either beforehand, as prayer for the worshippers and the leader of worship, or afterwards as a corollary to the thanksgivings and intercessions of the congregations. The prayer-meeting is sometimes a good place for the exercise of, for example, charismatic gifts for which public worship is not the best setting. Public services of envangelism have been sometimes modelled on the prayer meeting (e.g. the 'Camp-Meeting'), and so also have class-meetings and other fellowship gatherings.

P. R. Akehurst, *Praying Aloud Together*, 1972; C. Buchanan, *Encountering Charismatic Worship*, 1977; J. Gunstone, *The*

Charismatic Prayer Meeting, 1975; R. Petit-pierre, *Meeting for Prayer. A Practical Guide*, 1967; J. H. Ritson, *The Romance of Primitive Methodism*, 1909.

DAVID TRIPP

Prayer, Prophetic

Prophetic prayer is a term used by Friedrich Heiler* to describe a certain type of piety. Writers such as Nathan Söderblom, through whose influence Heiler eventually abandoned Roman Catholicism and became a Lutheran, distinguished two types of mysticism: the first was personality-denying, infinity-mysticism, mysticism of feeling; the second was personality-affirming, personal mysticism, mysticism of will, prophetic religion or religion of revelation. Heiler carried the distinction further by abandoning 'mysticism' as the generic term and describing the second type simply by the last two titles, prophetic religion and religion of revelation. In so far as it is best represented by the Bible and receives in the gospel of Jesus its classical form, it may also be called biblical or evangelical religion.

The prophetic religions of Zoroaster, Moses and in a certain sense Mohammed arose out of primitive religion; they were developed by the creative experiences of individual prophets, and grew into monotheism. But whereas Zoroastrianism and Islam hardened into rigid legalistic religions, the revelation to Moses led to a long line of development.

Prophetic religion is based on confident faith; it is life-affirming; it values faith and confidence rather than ecstatic experiences; it is naive rather than reflective, spontaneous rather than ascetic, masculine rather than feminine. It conceives of God as living, active, and merciful, revealing himself and bringing salvation in the midst of history. For it revelation is an objective, historical fact; the great biblical personalities are bearers of the revelation, and prophetic religion combines respect for the authority of revelation with personal freedom. Sin is breach of the God-ordained order of moral values; salvation is restoration of the broken fellowship; righteous action is itself fellowship with God. Prophets are called to act positively, to proclaim God's will, and to work for his kingdom; they build up fellowship. They take a positive view of human culture but look forward to a new heaven and a new earth. They embody dramatic dualistic tensions; they do not lose sight of the distance between God and man.

Accordingly prophetic prayer arises spontaneously from need and crisis. It includes complaints, questions, petitions and intercessions, not only for individuals but for the coming of the kingdom. It uses various ways of appealing to God's goodness, such as the recollection of his former benefits and the assertion of one's own piety; it expresses dependence, confesses sinfulness and includes trust, submission, thanksgiving and praise. It is often hostile to fixed forms. People of prophetic prayer know themselves to be children and friends of God, who is ever present to hear them.

Later Heiler came to prefer the term used by Rudolf Otto, 'faith-piety'. He also took a higher view of mysticism, but he still thought that for scientific study the distinction between two poles was necessary. His terminology has not had great influence. It is still often assumed that any profound spirituality must be on the road to mystical experience. The truth of this depends on the definition of mysticism, but it is certainly arguable that there is another type of spirituality which lacks the characteristics of mysticism as that is usually understood, and yet is equally genuine and valuable.

A. RAYMOND GEORGE

Prayer, The Psychology of

Prayer is an entering into communion with God and therefore belongs partly to a region beyond the competence of psychology to speak about. But it is also a human experience and as such is a valid subject for psychological scrutiny. C. G. Jung, a profoundly religious man, affirmed that there is an inherited tendency to give unconditional authority to God or to some person or cause which presents itself to the individual as bearing a divine or numinous quality. This tendency, or archetype as Jung called it, is quiescent until it is aroused by some symbol which triggers it into activity. One of the functions of public worship is to arouse this latent tendency; and prayer both arouses this yearning for God and expresses it when aroused.

Many symbols have been used to arouse this 'God-instinct'. For Christians the chief symbol is Jesus Christ himself. He is the powerful sign of the Creator reaching down into the welter of human weakness and sin, identifying himself with mankind in order to draw men and women into union with himself as his sons and daughters. No symbol, not even the manhood of Jesus Christ, can do more than hint at a reality that infinitely transcends it. Prayer is offered not to the symbol but to that which it represents. In prayer the individual looks through or away from the symbol to the Unknown to which it points. The words used in prayer are themselves symbols which direct the mind to a mysterious reality which they can express only in hints and suggestions made in stammering speech.

The experience of Christian prayer can be explored by looking at the well-known division: adoration, confession, thanksgiving, petition and intercession (*see* **Prayer**). Adoration is the acknowledgment of the overarching reality of God. Its function is partly to awaken, partly to express a sense of the divine reality. There is an element of abasement in it. The praying individual expresses his sense of nothingness in the presence of transcendent Godhead. But this abasement is balanced by his faith that the God he worships is the Father who loves him and sustains him in being. The abasement of adoration therefore turns naturally into delighted praise and a sense of heightened significance.

The prayer of confession is the articulation of an awareness of sin and is a cry for forgiveness and healing. It springs inevitably from a sense of estrangement from God. It gives voice to a feeling of corporate guilt as well as of personal sin. Modern psychological medicine has spread the knowledge that an exaggerated sense of guilt can be a morbid condition needing to be cured. This neurotic guilt may be partly due to the individual blaming himself unduly for corporate wrong-doing, for the unavoidable effects of membership in a selfish and unjust society. Yet penitence can be healthy and enriching. Jung has written: 'If only people could realize what an enrichment it is to find one's own guilt, what a sense of honour and spiritual dignity.' This enrichment springs from the fact that to acknowledge guilt is to affirm solidarity with the human race in its estrangement from its true life. The Lord's Prayer similarly emphasizes the individual's solidarity with his fellows.

'Forgive us our trespasses as we forgive those who trespass against us.' There need be nothing cringing in the human cry of penitence. The individual frankly though ruefully acknowledges his share in the human crimes of violence and cruelty, of greed and hate, as well as his own personal missing the mark.

Thanksgiving is the expression of both faith and gratitude. Its effect in proportion to its genuineness is to strengthen the sense of dependence on God and trust in him. Thanksgiving for all that is enjoyable in life strengthens the sense of creaturely dependence on the author of all that is good. But even in the midst of acute tribulation a person can give thanks for the love which is at work bringing good out of evil. The focus of thanksgiving for the Christian is Jesus Christ, crucified and risen. The figure of Christ in the believer's imagination releases a rush of gratitude and the energy to live for God and the kingdom. Thanksgiving for redemption, expressed corporately and sacramentally in the eucharist, colours all fully Christian prayer and gives it its characteristic note of joy.

The prayers of petition and intercession give voice to the confident trust in the power and willingness of God to intervene helpfully in human life. There is a naivety, a childlike quality, about petition which is apt to shock the sophisticated. But below the level of adult consciousness there exists a well of primitive feeling which resembles a child. Petitionary prayer awakens this childlike thing and involves it in prayer. Further, it seems that there are healing forces at work within us which the doubt and mistrust fostered by a sceptical society repress. Confident petition helps to break down the imprisoning wall of mistrust and so enables the life-renewing energy to flow out. The mysterious fact of telepathy which seems to imply that mind unconsciously touches and flows into mind independently of spacial proximity illuminates the corporate nature of private prayer. For it seems probable that the confident petition which opens the personality to its depths causes either distress signals or impulses of healing and encouragement to be sent out below the level of consciousness. This would shed light on some of the extraordinarily detailed answers to prayer which those who pray with confidence sometimes record.

C. G. Jung, *Collected Works*, vol X, para 461 ²1970; G. S. Spinks, *Psychology and Religion*, 1963.

CHRISTOPER BRYANT, SSJE

Preaching and Spirituality

A compelling sense of vocation is one of the most important factors in the spirituality of a Christian preacher. The 'prophetic call' narratives of the OT and some NT autobiographical passages illustrate both the divine purpose and the human response (Amos 3.7–8; 7.10–15; Isa. 6.1–8; Jer. 1.4–19; Ezek. 1.1–3.27; Acts 22.6–16; 26.12–18; I Cor. 9.16–27; 15.8–11). The psychological tension between dutiful willingness and natural reluctance is given some prominence in early Christian literature. Contrasting Isaiah and Jeremiah, Gregory the Great* reminded his mediaeval readers that 'there are those who laudably desire the office of preaching, whereas others no less laudably are driven to it by compulsion' (*Pastoral Care*, I, 7). Gregory believed some potential preachers suffered from 'excessive humility'. Those 'who can preach with good results, but shrink from doing so . . . are to be admonished' for 'hiding the medicine of life from souls that are dying' (ibid., III, 25). Gregory Nazianzen explains how he came to 'hold the balance between the fears, neither desiring an office not given to me, nor rejecting it when given'. He finds himself 'more timid than those who rush at every position, more bold than those who avoid them all' (Oration II, *In Defence of His Flight*, 112). Basil of Caesarea reminds Bishop Amphilochius at his consecration that God ensnares his servants within 'the inescapable nets of His grace' even when they are 'trying to escape' *Letters* CLXI).

More is required of a preacher than acceptable words; consistent example is of immense importance. Basil maintained that 'teaching a Christian how he ought to live does not call so much for words as for daily example' (*Letters* CLI). Gregory the Great asks 'with what presumption' does the preacher 'hasten to heal the afflicted while he carries a sore on his own face?' (*Pastoral Care*, I, 10). Centuries later the same truth was vividly expressed by Richard Baxter* in his *Reformed Pastor*: 'He that means as he speaks will surely do as he speaks' (cf. George Herbert*, *Priest to the Temple*, 2–3).

One of the preacher's dangers is that when he has preached about a thing he subconsciously imagines he has done it. Baxter warned about being 'hardened under the noise of our own reproofs'. Augustine* said that a preacher must take care to listen to his own sermon: 'For he is a vain preacher of the word of God without, who is not a hearer within' (Serm. 129, 1).

But listening is not enough; the preacher must pray. Lancelot Andrewes* shared the conviction of Fulgentius, the sixth-century North African bishop, that the preacher must realize he may do his work 'better by the piety of his prayers than by the fluency of his speech'. He must 'lift up to God a thirsty soul, that so he may give out what from Him he hath drunk in, and empty out what he hath drunk in, and empty out what he hath first replenished' ('A Caution and a Prayer before Preaching', *Preces Privatae*, 1648). Regular prayer not only reminds the preacher of his spiritual resources but makes him more sensitive to the needs of his congregation. Spurgeon described the poverty of preaching without praying. Genuine conviction is clearly necessary (e.g. Bunyan: 'I preached what I felt, what I smartingly did feel,' *Grace Abounding*, 1666), but the preacher must avoid bigotry. Experience of trouble is an aspect of life's spiritual resources of incalculable worth to the preacher. Even failure can have a sanctifying effect; it can prepare us 'for doing greater and higher work, for which we should not have been fitted unless anguish had sharpened our soul'. Humility of spirit is an obvious necessity.

A capacity for hard work will be a practical expression of the preacher's spirituality. The man with a fine vocabulary 'is not excused perpetual effort' since 'preaching is not a natural but acquired power, though a man reach a high standard, even then his power may forsake him unless he cultivate it by constant application and exercise. Hence the gifted need to take greater pains than the unskilful' (John Chrysostom, *On the Priesthood*, V. 5). The preacher's accountability to God will always be more important than the approval of the congregation. He is a steward, answerable for every aspect of his ministry.

W. E. Sangster, *The Approach to Preaching*,

1951; C. H. Spurgeon, *An All Round Ministry*, 1973.

RAYMOND BROWN

Proclus

The Neoplatonist* philosopher Proclus (412–485) spent most of his life as head of the Academy founded by Plato at Athens. One of his pupils there, Marinus, wrote an engaging biography which reveals him as energetic, cerebral and ascetic. He was also in an intellectual line of descent from Plotinus*.

As with Plotinus, Proclus' mysticism is the corollary of his metaphysics. Highest of all, beyond being, is the One; from it emanates everything, in increasing grossness and complexity. Proclus examined in greater detail than Plotinus the processes of cause and effect through which this system would work; he adumbrated hierarchies of principles which explained how higher powers could, by their activity, produce an effect at a lower level. These principles he was able to harmonize with the traditional classical pantheon.

He also thought it the business of serious men to purify their souls, raising them to the level of the higher simpler entities, and perhaps, to union with the One. To the contemplation advocated by Plotinus, Proclus added the practice known as theurgy, no mere magic or even preliminary rites of purification but a liturgy carried out with a clear purpose, that of creating, by a faith which goes even beyond intellect, the possibility of contact between men and the divine.

Proclus was a devout pagan; when Christians removed the statue of Athena from the Acropolis at Athens, the goddess appeared to him in a dream and said that she would henceforth make her home with him. However, Christians were strongly influenced by his work; in particular, probably in the generation after his death, his hierarchies of concepts were used as a metaphysical map by Denys the Areopagite*, one of the most carefully studied spiritual guides of the Middle Ages, both in the West and in Byzantium.

Proclus' works are copious and often hard to find. Recent editions include *The Elements of Theology*, ed and tr E. R. Dodds, [2] 1963; *Théologie Platonicienne*, ed with

French tr H. D. Saffrey and L. G. Westerink, 4 vols so far, 1968–. L. J. Rosán, *The Philosophy of Proclus*, 1949, summarizes his thought; J. Trouillard, *L'Un et l'âme selon Proclus*, 1972, considers it in a larger perspective.

OLIVER NICHOLSON

Providence

The word is derived from the Latin *providentia*, meaning 'foreknowledge'. Strictly, therefore, divine providence refers to God's prior knowledge and 'provision' rather than to his active involvement in the world, but in practice the word usually refers both to divine foreknowledge and divine government.

The primary source for a Christian doctrine of providence is the rule of God as this is portrayed in the Bible. It is possible to detect several elements in this overall rule, though the original writers would not always have recognized the distinctions that were later to be made. There is God's creative activity, especially as recounted in Genesis; there is the sustaining activity of God when he upholds the world or man (e.g. Isa. 41.10); there is the activity that came to be called 'general providence', that is the work of God in and through natural things, as when the rain falls on the just and on the unjust (Matt. 5.45); there is what some would later call 'special providence', when God speaks to a prophet, or works through some other specific action; finally, there is what some would later call 'miracle', when the specific action is one that must defy any purely natural explanation. In a broad sense all of these activities fall under providence, but in a narrower sense only the two that came to be called general and special providence.

In the OT God's rule is seen as universal, covering the realms of nature, as when he determines the weather; and the realm of man, as when pharoah's heart is hardened; and the realm of history, as when the outcome of a battle is determined by God (e.g. Josh. 6.2). Later, this view of universal providence raised acute problems because of its conflict or apparent conflict with human freedom, but as in the case of other ancient peoples, the Hebrews tended to accept both the view that God determines all things, and the view that man is responsible. In the NT a similar universal providence is implied, although the actual Greek word for providence, *pronoia*, is used only once, and then to refer to human forethought (Acts 24.2). However, there is an important change of emphasis. Nature appears to be seen as more independent, as when contrary winds hinder the spread of the gospel (Acts 27.7ff.), and more significantly, the stress throughout is more on the way in which God helps to change man, through his redemption, than on the way in which the world or history is changed directly. The kingdom of heaven is within, and the triumph of God is displayed in the cross rather than in the victory of Israel's armies. This suggests a new understanding of God's providential rule, although it is one that the late prophets had begun to see, as in the theme of the suffering servant.

Similarly, while the early church clearly accepted a theory of universal providence (as witnessed by Augustine's *Confessions*, in which God governs both Augustine's heart and the winds that drove him to Rome), the stress is again on God's activity in the redemption of mankind. This has profound implications for Christian spirituality, since God is held to be at work within the soul. This is explicit in St Paul's reference to the Spirit working with man as he prays (Rom. 8.26), and is a recurring theme in Augustine. Not only does God illuminate our thoughts, within the context of God's grace working within us 'we are fellow-workers with him' (*De natura et gratia*, XXXI, 35), so that, in an important sense, the Christian soul can actually share in the providential activity of God. Here there is a direct link between the Christian view of the spiritual life, and the Platonic tradition, with its theme of participation in the Good.

Within the mediaeval church gradual changes in the philosophy of nature had significant consequences for the doctrine of providence. Nature came to be seen more and more as an 'order' with its own relative autonomy or 'secondary causality'. Because it was the expression of the free creativity of its 'first cause', that is God, this order could not be discovered *a priori*, as in the Islamic-Neoplatonic philosophy of the time, but had to be discovered *a posteriori*, by empirical procedures. In due course this Christian philosophy paved the way for the scientific, empirical study of the world, but already in Aquinas it led to a sharp distinction between providence, wherein God works 'interiorily

in all things' (*ST* 1a, q.105, a.5), and miracle, which is 'something that happens outside the whole realm of nature' (*ST* 1a, q.114, a.4). Some mediaeval writers also distinguished a general and a special providence, along the lines already suggested, but Aquinas himself did not.

With respect to the manner of God's rule over man the Christian tradition has been divided. Calvinists, and others who follow Augustine's account of predestination, tend so to emphasize God's lordship that it is hard to make room for human freedom and responsibility, even though these have nearly always been affirmed. Aquinas and his followers, adopting a position that is found in Boethius and in the Neoplatonic tradition, try to solve the problem by insisting that God 'knows' human events only from his eternal standpoint, so that strictly speaking he does not '*fore*know'. Many contemporary Christians are more radical. For example, the Christian process philosophers see God's rule as persuasive rather than coercive, whether in respect to nature or man or history. Also, they frequently deny the total knowledge of God, thus allowing for a real contingency in human and historical events.

Contemporary Christian thought also includes radical accounts of other issues that affect one's view of providence. For example, Bultmann, and Christian existentialists generally, limit God's activity to the realm of persons, leaving nature and history as virtually autonomous. Many others deny the Thomistic distinction between providence and miracle, calling in question whether any event can be said to be 'beyond nature'.

These issues have important consequences for prayer. For example, on a view such as that of Bultmann, intercessory prayers concerning natural events or history seem inappropriate, except in so far as they express or arouse a personal encounter with God. On the other hand, those who are attracted to process philosophers with Christian convictions, such as A. N. Whitehead, can justify a more traditional approach to intercessory prayer, despite their unorthodoxy on the nature of God's sovereignty. In principle our prayers can alter the context in which God's persuasive power may be able to be effective.

Whatever view one takes of intercessory

prayer there is no doubt as to the importance of the doctrine of providence for the spiritual life in general. It includes the idea of a divine activity within the human soul which is a work of free grace and love, and which is at the same time a work that respects the integrity and freedom of the person.

Augustine, *De ordine*; Aquinas, *Summa theologiae*, 1a, qs. 19–25, 103–5; P. R. Baelz, *Prayer and Providence*, 1968; M. J. Langford, *Providence*, 1981; M. Wiles (ed), *Providence*, 1969.

M. J. LANGFORD

Psalms, The

Though its origins are lost in primitive religion, liturgical dances and coronation rites the Psalter, 'the hymn book of the second temple', is a legacy from Hebrew to Christian spirituality and from the first has been woven into its very fabric. Jesus himself quoted psalms, as his own prayers, in controversy, and as foretelling his own life, sufferings and God's purpose for him. The passion stories of the Gospels are all influenced by Psalm 22, which according to Mark and Matthew was on Christ's lips on the cross. Psalms have been constituents of Christian worship from the beginning, though it was in the monasteries that it became the custom to say or sing them in course over the week, the month, or even the day, using them as no hymnbook has ever been used except in a modern, money-raising 'sing-in'. This has produced a spiritual discipline of the prayer-wheel or treadmill type, which some have highly valued. The repetition of imprecations, 'highly-improper in the mouths of a Christian congregation' (John Wesley), has been an offence to some, while others have allegorized God's enemies as our sins, on whom the Divine vengeance should fall, or else have found in the Hebrew singer's vehemence either the force of the uninhibited enmities which we so often hypocritically suppress, or the model of that 'perfect hatred' which Christians should feel towards evil. Some have come to regard the psalms as too full of complaints, too lugubrious, self-righteous and self-pitying, to be worthy of those redeemed by Christ.

Some censorship is perhaps called for, and hymns*, which are often psalm-paraphrases, may in some instances be ap-propriate substitutes in spite of purist opposition. Yet for the Psalter not to be a staple of Christian private devotion would be a repudiation of a tradition which burst out of the monasteries to inspire the whole of Christian life in the world, Protestant perhaps even more than Catholic. Christian prayer as soliloquy, or colloquy with God, owes much to the Psalter and to the use Augustine * made of it in the *Confessions*. His experience could be expressed only in its language. 'It was the language of a man who addressed a jealous God, a God Whose "hand" was always ready to stretch out over the destinies of men. Like any gentleman of feeling in the ancient world, the Psalmist had a "heart"; but he also had "bones" – that is, a part of himself that was not just a repository of feeling, but was "the core of the soul", with which God dealt directly, in His rough way, "exalting" and "crushing" ' (Peter Brown). The Psalter has brought the Christian philosopher dwelling in a speculative heaven with his high and holy Theos, down to earth and to a God, such as that of Kierkegaard's * *Fear and Trembling*, for whom perhaps there is a 'teleological suspension of the ethical' and whom neither our moral nor our intellectual categories can contain. It has also brought comfort and strength to Bible-steeped believers like the Scottish crofters, who felt that in its pages were delineated the heights and depths of their own condition. They found help because they were able to relate many of the psalms to the life of David as well as to 'great David's greater Son'. In the Scottish Kirk the use of psalms, whether from the Bible or in metrical paraphrase at the communion seasons was especially prized, and the psalms had the effect of introducing a eucharistic and triumphant note, and of taking the community beyond the passion to the heavenly ascent. In our own time Thomas Merton * has written of those who have proved that the psalms are the perfect prayer because in them 'Christ prays in the Christian soul uniting that soul to the Father in himself'. Dietrich Bonhoeffer*, too, found that in the conditions of European war and Nazi tyranny, the 'whole Psalter' became a reality as 'the vicarious prayer of Christ for his church'.

Peter R. Ackroyd, *Doors of Perception: A Guide to Reading the Psalms*, ²1983; P. F.

Bradshaw, *Daily Prayer in the Early Church*, 1981; R. E. Prothero, *The Psalms in Human Life*, 1903.

EDITOR

Purgation, Purification
see **Catharsis**

Puritan Spirituality

The term 'Puritan' became current during the 1560s as a nickname for Protestants who, dissatisfied with the Elizabethan settlement of the church by the Act of Uniformity of 1559, would have subscribed to the contention of the *Admonition to Parliament* of 1572 that 'we in England are so fare of, from having a church rightly reformed, accordyng to the prescript of Gods worde, that as yet we are not come to the outwarde face of the same'. Those whom the sobriquet implicitly impugned as heirs of the mediaeval Albigensians or 'Cathari'* (Greek *katharos*, 'pure') never, however, belonged to a single sect or constituted a clearly defined party either within or without the established church. Puritanism, inspired originally by native Lollard traditions and the zeal of Marian exiles returning from Calvin's Geneva and Bullinger's Zurich, had no one founder, no recognized leader and no agreed policy. It embraced many forms and degrees of discontent with the *via media* of the Elizabethan church, from refusal to wear the surplice, to use the sign of the cross in baptism, or to kneel to receive communion in parish churches, to repudiation of the validity of episcopal orders and the gathering of congregations in separation from the established church. Its history is marked by the promulgation of, controversy over, and rivalry between a succession of models of reformed church government.

Presbyterianism had been the ecclesiastical aim of the majority of early Puritans, led by such Cambridge men as Walter Travers (*c.* 1548–1635) and Thomas Cartwright (1535–1603). The aspiration survived to become the official policy of the Long Parliament which, having abolished episcopacy in 1642, summoned the Westminster Assembly of Divines in 1643 to effect a new church settlement. Despite the publication of the Assembly's series of classic Presbyterian formularies (*Directory of Church-Government* (1644), *Directory of Public Worship* (1645), *Confession of Faith* (1647) and *Larger and Shorter Catechism* (1647)), its efforts were frustrated by opposition from within the Puritan movement itself. The polity known originally as 'Independency', but in New England and subsequently in England as 'Congregationalism' (cf. John Cotton, *The Way of Congregational Churches* (1648)), was, under the patronage of Oliver Cromwell (1599–1658), successfully championed by the New Model army with its watch-cry 'liberty of conscience'. Its principles were embodied in *The Savoy Declaration of Faith and Order* (1658), for which John Owen (1616–1683) was largely responsible. Thus, while for William Bradshaw (1571–1618) a Puritan was an Independent (*English Puritanism* (1605)), for John Geree (1601?–1649) he was a Presbyterian (*The Character of an Old English Puritan* (1646)).

There was, furthermore, division within the Presbyterian ranks, between such strict Presbyterians as Thomas Edwards (1599–1647), who saw toleration as tending to religious and civil anarchy, and a significant group of so-called 'Presbyterians' who favoured ecclesiastical compromise. Their leader, Richard Baxter* (1615–1691), who preferred the term 'Reconciler', declared 'You could not (except a Catholick Christian) have truelier called me than an *Episcopal-Presbyterian-Independent*'.

Cromwell's commitment to liberty of conscience, coupled with the hectic atmosphere of the Civil War and Interregnum, saw, in addition, the emergence of a great variety of radical sects. There had, since Elizabeth's reign, been in existence small separatist congregations which had abandoned the legislative effort for national reform (cf. Robert Browne (*c.* 1550–1633), *Of Reformation without Tarrying for Any* (1582)). Variously condemned as 'Brownists', 'Barrowists' (after Henry Barrow (*c.* 1550–1593)), 'Anabaptists' and 'fanatics', the disconcerting social implications of the extremism of their Interregnum successors, who came increasingly from the lower classes, attracted opprobrium for tending, all too literally, to 'turn the world upside down' (Acts 17.6). They included the Levellers of John Lilburne (1614?–1657), and such short-lived and amorphous groups as the Ranters, the Seekers and the Diggers led by Gerrard Winstanley (*fl.* 1648–1652), but from them came also the Baptists* and the

Quakers*, followers of George Fox* (1624–1691).

The Restoration Act of Uniformity (1662), which required episcopal ordination of every incumbent and his 'unfeigned assent and consent' to the entire Book of Common Prayer, deliberately excluded Puritans from the re-established church. Many of the 2,029 clergy, lecturers and university fellows ejected by 'Black Bartholomew Day' (24 August 1662) were unwilling nonconformists. Their hope of eventual comprehension within a broader national church was, however, finally doomed by the Toleration Act (1689), which, by granting the legal right to worship in non-episcopal congregations instead of liberalizing the 1662 settlement, ensured that henceforth nonconformity would constitute a religious tradition distinct from the Church of England. The old, general term 'Puritan' was therefore superseded by the more specific 'Dissenter'.

Puritan doctrine was as varied as Puritan ecclesiology. Many Puritans, such as Owen and John Bunyan* (1628–1688), did retain the Calvinist allegiance of the Puritan fathers, the 'English Calvin' William Perkins (1558–1602) and William Ames (1576–1633), but others, like Tobias Crisp (1600–1643), so stressed the unmerited free grace of Christ as to be denounced by Calvinists as antinomians. Amongst radicals, Titus 1.15 might push antinomianism into libertinism and amorality and the millenarianism which informed all Puritan thought was particularly pronounced with them. On the other hand, there were such divines as John Goodwin (1594?–1665) who rejected Calvinism for Arminianism. Some, like Baxter*, favoured the 'middle way' of Moise Amyraut's 'hypothetical universalism', while Peter Sterry (1613?–1672) could combine Calvinism* with Cambridge Platonism*. The courageous intellectual independence of Puritanism encompassed disciples of Jakob Boehme* ('Behmenists'), the heterodox theology of John Milton (1608–1674) and the unitarianism of John Biddle (1615–1662).

Such diversity has tempted some historians to deny there ever was a historical movement which can usefully be called 'Puritanism', but such a view mistakes the various manifestations of Puritan commitment for the commitment itself. Puritanism pursued ecclesiastical, political and intellectual reform as but a means to the end of spiritual and moral reform. Its essence therefore lies not in any church polity, liturgical practice or theological dogma, but in the distinctively Puritan conception of the Christian life which may inform any one of these. 'Truth,' wrote Milton, referring to Ps. 85.11, 'is compar'd in scripture to a streaming fountain; if her waters flow not in a perpetuall progression, they sick'n into a muddy pool of conformity and tradition.' What defines Puritanism is commitment to the continuing process of spiritual enlightenment and development. 'The true Christian,' wrote Baxter, 'sitteth not down contentedly in any low degree of grace' but 'presses towards Heaven … towards perfection'. This over-riding obligation was fulfilled not through any duties or dogmas in themselves, but through the sincerity of the conviction with which an individual, in the light of sustained biblical study, performed and professed them. Puritanism reinforced Protestantism's homiletic stress, as against the sacerdotalism of Rome, and it therefore also stressed the primacy of individual responsibility and faith (I Thess. 5.21). It was a constant theme of anti-Papist polemic that Rome allowed its adherents only an implicit faith. The scandal of this was compressed into Milton's paradox 'A man may be a heretick in the truth', which may be elucidated from Bunyan: we are not to take up 'any truth upon trust, as from this or that or another man or men but to cry mightily to God, that he would convince us of the reality thereof, and set us down therein, by his own Spirit in the holy Word'. This profound sense of the work of the Holy Spirit, which placed personal conviction at the centre of the religious life, explains the preoccupation of Puritan divines with soteriology, with the process of conversion and the marks of the saint, and their fondness for the Pauline imagery of light and darkness (e.g. Eph. 5.8, Col. 1.12–13, I Thess. 5.4–5; cf. Thomas Goodwin*, *A Child of Light walking in Darkness*, 1636, Bunyan, *Light for them that Sit in Darkness*, 1675). Individualism and fragmentation were the inevitable consequences. Since, in Milton's damning phrases, 'a gross conforming stupidity', 'the iron yoke of outward conformity', 'the ghost of a linnen decency' – in a word, hypocrisy – was conceived as the single most serious obstacle, compliance with any particular policy, rite or dogma advocated by external authority necessarily took second place. Its very diversity hence witnesses to Puritanism's distinctive spiritual zeal.

This dynamic conception of the Christian life was characteristically rendered in images of action and endeavour. For the many who had, in the 1630s, fled Archbishop William Laud's persecution in the 'Great Migration' to New England, or who, like Fox, had travelled England in search of spiritual assurance, or who had fought in the Civil War, journeying and combat had been spiritual experiences in biographical fact. There was a further incentive to the presentation of the Christian life in terms of warfare and itinerancy in the many Biblical battles and journeys, the many literal and metaphorical uses of 'way', culminating in the great assertion of John 14.6, and the Pauline imagery of the race (e.g. I Cor. 9.24, Heb. 12.1) and of armour and fighting (e.g. Eph. 6.11–13, I Tim. 6.12). Such titles as John Downame's *The Christian Warfare* (1609), William Gouge's *The Whole Armour of God* (1616), John Preston's *The Breast-Plate of Faith and Love* (1630), Arthur Dent's *The Plain Man's Path-way to Heaven* (1601) and Robert Bolton's *Directions for a Comfortable Walking with God* (1625) adumbrate Bunyan's allegorical development of these images in *The Pilgrim's Progress* (1678; 1684) and *The Holy War* (1682).

The Puritan hero, however, bore no resemblance to the questing knight errant of mediaeval chivalry, an ideal explicitly rejected in *Paradise Lost* (IX. 13–41). Puritanism challenged everyman to become a Christian hero in the context of his everyday domestic and commercial dealings. In a famous sentence, Milton scorned both coenobitic and eremitic monasticism: 'I cannot praise a fugitive and cloister'd vertue, unexercis'd & unbreath'd, that never sallies out and sees her adversary, but slinks out of the race, where that immortall garland is to be run for, not without dust and heat.' Mendicancy was similarly condemned. Puritan teaching gave a new dignity to marriage and employment, and, encouraging common people to see in the least circumstance of their lives an opportunity for Christian service, addressed itself deliberately to the 'vulgar'. This address was pragmatically realistic, sensitive to the complexity of

human nature and experience. Scholasticism was rejected as firmly as monasticism. The minute particularity of Puritan divinity analyses the psychology of conversion and temptation and immediate casuistical problems, not abstract propositions or traditional authorities. If Puritan divinity is, in consequence, moral rather than systematic, equally, distinctions between moral, ascetical and mystical theology will not apply to its devotional works, which refuse to divorce the 'private duties' of prayer and meditation from the 'public duties' of an active faith. Puritan treatises prefer the comprehensive term 'godliness' to the exclusive 'devotion', and have no conception of the 'spiritual' or 'religious' life as separate from daily, social life.

As the touchstone was individual sincerity, the most frequently enjoined spiritual exercise was self-scrutiny, to be carried out resolutely and often, for, in the oft-quoted words of Jer. 17.9, 'The heart is deceitful above all things.' On determining the crucial question of election (II Cor. 13.5), virtually every Puritan divine offered advice. The dangers attendant upon this self-analysis were complacency and hypocrisy on the one hand, anxiety and morbidity (even despair) on the other. In counselling either extreme divines, who might disagree on questions of perseverance and assurance, agreed on warning against the danger of isolating faith from works or vice versa (Prov. 23.26, Gal. 5.22–23, Phil. 2.12–13). Scrutiny was not, however, solely introspective. The Puritan's vital sense of providence * compelled him to observe, and interpret, personal, local and national affairs. He was, therefore, as habitually curious about the world around him as about his own inner life. 'True knowledge of Christ,' wrote Thomas Taylor (1576–1633), 'is experimental', and, in conversation, in testimonies before congregations and in a mass of autobiographical works, Puritans recorded, analysed and communicated their experience of what God 'hath done for my soul' (Ps. 66.16) for the guidance and encouragement of others and as a sacrifice of grateful praise (Heb. 13.15–16). Hence derive some of the classics of Puritan spirituality: Bunyan's *Grace Abounding* (1666), Fox's *Journal* (1694), Baxter's *Reliquiae Baxterianae* (1696), the poetry of Edward Taylor (1645?–1729).

Puritanism was, in consequence, a social

and comradely movement (Eccles. 4.9). As every household was to be 'a little church' (Perkins), so the Puritan meeting house retained the external appearance of a domestic dwelling, and its interior, without any division between chancel and nave, reflected the equal fellowship enjoyed within a society which respected the priesthood of all believers (I Peter 2.9, Rev. 1.6, 5.10), a society constituted not by act of Parliament or canon law but by the shared spiritual experience and willing commitment of its members (Matt. 18.20). Titus 2.14 prompted Perkins's definition of the church as 'a peculiar company of men predestinate to life everlasting and made one with Christ'. As the familiar and familial term 'Lord's Supper', in contrast to 'eucharist', testifies, worshippers did not passively 'look stupidly on' (Calvin, *Institutes*, IV. xiv. 4) a mysterious sacrifice, but, led by the minister, their 'spiritual tutor' (Bolton), participated in services which preferred extempore to liturgical prayers, reduced ceremonial to a minimum, centred on a plain-spoken and practical sermon, and used the metrical psalms of Thomas Sternhold (d. 1549) and John Hopkins (d. 1570) rather than non-scriptural hymns. The austerity of this worship characterized Puritan taste at large, which, in literary and fine art and social manners, preferred simplicity to the luxurious elaboration of Baroque styles. However, iconoclasm, rigid Sabbatarianism, anti-intellectualism and Philistinism were, like the extremes of social revolution, comparatively rare. The main thrust of Puritan thought was that the way to perfection lay not through abstinence and asceticism, but through the right admission and moderate utilization of the world and the flesh. The Puritan neither under-valued nor over-valued them: he sanctified them.

P. Collinson, *The Elizabethan Puritan Movement*, 1967; G. R. Cragg, *Puritanism in the Period of the Great Persecution 1660–88*, 1957; H. Davies, *The Worship of the English Puritans*, 1948; *Worship and Theology in England from Andrewes to Baxter and Fox*, 1975; W. Haller, *The Rise of Puritanism*, 1938; C. Hill, *The World Turned Upside Down*, 1972; U. M. Kaufmann, *The Pilgrim's Progress and Traditions in Puritan Meditation*, 1966; M. M. Knappen, *Tudor Puritanism*, 1939; P. Miller, *The New England Mind: the Seventeenth Century*, 1939; G. F. Nuttall, *The Holy Spirit in Puritan Faith and Experience*, ²1947; G. S. Wakefield, *Puritan Devotion*, 1957; M. R. Watts, *The Dissenters: from the Reformation to the French Revolution*, 1978.

N. H. KEEBLE

Pusey, Edward Bouverie

Together with John Keble* and John Henry Newman*, Edward Pusey (1800–1882) was a leader of the Oxford Movement* and the theological and spiritual guide of the Catholic Revival in Anglicanism after Newman joined the Church of Rome in 1845. A man of great learning and deep spirituality, in his early years he gained a first-hand acquaintance with German theology, forming links with German theologians in the pietist tradition, though subsequently repudiating the rationalist assumptions of much German critical theology. Possessing a wide knowledge of Oriental languages he was appointed to the Regius Professorship of Hebrew at Oxford as early as 1828, and held the chair until his death.

It was largely through his contributions to the *Tracts for the Times* that the *Tracts* became weightier theological documents, and the adherents of the Oxford Movement became known as 'Puseyites'. In his unpublished Lectures on Types and Prophecies he stressed the sacramental and symbolic character of Christian truth, and in his exposition of this in his sermons and other writings drew on his special acquaintance with the Syrian tradition as well as on the Greek and Latin Fathers. The doctrines of the indwelling of the Spirit, transfiguration and deification are central to Pusey's theology and spirituality. Baptism was the sacramental mystery of the Christian's regeneration in Christ; the eucharist was the gift of Christ's Real Presence. His teaching on baptism was expounded in Nos. 67–9 of the *Tracts for the Times*; his teaching on the eucharist in major sermons of 1843 and 1856, for the first of which he was suspended from preaching by the Oxford University authorities. In his eucharistic doctrine Pusey followed closely the teaching of St Cyril of Alexandria, and his concern for the teaching of the Fathers generally issued in the major series of translations in the *Library of the Fathers*, many of them by Pusey himself.

His sermons, many of which have

passages of an almost ecstatic quality, are often tapestries of quotations from scripture, the Fathers, and later spiritual writers, such as St Bernard*, Ruysbroeck*, St Catherine of Siena*, Surin and Avrillon. Pusey's appreciation of the last two writers has led to the suggestion that he ought to be seen in part as standing in the tradition of folly for Christ's sake.

Criticized both during his lifetime and subsequently for his self-deprecation and expressions of unworthiness, Pusey is misunderstood if he is not placed in the context of many similar expressions by Christian teachers of prayer profoundly aware of the overwhelming majesty and glory of God and man's sin and frailty. For Pusey himself sacramental confession was where true penitence was learned and the grace of sanctification was renewed, and it is to him above all others that the revival of sacramental confession in Anglicanism is due (see **Penitence**). He was much sought after as a confessor and spiritual guide, and played a prominent part in the revival of religious orders in the Church of England. Characterized by Brilioth as the *doctor mysticus* of the Oxford Movement, his sermons remain one of the richest, and surprisingly neglected, veins of Tractarian spirituality.

Y. Brilioth, *The Anglican Revival*, 1933; P. Butler (ed), *Pusey Rediscovered*, 1983; O. Chadwick, *The Mind of the Oxford Movement*, 1960; E. R. Fairweather, *The Oxford Movement*, 1964; H. P. Liddon, *The Life of Edward Bouverie Pusey DD*, 4 vols, 1893–1895; G. L. Prestige, *Pusey*, reissued 1982; G. Rowell, *The Vision Glorious*, 1983.

GEOFFREY ROWELL

Quaker Spirituality

The Quaker movement (also called The Society of Friends) originated out of the religious disorientation of the English Civil War and Interregnum. Its principle founder was George Fox* who, after a period of disillusion with all contemporary forms of religion, experienced in 1646–1647 a series of 'openings' which convinced him that paid ministries were deceits, and that true religion consisted in 'the divine light of Christ' in every man; those who acknowledged the light and lived in its power 'became the children of it, but they that hated it, were condemned by it'. He began to preach his mes-

sage to 'Seekers' and similar radical groups (e.g. 'shattered Baptists'). His preaching in north-west England – Westmorland ('the Quaker Galilee'), the Lake District and the West Riding from 1652 gathered large groups of converts, especially among yeomen and craftsmen. They were based at Swarthmoor Hall, under the protection of Judge Fell, whose widow Fox later married. In 1654, sixty to seventy missionaries spread in pairs to carry the new message, and groups sprang up in London, Bristol, East Anglia and other centres. It threw up many leaders, including women, some of whom were hardly less important than Fox – James Nayler, Francis Howgill, Isaac Pennington, Edward Borrough, John Audland, Thomas Aldams, Margaret Fell.

Their experience shares a common pattern. 1. A period of anguished searching for truth and holiness, and a conviction of sin – 'In this iron furnace I toiled and laboured, and none knew my sorrows and griefs.' 2. Recognition of the emptiness of existing churches – 'Christ saith, Believe them not, look not forth, for the Kingdom of Heaven is within.' 3. A transforming experience of exposure to the divine light within, which simultaneously 'beats down' the sinful self, and gives a new life of power, healing and joy. This experience the 'first publishers of Truth' often described in prophetic language, as a sort of 'internalized Armageddon'. Francis Howgill wrote: 'and as I bore the indignation of the Lord, something rejoiced, the serpent's head began to be bruised, and the witnesses which were slain were raised ... And as I did give up all to the judgment, the captive came forth out of prison, and I rejoiced and my heart was filled with joy. I came to see him whom I had pierced and my heart was broken and the blood of the prophets I saw slain, and a great lamentation. Then I saw the cross of Christ, and stood in it, and the enmity slain on it. And the new man was made.' 4. This internalized conflict and victory led to a mission to transform contemporary society by declaring the 'Lamb's War' on unrighteousness, on all 'who are in the fall and separation from God'. The Friends, convinced that Christ lived and spoke within them, that they were 'possessors, not professors', denounced contemporary formalism in religion, social and economic iniquities, and immorality, 'to cast out the enemy with all his stuff, and so subject the creature wholly to himself that he may form a new man, a new heart, new thoughts and a new obedience'. This conviction of the power of God in them 'over all' caused them to reject even scripture as a superior authority, and to use messianic language of themselves and their leaders. They interrupted sermons, denounced judges and justices, urging 'tenderness' and compassion, and performed acts of prophetic symbolism, sometimes of great eccentricity (going naked for a sign). A disciple wrote to Fox: 'Thou god of life and power, who is able to withstand thee?' In 1656 James Nayler brought disaster on the movement by riding into Bristol on an ass, his followers strewing his way and singing 'Hosanna to the Son of David'. Savage reprisals followed, and Nayler was disowned. Their refusal to swear oaths, pay tithes or to pay 'hat-honour' to social superiors made them suspect, but despite bitter persecution they survived the Restoration. Most of the constitutive elements of the Quaker movement can be paralleled elsewhere – refusal of 'hat-honour' among the Levellers, silent worship among the Seekers, refusal to use pagan names for days and months among the Baptists – but the Quaker blend of all this was uniquely powerful.

In the 1660s Fox took firm control of the movement and gave it organization in the form of a series of 'Meetings for church affairs'. The Monthly Meeting was a business meeting for pastoral care, membership and discipline. Quarterly Meetings were set up for counties and regions, and dealt with poor relief, and there was a general Yearly Meeting. In 1675 the Meeting for Sufferings to record and resist persecution was established. Fox's administrative measures were resisted as 'muzzling the Spirit', and led to division (the Wilkinson-Story separation), but they ensured the survival of the movement.

There was undoubtedly, however, a change in ethos. The earlier prophetic fire cooled, and holy indignation at pride, greed and injustice slowly modulated into a concern with personal integrity, simplicity and sobriety. Friends remained concerned with righteousness, but the messianic urgency had largely gone by 1700. These trends can be seen in the writings of William Penn* and in the *Apology for the True Christian Religion* (Latin 1676, English 1678) of the Scottish Quaker, Robert Barclay (1648–90). Expounding the doctrine of the Inner Light Barclay tamed it, and the systematic form of the *Apology* is worlds away from the spontaneous spirit of the early movement. By 1700 Fox's widow complained of the 'narrowness and strictness' which she felt was 'mangling poor Friends' with 'Jewism'. Quaker worship had long since settled into the familiar pattern of a largely silent Meeting with occasional exhortation or prayer (ecstatic singing had not been uncommon earlier).

Quakerism had spread in America as well as Britain. By the eighteenth century it had largely lost its missionary impulse and succumbed to Quietism*, though Quakers played a key role in the anti-slavery movement, and the work of John Woolman, Elizabeth Fry and Joseph Lancaster in the eighteenth and nineteenth centuries and that of the Rowntree and Cadbury families into the twentieth, are testimony to the continuing involvement of Friends with the gospel's bearing on social justice.

The essential sourcebook is Fox's *Journal* (best edn by J. L. Nickalls, 1952); see also H. Barbour and A. O. Roberts, *Early Quaker Writings*, 1973; Hugh Barbour, *The Quakers in Puritan England*, 1964; A. N. Brayshaw, *The Quakers*, 1921; W. C. Braithwaite, *The Beginnings of Quakerism*, [2]1955; *The Second Period of Quakerism*, [2]1961; G. F. Nuttall, *Studies in Christian Enthusiasm*, 1948.

EAMON DUFFY

Quietism

'It sometimes seems to be used of any author when teaching about contemplation what another author disapproves' (Owen Chadwick). The article in the *Dictionnaire de Theologie Catholique* published in 1937 includes under its disapprobation many 'heretics', even Luther. It should probably be confined to a small seventeenth-century group, the most notable of whom are Molinos*; Petrucci (1636–1701); Madam Guyon*; Fénelon*. For its doctrines see the appropriate articles and bibliographies.

EDITOR

Qur'ān see Koran

Radical Spirituality

Radical spirituality brings together two

things which seem to have little in common, which are normally thought of as alternatives, even as incompatible. 'Radical' here means politically radical. In this sense radical Christians are both politically conscious and active. Their social criticism leads them to expose, denounce and oppose what they regard as institutionalized evil in society. Such activism is normally undertaken through participation in groups, often college and university branches of national organizations. In Britain SCM, since the 1960s, is the most obvious example. However, local action is often taken in association with groups which are not necessarily religious, but are issue-oriented, e.g. CND. All this contrasts with the normal associations of the term 'spirituality'. Those who are deeply committed to the spiritual life would be expected to be older in age than the radicals, withdrawn from the arena of conflict, whether in attitude or even physically, perhaps in retreat centres or monastic houses. For them the spiritual life might be a private life from which the world is excluded; to lack critical consciousness about social issues might be regarded as a virtue. In the early 1970s the validity of both of these positions was challenged: radical spirituality represents the attempt to go beyond them, dialectically.

The period 1964–1970 saw new forms of idealism both in America and in Europe. Among young Americans central issues were life-styles and the values which were embodied therein. Vietnam was the logical outworking of the warfare state. In Europe the rediscovery of the young Marx led to alienation from 'bureaucratic' control, whether in the state, industry or education. Many young Christians became involved in these movements, indeed considered it part of their Christian responsibility to participate actively. However, by the end of the period there was growing unease about the situation. Young Christians were active, but there seemed to be no Christian in-put at a critical level. They were being carried along in a movement which was not Christian, yet they could not look for support from traditional forms of theology or spirituality. In many cases Christian traditions and institutions seemed to be part of the problem rather than aids to solutions. Yet social and political activism was not enough.

The experience of radical activism, it must be stressed, was not rejected, but now seen to be inadequate. At the same time traditional spirituality provided no alternative. Radically spirituality is a genuinely dialectical movement. Traditional spirituality did not include social and political action, which came to be regarded as a necessary part of Christian responsibility. At worst it would even be a religious distraction from Christian stewardship, the opiate of a rather effete form of Christianity. Radical spirituality is therefore a new synthesis of action and contemplation in which both are transformed. Activism has been transformed: political action for political ends is not enough. The 'seeds of resignation' are sewn wherever action fails to quickly produce change, or whenever the new order sadly patterns the iniquities of the old. How can faith continue in hope and overcome despair? Only if traditional spirituality is also transformed. Arguably the God of the Bible is less interested in religion than in the life of the world. A powerful model here is of Elijah the prophet commissioned by God to anoint kings and change the course of history, yet whose own strength will not be enough. 'Arise and eat, else the journey will be too great for you.' The new spirituality sees in the eucharist the resources to fulfil God's calling of Christians to responsible action. The development of the spiritual life is not for the benefit of the individual, for his or her salvation, but in order that God's will may be done on earth. Radical spirituality is a politicized spirituality. If political theology ends the privatization of religion in general, radical spirituality ends the privatization of the religious life. The eucharist is once again a corporate action. The scriptures hardly need to be 'searched' before the group is addressed, judged, called, commanded. In face of such demands prayer and contemplation are aids to obedience, reminiscent of Christ's retreat to the desert before his public ministry.

It is appropriate that this new spirituality should have become a source of Christian unity. In Europe and America it would be too schematic, though not entirely untrue to say that it is formed from a new meeting of Catholic piety and Protestant activism. There is some evidence that the Pentecostal movement in Latin America exhibits a similar breakthrough, so that the gifts of the Spirit are exercised not for the exclusive benefit of Christians, but to enable them to serve God in the community. This experience has provided a new basis for relations with traditional churches. It is also possible for the new spirituality to become a bond between Christians who might otherwise suspect each other. It would be a remarkable individual in whom both dimensions of the new spirituality were equally to be found. More often it is a group experience. But the relationship of Daniel Berrigan and Thomas Merton* is an important example of the complementarity of the activist and the contemplative. When both 'sides' in humility admit the inadequacy of their own emphases, then together they can move forward to a new and creative relationship.

See also **Liberation, Spirituality of.**

Tissa Balasuriya, *The Eucharist and Human Liberation*, 1977; Daniel Berrigan, *The Dark Night of Resistance*, 1971; *America is Hard to Find*, 1973; Chi-Ha Kim, *The Cry of the People*, 1975; Alistair Kee (ed), *Seeds of Liberation*, 1974; Thomas Merton, *Contemplation in a World of Action*, 1971; William D. Miller, *A Harsh and Dreadful Love*, 1973; Brother Roger, *Struggle and Contemplation*, ²1983.

ALISTAIR KEE

Rancé, A.-J. de *see* Trappists

Rastafarianism

Rastafarianism began in Jamaica in the 1930s among the poorer black population, spreading first to the English-speaking Caribbean and through Caribbean immigration to Great Britain and the USA. Its roots are in Christianity, Judaism and the new sense among Jamaicans of their African origins which developed at that time.

The Rastafarianism Movement takes its name from Ras (prince) Tafari (family name), the Ethiopian prince who in 1930 was crowned as the Emperor Haile Selassie I, and its adherents are known as Rastafarians, Rastamen or Rastas. Rastafarians believe Haile Selassie, 'King of Kings, Lord of Lords and Conquering Lion of Judah', to be God himself, who came to Zion (Ethiopia) to rule the true Jews, who were black. The ancient history of these 'chosen people' goes back to the scattering of the twelve tribes of Israel, when the spirit of the Lord, and Solomon, supposedly went to Ethiopia.

Rastas believe that Solomon and the Jewish tribes with him were black (they see this indicated in the Song of Solomon), proving the superiority of the black man over the white. Ethiopia, and Africa generally by extension, is Zion, the homeland, and black people elsewhere in the world are in Babylon, exiled as a punishment for past sins. White people are the agents of God's punishment; and exile, during which Rastafarians wait patiently for their repatriation, is spent under the rule of Rome, which Rastas see as the negation of everything they stand for. It is the destroyer and oppressor, the seat and source of the false white Christian churches which use the Bible and the promise of a better life beyond the grave to keep the black people in subjection and slavery.

For the Rasta God, in the person of Haile Selassie, is an object not of faith but of knowledge. He is known, seen, touched and spoken to, as he was on his state visit to Jamaica in 1966. He knows everything and prayers addressed to him are heard. He is so much the source of life that the true Rasta is forced to deny death. The deposing and death of Haile Selassie are less of an obstacle to Rastas than might be expected. There are those who refuse to believe that the Emperor is dead. Others, perhaps the majority, accept the end of his reign and his death. They see the Emperor as the seventy-second manifestation of God, who reminded black people of their true place in God's scheme of things. God will come and act again, and meanwhile black people prepare for the time when they will rule the world.

Rastas have a distinctive life-style, as peaceful warriors for the cause of Zion. Their awesome long hair, called dreadlocks, helps to identify them with the OT warriors and the Maasai tribesmen of Africa. To live in tune with nature means allowing hair to grow, so the Rasta's beard and locks show the seriousness of his commitment. Rastas are also vegetarian, believing that it is wrong to kill animals for food and that God has given enough to sustain his children in fruit and vegetables. Among these gifts is God's greatest gift, 'the leaves of the tree of life for the healing of the nations', ganja or marijuana, the Holy Weed. It is illegal to smoke ganja in Jamaica, as elsewhere in the Caribbean. Police make frequent raids to destroy ganja shrubs and ganja smoking is a source of conflict between Rastas and the police.

For the Rasta it has a quasi-sacramental value, and meetings begin with the passing of the ganja pipe around those present in a gesture of unity and healing.

Rasta use of the Bible is selective. The AV/KJV text is suspect, being a white king's translation and therefore a distortion of scripture. Only certain passages from the prophets, the Psalms, the law books, the Gospels and the book of Revelation are held to bear witness to the truth revealed in Ras Tafari; they alone can give the true black interpretation of the scriptures. The white version of the scriptures is designed to subject and enslave the black people. It is part of the hypocrisy of the white world.

Rastafarianism is a poetic interpretation of black Jamaican experience, an experience communicated first with the Rasta group and then more widely in myth, symbol and imagery and often by Reggae music. The ideology conveyed in the myths of anciency, punishment, exile, repatriation and in the person of Ras Tafari is a powerful expression of hope, search for identity and assertion of existence. A Rasta will add 'I' to his name to declare his allegiance to Ras Tafari; he becomes Frank-I or John-I. 'I' in the plural becomes not 'we' but 'I-n-I', a community of deciding individuals, the 'I' carries such weight that other words of importance in the Rasta vocabulary are remodelled to include that 'I'.

The social philosophy of Rastas is not revolutionary. They live in oppressed withdrawal, hoping for repatriation to Zion, which means either to Ethiopia or to some other African country. Rastas are contemptuous of other religions and will have nothing to do with the tribal religions brought over by the slaves from the West Coast of Africa, which Rastas consider false, since they deal in spirits. They consider all churches, with one exception, creations of Rome, designed to keep black people in subjection. The Pentecostal revivalist churches, although indigenous, are rejected because Pentecostalism is considered an emotional, other-worldly religion caught from the white churches. The exception to their general condemnation is the Ethiopian Orthodox, the church of Haile Selassie, and going back to before the time of Constantine.

Joseph Owens, *Dread: The Rastafarians of*

Jamaica, 1976; M. G. Smith, R. Augier and R. Nettleford, *The Rastafari Movement in Kingston, Jamaica*, 1960.

M. J. JACKSON

Reading, Spiritual

If spirituality may be defined as the sensing, absorbing, expressing and shaping of the awareness of God, spiritual reading finds its place in the Christian life as one of the classical methods of absorbing such awareness, as this has been embodied in great spiritual writing down the ages. To such writing every age and country makes its contribution, 'that', in George Herbert's words in *A Priest to the Temple*, 'there may be a traffick in knowledg between the servants of God, for the planting both of love and humility'.

The large place such reading occupies both within and beyond the Judaeo-Christian tradition derives from the structure and mechanism of the human psyche itself. Thus, though the mind is necessarily the primary instrument, the object of the exercise is not the acquisition of knowledge but the ravishing of the heart through the mind's delight, that quality of reverential delight echoed throughout Ps. 119, finally issuing in the moving of the will to the kind of action characteristic of 'love and humility'. The basic principle is contained in the phrase of Ps. 39.4: 'while I was thus musing the fire kindled'.

Yet although expression in enlightened action is the ultimate purpose of all such reading, it has three, more limited, functions vital to spiritual health. First, it acts as a dredger, gouging the silt out of the channels of our deepest affections, stretching our capacity to know both heights and depths, and so become fully alive. The regular careful recital of the psalms is the obvious example. Secondly, and it is here that spiritual reading approximates closely to meditation *, it is unfailingly effective in rendering specific doctrine real to the heart as to the mind. Doctrine being partly distilled experience, the thoughtful perusal of such experience through the mind of another, whether the author be scriptural or not, has the effect of rendering that experience palpable and therefore powerful, so that the cardinal doctrines become the furniture and formative structure of the mind.

Lastly, most significant in the Christian, and in the past particularly the monastic, tradition, spiritual reading, if slow, attentive and loving, provides the ideal preparation for contemplative prayer, in which the mind's disparate thoughts and perceptions fuse into a single track of intuitive sight, and the heart is riveted in an act of union (*see* **Contemplation**). *The Ancrene Riwle* * catches the essence: 'The remedy for Sloth is spiritual joy and the comfort of joyful hope, which comes from reading ... Often, dear sisters, you ought to say fewer fixed prayers so that you may do more reading. Reading is good prayer. Reading teaches us how to pray and what to pray for, and then prayer achieves it. In the course of reading, when the heart is pleased, there arises a spirit of devotion which is worth many prayers.'

Jean Leclercq, *The Love of Learning and the Desire for God*, 1974, ch v.

JOHN BYROM

Recusancy, Recusants

The English R C community was ill-defined for much of Elizabeth's reign. The phenomenon of recusancy (illegal abstention from parish worship) was slow to emerge, and probably consistent only among a small proportion of those sympathetic to 'the old religion' (*c.* 40,000 by 1603). For the first twenty years of the reign, priests were few and ill-organized, and devotion was largely 'traditionalist', strongest in remote rural areas (Lancashire, Wales). R C piety centred on the mass and rites of passage where there were priests, and on the annual cycle of feast and fast days (100 fasts annually). This 'separation of meats' and abstention from work on feasts served to define the community. Also crucial were the repetition of traditional prayers, the rosary *, the use of sacred objects (crucifixes, medals, relics, holy water), exorcism and in some areas religious pilgrimage to surviving shrines (e.g. St Winefrid's Well). Mediaeval works circulated such as the *Imitation of Christ* (translated in the 1530s by the Brigitine Richard Whitford), Latin or English *Primers* (the most popular of late mediaeval devotional aids) and a handful of works from Mary's reign. The most representative (and popular) devotion of this period was the *Jesus Psalter*. Probably originally the work of Whitford, More's and Erasmus' friend, this was a series of petitions worked

round the 150-fold invocation of the name of Jesus, with a refrain – 'Have mercy on all sinners, Jesu, I beseech thee: turn their vices into virtues, and make them true observers of thy law, and lovers of thee: bring them to bliss in everlasting glory.' Like the 150 Aves of the rosary, the petitions are gathered into fifteen decades, subdivided into three groups representing the stages of the spiritual life, purgative, illuminative, unitive *. Continually revised and modified, the *Jesus Psalter* remained in popular use throughout the recusant period, featuring in most subsequent prayerbooks.

From *c.* 1570, the mission was becoming more organized; the need for books of devotion adapted to English circumstances was met in 1583 by the appearance of the first edition of the *Manual of Prayers*. Based loosely on Verepaeus' *Precationes Liturgicae in Dies Septem Digestae*, the *Manual* was a wide-ranging collection of devotions and instruction for lay people, drawing from mediaeval sources but also from more recent writers (e.g. Thomas More). Running through eighty editions between 1583 and 1800, it was frequently modified. Typically it contained a calendar, brief summaries of R C belief, instructions for confession and communion, litanies, hymns, prayers and meditations arranged for the days of the week, prayers for times of the day or specific occasions. The *Manual* also normally contained the Gospels of the Passion, the penitential psalms, and the *Jesus Psalter*.

In 1599 the first *Tridentine Primer* in English was published. This Tridentine revision provided Catholics with a storehouse of liturgical piety, based on the offices of the Blessed Virgin, of the Dead, and Vespers for the Common offices. This book too remained in use throughout the period (forty editions by 1780). Together, *Manual* and *Primer* provided the backbone of R C religious observances even when no priest was available, and formed a link between mediaeval and Counter-Reformation piety.

R C piety in the later sixteenth century was dominated by the Jesuit *Spiritual Exercises* *. The organization of the mission by William Allen and Robert Persons facilitated the spread of Ignatian piety in England, and the last years of the century saw the publication of translations and original works in this tradition. Ascetic rather than mystical, these books inculcated the practice of systematic meditation in the manner of the *Spiritual Exercises*, and provided models. The most popular of such writers, among Protestants as well as Catholics, was the Spanish Dominican Lewis de Granada, whose *Of Prayer and Meditation* was translated in 1582 and his *Memoriall of a Christian Life* in 1586. The passionate and detailed evocation of incidents in the life of Christ found in such works were designed to move the heart and convert the will. They established in England as elsewhere the pattern of much of the best spiritual writing of the period. The best native example of this genre was Robert Persons' *Book of Resolution*, often called *The Christian Directory*. Published in 1582, this book was pirated and bowdlerized by the Protestant vicar of Bolton, Edmund Bunny, in 1584. '*Bunny's Resolution*' was one of the most influential works of the Tudor and Stuart period: Richard Baxter* was one of many converted by it.

These works mark the spread of a Counter-Reformation spirit among English Catholics, and contrast with the 'survivalist' Catholicism of many. The distinctive and intense piety of the gentry households where the 'seminary priests' and Jesuits settled as chaplains enshrined this newer spirit. Such households as that of Dorothy Lawson at Newcastle, or of Lady Montague at Battle, enjoyed a rich spiritual life involving intense personal direction, frequent confession and communion, veneration of the Blessed Sacrament, Ignatian meditation and spiritual reading. The translation of Canisius' catechism in 1578 and the appearance of such works as Gaspar Loarte's *How to meditate the Misteries of the Rosary*, designed to bring the use of the rosary into this meditative tradition, are indicative of the progress of the newer spirit. But the contrast between the two types of Catholicism – the intense household piety of the well-to-do, and the traditionalist, non-literate religion prevalent especially in the North and West – should not be exaggerated. There was no simple division between rich and poor, literate and illiterate. Dorothy Lawson had a Jesuit confessor and catechized local children, but she also distributed holy medals and brought relics to women in labour.

A distinctive English contribution to Counter-Reformation piety was a series of works springing from the experience of persecution. These included reissues of Sir Thomas More's *Dialogue of Comfort*, Robert Southwell's magnificent *Epistle of Comfort* (1587), and explicitly martyrological works such as Allen's *Briefe historie of the Glorious Martyrdom of XII reverend priests* (1582). Martyrological narratives circulated in manuscript, and relics of those who suffered under Elizabeth and her successors were preserved as objects of devotion.

Arguably the greatest literary product of recusant religious activity was Gregory Martin's Rheims–Douai Bible (NT 1582, OT 1609). Often dismissed for its excessively literal latinisms, it is in fact a work of considerable linguistic vigour which influenced the AV, and its notes provided a running refutation of Protestant doctrine. But although individual recusant writers (Gother, Challoner) show themselves saturated in the Bible, the Douai version never held the place in RC piety that the AV was to gain among Protestants.

In the early seventeenth century the Ignatian spirit gave way to that of St Francis de Sales*. The *Introduction to a Devout Life* was translated in 1613, five years after its first appearance; Francis' humane piety for men and women in every walk of life, rooted in mental prayer and obedience to a spiritual director, quickly established itself, especially among the secular clergy and their clients. The mission priests were now experiencing the revival of clerical ideals associated with Bérulle*and Vincent de Paul, and the English Seminary at Lisbon sent forth a stream of priests who encouraged piety on the Salesian model, aimed not only at gentry households, but also and especially at the poor. William Clifford's *Little Manual of the Poor Man's daily devotion* (1667) is representative here; it incorporated elements of the *Manual* with instruction in the method of Salesian meditation emphasizing its accessibility to the poor and uneducated. It is characteristically practical – 'Heaven is to be gained by action, and not by science or contemplation alone.'

The tradition embodied in such works found its most influential English expression in the writings of the Lisbon priest John Gother. His work included meditations in the form of instructions on all the Epistles and Gospels used at Mass, instructions and devotions for Mass and confession, and devotions for every walk of life, as well as works of counsel for 'timorous, fearful, melancholy and scrupulous Christians', linking English 'affectionate divinity' to Catholic treatment of the scrupulous conscience. The sober biblical tone of Gother's work, if without the geniality of Francis' own writings, contained little that would have alienated Protestant readers: there is little emphasis, for example, on the saints as intercessors. His work encouraged a more instructed and active Catholicism, the faithful being encouraged to follow the words of the Mass, rather than using its visible actions as triggers for meditation in the mediaeval manner. It marks the arrival of the pattern of RC practice which dominated the eighteenth century. This emphasized the need for catechizing, spiritual reading, regular confession and communion (at the eight 'Indulgences' or major feasts) and a rather discursive pattern of prayer (often in the form of litanies). This tradition in the eighteenth century informs the work of Richard Challoner*. By the end of the eighteenth century and of the recusant period, Catholic piety had been successfully democratized and the gap between the religion of rich and poor largely eliminated. Vernacular devotions adapted from the *Manual* or from authors such as Gother often preceded the Latin liturgy, encouraging a high degree of lay involvement, particularly in the use of litanies and responses, and a wide range of sober but ardent forms of private prayer. Suspicious of Baroque cults such as that of the Sacred Heart*, the recusant community had produced a distinctive English Catholic style which was to be largely obscured by the *Romanitas* of the nineteenth-century 'Catholic Revival'.

Mysticism made little headway among English Catholics at large, though it existed in the English religious houses abroad, and the families connected with them. The Benedictine Augustine Baker* was a mystical teacher of European stature: *Sancta Sophia*, a somewhat bowdlerized synthesis of his teaching, edited by his disciple Serenus Cressy, is a minor classic. Some of the creative vigour of the European renaissance of Catholic pastoral action showed itself in the evangelistic and educative work of Mary Ward's *Institute of the Blessed Virgin Mary*, which however encountered fierce clerical opposition. Perhaps the most distinctive

contribution of the Orders was their patronage of special indulgenced devotions with a wide appeal to laity; they include the Scapular (Carmelites), Rosary Confraternities (Dominicans and Benedictines) and the *Bona Morte* devotion for a holy death (Jesuits).

The court Catholicism of the wives of the Stuart kings provided a glimpse of the Baroque splendours of the Counter-Reformation, a liturgical opulence available elsewhere only in a handful of great houses or, in the eighteenth century, in the Chapels of the Catholic Ambassadors in London. Late Stuart Catholicism produced one devotional work with wide influence in John Austin's *Devotions in the Ancient Way of Offices*, now seeming impossibly prosy, but eagerly pirated and reprinted by Protestants, notably by the Nonjurors* and John Wesley*.

J. C. H. Aveling, *The Handle and the Axe*, 1976; J. M. Blom, *The Post-Tridentine English Primer*, 1982; J. Bossy, *The English Catholic Community*, 1975; P. Caraman, *The Other Face*, 1960; *The Years of Siege*, 1966; A. C. Southern, *Elizabethan Recusant Prose*, 1950.

EAMON DUFFY

Regula Fidei

Regula fidei ('rule of faith') is a theological concept first used by Irenaeus* and most significant in his theology and in Tertullian's*. The concept can also be expressed by other terms. *Regula fidei* means both the Christian's faith as normative, and a concise statement of the Christian's beliefs. *Regula fidei* always refers to what is original: the whole teaching of the church as it was proclaimed by the apostles and prophets and recorded in the scriptures. The fact that *regula fidei* and *regula veritatis* are synonyms makes this clear: there can be no rule for the truth; the truth itself is the norm. In this sense, the *regula fidei* is identical with the kerygma. Irenaeus writes: 'We have the truth itself as a rule'; and '[we] possess [God's] words as the rule of truth' (*Adversus haereses* 2, 28, 1; 4, 35, 4). Early writers assume that the *regula fidei* comprises not only doctrine but also moral principles, rites, and customs (see, for example, Eusebius, *Ecclesiastical History* 5, 24, 6).

The *regula fidei* is not identical with declaratory baptismal creeds, which developed later (mid-third century). Unlike creeds, the *regula fidei*, even as a concise statement of beliefs, had no verbally fixed form; the writer adapted it to his immediate needs and intent. Nor is the *regula fidei* the same as scripture, although it cannot contradict it. Rather, it guides the interpretation of scripture. Irenaeus writes that the Gnostics do not have the rule, and use obscure expressions to interpret the parables (*Adv. haer.* 1, 9, 4; 2, 27, 1; 3, 12, 6; 3, 15, 1). The *regula* is 'tradition' in the original sense of that word – that is, what has been handed on in the church from the beginning (*see 1 Clement* 7, 2: 'the norm [or rule] of our tradition'; cf. I Cor 11.23; 15.3). Seen historically, the *regula fidei* guided the formation of the NT canon.

In *Adv. haer.* 1, 22, 1, Irenaeus gives an extended statement of the rule, emphasizing the one God who is the creator of all things, and the God of Abraham, and the Father of Jesus Christ. Elsewhere he gives other, trinitarian, summaries of the rule (*Adv. haer.* 1, 10, 1; 3, 4, 2; 4, 33, 7; *Proof of the Apostolic Preaching* 3). Tertullian stresses the normative, binding character of the *regula fidei*: it is the single authentic norm of saving doctrine. *De praescriptione haereticorum* 13–14 is his clearest statement of the *regula*: one God the creator; the Word, his Son, who was seen by the patriarchs, heard by the prophets, made flesh in Mary's womb; who proclaimed a new law and a new promise, was crucified, raised, and exalted; who will come again as judge at the resurrection. Tertullian concludes: 'To know nothing against the rule is to know everything.' There are other statements of the *regula fidei* in *Adversus Praxean* 2 and *De virginibus velandis* 1; *see also De prae. haer.* 35–37; *De spectaculis* 4; *Contra Marcionem* 4, 5. The clarity of the concept of the *regula fidei* diminished as the significance of the canonical NT and of declaratory creeds grew.

There is a complete translation of Irenaeus' *Adversus haereses* in Ante-Nicene Fathers 1, and of his *Proof of the Apostolic Preaching*, by J. P. Smith, in Ancient Christian Writers 16, 1952. The complete works of Tertullian are translated in Ante-Nicene Fathers 3 and 4. See also D. van den Eynde, *Les normes de l'enseignement chrétien dans la littérature patristique des trois premiers siècles*, 1933; R. P. C. Hanson, *Origen's Doctrine of Tra-*

dition, 1954 (chs on the *regula* in Clement and Origen); *Tradition in the Early Church*, 1962 (esp ch 3, 'The Rule of Faith'); E. Flesseman-van Leer, *Tradition and Scripture in the Early Church*, 1953.

JOSEPH T. LIENHARD

Retreats

The term normally given to a period spent in silence and occupied by meditation and spiritual exercises, under a conductor who leads the worship, gives the addresses, and makes appointments with any retreatants who desire confession, counsel, or discussion. Michael Ramsey defines the essence of retreat as being 'with God in silence'. The forty days spent in the wilderness by Jesus constitute the authority for the Christian use of retreat. It is usual for a devout priest or lay-person in the catholic churches to make an annual retreat.

In her book *Worship* (1936), Evelyn Underhill * noted that 'In 1913 the Church of England had one retreat house. In 1932 it has twenty-two diocesan houses and over thirty belonging to religious communities. Some of these houses receive over one thousand retreatants yearly.' The first half of this century saw a phenomenal growth of spiritual life in England, and much of this was nurtured by retreats both inside and outside the newly established religious houses. The same is true in the USA, and the movement has also embraced Christians of the non-catholic traditions.

Canon James Wareham gave his whole ministry to the promoting and conducting of retreats and his book, *The Conducting of Retreats* (1950) is a definitive study. Historically retreats were introduced at the Counter-Reformation by the Jesuits who included them in their rule. The R C Church developed retreats subsequently and they were adopted by the Oxford Movement in the C of E in the nineteenth century, the first being held in Oxford in 1856.

In a normal retreat programme for a weekend or several days, the retreatants meet the conductor on arrival. Supper, evensong, and first address follow, and a silence begins which continues until the final meal. The eucharist is the focus of worship each day. Addresses are delivered and opportunity is given for quiet in chapel, lounges and garden. The traditional reading aloud of a spiritual classic at meals is sometimes replaced today by music. The overall experience of silence in retreat is unique.

Because the sudden movement into silence can be traumatic for some, experiments in open retreats have been conducted. A central parish church is used and people come in each day to spend the morning and afternoon in quiet and meditation. Experiments using music have been tried because for many music is a bridge leading into prayer. Similarly, plays, mime, dance and yoga have all been used. The current fascination with Eastern religions and relaxation emphasizes the complete offering to God of body, mind, and spirit.

Two other aspects of spiritual growth have been associated with retreats in the past: communication and training. Many people with a capability for prayer and spiritual growth discover a 'transfiguration experience' in retreat, and traditional addresses given in retreat often study Christ's transfiguration. The old words discipline, sacrifice, and mortification which were used in teaching addresses are explained today by speaking of training, giving, and being. This linking of the old with the new fosters a new and younger clientele who will come into retreat and happily discover for themselves the satisfactions of meeting *with* God instead of just talking *about* God.

Association for Promoting Retreats, *Retreats Today*, 1962; *Retreats Our Common Concern*, 1969; N. W. Goodacre, *Experiment in Retreats*, 1970.

N. W. GOODACRE

Rolle, Richard

Born at Thornton in Yorkshire, Richard Rolle (*c.* 1300–1349) studied at Oxford but broke off his studies when he was eighteen and became a hermit, first on the estates of his friend, John Dalton, then in various places in the north of England. He died at Hampole while living near a convent of Cistercian nuns. He was widely venerated as a preacher and mystic and was known in England as 'Blessed Richard, confessor and hermit' as late as the seventeenth century.

Rolle was a prolific writer in both English and Latin; the popularity of his best-known works, the *Incendium Amoris* and the *Emendatio Vitae* is shown by the wide circulation of their translations into Middle English. He is well known for his religious lyrics, which have a permanent place in the development of the vernacular. His experience of prayer has been treated more cautiously by commentators, and indeed was somewhat suspect in his own day. He is held to be an exponent of 'affective mysticism' and to depend unduly upon the sensible experiences of prayer. He described his own experience of prayer in terms of *calor, dulcor et canor*, 'heat, sweetness and song': 'In the beginning of my conversion and singular purpose, I thought that I would be like the little bird that languishes for love of his beloved but is gladdened in his longing when he that it loves comes and sings with joy and in its song also languishes but in sweetness and heat. It is said that the nightingale is given to song and melody all night that she may please him to whom she is joined. How much more should I sing with great sweetness to Christ my Jesus, that is spouse of my soul, through all this present life that is night in regard to the clearness to come, so that I should languish in longing and die of love.' Rolle uses the imagery of the senses in this way for the experiences of the spirit, and tries to translate into human terms the experience of prayer which overturned his own life and which in his eyes is the height of spiritual experience. But Rolle was not a theologian nor a theorist, and while as a mystical theology his work is certainly limited and incomplete, as a record of personal experience it is both sensitive and lucid. He should be treated not as a sure guide to prayer but as an example of the loving and praying person, who by reading the scriptures attains personal experience of that which is incommunicable.

English Prose Treatises of Richard Rolle of Hampole ed G. G. Perry, EETS xx, 1866; *Richard Rolle of Hampole and his English Followers* ed C. Horstman, 2 vols, 1895–6; *English Writings of Richard Rolle* ed H. E. Allen, 1931; *The Fire of Love* tr Clifton Wolters, 1972.

BENEDICTA WARD, SC

Roman Catholic Spirituality

A spirituality may be described as *fides quaerens cor suum*, faith yearning for the innermost source of its vitality. All Christians in some way acknowledge Jesus Christ as this source of their faith. Roman Catholics more specifically designate the Holy Spirit as the one who gives them new life by progressively incorporating members into the death and resurrection of Jesus Christ through Word and Sacrament. During the Second Vatican Council the church oriented her members more surely towards this abiding centre by engaging in a creative return to the earliest centuries of her existence (*see* **Vatican II Spirituality**). On 4 December 1963 the restoration of an adult catechumenate with appropriate revision and accommodation was solemnly decreed to replace the 1614 *Rituale Romanum* approved by Pope Paul V. A decade of critical research and pastoral experimentation followed before the *Rite of Christian Initiation of Adults* was issued on 6 January 1972. By re-directing attention to the centrality of the Holy Spirit's activity in the believing community the church has restored the liturgy to its privileged role as the primary locus in which spirituality is lived and interpreted.

This new *Rite* is a compendium of Catholic spirituality. It not only integrates the perennial principles of the past with insights developed during and after Vatican II but also provides a matrix within which life in the Spirit may be fostered and brought to maturity. The elements of this lived spirituality are expressed in rich biblical symbolism and integrated organically within the *Rite*. In transposing them into more abstract terms for the sake of systematic exposition of what is normative, one must bear in mind that a vital process can never be expressed in static concepts. Spirituality is in the first instance living in the Spirit; systematic reflection and interpretation of that lived experience is spirituality in a secondary sense.

This life in the Spirit which begins at baptism is both a communal mystery and a personal project. Catholic spirituality is embodied in a people as a corporate reality, historically visible and constituting the objective dimension of our redemption. Through this ecclesial body the Father is continually extending to all an invitation to accept his saving gift of love in Jesus Christ. By making a free and firm response to this invitation individuals are incorporated into the Body of Christ by the Spirit. There is a delicate interplay of divine grace and human generosity as each member assimilates the life-giving force of the Spirit and enters into the Paschal Mystery of Christ. Growth in

this life is effected in successive stages of conversion, illumination and transformation. The dominant image is one of movement and maturation since living in the Spirit is a vital process which is gradual, continuous and comprehensive. This experience of journeying in the Spirit towards the fullness of love which we call glory is not achieved in isolation; it is always part of the activity of an entire community which supports the conscious appropriation of each stage. One and the same Spirit abides in the community and enables each member to live its life more integrally and joyfully.

Conversion is the first step a person must take in this passage from death to life. It is effected by the Spirit who gives each person a share in the victory of Christ, but this divine initiative demands a faithful response. The Spirit, who is a Spirit of truth, can free individuals from the power of darkness only if they are willing to provide a suitable dwelling for him at the core of their being. Conversion remains a constant element at every stage of spirituality. Each member of Christ's Body is continually being called by the Spirit to turn away from all that is false and sinful in the surrounding culture in order to turn more consistently to the Father. This is not an indiscriminate rejection of the beauty of the Father's creation but a matter of entering into a distinctive way of living in the world, preferring at times the foolishness of Christ's gospel to the apparent wisdom of the world.

What is demanded is not only a change in mind and morals but a comprehensive renewal embracing the person at all levels: cognitive, affective and social. Living by the power of Christ's Spirit is not a matter of knowing him in a detached or speculative way. One must enter wholeheartedly into a new existence informed by faith, guided by hope and inspired by love. The Spirit wishes to effect a progressive transformation of the total person, touching and changing not only mind and memory but imagination and affections as well. Obviously the Spirit can work effectively only if persons are resolute in dissociating themselves from all disorder.

Such a continual conversion leading to increasing clarity of vision and vigour of commitment is a sublime ideal and a demanding challenge. Its actualization depends on the inspiration of the Spirit and patient personal effort which at times will be wanting. For this reason repentance and the desire for reconciliation are also constant features of Catholic spirituality. The Father who is rich in mercy readily grants pardon and peace through the ministry of the church which shares in the mission of the Son and the Spirit.

The Word of God in the form of scripture and sacrament is the instrument through which the Spirit effects this conversion and all subsequent growth. Since Vatican II the church has been deepening its appreciation of the Word as the inexhaustible source by which the Father's creative power enters into human history and enables it to reach its fulfilment. For Catholics Mary, the mother of Jesus and archetype of the church, has always served as the model of how one is to receive and respond to God's Word. She first welcomed the Word into her immaculate heart with total faith, then conceived him in her chaste womb by her obedient response and brought him forth into the world. In a similar way members of the church are called to embrace God's Word in prayer and worship so that they may cherish and embody it by reaching out to others in loving service and sacrifice. Listening to the Word and living in accordance with his way are complementary moments in the one mystery of divine grace and human generosity.

It is the Father's Word treasured in one's heart, moreover, that enables a person to stand without wavering beneath the cross. To become closely associated with God's Word is to be drawn more deeply into the mystery of his love. Inevitably this will entail embracing the cross, for it was on the cross that Jesus glorified the Father by revealing fully his fidelity and love. Since the Christian was signed by the cross at baptism he recognizes it not as a source of sadness but as the symbol of man's ultimate destiny: self-transcendence consummated in communion with the Father. Since the Lord in whom the Christian believes remains always a sign of contradiction, living in his Spirit will call for self-renunciation. Spirituality is the learning process which enables a person to rejoice 'to have had the honour of suffering humiliation for the sake of the name' (Acts 5.41).

The outpouring of Christ's Spirit at baptism and confirmation strengthens each member of his Body for engaging in this mission of witnessing to the world. In different ways and in varying degrees each is called to uphold the goodness of the Father's work in creation and witness to the transcendent character of Christ's death and resurrection. The richness of the Spirit is reflected in the variety of his gifts; his unity is manifested when those same gifts are encouraged and co-ordinated gracefully by the one entrusted with the office of preserving order in the church. It is the function of the Spirit to preserve a constructive vital tension within Christ's Body. Charismatic spontaneity and initiative as well as official guidance and tradition flow from one and the same Spirit. The peace and unity the Spirit inspires in Christ's Body flows from a dialectic of charisms.

In our contemporary world the complexity of life-situations confronts the Christian with crucial choices. The decisions to be made extend over a broad spectrum. They include not only personal matters such as determining a vocational state in life or the responsible expression of one's sexuality, but also global questions dealing with social justice and corporate power. How is the Christian to recognize the signs indicating the choice that God's Spirit is inspiring in order to advance his reign over the hearts of men? Discordant voices clamour for attention as diverse persons read the signs of the times differently.

Discernment, which is acknowledged as the *ars artium* in the spiritual life, has reassumed its critical role in the church. It is a prized charism and a respected acquisition necessary today more than ever in order to recognize what is authentically from God's Spirit. Awareness of this need for discernment has in turn restored the ministry of spiritual direction to its honoured place in spirituality after a period of neglect and undervaluation. Laity, religious and clergy alike are seeking out persons adept at guiding their fellow-pilgrims along the path of faith. This renewed interest does not indicate an abdication of personal responsibility but is the honest admission that members of Christ's Body need wise persons to direct them to the Spirit and teach them to understand what the Spirit is saying within the believing community and in each member's heart.

The celebration of the Holy Eucharist ranks supreme as the source and summit of

Catholic spirituality, for all the constitutive elements we have been considering are operative there. Individual members who are scattered abroad in their daily lives are gathered together in prayer and worship as a community of believers. They are called to conversion, to turn away from all that would make them unworthy to enter into this holy mystery. The Father illumines them with his Word proclaimed in their midst by the power of the Spirit. They respond by joining themselves to Christ in offering praise and thanksgiving to the Father, who in turn nourishes them by the body and blood of the Lord and deepens their unity by the Holy Spirit. Through this sacrament of the suffering and death of their Lord, his members manifest their willingness to go forth and suffer in the service of all in need, the distinctive sign of a Christian and the supreme manifestation of the Spirit. The trinitarian structure of Catholic spirituality is expressed clearly in the eucharistic celebration: in the Spirit, the church is led through Christ to the Father.

This revitalization of Catholic spirituality has restored a unity and balance characteristic of early Christianity. The spiritual theology that evolved during the middle ages arose in rural isolation and monastic regularity, and was systematized deductively in the lecture halls of the universities. From the doctrinal principles enshrined in scripture, tradition and magisterial teaching, theologians formulated certain laws which governed access to the summit of perfection. Spiritual guides were then to inculcate those tried and tested practices which could lead one to the heights of sanctity. Such a formal or structural approach to spirituality enjoyed conceptual clarity, coherence and comprehensiveness, but it easily became too abstract, rigid and individualistic since it had lost its trinitarian dynamism.

Contemporary Catholic spirituality is situating itself at the heart of modern life, amid the complexity of social, economic and political tensions. It takes a more inductive approach: what is actually necessary to enable the people in the parishes to live in the Spirit? How does the Spirit enter into their joys and sorrows, frustrations and failures, struggles and triumphs? The events that are shaping contemporary history and moulding the lives of individuals determine how contemporary spirituality is to be articulated. This more functional approach complements the earlier system by integrating its principles with the findings of the modern behavioural sciences and introducing the implications of a renewed christology, pneumatology, ecclesiology, anthropology and eschatology. The spiritual theology which has emerged is a vibrant one, bringing the triune God close to his people making its pilgrim way through distressing times. Millions have been displaced by flood and famine, war and the shifting of political power. Catholic spirituality enables its members to walk in hope by directing their hearts to the source of their faith: 'the Lamb who is at the throne,' whose Spirit provides them with 'living water' as he shepherds them toward the Father who 'will wipe away all tears' (Rev. 7.17).

Sacra Congregatio Pro Cultis Divino, *Rite of Christian Initiation of Adults*, 1972; Aidan Kavanagh, *The Shape of Baptism*, 1978; Karl Rahner, *Theological Investigations*, vols III, VII, XVI, 1974–1981; Pierre Teilhard de Chardin, *Le Milieu Divin*, 1960.

DOMINIC MARUCA, SJ

Rosary

A string of beads for counting prayers in a programme of prayer and meditation. In the Christian West there is evidence of various aids for counting prayers from as early as the fourth century. This familiar form begins to appear about the tenth century, and the Marian element in it in the eleventh. It consists of five sets of ten beads, each separated from the next by a larger bead. A short pendant is added to this circlet, formed by a large bead, three small ones, another large bead and a crucifix. Among various ways of using it, a popular one is to start with the crucifix at the end of the pendant, on which the Creed is said, and to use the five beads for the Lord's Prayer, three Hail Marys, and the Gloria. Where the pendant joins the round there is a large bead or medallion on which the Lord's Prayer is said. Then come ten small beads for ten Hail Marys. The large bead that follows is used for saying the Gloria to conclude the first decade and the Lord's Prayer to begin the next, and so on until the Lord's Prayer, ten Hail Marys and the Gloria have been said five times and the round is finished. The saying of these prayers is combined with a scheme of meditation on fifteen subjects drawn from the life of our Lord and Christian devotion to the Blessed Virgin Mary. These subjects are known as 'mysteries' and form three groups – the five Joyful Mysteries, the five Sorrowful Mysteries and the five Glorious Mysteries. While each decade of the Rosary is said one of these themes is held in the mind for meditation, so that each time the Rosary is prayed the mind will have considered five great Christian meanings. The fifteen mysteries figure twice a week in the daily use of the Rosary, the Joyful Mysteries on Monday and Thursday, the Sorrowful on Tuesday and Friday, the Glorious on Wednesday and Saturday. It is not possible to consider discursively the great themes of the mysteries and apply them to oneself and the world while actually praying the Rosary. One thought of God's presence in the life of men, of human existence as part of the passion, of the coming fulfilment of God's purpose, is as much consideration as most people can manage. Meditation, in the sense of detailed and personal consideration of the themes, is done outside the prayer, in reading the relevant passages of scripture with suitable helps to understanding and appreciation. The variety of meaning and personal significance to be discerned in each image of Christ is unlimited. To unfold it in detail is to admit him more deeply into one's life; and as a result of this work, the narrowly focused attention to the mysteries in prayer acquires the fullness of meaning that gives all wordless loving its intense depth.

The Rosary is usually considered a Roman Catholic devotion, but there is an Orthodox form of it, it has been and is present as a minor theme in Anglican spirituality and, under the mutual influences of twentieth-century ecumenical experience, it is not unknown now in Free Church private prayer. It is a devotional exercise which because of its practical simplicity and profundity and its warmth of personal character will always be popular.

In the repetition of the Hail Mary the mind implicitly renews through her image its joy in the Word made flesh, its sense of the church, and its reliance on the prayers of all those who believe that Jesus is the way to God. In its 'now and in the hour of our death' it simplifies life to the two realities that constitute the Christian's immediate concern, the present situation and the purpose of God through this and all other experience to bring us to himself. To pray in this way is to change life from being mere experience (whether happy or sad) into something dignified and made hopeful with Christian meaning.

The Gloria that ends each mystery endorses that mystery's content and implication with praise, though the praise will at times be 'unknowing' praise, the praise of faith and renewal of fidelity rather than of vision.

The 'Our Father' is Jesus' prayer. In praying the Rosary it may indeed have some intention related to present need or to the mystery next to be considered, but it is primarily a recall to the mind of Christ, to his understanding of what God does about human desires and griefs, and his insight into what matters are the appropriate substance of prayer.

A. Farrer, *Lord I Believe,* 1958; J. Neville Ward, *Five for Sorrow, Ten for Joy,* 1970.

J. NEVILLE WARD

Rosicrucians
see **German Spirituality**

Rules

1. *Canonical.* A rule is a document, usually composed by the founder of a monastery or religious order, that determines the particular ends of the foundation and the principal means by which these ends are to be attained, and contains norms and regulations that guide the life of members of the community. Modern canonical usage distinguishes 'rule' from 'constitutions'. Constitutions are particular laws that specify the practical application of the rule. Constitutions are subject to revision, whereas rules are not.

More particularly, rule can refer to one of the four major rules recognized by the church. The Second Council of the Lateran (1139) recognized three rules: those of St Benedict*, St Basil and St Augustine*; and the Fourth Council of the Lateran (1215) forbade the foundation of new Orders. This prohibition was understood to mean that no Order should be constituted under a new rule. Hence founders chose a rule already recognized by the church (St Dominic, for example, chose the rule of St Augustine) and added such prescriptions as were required for the application of the rule to their institutes. An important exception to this prohibition was the approval of the rule of St Francis*. Innocent III (in 1210) and Honorius III (in 1223) approved rules written by Francis of Assisi (the lost *Regula primitiva* and the *Regula bullata*, respectively), and the rule of St Francis became the fourth major rule recognized by the church. Orders and congregations founded since the sixteenth century (the Jesuits*, for example) generally do not have a rule, but only constitutions.

The rule of St Basil is respected in the East, but is not normative. The rule of St Benedict is followed by Benedictines*, Camaldolese, Carthusians*, Cistercians*, Trappists*, and others. The rule of St Augustine is followed by Canons Regular of St Augustine, Premonstratensians, Dominicans*, Hermits of St Augustine, and others. All Franciscan orders and congregations (and many other congregations) follow the rule of St Francis.

2. *Historical.* Asceticism*, which was always practiced in the Christian church, became monasticism* when ascetics separated themselves from other Christians and lived apart, either alone, or in groups around a freely chosen master. Younger hermits naturally enough sought advice from older or more experienced monks; such advice was the first step towards a rule. The author of the first monastic rule was Pachomius (d. 346). Pachomius was the founder of cenobitism: he organized the monks under a superior or abbot whom they were to obey. Pachomius codified his ascetical programme in writing, and the monks were obliged to obey this 'rule' under the abbot's leadership and guidance.

An ancient monastic rule often comprised three parts: instructions for the monks, an order of prayer, and disciplinary prescriptions. But the many documents extant from the early church and called 'rules' differ widely in length, content and character.

Pachomius's rule, written in Coptic before 346, is the only one extant from Egypt (and only in Jerome's Latin translation). The best-known Eastern rule is St Basil of Caesarea's (d. 379). The early version, called the *Asceticon parvum* (written before 370), is extant in Rufinus's Latin translation. The later version, the *Asceticon magnum*, is preserved in Greek. Basil's rule is a collection of ascetical principles and advice mostly for those leading common life. The Syrian church possessed three short rules by Rabbula of Edessa (d. 435).

The Augustinian tradition was crucial in the development of Western monastic rules. Three rules were attributed to St Augustine (d. 430), but none of them is authentic. Augustine's letter 211, written *c.* 423, contains regulations for a convent of nuns. The core of the *Regula secunda* or *Ordo monasterii* may have been written by Augustine's friend Alypius before 395; if so, it is the oldest Latin rule. The *Regula tertia* or *Regularis informatio* uses letter 211 and was probably composed in Italy in the fifth century. The *Regula prima* or *De regula puellarum* is a reworking of letter 211 and the second and third rules, perhaps made in Spain in the seventh century. The first four books of John Cassian's* (d. *c.* 435) *De institutis coenobiorum* are also essentially a rule. All further development of monastic rules in the West was strongly influenced by four authors: Pachomius, Basil, Augustine and John Cassian.

The traditions of the island-monastery of Lérins influenced many rules composed in Gaul in the fifth and sixth centuries: *Regula quattuor patrum*, *Regula Macarii*, *Regula patrum secunda* and *tertia* (all later fifth century); two rules by Caesarius of Arles (written in 499 and 512–534); two rules by Aurelian of Arles (d. 551); a rule by Ferreolus of Uzès (d. 581); and the *Regula Tarnatensis* (sixth century).

In Italy, the Augustinian tradition was strong. It influenced the *Regula orientalis* (late fifth century), *Regula Pauli et Stephani* (early sixth century), the *Rule of the Master*, and the *Rule of St Benedict*. The last is the most important rule in the history of the church. The *Rule of the Master* was long neglected as an odd and even perverse adaptation of the *Rule of St Benedict*, but since the 1930s a consensus has arisen that the author of the *Rule of St Benedict* used the *Rule of the Master* as a source, and even copied whole chapters from it. Both rules were probably written in Italy in the sixth century.

In Spain, rules were composed by Leander of Seville (d. 600), Isidore of Seville (d. 636), and Fructuosus of Braga (d. *c.* 665) and his circle. Finally, Irish monks who went to the continent composed rules in the tradition of harsh Irish monasticism; the most important authors are Columbanus* (d. 615) and his disciple Waldebert of Luxeuil (d. 670).

The Carolingian Renaissance was a turning-point in the history of monastic rules. At the request of Louis the Pious, Benedict of Aniane (d. 821) reformed the monasteries of the emperor's realm; and, under Benedict's influence, the synods of Aachen of 816 and 817 established the *Rule of St Benedict* as the sole rule for monks. Benedict also made a collection of other monastic rules (*Codex regularum*) and wrote a commentary on the *Rule of St Benedict* consisting of excerpts from other rules (*Concordia regularum*). After Benedict of Aniane no new monastic rules were written.

Besides monastic rules, there are also rules for canons regular, clergy who live the religious life. The oldest and best known is that of Chrodegang of Metz (d. 766); the synod of Aachen of 816 also promulgated a rule for canons. The eleventh and twelfth centuries saw a rich development of rules for canons regular.

Technical information on Latin monastic rules in E. Dekkers, *Clavis patrum latinorum*, 1961, and H. J. Frede, *Kirchenschriftsteller*, 1981. Translations: *The Ascetic Works of St Basil*, tr W. K. L. Clarke, 1925; Saint Basil, *Ascetical Works*, tr M. M. Wagner, 1950 (part of the *Asceticon magnum*); John Cassian in *Nicene and Post-Nicene Fathers* II, XI, 1894; *The Rule of the Master*, tr L. Eberle, 1977; there are many translations of the *Rule of St Benedict*, of which the most recent is *RB 1980: The Rule of St Benedict in Latin and English* ed T. Fry, 1981.

JOSEPH T. LIENHARD

Russian Spirituality

Dostoevsky affirmed that the Russian people 'recognizes sanctity as the highest value', and formal canonization in the Russian Church confirms popular, corporate veneration. Russian spirituality is especially illuminated in its saints. Saint Vladimir, Prince of Kiev (980–1015) and converter of Russia, instituted an emphasis on the social, corporate implications of Christianity. The first Russian saints to be canonized were his sons, Saint Boris and the childlike Saint Gleb, who were political victims, killed in 1015 by their brother, but not martyrs for their faith. Their sanctity was popularly perceived in their voluntary participation in Christ's passion, an intuition, through suffering, of the kenotic, humiliated Christ; subsequently the Russian church has especially loved and venerated a tradition of gentle sufferers, a feeling complemented by the power of belief in the resurrection and its universal application (the Russian name for Sunday is resurrection). A sense of the complete incarnation of the spiritual in the material is a fundamental theme in Russian spirituality; it is implicit in the Russian peasant's feeling for the earth, Holy Russia, and in the sense of divine presence in the icons*, crosses and other holy objects that are kissed and worshipped in the Russian church. The kenotic idea of Christ in his poverty and 'self-emptying', rather than his passion, is followed by Saint Theodosius (d. 1074), the founding image of Russian monastic sanctity. The ascetic ideal is humanized in him and he continues Vladimir's social emphasis; he used to wear patched and poor clothing, and the kenotic idea is expressed in a poverty and social humility that approaches folly for Christ. This folly, though not exclusively Russian, became prominent in mediaeval Russia and was cherished in the popular memory; the fool for Christ takes humiliation to an extreme, renouncing the social and intellectual ties of this world. The kenotic idea finds further expression in the life and writings of Saint Tikhon of Zadonsk (1724–1783), and has been given a doctrinal base in modern Russian thought, most thoroughly by Sergius Bulgakov, for whom it is founded and realized in Holy Wisdom (Saint Sophia). Bulgakov also discerned a 'purely Russian manner of the artistic interpretation of Christ's image', and the ideal of humility recurs both in the folk tradition and in such writers as Tyutchev, Tolstoy, Dostoevsky, Leskov.

Saint Sergius of Radonezh (?1314–1392), the greatest national saint and 'Builder of Russia', was the guiding spirit of a movement, eremitic but by extension also colonizing, into the 'desert', the forests of Northern Russia. After some years of solitude a community grew up around him and the chapel he had built (he was a great carpenter); this became the Monastery of the Holy Trinity. In his coarse clothing, lack of exterior authority and social humility, Sergius refined the Theodosian kenotic image, but, akin to the contemporary Hesychast movement in Byzantium, he also deepened Russian spirituality through his experience of mystical prayer and heavenly visions. There was now a golden age of Russian spirituality and religious art, and perhaps the finest of all icons, the *Holy Trinity* by Saint Andrei Rublev (?1370–?1430), was painted in honour of Saint Sergius. The Russian icon has been called a 'concrete example of matter restored to its original harmony and beauty ... part of the transfigured cosmos', and Rublev, in the words of Saint Joseph of Volotsk (1439–1515), 'elevates mind and spirit to the immaterial divine light'. The Russian preference for the *Vladimir* icon of the Mother of God, known as *Umilenie* (tenderness), rather than the *Odigitriya* (queen type), strikes a deep chord in Russian spirituality: the Russians especially love and venerate the Mother of God as Mother, the one human being who achieved an ideal harmony of spirit and body to become the genuine, free partner of the Creator.

In the sixteenth century the social and mystical themes, united in Saint Sergius, separate, a separation associated with Saint Joseph of Volotsk and Saint Nilus of Sora (?1433–1508). The former tradition – social, liturgical – was associated with the messianic idea of Moscow the Third Rome and for some time reigned supreme, while the tradition of Nilus was eremitic, mystical, and renounced worldly possessions. Nilus, exceptionally, rejects the aesthetic response to worship which is a characteristic feature of Russian spirituality and which, according to the Chronicle story, was decisive in the very adoption of Orthodoxy when the Russians, in search of the true religion, were overcome by the beauty of the Divine Liturgy in the great church of Holy Wisdom in Constantinople. The renunciation of worldly possessions can lead, however, to *strannichestvo*, the tradition of wandering; this too is a characteristic tendency in Russian spirituality, and in the nineteenth century *The Way of a Pilgrim*, a book which describes the wandering life of a peasant who practised the Jesus prayer under the guidance of a *starets*, achieved a great popular following.

The nineteenth century in Russia is the golden age in Orthodoxy of the *starets*, the spiritual guide. The first and greatest of these *startsy* was Saint Seraphim of Sarov (1759–1833), in whom the eschatological tendency in Russian spirituality, ever directed towards the future city, could see a progression to a new form of spirituality, an image of transfiguration through voluntary love and suffering. Seraphim withdrew into the desert (at one time he spent a thousand nights in continual prayer, standing motionless on a rock) and then into the silence of the recluse, before returning, on the instruction of the Mother of God, as healer, seer and spiritual guide in the last seven years of his life. He defined the goal of the Christian life as the acquisition of the Spirit, and his body, as witnessed by his 'spiritual child' Motovilov, could be visibly transfigured by the Divine Light: 'Imagine in the centre of the sun, in the dazzling light of its midday rays, the face of a man talking to you.'

The main centre of the *starets* tradition through the rest of the century was at the hermitage of Optino. A sequence of writers and thinkers found spiritual guidance there, and so the *starets* provides a direct link to the rich tradition of Russian writing and thought in the nineteenth and twentieth centuries. Some of the writers in this tradition are centrally concerned with the specific themes of Russian spirituality, while others, such as Tolstoy, Dostoevsky, Rozanov, Shestov, Berdyaev (often those with a personalistic emphasis), may be more neutral in respect of these themes.

Whereas Tolstoy approaches a moral maximalism devoid of any mystical sense, Dostoevsky is fundamentally concerned with the problem of religious consciousness and explores the dialectic of good and evil in the human soul. In Rozanov, a follower of Dostoevsky and a writer of natural genius, personalism has a cosmocentric, not ethical, emphasis. His feeling for the truth of this world is inseparable from an intimate sense of God the Father, and, by linking God with procreation, he develops a spiritual interpretation of the elemental process of cultural creativity. In this century Dostoevsky's inspiration is keenly felt in both Shestov and Berdyaev. Shestov maintains absolute irrationalism in order to restore to man his right to freedom and to God, while Berdyaev is the insistent defender of personalism in the name of freedom and creativity: his hope in the creative ethical freedom released in man by Christ's redemptive work is imbued with the eschatological theme, the 'Russian idea' of universal and complete transfiguration.

The specific themes of Russian spirituality are established in the middle of the nineteenth century by the Slavophiles, with Ivan Kireevsky and Khomyakov at their head. Khomyakov it is who gives the name to the theme of *sobornost'*, the theme of integral wholeness, organic unity, with an implication of some social content. Following Kireevsky, he integrates faith and reason in integral reason, but the individual can only comprehend truth through the organic togetherness of the church, which is a living social organism held together by love. History for Khomyakov is thus a spiritual process, and in its universal development he sees a special path for Russia. Among the later Slavophiles Leont'ev relates spirituality and politico-cultural types, but from a pessimistic, almost apocalyptic stance.

In the last quarter of the nineteenth century the great Russian thinker Vladimir Solov'ev gave (or returned) the name of Holy Wisdom (Saint Sophia) to Russian spirituality. The fundamental Russian themes of the complete incarnation of the spiritual in the material and the unity of the whole creation come together with the hope for universal transfiguration under the name of Holy Wisdom. The mystical vision of Sophia was the inspiration of Solov'ev's life and work. He realized the need for a religio-spiritual grounding for the social ideal, and attempted an organic philosophical synthesis based on the idea of God-manhood. Sophia is for him the hidden soul of the created world, and the history of man, mankind as a whole, is directed towards the God-man realized in Christ. He tends to assimilate Sophia and the Mother of God, and sees support for this in Russian churches and iconography*. In the middle of his life Solov'ev hoped for a reconciliation of Orthodoxy and Rome in order to realize a free theocracy, but towards the end of his life he developed an apocalyptic, prophetic vision.

A singular but emblematic Russian thinker in the second half of the nineteenth century is Fedorov, whose major work was put together after his death as *The Philosophy of the Common Task*. His thinking was inspired by the desire for the kingdom of God and the salvation of the world, and for him the collective task in history of the Christian life is to achieve universal redemption – victory over disease, disunity and death through the resurrection, transfigured, of all men.

The Sophianic direction given to Russian spirituality by Solov'ev is developed in this century by Pavel Florensky and Sergius Bulgakov. Florensky was a brilliant mathematician as well as theologian and priest. He grounded his approach to religious dogma in living religious experience, and his major work, *The Pillar and Foundation of the Truth*, is rich and vivid with this experience, with quotations from the lives of the saints and liturgical texts, even with iconographic material. Florensky's mystical perception of the cosmos as a living whole leads to a doctrine of created Sophia, the 'root of the totality of total created being', which brings created being within the infra-trinitarian life of God; he assimilates Sophia to the church and also – following Solov'ev – to the Mother of God.

This move into the theology of Sophia leads, finally, to Bulgakov. He passed through Marxism and idealist philosophy on his way to the Orthodox priesthood, and his fundamental idea is the revelation of God in everything, his source the church life as a whole. Bulgakov first came to the Sophiological problem under the influence of Florensky. He developed the idea of Sophia beyond cosmology into theology, and set out to formulate the doctrine of God-manhood and the inner unity between the divine and created Sophia. Holy Wisdom is the link which unites God and the world, and it is through the church that Sophia becomes manifest in the world; the church is Sophia in process of becoming until, in the eschatological fulfilment of all things, Divine Wisdom is fulfilled in the created.

N. Berdyaev, *Dream and Reality*, 1948; *The Russian Idea*, 1948; S. Bulgakov, *A Bulgakov Anthology*, ed J. Pain and N. Zernov, 1976; G. P. Fedotov, *The Russian Religious Mind* (2 vols), 1946–1966; *A Treasury of Russian Spirituality*, 1950; N. Gorodetzky, *The Humiliated Christ in Modern Russian Thought*, 1938; P. Kovalevsky, *St Sergius and Russian Spirituality*, 1976; P. Pascal, *The Religion of the Russian People*, 1976; V.

Solov'ev, *A Solovyev Anthology*, ed S. L. Frank, 1950; T. Ware, *The Orthodox Church* (revd edn) 1980; V. Zander, *St Seraphim of Sarov*, 1975; N. Zernov, *The Russians and their Church*, 1945; *The Russian Religious Renaissance of the Twentieth Century*, 1963 (includes an extensive bibliography).

ROBIN AIZLEWOOD

Rutherford, Samuel

Samuel Rutherford (*c.* 1600–1661) was a leading figure in the second generation of post-Reformation churchmen in Scotland. Before the age of thirty he became minister of the parish of Anwoth in Galloway (the Stewardry of Kirkcudbright), and it was the pastoral office which developed his devout and prayerful way of life and built up his great spiritual influence in Scotland. Early morning study and prayer undergirt assiduous pastoral care and visitation of his people, who were also nurtured by his preaching which held his flock spell-bound as he spoke of the loveliness of Christ. His theology was the current Calvinism* of the time, and he accepted verbal inspiration of the Bible. He affirmed the Word of God in the holy scriptures to be the supreme rule of faith and life for Christians. His ministry was marked by a passionate desire that the gospel should shape the character and life of his people. Anne Ross Cousin's well-known hymn (published in *The Christian Treasury*, 1857) is a skilful mosaic of phrases from Rutherford's writing:

> The sands of time are sinking;
>   The dawn of heaven breaks . . .
> O Christ! He is the fountain,
>   The deep, sweet well of love;
> The streams of earth I've tasted
>   More deep I'll drink above.

In 1639 Samuel Rutherford became Professor of Divinity and later Principal at St Mary's College, St Andrews, teaching and writing as one of the great protagonists of Presbyterianism, and being sent as one of the eight Scottish Commissioners present during the effective years of the Westminster Assembly (1643–1647). His writings attacked monarchical absolutism in the state while at the same time enunciating and defending a most rigid Presbyterian Church polity in the ecclesiastical sphere. Completely identified with the controversies about church and state and presbytery and

episcopacy in the troubled years following the National Covenant of 1638, nevertheless Rutherford's devotional life and also his devotional writings were sustained on the foundation of the pastor's heart and mind evolved when he was parish minister at Anwoth. Believing in the divine right of Presbytery, he also stressed a kind of apostolic succession of pastor to pastor in the parish, regarding the presence of a minister of word and sacrament serving in every parish as more important than any issue of church polity. The 'cure of souls' understanding of the local community, unaltered by the Reformation, was at the heart of his spirituality.

In Scottish homes for some two centuries the most widely read devotional classic, apart from the Bible, was Rutherford's *Letters*, the first edition being published within three years of his death. The tenderness of his devotional writing has affinities with the nuptial mysticism of some Catholic hymnology, e.g. Jesu dulcis memoria (printed in *Lyra Catholica*, 1849). This strand in his piety infused a gentle and tenderhearted quality into evangelical faith which so easily became rigid and legalistic, for instance in the understanding of Christ's atoning sacrifice. Rutherford's wide influence engendered a spirituality of ardent and almost passionate love, with a Jesus-centred yearning for heaven. His *Letters* were regarded by C. H. Spurgeon (1834–1892) as 'the nearest thing to inspiration which can be found in all the writings of mere men'.

A personal and affectionate love for Jesus and a longing for heaven are the essence of the spirituality of Samuel Rutherford and partly explain his lasting influence. This spiritual quality is exemplified in his own words: 'I know no wholesome fountain but one. I know not a thing worth the buying but heaven; and my own mind is, if comparison were made betwixt Christ and heaven, I would sell heaven with my blessing and buy Christ . . . I would frist (postpone) heaven for many years, to have my fill of Jesus in this life, and to have occasion to offer Christ to my people, and to woo many people to Christ.'

Joshua Redivivus or Mr Rutherford's *Letters* ed A. A. Bonar, 1848 and 1891; A Collection of *Sermons* preached at Sacramental Occasions, on several Subjects and in Dif-

ferent Places, 1802; *Quaint Sermons* of
Samuel Rutherford, 1885; see also Adam
Philip, *Devotional Literature of Scotland*
1922.

R. STUART LOUDEN

Ruysbroeck, Jan van

Ruysbroeck (1293–1381) spent many years
in Brussels, chiefly connected with the collegiate Church of St Gudule. Mystically
inclined from youth, it was said that 'he went
about the streets of Brussels with his mind
lifted up to God'; but he came into conflict
with various mystical sects such as the
so-called Brethren of the Free Spirit, who
were independent of church authority and
inclined towards pantheism. In 1343 he left
the collegiate Church, and, with his uncle
and a fellow priest established a contemplative community in the country, which
later adopted the rule of the Augustinian
canons.

Ruysbroeck's spirituality is couched at
times in highly metaphysical language. It is
not derived from an openness to the outward world of nature, or from a study of the
scriptures, though he found the Johannine
writings especially congenial. It is a spirituality of the interior, introspective life,
born out of self-examination, awareness and
discovery. It looks within and also down –
down to God the ground of all being, who is
a 'fathomless abyss'. It demands a stripping
of all concepts and pre-conceived ideas.
'Sink down to that imageless nudity which
is God.' This sounds not only devastating
but dangerous; it is, in fact, the way to freedom from the false props and stays which
come between us and God and hamper our
movement towards perfect union. There is
an essential unity with God by virtue of our
humanity. 'This unity makes us neither
saints nor blessed, for all men have it in
them, the bad as well as the good; but it is
the first cause of holiness and bliss; and this
is the meeting and the unity of God in our
spirit, our bare nature.' There is also an
'active' unity which results from the essential
unity and learns its guiding principle
directed by the Spirit of God, and through
the work of the Augustine-like Trinity of
memory, intelligence and will. This leads to
the 'super essential unity', beyond the active
and beyond the interior, 'the unity from
which we flowed out when we were created,
and where we abide according to our es-

sence, and towards which we endeavour to
return by love'. This is contemplation*, 'the
God-seeing life'; but Ruysbroeck does not
only use the language of vision. As the quotation shows, he is even fonder of metaphors
drawn from water, rivers and fountains, outpouring, flowing, immersion, the 'downsink-
ing of our being'. Eternal blessedness is 'an
eternal going out from ourselves'. 'Down
into God' is the direction of our true life,
but the unity we seek does not mean that we
are so absorbed in him that we are (pace
later attacks by Jean Gerson*) no longer
other than he. 'And we must go forth from
ourselves' not only towards God, 'but towards all good men with loyalty and
brotherly love'.

Ruysbroeck was one whose spirituality
did not conflict with his ecclesiology (*see*
Ecclesiology and Spirituality). Outward
obedience and discipline must accompany
the inward life and the bridegroom with
whom we desire interior union comes to us
every day in the sacrament by which he takes
and gives all.

Texts: Eric Colledge (tr), *The Spiritual Espousals*, 1952; C. A. W. Dom (tr), *The Adornment of Spiritual Marriage, The Sparkling
Stone, The Book of Supreme Truth,* 1916;
John Francis (tr), *The Twelve Beguines*,
1913; P. S. Taylor (tr), *The Seven Steps of
the Ladder of Spiritual Love*, 1944; see also
Ray C. Petry (ed), *Later Mediaeval Mysticism* (LCC XIII), 1957, pp. 285–320;
Evelyn Underhill, *Ruysbroeck*, 1915.

EDITOR

Sacramentalism

This is to be distinguished from a spirituality
based on the eucharist* as the central and
normative act of Christian worship and
hence of life. There have been many of a
Platonic spirit and a Monistic theology who
have seen the phenomenal world as a veil
concealing the glory of God which yet shines
through it. There are many illustrations in
e.g. English romantic poetry, Wordsworth
most notably, but Shelley also and Elizabeth
Barrett Browning's 'Earth's crammed with
heaven/and every common bush aflame with
God'. This is closely linked with Nature Mysticism* and is found in Gerard Manley Hopkins*, but it is often cold towards institutional Christianity, which by authoritarianism and austerities kills the im-

agination and dulls sensitivity to the glory outside the revelation confined within the church. Modern Quakers* have been among its exponents, with their inherited disuse of the ecclesiastical sacraments somewhat reinterpreted to serve the belief that all life is sacramental. C. E. Raven (1885–1964), at any rate in his youth, was sensitive to the Shekinah, in the Lakeland hills, in the lovemaking of a young couple in the park, in the serving of fish and chips in a drab Liverpool slum, and to the Risen Christ himself in the squalid room of a sick friend. This accounts for his great interest in biology and ornithology, his refusal to think of God in Christ as a divine invader from outside the evolutionary process, or of the world as simply a stage for the drama of redemption; and his work for the reconciliation of religion and the natural sciences.

Anne Fremantle (ed), *The Protestant Mystics*, 1964; W. R. Inge, *The Platonic Tradition in English Religious Life*, 1926; C. E. Raven, *Natural Religion and Christian Theology*, vols I and II, 1953; *A Wanderer's Way*, 1928; Pierre Teilhard de Chardin, *Le Milieu Divin*, 1960.

EDITOR

Sacred Heart

Devotion to the Sacred Heart of Jesus began in the twelfth century Western church in an age when human feelings burst the bonds of a rigid social order and yearned for a God, who in spite of the impassibility theologians averred, shared our human nature, and a Christ, seen not in iconic majesty, but as the meek and suffering Jesus. It derived from meditation on the wound in Christ's side. The Franciscan theologian, Bonaventure*, gave it expression. In the Middle Ages, it seems to have been practised chiefly in the monasteries, and was the subject of the visions of nuns such as Mechtilde of Magdeburg. In Julian of Norwich's* tenth Revelation, her understanding is drawn into the side of Christ and the Lord shows 'his blessed heart split in two'. This is no grisly and repulsive sight but the inspiration of an unspeakable joy. The open side and broken heart are the infallible signs of Christ's tender and unceasing love, as well as our security and salvation – 'concealed in the cleft of thy side/eternally held in thy heart', as Charles Wesley* wrote later.

The devotion continued but became genuinely popular in the seventeenth century. It is found in the writings and testimonies of St Francis de Sales*, who longed that in the holy communion, his heart might leave his body and be replaced by Christ's, and who taught that we must love our neighbour in spite of his faults because he is 'right in our Divine Saviour's heart'. In 1646, St John Eudes instituted the feast of the Holy Heart of Mary and, in 1672, that of the Sacred Heart of Jesus, but without much response. Between 1673 and 1675, St Marguerite-Marie-Alacoque received revelations at Paray-le-Monial, which in return for certain liturgical observances, including a holy hour on Thursdays, gave promise of rich rewards.

Henri Bremond* has distinguished between the Eudist devotion and that of Paray. The former is theocentric, directed to the heart of Jesus as embodying his '*intérieur*'; the latter is obsessed with the ruptured organ of his human body and has had great popular influence in the Roman Church, faithful homes being frequently adorned with pictures of Jesus, his heart exposed. The liturgical observance was not authorized until 1765. Pius IX (1856), Leo XIII and Pius XI all extended it. Leo XIII, after much consultation of theologians, yielded to the request of another visionary nun, Sister Droste-Vishering, and in 1899, consecrated the whole world to the Sacred Heart of Jesus. In 1960, the Octave was abandoned, but in 1969, the observance was classed as a 'solemnitas', a feast of greatest importance.

Though some may be repelled by what appear to them the carnal excesses of the popular cult, the devotion unites too closely human longing for evidences both of a compassionate God and the humanity of man with profound Christian theology for it not to have wide appeal in certain periods. After the death of the French revolutionary, Marat, in 1793, his heart was translated to the Cordelier's Club room, 'where it was suspended in an urn from the roof, amidst applause'. One orator cried 'O cor Marat, O cor Jesus', not to divinize Marat, but to humanize Jesus.

The English Puritan theologians wrote of the heart of Jesus, and of the 'mighty flame of love that burns in it' (Isaac Ambrose). Richard Baxter* declares: 'If thou know him not by the face, the voice, the hands, if thou know him not by the tears and bloody sweat, thou mayest know him by the heart; that broken healed heart is his; that soul pitying, melting heart is his, doubtless it can be none's but his, love and compassion are its certain signatures.' Most important of all, there is Thomas Goodwin's * treatise, *The Heart of Christ in Heaven towards Sinners on Earth* (1643), which seeks 'to lay open the heart of Christ as now he is heaven'. He begins with a commentary on the farewell discourses of the Fourth Gospel, which reveal the love of Christ for his own, which extends even beyond his passion, so that John 17 is the 'platform' of Christ's intercession for us in heaven. The second part goes deeper still. Why did the Son of God take our nature upon him, have a human heart and retain it in his glory? Because he needs the fullness not only of divine but of human nature. He must love as a man to kindle our human love. 'As he is a true man, and the same man that he was, both in body as well as in soul (or else it had not been a true Resurrection), so he hath still the very same truly humane affections in them both'. Our spiritual growth, obedience and increased strength gladden Christ's heart.

In 1874, a writer in the *Edinburgh Review* posited a link between Goodwin and Roman Catholic devotion, through Père Claude la Colombière. But there is a fundamental difference between such spiritual theology and a cult of the Sacred Heart.

Modern Roman Catholic theologians have treated of the devotion, notably Hans Urs von Balthasar in *Das Herz der Welt* and Karl Rahner in his *Theological Investigations* (III, pp. 321–54). Von Balthasar's meditations grapple with the whole problem of suffering in God. The devotion should be no unhealthy deviation from Christian theology into an unreal, nauseating realm of soft sentimentality. It raises the awesome question of how we may see the transcendence of God in the wounds of Jesus.

Karl Rahner analyses the word 'heart', which is primordial, beyond definition and irreplaceable. The physiological heart, what the anatomist studies, is but the symbol of the reality. We must know what we mean by heart, the source and unity of our human being, before we can understand the Christian good news that 'the eternal logos of God has a human heart, he risked the adventure of a human heart, until pierced by the sin of the world, it had flowed out, until it had suffered to the end on the cross the uselessness and powerlessness of his love and become thereby the eternal heart of the world'. Rahner warns against the pseudo-religiosity, which may attach itself to the cult in the contemplations of the holy hours, as well as the sheer bad taste. Devotion to the Sacred Heart is primarily devotion to the Person of Christ. Ideas of 'reparation' and 'consoling' the Lord need to be saved from error. It is not our reparation to Christ for our sins but our share in his one sufficient reparation to the Father that is the concern of our prayer; while our seeking to console Christ in his sufferings may make us unmindful both that he is now glorified, and that 'the sight of our "good" deeds made him suffer almost as much in his torn wretchedness as the sight of our sins'. Christ may be consoled by the co-suffering of his mystical body even when there is no such deliberate intention. He participates in all that has happened and will happen through the whole of history in all the members of his body, but this is rather different from the childish belief that my prayers may staunch his wounds or heal his broken heart.

In addition to the works referred to see Dietrich von Hildebrand, *The Sacred Heart*, 1965, and the accounts in Louis Bouyer, *A History of Christian Spirituality*, 1963–1969, vol II *passim*, vol III, pp. 140ff.

EDITOR

Sacred Humanity

A devotion which appears in the Western church around the twelfth century and which is particulary associated with Bernard of Clairvaux * and Francis of Assisi *. It was in reaction to the Byzantine preoccupation with Christ's Divine Majesty. There was longing for tenderness, compassion, for the human face and heart of God. Hence interest in the childhood of Christ (e.g. Bonaventure *), the scene in the stable, the Mother and the Holy Name, fascination with the cross, the five wounds, the torn heart. But Bernard and the mystics usually imply that this devotion is but the preliminary to imageless contemplation of the Majesty which transcends the life of the Incarnate, and knows Christ no longer after the flesh. This seems Neoplatonist rather than scriptural. For the NT, Christ is 'the image of the invisible God' and he is not a disembodied spirit even in the resurrection. It is possible to assert as Christian mystics did, that the manhood and the passion of Christ are the door to union with him in God – but is the door passed through without return as the soul ascends? (*See* **English Mystics, The.**) The question caused much controversy in, for example, seventeenth-century France.

There is an obvious danger of sentimentality in devotion to the sacred humanity which has persisted into the icing sugar of much devotion to the Blessed Sacrament and the Virgin, as well as into liberal Protestantism. Leonardo da Vinci's fresco of the Last Supper, though not of such a genre, is dramatic and psychological rather than sacramental, and has been thought, in spite of its genius, to mark a decline in religious art. It is a human interest drama – 'Lord, is it I?' The attention is directed away from Christ to the disciples and, in front of Judas, the salt-cellar is spilled.

EDITOR

Saints, Sanctify

In the NT 'the saints', i.e. 'the holy ones' is a designation of members of the church, especially in the Pauline writings, though also in Hebrews and Revelation, and occasionally elsewhere. It is hardly ever used in the singular. The NT knows nothing of a *Saint* Peter or *Saint* Paul, except in so far as they are incorporate in the 'communion of the saints'. Individual holiness is derived from the fellowship of believers, whose sanctity consists in their being 'in Christ', the Holy, the Saint (Mark 1.24; John 6.69; Acts 3.14; Rev. 3.7), and also the Sanctifier, the one who calls and consecrates the saints (Heb. 2.11; John 17.17–19; I Cor. 1.30). The concept has OT origins. It means *inter alia* that the church is the New Israel, also the eschatological community, quickened and possessed by the Holy Spirit, in which the life of the age to come is already manifest on the earth. This 'communion of the saints' is separate from the world, though it is not taken out of the world, and has a mission to the world. It transcends barriers of race, sex and social distinction, and is characterized by intense loyalty and mutual love. It is a priestly, worshipping community, which is summoned to the single-hearted quest of the divine perfection, the goodness and mercy of God himself.

It seems a far cry from this to the cult of the saints as it grew throughout the centuries, and to the attribution of especial holiness to departed individuals, whose intercession is believed to be of particular efficacy, and who each receive a day in the church calendar and commemoration in propers of the liturgy. But scriptural foundations can usually be unearthed for most of the practices of piety, if the digging is deep enough, and in II Maccabees 15.12, there is Jewish precedent, when Judas Maccabaeus sees in a dream Onias a former high priest, 'praying with outstretched hands for the whole body of the Jews', and joined by the prophet Jeremiah, who is said to pray much 'for the people of the holy city'. NT support would lie in the doctrine of the church as Christ's body in which the members work together and support each other in their different functions. The cult of the saints carries this beyond the grave.

The grim fact of death is decisive in the development of devotion to the saints. In the history of Christ's people in a continuing world, there has always been a tension in Christian faith and worship between joyful affirmation of Christ's victory, and awareness that still 'in the midst of life we are in death' and that the resurrection has not visibly transformed the terrible ravages of the last enemy, or the human agony of bereavement. The tension is as strong today as ever. Should a Christian funeral be a paean of triumph – (when it is, the celebration is more often thanksgiving for the life of the departed about whom the whole truth cannot be known, than the glory in what God has done by raising Jesus from the dead)? Or should there be a real expression of our griefs and fears and a solemn remembrance of mortality? And is there any joy or consolation to be found in the death of a child, unless the young life is so distorted and deformed as to have no hope in this world? These questions were not mute among the Christians of the immediately post-apostolic centuries. And they retained their hope, not only because of the forsaken grave of Christ but because the shrines of their holy ones, particularly 'the very special dead', the martyrs*, seemed places of the divine presence and power, where the veil between earth and heaven was rent. There were terrible fears made worse by the

Augustinian doctrine of election. To interr your own, unheroic loved one near to the shrine of a saint or martyr might make appallingly clear the distinction between the saved and those whose destiny was less certain. Yet there is discernible in the sixth century, in Gregory of Tours and Venantius Fortunatus, 'a carefully maintained crescendo of beauty in poetry, in ceremonial and in shimmering art around a new and obsessive theme ... Both men turned the *summum malum* of physical death preceded by suffering into a theme in which all that was most beautiful and refined in their age would be compressed' (Peter Brown).

The cult of contemporaries and those whose stories were handed down from the great persecutions preceded that of biblical saints, partly because they had no shrines or associations of place in the local churches, apart from SS Peter and Paul at Rome. Devotion to Mary, the *Theotokos*, sprang directly from the christological controversies of the fourth century and their resolution in the Catholic creeds. The Eastern Church, in spite of the prominence it gives to Mary throughout its worship, has always insisted that Mary is venerated because of the child she bore. 'Mother and Son are not to be separated, but Mariology is to be understood as an extension of Christology' (Kallistos Ware). OT saints followed those of the NT in devotion. (*See also* **Marian Devotion.**)

In the Western church, there were no new canonizations in the 600 years between Gregory the Great* and Thomas Beckett (1170). After that cults proliferated and popular devotion, which the church fostered, lost touch with historical reality and what a later age would deem scientific truth. Bogus relics, legendary miracles, and fictitious saints abounded; the great themes of Christian worship were overlaid by the number of saints' days. The abuses and superstitions were such that the reaction of the Protestant Reformers in sweeping many cults away wholesale and returning to scripture alone is entirely understandable. Pius V in reforming the Divine Office in 1568 and the Missal in 1570 reduced the number of saints' celebrations to 158, mostly from the city of Rome itself, but by the time of the Second Vatican Council they had increased to 338. In 1969, there was a drastic revision and the Roman Calendar now includes 191 saints of whom 95 may be ignored if local communities so desire. The list is now more universal and international. Sunday is reasserted as the Feast of Our Lord and it is rare for this to be displaced by the commemoration of any saint.

The Roman Church continues to canonize in the belief that sanctity did not die with the apostles. But the process is long and legalistic and there must be evidence of a sanctity supernaturally manifested (though in the case of St Thomas Aquinas* his theological writings were accounted miraculous), and of distinctively Christian virtues such as joy.

The Orthodox Churches have a simpler, more homely method, less formal, which makes it easier to canonize local saints who need not be included in a universal calendar. The Orthodox have also, though by no means exclusively, made much of the sanctity of the simple and uneducated, the 'holy fools'. This is very much in the spirit of Matt. 11.25, and is illustrated in Tolstoy's story of 'The Three Hermits', who could not learn the Lord's Prayer but could walk on the water. Rational Protestantism remains somewhat uneasy at this point. Childlike simplicity is of the kingdom of Heaven and God's wisdom has in it an element of folly and those who are mentally retarded may teach us of his love. They are not to be despised, much less liquidated, and the saint is not the superman of Nordic blood, or genetic engineering. But although most saints have had a touch of eccentricity by the standards of rational calculation, insanity is fearful if not tragic and should not be glorified in itself, even if some saints have known periods of mental stress and depressive illness.

Protestantism has been sorely deprived if saved from excesses by its suspicions of the cult of the saints, and, as the Methodist historian, H. B. Workman (d. 1955) once said, it 'has too often driven out the eagle to save the sparrows'. It has also meant that the unseen world has become less real since the Reformation. Yet it has been more in liturgy than in spirituality that the saints have been ignored. Verses such as Richard Baxter's* 'He wants not friends that hath thy love' are hardly deficient in affirming the reality of the *communio sanctorum* and many a Puritan congregation had its own calendar more after the Orthodox than the Roman fashion, in which the departed saints of the fellowship were remembered along with the patriarchs of old. Prayer *to* the saints was felt to assail the glorious comfort of the sole mediatorship of Christ; prayer *with* the saints was a daily experience.

But the whole history of the cult of the saints illustrates the undoubted, though disturbing truth, that God, the high and holy Redeemer, is not sufficient for us in his transcendent majesty. We need, in life and most of all in death, human faces, and although we have Jesus, he may be lost in the mists of antiquity if not in the clouds of heaven, unless he brings us into the companionship of our friends and his, and we see his 'countenance divine' in the lineaments of those who in their time on earth have revealed to us his love.

Peter Brown, *The Cult of the Saints*, 1981; Pierre-Yves Emery, *The Communion of Saints*, 1966; Owen E. Evans, *Saints in Christ Jesus*, 1975; Geoffrey F. Nuttall, *Visible Saints*, 1957; John Saward, *Perfect Fools*, 1980.

EDITOR

Sangster, William Edwin   *1960.*

A Methodist preacher of great power and popularity, Sangster's (1900–1959) essential message, driven home by an amazing gift of illustration and many histrionics, was holiness. Minister of the Central Hall Westminster from 1939–1955, he did notable work in the air-raid shelters during the Second World War, but his principal study was sanctity, and his most typical book *The Pure in Heart* (1954). Written in his characteristic pulpit style, the book shows how the desire for holiness unites all Christians, whatever their history, period, church tradition or social status, in the divine love. The examples used and examined are from an enormous range of spiritual history, as the author attempts to say what sanctity is and to describe it in particular by study of the fruits of the Spirit. The book is a summons to the adventure of holiness for all. 'Far above us we see the saints moving on the snowy whiteness ... and we follow after. *Any* man may climb.'

Paul Sangster, *Doctor Sangster*, 1960. *1962.*

EDITOR

Satan *see* **Devil, The**

Scottish Spirituality

Anyone acquainted with the intellectual argumentative character of Scottish Calvinism might wonder if any flower of spirituality could grow on such a rocky soil. Yet from the beginning one finds side by side with the fierce outpourings of theological controversy or the arid summations of Calvinist orthodoxy a deep, tender, loving, at times almost sentimental devotion to the person of the Saviour, expressed in hymns and songs and ever and again in personal letters. If one looks for the soul of Scotland one must remember this second aspect, and not think that the first is all. Thrawn, contentious and intolerant as they may have been (though not more so than their opponents), the Scottish Covenanters did not give their lives for an intellectual argument, but committed them to a Saviour.

An Anglican divine, writing of the growth of moral and spiritual conscience in the sixteenth century, could say, 'The Reformation brought, in some sense, mere loss.' Nothing better illustrates the difference between the English and the Scottish experience. For the Scot, the Reformation was sheer gain, because it was the rediscovery of the gospel. The most eloquent, joyful and still delightful testimony to this is *The Guid and Godlie Ballatis*, compiled by the brothers James, John and Robert Wedderburn, and first published some time between 1542 and 1546. This was the unofficial song-book of the Scottish Reformation. James Melville relates how, as a schoolboy in Montrose in 1570, he first saw 'Wedderburn's Songs, wharof I lerned diverse *par ceur*, with great diversities of toones'. The book contained verse translations of the Psalms and other passages of scripture, translations of some of Luther's hymns, as well as original polemical, didactic and devotional verse. The didactic verses follow the style of the mediaeval carol, in telling the story of salvation. The polemical are never without humour, as in the mischievous 'God send everie Preist ane wyfe, And everie Nunne ane man.' The translations of the Psalms are perhaps the least inspired in the collection, though some have a deeply moving quality. Of the other songs, some seem to be adaptations of secular love-songs. Here love, joy, comfort, trust in the Saviour is expressed in simple and moving imagery. The theology is the theology of justification by grace. The hymns are the response of the Christian soul to the Gospel.

The language of the *Ballatis* is the purest Scots. Such was not for long to be the language of Scottish spirituality. The Scots never had an approved version of the Bible, nor yet a service-book, in their own tongue. The Geneva Bible and Knox's Genevan Service-book were in English; and when they were superseded it was by the Authorized Version of 1611 and the Westminster Directory of 1645. Bible-reading and prayer went together, in Kirk and in home. The head of the household who opened the book to lead the worship of his family, passed at that point from the use of his native tongue to the English of the Authorized Version; and since the language and imagery of the Bible was also the language of prayer, his prayers would tend to be in his own version of the same.

Samuel Rutherford* (1600–1661) illustrates perhaps better than any other the co-existence of hard intellectual theology and emotional, indeed erotic, spirituality. Calvinist, Covenanter, author of *Lex Rex*, he was in the heart of the religious and political struggles of the seventeenth century. But in his letters he pours out the religion of his heart. It is difficult to determine how healthy is the erotic imagery of Rutherford's devotion, or what notes of anxiety may lie behind his reiterated protestations.

Family worship was intended by the Kirk to be the pivot of Scottish devotion, and there were frequent attempts to encourage and assist the practice. The General Assembly of 1647 approved Directions for Secret and Family Worship, regarding these as the right preparation for all other duties. Models of prayer were provided, and suggestions for family conference on the passage of scripture read. The insistence was that worship was to be in families, with the head of the family presiding, and not in any self-selected groups with self-appointed leaders. The schismatic potential of the prayer élite was greatly feared. Nevertheless, and partly as a development of the fellowship meetings of the Kirk Session, 'praying societies' began to develop, and become the nurseries of evangelical religion, especially in parishes where the incumbent was 'Moderate'. In the Lowlands such groups were frequently the nucleus of Secession congregations. In the Highlands they remained within the Establishment, at least until 1843, and the lay leadership of 'the Men' provided a powerful evangelical, spiritual and disciplinary force. They alone spoke and prayed in public in fellowship meetings, and they in particular maintained the discipline of the Lord's table and of the weekly Sabbath. That such a discipline became in time harsh and Pharisaical is clear; it had also the Pharisaical virtue of seeing spirituality not as a department of life, but as the whole of it.

As the nineteenth century developed it saw the emergence of a warmer, more liberal evangelicalism, which was perhaps more in tune with the traditional spirituality of the Scottish people, in its devotion to the Saviour. Influences from across the Border were considerable, and many homes contained an edition of Matthew Henry, and Doddridge's* *Rise and Progress of Religion in the Soul*. The hymn books which came into use became manuals of private devotion in a church which had no set forms and few aids to prayer, and hymn books are always an ecumenical influence.

The sacrament of the Lord's Supper was, and still is, celebrated infrequently in the Scottish Church. It would be a mistake to deduce from this that Scottish spirituality is not sacramental. The characteristic and stubborn Scottish insistence that communion is to be received sitting at a table arose from the conviction that here we are the guests of the Lord, sons of God, kings and priests, called by grace into his banqueting-house and set at his table. The infrequency of the occasion was the measure of its importance, and the whole of the discipline of the church, in its preaching week by week, and at the family table day by day, was designed to bring around the table of the Lord a community that was joyful, believing and obedient.

No ideals are safe from corruption, and this could, and did, degenerate into 'The Holy Fair'. Today the old discipline of 'the Communion season' is mostly gone. Communion services have become more frequent and more informal, and there is great gain in this. But the sense of the family occasion always remains. At the heart of Scottish spirituality is the ideal of a family gathered at a table – the table of the Lord. *See also* **Calvinist Spirituality.**

JAMES A. WHYTE

Scupoli, Lorenzo *see* **War, Holy**

Self-Control *see* **Fruit of the Spirit**

Seuse, Heinrich *see* **Suso, Heinrich**

Sexuality

Historically, human sexuality always assumes a meaning in a particular cultural and religious context. Hence the role sexuality plays in Christian spirituality originates in distinctive cultural and theological perspectives.

1. Although both the Hebrew and the Christian scriptures present human sexuality in a positive light as a divine gift proclaiming companionship and procreation as necessary for human life, the Bible also contains other less positive connotations as well. Sex, for example, for the author of Deuteronomy was seen as a taboo (Deut. 15, 17, 21), a human phenomenon to be put aside at times lest one be rendered ritually unclean through sexual contact. The eschatological thrust of much of the NT implied that all human realities, including sex, be assigned importance relative to the final coming of the Lord.

By the second and third centuries Christians tended to interpret the biblical data in a less positive vein. At times an extreme expression of asceticism resulted in the founding of sects which eschewed sexual contact and therefore even marriage. The Manichean heresy viewed sexuality as one of the deepest sources of human sinfulness. Augustine's attitudes, though avoiding such extremes, betrayed a strong discomfort with and suspicion of human sexuality. Augustine's views on sex exercised a powerful influence on Christian spirituality during mediaeval times and even in later centuries.

As monasticism found expression as a Christian life-style, the three vows of poverty, chastity and obedience became prominent features of Christian spirituality. Monasticism intended to witness to the eschatological dimension of Christianity and hence to the need for singleminded dedication to the kingdom. To be sure, this insight represents the genius of the monastic movement. In time, however, coupled with the deep distrust of 'worldly affairs' among Christians, this *fuga mundi** (flight from the world) became the paradigm for all of Christian spirituality. This expression of spirituality found ready expression in a Neoplatonism which had been adapted to the Christian experience even before Augustine.

The role of sex in this spirituality followed with rigorous logic. The norm for those striving for perfection was vowed chastity. Marriage, while officially extolled by the church as a praiseworthy Christian life-style, was in practice seen as a lesser way to ascend the ladder of perfection. This understanding of the human reality of sex has dominated much of Christian spirituality since mediaeval times.

In the sixteenth century Martin Luther and other reformers effected a dramatic break from this viewpoint by reaffirming marriage as the normal way of Christian holiness. Yet Christians continued to display their ambivalence towards sexuality. Attitudes antithetical to the sense of the sacredness of the human body have appeared in nearly every Christian faith community. In another sexually related area, women have been relegated to a secondary, if not a subservient status among Christians in every era. Sexism has been one of the oldest offsprings of the Hebrew patriarchial period.

In the theological framework described above, therefore, sexuality, seen principally as a physical reality, has been considered at least a serious hindrance to a Christian spiritual life.

2. A radically different view of sexuality claims its roots in the lyrical description of human creation in Gen. 1.27: 'So God created human beings, making them like himself. He created them male and female.' Here the emphasis is placed on human sexuality as a God-given gift affirming that human beings image God when they join together to complement each other. Sex must be distinguished from sexuality; the latter refers to the human capacity to enter into relationship as body-person. Sex is seen as the genital expression of sexuality, the very language of sexuality.

This view of human life equates human wholeness with holiness. The Christian quest for holiness is a call to total human integration. Through the life, death and resurrection of Jesus Christ human beings are summoned to mirror more closely the image of God in which they are created. Spirituality is the style by which the believer integrates all aspects of life. Clearly, then, sexuality, the human capacity to establish relationships with others as body-persons, assumes a key role in this life journey towards holiness. The call to holiness demands that the Christian embrace his/her sexuality, try to understand it and grow into the full potential which this gift of sexuality promises. This theological orientation is therefore positive, profoundly humanistic.

Historically this view of sexuality traces its roots not only to the Genesis creation account, but also to the Song of Songs *, the unusual piece of biblical literature which has been the subject of considerable controversy through the centuries. Contemporary commentators see this poem primarly in its first meaning as a human love song and only secondarily as an allegory describing God's relationship with his people. The Song of Songs, according to this understanding, merits a place in the canon of scripture precisely because it narrates the most sacred of human events, the love between two people. Rather than being an embarrassment, the vivid sensuousness and even eroticism of the Song portray a celebration of sexual love. That this literal interpretation met strong opposition among both Jewish and Christian commentators testifies to the deep impact of the negative view of sexuality.

With this more positive approach in mind, some present-day NT scholars do not hesitate to address the previously taboo topic of the sexuality of Jesus himself. Here the discussion focuses not on Jesus' sex-life, about which nothing substantial can be said with biblical evidence, but rather on Jesus' capacity to enter into relationships. Indeed, observing the movement of Jesus' life, one is struck by the Son of man's ability to establish deep, trusting relationships with people of both sexes and from all walks of life. From prostitute to law-abiding Jew, from fisherman to tax collector, all were drawn to this appealing personality. The person of Jesus, in fact, became the occasion for their entry into the process of metanoia, 'seeing things anew', and hence accepting God's salvation. The sexuality of Jesus, therefore, is not an obscure, peripheral factor in his redemptive work.

To a great extent this positive view of sexuality adopts the insights drawn not only from biblical studies, but also from humanistic psychology with its studies on the developmental process of human beings. Men and women grow to wholeness in relationship to others. The personal, inner search, though essential, finds its necessary complement in one's growth in intimacy with others. Awareness of sin and of personal inadequacy finds a balance in self-acceptance as a body-person. Celebrating the body through a healthy sensuousness and achieving a freedom from fear-imposing sexual taboos represent milestones on the sexual-spiritual journey. Finally, the studies of Jungian psychology have added the notion of androgyny, the integration of both masculine and feminine traits in the person who would be truly whole and holy. In discovering the fullness to which one is called in the act of creation, a person discovers the loving, ever-creating God as well. This incarnational principle is essential in Christian spirituality.

This view of the role of sexuality in spirituality includes the distinctive life-styles of single, married and celibate people. All are called to the basic task of discovering their true selves and God within the setting of their sexuality. Although this view claims biblical origins, it represents a relatively recent development in the history of Christian spirituality.

E. Dufresne, *Partnership: Marriage and the Committed Life*, 1974; H. Gollwitzer, *Song of Love*, 1979; R. Haughton, *The Mystery of Sexuality*, 1972; *Transformation of Man*, 1967; U. Holmes and R. T. Barnhouse (eds), *Male and Female: Christian Approaches to Sexuality*, 1976; A. Kosnik et al, *Human Sexuality*, 1977; J. Nelson, *Embodiment*, 1978; J. Ohanneson, *And They Felt No Shame*, 1983.

DANIEL DIDOMIZIO

Silence

'There was silence in Heaven for what seemed half an hour': this text from Rev. 8.1 is not easily explained but it does suggest reverence in the presence of God. *Elected Silence* (1949) was the title of Thomas Merton's autobiographical account of his choice of silence in the life of a Trappist monk. The catch phrase 'silence is golden' suggests the deep value of silence.

Ladislaus Boros in *God is With Us* (1967),

discerns three kinds of silence used by Jesus. 1. A 'test', in John 8.1–11, when silence moved people to shame; 2. 'Knowledge', in Luke 22.63–65, when the mocking words 'who hit you?' was met by silence; 3. 'Mercy', in Luke 22.54–62, when at Peter's denial, Jesus turned and looked silently at him.

Silence has always been an integral part of worship. In the Middle Ages 'secret prayers' and private devotions were added to the liturgy. These were dropped by the reformers who recited the whole eucharistic prayer aloud in English. The Tractarians reintroduced 'secret prayers' which were also used in the Roman *Ordo* up to 1966. The Alternative Service Book 1980 returned to the printed spoken word with directives to silence in all the services. The chief purpose of silence in worship is to be attentive to God. The monks at Taizé in France make a practice of keeping silence after the reading of scripture. The Community of the Resurrection at Mirfield do the same. These silences are felt to be active and dynamic. They constitute a genuine 'waiting upon God' in corporate prayer. The absence of such creative use of silence in church services today may be in part responsible for the considerable lack of interest in church worship by the young. We think that 'by our much speaking' we shall make a successful relationship with God. Not so. Anglican and Free Church worship is full of busyness: Roman Catholics do rather better as their churches are open and people learn to use them for silent prayer.

Spiritual life and growth flourish when silence becomes part of human life. Retreats* for spiritual training and refreshment offer unique opportunities to experience silence. St Benedict* differentiated between *silentium*, absolute silence, and *taciturnitas*, relative silence. We move only slowly into deep silence as we become aware of the numinous presence of God. Prayer then becomes a combination of quiet and talk, until we reach the stage when meditation and contemplation take over and the spiritual life is 'hidden with Christ in God'.

Today many look to Eastern religions and to their gurus in an endeavour to escape from the noise and bustle of a secular world. A common concern for silence draws Eastern and Western Christendom nearer together. Aspirants are able to study the masters of spirituality in Christianity and in other faiths. The art of contemplation can be learnt in all faiths. For Christians the writings of John of the Cross*, Francis de Sales*, Père Grou, Evelyn Underhill*, Staretz Silouan, R. Somerset Ward* and many others all emphasize silence in the interior life of the soul. God raises up spiritual directors and counsellors to illuminate this study and prayer (*see* **Direction, Spiritual**). Michael Ramsey writes, 'the only initiation into silence is silence. And when the silence is continuous it ceases to be merely negative – not talking – and it begins to have the quality of depth.'

Silence has to be built into the spiritual life in a realistic way. Quaker worship has learnt to do this. In silence we learn to ask the right questions about God, about the world, and about ourselves. Without silence we become so many 'tinkling gongs and clanging cymbals'.

William Johnston, *Silent Music*, 1974.

N. W. GOODACRE

Society of Friends
see **Quaker Spirituality**

Society of Jesus *see* **Jesus, Society of**

Song of Songs, The

A collection of love poems, generally dated from the third century BC, richly sensual, though in no way salacious or pornographic. Its place in the Jewish canon puzzled some Rabbis, but it was defended by the explanation that it was the 'Song of Songs' i.e. the loveliest, and analogous to the Holy of Holies. This led to allegorical interpretation, which Christians, inheriting the book along with the rest of the OT, adopted too, though from Theodore of Mopsuestia (d. 428) onwards there have been those who insisted that it should be taken *au pied de la lettre*. Jewish allegory applied the lovers' language to the relation of God to Israel, in the spirit of Hosea. It was eventually incorporated into the Paschal liturgy, though perhaps not until the Middle Ages. The Christian Hippolytus (*c.* 215) expounded 3.1–4 at Easter and like the AV of the English Bible interpreted the Song as of Christ and the church. Origen*, while not by any means losing this, began the long tradition of treating the Song as an account of the mystical union of Christ and the soul.

Origen finds seven songs in the OT, corresponding to seven stages of the Christian life. The first is baptism typified by Israel's crossing of the Red Sea; the last is the Song of Songs, the crown and climax of the spiritual journey. Origen is not disturbed by the literal meaning. There are spiritual senses corresponding to the physical, and his Platonism means that even the incarnation is but a glass through which we see darkly until at last we behold God face to face. His exegesis does not teach a mysticism of absorption or ecstasies. He is aware from his own experience both as a scholar and a man that the divine lover comes and goes, and that love bears wounds through the ardour of desire – intellectual desire – not completely fulfilled. But there is no un-relieved darkness.

Gregory of Nyssa's commentary differs from Origen in that the consummation is itself wounding in that it pierces the soul with ever more intense desire. The soul is always following after God, always ascending. And the ascent is never solitary. Like the bride with her maidens, the soul is always accompanied by those who are drawn to her for God's sake.

We must not conclude that the Christian mysticism of the Song is ever unmindful of the church. Bernard of Clairvaux's* exposition is the most famous and influential of all. The allegory may at times be quaint, but the psychology is profound. He swings delicately between the interpretation of the Bride as the church and the Bride as the individual giving countenance to no un-healthy eroticism in personal religion. There is an impressive unity of contemplation and action and strong moral tone; but over all is the love of Jesus, glorified, but still 'known in that humanity in which he walked the earth' (K. E. Kirk), who in his labour and sufferings lies as a bundle of myrrh between the breasts, not a burden borne on our shoulders, but before our eyes, through whom we bear our own burdens and find our delight in God, and his in us. John of the Cross* also drew extensively on the Song's imagery in his writing (*see* **Spiritual Canticle**).

No divines were more prolific in their writing on the Song of Songs than the seventeenth-century English Puritans*, who much revered Bernard, and drew on his work. The mainstream Puritans are more cautious in their use of the Song's language than those of a more independent turn. Richard Sibbes (1577–1635) insists that the Bride is the church, though since 'all Christian favours belong to all Christians alike ... every Christian soul is the Spouse of Christ as well as the whole church'. The divine lover's kisses are Christ's presence in the ordinances; the sacraments are his love tokens, and though the soul longs for Christ and every taste whets her appetite the more, she receives him in his appointed ways, and not, as a rule through special and private raptures. The Cornish layman, Francis Rous (1579–1659), Speaker of the House of Commons, and one who passed from the Presbyterians to the Independents, in his treatise on *The Mysticall Marriage* is concerned much more with individual spirituality and his language is less restrained than that of Sibbes – or Baxter* or Bunyan*. But his book is emphatically ethical and full of wise counsels of contemplation. Nor does he encourage spiritual indulgence, or a living from one consolation to another. Christ and his love 'are thine when thou seest or feelest not that they are thine . . . He and his love are better than the seeing and feeling of him and his love.'

There is no better epitome of the traditional understanding of the Song than Charles Wesley's* remarkable lyric based on 1.7, 'Thou Shepherd of Israel and mine', which relates the individual's communion with Christ to life in the company of believers, and by associating the 'noon' of the shepherd's repose in the Song with Cavalry finds the secret of ecstasy in the fellowship of Christ's sufferings and the power of his resurrection.

Modern exegesis deserts allegory, and it is doubtful if the Song looms large in devotion today, but its natural meaning is valued by many, its place in scripture prized as witness to the fact that God made sex, and its celebration of mutuality between male and female may have 'something new to teach us about how to redeem sexuality and love in our fallen world' (Marcia Falk). Karl Barth regarded it as the apogee of scripture.

Marcia Falk, *Love Lyrics from the Bible*, 1982; Kenneth E. Kirk, *The Vision of God*, 1931; Andrew Louth, *The Origins of the Christian Mystical Tradition*, 1981; H. H. Rowley, *The Servant of the Lord*, 1952, pp.

189–234; G. S. Wakefield, *Puritan Devotion*, 1957.

EDITOR

Spirit, Holy

In matters of spirituality as concerning the Spirit it is important and wise always to bear in mind the earliest understanding of the Spirit in Judaeo-Christian belief, as well as the earliest specifically Christian teaching.

'Spirit' is the word used from the earliest traditions behind the OT to denote the mysterious invisible power of God, manifested in the wind (e.g. Ex. 10.13, 19), in the breath of life (e.g. Gen. 6.3; Ps. 104.29–30) and in the ecstatic power of charismatic leader and prophet (e.g. Judg. 6.34; 13.25; I Sam. 10.6, 10). In particular the sense of continuity between the creative energy of God and man's own inner vitality is fundamental to all spirituality – the awareness that one's life in this three-dimensional world is sustained, can be influenced and animated at hidden depths of the human being by the cosmic power of God. It is this recognition of continuity between God's creative power and man's inner being which explains the difficulty of knowing whether to translate 'Spirit' (of God) or 'spirit' (of man) at several points in the Bible. But continuity is never allowed to become identity. In so far as man is recipient of God's Spirit, it never becomes simply man's spirit. The spiritual person is always conscious of his dependency on the Spirit as God's: 'Take not your holy Spirit from me' (Ps. 51.11); 'Where can I escape from your Spirit?' (Ps. 139.7).

In Judaism the Spirit has been typically and pre-eminently the Spirit of prophecy (e.g. Neh. 9.20, 30; Isa. 59.21; Ezek. 2.2; Mic. 3.8), 'prophecy' being understood not simply as a foretelling of the future or as a speaking out in forthright manner on controversial issues, but as a speaking and acting under inspiration. It is this sense of a divine compulsion overriding other considerations which marks out the ancient prophet (e.g. Jer. 20.9; Amos 3.8). The same combination of inspiration and compulsion is evident in the consistent NT emphasis on the Spirit as the Spirit of mission (John 20.21–22; Acts 1.8; I Cor. 2.4–5; Heb. 2.4; I Peter 1.12).

Christianity began within this prophetic tradition. The first Christians believed that the prophetic hope of one anointed by the Spirit had been fulfilled in Jesus (Isa. 11.2; 61.1–3), and of a wider dispersion of the Spirit on all God's people at Pentecost (Joel 2.28–29; Acts 2). Both these assertions are fundamental to Christian spirituality, since both mark for Christians the beginning of a new epoch in God's dealings with humankind.

1. Jesus is the uniquely conceived and anointed one (Matt. 1.18; Mark 1.10–11), whose anointing brings to concrete expression the power of God's final rule on earth (Matt. 12.28) and has in view the broadening out of God's saving purpose to all the world (Matt. 12.18–21; Luke 4.16–27). But as such his anointing becomes archetypal for those of the Spirit in future generations (John 3.34), so that the Spirit can be more clearly defined as 'the Spirit of Jesus' (Acts 16.7; Phil. 1.19; I Peter 1.11), and the mark of the Spirit's inspiration and grace becomes the quality and character of Jesus' own spirituality.

2. So, too, the decisive act of faith through which one enters into the company of Jesus' disciples in the new age is from the first understood in terms of the Spirit – the gift of the Spirit, receiving the Spirit, being baptized in the Spirit, etc. (e.g. John 7.37–39; Acts 2.38, 11.15–17; Rom. 8.9; Gal. 3.2–3; Heb. 6.4). Fundamental here is the recognition that this gift is only the first fruit, the first instalment of God's complete salvation (Rom. 8.23; II Cor. 1.21–22; Eph. 1.13–14; Phil. 1.6). Since the believer in the interim still belongs to this world his experience as a believer is inevitably one of spiritual tension between the life of the Spirit and his belongingness to this age, of warfare between Spirit and flesh (Gal. 5.13–26). Such tension is the mark of life, not of disease, and even suffering and defeat (when experienced as defeat) can be a sign of hope (Rom. 5.3–5; 7–8; II Cor. 4.7–5.5).

The experiential character of the Spirit's coming and presence in the believer's life is given considerable prominence in the NT. Luke particularly emphasizes the ecstatic quality of this earliest experience of the Spirit (e.g. Acts 2.1–4; 4.31; 19.6). Prophets, speaking under immediate inspiration, evidently played an important role in the earliest churches (e.g. Acts 11.27; I Cor. 14; Eph. 2.20; I Thess. 5.19–20; Rev. 1.3; 19.10; Did. 11–13). For Paul the community of faith grew out of the shared experience of the Spirit (I Cor. 12.13; II Cor. 13.13; Eph. 4.3; Phil. 2.1–2) and the body of Christ in each place was essentially charismatic, depending on the Spirit to prompt individuals with particular words and actions which constituted the functions of the body (Rom. 12.3–8; I Cor. 12.4–26). Not least of importance was the belief that the prophetic hope of a more vividly real and immediate relation between God and the believer had been realized (e.g. John 4.13–14; II Cor. 3.3–6; Heb. 8), so that the believer could be encouraged to walk or be led by the Spirit, in contrast to a spirituality and conduct dependent on a written code (Rom 7.6; 8.4; Gal. 5.16, 25).

The emphasis on the Spirit as the Spirit of prophecy within the biblical tradition is accompanied by a recognition of the danger of false prophecy. The attempt to 'tune in' to the power of God on the dimension of the spirit can evidently result in all kinds of self-deception and spiritual arrogance, as the individual convinced of his own inspiration seeks to impose its authority on others. The believer must constantly remember that the line between walking according to the Spirit and according to the flesh is often very narrow indeed (Rom. 8.12–14; 12.2). Paul in particular was very much alive to this danger and his counsel regarding it is of perennial value. Hence the claim to inspiration must always be tested (I Cor. 14.29; I Thess. 5.19–22). One test is whether the inspired utterance accords with the basic axioms of the gospel (I Cor. 12.3). Another is whether the claimed inspiration is exercised in and produces a love genuinely unconcerned for self – the gifts of the Spirit and the fruit of the Spirit can be pulled apart only at considerable peril (I Cor. 13; Gal. 5.16–23). Another is the recognition that spiritual gifts are given for service of others, not for personal aggrandisement (I Cor. 12.5, 7; 14). Even prayer in the Spirit (cf. Rom. 8.26) within the community of faith must be subject to the test, does it benefit my neighbour? (I Cor. 14.12–19). Not least, he who claims to be led by the Spirit or to special experiences from God should never forget that the test of all spirituality is whether it advances in the believer the relationship with God which Jesus enjoyed (Rom. 8.14–17), and whether it conforms the believer to Christ's pattern of life

through death, strength through weakness (II Cor. 12.1–10; Phil. 3.8–14).

In the Johannine writings the understanding of the Spirit is very similar: the immediacy of the Spirit (I John 3.24, 4.13) in worship and teaching (John 4.21–24; 14.26; I John 2.27) must be held in tension with the truth already revealed in Christ (John 16.13–15; I John 2.24). The Spirit is the 'other Paraclete' or Counsellor, the presence of Jesus now that Jesus is no longer in the flesh, whose inspiration reveals its continuity with the incarnation (John 14.16; I John 4.1–3).

Where the Spirit is active there will always be tension – tension between older traditions and immediacy of fresh inspiration, between institutional office and individual prophet, between flesh and Spirit. It is hardly surprising that in the history of the church those movements which most emphasized the Spirit have tended always to be regarded as suspect – whether Montanists or Messalians in early centuries, or Radical Reformers and Pentecostalists more recently. The answer is not to suppress such aspiration after greater directness and richness of spiritual experience, but rather to encourage it within a context which recognizes that diversity of the Spirit's gifts must be both sustained and checked by the maturity of love if the body is to function as one.

H. Berkhof, *The Doctrine of the Holy Spirit*, 1965; J. D. G. Dunn, *Baptism in the Holy Spirit*, 1970; *Jesus and the Spirit*, 1975; T. Hopko, *The Spirit of God*, 1976; C. F. D. Moule, *The Holy Spirit*, 1978; A. M. Ramsey, *Holy Spirit*, 1977; E. Schweizer, *The Holy Spirit*, 1981; T. A. Smail, *Reflected Glory*, 1975; L. J. Suenens, *A New Pentecost?*, 1975; J. V. Taylor, *The Go-Between God*, 1972.

JAMES D. G. DUNN

Spiritual Biographies, Combat, Direction, Journal, Journey, Ladder, Marriage, Reading

see under second word

Spiritual Canticle

The title commonly given to the longest poem by St John of the Cross* and one of the greatest lyrical poems in Spanish literature; also to his prose commentary on it. Both poem and commentary come in two versions. The original poem has thirty-nine five-line stanzas and the revision forty, but in a significantly changed order. Begun during his imprisonment (1577–1578), it was completed after his escape, alongside the first expositions of certain verses. These he turned into a complete commentary on the poem, which was later revised so that its teaching would more closely accord with the traditional three-fold way of purgation, illumination and union.

The poem's two sources are St John's mystical experience and the Bible, notably the Song of Songs*, from which it derives its erotic and natural imagery (lovers, stags, hills, flowers, spices, breezes, night) and its format, an impassioned dialogue between the Bride and Bridegroom. All these elements are freely reworked, and there are also signs of more secular, Spanish influences. It weaves an intensely rich, beautiful and mysterious atmosphere around a fragmented narrative, which begins with anguished questions and exclamations as the Bride seeks her absent Beloved. His brief appearance releases an outpouring of images in which she celebrates his beauty, and his reappearance heralds their union, the theme of the closing stages of the poem.

The second, somewhat longer redaction of the commentary is generally held to represent St John's final intention, though some scholars have doubted its authenticity. It expounds the imagery in detail, and with extensive biblical references relates it to the life of prayer under the controlling symbols of betrothal and marriage. The style is analytical, the dominant theology scholastic, though there are lyrical moments. Some of the allegory seems arbitrary today, especially when one image bears a multiplicity of sometimes contradictory meanings; but behind it stands the ancient and authoritative tradition of the Song of Songs as a love-song between Christ and the soul. Occasionally St John gives a more systematic account of the teaching implicit in the poem: stanzas 1–5 deal with the purgative way, meditation and mortification; 6–13 with the illuminative way, leading to the spiritual betrothal and its effects; and 14–21 with the unitive way, culminating in the marriage. This is preceded by a tormenting sense of the absence of God, as more fully expounded in his *Dark Night of the Soul*. The final verses look to the eternal enjoyment of

God in the beatific vision, and contain important passages on the equality of love between God and the soul, and the transformation of the soul in God.

The commentary is not a systematic mystical treatise like the *Ascent of Mount Carmel* and the *Dark Night*, because it is bound to the poetic text, but it should be read in conjunction with them and the *Flame* to appreciate his teaching fully. The poem remains a witness to the great literature which the highest spiritual experience can inspire, and continues to move many who know little of its author's intended meaning.

The Poems of St John of the Cross, tr Roy Campbell, reprinted 1979; D. Alonso, *La poesia de San Juan de la Cruz*, 1942; E. Pacho, *Cántico espiritual*, 1981; C. P. Thompson, *The Poet and the Mystic*, 1977.

COLIN P. THOMPSON

Spiritual Exercises

The name given to a manual of religious exercises composed by St Ignatius of Loyola*. It is also used to designate retreats conducted according to the plan suggested in the manual. Ignatius began making notes during his stay at Manresa following his conversion in 1521. He added to these jottings over the years. The book was first published in 1548.

The text of the *Spiritual Exercises* was not meant to be read, but to be used as a guide to assist the director who would lead an exercitant through the course of this experience. Much effort has been expended in an effort to discover the sources of the work. Surely his spirituality shows similarities to the *Devotio Moderna*. We know too of his very high regard for *The Imitation of Christ* (see **Thomas à Kempis**). Still, Ignatius's own work has an originality born of his own studies and experience. He tells us that he wrote down 'things that he observed in his own soul and found useful and which he thought would be useful to others'.

The spiritual exercises are primarily a series of religious activities undertaken at the direction of an experienced guide. To experience the complete spiritual exercises requires approximately thirty days. Ignatius allows for and recommends a great deal of flexibility in adopting the experience to the needs, talents, etc. of the individual. The strictest form of the exercises is in the form of a retreat of thirty days prayer in complete silence and apart from a person's ordinary activities and surroundings. In a typical day of such a retreat the exercitant has an interview with his director and spends four or five hours in prayer in addition to attendance at daily liturgy.

The spiritual exercises are divided into four sections which are called Weeks, but which Ignatius reminds us need not occupy a period of seven days each. The First Week is preceded by a kind of preamble called First Principle and Foundation. This is a consideration concerning creation, the purpose of life, and the proper relationship of a person to the rest of creation. The First Week is devoted to prayer about sin and its consequences. The process moves from the history of sin in the world to the individual's involvement in sin and God's mercy towards the sinner. The Second Week begins with a contemplation of Christ's kingship over the world. There follows a series of contemplations on the mysteries of Christ's life up to the Last Supper. During this week various exercises are proposed to assist the retreatant to make choices about the direction of his or her life or about a better fulfilment of choices already made. The Third Week brings the retreatant to share in the sufferings and death of Jesus and to appreciate his saving love in the passion. Finally, the Fourth Week leads the retreatant to an experience of the joy Jesus shared with his followers in his Risen life. The concluding exercise is a profound and intimate experience of the many gifts of God's love to the individual and an invitation to an appropriate response of love in return.

See also **Indifference; Jesus, Society of.**

D. L. Fleming (ed), *The Spiritual Exercises of St Ignatius*, 1978; D. M. Stanley. *A Modern Scriptural Approach to the Spiritual Exercises*, 1967.

GERARD J. CAMPBELL, SJ

Spiritualism

1. In philosophy, one of various doctrines which identify Spirit as the only or major reality. 2. In history, a movement which arose in New England in 1848 and spread worldwide, proclaiming communication with the dead through mediums. The term 'Modern Spiritualism' distinguishes it from

mediumship found in ancient cultures, and today in primitive societies studied by anthropologists such as Beattie and Middleton. In R C countries, it takes the predominant form of Spiritism, a system formalized by Allan Kardec (1803–1869). Kardec taught reincarnation, which was initially opposed by 'Anglo-Saxon' Spiritualists, though reincarnation has gradually become widely accepted by them. Some Christian writers also employ the term Spiritism to repudiate any suggestion of spirituality in the worldwide movement; but as Thurston points out, the term Spiritualism was in use by adherents by 1852.

Spiritualism is an amorphous, protean and syncretistic influence, which reflects the notions of the surrounding culture, especially optimism about human nature, science and social improvement. Apart from fashionable centres in major cities, organized Spiritualism has been mainly a working-class movement, and anti-Christian rhetoric in the movement has been similar to 'protestant' criticism of established religion. Spiritualist activists commonly reject what they believe to be the full Christian scheme – the Trinity, Incarnation, Fall, Atonement, and settling of the fate of the soul at death. The unique status of Jesus Christ is denied by some Spiritualist authorities, and not mentioned by others, though Spiritualist churches may be very similar to mainstream Free Churches in architecture and procedure. There is also an explicitly Christian Spiritualist minority, which makes more use of the Bible and of rites such as baptism.

It quickly became apparent after 1848 that 'mental phenomena', information supposedly communicated by spirits through mediums in trance and by other means, could not be taken at face value; and that 'physical phenomena' the paranormal exertion of force to move objects, could be simulated. Scientific and other serious intellectual interest led to the formation of the Society for Psychical Research in London in 1882. A further century of investigation, including the sustained study of some mediums, has not led to decisive evidence that the dead are involved in the phenomena, though equally the evidence is too strong and diverse to be ignored. The validity of electronic devices said to facilitate communication with the dead is not admitted by scientific observers. Much of the material offered by a medium may originate in the minds of the medium and of others present – or even the minds of others absent, such is the complexity of the human psyche and the limits, so far unknown, of its telepathic abilities.

Christians responded immediately to the rise of Modern Spiritualism, pointing out its evidential flaws, the incidence of fraud, and the possible role of the revival of one of the sins of King Saul (I Sam. 28) as a sign of the approaching End. Christian criticism grew when war bereavement increased recruitment to Spiritualism, and during the post-1960 growth of occultism; though organized Spiritualism, with its Victorian image, has not been as successful as some new cults which also use psychic powers.

A severe warning about the dangers of psychic involvements, such as mediumship, to the spiritual life, is a widespread feature of world religion. The Spiritualist Movement overlaps at many points with the occult, and prohibitions of involvement with occult practitioners are found throughout scripture (Deut. 18; Acts 16.16, 19.19; Gal. 5.20; Rev. 21.8). Spiritualist involvement is likely to bring contact with non-Christian ideas and practices (for example, yoga* or oriental meditation), and to stir doubt about Christian authority. The charismatic renewal of 1960–1980 reminded the church of need for discernment of spirits*, and although Spiritualism is not the main focus of evil in the contemporary world, there is a steady stream of casualties from unwise psychic exploration known to diocesan advisors and others with pastoral responsibility, especially among the young.

Final assessment of Spiritualism will depend on our eschatology, and whether it theoretically permits the dead to return (as some Catholic and many Evangelical theologians have denied). Recent theological accounts of the Last Things take account of the problem of Spiritualist evidence. For those whose theology permits post-mortem return (in presence at the eucharist, in dream, or vision) it is wise not to deny the possibility of involvement by the dead, the non-Christian dead in particular, in the production of some communications through mediums, though there is also evidence of non-human entities assisting in 'physical phenomena'. The modern church has gone some way towards reviving the healing

ministry, which has been a prominent factor in Spiritualist recruitment. But care of the bereaved is inadequate in parts of the church, and until this is enhanced, the appeal of Spiritualism cannot be contained.

It should be added that Christian responses to Spiritualism should not exaggerate, distort or dehumanize Spiritualists. In large measure, Modern Spiritualism is a protest movement (against lifeless congregational life, distant leadership, uncomprehended theology and other blemishes) and most Spiritualists can eventually find their way back to the church. Moreover God does use deviant religious movements (such as the Samaritans in the NT) to remind the church of areas and insights overlooked.

John Beattie and John Middleton, *Spirit Mediumship and Society in Africa*, 1969; Slater Brown, *The Heyday of Spiritualism*, 1970; Alan Gauld, *The Founders of Psychical Research*, 1968; *Mediumship and Survival*, 1982; G. K. Nelson, *Spiritualism and Society*, 1969; Herbert Thurston, SJ, *The Church and Spiritualism*, 1933.

LESLIE PRICE

Spirituality

This is a word which has come much into vogue to describe those attitudes, beliefs, practices which animate people's lives and help them to reach out towards super-sensible realities. It has not always had this meaning in English. In the fifteenth and sixteenth centuries, it stood for the clergy as a distinct order of society, and sometimes for ecclesiastical property or revenue. Later, it distinguished the spiritual from the material or bodily. Its modern meaning was covered by 'Piety' or Jeremy Taylor's 'The Rule and Exercise of Holy Living'. 'Spiritualité' was used in seventeenth-century French, though in a pejorative sense at first. 'La nouvelle spiritualité' of Madame Guyon* was a type of mysticism to be condemned because *inter alia* it was too refined, rarefied, insufficiently related to earthly life. But it was no large step from this for spirituality to become an irreproachable term defining the life of prayer and discipline with perhaps a hint of 'higher levels' and mystical elements. The Abbé Pourrat divided theology into three branches – dogmatic, moral and – 'above them but based on them' – spiritual. In this last, R. Newton Flew's *The Idea of Perfec-

tion in Christian Theology (1934) claims to be an essay. He would, however, disagree with Pourrat's statement that spiritual theology is founded on the rational formulations of the other two. 'I would rather say that the *Theologia Dogmatica* of the future may be built on the *Theologia Spiritualis* of the past' (p. xi).

What is not always recognized is that 'spirituality' need not necessarily be Christian, i.e. derived from and inspired by the revelation of God in Christ. All religions have their spiritualities. And 'spirituality' is not always good. Adolf Hitler was a spiritual being, a man, more than most, 'possessed'; yet his spirit was surely evil.

Alexander Schmemann, the Orthodox theologian, would substitute 'Christian life' for 'spirituality', 'because the latter term today has become ambiguous and confusing. For many people it means some mysterious and self-contained activity, a secret which can be broken into by the study of some "spiritual techniques".' The prevalent restless search for 'spirituality' and 'mysticism' may be unhealthy. 'Spiritual sobriety' has been the 'source and foundation of the truly Christian spiritual tradition', not corybantic excitement, or abnormal phenomena, or even special revelations. 'Too many self-appointed "elders" and "spiritual teachers", exploiting what may be a genuine spiritual thirst and hunger, in fact lead their followers into dangerous spiritual dead ends.' Christian spirituality 'concerns and embraces the whole life'. Paul's 'new life' is not another life, but the life which God has given us 'renewed, transformed and transfigured by the Holy Spirit' (*Of Water and the Spirit*, 1976, p. 107).

This means that Christian spirituality is not simply for 'the interior life' or the inward person, but as much for the body as the soul, and is directed to the implementation of both the commandments of Christ, to love God and our neighbour. Indeed, our love, like God's, should extend to the whole creation. Christian spirituality at its most authentic includes in its scope both humanity and nature. There is need for asceticism*, for control of natural appetites, for mental discipline, self-denial and sometimes for renunciation of a lesser for the greater good. But even St John of the Cross*, whom Reinhold Niebuhr condemned for his harsh detachment – 'Live in this world as though there were in it but God and thy soul, so that thy heart may be detained by naught that is human' – also declares that 'He who loves not his neighbour hates God' and says 'the deeper our love for God, the deeper is our love for our neighbour. For when love is rooted in God, the reason for all love is one and the same, the cause of all love is one and the same.' And in his poetry, there are many images from nature. It is as though what is given up for the love of God is received back to be enjoyed by spiritual senses which are constantly quickened.

Orthodox spirituality*, too, particularly in such a writer as St Seraphim of Sarov (1759–1833), exults in this world and believes that all creatures, every tree and every animal, are to be enjoyed, rather as Thomas Traherne* perceives the corn as 'orient and immortal wheat' and sees the children playing in the streets as 'moving jewels'. Nor is Richard Sibbes, the Puritan, alone of his kind in believing that' the world is the theatre of God's glory'.

The quotation from Sibbes reminds us that those Protestant and biblical theologians who are suspicious of scholastic and mystical spirituality and fear that the Carmel we are bidden ascend may be the Sinai of bondage and all our asceticism dead works, are not as pessimistic about the realm of nature as is often popularly supposed and believe that it has place in the Christian life. Sir Edwyn Hoskyns (1884–1937), though brought up in the tradition of the Oxford Movement*, was temperamentally allergic to pietism and religiosity of all kinds. He dreaded the escape into 'spirituality' which was causing contemporary Anglo-Catholics to ignore historical and critical issues and, indeed, ethics; 'devotion' seemed more important to them than either truth or conduct. He preferred *The Farmer and Stockbreeder* to precious manuals of self-examination. The Gospel proclaims the futility of our good works as much as of our sins and yet announces a new heaven and a new earth. '. . . At the supreme point, at Jerusalem where the Lord was crucified, the whole world – please notice, the *whole world* – comes back to us in all its vigorous energy, shining with the reflected glory of the God who made it and us, and with the reflected love of the God who made both it and us'. (*Cambridge Sermons*, p. 93).

There is, then, a difference between Catholic and Protestant spirituality, in that the one will lay more emphasis in our own effort towards God, of union consummating purgation and illumination, whereas for the other all is of God's justifying mercy and this begins the mystical union, which is the first work of saving grace in our hearts. For the Protestant evangelical everything starts with the joyful experience of sins forgiven which for the Catholic may be fully realized only at the end; while sanctity is not attained so much by a deliberate rule supervised by a priestly director, as by the disciplines which life itself imposes and the grace to discern God's providence in all the events and struggles of the spiritual journey through the world and its changing scenes. For this, pastors and spiritual guides are essential; they are often preachers. Bunyan's pilgrims had their Greatheart and, earlier, Christian had Evangelist, the Interpreter and his companions. They are not lords of faith but helpers of joy.

It is wrong to exaggerate the differences between Catholic and Protestant spirituality. The Reformers did not abandon the Western mediaeval tradition, and they believed that saints such as Augustine* and Bernard of Clairvaux* would have been on their side in the great debate. John of the Cross* was in some ways a Protestant among Catholics, and affinities have been pointed out between him and Luther* and Kierkegaard* in their understanding of the soul's relation to God. In our own time a theologian of spirituality such as Karl Rahner well understands the doctrine of justification by faith alone. But there are differences of culture and of ecclesiology; and, above all, over the nature of authority.

Christian spirituality is itself a synthesis and has undergone many developments. In the first millenium it was profoundly influenced by Neoplatonist* philosophy and monasticism*. Some twentieth-century Protestant scholars, such as the Lutheran Anders Nygren in *Agape and Eros*, have sought to return to a supposedly biblical purity based firmly on Hebraic understanding, almost echoing Tertullian's* question 'What has Athens to do with Jerusalem?' This attempt fails for two reasons – first, a living, organic religion must develop even though in different directions and at the price of variety and controversy and one cannot go back completely to the beginning, while secondly, recent scholarship, with the Dead Sea Scrolls and a great deal of OT and NT background material at its disposal, is unwilling to isolate one authentic 'biblical' strand from what is a confused, if rich, tapestry. The unity of the Bible is a myth.

The relation of Christian spirituality to that of other religions is a matter which is likely to loom ever larger in the next decades. There have been influences, there are similarities. John of the Cross* writes like a Buddhist at times, and some Christians may be drawn to Judaism*, Buddhism* and Islam* especially when they encounter their finest teachers and exemplars. The 'fundamentalists' of Judaism, Islam and Christianity are less hospitable to other faiths and less attractive to sensitive, intellectual seekers. A Logos theology would maintain that the Divine Word, incarnate in Christ, is present wherever there is goodness and truth, and those influenced by a thinker such as F. D. Maurice (1805–1872) would want to assert that Christ is head of all mankind and even those who do not know him are not excluded from his redemption. But there are differences too radical to be smoothed over at summer schools.

Christian spirituality may seem to suffer from an embarrassment of riches. Confused syncretism and retreat into 'pietistic' and bigoted sentimentality are both to be deplored. Let heart speak to heart, but there must also be an enlargement of the mind, which demands its own asceticism. Mutual indwelling with God in Christ is at once the means and the end; but this is a being caught up into the paschal mystery, not absorption into the infinite, and it cannot deliver us from the sometimes unbearable tensions, dangers and sufferings of 'the world of action'.

L. Bouyer, et al, *A History of Christian Spirituality,* vols I, II and III, 1968, 1982; Peter Brooks (ed), *Christian Spirituality*, 1975; V. A. Demant, *A Two-Way Religion*, 1957; F. Heiler, *Prayer*, ET 1932; A. L. Lilley, *Prayer in Christian Theology*, 1924; Andrew Louth, *Discerning the Mystery*, 1983; Anders Nygren, *Agape and Eros*, ET 1953; Rowan Williams, *The Wound of Knowledge*, 1979; P. Pourrat, *Christian Spirituality*, 3 vols, 1922–1927; R. C. Zaehner, *Mysticism Sacred and Profane*, 1957.

EDITOR

Steiner, Rudolf
see **German Spirituality**

Sufism
The early development of mystical movements in Islam * is one of the most remarkable features of this prophetic and conquering religion. The name Sufi, which came to be applied to all Muslim mystics, was formed from the word *suf* used of a cloak of white wool which was worn after the model of Christian monks. From this the act of devoting oneself to a mystical life was called Tasawwuf. Suggestions that Sufi came from the Greek *sophia* are now generally rejected.

That Muhammad was a mystic is claimed by Sufis and denied by their critics. This prophetic figure, a successful soldier and administrator, claimed profound religious experiences but whether they can be regarded as mysticism depends largely on whether radical distinctions are made between a devout religious life and the mystical way. When Muhammad reached the age of forty he came to love solitude and went at times to a cave on Mount Hira near Mecca to pray and there Gabriel brought him the command of God to prophesy. He covered his head with a robe in receiving revelations, had auditory and probably visual experiences, spoke of the greatness of God but also of his nearness, 'closer than the jugular vein', the Face of God being wherever one may turn. Sufis interpret Muhammad's visionary ascent to heaven as an image of the ascent of the soul to God.

Christian influence upon the emergence of Sufism has been traced by Margaret Smith in *The Way of the Mystics* (1976). Islam developed in the Near and Middle East where there were many hermits and monks. The Koran * itself speaks of Christians as 'those who are nearest in love' to Muslims, 'because among them there are priests and monks' (5, 85). But commentators differed in interpretations of another text which seemed to state either that God had given Christians 'monasticism' or 'that they had invented it' (57, 27). The Islamic principle that People of the Book should be free to practise their religion meant that when Islamic armies came Christians were generally spared. Christian monasteries were open to early Islamic mystics and they could study their devotional books. Later the lines between the religions were drawn more rigidly and only in modern times have Christians and Muslims shared again in devotional conferences and retreats.

Western writers have often concentrated upon individual Sufis, but J. S. Trimingham in *The Sufi Orders in Islam* (1971) emphasizes the organizational aspect of these orders, their practical discipline and ritual performances. A *faqir* was the Arabic name for a religious mendicant which in Persian was a dervish (*darwesh*) as a member of a religious fraternity. Sufis taught a Way (*tariqa*) of organization and worship in a relation of master (*murshid*) and disciple (*murid*). Each brotherhood had forms of 'recollection' (*dhikr*), glorifying God by repeating words or phrases, sometimes with special breathings or the use of prayer beads, and seeking to advance by 'stages' to experiences of divine reality. Early mystical groups were loose, with members travelling from one master to another, but houses for such wanderers developed into monasteries and convents though they were more open than Christian enclosed or fortress monasteries. A saying attributed to Muhammad, 'there is no monkery in Islam', is now known to be apocryphal, but although there were celibates in Sufism yet Islam like Judaism has prized marriage and the sense-world, and Sufi masters were often married.

Women as well as men followed the Sufi way and one of the most famous early mystics was a celibate woman, Rabi'a of Basra. Like other Sufis she taught the indifferent love of God or the ardent desire of the lover of God which led on to 'unity' (*tawhid*) which became a central technical term. The Persian Abu Yazid in the third Islamic century spoke of the 'body of unity' and the 'tree of unity', but this apparent pantheism was opposed by Junayd of Baghdad. The mystic sought 'oblivion' or 'annihilation' (*fana*) in God, though Junayd claimed that the soul is united to God without being annihilated. The Persian mystic Hallaj declared 'I am the Real' which was taken as blasphemous deification and he was martyred in Baghdad in AD 922. Apparent pantheism or monism in Sufism has been claimed as influence from non-dualistic Hindu philosophy, but the evidence adduced has been strongly disputed.

The biographers of Hallaj claimed that he followed the example of Jesus and prayed like him for his executioners. Jesus was often taken as a pattern of mystical life and his poverty was emphasized, with his purity giving him the title 'seal of the saints'. There were many great Persian mystics. Hafiz, Attar and other poets celebrated divine and human love, and this can be traced in the verses of Omar Khayyam. The philosopher Ghazali in the twelfth century is said to have made mysticism orthodox, teaching *tawhid* as the unity of God. One of the most famous Persian mystics was Rumi in the thirteenth century whose Mathnawi, 'rhyming couplets' in six books, has been called 'the Koran in the Persian tongue'. He taught that the one light of God appeared in different religions and that all creatures will be saved through the love of God. Rumi is said to have founded the Whirling or Dancing Dervishes who still give slow circular dances to music (which is banned in mosques) and go into trance.

Some of the mystical orders became corrupt or superstitious and they have been attacked by Muslim modernists. They were banned in secular Turkey, yet new movements such as the Nurculars, 'children of light', have arisen and the Whirling Dervishes survive in Turkey. There have been revivals of militant fundamentalist Islam and semi-mystical Muslim Brotherhoods, from Iran to Egypt and beyond, and also of more spiritual Sufism. J. S. Trimingham concludes that the Path is for the few who are prepared to pay the price, but it remains vital for the spiritual welfare of mankind.

In addition to titles mentioned in the text, see Kenneth Cragg, *The Wisdom of the Sufis*, 1976; Geoffrey Parrinder, *Mysticism in the World's Religions*, 1976; R. C. Zaehner, *Hindu and Muslim Mysticism*, 1960.

GEOFFREY PARRINDER

Sunday

1. *Names*. (i) In Jewish tradition and in the Gospels (Mark 16.2 par.; John 20.19) Sunday is termed 'the first day'. The Christian week also begins with it; that should be stressed, in spite of the modern tendency to make Sunday the end of the week. (ii) The new Christian name for Sunday, 'The Lord's Day', appears as early as Rev. 1.10; it is still used in Slavonic and Romance languages. This designation brings out the fact that Sunday belongs to the risen Lord and presumably also that the Lord's Supper is celebrated on it (cf. I Cor. 11.20). (iii) Even in antiquity the days of the week were also named after the seven planets (which at that time also included the sun and the moon). The Christian church took over these pagan names without too much hesitation; in the case of Sunday the adoption of this terminology could bring with it a rich symbolism: Christ is the true sun (Christmas Day on 25 December is a parallel case). (iv) Occasionally we also find the designation 'the eighth day'.

2. *Origin and content of its observance*. (i) It is occasionally claimed that the Christian observance of Sunday has a pagan origin (the cult of the sun) or derives from Judaism (Qumran). So far no historical evidence has been found for this. Therefore the observance of Sunday is most probably Christian in origin (the earliest allusions are in I Cor. 16.2; Acts 20.7; cf. the Easter stories). It is rooted directly in the Easter event. (ii) Christian Sunday celebrations originally took place in the evening. Historians in fact differ as to whether these celebrations took place on Saturday evening (when the Sabbath was ended) or on Sunday evening (in remembrance of the meals in which the Risen Lord was present with his disciples). In either case these celebrations included a eucharist, within the framework of a meal (Acts 20.7; Didache 9–10; 14; Pliny the Younger, Letters X, 97, 7). (iii) During the course of the second century the celebration was moved to early on Sunday morning. Justin Martyr (d. 165) gives us the first detailed description of worship which already comprised readings (from OT and NT), a sermon, prayer, eucharist and collection. The continuity of the liturgical tradition down the centuries is amazing!

3. *Sunday as a day of rest*. In the first centuries Christians had to work on Sunday like everyone else, which is why they gathered together in the evening or in the early morning. The change came – as in many things – when the Emperor Constantine was converted to Christianity; in 321 he declared Sunday to be the official day of rest in the Roman Empire (Cod. Justinian III, 12, 2). The advantage of this was that people could now gather for worship at their

leisure; however, it also brought with it the dangers of idleness. To obviate this problem, from then on the OT sabbath legislation was increasingly transferred to Sunday. Unfortunately, however, over the course of history this led to the observance of Sunday becoming legalistic, repressing the joy over this day of worship which was originally its central feature. Nowadays we should certainly recall that the justifiable concern for organized rest from work was not originally connected with Christian joy at celebrating the day of resurrection.

S. Bacchiocchi, *From Sabbath to Sunday*, 1977; R. T. Beckwith and J. W. Stott, *This is the Day: The Biblical Doctrine of the Christian Sunday*, 1978; P. K. Jewett, *The Lord's Day: A Theological Guide to the Christian Day of Worship*, 1971; F. A. Regan, *Dies dominica and dies solis. The Beginnings of the Lord's Day in Christian Antiquity*, 1961; W. Rordorf, *Sunday*, 1968.

W. RORDORF

Suso, Heinrich

Heinrich Suso (German Seuse) was born about 1295 near Lake Constance, probably in Constance itself, and died on 25 January 1366 at Ulm on the Danube. With Meister Eckhart* and Johannes Tauler*, he is one of the chief representatives of German mysticism. When he was only thirteen, his parents entrusted the upbringing of their sensitive child to the Dominicans of Constance. Suso also became a Dominican monk. His first religious ascetical ideal was to expose himself to the harshest physical chastisement. However, he soon had to recognize that asceticism of this kind did not lead to inwardness. As preacher and pastor he communicated this insight in Dominican convents. This activity brought him into contact with numerous nuns of the Order who were in search of spirituality, above all in the Dominican convents of St Katharinenthal near Diessenhofen and in Töss near Winterthur in Switzerland. It was here that Elsbeth Stagel lived, herself a pious mystic, and the biographer of Suso, who was her spiritual director.

Between 1348 and 1366 Suso lived and worked in the Dominican monastery in Ulm. Here he found the leisure he needed to gather together his writings, some of which had been composed previously, into a kind of Collected Works, the so-called *Exemplar*. This is in four parts: 1. The *Vita*, the life of Suso; 2. The Little Book of Eternal Wisdom (Sapientia); 3. The Little Book of Truth; 4. The Little Book of Letters. Other texts by Suso were not taken up into the *Exemplar*, including some sermons and the large Book of Letters.

In contrast to his teacher, Meister Eckhart, and to his Dominican brother Johannes Tauler, Suso has a distinctive spirituality. With him we find unfolding all the riches of his mystical experiences. He transposes what he thinks into activity of the soul. His writings express a joyful, yet painful fellow-feeling with human beings and creatures. As a spiritual guide he counselled soberness. In his view, the aim of mystical striving is not visions or powerful feelings of ecstasy. So he suggests for example to his disciple Elsbeth Stagel that in her striving she should 'raise herself above the comfort of images enjoyed by the beginner'. All imagery, however profoundly religious it may be, is nourished on conceptions which are taken from creation. The experienced, i.e. spiritually mature, person therefore longs for a 'vision without images'. What is meant is immersion in the pure being of the deity, in sheer 'nothingness', as Eckhart put it, here agreeing with the older masters of mysticism. Suso's mystical teachings extend to the point where the spiritual director makes himself superfluous, where he can happily keep silent because his disciple on the inward journey receives real direction through God himself or through Christ. Hence Suso's invitation: 'Say farewell to the creature and in future let your questions be. Simply hearken to what God says in you!'

Because of his poetic language, full of many images and similitudes, Heinrich Suso has sometimes been called the troubador of the German mystics. Because of his own experiences he appeals to those who are in danger of damaging themselves on the journey inwards by harsh asceticism, though the forms of such asceticism have changed considerably since the days of German mysticism.

Heinrich Suso, *Deutsche mystische Schriften*, ed George Hofmann, 1966. *See* Louis Cognet, *Gottes Geburt in der Seele. Einführung in die deutsche Mystik*, 1980; Gerhard Wehr, *Deutsche Mystik, Gestalten und*

Zeugnisses religioser Erfahrung von Meister Eckhart bis zur Reformationszeit, 1980.

GERHARD WEHR

Syrian Spirituality

During the early centuries of Christianity Syria was a centre of creativity in several different fields, producing a literature on spirituality in both Greek and Syriac (a dialect of Aramaic). Three main periods may be distinguished, to *c.* A D 400, fifth and sixth centuries, and seventh and eighth centuries. The christological controversies of the fifth century divided Syriac Christianity into two main bodies, the Church of the East and the Syrian Orthodox; mystical writings, however, were unaffected by ecclesiastical boundaries.

1. *To* c. *AD 400.* The main Syriac writings are: the Odes of Solomon, a group of short religious lyrics of the late second century; the Acts of Thomas (third century), giving expression to an encratite form of Christianity; the Demonstrations of Aphrahat (mid-fourth century), which include pieces on prayer (no. 4) and the indwelling of the Holy Spirit (no. 6); the extensive works (largely hymns) of Ephrem (*see* **Ephrem Syrus**); and the thirty homilies on the spiritual life known as the *Liber Graduum* (Book of Steps, or Ascents), perhaps originating from the same sort of milieu as the Macarian Homilies (*see* **Macarius the Egyptian**).

Syriac Christianity of this period is at its most semitic in character, and is as yet little influenced by Greek thought patterns. It developed its own distinctive form of protomonasticism, based on small groups of ascetics ('members of the covenant') living together; Egyptian-style monasticism does not make itself felt until the end of the fourth century.

The ideal of the Christian life as an imitation of Christ is recurrent in various forms. A strong emphasis on virginity was encouraged by viewing baptism as the betrothal of the soul to Christ, and by the view that the Christian life should imitate the marriageless life of angels. Baptism was regarded as the re-entry into paradise and the recovery of the 'robe of glory' lost by Adam (humanity) at the Fall; this is not, however, a cyclical process, since the righteous will be rewarded in the eschatological paradise with divinization.

The *Liber Graduum* offers some distinctive doctrines, such as the distinction between the 'upright' who keep the 'lesser commandments' (active charity) and the 'perfect' who observe the 'greater' as well (total renunciation of the world); also notable is the teaching on the three churches, the visible, and the invisible, of the heart, and in heaven.

2. *Fifth and sixth centuries.* The most important texts are: the Macarian Homilies, written in Greek and the Syriac writings of John the Solitary, Philoxenus and Stephen bar Sudhaili.

During this period Syriac writers come under the strong influence of certain Greek works in Syriac translation, notably the Egyptian monastic literature, the Macarian Homilies, Evagrius and the Writings attributed to Denys the Areopagite *. Evagrius' intellectualist spirituality proved particularly influential on all Syriac writers, from Philoxenus onwards, and several of his works, lost in Greek due to his condemnation for Origenism in 553, are preserved only in Syriac (and Armenian) translations.

John the Solitary (or John of Apamea; probably early fifth century) is the author of several dialogues and letters on the spiritual life. His threefold classification of this life into the stages 'of the body, of the soul, and of the spirit' was to prove influential among later writers. Throughout he lays great emphasis on baptism as an anticipation of resurrection. His is very much a 'mysticism of hope'.

Philoxenus, the great Syrian Orthodox theologian (d. 523), wrote several works on spirituality, notably thirteen discourses, which concentrate on the early stages. He offers an original synthesis of Greek and native Syriac elements; characteristic of the latter is his emphasis on baptism, and on the need for co-operation between the human will and the grace of the Spirit. He follows a two-stage pattern of the spiritual life.

Stephen bar Sudhaili (*fl. c.* 500) was probably the author of *The Book of the Holy Hierotheos,* which claims to be by Denys the Areopagite's teacher, but which is certainly later than the writings attributed to Denys. It is a markedly Evagrian work on the ascent of the mind, and is notable for its eschatological pantheism.

3. *Seventh and eighth centuries.* The

writers of this period belong to the Church of the East which experienced an impressive monastic revival in the sixth century. Of the many authors four may be singled out: Martyrius, Isaac of Nineveh, Joseph Hazzaya ('the seer') and John of Dalyatha.

Martyrius (or Sahdona; early seventh century) was expelled from the Church of the East for his Chalcedonian christology. His Book of Perfection stands apart from other writings of this period for its strongly biblical emphasis, and for the centrality he gives to the heart (as opposed to the mind) as the spiritual centre.

Isaac of Nineveh (or 'the Syrian'; fl. second half of seventh century) is the best known of the Syrian mystics, thanks to the translation of his works into Greek in the ninth century. Like most of his contemporaries he draws both on the intellectualist traditions of Evagrius and the writings attributed to Denys the Areopagite and on the more experiential ones of the Macarian Homilies and the native Syriac writers (especially John the Solitary). Great stress is laid on the need for absolute renunciation of the 'world' (which includes the 'self') and for humility. There are several remarkable passages describing the workings of the Holy Spirit.

Joseph Hazzaya (eighth century), a convert from Zoroastrianism, is probably the author of a systematic exposition of the three stages of the spiritual life (wrongly attributed to Philoxenus); this provides a synthesis of the various threefold classifications of John the Solitary, Evagrius and the writings attributed to Denys the Areopagite. Some of his other writings are attributed to his brother Abdisho.

John of Dalyatha (or Saba, 'the Old Man'; eighth century), like his predecessors, belonged to the monastic circles of northern Iraq. His main works are collections of homilies and letters; the latter contain several descriptions of mystical experiences.

It is likely that early Islamic Sufism * was influenced by East Syrian mystical circles, but the precise extent is still very unclear.

Among later writers one stands out, the polymath Barhebraeus (d. 1286). In old age he compiled a systematic set of directives for Christian living (lay, as well as monastic), entitled the *Ethicon*, and The Book of the Dove, intended to assist monks who did not have the benefit of a spiritual director.

These writings show some influence from the Muslim mystic al-Ghazālī.

───

Texts: R. Beulay, *La Collection des lettres de Jean de Dalyatha* (Patrologia Orientalis 39), 1978; E. A. W. Budge, *The Discourses of Philoxenus*, 1894; F. S. Marsh, *The Book of the Holy Hierotheos*, 1927; A. Mingana, *Early Christian Mystics*, 1934; A. J. Wensinck, *Mystic Treatises by Isaac of Nineveh*, reissued 1969; *Bar Hebraeus' Book of the Dove*, 1919. Studies: S. P. Brock, *The Holy Spirit in the Syrian Baptismal Tradition*, 1979; A. Guillaumont, *Les 'Kephalaia Gnostica' d'Evagre le Pontique et l'histoire de l'Origenisme chez les grecs et les syriens*, 1962; R. Murray, *Symbols of Church and Kingdom*, 1975; A. Vööbus, *History of Asceticism in the Syrian Orient*, I, II, 1958, 1960.

SEBASTIAN BROCK

Taizé

Creating a community in Taizé had no other purpose than to bring together men who would commit themselves for life to celibacy and to life together, in order to be a sign of the communion of the People of God.

A life in community is a microcosm of the church; it offers a reduced image of the reality of the whole People of God. More than ideas, today's world needs images. Ideas only become credible when they are supported by a visible reality – otherwise they are only an ideology. What we have always been passionately seeking is something very concrete: a parable of communion incarnate in the lives of a few men. When I settled in Taizé in 1940, I already had that idea: as a way of responding to the ecumenical vocation, let us, by our lives, insert a ferment of communion in the dough of the divided churches.

The fact that some of us belong to different confessions which arose from the Reformation, or to the Anglican communion, and that it is possible to have Catholic brothers as well, in no way implies that there is a separation in our life. Communion in the faith takes shape through the prayer of the liturgy, in a slow process of growth. We have never wanted simply to integrate monastic life into the churches of the Reformation alone: that would merely have consolidated the parallelism between denominations which blocks communion among Christians to such an extent. The gospel calls upon Christians to be reconciled immediately, without delay. Personally, I can say that I have found my own identity by reconciling within myself the current of faith of my Protestant origins with the faith of the Catholic Church, without being a symbol of repudiation for anyone.

With the freedom given by our situation, we might well have taken no account of those who preceded us in the vocation to common life. Being attentive to the mystery of the church has led us to consider that Taizé is only a simple bud grafted on a great tree. In this regard it is undoubtedly significant that our village lies between Cluny and Cîteaux. On the one side is Cluny, the great Benedictine tradition which humanized everything it touched. Cluny, with its sense of moderation, of visible community built up in unity. Cluny, the centre of attraction for men consciously or unconsciously seeking their own inner unity and a reconciliation. On the other side is Cîteaux: there, Saint Bernard foreshadowed all the reforming zeal which was to explode in the sixteenth century. He refused to compromise the absolute of the gospel in any way. He spoke the language of a reformer. He was more concerned with the demands of the present moment than with historical continuity. For us, fusing the sense of urgency with a sense of the continuity assured by several generations is an incomparable factor permitting a common creation.

From the very beginning we have been convinced of one thing: the more someone wishes to live an absolute of God, the more essential it is to live out this absolute in a situation of human distress. When I was still alone, I offered shelter and hiding to political refugees, particularly Jews: it was war time. Later on, when we were a few brothers, we started small fraternities in the poorest parts of the world, in Asia, Africa, North and South America. This presence of brothers on every continent is never in order to re-activate the process which consists in bringing Western solutions, however valuable these may be. If we go, it is to live a presence with no ulterior motives.

Since the 1960s we have been unexpectedly led to welcome the tens of thousands of young adults who visit our community; they come from a great many different countries. Today, young people everywhere are searching for God, often after having apparently given up living a life of faith. These young people are going through a time of disenchantment, a great void. Previously they had hope, a fine human hope for justice. But we have to admit that what had been hoped for most has not come about, that the human community has evolved differently than many wished. These young people are aware that world peace depends in part on an equal confidence shown to all the peoples of the earth, and that it depends as well on a fairer distribution of material goods between rich and poor countries.

In the end, what captivates us most is the reconciliation of the entire human family. If Christians are seeking reconciliation within the church, that is not in order to become stronger against others, it is so as to stand together as a ferment of peace in the places where the human family is being torn apart. When they are reconciled, even just a few of them, Christians can reverse the determinisms of hatred and war, and give renewed human hope to those who are sunk in passivity, discouragement and a life without meaning.

Brother Roger, *Dynamic of the Provisional*, 1981; *Festival without End*, 1983; *A Life We Never Dared Hope For*, 1980; *Living Today for God*, 1980; *Parable of Community*, 1980; *Rule of Taizé*, 1965; *Struggle and Contemplation*, [2]1983; *Violent for Peace*, 1981; *The Wonder of a Love*, 1981; see also *Praise: Prayers from Taizé*, 1979; *Praise in All Our Days*, 1979; José Balado, *The Story of Taizé*, 1981; Rex Brico, *Taizé: Brother Roger and his Community*, 1978.

BROTHER ROGER

Talmud *see* Jewish Spirituality

Taoism

Both a philosophy and a religion, which has been an important influence on Chinese thought. It takes its name from the Tao, which is regarded as the basis and source of all things. The Tao itself is often regarded as non-being, a state of emptiness or oneness from which beings derive. Behind the changing phenomena which we perceive with our senses there is an unchanging principle, and this is called Tao. Various terms are used to express this subtle idea. As the source of creation, Tao is 'wu', or nothing; as creator, Tao is non-being; and as creation itself, Tao is 'yu', which means 'to exit'. The Tao Tê Ching says of the Tao: 'There is a thing, formless yet complete . . . It is all pervading and unfailing. We do not know its name, but we call it Tao.'

Taoism developed alongside Confucianism in China, and in the process incorporated a number of different elements. Philosophical Taoism was much concerned with the principle characteristics of the Tao, which were thought to be change, spontaneity, non-purposiveness, and reversion to origins. It taught that these characteristics are to be incorporated into the life of society. So the principle of spontaneity, for example, has been taken to suggest that conduct should be intuitive. Other elements contributing to Taoism were the hygiene school, which sought longevity by means of exercises and respiratory techniques; and a search for the elixir of life, for Taoism has been much concerned with the pursuit of immortality. It is believed that longevity can also be encouraged by holding together the yin (the principle of rest, or what is dormant) and the yang (the active principle, or what is creative).

Religious Taoism has paid particular attention to the search for immortality and to the balance and interaction of yin and yang. Taoists do not regard matter and spirit as essentially different and separate, and so immortality is to be found through transformation rather than by an attempt to release the soul from bondage to matter. During the course of its development religious Taoism absorbed many popular ideas and practices.

Taoist temples flourished in China. They are of two main types: the great public temples which have been major monastic centres open to tao-shih (monks or priests) of any school; and hereditary temples, in which control is retained in the hands of a particular sect or sub-sect. Two major sects are T'ien-shih Tao (the way of the Celestial Masters) and Ch'üan-chen Chiao (the doctrine of Complete Perfection). Ch'üan-chen Chiao was influenced by Ch'an (or Zen) Buddhism, although Taoism generally has itself exerted considerable influence on Buddhism in China.

Taoism is known in the West chiefly through the Tao Tê Ching ('the way and its power') which is traditionally attributed to Lao Tzu, an older contemporary of Confucius. The Tao Tê Ching teaches the benefits of self-abnegation, non-action, and conformity to nature as means of becoming like Tao, and therefore indestructible. The classic also expounds upon Tê, the virtue or power of Tao, which can extend Tao into the existence of each individual.

W. Eichhorn, 'Taoism', in R. C. Zaehner (ed) *The Concise Encyclopaedia of Living Faiths*, [2]1971; D. H. Smith, *Chinese Religions*, 1968; H. Welch & A. Seidel (eds) *Facets of Taoism*, 1979.

PETER D. BISHOP

Tauler, Johannes

Tauler was born in Strasbourg *c*. 1300 and died on 16 June 1361. With Meister Eckhart* and Heinrich Suso* he is one of the most important representatives of German mysticism. He entered the Dominican Order at the early age of fifteen. Round about 1330 he was active as a preacher and monastic teacher (lector) in Strasbourg. He then spent some years in Basle, but Strasbourg was the centre of his further work as a preacher and pastor. From there he travelled to many places, including the Netherlands, where he probably met the mystic Jan van Ruysbroeck* (Ruusbroec) in Groenendaal. In Strasbourg Tauler had associations with the so-called 'Friends of God', including Rulman Merswin, an active writer, who had chosen Johannes Tauler as his spiritual director. A tradition circulated widely to the effect that Tauler had undergone an inner conversion about the age of forty. This fundamental change in his whole being was said to have been brought about by an anonymous 'Friend of God from the Oberland', a simple but deeply spiritual layman. In the first printed edition of Tauler's sermons, which appeared in Leipzig in 1498, this story is given as *Historia Tauleri*. Research in Tauler has not in fact succeeded in confirming it, especially as an early form of the text speaks only of an anonymous 'Master (magister) of theology' and not of Johannes Tauler, who did not have this distinction. However, this does not exclude the possibility that Tauler underwent such an inner conversion about the middle of his life.

If Meister Eckhart is the most significant and boldest representative of speculative mysticism in the German language, and Heinrich Suso stands out by the depth of his feeling, Johannes Tauler can be seen as a mystic who is close to life. He is concerned to demonstrate the two-fold path of the *vita activa* and the *vita meditativa*, i.e. the active and the meditative life. In one sermon he tells of a farmer who for more than forty years had been wrapped up in his everyday work. This man asked God whether he should stop his work and go to church. God said, No, he should not do that; he should go on working for his bread by the sweat of his brow, in honour of the precious blood of Christ. Here Tauler clearly showed the high value which attaches to any human activity, if only it is performed with the right degree of sacrifice. So Tauler's sermons, of which more than eighty transcriptions are regarded as authentic, testify that the meditative journey inwards and active concern for the duties of everyday life must be kept in constant equilibrium. Numerous impressions saw to it that Tauler's sermons were read over the centuries: 1498 in Leipzig, 1521/22 in Basle, 1543 in Cologne; further editions and translations followed.

Martin Luther in particular was concerned to make Tauler known. Of the preacher-monk he said: 'I have found more true theology in him than in all the doctors of all the universities.' The *Theologia Deutsch* (called *Der Frankfurter* or *Theologia Germanica**), which was edited anonymously by Luther, also brought the Reformer into touch with Tauler's spirituality. Very different figures, like Thomas Muntzer, Luther's opponent, or the Jesuit Petrus Canisius, also treasured Tauler's sermons. Both Luther's Reformation and sixteenth-century Catholicism drew on the spirit of German mysticism. The effect of this, as of Tauler, is still with us today.

Johann Tauler, *Predigten*, ed Georg Hofmann, 1980; *Theologia Deutsch. Eine Grundschrift deutscher Mystik*, ed Gerhard Wehr, 1980. See also Louis Cognet, *Gottes Geburt in der Seele. Einführung in die deutsche Mystik*, 1980; Friedrich Wilhelm Wentzlaff-Eggebert, *Deutsche Mystik zwischen Mittelalter und Neuzeit*, 1969; Gerhard Wehr, *Deutsche Mystik. Gestalten und Zeugnisse religiöser Erfahrung von Meister Eckhart bis zur Reformationszeit*, 1980.

GERHARD WEHR

Taylor, Jeremy

Jeremy Taylor (1613–1667) was educated at Gonville and Caius Cambridge, ordained 1633 and became Rector of Uppingham in 1638. Through the influence of Laud, he became domestic chaplain to Charles I. He was imprisoned by the Parliamentarians in Cardigan in 1645 and after his release spent the next ten years under the patronage of the Earl of Carberry at Golden Grove, Carmarthenshire. He moved to Ireland in 1658. After the Restoration he was consecrated Bishop of Down and Connor and later 'overseer' of Dromore. His time in Ireland was unhappily controversial.

Taylor confesses that he 'was weary and toiled with rowing up and down on the seas of questions' (*The Great Exemplar*, 1649) and his temper (charitable though not doctrinally casual) and his great literary gifts are best expressed in his devotional writings. *The Great Exemplar* is partly a narrative life of Christ (the first in English) and partly a book of devotional explication, meditation and application. Taylor warmly recounts the story of the nativity but there are curious though comprehensible shifts of tone as he moves from a panegyric to the Virgin to the chapter of application, 'Of Nursing Children'.

Extracts from his work always mislead for he can on the one hand produce long richly-patterned sentences and paragraphs with widely-ranging imagery that move and exult the reader, and on the other passages of sensible, prosaic advice for decent behaviour.

Holy Living (1650) and *Holy Dying* (1651) are practical manuals which draw on a wide range of classical as well as Christian writing. Each chapter concludes with suggested prayers. Taylor, of fundamentally eirenic outlook, is one of the greatest composers of prayers in English, for 'anger is the perfect alienation of the mind from prayer' (*Sermons*, 1653). Taylor is always aware of the lamentable lapses of human concentration and makes wise suggestions about combating them. Similarly *Holy Dying* contains not only great meditations on death but practical 'psychological' advice for the sick person. Taylor's insight serves him well in *Doctor Dubitantium* (1660).

He believes that 'private devotions and secret offices of religion are like refreshing of a garden with the distilling and petty drops of a water-pot' but 'addresses to the temple and serving God in the public communion of saints, is like rain from heaven' (*Great Exemplar*). Taylor's liturgies, devised as alternatives to the banned Book of Common Prayer, show the influence of the Eastern tradition. He is sadly though perceptively aware of the divisions of opinion about the eucharist, analysing the differing emotionally charged terminologies, but his main aim is 'not to confute anyone, but to instruct those that need, not to make a noise, but to excite devotion' (*The Worthy Communicant*, 1668).

R. Heber (ed), rev C. P. Eden, *Whole Works of Jeremy Taylor*, 10 vols, 1841–1872; L. Pearsall Smith (ed), *The Golden Grove* (selected passages from Taylor), repr 1955; H. T. Hughes, *The Piety of Jeremy Taylor*, 1960; F. L. Huntley, *Jeremy Taylor and the Great Rebellion*, 1970; H. R. McAdoo, *The Structure of Caroline Moral Theology*, 1949; C. J. Stranks, *Life and Writings of Jeremy Taylor*, 1952.

ELUNED BROWN

Teilhard de Chardin

Pierre Teilhard de Chardin, the Jesuit priest and paleontologist whose religious thought has so greatly influenced Christian spirituality since his death on Easter Day 1955, was born in 1881 into a traditionally pious French Catholic family in Clermont. He entered the Society of Jesus* at the age of seventeen, and was ordained a priest after thirteen years of training. He continued his studies, then served in the First World War, and studied and taught geology and paleontology in Paris. He was soon exiled from France by Jesuit superiors for his interpretations of Catholic dogma and forbidden to publish his religious views. His spiritual teaching could not find a wide audience until the publication of his theological and spiritual writings in the two decades after his death.

Considered somewhat unorthodox by church officials during his lifetime, and afterwards appreciated by many Christians for his understanding of the doctrines of the incarnation, the resurrection, original sin and the relationship between nature and grace, Teilhard has finally emerged as a great spiritual writer, important in Christian thought mainly for his spiritual doctrine.

Both a priest and a scientist, Teilhard lived at the intersection of two worlds, the world of science and of contemporary scientific culture at its most intense, and the ecclesiastical world of the official church. He knew the patterns and the idioms of both these worlds, and he was at home in both. By profession and by background he was unusually well-equipped both to explain Christianity to the modern world and to relate traditional Christian teaching to life in the world today.

Teilhard's spirituality answers what he considered the chief religious problem of our times, a problem of two faiths that seem opposed: faith in the world and faith in Jesus Christ. The problem is this: how can we reconcile Christian detachment and attachment to human progress, how reconcile love of God and love of the world, how reconcile the doctrine of the cross and belief in the fullest possible development of human potential? Teilhard calls this 'the problem of the two faiths'.

It applies particularly to Christians. The two faiths can be found almost always in some conflict in every truly contemporary Christian: an upward impulse in the direction of faith in God, of faith in Jesus Christ, of worship and adoration; and a forward impulse in the direction of faith in humanity and in the world that the human race is building up in the course of progress. Both these impulses, the 'upward' and the 'forward', appear deserving of all our dedication and efforts. But they seem two different directions; today's Christian stands caught in a spiritual dualism, torn in two directions. Some end the conflict by giving themselves totally to the world. Others renounce the world completely to give themselves to God. Most try to go in both directions at once, limping badly, never achieving a workable synthesis between the two faiths.

How can faith in the world and faith in Christ be shown as not opposed but mutually necessary and complementary? Teilhard's efforts to formulate a solution to the problem fall into three steps or phases; he worked on all three phases simultaneously, but they nevertheless form three distinct levels of his thought. Taken together, they comprise his overall Christian vision.

Teilhard first develops a theory of evolution that provides a framework for his theology of Jesus Christ risen. At a second level of thought, Teilhard's christology discovers that, in the light of Christian doctrine, the future focal centre of all evolution, including human history and progress, is the risen Christ. Christ risen, the focus of the world's forward movement, stands as the God of both the 'forward' and the 'upward'. In him, therefore, the seeming opposition between faith in the world and faith in God finds its resolution. Jesus Christ risen is the personal principle of synthesis of Christian life in the world because every personal history and all history as a whole is evolving towards him. Christ risen, because of his transcendence, makes the Christian's ultimate future present now, and so Christ acts as the basis of Christian hope in the future.

At a third level, building on his christology, Teilhard works out a contemporary Christian spirituality, a positive moral teaching that takes the form of a mysticism of involvement in the world through love and through the unification and the progressive reconciliation of all things in Christ. The cross is no longer a sign simply of expiation, but the symbol of growth and progress accomplished in pain and through suffering. Detachment means not to reject but to work through. Resignation becomes the final form of the fight against evil, the final transformation in Christ of inevitable defeats. Christian faith includes faith in the world. Christian hope involves us more deeply in this life. And Christian love moves us to build a better world. Teilhard's central contribution to Christian spirituality is a contemporary understanding of the age-old problem of the antithesis between prayer and action, and the solution to that problem: a vision of Christian life centred on Jesus Christ risen in a world moving towards him.

P. Teilhard de Chardin, *Le Milieu Divin*, 1960; *Hymn of the Universe*, 1965; Robert Faricy, *All Things in Christ: Teilhard de Chardin's Spirituality*, 1981; Ursula King, *Towards a New Mysticism: Teilhard de Chardin and Eastern Religions*, 1980.

ROBERT FARICY, SJ

Temple, William

William Temple (1881–1944) was, by general consent, both a great and a good man. Endowed with a rich variety of talents and natural advantages, he would have risen to the top of whatever career he had followed, but he was without any trace of pride or pomp and the attractiveness of his personality won him a host of admiring friends wherever he went.

Born in an episocpal palace and having received the finest available education, he became a philosophy don at Oxford, then a headmaster and a canon of Westminster, and after that successively Bishop of Manchester, Archbishop of York and (like his father, Frederick Temple) Archbishop of Canterbury. His premature death prevented him from achieving all that had been expected of him in that office. Nevertheless he influenced multitudes of people, especially young people, as a lecturer, preacher, missioner and author. He was also in constant demand as a chairman for commissions, conferences, etc., because of his understanding sympathy with many different points of view and his ability to harmonize or synthesize apparently conflicting beliefs and claims. He was a pioneer of the ecumenical movement and a dedicated church reformer.

Because of the wide range of his interests and sympathies it is not possible to label him or to identify him with any particular school of thought or ecclesiastical standpoint. While as a philosophical theologian he always confessed his indebtedness to the metaphysical idealism of Edward Caird and to the incarnational theology of Charles Gore and his friends, which were prevalent at Oxford when he was young, his teaching and way of thinking never became hard and fast and he was seeking to come to terms with new ideas and disconcerting developments till the end of his life. His prophetic qualities were most evident in his leadership of Christian social movements where he had a role similar to that of Maurice and Kingsley in the middle of the nineteenth century, and to that of Gore and Scott Holland in the generation preceding his own.

Some of the characteristics of his teaching may be indicated by saying that he was a Platonist rather than an Aristotelian and a disciple of St John rather than of St Paul.

Moreover, like Coleridge, he held that people were mostly right in what they affirmed and wrong in what they denied. Thus he said that 'in our dealings with one another let us be more eager to understand those who differ from us than either to refute them or to press upon them our own tradition'. The best introduction to his spirituality is his *Readings in St John's Gospel* (1945), in which all his insights find expression, notably his sense of the sacramental nature of the universe and of Christ's universal lordship. He attached great importance to the Logos-doctrine of the Fourth Gospel. 'All that is noble,' he wrote, 'in the non-Christian systems of thought, or conduct, or worship is the work of Christ upon them or within them.'

He naturally had his limitations. He himself was so integrated a personality and so unshaken a believer that he could not really sympathize with the scepticisms that perplex and bewilder many minds, including Christian minds, and his innate goodness and kindliness caused him to judge other people much too benevolently. He found it hard, and perhaps did not much try, to cultivate the astringency and severity that are also required in Christian leaders.

Joseph F. Fletcher, *William Temple, Twentieth-Century Christian*, 1963; F. A. Iremonger, *William Temple, Archbishop of Canterbury*, 1948.

A. R. VIDLER

Teresa of Avila, St

Teresa de Cepeda y Ahumada was born 28 March 1515 in Avila, and entered the Carmelite Convent of the Incarnation there *c.* 1535. She suffered long periods of serious illness, especially 1538–1539, when she was deeply influenced by the *Third Spiritual Alphabet* of the Franciscan Osuna and its teaching on recollection and the prayer of quiet. Living under the mitigated rule for some years, she had occasional supernatural experiences, but it was not until her 'second conversion' *c.* 1555 that her inner life took a specifically mystical direction. Her confessors believed her increasingly frequent visions and raptures were diabolically inspired, but after an exhausting struggle she became convinced of God's leading and in 1559 experienced the transverberation, a series of intense visions in which

Christ pierced her heart with a spear.

At this time St Peter of Alcántara gave her encouraging spiritual counsel and supported her project for a Discalced Carmelite house following the strict primitive rule and devoted to the contemplative life. She founded St Joseph's, Avila, in 1562, and at the behest of her spiritual directors began her *Life*, a remarkable autobiography, best known as a devotional work for its image of the 'four waters', in which the life of prayer is likened to four ways of watering with a progressive lessening of human effort: a well, a water-wheel, a stream and rain. The *Way of Perfection*, written for her nuns 1565–1566, includes a contemplative commentary on the Lord's Prayer. From 1567 she began to found further Discalced houses, seventeen in all, and her *Book of Foundations*, 'the biography of her convents' (Peers), recounts her attendant tribulations, particularly burdensome after 1575. Meanwhile she had persuaded John of the Cross * to begin the Reform among the Carmelite friars, and a strong mutual regard grew up between them.

Her most important work on prayer is undoubtedly the *Interior Castle*, conceived following a vision. The soul progresses from the outer courtyard of a crystal globe in the form of a castle to the innermost of its seven mansions. Prowling beasts symbolize the obstructions and distractions of the earlier stages, but their power recedes as the soul approaches its centre. The first three mansions correspond to the purgative way and the fourth teaches the prayer of recollection, which precedes the prayer of quiet. The fifth leads to the prayer of union and the spiritual betrothal, and contains the beautiful picture of the soul as a silkworm emerging from its cocoon as a white butterfly. The last two mansions progress beyond the stages described in her earlier works and introduce afflictions similar to St John's dark nights; but the seventh brings the spiritual marriage and a more or less permanent state of union with God in the centre of the soul. Detailed analyses of visions, locutions and raptures occur in these later chapters.

Teresa died in 1582, was beatified 1614, canonized 1622 and proclaimed a Doctor of the Church 1970. Her first editor, Luis de León, wrote (1588) of her 'unaffected elegance, which is delightful in the extreme'. Her writing, direct and personal, reveals a vigorous, down-to-earth character whose long involvement in the active life was uniquely joined with the loftiest experiences of the contemplative.

The Complete Works of Saint Teresa of Jesus tr E. Allison Peers, 1963; E. Allison Peers, *Mother of Carmel*, 1945; E. W. Trueman Dicken, *The Crucible of Love*, 1963.

COLIN P. THOMPSON

Tertullian

In dogmatic theology and apologetic Tertullian (*c.* 160–225) may be called the father of Western Christianity. The flavour and content of his underlying religious and ethical teaching have become imprinted by his literary genius on one constant element in the Western tradition – the ascetic, the un-compromising, the legalist pattern of God as judge, the gospel as *lex proprie nostrum* and salvation as *salutaris disciplina*. In this respect his 'conversion' to Montanism (or 'Tertullianism') did little more than intensify a persisting spirituality of guilt, fear, compensation and satisfaction (key-words to be understood throughout *coram Deo*, in Luther's phrase).

1. Standing at the opposite pole to the Greek Apologists and the Alexandrians, Tertullian (like Tatian) rejects any accommodation between philosophy and the gospel ('What has Athens to do with Jerusalem?'); yet no Father has a greater proportion of *argumentative* content, nor does he (one suspects) convince even himself that the similarities between Greek speculation and Christianity result from the purloining of such ideas from the O T, especially as Tertullian is himself a half-confessed Stoic in much of his teaching on God, the soul and ethical principles and practices. Nor is it clear why human philosophy should be alien to the gospel, while human law is its unfailing servant (and at times its master).

2. The famous *testimonium animae naturaliter Christianae* hints at the Stoic doctrine of the soul as a microcosm of the universe, and although hardly consistent with Tertullian's insistence that Christians are made, not born, it is intended to ground Christian evidence in unspoilt and unsophisticated intuition. In the treatise *On the Soul* Tertullian accepts against the Platonists the Stoic identity of soul and spirit (of which mind is but a function) as corporeal in essence, how-

ever subtle and rarefied; but he insists on the freedom of the will and the fundamental right of freedom of conscience, especially in religion. In *Adversus Praxean* Tertullian offers the analogy between the functions of the soul and the Holy Trinity of which Augustine was to make such elaborate use.

3. Tertullian's doctrine of sin and forgiveness becomes notably more severe in his later writings: in *De Pudicitia* he introduces the distinction between 'remissible' and 'irremissible' sins (fornication, idolatry, murder), for which neither the church nor even the intercession of the martyrs can avail. He forbids Christians to attend public games or contests, which originated from idolatry (*De Spectaculis*); military service is banned, as are offices of State in general, and Tertullian excludes from the church any art or profession (even professors of literature and mathematics) which is dependent on the heathen establishment (*De Idolatria*). Immodesty or artificiality in women's apparel obscure the distinction of Christian from pagan: the only suitable attire for the daughters of Eve, through whom sin came into the world, is the garb of penitence (*De Cultu Feminarum*), and Tertullian insists on the veiling of virgins, both inside and outside the church (*De Virg. Vel.*). His teaching on marriage grows gradually more severe, until second marriage after the death of a partner is forbidden and virginity and continence are exalted above the marriage state itself (*Ad Uxorem, De Exhortatione Castitatis, De Monogamia*). On the positive side Tertullian commends Christian patience, while honestly admitting he lacks the virtue himself (*De Patientia*), and penitence – allowing, at least in his earlier period although even then with hesitation because of its psychological dangers, the 'second penance' with due public confession and absolution.

4. In his *Apology* Tertullian gives a well-known picture of Christians at worship, where hope and judgment are nicely blended, and the voluntary offerings are for the poor, the slaves, the prisoners. To this should be added his treatises on *Prayer* – practical and disciplinary, although with the earliest known exposition of the Lord's Prayer – and *Baptism*, which discourages infant baptism ('let them become Christians when they are able to know Christ'), and allows only one exception to baptism with water – 'baptism of blood', or martyrdom,

which he exalts to a supreme degree in his treatise *Ad Martyras*. It is the climax of world-renunciation, and in line with Ignatius and the *Passion of Perpetua and Felicitas* (which he perhaps edited), Tertullian glorifies this 'escape from the world's prison' in terms hardly consistent with his own incarnational theology.

5. Tertullian's christology, his Mariology ('the second Eve'), his doctrine of the church ('our mother'), his eschatology (with its adumbration of purgatory), as well as his doctrine of the paraclete (especially in his later writings), while of capital significance in the history of doctrine, are only of indirect value for evidence of his spirituality and ethics.

Eng tr of works by P. Holmes and others in *ANCL* vols VII, XI, XV, XVIII, 1868–1870; see also T. D. Barnes, *Tertullian*, 1971; R. D. Sider, *Ancient Rhetoric and the Art of Tertullian*, 1971.

BENJAMIN DREWERY

Thanksgiving
see **Prayer (5) Thanksgiving**

Theologia Germanica

A mystical treatise, composed about 1350 by an anonymous author from the circle of 'The Friends of God', probably in Frankfurt-am-Main; discovered in 1516 by Luther, and printed at his instigation, and reissued on the basis of a longer MS in 1518. A longer, stylistically smoother and probably later recension was printed in 1497 (Wurzburg); this recension was reprinted by Pfeiffer (1851, 1855) and translated into English by Susanna Winkworth (1874). Both recensions are provided with chapter headings which attempt to modify the doctrine of the treatise and to re-align it with the mysticism of Denys the Areopagite*. The title ('A German Theology') is due to Luther, and the work, which certainly influenced him deeply, is often quoted as if it were his own.

The mystical quest, with its classical pattern, is taken for granted: '. . . note that no one can be illuminated before becoming purified, chastened, and liberated. By the same token, no one can become united with God if he has not before been illumined. That is what the three stages are for. First comes the purification, then the illumination, and third the union' (ch 12). The mys-

tical quest's dangers are acknowledged. The seeker may too readily leave off the exercise of outward duties (12), and can so deceive himself that he is dominated by an evil spirit while he thinks he is ruled by the Holy Spirit; there is true light and false light (20). The source of this delusion is self-reliance. Despite its perils, the mystical quest for union with God *is* possible. The mystic can know the essence of deity – 'as God is simple goodness, inner knowledge and light, he is at the same time also our will, love, righteousness and truth, the innermost of all virtues' (30). God can be loved for himself.

The *Theologia* sets this confidence in a distinctively Christian context by stressing two factors – sin and christology. 'What else did Adam do but precisely this thing? . . . because of his presumption and because of his I and Mine, his Me and the like . . .' All activity that I call 'mine' is doomed to be a re-inforcement of my disobedient state. At the same time, God does not act without me. 'No great works and wonders God has ever wrought or shall ever do in or through this created world, not even God himself in his goodness, will make me blessed if they remain outside of me' (9).

Christ as the new Adam is the resolution of this dilemma. Christology is a doctrine about *God*. 'He became humanized and man becomes divinized' (3). In Christ the divided loyalties of humanity are reconciled (7). He turns the path through hell into a triumphal progress (11). He renewed humanness: 'Everything that perished and died in Adam was raised again and made alive in Christ. And everything that was raised and made alive in Adam perished and died in Christ' (13).

The essential decision is faith, that renounces self-trust. Needed in the first place is keen yearning for, diligence in and steadfast resolve about the way to prepare for the Lord. This is the way of the cross. 'If you wish to follow Him you must take the cross upon you. The cross is the same as the Christ life and that is a bitter cross for natural man' (52). It is also acceptance of hell: 'Christ's soul had to visit hell before it came to heaven. That is also the path for man's soul.' '. . . God must become humanized in me. This means that God takes unto Himself everything that is in me, from within and without, so that there is nothing in me that resists God or obstructs his work' (3).

The surrender of self allows God to work in and through the soul. Even the troublesome self finds a purpose. Inner surrender gives the soul stability – 'When true union with God takes place deep in our being the inner man is enduringly rooted in that union' (26) – and hope, both of present growth – 'Whoever wants to know must wait until he becomes what he knows' – and of eternity: 'finally hell departs but the kingdom of heaven will remain' (11).

B. Hoffmann, *The Theologia Germanica of Martin Luther* (Classics of Western Spirituality), 1980; S. Winkworth, *Theologia Germanica*, 1874.

DAVID TRIPP

Thérèse of Lisieux, St

Marie Françoise Thérèse Martin was born at Alençon, Normandy on 2 January 1873. From the age of five she lived in Lisieux where she entered the Carmelite monastery when only fifteen, receiving the religious name of Sister Thérèse of the Child Jesus and the Holy Face. Completely unknown, she died on 29 September 1897, aged twenty-four. The Carmelite custom was to send other Carmels a short biography of each sister who died. Under obedience, Sister Thérèse had written her own spiritual autobiography before she died, so this was passed round in 1898, spread beyond Carmel and had an immediate impact. By 1925 her autobiography was known throughout the world and on 17 May of that year she was canonized by Pope Pius XI.

Thérèse seemed in Carmel only remarkable in her simplicity and ordinariness. But on 16 July before she died, she said to her sister, Mother Agnes: 'I feel my mission is soon to begin, my mission to teach souls my little way.' Mother Agnes asked: 'What is this little way which you would teach souls?' 'It is the way of spiritual childhood, the way of trust and absolute surrender.' Different writers have suggested her unique spiritual contribution is based on simplicity, spiritual poverty, confidence, love or a collection of virtues. But spiritual childhood is a fundamental attitude from which spring virtues. She explains:

It is the way of spiritual childhood, the way of confidence and abandonment to God. I want to teach them the little means which have proved so perfectly successful for myself . . .
It means that we acknowledge our nothingness; that we expect everything from the good lord, as a child expects everything from its father; it means to worry about nothing, seeking only to gather flowers, the flowers of sacrifices, and to offer them to the good lord for his pleasure. It also means not to attribute to ourselves the virtues we practice, not to believe we are capable of anything, but to acknowledge that it is the good lord who has placed that treasure in the hand of his little child that he may use it when he needs it, but it remains always God's own treasure. Finally, it means that we must not be discouraged by our faults, for children fall frequently (*Novissima Verba*).

Thérèse said the way was short, straight and new. There were no complexities, for we recognize our spiritual poverty and accept it. It is short because straightway we go to God as infinite love and he accomplishes in us what we cannot. It is new because it relies totally on the merciful love of God.

There are numerous translations of the autobiography under different titles, e.g. *Autobiography of a Saint* tr R. A. Knox, 1958; *The Story of a Soul* tr M. Day, 1973; also her *Collected Letters*, 1979; see also A. Coombes, *Introduction à la spirtualité de Saint Thérèse de l'enfant Jesus*, 1948; François Jamart, *Complete Spiritual Doctrine of St Thérèse of Lisieux*, ET 1961.

MICHAEL HOLLINGS

Thomas Aquinas, St

Dominican theologian (*c*. 1225–1274). Like his teacher, St Albert (*c*. 1200–1280), he espoused an intellectualist view of life. Our final union with God is essentially the union of our minds with the First Truth in love. Contemplation is the ascent of the mind to God, through the ordinary ways of human thought, including metaphysics, enlightened by revelation and the Holy Spirit. It grows out of the curiosity which is innate in human beings. 'Contemplatives', as such, are likely to love God less than 'actives', Thomas warns; but they are closer to the goal of human life, which is 'to know God' (John 17.3). Like everything else, contemplation needs to be motivated by charity, but, against the prevailing voluntarist interpretation of Denys the Areopagite*, Thomas insists that love by itself cannot unite us with God. Love motivates the mind to approach God. But Thomas also insists on the incomprehensibility of God. By clarifying all that can be understood, we come face to face with the mystery of God. Shortly before his death, Thomas underwent some strange experience, after which he abandoned writing and teaching and declared that all that he had written was 'straw' by comparison with what he had seen. But this was not a repudiation of all his previous work, it was its fulfilment. The simple, inexpressible, vision presupposes the hard intellectual work which leads up to it.

Perfection, for Thomas, means the perfection of charity. He offers a purely functional account of 'states of perfection'. No external situation, as such, constitutes a perfection; a public commitment by vow to the three evangelical counsels puts a person in a 'state', in which he or she practises three valuable aids towards the perfection of charity, but poverty, chastity and obedience are means, not ends.

Prayer (meaning primarily petition, as it does in most of the older traditions) is seen as the expression of the mind's readiness to submit its plans to God and to acknowledge that all good comes from him. In principle, it ought to be present in all that we seek to do or obtain. Since we cannot in practice pray always, Thomas recommends frequent, brief prayer. He warns against prolonging prayer beyond the point where we lose interest. He stresses the value of bodily prayer and worship. (He accepts the Aristotelian doctrine of the soul as the form of the body, which means that the body is necessarily involved in our spirituality.)

As a child, Thomas asked his teacher, 'What is God?'. His spirituality is theocentric, and the doctrine of creation in particular is central to his thought. The absolute primacy of God's act, even in our own free acts, allows him to develop a strong doctrine of grace as moving our wills from within (a doctrine later fiercely controverted by the Jesuits).

He made an important contribution to the theology of the sacraments and was known for his devotion to the eucharist. He composed the Office for the Feast of Corpus Christi.

K. Foster, *The Life of St Thomas Aquinas – Biographical Documents*, 1959; E. Schillebeeckx, *Christ the Sacrament*, 1963; G. Vann, *Morals makyth Man*, 1937; J. A. Weisheipl, *Friar Thomas d'Aquino*, 1975.

SIMON TUGWELL, OP

Thomas à Kempis

Thomas à Kempis (1379/80–1471) was born near Cologne and spent the rest of his life in the Netherlands. He was powerfully influenced by an informal monastic community, the Congregation of the Common Life, which had been founded by Geert Groote. His many writings commending the monastic life to his contemporaries have been overshadowed by *The Imitation of Christ* which is commonly ascribed to him. This work belongs to a genre of spiritual guides popular in the late fourteenth and fifteenth centuries and has become one of the Christian spiritual classics, although it is neither an extended treatment of the ideal of the imitation of Christ (in spite of its title) nor a specially original presentation of the pattern of Christian living. In spite of its monastic origins and content it has been continuously very popular with lay people; Maggie Tulliver in George Eliot's *The Mill on the Floss* speaks of it as 'a lasting record of human needs and human consolations'.

Christ is to be imitated by mediating on his life and especially his passion and death. 'The whole life of Christ was a cross and a martyrdom', says the author and the Christian life takes the shape of the 'royal road of the holy cross' (II 12). This is the path to resignation and other-worldliness which throughout the book is interpreted in a world-renouncing way.

The Imitation of Christ is in four books, the first ('Counsels on the Spiritual Life') concerned with growth in self-knowledge on the part of the follower of Christ and a progressive detachment from secular values. The author is particularly severe in his strictures on loveless scholarship and learning. Book 2 ('Counsels on the Inner Life') develops the theme of the interior life as a tracing over the passion of Christ. Book 3 ('On inward consolation') is a series of dialogues between Christ and the disciple and these are important as showing that for

Thomas à Kempis the imitation of Christ is not based on Jesus as only a figure of past history but as a present reality exercising a formative influence on the growth of the spiritual life of the Christian in the present. Book 4 is concerned with the eucharist and is again a series of dialogues between Christ and the disciple, emphasizing the need for careful and ordered preparation and the value of frequent reception of the sacrament. This book on the eucharist displays no narrow sacramentalism; in fact the Bible and eucharist are pictured as 'two tables set on either side the treasury of holy church'.

The Imitation of Christ will continue to have popularity far beyond the monastic circles for which it was originally intended. The basis of this popularity is its lucidity of style and psychological perceptiveness.

A convenient English edition of *The Imitation of Christ* is edited by L. Sherley-Price, 1952.

E. J. TINSLEY

Thomas Traherne

Born and brought up in Hereford, Thomas Traherne (1637–1674) came up to Brasenose College, Oxford, in the 1650s, was ordained in 1660 and became parish priest of Credenhill outside Hereford (to which he had previously been appointed under the Commonwealth) in 1661. In 1667 he moved to London as chaplain to Sir Orlando Bridgeman, the Lord Keeper of the Great Seal, serving also as 'minister' of Teddington, where he was buried on his death in 1674.

Traherne published almost nothing during his lifetime, but his *Christian Ethicks*, subtitled *The Way to Blessedness*, appeared in 1675 a few months after his death. His poems remained in manuscript until 1903, and his most famous work, *Centuries of Meditation*, was not published until 1908, having for long been lost in an anonymous manuscript.

Described as being of 'a cheerful and sprightly temper', Traherne's spirituality is pervaded by an optimism which has been both remarked upon and criticized. From the standpoint of a Calvinistic Puritanism with a dark view of man such criticisms may be justified, but Traherne stands in a long tradition of Christian Platonism, and one

which by no means sacrifices scripture to Platonist speculation, even though he quotes substantially from the Renaissance Platonist, Pico della Mirandola, and shows knowledge of the Neoplatonist writings of Hermes Trismegistus. In his *Ethicks*, as a recent editor has commented, there is a 'preoccupation with the beauty of holiness' and man's restoration to spiritual wholeness is understood in terms of 'recovery of vision, rather than conquest of sin.' In the *Centuries* Traherne shows that he shares with St Augustine* a deep understanding of want and desire as the way in which man be led to God, and Martz has also discerned the influence of Bonaventure's *Itinerarium mentis ad Deum*. Like Augustine, Traherne sought to convey his meaning by the technique of repetition, bringing to light the divine image and leading man to the paradise within. The cross is seen as the revelation and communication of the love of God, the ligature of the whole creation. Sharing much with the contemporary Cambridge Platonists* and poets like Henry Vaughan*, Traherne is a supreme exponent of the affirmative way whose vivid sense of the divine glory transfiguring creation is expressed in rich and moving prose.

Thomas Traherne, *Poems, Centuries and Three Thanksgivings* (ed A. Ridler), 1966; *The Way to Blessedness* (ed M. Bottrall), 1962; L. L. Martz, *The Paradise Within: Studies in Vaughan, Traherne and Milton*, 1964; G. I. Wade, *Thomas Traherne, A Critical Biography*, 1944.

GEOFFREY ROWELL

Thomist Spirituality
see **Thomas Aquinas, St**

Tractarians
see **Oxford Movement, The**

Transcendental Meditation
see **Meditation, Transcendental**

Transfiguration

The episode in the Synoptic Gospels known as the Transfiguration has had much influence upon Christian spirituality through the centuries, and the verb transfigure has come to describe an aspect of the Christian life. Inspired as they have been by the gospel story these spiritual trends have sometimes been only loosely related to the exact exegesis of the story.

In Mark's narrative (9.2–8) the episode is described as happening six days after Peter's confession and the first prediction of the suffering and death of Jesus. Jesus takes Peter and John and James up a high mountain and there he is 'transfigured' before them; they see him in an intense bright radiance. Moses and Elijah are seen in converse with him, a cloud (apparently the cloud of the divine presence as in the Book of Exodus) appears enveloping all, and a voice is heard proclaiming the unique sonship of Jesus and summoning the disciples to hearken to him. The scene appears to convey that in spite of his coming suffering and death Jesus is seen in glory, perhaps in anticipation of the glory which will be his in his predicted return. Matthew's account follows Mark's and emphasizes the contrast between Moses on Mount Sinai and Jesus on the mount where he is now seen. Luke's account diverges a little from the others. The word 'transfigure' is avoided, as perhaps suggesting some pagan concept. Luke says that Jesus is praying when the scene happens, and Moses and Elijah are described as speaking about 'the Exodus which Jesus will fulfil in Jerusalem': no doubt the word suggests not only the death of Jesus but his departure through death to glory. In II Peter 1, probably a late document amongst the NT writings and not one of Petrine authorship, there is a brief account of the transfiguration scene. It is thought by some scholars that the words of I Peter 5.1, 'a witness of the sufferings of Christ and a sharer in the glory that is to be revealed', refer to the writer's experience in the event of the transfiguration.

The story of the Transfiguration has inspired a number of themes of Christian spirituality. Christians have been drawn by the story to the contemplation of Jesus in glory on the way to suffering and death, and here the language of Heb. 2.9 is comparable. Some have contrasted Peter's desire to linger in the presence of the glory on the mountain and the call of Jesus to return to the plain and to follow the path to death where glory will be in the end no less apparent. Some have emphasized the prayer of Jesus on the mount as an instance of the bodily transformation which has sometimes accompanied union with God in prayer, and

have cited the stigmata of St Francis of Assisi * as another instance.

The idea of transfiguration as a description of the Christian life has recurred in Christian teaching. Several instances of this occur in NT writings without explicit relation to the transfiguration story. Thus in II Cor. 3 St Paul describes the Christians as beholding the glory of God reflected in Jesus as in a mirror, and while they do so being changed into his likeness from one degree of glory to another by the indwelling Holy Spirit. So in I John 3.1–2, the Christians are described as becoming like Jesus and seeing him as he is. In both passages there is the link between the vision of Jesus and the growth into his likeness. In Rom. 12.1–2 St Paul, without any reference to vision, describes the transfiguring of Christian lives in a searching way.

In Eastern Orthodox Christianity the Transfiguration has special prominence. Thus the festival of the Transfiguration, observed on 6 August both in the East and in the West, is in the East one of the great celebrations of the Christian year alongside Epiphany and Easter. It was taught by many of the ancient fathers and by later Eastern mystical writers that the light which the disciples saw on the mount was the uncreated light of deity, and in virtue of the light the transfiguration tells of the recreation both of humanity and of the cosmos into the divine likeness. This theme found in some of the ancient Fathers was specially drawn out by St Gregory Palamas * and his school from the fourteenth century.

A. M. Allchin, *The World is a Wedding*, 1975; V. Lossky, *The Mystical Theology of the Eastern Church*, ET 1957; A. M. Ramsey, *The Glory of God and the Transfiguration of Christ*, ²1967.

A. MICHAEL RAMSEY

Trappists

The word derives from the abbey of la Trappe (Orne) reformed by Armand-Jean de Rancé (1626–1700), who, after a notable conversion in 1657, became regular abbot in 1664. Though juridically subject to the Cistercian Order, and part of the Strict Observance, he soon formulated a rule (first, unauthorized, edition 1671, as *Réglements de la Trappe*) going beyond that of the Strict Observance but applicable solely to his own abbey. This autonomy continued until the French Revolution when, alone of all French Cistercian communities, that of la Trappe went into exile as a body, albeit depleted, under the leadership of Dom Augustin Lestrange (elected abbot 1794). This group became the nucleus of Cistercian survival and after travelling as far as Russia and America returned to la Trappe in 1815, accompanied and followed by other communities formed in the course of their odyssey. Until Cîteaux was repopulated and restored as mother-house in 1898 la Trappe was *de facto* the centre of Cistercian expansion throughout the world, though the Strict Observance (by then popularly known as Trappists) only achieved canonical independence from the Common Observance (almost obliterated in France and surviving much altered elsewhere) in 1892. The various groupings of monasteries united finally in 1892 followed Rancé's originally domestic prescriptions with only local variations. Thus the striking success of Rancé's initial reform, its persistence after his death, and then the heroic leadership of Dom Lestrange, whose emergency rule of 1794 saved the Cistercian Order at the price of ferocious austerity, strengthened the claims of a monastic ideal, constantly attacked as excessive, but justified by events. This triumphant vindication did not encourage Trappists to compromise thereafter.

The external features of the rule (mitigated since Vatican II *) are the best known, and the most apparent: perpetual abstinence from meat, fish and eggs (except for the sick), rigorous silence and enclosure, some seven hours a day in choir, rising for the night office, manual labour for all, dormitories and not cells. Rancé saw these as means to an end, validated only by inward dispositions, and he warned against the dangers of mere external observance leading to spiritual pride. The essence of Trappist life is penitence, a single-minded love of God built up from destruction of self-love through physical mortification, intellectual humility (whence Rancé's ban on monastic studies) and spiritual renunciation of all earthly ties. While the peace in this life and joy hereafter offered by such a rule is stressed, there is always more emphasis on the negative, pessimistic aspects, and especially during the nineteenth century rigidity of observance seemed almost to become an end in itself. Rancé always appealed to the Rule of St Benedict, and its renewal by the Cistercian founders, particularly St Bernard *, to justify his own practice, but the ascetic teaching of the Desert Fathers *, above all St John Climacus *, played a decisive part in his spirituality. His own theology was Augustinian, but he discouraged theology in his monks, nor did he compensate with any special teaching on prayer. During this century reaction against Rancé has been strong, and Trappists look back instead to their original Cistercian heritage, and now even to non-Christian systems like Zen.*

See also **Cistercians**.

A. J. Krailsheimer, *A.-J. de Rancé, Abbot of la Trappe*, 1974.

A. J. KRAILSHEIMER

Underhill, Evelyn

Prolific writer on the spiritual life and guide to many devout people, she was born in 1875 into a cultivated upper middle-class family in which, by her own account, she was 'not brought up to religion'. Her earliest publications, however, consisting of poetry and novels, give evidence of an immanentist theology tinged with Christian imagery; and a visit to a convent of perpetual adoration in 1907 contributed towards her conversion to an incarnational and sacramental faith with worship at its heart. It seemed at first to be leading her to the Roman Catholic Church, but her disapproval of Rome's treatment of modernist writers and consideration for her husband's wishes (she married Stuart Moore in 1907) persuaded her to remain in the Church of England although she did not become a fully practising Anglican until 1921, the year in which she formally placed herself under the direction of the Baron von Hügel *. He encouraged a christocentric piety and as wide a range of interests as possible. In her contribution to *Essays Catholic and Missionary* (1928) she sought to establish the uniqueness of Christianity among the world religions, arguing that the gospel cut across them. 'In the depth of reality revealed by the cross, Christianity stands alone.' It was in personal religious experience that other faiths were closest to Christianity and she blamed contemporary Christianity for its lack of quietude and failure to apply religion to social life. In 1936,

Worship, perhaps her finest book, witnessed to an increasingly deep ecumenism and appreciation of corporate liturgical worship.

Her own contribution to spirituality lay in three main areas. Almost self-taught in the early 1900s, she made herself an authority on the literature of Western mysticism. In one big book, *Mysticism* (1911), and in numerous smaller works she related it to contemporary psychology and philosophy, and with discriminating editorship introduced to her readers the texts of such writers as the Italian Franciscan Jacopone da Todi, the Flemish Ruysbroeck *, and the English mystics Walter Hilton, Richard Rolle * and *The Cloud of Unknowing* * (*see also* **English Mystics**). She had always, ever since a girlhood declaration of socialism, been sensitive to the cause of social justice and the sufferings of the poor, and as the Second World War approached she embraced, with anguish, a complete pacifism, seeing it as implicit in her teaching and experience of the mystical tradition. She published a pamphlet, *The Church and War* not long before her death in June 1941.

The second area lay in her vocation to a ministry of spiritual direction *, in which she made herself available to anyone who sought counsel in the art of prayer and in relating it to everyday life. Her time was at her own disposal and she could carry on the work in her own home by interview and correspondence. Her direction was sane, practicable, encouraging and adapted to the needs of the individual.

Allied to her work of direction but distinct from it was the third area, from 1924, of the conduct of retreats *, mostly at Pleshey, in Essex, a place for which she came to have a special devotion. She took great trouble over the preparation of addresses and especially the introductory ones composed for the guidance of those unused to the silence of retreat. Many of the courses of addresses were subsequently published, and contain some of the most enduring parts of her life's work.

Margaret Cropper, *Evelyn Underhill*, 1958; Lucy Menzies (ed), *Collected Papers of Evelyn Underhill*, 1946; Charles Williams (ed), *The Letters of Evelyn Underhill*, 1943.
REGINALD CANT

Union *see* **Mysticism**

Unitive Way

The unitive way, the so-called way of the perfect, is the third and final stage of the spiritual journey as it was understood by many ancient spiritual guides. The other two stages are the purgative way, the way of beginners, and the illuminative way, the way of the proficient. Modern spiritual writers tend to regard this scheme as altogether too rigid. For the special characteristics which give their name to the three stages, the deepening of repentance, the enlargement of faith and vision, the growth in love for God and neighbour, are present and important throughout the spiritual journey. Further, individuals are led in many and differing ways, according to temperament, early experience, present circumstance and special vocation. Like a river which winds and loops and bends back upon its course, a person may sometimes travel by strange and twisting paths to reach his journey's end in God. However, if this is borne in mind and the scheme is understood flexibly, it can help the spiritual guide. For people do pass through stages; there are spiritual beginners, there are the experienced and there are those far advanced on the Godward journey, and their needs will tend to differ.

The unitive way might be described as a set of motives and aims especially characteristic of those well advanced on the spiritual journey. A dominant aim of the spiritual life is to grow into oneness with God and his will. The Christian is urged by many motives; the fear of sin and guilt, the longing for inner freedom and peace, gratitude for grace received and a feeling of obligation to respond to it, the desire to please God. As he progresses a feeling of love towards God and the desire to please him, not primarily for the sake of reward either in this world or the next but out of a kind of friendship, begins to predominate over the other motives. This master motive does not destroy the lesser motives but slowly transforms them so that they conform to the desire for oneness with God and harmony with his will. The love for God is not the rival of the love of husband for wife and wife for husband, of parents for children and children for parents, or the love between friends. Rather, love for God tends to reduce the selfish and possessive elements in loving and so to strengthen genuine love. As an individual's sense of friendship for God grows he tends to see and feel all men and women, indeed the whole world of nature, as belonging to God his Friend, and he begins to share the divine concern for the whole created universe.

This love for God which overflows in love for all creation is in T. S. Eliot's * words a gift from God, 'something given/And taken, in a life-time's death in love,/Ardour and self-lessness and self-surrender' ('The Dry Salvages'). 'We love because he first loved us.' God's love awakens an answering love once we become aware of it. One of the disciplines of the unitive life is the endeavour to strengthen this realization. The Christian wanting to grow in love will read and ponder the Gospel story and especially the scenes and symbols that most powerfully express God's love. He is likely to be especially drawn to the story of the passion and death of Christ and to the figure of the crucified in which he can contemplate God's love for mankind exposed nakedly on the cross.

In the unitive life prayer will have the central place. An attitude of loving trust in God will express itself in the whole of a Christian's life and the specific times of prayer will focus and strengthen this Godward orientation. The typical prayer of the unitive life is that of contemplation *, which has been described as a prayer of loving attention to God or as 'looking and loving'. It is an exercise of intuition, a waiting on God, a listening, a looking towards a reality which utterly transcends the mind's grasp. Contemplation is a gift, a grace, which cannot be commanded but must be waited for in patience. It is impossible for anyone whose heart is not strongly engaged in the quest for closer oneness with God and his will.

At every stage of the spiritual journey the individual who seeks a closer walk with God will find the cross in some shape or form. Christ's saying about losing life in order to gain it applies from beginning to end of the Godward journey, but is especially true of the unitive life. Genuine love for and trust in God creates a sense of inward security which enables and persuades the individual to relax his defences against the forces which threaten his peace. In consequence he becomes vulnerable in diverse ways. He finds it impossible to resist the demands that others make on him or refuse the burdens they place on his shoulders. Yet despite his voluntary servitude to the needs and demands of others he feels freer than ever before. A worse trial has its source in himself, as emotions, rooted in painful infant experience and long repressed, are released. For the relaxing of his defences leaves him open to feelings of loneliness and rejection, of fear and rage, of crude sexual cravings, of depression, which rise up into consciousness in the shape of disagreeable fantasies and black moods. Questions as to the reality or goodness of God are liable to invade the mind. Self-confidence is being destroyed in order to be reborn as a rock-like confidence in God. The individual is inwardly broken in order to be remade. He learns to rejoice in both triumph and disaster, whether in his outward circumstances or in the sphere of his inner life. For he knows with the certainty of faith that the almighty Love is present in everything and working for the everlasting good of himself and everyone else.

Christopher Bryant, *The Heart in Pilgrimage*, ch 5, 1980.

CHRISTOPHER BRYANT, SSJE

Unity *see* Ecumenical Spirituality

Upanishads

A collection of Hindu * writings, dating from the period between 800 and 300 BC. Upanishad is a composite word which conveys the meaning of a pupil sitting down beside his guru in order to receive instruction. The Upanishads are said to constitute the conclusion to or to indicate the purpose of the whole corpus of Vedic literature, and for one of both of these reasons they are known as Vedānta, 'the end of the Vedas'. In origin they were remarkably varied writings, and the unity implied in attributing the single name Upanishads to them all was imposed upon them by later commentators.

Traditionally there are said to be 108 Upanishads, although it is probable that even more were composed. But the more important ones are limited to between ten and fourteen (authorities disagree on how many principal Upanishads there are). The early Upanishads, including the Brihadāranyaka and the Chāndogya, were written in prose and in dialogue form. The later Upanishads are in verse.

The Principal Upanishads have been widely translated. They are important as sources for much Indian philosophy and because they represent the earliest literary source for many significant and widespread Hindu ideas.

It is in the Upanishads that we find the first clear references to the ideas of transmigration and karma, which suggest that at death souls are reborn and go through an almost endless cycle of rebirths, and that the condition of an individual's rebirth will depend upon actions performed during previous existences. Since the time of the Upanishads the ideas of karma and transmigration have been found in almost all varieties of Hindu religion.

The Upanishads also show development, or change, from the earlier Vedas in their teaching about Ultimate Reality, or Brahman. The Upanishads emphasize the all-prevailing presence of Brahman, who is regarded as the one true reality, rather than the earlier Vedic belief in many gods. People are generally unable to perceive Brahman's reality and operation in the world because of māyā, a word which signifies something like illusion or deception. When the ignorance in which māyā enfolds man is dispelled, and he is able to experience his essential oneness with Brahman, he will find release or liberation (moksha) from the cycle of birth and rebirth. The identity of the individual soul (ātman) with Brahman is an important element in the teaching of the Upanishads, and is summarized in the statement 'Thou art that' (tat tvam asi). In some Upanishads, especially the relatively late Śvetāśvatara and also the Īśa and Katha, the possibility of the appearance of the Absolute within the flux of the phenomenal world is conceded in references to Īśa or Īśvara, the personal God and Creator who may be an object of worship.

The more important Upanishads include: Aitareya, Brihadāranyaka, Chāndogya, Īśa, Kauśītaki, Kena, Katha, Mahānārāyana, Maitri, Māndūkya, Mundaka, Praśna, Śvetāśvatara, and Taittirīya.

The Upanishads have had some influence on Western ideas since the nineteenth century, particularly through Schopenhauer and later through Western Advaitists.

A. L. Basham, *The Wonder that Was India*, [3]1967; P. Deussen, *Philosophy of the Upanishads*, 1966; S. Radhakrishnan, *The Principal Upanishads*, 1968; R. C. Zaehner, *Hindu Scriptures*, 1978.

PETER D. BISHOP

Vatican II Spirituality

The Second Vatican Council aimed at *aggiornamento*: bringing the Roman Catholic Church up to date. In both the conciliar documents and developments after the Council, *aggiornamento* mainly came to mean taking a more responsible and hopeful attitude towards the modern world. The most influential conciliar documents – *Lumen Gentium, Gaudium et Spes*, and *Dignitatis Humanae* – developed this theme, stressing that all Christians have ministerial and missionary roles to play. The result was a significant change in the stance of Roman Catholicism, and through Roman Catholicism a significant change in the stance of Christianity overall. Hand in hand with a return to the scriptural and liturgical sources, Vatican II's openness to the modern world sketched a sacramental spirituality in which Christian life might symbolize the fulfilment which God's grace labours to bring to all human beings.

Twenty years after the Council, this sacramental spirituality stood forth in clearer lines. Experience had shown that 'spirituality' had to become synonymous with a deep life of faith, and that a deep life of faith co-ordinates contemplative love of God and political love of neighbour. When they accepted the Council's invitation to probe the mystery of the church, renew their formation by scripture, and participate more fully in the divine liturgy, Christian religious and laity alike grew hungry for a deeper life of prayer. No longer did prayer seem the exclusive prerogative of priests and nuns, for all Christians who studied the Bible found an injunction to pray always, an invitation to taste and see the goodness of the Lord.

With time this hunger for a deeper life of prayer led to an increased interest in retreats*, spiritual direction*, and classical works on simple contemplation such as *The Cloud of Unknowing**. Greater contact with Eastern religions revealed the spiritual power of yoga* and zen*, while ecumenical contacts brought Eastern Orthodox practices such as the Jesus Prayer* and charismatic emphasis on the gifts of the Spirit* closer to the Western mainstream. Religious education developed a fresh view of the married and lay vocations, seconding the Vatican II instinct that holiness is possible in the midst of the world, so belatedly Roman Catholicism found itself accepting many of the sixteenth-century Protestant Reformers' intuitions and returning to the biblical sense that the earth should be the Lord's and the fullness thereof.

On the political side, Vatican II came to be seen as a call to a wholesale promotion of social justice. In matters of race, sex, economics, and war-making, the opening of the Council to the modern world revealed a great many injustices crying out for redress. With an increased appreciation for many of the insights of Karl Marx, political theologians in Europe and liberation theologians in Latin America (*see* **Liberation, Spirituality of**) led a movement to focus Christian faith on the service of the world's poor, arguing that to know God one must do justice to one's neighbour. The Roman Catholic hierarchy often was uneasy with liberation theology, but both Pope Paul VI and Pope John Paul II put social justice high on their agendas. So long as political theology did not ignore the realm of transcendence and grace, the popes approved it as speaking forth the true message of the Sermon on the Mount, the true Christian tradition that the goods of the earth are for all the earth's people.

By the early 1980s the dominant political focus had become nuclear war. Realizing that the threat of war coloured all contemporary life, Christians formed by Vatican II began to pressure for a widespread conversion to peace-making. Combining prayer vigils and political marches, they contrasted the life-giving character of their God with the death-dealing character of many modern institutions. In this movement they joined many secular humanists, who had come to question the modern assumptions about the death of God and the blessings of technology. As economic disparities, ecological crises and nuclear stockpiles all mounted, people of spiritual awareness around the world were calling for a new set of priorities.

However, as it became clear that wholesale conversion to a new set of priorities faced immense opposition, because it threatened all the dominant regimes, Christians and aroused humanists began to contend with evil and suffering on a new level. Without retracting their love of the world, they began to remind themselves of Jesus' crucifixion. Throughout the world, the body of Christ, the assemblies of grace, would be praying and labouring in hope more than vision. To find the life of God, they would have to lose many this-worldly securities. So Vatican II spirituality led to the challenge to believe deeply enough, live intensely enough, to find God in the midst of counter-cultural trial and suffering.

J. Carmody, *Reexamining Conscience*, 1982; L. S. Cunningham, *The Meaning of Saints*, 1980; J. Deretz and A. Nocent, *Dictionary of the Council*, 1968; R. P. McBrien, *Catholicism*, 2 vols, 1980; K. Wojtyla, *Sources of Renewal*, 1980.

JOHN CARMODY

Vaughan, Henry

Henry Vaughan (1621–1695), the elder of twin brothers, was born in Breconshire and educated locally and then most probably at Jesus College, Oxford and at one of the Inns of Court. His legal aspirations were frustrated by the Civil War but there is no certain record of his service as a Royalist soldier nor of his qualifications as a doctor, his eventual profession. He lived in Breconshire after the Royalist defeat and adopted the appropriate title 'Silurist' after the ancient British tribe of that county. He translated numerous prose treatises mainly on retirement and solitude, wrote a devotional book, *The Mount of Olives*, and published his greatest poetry, *Silex Scintillans*, in 1650 (enlarged 1655). He acknowledges in its preface the deep religious and literary influence of George Herbert* and consciously 'baptized' his Muse, simultaneously achieving a massive increase in poetic power. The new intensity was reinforced by personal loss (his brother's death; the eviction of another brother and other clerical friends from local livings) as well as by his study of books of devotion and the Hermetic writings. How deeply Vaughan was affected by Hermeticism is a matter of debate, but it is certain that nothing separated him from his allegiance to the Anglican tradition.

The Mount of Olives or Solitary Devotions (1652) is not a manual of instruction but a collection of prayers and meditations primarily addressed to Anglicans deprived of the Book of Common Prayer and the familiar services. The prayers incorporate complex biblical allusion and are arranged according to the key moments of the day or in the Christian life. Vaughan sometimes allows his own despair to break through, giving the meditations considerable though strictly contemporary intensity.

A sense of loss and deprivation informs many of the greatest poems in *Silex Scintillans*. Vaughan longs for the familiarity with God enjoyed by the Patriarchs ('Religion'), or in childhood ('The Retreate'), but principally he speaks with longing of the dead's enjoyment of the 'world of light' ('They are all gone'). The natural world, though but 'masques and shadows', still speaks of 'thy sacred way' but Vaughan awaits the vision without 'mists' or 'veils'. Many poems look forward to the Day of Judgment as restoring and fulfilling the natural world. Nature is sometimes treated allegorically or as a 'hieroglyph' of glory, but Vaughan has the especial gift of showing life as 'a quicknes, which my God hath kissed' ('Quickness'). He asks 'When thou shalt make all new again .../Give him amongst thy works a place/Who in them lov'd and sought thy face' ('The Book'). At this moment the light of God will 'through thy creatures pierce and pass/Till all becomes thy cloudless glass' ('L'Envoy'). Many poems are more coolly meditative, more conventionally didactic, but his vision of vitality, of blazing light, of the 'great Chime/and Symphony of Nature, although most individual and private, remains most universally available.

L. C. Martin (ed), *The Works of Henry Vaughan*, revd edn 1957; R. Garner, *Henry Vaughan Experience and the Tradition*, 1959; F. E. Hutchinson, *Henry Vaughan. A Life and Interpretation*, ²1971; L. Martz, *The Paradise Within*, 1964; E. C. Pettet, *Of Paradise and Light*, 1960; A. Rudrum, *Henry Vaughan*, 1981; J. D. Simmons, *Masques of God*, 1972.

ELUNED BROWN

Vianney, Jean-Baptiste-Marie
see Ars, Curé d'

Victorines, The
The Abbey of St Victor was in Paris and in the twelfth century it produced among its canons regular scholars and spiritual theologians of great ability and influence. Adam (d. *c.* 1185) was a composer of liturgical sequences; Hugh (d. 1142), from Saxony, was a prolific writer, 'rich in new ideas and fresh presentations of old ones' (Aelred Squire); Richard (d. 1173), who came from Ireland or Scotland, was the most mystical and ecstatic.

The original contribution of the Victorines to spiritual theology was in the place they accorded to meditation. They distinguish three stages of prayer; reflection which may be no more than reverie, 'idle thoughts of an idle fellow', in Jerome K. Jerome's title; meditation; and contemplation. Richard, with a hint of Isaiah 40.31, describes reflection as wandering, rather aimlessly; meditation as a search for the heights, 'with intense concentration of purpose'; contemplation as a mounting up with wings like an eagle to that empyrean where all may be surveyed in a single glance.

In their stress on meditation, the Victorines not only introduced orderliness into prayer without quenching individuality (Kirk); they obliterated the false distinction between prayer and the intellectual quest. Natural knowledge is not to be despised, godliness and good learning are not incompatible. Says Hugh, 'Learn everything: thou shalt find in the end that nothing is superfluous.' Any discipline of the mind may be preparatory to contemplation. Behind all this is the doctrine of creation, and of the incarnation, too, for the Word was with God in the beginning and became flesh in Christ. Hugh widens meditation from the concentration on the sacred humanity* which dominated the spirituality of Bernard of Clairvaux*. There is a foretaste here of the theology of the Cambridge Platonists*, and in the twentieth century of F. R. Tennant and C. E. Raven, who have denied that natural theology and the Christian revelation are opposed and that we can learn nothing of the God and Father of Jesus Christ from the world around us.

Richard is an allegorist, with his interpretation of the story of Benjamin as illustrative of the stages of the mystic way. There are for him six degrees of contemplation and the first three which concern natural knowledge are lower and preliminary. Martin Thornton has described them as simple awareness of things, which may lead to worship; the aesthetic stage, a deeper awareness of beauty and design in creation; the sacramental stage, wherein the inner reality of creatures is sought and perceived. Then Denys takes over, the natural faculties are gradually discarded and we apprehend truths above reason, and truths contrary to reason. At the last, natural knowledge seems to be vain if we are to share the Divine ecstasy. Yet it is not so. It teaches us discipline in the search for a God who is not of confusion but of peace, while 'it is better to meditate on the true good in any fashion whatever, and thereby inflame the heart's longing for it, than to fix the thoughts on false and deceptive goods'.

Clare Kirchberger (ed), *Selected Writings on Contemplation*, 1957; Kenneth E. Kirk, *The Vision of God*, 1931; Martin Thornton, *English Spirituality*, 1963; F. Vernet, 'Hugues de Saint-Victor,' *DTC*, VII, cols 240–308.

EDITOR

Vision of God

One of the classic definitions of the *summum bonum*, the goal of the spiritual life. Platonist rather than Christian in origin, though found in most of the world's great religions, it has been considered by some to be an inadequate, if not dangerous expression of the final beatitude, almost as dangerous, and as infrequent in the NT, as deification*. K. E. Kirk has to admit that the beatitude 'Blessed are the pure in heart for they shall see God', 'stands without echo in the synoptic tradition', while in the OT Yahweh says, 'No one can see my face and live,' though Job concludes, after all his trials and his painful re-education, 'I had heard of thee by the hearing of the ear, but now mine eye seeth thee.' The vision leads him, as Isaiah in the temple, to penitence.

During the heyday of biblical theology, 'the Word' was the paramount symbol. It still asserts itself as in the sociologist David Martin's rejection of mysticism* as providing the exclusive definition of religion. 'Man does not retire to the interior castle or live by illumination. He lives by the Word: *logos*, reason, embodiment.' And the Word demands obedience, an act of will (more of the Hebrew ethos than the Greek). There has been a parallel debate in philosophy. G. E. Moore used the quasi-aesthetic imagery of

vision in considering the good, conceiving it on the analogy of the beautiful, and making the moral agent a contemplative, whereas some would maintain that 'he is essentially and inescapably an *agent*', willing and doing the good. In *The Sovereignty of Good* (1970) Iris Murdoch, quoted in the above sentence, seeks to rehabilitate the language of vision and the metaphor of sight, for man is not simply a will, but 'a unified being who sees' and anyone without philosophical prejudice would describe a change of attitude in terms of sight. We come to love and admire a person whom we had disliked by 'seeing' him/her differently.

To describe the *summum bonum* as the vision of God implies the promise that we shall see him who is invisible. The vision then is intellectual not physical, and is only attained by a detachment from the appetites and desires of sense involving not only mental discipline but bodily austerity and a harsh rigorism of ethical judgment. This again has caused Christian theologians to demur, for not only is that profoundly unhebraic but it could be anti-incarnational as well, implying a spirituality in which the human Jesus is but a stage on the way to God, Calvary but one place on a long journey, and human relationships so great a distraction from the Divine that love of neighbour may become very much the second and subordinate command. That this has been so in the history of Christian spirituality is undoubtedly true, but the modern debate in philosophy should reassure us. Iris Murdoch is seeking to refute those linguistic philosophers who, however cathartic the astringency of their analysis, have in the extremes of their logic been the progenitors, not simply of anti-religion, but of nihilism and meaninglessness. Also she is trying to base her moral philosophy on a truly human psychology in a counter to behaviourism and she draws from aesthetic experience and not simply from science. True the former may imprison us in the sensual, and Iris Murdoch has also confronted the uncomfortable fact that Plato banished the artists (*The Fire and the Sun*, 1978). Perhaps it is Christianity alone which does full justice to the concept of vision as the *summum bonum*. Vision takes us beyond ourselves; we look away from ourselves to God; in particular for Christians it is christocentric, a looking to Jesus not simply in the wonder of his own person, but in his compassion for the world, and it unifies our whole being in worship and implies not merely being told what is truth, but seeking one's own 'insight', not merely 'gaze' but participation. It also beckons us ever onward to what is yet unattainable. 'This truly is the vision of God: never to be satisfied in the desire to see him. But one must always, by looking at what he can see, rekindle his desire to see more. Thus no limit would interrupt growth in the ascent to God, since no limit to the God can be found nor is the increasing desire for good brought to an end because it is satisfied' (Gregory of Nyssa, *Life of Moses* 239).

Dorothy M. Emmet, *The Moral Prism*, 1979; Kenneth E. Kirk, *The Vision of God*, 1931; Vladimir Lossky, *The Vision of God*, 1963; John Macquarrie, *Paths in Spirituality*, 1972, pp. 120–6.

EDITOR

Vives, Juan Luis

A prolific writer, not least on education, Vives (1492–1540), known also as Ludovicus, was born in Valentia, but brought over to England from Bruges by Henry VIII to be tutor to Princess Mary. He also taught at Oxford. He fell foul of the monarch for opposing his divorce, but withdrew his support for Queen Katherine on his release from prison, though was wise enough to live mostly back in Bruges thereafter. His importance in spirituality lies in his prayers *Exitationes Animi in Deum* which are found both in Catholic and Protestant primers and had especial vogue in Reformed collections, where they recur until well into the next century. John Bradford, the martyred English reformer, used them, which ensured their provenance, and they are found in Lewis Bayly's phenomenally popular *The Practice of Piety* (1610). The feature most prominent from Vives in Puritan and German Pietist guides to Godliness is the advice that the simple tasks of mundane life should be associated with the solemnities of scripture and mortality. The bed is always to remind the sleeper of his grave, his rising of the resurrection from the dead. Should he hear the cockcrow, he must remember Peter's denial and penitence with many tears. The putting on of clothes is to carry the mind back to man's primaeval innocence

and fallen shame. The sun streaming through the windows is to be a sign of the Sun of Righteousness, risen with healing in his wings. Vives is somewhat joyless, but his method is still advanced in spiritual counselling today.

C. J. Stranks, *Anglican Devotion*, 1961; Foster Watson, *Vives on Education*, 1913.

EDITOR

War, Holy

The NT itself portrays the disciple as a soldier, though the language of war and of athletics is apt to get confused. Sometimes it is the wrestling ring, or the race that is in mind rather than military engagement, and the early ascetics were the athletes rather than the soldiers of Christ (*See* **Asceticism**). There are of course many NT passages which clearly concern soldiery, such as the summons to put on the whole armour of God (Eph. 6.13). And the conversion of Constantine meant that the Roman army was henceforth nominally on the side of the church and analogies of military service could be more appropriately drawn. In the period of warfare in Western Europe which preceded the establishment of the Holy Roman Empire, Christ himself was seen as the Divine Son arming himself for fight, his royal banners advancing (e.g. the hymns of Venantius Fortunatus *c.* 600). The Crusades too led to the Christian life being regarded as a Holy War, as certainly did the religious conflicts and the breaking out into the world of the sixteenth century. The 1552 Prayer Book intercessions at communion are for 'the church militant here in earth' (though there is a polemical contrast to the church triumphant in heaven for which we do not pray). Ignatius Loyola * had been a soldier and at the beginning of his *Spiritual Exercises* * the retreatant is asked to imagine the two hosts of Christ and of Evil in confrontation, a picture which is also drawn, though more gently, in Francis de Sales' * *Introduction to the Devout Life*. Bunyan * arms Christian as he proceeds on his pilgrimage, his burden rolled away. He also wrote the *Holy War*, less of a work of genius than *Pilgrim's Progress*.

Lorenzo Scupoli wrote *The Spiritual Combat* in 1589. This is on Christian Perfection, to achieve which 'you must wage a constant, cruel war with yourself'. The volume is very much in the Western six-teenth-century tradition, in which mental prayer predominates. This treatise fell into Orthodox hands and was edited by Nicode-mus the Hagiorite (1748–1809) who, in 1796, published it together with another work of Scupoli, *The Path to Paradise*, under the title of *Unseen Warfare*. In the next century this work was extensively revised by Theophan the Recluse (1815–1894). The changes from Scupoli's original work in *Unseen Warfare* both point the Orthodox criticism of the Counter-Reformation and the difference between the spiritualities of East and West. There is much more 'mental fight' in the West, direct organization of the faculties of the mind; in the East, prayer is not so much a weapon in the Christian's armoury essen-tial to a long and planned campaign as life itself. It is pure prayer, contemplation rather than meditative analysis. As Theophan is fond of saying: 'The principal thing is to stand with the mind in the heart before God, and to go on standing before him unceas-ingly day and night, until the end of life.' The Jesus Prayer * is central to this. There is much less emphasis on struggle and conflict.

It may be questioned whether the imagery of war is appropriate to the Christian life in an age when swords are beaten into bomb cases, and pacificism has probably greater influence in the church than has been tradi-tional. But modern psychology has under-taken much analysis of human aggression and in the personal sphere the concept of Holy War, as well as of wrestling both with ourselves and with God, may be valid and illuminating; while evil in the soul and in society needs to be 'flushed out' and fought, though with spiritual weapons.

E. Kadloubovsky and G. E. H. Palmer (ed), *Unseen Warfare*, ET 1952; T. R. Glover, *The Disciple*, 1942.

EDITOR

Ward, Reginald Somerset

Many men and women who came under the direction of Reginald Somerset Ward (1881–1962) trace a new pattern in their spiritual lives from the moment he 'took them on'. Those he directed saw him three times a year at one of some twenty centres in Britain, or at Ravenscroft, his home in Farncombe, Surrey. In interviews lasting half-an-hour 'on tour', rather longer at his home, there

was time for confession, counsel, talk about the spiritual life and particular problems. From the end of the First World War he wrote a monthly *Instruction* on prayer. The last one, number 457, closed a period of publication covering forty years. 'RSW' corresponded with hundreds – many of them clergy – on every aspect and problem concerning the spiritual life.

The possessor of an excellent brain, a good organizer, lecturer, writer and prea-cher, Ward was content at God's call to relinquish his living and give himself com-pletely to spiritual counselling. Ordained priest in 1904, from 1909–1913 he was organizing secretary for the Sunday School Institute, and from 1913–1915, Rector of Chiddingfold. His answer to God's call was met by the anonymous provision of a house and financial support, enabling him to set out on the lonely road of peripatetic spiritual direction in 1915 with the ap-proval and blessing of the then Bishop of Winchester and to follow it faithfully until his death. Centres visited three times a year on north-west, north-east, midland and southern tours included Manchester, New-castle, Leeds, Birmingham, Bristol, Not-tingham, Portsmouth, and there were re-gular days in London throughout the year.

It is the special gift of a spiritual director to possess insight into the needs and condi-tions of souls, and in his long ministry Ward emphasized several truths. First the neces-sity to approach spiritual direction as a physician of souls and not as a dictator. His 'contribution' to Anglican counselling may well turn out to be his emphasis on the joint hindrances of fear and sin. He had the good priest's horror of sin. His knowledge of fear and its ravages in life led him to accept the best in psychology. 'One pound of spiritual direction', he used to say with a twinkle, was made up of 'eight ounces of prayer, three ounces of theology, three ounces of common sense and two ounces of psy-chology.' In his teaching he emphasized the importance of time. 'A rule of life is primar-ily concerned with time, the only possession we have in this world.'

The majority of those who used RSW's ministrations were leaders in the church. They were Christians who wanted to follow 'the way'. His writings, e.g. *The Way* (1922); *Following the Way* (1925), *The Way in*

Prayer (1932), some twenty in all, were, with the single exception of *Robespierre* (a historical study in deterioration), written under the pseudonym of 'The Author of the Way'. Much of his notable and distinguished contribution to the corpus of mystical theology is as yet only in private circulation amongst those he trained for the mystical road.

Over the years R S W developed 'cells' for leaders in the church where emphasis on prayer and discussion was equally divided. Always the stress was upon God and the immediate and ultimate importance of waiting upon him rather than upon the intellectual cleverness of man.

Reginald Somerset Ward commended hobbies. He persuaded his people to develop activities of a relaxing kind to counter-balance any possible idolatry of work. He frequented his own workshop on many afternoons, making games and toys. During his last two years when his health was not so good he continued to see people at his home. About that time he was given a Lambeth D D by Archbishop Ramsey. He died on 9 July 1962 at the age of eighty-one.

See also **Direction, Spiritual.**

E. R. Morgan, *Reginald Somerset Ward: Life and Letters*, 1963.

N. W. GOODACRE

Water

Water, essential to human life, is one of the four ancient elements constituting the universe. It is a natural symbol principally signifying purification and life. Paradoxically, water is destructive as in floods and also a source and sustainer of life. Water is used ubiquitously in the rituals of the religions of the world, e.g. the washings by the Hindus in the Ganges River and the ablutions that precede Islamic daily prayer. Water has a prominent role in the OT. In the beginning the Spirit of God moved over the face of the waters (Gen. 1.2). Rain is God's gift (Gen. 2.5) but it is also an instrument of God's chastisement as in the deluge (Gen. 6.5–9.17) when the waters of chaos return as a purification of the wickedness that God saw on the earth (Gen. 6.11–12; see also Wisdom 5.22). The flood is a purification that issues in a covenant between God and 'all flesh' (Gen. 9.17). The God of Israel is the source of living waters that give life (Ezek. 47.1–12).

Just as God in the OT is lord of the waters, so Jesus is lord of the waters in the NT (Matt. 8.23–27; Mark 4.35–41; Luke 8.22–25). Jesus even walks upon the waters (Matt. 14.22–23; Mark 6.42–52; John 6.16–21). Water has an important and highly symbolic place in the life of Jesus. He seeks a baptism in water from John the Baptist (Matt. 3.13–17; Mark 1–9–11; Luke 3.21–22; John 1.29–34). At Cana Jesus changes water into wine, an event which is the 'first of his signs' (John 2.1–11). The teaching on baptism in John 3 is followed by the story of the Samaritan Woman at Jacob's Well, where Jesus says to her, 'Give me a drink' (John 4.7). At the Last Supper Jesus serves his followers in the washing of their feet. The NT is filled with such references to water and to Jesus from whose side 'there came out blood and water' (John 19.34). In his doctrine on baptism, St Paul sees water as both death-dealing and life-giving (Rom. 6.3–11). Baptism in the early church washes away sin (1 Cor. 6.11; Acts 22.16), and also brings new life through re-birth (John 3.5–8). Holy water in fonts and a liturgical asperges in some Christian churches are a reminder of the waters of baptism; yet, the recovery of a consciousness of baptism as the initiation into the life of the Spirit and as a source and centre of the spiritual life poses a major pastoral challenge, made more tenuous by the loss of the sense of symbolism.

Water is a prominent symbol among Christian spiritual authors. Francis of Assisi* in his 'Canticle of the Sun' praises the Lord for 'Sister Water, who is useful and humble, Precious and Pure'. Water is a frequent image for John of the Cross* and especially for Teresa of Avila* who says: 'For I don't find anything more appropriate to explain some spiritual experiences than water . . . and [I] am so fond of this element that I have observed it more attentively than other things' (*The Interior Castle*, IV, 2, 2). Best known is Teresa's imagery of the four waters as a way of passing on an understanding of growth in prayer (*The Book of her Life*, 11–22). The gift of tears, water as a physical and symbolic reality, while not much appreciated in modern spirituality, deserves a thorough examination.

Water has long been appreciated for its curative effects, as in 'taking the waters', but spirituality has not as yet paid sufficient attention to the healing quality of water.

Carl Jung sees water as a common symbol for the unconscious. Water is also a feminine symbol, a sign of fecundity and birth. Spirituality needs to recover the feminine character of water as there has been an unbalanced emphasis on the purificatory aspects of water. The psalms, religious songs and poetry find water a basic symbol; thus, T. S. Eliot* writes: 'The river is within us, the sea is all about us' (*Four Quartets*, 'The Dry Salvages', I, 15). The poet's affinity for water has much to offer by way of imagery to the spiritual life. Most remarkable for Christian spirituality is the symbolism of living water as signifying the Holy Spirit (John 7.38–39), the architect of the spiritual life.

F. Cabrol, 'Eau, usage de l'eau dans la liturgie; eau bénite', *Dictionnaire d'Archéologie Chrétienne et de Liturgie*, 4–1, 1921, cols 1680–90; J. Gaillard, 'Eau', *DS*, 4–1, cols 8–29.

KEITH J. EGAN

Watts, Isaac

A Nonconformist Divine, Watts (1674–1748) was mostly famed as the first of the great English hymn-writers, whose compositions have been sung throughout Western Christianity and one of which, 'O God our help in ages past', has been itself something of an event in British history. Watts had an undoubted gift of poetry, though he claimed only to have 'just permitted my verse to rise above a flat and indolent style ... because I would neither indulge any bold metaphors, nor admit of hard words, nor tempt the ignorant worshipper to sing above his understanding'. Despite this, Watts' hymns convey a sense of the Divine transcendence, the glory and majesty of God before whom angels veil their faces. Many are psalm paraphrases. Some, particularly communion hymns, declare that all the wonders of creation are as nothing to the grace that rescued man in the cross of Christ.

Watts was not only a hymn-writer but a 'guide to godliness' in the seventeenth-century Puritan* succession. Though as a speculative theologian he strove for free thought and in his later years inclined towards Unitarianism, his *Guide to Prayer* is a judicious volume. Chiefly concerned with public prayer, it offers a rigorous and very full analysis of the parts of prayer. Watts found eight rather than the usual four or five: 1. Invocation. 2. Adoration. 3. Confession. 4. Petition. 5. Pleading with God, which is not easy to distinguish from (4) yet is so large that it demands separate treatment. 6. Self-dedication. 7. Thanksgiving. 8. Blessing God, which is the peculiar work of the saint, whereas all God's works praise him. There are wise counsels on 'the Use and Abuse of Book Prayers' and on posture in prayer.

A. P. Davis, *Isaac Watts*, 1948; Donald Davies, *A Gathered Church. The Literature of the English Dissenting Interest 1700–1930*, 1978; John Laird, *Philosophical and Literary Pieces*, 1940.

EDITOR

Weatherhead, Leslie Dixon

A Methodist minister, Weatherhead (1893–1975) was 'permitted to serve' the City Temple (Congregationalist) in London from 1936–1963. A broadcaster over four decades, he was also a pioneer in the use of psychiatric techniques in pastoral work. As a preacher, he had the supreme gift of being able to make individuals in a congregation of thousands feel that he was identifying with their lives and speaking directly to their needs. He was also a teacher of prayer both in the periods assigned to it in public worship and in the publication of private guides. His prayer card, 'Ten Minutes a Day', enabled busy people, who would never regard themselves as mystics, to learn something of the many aspects and vast scope of the activity, while in *A Private House of Prayer* (1959) he brought the classic techniques into the lives of twentieth-century people, many of them from the non-Catholic tradition. His underlying theology began with the liberalism and interest in the human Jesus of the 1920s and 30s, and with concern about problems, especially suffering. It stiffened somewhat during the war in a Pauline and doctrinal direction and then became more than ever sensitive to people's doubts and questionings as radical theology made its inroads and the problems of growing old beset him. *The Christian Agnostic* (1965) was somewhat heterodox but showed an open and still youthful mind aware of the needs of those who could turn neither to orthodox formulation nor academic theology for help, but who felt that Christianity might offer them faith and hope if it could accommodate their doubts and not crush speculation prompted by a modern understanding of the universe.

Kingsley Weatherhead, *Leslie Weatherhead: A Personal Portrait*, 1975.

EDITOR

Weil, Simone

Born in 1909 in Paris to a secularized Jewish family, Simone Weil studied philosophy at the Ecolé Normale Supérieure from which she graduated (along with Simone de Beauvoir) in 1931. In the early 1930s she taught philosophy in a number of provincial schools in France while being active in social and political causes both on an intellectual level (she wrote for a number of socialist and communist periodicals) and as an activist (she did factory work for a period and also served with the forces of the Left in the Spanish Civil War). A series of intense religious moments culminating in a mystical experience while she was a guest at the Benedictine abbey of Solesmes in 1938 ('Christ came down and siezed me,' she later wrote to a friend) led her to a passionate interest in Catholic Christianity, although she never sought baptism or formally joined any Christian denomination. In 1940–1941 she lived in and around Marseilles where she enjoyed the close spiritual friendship of Father J. M. Perrin, OP, and Gustave Thibon, a Catholic lay thinker and writer. In May 1942, along with her family, she fled the Vichy anti-semitic laws by sailing via North Africa for the United States. In late 1942 she got to London where she worked with the Free French. She died of starvation and pulmonary tuberculosis in a Kentish sanatorium on 24 August 1943. Despite her grave illness, she refused to eat to show solidarity with the French under German occupation.

The posthumous publication of works like *Waiting on God* (1951); *Gravity and Grace* (1952), *The Notebooks* (1956) and later publications reveal a deeply religious, albeit eclectic, spiritual vision nourished by her profound love for Greek culture, Hindu religion, the gospels, and the Christian mystics as well as her antipathy for much of the OT and all of Roman culture. Her spiritual emphases include the separation of God from creation, the spiritual value of suffering, the gulf between our created world and the reality of God, the symbolic value of the cross, and her notion of 'waiting in patience' for God in an age of atheism. Weil's influence has been profound on both social activists and religious thinkers. Although much of her published work is culled from random essays, notebook jottings, projects for fuller works, and so on, she is highly regarded both for the lucidity of her prose style and her high intellectual seriousness. Those not convinced of her Christian orthodoxy have noted her strong interest in the Neoplatonists* and the Manichees*. Her defenders have underscored her tentativeness and the eccentric nature of her vocabulary. The very complexity of her thought helps explain why her influence has extended to commentators as diverse as Daniel Berrigan and T. S. Eliot*.

Jacques Cabaud, *Simone Weil: A Fellowship in Love*, 1964: Simone Pétrement, *Simone Weil: A Life*, 1976; Richard Rees, *Simone Weil: A Sketch for a Portrait*, 1966; E. W. F. Tomlin, *Simone Weil*, 1954; G. A. White (ed), *Simone Weil: An Interpretation*, 1981.

LAWRENCE S. CUNNINGHAM

Welsh Spirituality

The record of Welsh spirituality is to be traced in the literary tradition of a country which absorbed outside influences into a distinctive culture and gave them expression in a native language which by the sixth century was beginning to acquire literary form. Evidence of an established Christian tradition is suggested by the casual reference of the sixth-century poet, Aneirin, to soldiers going to churches for shriving on the eve of battle; and that in a language which with little annotation is intelligible to a modern speaker of Welsh.

The Church in Wales before 1066 was poor and isolated. Its *scriptoria* were few, as are the surviving manuscripts. It was dragged from its isolation by the Norman conquerors. During the Middle Ages many devotional works were produced in the Welsh language. They were translations from contemporary writings. One exception is *Y Gysegrlan Fuchedd* (The Holy Life) but of this it has been said that its imagery becomes intelligible only when it is placed in the context of earlier mediaeval religious writings. The significance of these works is that they introduced much of the language of contemporary mysticism into Welsh.

The mediaeval poets gave expression to the spirituality which is evidenced by the prose writings. It included a devotion to the many native saints whose lives were being written at this time. It was nurtured by pilgrimages for which there were many notable centres. Two journeys to St Davids was the equivalent of one to Rome, while three equalled a pilgrimage to Jerusalem. The numerous holy wells of Wales also had their devotees. Devotion to the Blessed Virgin Mary is indicated by the large number of churches dedicated to her; by the many wild flowers which were given her name, the foxglove for example being called *Gwniadur Mair* (Mary's Thimble) and by the poets of the period. They saw her as the embodiment of all that is tender and good, but they derive the details of her life from apocryphal sources well known in Wales from the document *Buchedd Mair* (Life of Mary). She was 'the lady of the seas' who brought voyagers safely home and her healing powers attracted large numbers to her shrines. An anonymous carol describes her as *brydferthaf o ferched y byd* (fairest of the women of the world). She was the great mediatrix, for she was *morwynig frenhines y nefoedd* (virgin queen of the heavens). Echoes of these phrases recur in the poetry of Henry Vaughan* (1621–1695): 'Bright Queen of Heaven/God's Virgin Spouse/The glad world's blessed maid'. Vaughan wrote in English but he inherited the Welsh tradition which he learned at his mother's knee. The mediaeval poets loved to dwell on the significance of the passion. There were a number of famous roods, for example at Brecon, Llangynwyd and Tremeirchion. They also stressed the importance of the sacraments and they derived from the prose writings the five blessings for hearing the Mass and the seven blessings for receiving the sacrament.

In the post-Reformation period the translation of the Bible and the Book of Common Prayer into Welsh ensured that Welsh spirituality would have a firm scriptural base. There was considerable stress on devotion within the family circle. Devotional books were provided for that purpose and also to wean the people from the 'superstitions' that lingered on from the past. A large number

of the most popular and influential English devotional books were translated into Welsh, such as *The Practice of Piety, The Whole Duty of Man*, and *Holy Living*, a much esteemed book which Jeremy Taylor* wrote during his sojourn in Wales. Meanwhile Griffith Jones (1683–1761) by means of his circulating schools taught almost a whole nation to read the Bible and the Prayer Book.

The influence of the prose translations is reflected in religious verse. A pattern had been set by the metrical psalms of Edmund Prys (1544–1623). Significant if only for the quantity of editions was Vicar (Rhys) Prichard's *Canwyll Y Cymry* (The Welshmen's Candle). The long tradition of carols was maintained in the *cwndidau* and *halsingod* of the period. Both words may be translated as 'carols' but there is a subtle difference, for the *halsingod* were verse renderings of biblical and doctrinal themes.

Welsh Methodism at the outset owed nothing to English influences for it was an independent growth and it took the Calvinistic form. The movement threw up a large number of hymn writers. William Williams, Pantycelyn (1717–1791), was the most prolific and influential but his spirituality was that of the movement he served. The pilgrimage of the Christian life, the goal and its approach are the dominant themes in which the imagery of the Bible is set against the landscape of Wales, the hills and the changing weather. The hymns of Ann Griffiths (1776–1805) are few but significant. She has been compared to the great mystics of the past such as St Teresa of Avila*. But there is no distinctive school of Williams' or Griffiths' spirituality. Ann Griffiths' verse is a product of the Bible and the Prayer book, perhaps also the seventeenth-century books of devotion, reflected in a life lived in the light of eternity.

A firm hold on the doctrine of the incarnation and a love for the sacrament enabled Ann Griffiths to avoid the overemphasis on the atonement which characterized the evangelical movement of which Methodism was part. The Tractarians set out to counter-balance this tendency and their influence in Wales has been considerable. *Emynau'r Eglwys* (1946), the hymn book of the Church in Wales, reflects this influence. In addition to native productions it contains a large number of translations from English and Latin sources. The sections on the sacraments and the saints were designed to fill a vacuum which had been evident in Welsh spiritual life since the sixteenth century. It is indicative of a renewed interest in the older devotional tradition. Somewhat elusive, semi-mystical, owing little to any particular school of spirituality, it began in the age of the Welsh saints of the fourth and fifth centuries; found literary expression in the Middle Ages and at intervals in the centuries that followed, and still appears in the verse of modern writers such as Saunders Lewis, Gwenallt Jones, Waldo Williams, Euros Bowen and R. S. Thomas.

A. M. Allchin, *Ann Griffiths*, 1976; Geraint H. Jenkins, *Literature, Religion and Society in Wales 1660–1730*; Gwyn Jones (ed), *Welsh Verse in English*, 1977; R. Gerallt Jones, *Poetry of Wales 1930–1970*, 1974; Glanmor Williams, *The Welsh Church from Conquest to Reformation*, 1962.

OWAIN W. JONES

Wesley, Charles

Charles Wesley (1707–1788) was the partner of his brother John* in the Methodist Revival, but his importance for spirituality lies in his hymns. Fifty or so of these have become the common possession of all denominations, but hundreds more shaped the devotion of Methodists until our own time. The Collection of 1780 contains 480 out of 525 hymns by Charles Wesley. It was arranged by John Wesley in the form of a spiritual autobiography of a 'real Christian', an exercise in 'experimental and practical divinity'. It was intended for the worship of a society rather than that of an independent denomination, which Wesleyanism had become by 1850. The hymns are charged with orthodox doctrine, 'lex orandi is lex credendi', the mysteries of faith are 'made friendly'. There is a passionate sense of personal experience, and a mysticism, which is neither absorption nor a 'flight of the alone to the alone'. Evangelical and written for evangelists, the hymns trace the pilgrimage of faith from conversion to the attainment of perfect love. But they never neglect the means of grace. In 1744 the Wesleys had published *Hymns on the Lord's Supper*, a paraphrase of Daniel Brevint's *The Christian Sacrament and Sacrifice*, redolent of the High Anglican Doctrine of the Caroline

Divines*. All the hymns are masterpieces of scriptural allusion from almost every part of the Bible. Perhaps one reason why they do not speak to the hearts of this generation as of old is fading knowledge of scripture combined with the bewildering variety of modern versions.

F. Baker, *Representative Verse of Charles Wesley*, 1962; J. E. Rattenbury, *The Evangelical Doctrines of Charles Wesley's Hymns*, 1941; *The Eucharistic Hymns of John and Charles Wesley*, 1948; F. Whaling (ed), *John and Charles Wesley. Selected Writings and Hymns* (Classics of Western Spirituality) 1982.

J. MUNSEY TURNER

Wesley, John

John Wesley (1703–1791) was a priest of the Church of England, and with his brother Charles*, founder of the Methodist societies whose chief aim was 'to spread scriptural holiness through the land'. Fundamentally, this was a spirituality of the Great Commandments. Where other traditions emphasized either the direct, contemplative love of God, or the development of love of neighbour and personal holiness of life, Wesley kept a balance. The two biblical laws provided him with a corrective to a righteousness of either faith or works, to the extremes of mysticism and activism.

He drew on many sources to inform his prayer and mission, and in the end it is futile to try to make particular attributions. His home life, and especially the influence of his mother Susanna, was of great importance. The Epworth Rectory was notable for its discipline of family prayer. Here the Bible and the Book of Common Prayer (1662) provided a daily diet of reading and laid the foundation of his claim to be *homo unius libri*, a man of one book. He drew on his Anglican inheritance further in the *Homilies* and the stern advice of Jeremy Taylor*, and of the nonjuring divines, especially William Law (*see* **Nonjurors**). But unlike the parochial practice of the time, he placed a high value on preaching, on frequent holy communion, and on the use of extempore prayer. The influence of his Puritan* forebears may be seen in such practices as the making of rules of life both for individuals and for societies, in a service for renewing the covenant with God, in the keeping of a journal, in the strict observance of the Lord's Day, in simplicity of life and in regular examination of conscience. Puritan authors form the greater part of the *Christian Library* (50 vols, 1749–1755), the *lectio divina* he prepared for his preachers.

He read avidly the classics of spirituality: the early Fathers of East and West, Basil, Chrysostom, Augustine* and Jerome*. He valued the somewhat obscure Ephrem Syrus* and 'Macarius the Egyptian'* (a disciple of Gregory of Nyssa). These writers confirmed him in his search for Christian Perfection or Entire Sanctification, whereby God dwells completely in the believer and enables full love of God and neighbour.

Thomas à Kempis* and Roman Catholic writers of the Counter-Reformation (again including rather less central exemplars: the Mexican hermit Lopez, the Spanish Quietist Molinos*) provided him with instances of holy and dedicated lives and yet forced him to define his attitude to mysticism. In the French Count de Renty he found both a saint and a philanthropist.

Ironically it was the 'quietism' of his Moravian friends which disturbed him most, since he feared any religion which did not issue in 'social holiness'. Yet to these German Pietists* he owed a particular debt: the translation of his prodigious spiritual reading into a personal 'experimental' faith, marked by his experience at a society meeting in Aldersgate Street, London on 24 May 1738. There, he recorded, 'I felt I did trust in Christ, Christ alone for salvation: and an assurance was given me that he had taken away *my* sins, even *mine*, and saved me from the law of sin and death.' Though he differed from the Moravians* theologically, he was impressed by their sanctity and pious practices. He saw examples of these when he visited Herrnhut in August 1738. These observations, together with material culled from many other sources, provided the basis for the Methodist organization into which every believer was drawn, a network of classes and bands designed specifically to promote growth in holiness.

See also **Methodist Spirituality**.

R. Davies and E. G. Rupp (eds), *A History of the Methodist Church in Great Britain*, vol 1 1965; A. C. Outler, *John Wesley*, 1964; G. S. Wakefield, *Fire of Love*, 1976.

R. W. GRIBBEN

Whyte, Alexander

A minister of the Free Church of Scotland, Whyte (1836–1921) from 1870 to the middle years of the First World War was based at St George's West Church, Edinburgh. A dramatic preacher of poetic imagination, born in the north-east of Scotland, Whyte supported Robertson Smith, whose critical OT scholarship led to fierce controversies and dismissal from his chair in 1881. But though he always contended for academic freedom in the quest for truth, Whyte's own preaching owed little to the results of the higher criticism, since he used scripture to deal with 'man, the heart of man and human life', and made the Bible characters windows into the souls of his contemporaries, his attitude to ministry being Shakespearian rather than scientific. It may have been this which made him so remarkably catholic in his spirituality and so warm towards all those who had a sense of God and of the needs of the human heart, irrespective of period or churchmanship. Reared in the *gravitas* of the Scottish Reformed tradition, he early discovered the English Puritan, Thomas Goodwin*, and to the end believed that the study of his work was the best preparation for ministry. He was a great expositor of Samuel Rutherford* and John Bunyan*, but in the course of his life he formed friendships far beyond the bounds of the Kirk including J. H. Newman*, Henri Bremond*, and the Russian Orthodox, Father John of Kronstadt. He published anthologies and appreciations of Dante, Jakob Boehme*, William Law, Teresa of Avila* and an edition of Lancelot Andrewes'* *Preces Privatae*, and in famed classes of instruction dealt year after year with the lives of spiritual guides of many traditions, some whose orthodoxy had been questioned. Of his own public sermons, the course *Lord, Teach us to Pray* (delivered in the 1890s but published posthumously) is outstanding, and the meditation on Christ in the Garden of Gethsemane must rank as one of the greatest sermons ever preached in the whole history of the Christian pulpit.

G. F. Barbour, *Life of Alexander Whyte DD*, 1923.

EDITOR

William of Saint-Thierry

William (1070?–1147/1148), the Abbot of Saint-Thierry, near Reims, entered monastic life from the schools. Meeting Bernard of Clairvaux* c. 1120 and seeing in him and in the Cistercian* movement the primitive desert spirit rekindled, he began under their influence to explore the stages of man's return from unlikeness to the image of God.

Drawing on his Augustinian training, William set out in his Benedictine works the basic pattern which, with variations in detail, he thereafter followed. Created in the image of God and endowed with the trinitarian impress of memory, reason, and will, man has turned away from God, and by his attachment to created things has made himself less than fully human, i.e. less that God created him to be. Pulled by his own nature and provoked by Christ's love, man may choose to respond to God's persistent call (with one exception, William always begins his ascent with this choice of the will, and does not discuss those who never make it). As the will grows fervent, it becomes love. Human love, balanced by reason, then grows into charity, God's own love. Within charity man achieves wisdom, the experience of God, which William liked to call 'the vision of God face to face' (De natura et dignitate amoris = On the Nature and Dignity of Love).

Transferring to a Cistercian abbey in midlife (1135), without the blessing of Bernard which had been asked and refused, William composed scriptural commentaries which express variations on this theme until an encounter with Peter Abelard's Theologia 'scholarium' caused him to clarify points of doctrine and, in doing so, to reconsider the means by which, and the extent to which, man can know God in this life.

Two post-Abelardian works, The Mirror of Faith (Speculum fidei), and The Letter to the Brothers of Mont Dieu (Epistola ad fratres de Monte Dei), contain the most systematic presentations of his mature spirituality. In them he treats man in three stages: animal man (the stage of faith); rational man (reason); and spiritual man (love). Animal – besouled, not bestial – man, having willed to turn back to God, must choose also to believe what God has revealed in scripture. For his knowledge of God, he depends upon his physical senses and his imagination. Not only must he discipline these senses, but as a composite being, he must integrate his physical with his spiritual nature. This necessary foundation stage must be surpassed, however, for humankind's uniqueness lies not in the senses, but in reason. Devout rational inquiry allows one to perceive a reality beyond the corporeal and permits therefore man's first recognition of the divine ideas. Yet in its turn, reason must yield to a still greater cognitive faculty, the one most like God himself, love. Human love, in reaching out to God singlemindedly, encounters God who is love, and love conforms the soul to God. It is this likeness of being which provides the fullest possible understanding of God in this life.

Despite William's ascents, he warns readers from his first work to his last that growth in understanding occurs not in successive stages so much as in an ever deepening realization of the presence of God who forever envelops and sustains each person. The unnatural disorder into which sin, self-deceit and absorption with trivia have cast man blinds him to the divine in-dwelling; discipline, provided by the monastic life, dislodges these distractions and lets the person be reformed to the divine Image.

From the monastic tradition William inherited a love for words which, if carefully pondered, communicate a hidden meaning which they, as signs, somehow share. With his contemporaries he shared a love for logic which led him to posit distinctions which, even though they are not consistent from work to work or carried throughout a single work, lend precise clarity within the passage where they appear. (Indeed, one of William's objections to Abelard's methodology was the scholar's inflexible refusal to abandon a definition once it had served its purpose.) From his association with the Cistercians, he learned to interpret traditional teaching in terms of personal experience, and to esteem solitude, simplicity, and self-knowledge.

Although William's favourite metaphor for the experience of God was 'to see', he was not a visionary in the later mediaeval sense. To a man convinced that sensory vision and imagination were among the most elementary faculties, 'visions' would have been as inconsistent as sculpted capitals to Bernard's theory of monastic architecture.

Similarly, although William thought rational investigation incumbent upon all persons capable of it, and although he was a meticulous and exacting theologian, he held that rational explanations of supra-rational reality must be regarded as vehicles to be used and then left behind, not as immutable truths to be idolized. Even meditation on the Word of God in scripture, without which one cannot learn of God more than his existence, even meditation on the Word of God incarnate, without which one cannot apprehend God's love, must be abandoned as one more nearly approaches the indivisible, eternal, triune God. Only by rigorous physical, mental, and spiritual asceticism can the human person come to participate in the love between Father and Son which is the Holy Spirit. This 'unity of Spirit' brings to its fullness the likeness of God which is both innate to man and increased by likeness of will. Not only is it the work of the Spirit, 'it is the Spirit itself, the God who is charity'. Within that divine love, man 'becomes by grace what God is by nature' (*Epistola aurea*).

Scholarship on William has flourished in the past half century, concentrating first on his mystical theology and, most recently, on the chronology of his life, and on his sources, particularly on his use, or non-use, of Greek sources not commonly utilized by his contemporaries.

There are translations into English of William's works in the Cistercian Fathers Series, Cistercian Publications, 1971ff.; see also D. N. Bell, *The Image and Likeness. The Augustinian Spirituality of William of Saint-Thierry*, 1983.

E. ROZANNE ELDER

Wyon, Olive

Olive Wyon was born on 7 March 1881 in Hampstead, London, the eldest of five children in a cultured Victorian home with deep church loyalties. In her English Free Church background she was also familiar with and devoted to Anglican sacramental practice. Dr Wyon came into prominence in the churches of Great Britain as a competent translator of German theological writings. English speaking Christianity was deeply indebted to her in particular for splendid translations of Emil Brunner's *The Mediator* (1934) and *The Divine Imperative* (1937).

This theological work was built on her early call to missionary service through the London Missionary Society, and subsequent missionary training in Edinburgh at what was to become the St Colm's Missionary College of the Church of Scotland. Over forty years later Olive Wyon was invited to serve as Principal of St Colm's for three years in 1951, a final church appointment for which wide ecumenical service and experience had prepared her well.

The ecumenical contacts of a life of varied Christian service, including the World Council of Churches in Geneva, deepened Olive Wyon's almost mystical spirituality which can be described and understood only in terms of community and ecumenical facets.

Particularly significant was her contact through Geneva with the Community of Grandchamp, where in 1931 a small group of women of the Reformed Church had begun to build up a centre for prayer, silence and meditation which developed into a Protestant Women's Religious Order which adopted the Taizé* Office for its pattern of worship. Dr Wyon's own *Living Springs* (1963), dedicated 'in memory of Mère Geneviève Foundress of Grandchamp', expounds the element of community in any vital Christian spirituality.

In her study of such modern movements as the Iona Community, the Michaelsbruderschaft, and the Grail Society, she observed that structured Christian fellowship and community are vital for the development of prayer life. She stressed 'a right relation between prayer and action'; 'the need for and the value of solitude and silence'; and a community where 'men and women find each other in Christ and begin to pray and work as never before for the extension of the spirit of unity'.

Further, from the Protestantism and missionary challenge towards 'the evangelization of the world in this generation' characteristic of her youth, her theology developed evermore ecumenically. She believed that we are challenged 'to live more truly as members of the One, Holy, Catholic Church: that is, in unity, holiness, mission – and the three are one'.

Personally attracted to a more liturgically ordered and sacramental tradition in Christian worship than had yet developed in the English Nonconformity where she was nurtured, Olive Wyon delighted in common and community worship, and she mediated a joyful spirit of shared devotion and prayerfulness with an almost mystical quality. Yet her spirituality was earth-rooted and marked by happiness verging into fun.

On her death in Edinburgh on 21 August 1966 Bishop Kenneth Carey wrote: 'There can be few people who have ever been so ready for eternal life. She had lived in it and by it for so many years, and by her writings, her work, and, most of all, by what she was, she had helped so many people to realize the glory of being a Christian.'

Olive Wyon, *The School of Prayer*, 1943; *The Altar Fire*, 1954; *Prayer for Unity*, 2 vols, 1955–1956.

R. STUART LOUDEN

Yoga

The word has a number of uses. Yoga is one of the six main philosophical schools of Hinduism*. In common with Sāmkhya, Yoga philosophy regards both spirit and matter as real, and traces the whole of the physical universe to a single source, Prakriti. Spirit, or personality, is Purusha, and it is Purusha alone which gives meaning and purpose to Prakriti. Man's predicament is thought to be caused by his ignorance, and particularly by his lack of awareness of what constitutes true reality, by his egoism, and by his clinging to life. In ignorance, man comes to regard Prakriti rather than Purusha as the true reality. The aim of Yoga is to obtain liberation for Purusha from Prakriti, and the great contribution of the Yoga school of philosophy was to suggest a system of physical, mental, and spiritual discipline which could reassert the supremacy of Purusha over Prakriti.

The root meaning of the word yoga is 'to join together', but the yoga system as it developed came to emphasize liberation, or isolation, rather more than union with God, although such union remains a possibility.

The great text of classical Hindu Yoga is Patanjali's Yoga Sūtras, written between A D 300 and 500. The Yoga Sūtras are divided into four sections, the first concerned with concentration, the second with the means of attainment, the third with supernormal powers which it is claimed can be conferred by the practices, and the fourth with an account of the state of liberation.

It is the second section, the Sādhanā Pada, which contains the heart of the system. Here Patanjali describes the eight limbs, or parts, which are regarded as essential to the successful pursuit of yoga. The eight limbs are:

Yama – moral obligations which include truthfulness, chastity, non-violence and refraining from stealing or covetousness.

Niyama – ritual purity in matters of eating and drinking, purity of thought, self-denial and contentment with one's lot.

Āsana – postures and exercises aimed at the control of the body.

Prānāyāma – breath control, often practised in conjunction with the exercises of āsana in order to subordinate physical concerns to mental and spiritual activities.

Pratyāhāra – withdrawal of the mind from preoccupation with the concerns of everyday life.

Dhārana – concentrating the mind on a particular object.

Dhyāna – contemplation, in which thoughts should deepen and extend on the object of concentration.

Samādhi – trance, or mystical awareness.

The eight limbs are not simply stages to be discarded when the next step is reached, but a coherent system in which moral, physical, mental and spiritual activities all contribute to the attainment of the goal of liberation. The complete system of yoga is often referred to as Rāja Yoga. In modern practice, especially in the West, some elements of yoga may be emphasized more than others or divorced entirely from the system of the Yoga Sūtras. Hatha Yoga, which is concerned with the physical aspects, particularly with the exercises and breathing, is often taught as a complete system of self-improvement.

Another use of the word yoga is found in the Bhagavad Gītā*, which considers three possible methods of obtaining liberation or salvation. Yoga is used in connection with all three methods, and so in the Gītā yoga becomes a synonym for 'way' or 'method'. The three are:

jnāna yoga – the way of knowledge or wisdom;

karma yoga – the way of action, particularly in performing the duties, or dharma, appropriate to one's own caste;

bhakti yoga – the way of devotion to a personal God.

The popularity of yoga in the West in recent times has been encouraged by Hindu teachers who have offered precise methods of training in spiritual discipline as an attractive alternative to institutionalized Christianity, whilst Hatha Yoga has flourished as a novel way of engaging in physical exercises and as a method of relaxation. But aspects of yoga also lend themselves to reinterpretation in association with the teaching of other religions, including Christianity. The calm and deliberate movements of āsana can be used to encourage a peaceful state of mind, and physical postures associated with particular kinds of prayer. Prānāyāma, or breath-control, in Indian yoga is often used as a framework for prayer, the words of a mantra or short prayer being incorporated into the pattern of breathing. Some Christian teachers of spiritual discipline (St Ignatius Loyola*, for example) have advocated breathing techniques in association with spiritual exercises, and there are many appropriate short prayers that the Christian may use in this way. Similarities may be found between Pratyāhāra and the Prayer of Simplicity or Prayer of Quiet in the Christian tradition. Dhārana may be interpreted by the Christian in concentrating upon a religious object, such as a cross, or upon a short passage of scripture.

To make too close an analogy between yoga and Christian devotion would be misleading. But some of the techniques of yoga are increasingly coming to be incorporated into Christian as well as Hindu prayer, and such techniques may be employed profitably in devotion and meditation whatever the doctrinal assumptions may be.

P. Bowes, *The Hindu Religious Tradition*, 1978; J.-M. Dechanet, *Christian Yoga*, 1960; M. Hiriyanna, *The Essentials of Indian Philosophy*, 1949; S. Radhakrishnan and C. A. Moore, *A Sourcebook in Indian Philosophy*, 1957; J. H. Woods, *The Yoga System of Patanjali*, 1966.

PETER D. BISHOP

Zen

The best known form of Buddhism* in the West, popularized especially in America during the first half of this century by the writings of D. T. Suzuki and Alan Watts. Zen became even more visible after the Second World War with extensive cultural contact between Japan and America. Zen centres were established in major urban areas throughout the United States. California proved to be especially hospitable to teachers of Zen thought and practice. Literary figures associated with the 'Beat Generation' and the 'San Francisco Renaissance', e.g., Jack Kerouac, Alan Ginsberg, Gary Snyder, became involved in Zen. Snyder spent several years in Japan studying and practising Zen. Zen meditation centres have since been established in the mountains of California, Colorado, New York, New England and elsewhere. Zen has also attracted considerable interest among Christians, especially Roman Catholic religious orders. Thomas Merton*, the famous Trappist monk, spoke and wrote appreciatively of Zen. What is Zen, and why have thoughtful Christians been attracted by it?

1. *Practice.* Zen is, foremostly, a practice. The word is the Japanese rendering of *ch'an*, the Chinese word for *dhyāna* (Sanskrit), meaning a meditative state of consciousness. In the broadest sense, then, Zen is not a sect or a school of Buddhism, but a way to understanding, insight and enlightenment (Japanese: *satori*), the key to which is meditation.

Monastic training focuses on meditation not primarily as a means of controlling the mind, but as a way of coming to know the truth of the true nature of things. Forms of meditation vary, but all involve long periods of sitting quietly and concentratedly in a meditation hall under the direction of an accomplished master (Japanese: *roshi*). Included among the subjects for meditation may be an enigmatic or paradoxical mind-twister (Japanese: *koan*) such as 'What is the sound of one hand clapping?' or 'Does the dog have Buddha nature?' These *koans* have been collected and commented upon (e.g., the *Mumokan*, the *Heikiganroku*), although originally they were simply sayings which grew out of stories about famous Chinese and Japanese Zen masters. In fact, these narratives may be thought of as constituting the core of the Zen textual tradition rather than those Indian Buddhist texts which are also highly regarded in Zen, e.g., the *Laṅkāvatāra Sūtra*, the *Prajñāpāramitā Sūtras*. Authority in Zen, therefore, does not rest in scripture or an institution but in persons of transforming vision. The history of the tradition, from this perspective, becomes the history of the lives of the Zen masters, saints or patriarchs. The heart of Zen training lies in the relationship between these accomplished beings and their students. They impart a wordless wisdom not limited to a sacred text, a skilful means derived from their own insight into the nature of reality. How does Zen understand the human condition and the nature of reality?

2. *Teaching*. Zen, like other forms of Buddhism, can be said to be about overcoming the basically unsatisfactory (Sanskrit: *duḥkha*) character of mundane existence. Why is life plagued with dissatisfaction? Basically, because of our proclivity for making life into something it is not; for attributing to it stability and permanence when in reality life continually changes; for isolating ourselves as subjects from objects to which we attribute a singular independence when, in fact, existence has a much more interdependent character. Futhermore, and more importantly, life has a subtle or sacred nature to it not readily discernible to common sense experience. The true nature of things cannot be learned out of books, nor can it be taught in any conventional sense. Such knowledge is discovered, an intuition (Sanskirt: *prajñā*) of a shared depth of experience, a universal reality (Sanskrit: *śunyatā*) which everything in the world expresses in its own particularity or uniqueness. A tree is not merely a tree, any more than a mountain is merely a mountain or a person merely a person. Being attached to an outer form one misses a deeper, hidden meaning, a meaning discovered in an awareness of the ultimate interconnectedness of all things. To be myself I must realize my own Void (*śunya*) nature, that ultimately in the Void I discover both myself and the universe. With this realization I become a means of grace or compassion (Sanskrit: *karuṇā*). In the language of the Zen tradition, I become a *bodhisattva*, a saint or fully realized human being.

3. *History*. India gave birth to Buddhism, including much that we consider to be a part of Zen. Yet, Zen as a distinctive tradition was nurtured and developed in China, Korea and Japan. Zen attributes the founding of the tradition to Bodhidharma who reputedly came from India to China about AD 520. Legends of his life and other patriarchal figures express many characteristics of Zen, as well as relate its historical development in narrative form. For example, Bodhidharama is said to have approached the Emperor Wu of Liang, a pious supporter of Buddhism, admonishing him that all his religious good works were of no spiritual benefit. Bodhidharma then departed for north China where he meditated in intense concentration for ten years. Hui-k'o (486–593?), the second patriarch of Zen, proved his sincerity and dedication to Bodhidharma by cutting off his left arm; Hui-Neng (637–713), the sixth patriarch, became famous for his teaching of no-mind (Chinese: *wu-hsin*); Hakuin Zenji, the eighteenth-century reformer of Zen in Japan systematized *koan* training. In this manner the lineage of great teachers tells the story of Zen, a tradition rooted in transformative experience transmitted from 'mind to mind'.

Heinrich Dumoulin, *A History of Zen Buddhism*, 1960; Thomas Hoover, *Zen Culture*, 1978; Thomas Merton, *Zen and the Birds of Appetite*, 1968; Nancy Wilson Ross, *The World of Zen*, 1960; D. T. Suzuki, *An Introduction to Zen Buddhism*, 1949.

DONALD K. SWEARER